PROCLAIMING THE TRUTH

Second Edition

An Illustrated History of ASHRAE

This publication was prepared under the auspices of ASHRAE's Historical Committee.

Edited by W. Stephen Comstock

First edition written by W. Stephen Comstock and B.J. Spanos
Second edition updates written by W. Stephen Comstock
First edition researched by Emily S. Walker and Patricia Mathis
Second edition researched by W. Stephen Comstock
First edition manuscript contributions by John Janssen, Frank H. Faust, Andrew T. Boggs, Adele Brandstrom, William R. Coker
Second edition manuscript contributions by H. Michael Newman, Steven T. Bushby, Bruce D. Hunn, J. Richard Wright, Michael Vaughn, and Thomas A. Gilbertson

Updates and errata for this publication will be posted on the ASHRAE website at www.ashrae.org/publicationupdates.

PROCLAIMING THE TRUTH

Second Edition

Completed in celebration of ASHRAE's 125th anniversary

ASHRAE® CELEBRATING 125 YEARS

ISBN 978-1-947192-45-4 (paperback)
ISBN 978-1-947192-46-1 (PDF)

1791 Tullie Circle, NE
Atlanta, GA 30329
www.ashrae.org

Library of Congress Control Number: 2019955534

ASHRAE STAFF

SPECIAL PUBLICATIONS	Cindy Sheffield Michaels, Editor James Madison Walker, Managing Editor of Standards Lauren Ramsdell, Associate Editor Mary Bolton, Assistant Editor Michshell Phillips, Senior Editorial Coordinator
PUBLISHING SERVICES	David Soltis, Group Manager of Electronic Products and Publishing Services Jayne Jackson, Publication Traffic Administrator
DIRECTOR OF PUBLICATIONS AND EDUCATION	Mark S. Owen

Dedication

To the Thermal Engineer who "...is privileged more than the historian, theologian, or poet, to consider some of the great questions of the universe. The nature of the force he is harnessing calls forth his imaginative powers."—Willis H. Carrier, 1928

"Let us have the faith that right makes might and in that faith let us always strive to do our duty as we understand it." — Abraham Lincoln, 1860, as quoted by ASHRAE President James Hill, June 1997.

Vision Statement

1995

ASHRAE

- *will be the global leader in the arts and sciences of heating, ventilation, air conditioning and refrigeration;*
- *will be the foremost, authoritative, timely and responsive source of technical and educational information, standards and guidelines; and*
- *will be the primary provider of opportunity for professional growth, recognizing and adapting to changing demographics, and embracing diversity.*

2020

A healthy and sustainable built environment for all

Contents

Acknowledgments

The publication of the first edition of *Proclaiming the Truth* marked the centennial celebration of the founding of the American Society of Heating, Refrigerating and Air-Conditioning Engineers, known today as ASHRAE.

Initiated by 1993–94 ASHRAE President Richard A. Charles to be a permanent record of the Society's 100 years of progress and accomplishment, the first edition was prepared under the guidance of the ASHRAE Centennial Committee: Louis F. Flagg, chairman; David S. Butler, Sr.; Richard A. Charles; William J. Collins, Jr.; Robert W. Crosby; Richard Rooley; and Thomas J. White. Charles monitored project completion on behalf of the committee.

The second edition of *Proclaiming the Truth* was published to add ASHRAE's progress and accomplishments from 1995 to 2020, as a commemoration of the Society's 125th anniversary.

Frank H. Faust and John E. Jansen formed the basis of Chapters 6 and 9, respectively, written for the first edition. Manuscripts on ASHRAE history by Bernard A. Nagengast and Alfred Greenberg are sources of information found throughout the book. Review and comment on manuscripts was provided by Richard A. Charles, Mervin W. Dizenfeld, Louis F. Flagg, John C. Fox, William L. Holladay, Burgess H. Jennings, Roderick P. Kirkwood, and J. Richard Wright. Appendix B, "The Show," was based on an article authored by Andrew T. Boggs.

In the second edition, H. Michael Newman's book *BACnet: The Global Standard for Building Automation and Control Networks* was a source for updating ASHRAE standards work in Chapter 4 and Thomas A. Gilbertson's article for the Golden Gate Chapter's newsletter on Title 24 was used to update Chapter 8. J. Richard Wright, Bruce D. Hunn, and Michael Vaughn provided their perspectives on the evolution of ASHRAE Research.

The papers from ASHRAE's archives for the years 1895 through 1994 listed in Appendix K were selected by Louis F. Flagg, Raymond Cohen, Guy W. Gupton, George B. Hightower, Gershon Meckler, Donald E. Nichols, Joseph B. Olivieri, Ronald L. Shelton, and Hans O. Spauschus. ASHRAE Handbook Associate Editor Adele Brandstrom assisted in the preparation of the abstracts listed for each paper.

The papers for the years 1995 through 2019 were selected by Eric Sturm, Steven F. Bruning, Charles E. Henck, James E. Hill, Gordon Holness, David Knebel, Ronald Shelton, Branislav Todorovic, and David Underwood. ASHRAE Librarian Emily Sigman assisted in the shepherding of the selections.

Appendix J, which gives the reflections of Presidential Members on the Society, was assembled by Emily Sigman for the entries from 1894 to 1994. She, along with Communications and Publications Administrative Assistant Patricia Mathis, researched and gathered many of the facts and illustrations used in the book. W. Stephen Comstock assembled the reflections of Presidential Members from 1995 through 2019.

Many *ASHRAE Journal* covers are reproduced in this volume. Most were created by Lawrence H. Darrow, who was the Journal's art director from 1975 through 1994. These covers graphically portray the issues which were dealt with by the Society during these years.

Most of the content used to update *Proclaiming the Truth* to celebrate ASHRAE's 125th anniversary in 2019–2020 are from original source speeches, news reports, Board reports, and articles published in *ASHRAE Insights*. Woven together, they tell the story of ASHRAE as it entered, evolved, and prospered in the twenty-first century.

W. Stephen Comstock

Introduction

Why entitle this illustrated history of ASHRAE *Proclaiming the Truth*? To John E. Starr, the first president of The American Society of Refrigerating Engineers (ASRE), "finding the truth" was the principal responsibility of the technical society. He stated this eloquently in 1905: "The Association has a weight in any utterance which is many times greater than those of any individual. The public recognizes that such utterance was made in an arena where, if it could have been intelligently questioned or differed from, it would have undergone that ordeal then and there."

Of The American Society of Refrigerating Engineers, he said, "We have undertaken the responsibility of speaking with authority, of finding the truth, and proclaiming it, and a critical world will hold us to our task or pass us by as unworthy."

Starr's words reappeared often, such as under the Society logo on its Circular No. 1, "Heat Transmission of Insulating Materials."

To us, the phrase represents all that is good about ASHRAE. It reminds us that ASHRAE places technological advancement before commercial advantage. It reinforces the notion that the work of ASHRAE is for the benefit of the public. It tells us that ASHRAE members recognize that their obligation to humanity is to scrutinize, to contribute, and to participate.

This resolve to do good is why the work of ASHRAE and the spirit of ASHRAE are as relevant today as was the case 125 years ago when engineers seeking technical truths formed the American Society of Heating and Ventilating Engineers (ASHVE).

James E. Hill, 1996–97 ASHRAE President, saw the good works of ASHRAE reflected in the words of Abraham Lincoln. Hill often quoted a Lincoln speech given at Cooper Union in New York City before the future U.S. president had secured the nomination of his party. "Let us have the faith that right makes might and in that faith let us always strive to do our duty as I understand it," Lincoln said. Hill used that phrase to describe ASHRAE. He noted that within a year of ASHRAE's founding the Society formed a committee to develop a standard of innovation for New York City schools.

The engineers of that long-ago time showed remarkable resolve and foresight. Those who followed, to paraphrase 1994–95 ASHRAE President Billy R. Manning, have "Built on the Shoulders of Giants." Their work continues. This record of accomplishment, as chronicled in the pages which follow, has improved immeasurably the quality of life.

There are several notes that will prove valuable to readers as they ponder the beginnings and growth of ASHRAE:

Both ASHVE and ASRE had their first annual meetings at the American Society of Mechanical Engineering offices. ASHVE refers to the meeting room as the "chamber" and ASRE refers to the meeting room as the "hall." It is one and the same as near as we can figure.

Neither organization used an acronym for its name until sometime after its founding. Actually, the use of acronyms in place of organizational names had not yet been invented. At its birth, ASHVE was referred to as "this society" in its Transactions, while ASRE was called "the Society." By the 1930s, the terms A.S.H.V.E. and A.S.R.E. had begun to appear with greater frequency in the literature. In the 1940s, use of periods fell out of general favor. In some eras, the "The" preceding "American" was considered a formal part of the name by both organizations. Usually, but not always, members of both organizations capitalized the "S" when writing of the "Society." Most often in this book, references were used in each chapter that were appropriate for the time to which they refer. But in some cases, ease of reading required use of acronyms. No doubt, the casual reader will consider this use of capitalization and acronyms inconsistent and in error. Hopefully, the choices illustrate the variety of styles used.

The ASHVE research laboratory was called the Research Bureau, perhaps because it was first located at the U.S. Bureau of Mines. The committee charged with monitoring research was called the Committee on Research Bureau. Later, the committee became known as the Committee on Research.

The dedication "To the Thermal Engineer" that appeared in the first edition of this book is taken from an address delivered by Willis H. Carrier in 1928. Carrier's description of a "thermal engineer" is appropriate today, and all who contributed to this book—first or second edition—share his respect for the profession.

Enjoy your trip through time. If along the way you find errors or omissions, let ASHRAE know. While the research was painstaking and exhaustive, some readers no doubt will recall a different memory or will be able to provide an undiscovered fact. But you have the historian's assurance that any communicated correction will be stored safely away for those who will prepare ASHRAE's 150th anniversary publication in 2044. Errors and significant omissions will also be posted on the Internet—for however long there is an ASHRAE home page and an Internet.

Disclaimer for the ASHRAE Story

ASHRAE has accomplished much more than the number of pages allotted for this publication allows. ASHRAE's story has been written by the hundreds of thousands of volunteers who over the course of the past 125 years have served on committees, participated in chapters, and used ASHRAE published literature in their work and studies. They are the authors of the ASHRAE story. That story continues to be written today, literally 24/7 as ASHRAE membership and influence expands globally.

Consider this historical work a collection of stories driven by vision, connected by threads created by the needs of humankind, and woven by ASHRAE volunteers who dedicate their work to improve the quality of life.

Most of the words in *Proclaiming the Truth*, especially those in the second edition, which adds chronicles of ASHRAE from 1995 through 2020, are words that were spoken at the time. There were more voices than could be accommodated, more needs than could be recorded, and most importantly, more solutions than could be cited.

W. Stephen Comstock

ASHVE

Chapter 1

A Long, Strong Pull Together

"I now charge you, as you love the cause in which you have so recently launched your bark, to look well to your applications for membership, as the growth and perpetuity of this society rests upon this fully as much as on any other proposition."

Edward P. Bates
1894

In the late nineteenth century, the science of heating and ventilation was not well understood. When installing heating and ventilating systems, most contractors based their calculations solely and unquestionably on data in fan manufacturers' catalogues. Only a few contractors were educated and had formal training in engineering.

Perhaps the best summary of the late 1890s was written by Stewart A. Jellett, a charter member and the second president of The American Society of Heating and Ventilating Engineers. He explains:

"Until about 1890 the business of heating and ventilating had been largely based on the most ancient rule known to engineers, the rule of thumb...I believe it was the stress of competition, the commercial side of the business, that finally forced the recognition of the necessity for more scientific consideration, both in regard to the manufacture of the apparatus and in its application for regular work.

"Between the so-called 'Heating and Ventilating Engineer,' who did not understand his business, and the heating and ventilating engineer who was 75 per cent. fakir [sic], the public was getting but a poor return for its money. There was general ignorance on the subject of heating and ventilation, and there were any number of contractors who had patented schemes, designed to give all the heat desired at practically no expense for fuel; in fact, after reading some of the descriptive matter, one felt that a coal bin had ceased to be a necessary adjunct to any building.

"The results of the efforts of contractors and engineers of this class was that the installation of steam and hot water heating apparatus was so generally unsatisfactory that the outlook for business was not favorable."

Matters of Business vs. Engineering

In 1889 the Master Steam and Hot Water Fitters Association was formed to protect the interests of the contractors. Also at this time, more sophisticated scientific approaches to heating and ventilation were being imported from Europe and, in particular, England.

In response to the wishes of members who were interested in learning more about these scientific approaches, a few technical papers were presented at the Association's meetings. But the majority of members were business and sales men, and they were not particularly interested in the arts and sciences of heating and ventilation. In fact, according to Mr. Jellett, they felt that "the conventions were principally for the discussion of business matters, and but scant courtesy was given to the reading of these papers, and practically no discussion followed." This conflict led to the organization of The American Society of Heating and Ventilating Engineers.

NATIONAL ASSOCIATION OF MASTER STEAM AND HOT WATER FITTERS

During the Association's 1894 National Convention, three technical papers were scheduled to be presented by David M. Nesbit, of London, England; Edward P. Bates, of Syracuse, New York; and Arthur Walworth, of Boston, Massachusetts. The reception of these papers "very much disgusted" the members who were at the Convention to hear and discuss them, and inspired one member, Hugh J. Barron, to write a critical article, which appeared in the July 15, 1894 issue of *Heating and Ventilation*:

David M. Nesbit
The tepid response of the Master Fitters convention in 1894 to a paper delivered by English heating engineer David Nesbit was one of the factors that led to the formation of an engineering society in the field.

"There was one thing conclusively shown by this Convention, and that was that engineers are in a decided minority; the majority are more anxious about getting work and money than about the mere art of heating. Imagine any other society in the world inviting men to give them the results of their thoughts, and one gentleman actually coming three thousand miles to do so, and having a resolution passed that, in the future, papers must only take ten minutes to read.

"The facts are that the majority of American heating and ventilating engineers are not members of the Master Steam and Hot Water Fitters' Association, and that a majority of the Association are really businessmen only…It is a pity that there were not at least a thousand present to hear Mr. Nesbit's paper, and to intelligently discuss it, as English societies of engineers would discuss a paper presented to them by an American engineer of equal eminence."

Hugh J. Barron

Mr. Barron's article was submitted to Louis H. Hart, business manager of Heating and Ventilation. During a meeting with Mr. Barron to discuss its publication, Mr. Hart talked with him about forming a society to give consideration to engineering matters connected with heating and ventilation only. Following this meeting, Mr. Hart spoke with and inspired William M. Mackay. Mr. Hart then took it upon himself to ask the opinions of fifty to seventy-five engineers known to be much interested in their chosen line of work, as to the advisability of forming such an organization. He received many favorable replies.

William MacKay

Louis Hart

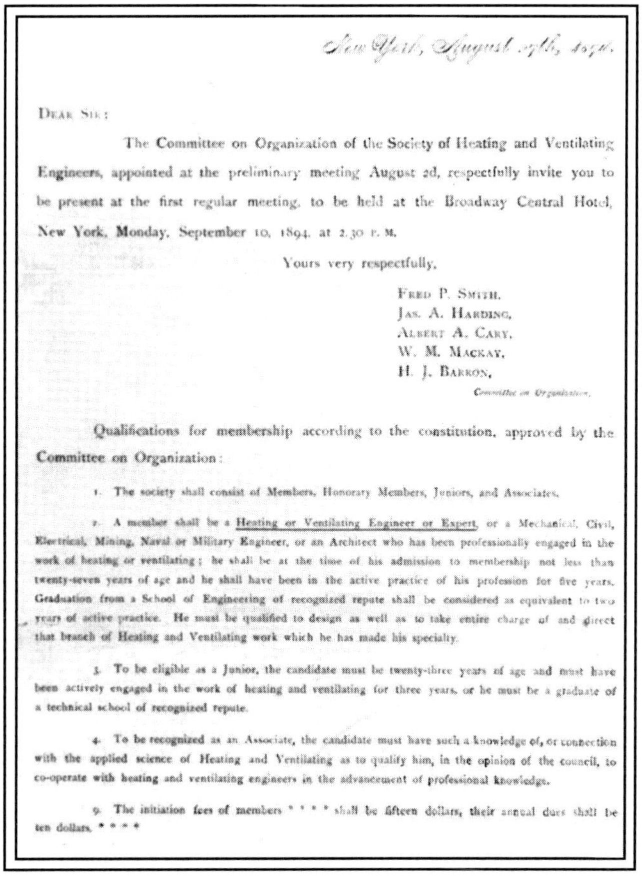

New York, August 27th, 1894.

Dear Sir:

The Committee on Organization of the Society of Heating and Ventilating Engineers, appointed at the preliminary meeting August 2d, respectfully invite you to be present at the first regular meeting, to be held at the Broadway Central Hotel, New York, Monday, September 10, 1894, at 2.30 P. M.

Yours very respectfully,

Fred P. Smith,
Jas. A. Harding,
Albert A. Cary,
W. M. Mackay,
H. J. Barron,
Committee on Organization.

Qualifications for membership according to the constitution, approved by the Committee on Organization:

1. The society shall consist of Members, Honorary Members, Juniors, and Associates.

2. A member shall be a Heating or Ventilating Engineer or Expert, or a Mechanical, Civil, Electrical, Mining, Naval or Military Engineer, or an Architect who has been professionally engaged in the work of heating or ventilating; he shall be at the time of his admission to membership not less than twenty-seven years of age and he shall have been in the active practice of his profession for five years. Graduation from a School of Engineering of recognized repute shall be considered as equivalent to two years of active practice. He must be qualified to design as well as to take entire charge of and direct that branch of Heating and Ventilating work which he has made his specialty.

3. To be eligible as a Junior, the candidate must be twenty-three years of age and must have been actively engaged in the work of heating and ventilating for three years, or he must be a graduate of a technical school of recognized repute.

4. To be recognized as an Associate, the candidate must have such a knowledge of, or connection with the applied science of Heating and Ventilating as to qualify him, in the opinion of the council, to co-operate with heating and ventilating engineers in the advancement of professional knowledge.

9. The initiation fees of members * * * * shall be fifteen dollars, their annual dues shall be ten dollars. * * * *

Invitation sent to prospective charter members of the new society. The first regular meeting was held on September 10, 1894 in New York City.

Organizational Meetings

As a result, about 25 invitations were sent to engineers in New York City to attend a meeting at the offices of *Heating and Ventilation* on Thursday, August 2, 1894. Sixteen attended: A.A. Cary, James A. Harding, George B. Cobb, Hugh J. Barron, H.M. Swetland, William M. Mackay, W.A. Russell, W.B. Wilkinson, Thomas Barwick, F.R. Smith, Albert A. Cryer, Edward A. Munro, Percival H. Seward, O.C. Breckenridge, Morris S. King, and Louis H. Hart. They became known as the Committee of Sixteen.

Fred P. Smith was elected temporary chairman to run the meeting, and Mr. Hart was elected temporary secretary. After discussing the best way to form the society, Mr. Barron moved that a Committee on Organization be selected. Appointed to serve on the Committee on Organization were Messrs. Smith, Barron, Harding, Mackay and Cary. All those present, by motion of Mr. Cary, were made charter members. The meeting was then adjourned to September 10, 1894.

During the next six weeks, the Committee on Organization met five times. Invitations to become a charter member were sent to 157 engineers, and circulars explaining the necessary qualifications were sent out with the invitations. The Committee also worked on drafting a constitution and by-laws.

The first regular meeting, which was purely a business meeting, was called to order at 3:00 P.M. on September 10, 1894 at the Broadway Central Hotel, New York, New York; seventy-five persons accepted the invitation and became charter members. Mr. Smith chaired the meeting, and Mr. Hart was secretary.

In his opening remarks, Mr. Smith defined the objects, advantages and policy of this proposed society. He spoke at length about the importance of good fellowship to the society's success, especially with respect to discontinuing the practice of discrediting another engineer's work when presenting a competitive bid.

"It is only through the united efforts of the members of the society that we may expect to attain that improvement for which we are looking," said Mr. Smith. "There is no reason in the world why the society cannot, if properly managed, aid us in raising a high standard of work, and regulate the price we ought to get for our work. What we want is a long, strong pull together, and that is exactly what I meant when I spoke of good fellowship."

The first order of business was to choose a name for this new society. Mr. Jellett recalls the debate:

"The Committee on Constitution and By-Laws suggested 'The Society of Heating and Ventilating Engineers' as a title for the new society. The debate that followed this suggestion was a spirited one. One member objected to the proposed name and wanted a more definite title, while another thought the name was all right; that other societies might be founded, but they would not count for much, and that the word 'THE' in large letters expressed his ideas of what the society was bound to become. Still another member, our Secretary, Mr. Mackay, suggested that the society be called 'The International Society of Heating and Ventilating Engineers,' inasmuch as foreign engineers had been invited to become members. Mr. Mackay's idea seemed to be to take in the entire world and prevent infringements, on the general idea expressed by the first members, that we were 'The' society with a capital T.

"After a long discussion...the members reached the conclusion that the heating and ventilating engineering required in America would be a sufficient tax on the society for some years to come, and when Mr. Harding, and Mr. Barron seconded, the motion that the society be called 'The American Society of Heating and Ventilating Engineers,' the motion prevailed."

They next read and discussed the proposed Constitution and By-Laws section by section. This discussion was also spirited, and after a number of revisions, it was adopted. Section 4 in Article 1 of the Constitution clearly stated eight objects of the Society that would guide its work in years to come:

- The promotion of the arts and sciences connected with heating and ventilation, and to encourage good fellowship among its members.
- Improvement in the mechanical construction of the various apparatus used for heating and ventilation.
- The maintenance of a high professional standard among heating and ventilating engineers.
- To establish a clearly defined minimum standard of heating and ventilation for all classes of buildings.
- To favor legislation compelling the ventilation of all public buildings in accordance with the standard of this society.

STEWART A. JELLETT.
1895 - 1896.
EDWARD P. BATES.
1894 - 1895.
ROLLA C. CARPENTER.
1896 - 1897.
WILTSIE F. WOLFE.
1898 - 1899
WILLIAM M. MACKAY.
1897 - 1898.
HENRY ADAMS.
1899 - 1900.
JOHN H. KINEALY.
1901 - 1902.
DAVID M. QUAY.
1900 - 1901.
ALFRED E. KENRICK.
1902 - 1903.
PRESIDENTS of the AMERICAN SOCIETY of HEATING and VENTILATING ENGINEERS.
HARRY D. CRANE.
1903 - 1904.

- To encourage legislation favorable to improvement in the arts of heating and ventilation, and to oppose legislation inimical to the business of the engineer.
- The reading, discussion, and publication of professional papers, and the interchange of knowledge and experience among its members.

To establish a uniform scale of prices for all professional services.

The final order of business was to elect officers to serve until the annual meeting. The Constitution and By-Laws stated that the affairs of the Society would be managed by a Board of Managers and a Council that would review membership applications. Those elected were:

President	E.P. Bates
First Vice President	W.M. Mackay
Second Vice President	W.F. Wolfe
Third Vice President	C.S. Onderdon
Secretary	L.H. Hart
Board of Managers	P. Smith, H.J. Barron, A.A. Cary, J.A. Harding, and Henry Adams
Council	Charles W. Newton; R.C. Carpenter; A.A. Cryer; F.W. Foster; V.G. Halley; E.P. Bates, president; and L.H. Hart, secretary.

First Annual Meeting

The Society was incorporated in the state of New York on January 24, 1895. To comply with the laws of this state, the date of the annual meeting was specified in the Constitution as the last week in January. Accordingly, the charter members agreed to have their first annual meeting in January 1895, at which time papers on heating and ventilation topics would be read and discussed. The Constitution also specified that the Society would have a Semi-Annual meeting as well, though the first one would not occur until 1897.

The dates of January 22-24, 1895 were confirmed for the first Annual Meeting, and President Bates called the meeting to order at 10:50 A.M. on January 22, 1895 in the hall of the American Society of Mechanical Engineers (ASME), 12 West 31st Street, New York.

In his opening address, President Bates commented on the potential and the importance of the

CHARTER MEMBERS OF THE SOCIETY

Henry Adams, Washington, D. C.	C. F. Gessert, New York, N. Y.	Charles W. Newton, Baltimore, Md.
Homer Addams, Washington, D. C.	Judson A. Goodrich, New York, N. Y.	Theodore C. Northcott, Elmira, N. Y.
Newell P. Andrus, Brooklyn, N. Y.	John Gormly, Philadelphia, Pa.	Charles S. Onderdonk, Philadelphia, Pa.
Hugh J. Barron, New York, N. Y.	James A. Harding, New York, N. Y.	John A. Payne, Providence, R. I.
Thomas Barwick, New York, N. Y.	L. H. Hart, New York, N. Y.	John H. Petherick, Chattanooga, Tenn.
Edward P. Bates, Syracuse, N. Y.	Charles F. Hauss, New York, N. Y.	Geo. W. Plastow, Jersey City, N. J.
Geo. C. Blackmore, Pittsburgh, Pa.	Jno. D. Hibbard, Chicago, Ill.	Henry B. Prather, Buffalo, N. Y.
J. J. Blackmore, New York, N. Y.	William H. Hill, New York, N. Y.	Leon H. Prentice, Chicago, Ill.
L. R. Blackmore, New York, N. Y.	Geo. D. Hoffman, Chicago, Ill.	D. M. Quay, Chicago, Ill.
Samuel Burns, New York, N. Y.	Charles S. Hopkins, Rochester, N. Y.	Wm. A. Russell, New York, N. Y.
B. Harold Carpenter, Wilkes Barre, Pa.	Alfred A. Hunting, Boston, Mass.	U. G. Scollay, Brooklyn, N. Y.
R. C. Carpenter, Ithaca, N. Y.	Stewart A. Jellett, Philadelphia, Pa.	Percival H. Seward, New York, N. Y.
Albert A. Cary, New York, N. Y.	J. H. Kinealy, St. Louis, Mo.	Le Roy B. Sherman, New York, N. Y.
Robert C. Clarkson, Philadelphia, Pa.	Jos. A. Langdon, Pittsburgh, Pa.	Fred P. Smith, New York, N. Y.
Geo. B. Cobb, New York, N. Y.	Chas. W. Light, Saginaw, Mich.	B. F. Stangland, New York, N. Y.
H. D. Crane, Cincinnati, Ohio	H. E. Light, Saginaw, Mich.	Geo. P. Steel, Philadelphia, Pa.
Albert A. Cryer, New York, N. Y.	Chas. C. Lincoln, New York, N. Y.	Joseph M. Stoughton, Yonkers, N. Y.
T. B. Cryer, Newark, N. J.	C. K. Longenecker, New York, N. Y.	H. M. Swetland, New York, N. Y.
Mark Dean, Boston, Mass.	James Mackay, Chicago, Ill.	Geo. H. Underhill, Boston, Mass.
John Demarest, Boston, Mass.	Wm. M. Mackay, New York, N. Y.	T. J. Waters, Chicago, Ill.
Thos. J. Douglass, Norwich, Conn.	A. S. Mappett, New York, N. Y.	J. R. Wendover, New York, N. Y.
A. C. Edgar, Philadelphia, Pa.	Wm. McMannis, New York, N. Y.	W. B. Wilkinson, New York, N. Y.
Hermann Eisert, Baltimore, Md.	George L. Mehring, Chicago, Ill.	James R. Willett, Chicago, Ill.
John A. Fish, Boston, Mass.	Edward A. Munro, Brooklyn, N. Y.	J. J. Wilson, Troy, N. Y.
Frank W. Foster, Boston, Mass.	Robert Munro, Pittsburgh, Pa.	Wiltsie F. Wolfe, Boston, Mass.

The roll call of the first Society meeting showed that seventy-five persons had become charter members.

Society's work, "The purposes for which this society was formed are commendable in every respect. If we carry out the wise provisions named in the preamble to our Constitution and By-laws, we shall be public benefactors...Our work, however, will not stop with any class; it will benefit all classes, and the amount of benefit received will be commensurate with the labor expended."

He also spoke about maintaining a high standard of members, "We need to gather about us men devoted to the work; men of character and reasonably ambitious of success; men who will think, study, and work until they see the fruition of their hopes. We need also, in this infantile state, to avoid adding to our number any who are not really engineers in our acceptation of the word."

In conclusion, President Bates said, "In order to carry out the objects of the Society, we shall need, first, the hearty cooperation of all its members; we shall need, further, a practical, intelligent devotion to the purpose for which we are organized. With these points carefully covered by each member, there is a work before us, which never has been thoroughly done, but will be accomplished by the members of this Society, to the credit and the good of the race."

Eight papers were presented during the three-day meeting, along with a series of topical discussions. Among them was a learned exchange about the future of electric heat, about which those attending concluded was too expensive even for trolley cars. The members also talked about wooden air conduits, but the discussion was cut short when they learned that galvanized iron had generally replaced wood. As a result of comments made by Mr. Jellett, a lengthy debate ensued over whether steam heating contractors and engineers should get paid for preparing plans and specifications for architects. This debate was the start of an argument about conflict of interest that would rage on for many years.

Secretary Hart reported that the Society had seventy-five members, and in the absence of Treasurer J. A. Goodrich, he reported that since its founding, the Society had received $750.00 and had expended $256.82 for a total of $493.18 cash on hand. President Bates then reported that after December 1, 1894, the Society's business offices would be located at ASME headquarters, 12 West 31st Street, New York City.

Year	Receipts	Expenses	Number of Members	Income per Member	Expense per Member
1894	$ 750.00	$ 256.82			
1895	1,112.28	992.36	88	$12.64	$11.28
1896	845.65	1,042.63	109	7.76	9.57
1897	1,109.25	958.18	129	8.60	9.43
1898	1,878.72	1,900.77	153	12.28	12.42
1899	1,408.09	1,680.38	121	11.64	13.89
1900	1,327.07	1,274.15	126	10.53	10.11
1901	1,619.84	1,625.24	137	11.82	11.86
1902	2,460.34	2,086.88	158	15.57	13.20
1903	2,423.93	2,334.13	198	12.24	11.70
1904	2,414.99	2,274.20	211	11.45	10.78
1905	2,542.75	2,593.00	231	11.01	11.23
1906	3,710.62	2,549.66	261	14.22	9.76
1907	3,912.41	3,662.45	301	12.99	12.20
1908	3,928.93	4,025.84	335	11.73	12.00
1909	3,952.14	4,687.41	357	11.07	13.13
1910	4,324.10	4,269.83	377	11.47	11.36
1911	4,953.54	4,823.08	405	12.23	11.83
1912	4,717.40	5,073.19	437	10.79	11.47
1913	5,272.02	4,532.06	455	11.59	10.81
1914	6,362.49	6,487.66	485	13.12	11.52
1915	9,256.05	9,071.33	571	16.21	10.59
1916	9,512.79	8,136.97	683	13.93	12.21
1917	11,809.47	11,098.28	784	15.06	14.01
1918	11,231.35	11,881.01	839	13.39	14.16
1919	18,127.40	17,847.42	993	18.26	17.97
1920	26,234.82	28,738.68	1,192	22.01	24.11
1921	34,555.64	30,984.97	1,388	24.90	22.32

This chart summarizes the growth of the American Society of Heating and Ventilating Engineers from financial and membership perspectives for the years 1894 to 1921.

The members then elected officers, Board of Managers and Council for 1895-96:

President	Stewart A. Jellett
First Vice President	William M. Mackay
Second Vice President	C.S. Onderdonk
Secretary	Louis H. Hart
Treasurer	Judson A. Goodrich
Board of Managers	James A. Harding, chairman; B.F. Stangland, Geoffrey B. Cobb, U.G. Scollay, William McMannis, Stewart A. Jellett, president; and Louis H. Hart, secretary.

"I will say that…it is especially important, therefore, that each member should be encouraged to put his knowledge where it may be used by all the others and the most important work of the society in my opinion is this collecting of individual knowledge and putting it on record for use of all." (From *Heating and Ventilation,* October 15 and November 15, 1894.)

Charter Member John Kinealy, professor, Washington University, St. Louis, Missouri

"Another point of advantage to our society would be to have a neat card, with the name and address of our society and each member's name and address, sent to the offices of the architects of the United States, and sent yearly as their membership changes by death, withdrawn or election. For our own office, we should have a neat certificate of membership, framed and hung conspicuously, to let the work know 'we are it' for business and pleasure and proud of it." (From *Heating and Ventilation,* October 15 and November 15, 1894.)

Charter Member John Gormly of Philadelphia

"… members will have the opportunity of forming acquaintances, exchanging theories and experiences, and through these associations promulgate a feeling of perfect freedom in consulting one another when in doubt on a subject…." (From *Heating and Ventilation,* October 15 and November 15, 1894.)

Charter Member Harrie Crane of Cincinnati, Ohio

"I would suggest that the object of such a society should be as far as possible, to embrace all sections of this continent, and it should not be in any sense what might be termed a local organization." (From *Healing and Ventilation,* October 15 and November 15, 1894.)

Charter Member James Mackay, American Boiler Co., Chigago, Illinois

Membership

The Constitution and By-Laws established four levels of membership: Members, Honorary Members, Associates and Junior. Members and Associates were required to pay an initiation fee of $15.00 and annual dues of $10.00. The initiation fee of Junior members was $10.00 and their dues were $10.00. A Junior member, being promoted to full membership, paid a further initiation fee of $5.00. Honorary Members were defined as "distinguished persons elected by the society." Within two years, membership rose from 75 to 109 members.

In his short history of the Society, published in 1904, Mr. Jellett pointed out that the membership roles listed quite a few more names than those counted as active members. This is in part due to deaths and in part due to some joining for commercial reasons.

As Mr. Jellett said, "It did not take a very great length of time to disabuse their minds of this idea and to clearly impress upon them the fact that the commercial side of the business of heating and ventilation was to be left to the Master Steam Fitters' Association. This fact accounts for the disappearance during the first three or four years of a large number of names from the list of members."

Issues of the Day

The work of the Society began during the First Annual Meeting. President Bates called the members to action in his address by clearly defining the Society's priorities:

"I believe we should not cease our labors when public buildings are thoroughly warmed and ventilated, but our zeal for a good cause should eventually take us into every building which shall be constructed for any purpose...There are cases where factories and work shops are fairly well ventilated, but in comparison they are rare...Every family has the right to have an abundance of good fresh air, even if it is not aware of its rights."

The members responded to his inspiring words and to the lively discussions during the meeting by appointing various committees:

- The Committee on Tests "for the purpose of making such tests as may be for the interest of the society"
- Committee on Standards "to establish a clearly defined minimum standard of heating and ventilation for all classes of buildings"
- Committee on Compulsory Legislation "to favor legislation compelling ventilation of all public buildings in accordance with the standards of this society"
- Committee on Uniform Contract and General Conditions of Governing Specifications "to establish a uniform scale of prices for all professional services"
- Committee on Compulsory Legislation "to favor legislation compelling ventilation of all public buildings in accordance with the standards of this society"
- Committee on Uniform Contract and General Conditions of Governing Specifications "to establish a uniform scale of prices for all professional services"
- Nominating Committee for the purpose of identifying and nominating candidates for officers, Board of Managers and Council

Each year, beginning in 1895, the Society documented its work by publishing the proceedings, papers and discussions from the annual and semiannual meetings in *Transactions of The American Society of Heating and Ventilating Engineers.*

President Bates said of this new society and the work to be done, "We need to look backward but a very few years to find that our profession was unknown. The rapid strides of modem civilization have created many new professions, and ours among them. There is a wide field open before us, and it yet remains to be seen how well we shall occupy it. The child is born, and it gives great promise of a grand future."

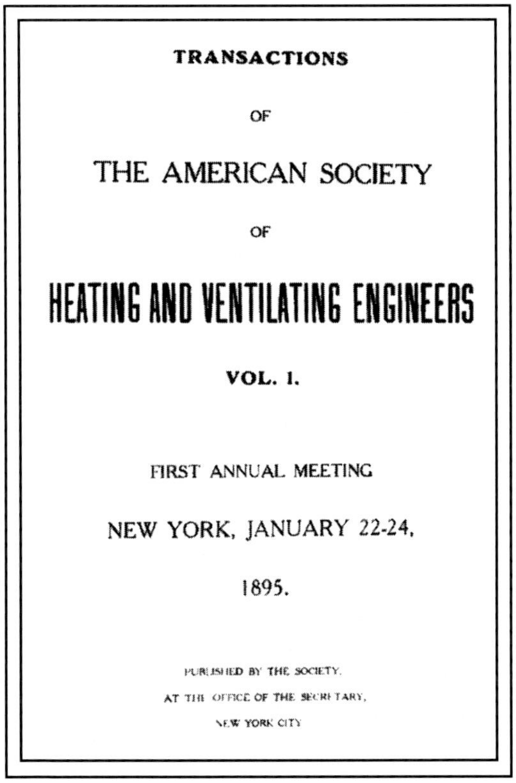

TRANSACTIONS

OF

THE AMERICAN SOCIETY

OF

HEATING AND VENTILATING ENGINEERS

VOL. I.

FIRST ANNUAL MEETING

NEW YORK, JANUARY 22-24,

1895.

PUBLISHED BY THE SOCIETY,
AT THE OFFICE OF THE SECRETARY,
NEW YORK CITY

Transactions of the first Annual Meeting

Annual Meeting, 1906

The Twelfth Annual Meeting took place in New York at the rooms of the American Society of Mechanical Engineers.

Annual Meeting, 1908

The Annual Dinner at the 1908 meeting was held at the New Grand Hotel, New York. After the cigars were lighted, the retiring president, C.B.J. Snyder, acting as toastmaster, introduced Professor William Kent as the first speaker of the evening, who responded to the toast "Training the Engineer." Other speakers and the toasts included: Gilbert Evans, managing editor of the Brooklyn *Eagle* who responded to "The Problems of Life That Are Unsolved;" C.V. Kellogg to "Our Associates, the Manufacturers;" Andrew Harvey to "The Ladies;" James Mackay to "Summer Meetings;" and John F. Hale to "The Chapter."

Semi-Annual Meeting, 1917

The convening of semi-annual meetings was a provision of the Society's Bylaws when they were written in 1894, but the first summer meeting was not held until 1897, when the Society met in New York. Cities such as Chicago, Detroit and Buffalo soon became favored summer meeting sites in that they afforded members from the west greater opportunity for attendance. The Semi-Annual Meeting of 1917 was held in Chicago, where the Chicago Yacht Club was the scene of the meeting dinner. The Semi-Annual Meeting of 1906 also in Chicago was the first semi-annual meeting to which ladies were invited to meeting functions.

Annual Meeting, 1919

The 25th Annual Meeting of the American Society of Heating and Ventilating Engineers was held in New York, New York in the United Engineering Societies Building on January 22-24, 1919. The annual banquet was held at the Hotel McAlpin. It was perhaps the most notable meeting in the history of the Society, as it was not only the Society's Silver Anniversary, but it also marked two epochs of great importance, namely the passing of the 1,000 mark in membership and the announcement of the establishment of the proposed Research Bureau.

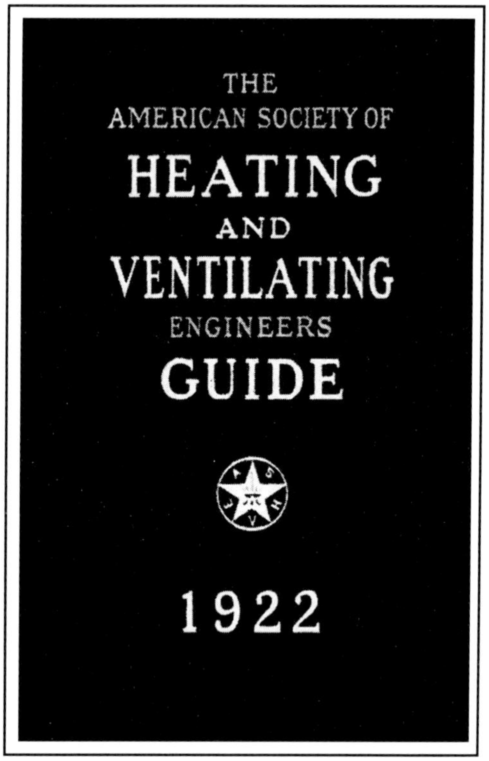

The American Society of Heating and Ventilating Engineers Guide was introduced in 1922.

The Synthetic Air Chart was developed by Dr. E. Vernon Hill and adopted by The American Society of Heating and Ventilating Engineers for the purpose of comparing the air conditions in any room with the ideal or standard conditions. The 1922 issue of *The Guide* presented the chart along with a description of its method of application, which was worked out by the Society's Research Bureau. The Bureau stated that the Synthetic Air Chart offers a means of determining the percentage of perfect ventilation by considering all the known factors that make up the air conditions in a room.

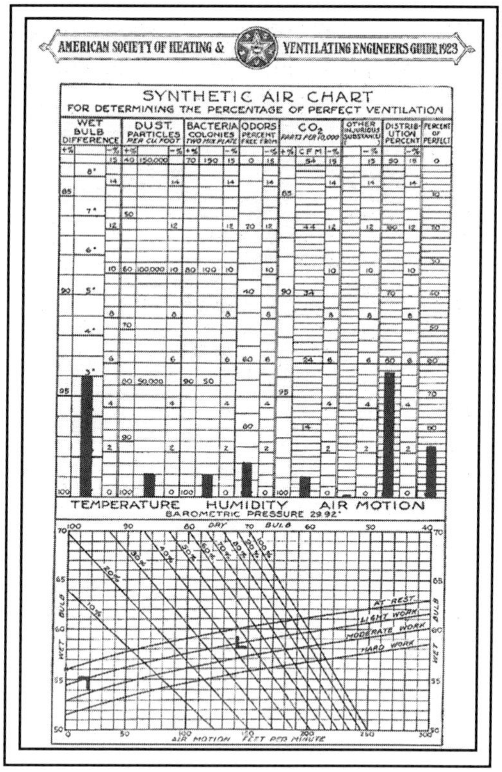

ASHVE's **F. Paul Anderson Award** was first presented in 1932 to Dr. Willis H. Carrier. The award was named for F. Paul Anderson, ASHVE president in 1927 and an ASHVE laboratory director from 1921 to 1925. As stated in an article documenting the presentation, the award "was given by the American Society of Heating and Ventilating Engineers in recognition of work done and meritorious services performed in the field of heating, ventilation or air conditioning."

"Attention is called to your privilege as a member of wearing the Society's emblem." (1925)

Past Presidents Dinner, 1944

From left o right around table: John Howatt, F.B Rowley, II.M. Hart, G.L. Larson, W.T. Jones, Thornton Lewis, H.P. Gant, W.H. Carrier, W.H. Driscoll, C.V. Haynes, E. Holt Gurney, J.F. McIntire, W. L. Fleisher, E.O. Eastwood, S.E. Dibble, F. EE. Giesecke.

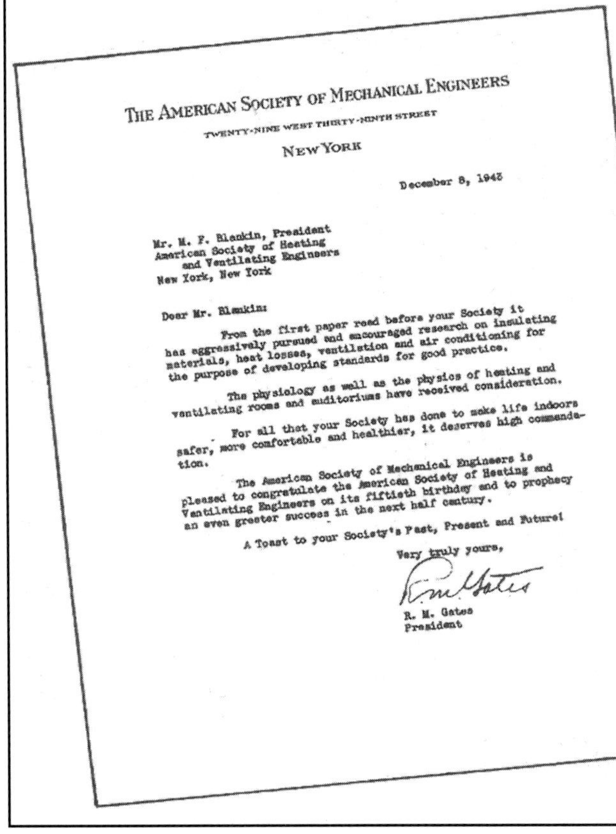

THE AMERICAN SOCIETY OF MECHANICAL ENGINEERS
TWENTY-NINE WEST THIRTY-NINTH STREET
NEW YORK

December 8, 1943

Mr. M. F. Blankin, President
American Society of Heating
and Ventilating Engineers
New York, New York

Dear Mr. Blankin:

From the first paper read before your Society it has aggressively pursued and encouraged research on insulating materials, heat losses, ventilation and air conditioning for the purpose of developing standards for good practice.

The physiology as well as the physics of heating and ventilating rooms and auditoriums have received consideration.

For all that your Society has done to make life indoors safer, more comfortable and healthier, it deserves high commendation.

The American Society of Mechanical Engineers is pleased to congratulate the American Society of Heating and Ventilating Engineers on its fiftieth birthday and to prophecy an even greater success in the next half century.

A Toast to your Society's Past, Present and Future!

Very truly yours,

R. M. Gates
President

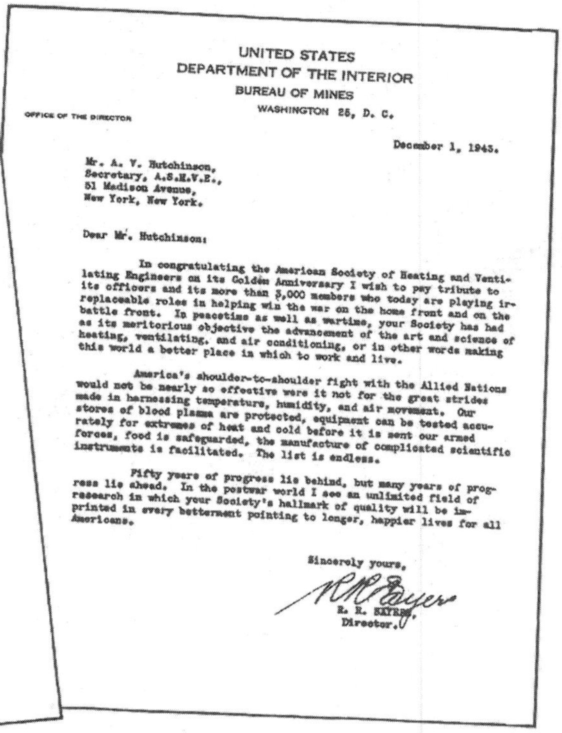

UNITED STATES
DEPARTMENT OF THE INTERIOR
BUREAU OF MINES
WASHINGTON 25, D. C.

OFFICE OF THE DIRECTOR

December 1, 1943.

Mr. A. V. Hutchinson,
Secretary, A.S.H.V.E.,
51 Madison Avenue,
New York, New York.

Dear Mr. Hutchinson:

In congratulating the American Society of Heating and Venti-
lating Engineers on its Golden Anniversary I wish to pay tribute to
its officers and its more than 3,000 members who today are playing ir-
replaceable roles in helping win the war on the home front and on the
battle front. In peacetime as well as wartime, your Society has had
as its meritorious objective the advancement of the art and science of
heating, ventilating, and air conditioning, or in other words making
this world a better place in which to work and live.

America's shoulder-to-shoulder fight with the Allied Nations
would not be nearly so effective were it not for the great strides
made in harnessing temperature, humidity, and air movement. Our
stores of blood plasma are protected, equipment can be tested accu-
rately for extremes of heat and cold before it is sent our armed
forces, food is safeguarded, the manufacture of complicated scientific
instruments is facilitated. The list is endless.

Fifty years of progress lie behind, but many years of prog-
ress lie ahead. In the postwar world I see an unlimited field of
research in which your Society's hallmark of quality will be im-
printed in every betterment pointing to longer, happier lives for all
Americans.

Sincerely yours,

R. R. SAYERS,
Director.

"Greetings for Our Golden Anniversary" were published in the January 1944 *ASHVE Journal.* The Society received greetings from, among others, the American Society of Mechanical Engineers, Kiwanis International, and the United States Department of the Interior, Bureau of Mines.

1894  1944

Alfred J. Offner
General Chairman

Alfred Engle
Chairman
Banquet

A. C. Buensod
Chairman
Special Events

COMMITTEE ON ARRANGEMENTS

Alfred J. Offner, *General Chairman*

Honorary Chairmen—Homer Addams, W. H. Carrier, W. H. Driscoll, W. L. Fleisher, D. D. Kimball.

Vice-Chairmen—R. H. Carpenter, J. C. Fitts, W. E. Heibel, C. S. Koehler, A. E. Stacey, Jr., R. A. Wasson.

Banquet—Alfred Engle, *Chairman;* Russell Donnelly, *Vice-Chairman;* E. E. Ashley, R. W. Cumming, M. C. Giannini, Joseph Wheeler, Jr.

Finance—W. M. Heebner, *Chairman;* H. W. Fiedler, *Vice-Chairman;* R. R. Ferguson, G. E. Olsen.

Hospitality—H. S. Wheller, *Chairman;* W. J. Olvany, *Vice-Chairman;* T. N. Adlam, F. E. W. Beebe, H. H. Bond, Ernst Graber, E. B. Johnson, C. A. Miller, L. L. Munier, J. R. Murphy.

Inspection—C. S. Pabst, *Chairman;* P. B. Gordon, *Vice-Chairman;* H. L. Alt, J. A. Heller, M. H. Hirsch, F. D. Lawrence, Rudolph Pollak.

Ladies—Mr. and Mrs. H. J. Ryan, *Co-Chairmen;* H. S. Johnson, Mrs. R. H. Carpenter, Mrs. H. W. Fiedler, Mrs. W. L. Fleisher, Mrs. O. E. Frank, Mrs. A. V. Hutchinson, Mrs. C. S. Koehler, Mrs. G. E. Olsen, Mrs. R. A. Wasson.

N. Y. Chapter Special Committee—C. F. Roth, *Chairman;* J. G. Eadie, J. C. Fitts, C. S. Hoffman, H. C. Meyer, Jr., G. M. Scott.

Publicity—R. V. Sawhill, *Chairman;* Clifford Strock, *Vice-Chairman;* A. A. Bearman, C. H. B. Hotchkiss, O. O. Oaks, W. J. Osborn.

Sessions—E. J. Ritchie, *Chairman;* C. H. Flink, *Vice-Chairman;* E. E. Adams, S. R. Apt, Thomas Baker, P. G. Griess, G. D. Guler, C. R. Hiers, H. P. Waechter.

Special Events—A. C. Buensod, *Chairman;* A. F. Hinrichsen, *Vice-Chairman;* V. J. Cucci, C. A. Fuller, F. D. McCann, M. F. Rather, H. J. Rose, W. A. Sherbrooke.

W. M. Heebner
Chairman
Finance

C. F. Roth
Chairman
N. Y. Chapter Special Committee

H. S. Wheller
Chairman
Hospitality

R. V. Sawhill
Chairman
Publicity

A GREAT PAST A GREATER FUTURE

C. S. Pabst
Chairman
Inspection

Mrs. H. J. Ryan

H. J. Ryan

Co-Chairmen
Ladies' Committee

E. J. Ritchie
Chairman
Sessions

Program and Committee on Arrangements for the fiftieth Annual Meeting of The American Society of Heating and Ventilating Engineers was held at the Hotel Pennsylvania in New York, New York on January 30 - February 2, 1944. This meeting established a registration record, with a total registration of 920, of which 540 were Society members, 258 guests, and 122 ladies. Of the Society's twenty-three living past presidents, nineteen attended.

"It is my pleasure through the courtesy of the Westinghouse Electric and Mfg. Co., to be permitted to briefly speak for a great industry, which contributed so much to our comfort, health and happiness," began ASHVE President L.A. Harding in a 1930 radio broadcast to 31 cites.

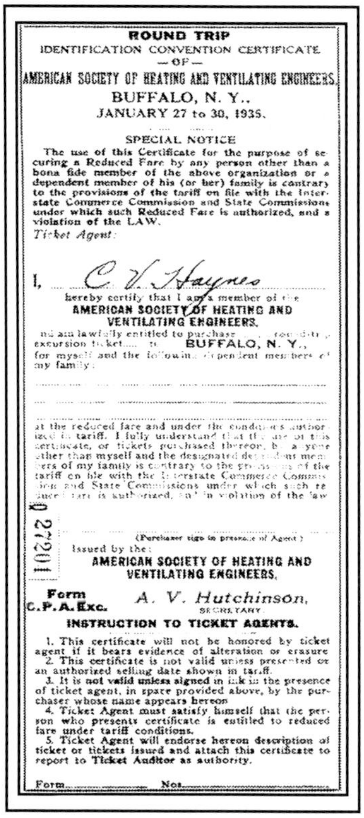

ROUND TRIP
IDENTIFICATION CONVENTION CERTIFICATE
—OF—
AMERICAN SOCIETY OF HEATING AND VENTILATING ENGINEERS,
BUFFALO, N. Y.,
JANUARY 27 to 30, 1935.

SPECIAL NOTICE
The use of this Certificate for the purpose of securing a Reduced Fare by any person other than a bona fide member of the above organization or a dependent member of his (or her) family is contrary to the provisions of the tariff on file with the Interstate Commerce Commission and State Commissions under which such Reduced Fare is authorized, and a violation of the LAW.
Ticket Agent:

I, C. V. Haynes hereby certify that I am a member of the AMERICAN SOCIETY OF HEATING AND VENTILATING ENGINEERS, and am lawfully entitled to purchase [illegible] excursion ticket [illegible] to BUFFALO, N. Y., for myself and the following dependent members of my family:

at the reduced fare and under the conditions authorized in tariff. I fully understand that the use of this certificate, or tickets purchased thereon, by anyone other than myself and the designated dependent members of my family is contrary to the provisions of the tariff on file with the Interstate Commerce Commission and State Commissions under which such reduced fare is authorized, and in violation of the law.

0 27201

(Purchaser sign in presence of Agent.)

Issued by the:
AMERICAN SOCIETY OF HEATING AND VENTILATING ENGINEERS,

Form C.P.A. Exc.

A. V. Hutchinson,
SECRETARY.

INSTRUCTION TO TICKET AGENTS.

1. This certificate will not be honored by ticket agent if it bears evidence of alteration or erasure.
2. This certificate is not valid unless presented on an authorized selling date shown in tariff.
3. It is not valid unless signed in ink in the presence of ticket agent, in space provided above, by the purchaser whose name appears hereon.
4. Ticket Agent must satisfy himself that the person who presents certificate is entitled to reduced fare under tariff conditions.
5. Ticket Agent will endorse hereon description of ticket or tickets issued and attach this certificate to report to Ticket Auditor as authority.

Form .... Nos. ....

Reduced Rail Fares for Annual Meeting

(1) The rate of one and one-third fares for the round trip is guaranteed to all Society members under the Identification Certificate Plan.

(2) On January 2nd certificates will be mailed to all members in the United States and Canada.

(3) The identification certificate must be presented to the local ticket agent at the time of buying round-trip ticket to Buffalo.

(4) One identification certificate may be used by a Society member and his family.

BATTLE CRY OF THE A.S.H.V.E.

"We're here to sing the glory
Of the A-S-H-V-E,
How from hot and humid weather
It hath made all mankind free.
Thanks to air conditioning
Can everyone in comfort be.
Its joys are everywhere.

Chorus:

Hail our heating engineers,
Ventilating engineers,
Hail to A.S.H.V.E.
Our works are everywhere."

To the music of the Battle Hymn of the Republic (words by Washington Chapter, performed at 1940 Annual Meeting in the District of Columbia

Be a GUIDE Booster

Work on THE GUIDE, 1924, has progressed to such an extent that some important announcements of interest to the members can be made. The Guide Publication Committee has mapped out a strenuous program and

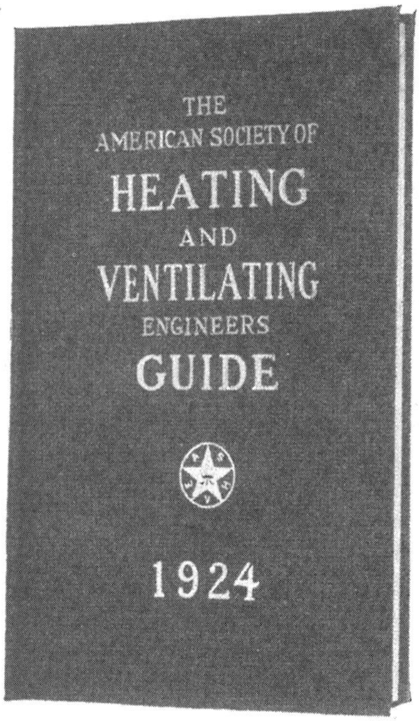

HELP MAKE IT A SUCCESS

is aggressively enlisting the cooperation of the heating and ventilating industry so that this third edition of THE GUIDE will be the best yet.

It is the Committee's desire that every member use and recommend THE GUIDE on every possible occasion for only in that way can it be most effective in spreading the idea of more and better heating and ventilating. So that the membership will be thoroughly familiar with the progress of THE GUIDE work an outline of what has already been accomplished and what is in store will be given briefly. It is believed that these facts will assist them in recommending the use of THE GUIDE to their own firms or to those who supply them with apparatus.

Some additional chapters will be added to the text section and a complete list of the contents which the Committee desires to publish is as follows:

HEATING

Steam and Hot Water Systems
Indirect and Warm Air
Gas and Oil
Heat Losses
Infiltration
Pipe Sizes
Insulation
Automatic Heat Control
Pumps for Heating Service

VENTILATION

Synthetic Air Chart
Comfort Zone
Ventilation Requirements of Buildings
Air Duct Sizes
Drying
Air Conditioning and Cooling
Humidifying and Dehumidifying
Exhaust and Collecting Systems
Mechanical Draft
Ventilators

For the catalog data section space reservations have been rapidly coming in and at this writing 60 firms have sent in their contracts. It is the Committee's desire to have 150 or more firms represented in order to make THE GUIDE most complete and useful to the architects, engineers, contractors, and their draughtsmen and estimators who use it in designing and buying. This year our plan is to print 7500 copies, an increase of 1000 over 1923, for the Committee confidently believes that THE GUIDE has established itself so firmly that their faith in getting this additional distribution is thoroughly justified. The large sale of copies this year indicates that a greater demand for this official and authoritative reference data book will logically result.

Every member should be proud of the Society's effort to advance the science of heating and ventilating by placing the best available design data in the hands of over 7000 men who are responsible for a large amount of the heating and ventilating work done in this country. It should be a privilege to lend your assistance in making THE GUIDE, 1924 a success.

Center — The Boardwalk Interpreted by R.C. Bolsinger

Upper — J.M. Frank and R.L. Gifford, Chicago — J.A. Donnelly and W. C. Donnelly

Lower — E.J. Ritchie and Miss Pauline Kurland, New York; A.J. Nesbit, Atlantic City, W.J. Olvany, New York

Upper — D.H. Faulkner, A. Engle, G.A. Dornheim and R. Donnelly, all of New York

Lower — W.H. Riblet, New York; John D. Cassell, Mrs. Hackett and Charlie Hackett, Philadelphia

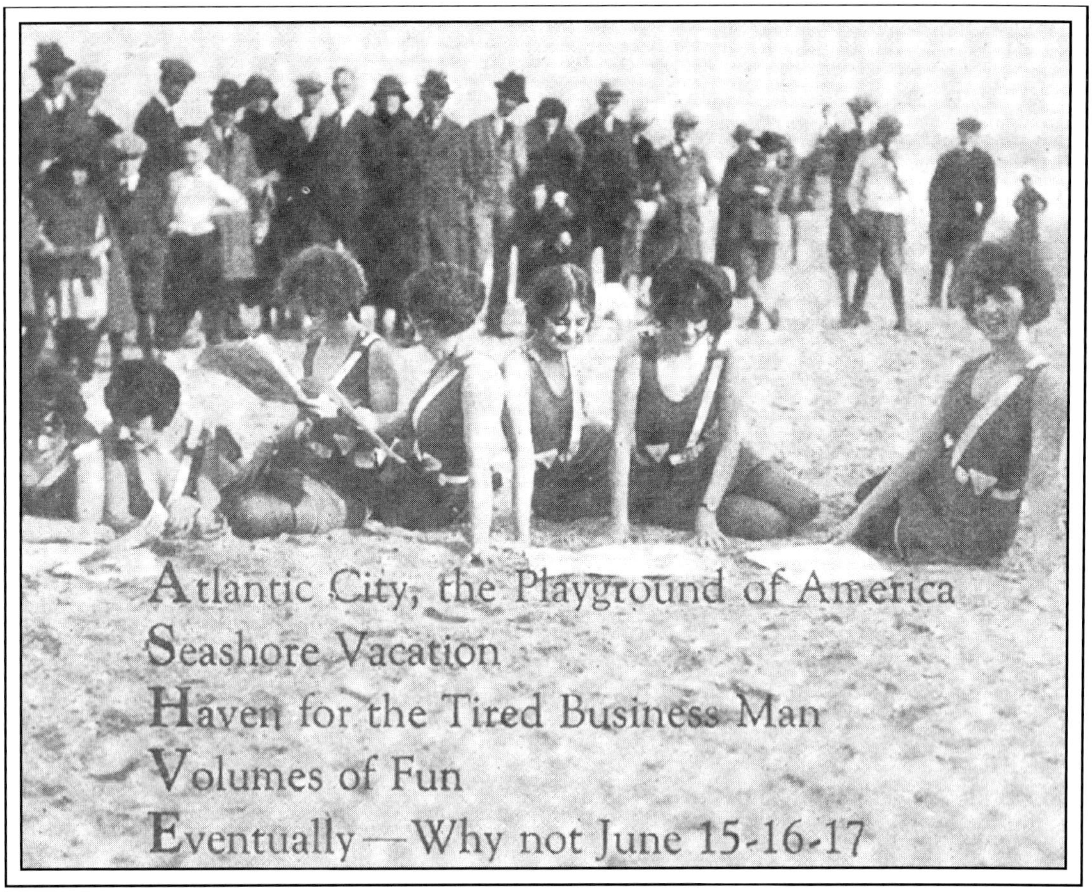

Semi-Annual Meeting, 1925

At the 1927 Semi-Annual Meeting, Thornton Lewis cited the 150th anniversary of "an act which made possible the foundation of our great Republic." Mr. Lewis referred to the signing of the treaty between the American Colonies and France, by in Mr. Thornton's words, "one of the greatest men the world has ever known, and strange to say the same gentleman, Benjamin Franklin was also a heating and ventilating engineer." Franklin, Thornton said, invented a device that would consume and take care of smoke, and while all the world slept at night with their windows closed, he was the first to advocate opening them. By resolution of the Council, Franklin was designated the patron saint of A.S.H.V.E. and all assembled pledged themselves to honor his memory on all suitable occasions.

THE AMERICAN SOCIETY OF REFRIGERATING ENGINEERS

ASRE

Chapter 2

First and Last—The Truth

"We have started on a mission similar to that which other great societies in the engineering world are so ably accomplishing, and considering that our particular scope of operation touches on almost every department of human interest, our aims, if attained at all, must be reached by manful, honest effort. The Grail of the engineer must be first and last – The Truth."

John E. Starr
1904

Refrigeration as an industrial practice was already established by 1885. In the United States, which was a recognized world leader in refrigeration at this time, the main applications were the production of ice and beer and cold food storage. Australia and New Zealand were also industry leaders. Their primary uses were mechanical refrigeration for food preservation, for shipping frozen meats to other countries and for producing beer.

By 1900, manufactured ice in the United States could be made for the same low cost as storing natural lake ice, and it was not weather dependent. One contributing factor was due to polluted lakes and rivers near metropolitan areas, ice harvesters had to go further away to obtain their supplies, which increased their shipping costs and provided ice manufacturers' with claims that their product was purer.

Ploughing and storing ice on the Hudson River above New York City in 1870s.

"Volumes were written by the two sides as between the merits of lake and machine-made ice....Much that was written was technically unsound as reported from both sides," wrote Willis R. Woolrich in 1969. Those who harvested and sold natural ice touted it as having a greater cooling capacity. Those who manufactured ice said there was no difference, except manufactured ice was made from distilled water.

For many years, there was an intense competition for the ice market. With the invention of electric and gas household refrigerators, the market changed for household ice and the natural ice market virtually disappeared by 1950.

Air conditioning or comfort cooling, as it was known then, was not used in every day practice in 1904. There were a few installations, however, which were used primarily to keep valuable records and manuscripts.

Many other uses of refrigeration that are considered modern conveniences were also common in 1904. These include artificial skating rinks, bakery and candy cooling, fur storage, cooling of drinking water and the use of refrigeration in the making of camera film and ice cream.

Other industries that looked to refrigerating engineers to help make their businesses more cost effective included textiles, tobacco, perfume production, chemicals, and mining. Civil engineers sought the expertise of refrigerating engineers in the building of shafts and tunnels.

Issues Leading to Organization

In the United States the only engineering organization suitable for engineers interested in refrigeration was the American Society of Mechanical Engineers (ASME). Although some very outstanding papers had been presented at ASME meetings from 1889 to 1892, by the turn of the century, ASME members interested in refrigeration "found very little on the programs bearing directly on their professional work," recalled Harry Sloan from Vilter Manufacturing Company. They "had been in a huddle in a corner discussing their problems, but with a new society the whole program would be of interest."

Another factor that inspired the organization of a society of refrigerating engineers was the formation of the American Ice Machine Builders Association in 1903. The work of the American Ice Machine Builders Association, whose members were primarily manufacturers, pointed out the advantages of working together, cooperating with other organizations, and of sharing information. More than one-half of the men who would join the refrigerating engineer's society were also members of this association.

In addition, technological advances and new applications were prompting a need for fundamental data on which to base standards within the refrigeration industry. Some engineers felt that it was time to form a scientific society to meet this need.

The Society Organizes

William H. Ross, who was employed by *Cold Storage and Ice Trade Journal* and was secretary of the Eastern Ice Association, organized a meeting of thirty to forty refrigeration engineers on April 2, 1904 at the ASME headquarters in New York City to discuss forming a new society. John E. Starr was elected temporary chairman to run the meeting, and Mr. Ross acted as secretary.

William Ross

Mr. Sloan recalls the meeting: "He [Mr. Starr] opened the meeting with a carefully prepared talk pointing out the needs of such a society, and predicting a rapid growth and secure future for the refrigerating industry. This coming from the leading consulting engineer, who had engineered many large projects, such as cold storage warehouses, distribution of refrigeration by pipe lines through city streets, etc., presented in a very earnest and convincing manner, resulted in carrying the unanimous favorable action of the meeting. I do not remember a single dissenting voice when the subject was opened for discussion."

Following the discussion, a committee was appointed to draft a constitution and by-laws. The committee consisted of L. Howard Jenks, chairman; John E. Starr; W. Everett Parsons; James Wills; Henry Torrance, Jr.; William H. Ross; and George Richmond. Mr. Richmond died before the committee's work was completed. E.L. Phillips took his place.

John E. Starr

On December 4 and 5, 1904, in New York City, these engineers met again to adopt the Constitution and By-Laws and to elect officers, thus forming The American Society of Refrigerating Engineers—the only engineering society in the world solely dedicated to promote the arts and sciences connected with refrigerating engineering.

There were seventy-four charter members of this new society. The officers and directors elected at the meeting were:

President	John E. Starr
Vice Presidents	P.DeC. Ball and H.B. Roelker
Treasurer	Walter C. Reid
Directors	W. Everett Parsons; Henry Torrance, Jr.; E.L. Phillips; S. Jacobus; Howard Jenks; Louis Block; Edgar Penney; W.T. Robinson; and Thomas Shipley

OFFICERS

OF

THE AMERICAN SOCIETY OF REFRIGERATING ENGINEERS.

1904–1905.

PRESIDENT.

JOHN E. STARR...New York, N. Y.

VICE-PRESIDENTS.

H. B. ROELKER...New York, N. Y.

Term expired at Annual Meeting of 1905.

P. D. C. BALL...St. Louis, Mo.

Term expires at Annual Meeting of 1906.

DIRECTORS.

LOUIS BLOCK...New York, N. Y.
W. EVERETT PARSONS...New York, N. Y.
EDGAR PENNEY...Newburgh, N. Y.

Terms expired at Annual Meeting of 1905.

ELLIS L. PHILLIPS...New York, N. Y.
D. S. JACOBUS...Hoboken, N. J.
W. T. ROBINSON...Philadelphia, Pa.

Terms Expire at Annual Meeting of 1906.

HENRY TORRANCE, JR...New York, N. Y.
THOMAS SHIPLEY...York, Pa.
L. HOWARD JENKS...New York, N. Y.

Terms Expire at Annual Meeting of 1907.

TREASURER.

WALTER C. REID...New York, N. Y.

SECRETARY.

WILLIAM H. ROSS...New York, N. Y.

The business affairs of the Society were managed by a committee called the Council. It consisted of the Society's president, two vice presidents, treasurer and nine Members or Associate members.

The secretary was permitted to take part in the Council's deliberations but could not vote.

During the first meeting of the Council, held on January 14, 1905 in New York City, William H. Ross was appointed as secretary of the Society at a salary of $25.00 per month, out of which all office expenses would be deducted. President Starr appointed standing committees on finance, publications and membership, and the Council voted to have the Society incorporated under the laws of the State of New York, which was done on August 30, 1905. In addition, the Council voted to locate the Society business offices at 258 Broadway, New York City.

First Annual Meeting

Exactly one year after the December 1904 organizational meeting, the Society convened its First Annual Meeting in the chambers of ASME in New York City on December 4 and 5, 1905. Eight papers were presented and debated on such topics as plate and can systems for manufactured ice, pipe line refrigeration, and carbonic acid and refrigerating machines.

Characterized as the "dean of refrigerating," John Starr was the most respected refrigerating engineer in the first half of the 20th century.

To comply with the laws in the State of New York, the date of the annual meeting was specified in the Society's Constitution and By-Laws. The founding members specified that the date "shall be on the Monday before the first Tuesday in December" so the Society meeting would be held as close to the ASME meeting as possible, thus allowing out-of-town members of both societies to conveniently attend both meetings.

The Refrigerating Engineers in Session, President Parsons Has the Floor and Vice-President Starr Backs Him Up

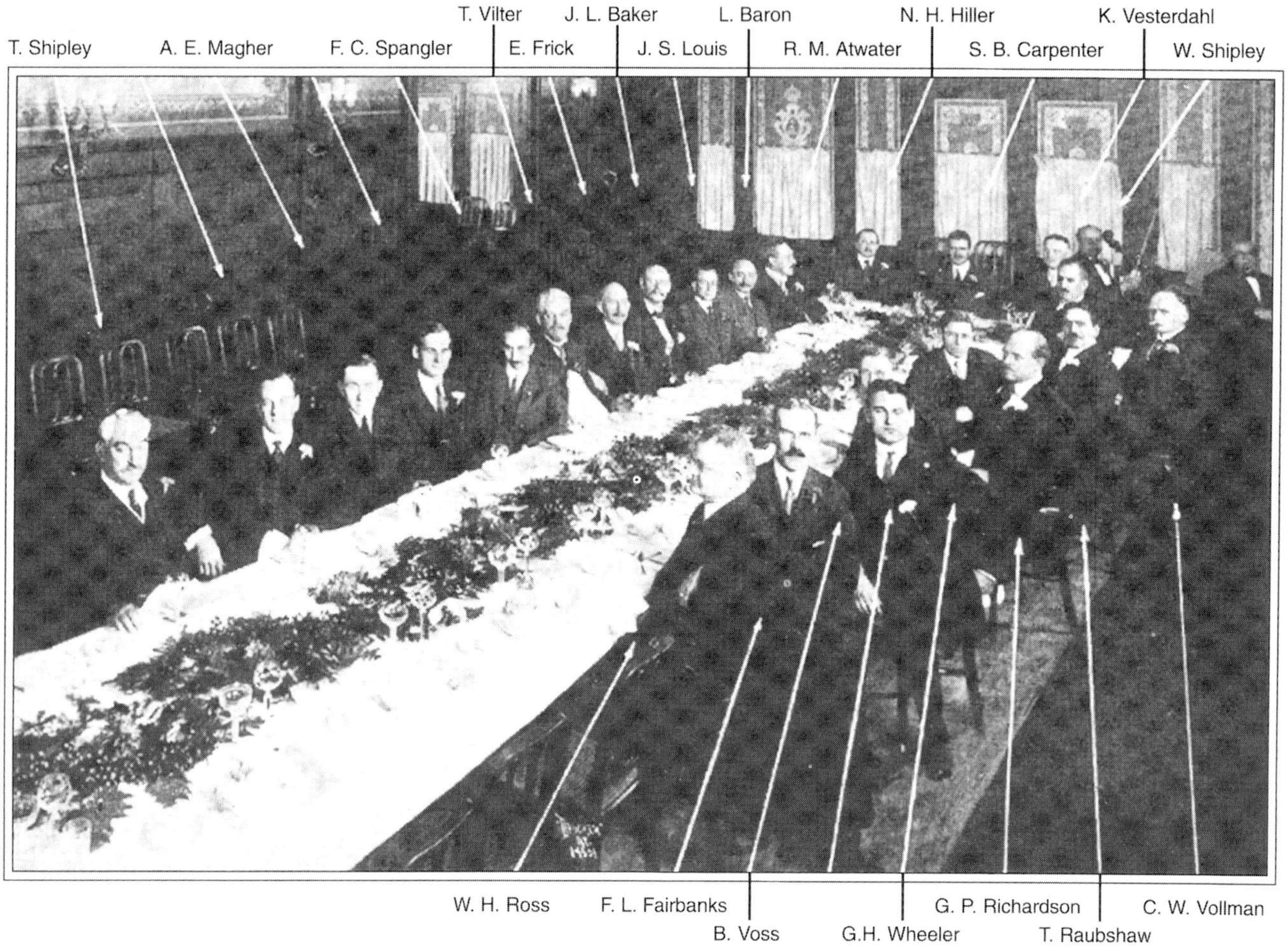

This photograph has long been identified as a view of the Society's first annual dinner at Luchow's Restaurant in New York. It is actually a view of a Refrigerating Machinery Contractors Association dinner of about the same date (1905). Some of the men present, however, are the same refrigeration leaders who founded the American Society of Refrigerating Engineers in 1904.

Charter Members

The American Society of Refrigerating Engineers

Joseph E. Aue
P. De C. Ball
Victor H. Becker
Carl Balm
George E. Berna
J.C. Bertsch
Louts Block
Samuel H. Brubaker
Martin B. Carpenter
B.C. Carpenter
Albert A. Cary
Charles L. Case
Fred B. Church
Harold W. Cole
John Glenn Collins
Madison Cooper
A.P. Criswell
I.J. deKinder
John B. DeHart, Jr.
M. Dennedy
Charles Dickserman
Frank J. Flocke
Ezra Frick
Edward N. Friedmann
J.C. Goosmann
Oswald Gueth
Harry M. Hasan
David J. Havenstrite
N.H. Hiller
D.L Holden
D.S. Jacobus
L. Howard Jenks
Rockwell King
Charles L Krum
John M. Larsen
John Levey
J.S. Louis
George L. McCarthy
W.H. Manns
F.E. Matthews
Peter Neff
J F. Nickerson
L.C. Nordmeyer
C.C. Palmer
W. Everett Parsons
Edgar Penney
Ellis L. Phillips
F.W. Pilsbry
Thomas L. Rankin
Walter C. Reid
W.T. Roblnson
H.B. Roelker
William H. Ross
Samuel J. Rowe
Louis M. Schmidt
Samuel J. Shipley
Thomas Shipley
Alfred Siebert
John E. Starr
Henry Torrance, Jr.
Alfred P. Trautwein
Karl E. Vesterdalh
Henry Vogt
Carl W. Vollmann
Gardner T. Voorhees
Bernhard Voss
John C. Walt
Karl Wogemann
Robert A. Whelan
Frank H. White
L. Williams
James Wills
Fred W. Wolf. Jr.
Otto C. Wolf

During his address, President Starr eloquently defined the Society's guiding principles:

"To define our field in a word, I may say that we claim as our own all that relates to the production of temperatures, below the ordinary, for useful purposes....

"We have undertaken the responsibility of speaking with authority, of finding the truth, and proclaiming it, and a critical world will hold us to our task or pass us by as unworthy.

"Our forum, however, must be a forum for all the membership, and its discussion for the good of all. The truth is our aim and the seeking of it our work. Within our doors a perpetual truce should prevail, and the sword and buckle of everyday strife is to be laid aside at the threshold."

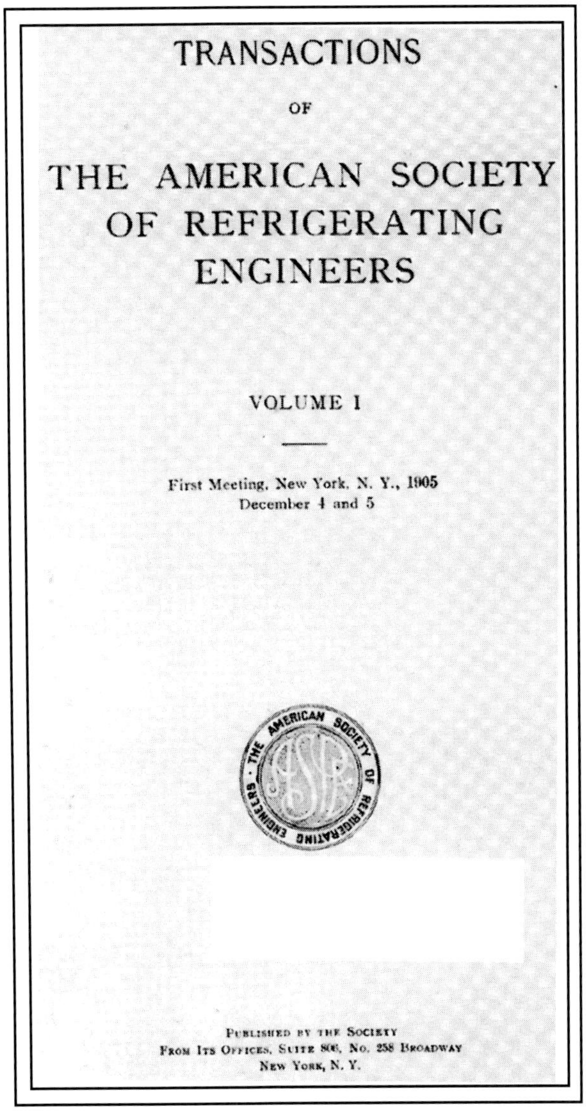
TRANSACTIONS

OF

THE AMERICAN SOCIETY
OF REFRIGERATING
ENGINEERS

VOLUME I

First Meeting, New York, N. Y., 1905
December 4 and 5

PUBLISHED BY THE SOCIETY
FROM ITS OFFICES, SUITE 806, NO. 258 BROADWAY
NEW YORK, N. Y.

The Society immediately began publishing the papers read at its meetings in the Transactions of The American Society of Refrigerating Engineers. The Transactions also included minutes of Society meetings.

In echoing the theme of cooperation and exchange of information that inspired the founding members of the Society, President Starr said, "In carrying out our work... there will be no feeling of jealousy between ourselves and our brother organizations... whose field embraces our own, unless it be that fair and honest emulation to be of use to the world."

The financial report, given by Treasurer Walter C. Reid was very encouraging. The Society had received \$1,495.10 in revenue during its first year and expended \$892.93, for a surplus of \$602.17 cash on hand.

Membership

The Society's Constitution and By-Laws established three levels of membership: Member, Junior and Associate. Each member paid an initiation fee of \$5.00, and membership dues were set at \$10.00 for Members and Associates and \$5.00 for Junior members for the first six years of membership, after which their dues would be the same as Members and Associates.

Each member received a membership certificate and could purchase an emblem pin, with a different color defining each level of membership—dark blue for Members, white for Associates and light blue or turquoise for Junior members. The emblem was the seal of the Society and measured 5/8 inch in diameter.

Although the Society was organized as a national institution, by 1906 it already had members from Canada, England, India, the Argentine Republic, Australia and New Zealand. Membership in 1906 totaled 146.

Primary Issues and Early Actions

The objective of the Society was to conduct research, develop standards, hold technical meetings and present and publish technical articles in journals and handbooks. The founding members of the Society immediately went to work to meet these objectives and the greatest need of refrigerating engineers: the search for fundamental data upon which more accurate data could be published and standards developed.

In an effort to share information, the proceedings of the Society's annual meeting were published and made available for sale each year in a bound book, titled *Transactions of The American Society of Refrigerating Engineers*. It was distributed to other technical publications that might find the technical papers published therein of interest.

Early actions of the Society reflected the members' earnest desire to meet the stated objectives of their society. During the First Annual Meeting, for example, members unanimously passed a resolution recommending that the U.S. Congress appropriate sufficient funds so the U.S. Department of Agriculture could equip and maintain a cold storage plant for the purpose of research. In addition, the Society responded to the issue of establishing a standard unit or "ton" of refrigeration by appointing a committee of five to work with other engineering organizations.

Another example of an early action by members is that at the January 14, 1905 meeting of the Council, members voted to accept an invitation from Thomas Shipley, chairman of the York Manufacturing Company of York, Pennsylvania, to visit the company's test plant to conduct tests on mechanical refrigeration.

The actions taken during the Society's first meetings, as well as the members' dedication to the work of the Society, planted the seeds of research and committee efforts that would provide significant results and benefits to the refrigerating industry for years to come.

1916 Beefsteak Dinner

The "old fashioned beefsteak dinner" in 1916 was held at Murray's Restaurant on December 5.

In 1917, the *Journal of The American Society of Refrigerating Engineers* reported tests to determine the elastic deformation of balsa wood. They were part of a study on the properties of balsa as an insulation material.

1	西村與志秋	15	上西 威	29	杉村伊兵衛	43	加茂正雄
2	Janson, A. J.	16	水志正直	30	米元晋一	44	齋藤道三
3	小栗八郎	17	齋藤省三	31	宮副条市	45	陣道文藏
4	今井文平	18	釜 惣三郎	32	丹羽重光	46	松野高一
5	篠原史郎	19	長野·愷介	33	伊澤幾次郎	47	臼井孝雄
6	McCormick, E.J.	20	Vilter, E. F.	34	關山 延	48	畔柳健太郎
7	細井圓太郎	21	Vilter, Emil.	35	岩城敏夫	49	柴垣鼎太郎
8	Fay, Charles, H.	22	菊池武一	36	和合英太郎	50	藤村源藏
9	Babbitt, H. E.	23	星野三郎	37	小林正規	51	澁谷乙彥
10	北浦重之	24	西原脩三	38	寺田重登	52	大堀正一
11	Bartow, Edward.	25	經塚茂一	39	本山重壽	53	曾根田又雄
12	Carrier, W. H.	26	濱本信一	40	大澤一郎	54	淺野定次
13	Binnie, W. J. E.	27	木村寛六	41	真野文二		
14	柳町政之助	28	楚南元暎	42	池田 進		

The Japanese Society of Domestic and Sanitary Engineers hosted Refrigerating Engineers in 1930 during a visit to the World Engineering Congress.

A true to scale model of a cold storage plant with more than 2,000 individual castings was conceived by an ASRE committee and built by Berthold Audsley in 1931. The model showed the insulation, refrigerating system, elevators, and power plant equipment. The model was loaned to the Chicago Museum of Science and Industry.

To record the progress of refrigerating engineering, the members of ASRE sealed a time capsule on November 29, 1954 on the occasion of the 50th Anniversary of the organization's founding. The capsule received its last paper from Society President A. J. Hess. A.C. Carlton (left) from The Franklin Institute, J.S. Burlew and past ASRE President Edward Simons (right) observe.

Dr. Edgar Ross (left) and T.H. Silary of the Philadelphia Section emplace the time capsule. The year of opening is set for 2004, the 100th Anniversary of ASRE's founding.

April 8, 1955, ASRE held dedication ceremonies at The Franklin Institute in Philadelphia and formally transferred their time capsule to the custodianship of The Institute. Edward Simons, chairman of the Fiftieth Anniversary Committee, delivered the dedicatory statement: 'The work here emplaced in record has been accomplished toward the betterment of mankind. Dedication lies with the very doing. We here, and those for whom we stand, hold ourselves ready for the years to come and solemnly pledge ourselves to work truly and well that there may be those who shall give of themselves to the fullness of their talents in the growing of this age." Pictured left to right are Leon Buehler, Jr.; A.J. Hess; H.F. Spoehrer; J.F. Stone; C.S. Leopold; R.C. Jordan; R.C. Cross; M.C. Turpin; Edward Simons and Edward Simons, Jr.

In 1959, three bronze plaques were completed honoring pioneers in the field of refrigeration and refrigerating equipment. The two men individually honored are John Gorrie and Alexander Twining. The third plaque listed 12 additional American pioneers. The plaques now hang at the International Headquarters of ASHRAE in Atlanta.

Chapter 3

The Research Bureau

Eight Steps in an ASHVE Research Project:

***R**eview of past work*
***E**valuation of available information*
***S**tudy of methods of attack*
***E**xperimental investigation and analytical study*
***A**nalysis of results*
***R**eview of technical advisory committees*
***C**ompiling of practical, usable data for publication*
***H**eating, ventilating and air conditioning benefits*

Annual Report
1944

In describing the state of the industry in the early years of the Society, Presidential Member and former director of the Research Bureau Burgess H. Jennings wrote in 1969, "the lack of standards and the uncertainty of the data required for rational design, manufacture, and application created urgent needs. The practice of heating, ventilating, and air conditioning was then more art than science. Although fundamental concepts were known, the confusion, which resulted from the conflicting claims of commercial interests, was widespread."

In 1918, *Heating and Ventilating* magazine explained that "the science on this subject did not develop very rapidly.... Some very simple facts and theories were literally dragged forth from obscurity by repeated failures in obtaining uniform results, because of the fact that physical laws had been overlooked."

To compensate for the lack of reliable data, heating and ventilating engineers relied on their individual experience. In addition, many companies kept files on their engineers' efforts. Historian Gail Cooper adds, "The existence of such company files, which collected individual engineering expertise in an institutional form, is indicative of the distinctly commercial character of engineering

Committee Chairmen
Chairmen, Committee on Research, A.S.H.V.E., 1919 to 1931 (left to right, starting at the top) George W. Barr, 1917; J. Irvine Lyle, 1918-19; Perry West, 1917; Fred R. Still, 1920; J.R. McColl, 1921; Thornton Lewis, 1922; C.V. Haynes, 1931; E.E. McNair, 1923; W.H. Driscoll, 1924-25; H.P. Gant, 1926; S.R. Lewis, 1927-28; L.A. Harding, 1929; F.B. Rowley, 1930.

knowledge [at that time]. It was often proprietary knowledge, gained through company research and sometimes maintained as a commercial secret, particularly in the case of non-patentable data."

In many cases, the "textbook sections" in manufacturers' catalogs were the only source of engineering information. The lack of information or information only available from manufacturers and the conflicting claims by manufacturers contributed to the overall problem of obtaining consistent, reliable results.

Historian Cooper explains, "In the heating and ventilating industry, engineering expertise was in some cases more important for commercial success than new products. That was particularly true for consulting engineers who sold their expertise in estimating and designing installations.... This uncertain grasp over a specialized body of knowledge struck at the roots of their claim to professional expertise.

"The importance of producing consistent results only increased with the invention of air conditioning, for most companies gave their customers atmospheric rather than mechanical warranties...air conditioning companies were in the forefront of engineers concerned with effective engineering practice."

Issues Leading to Organization

The need to transform commercial engineering into scientific engineering knowledge resulted from three primary issues. One issue was the lack of cooperation from company to company in sharing engineering knowledge. In addition, manufacturers used technical papers to promote their products.

Another issue was the challenge in the public arena by health professionals who pushed to change state and municipal ventilation ordinances, which were favorable to the industry. In fact, ventilation of schools had become a lucrative specialty within the industry.

"The potential threat of government legislation to the industry, however, became clear in 1911 to 1913 when new experimental evidence convinced the medical community that the build up of carbon dioxide in densely occupied rooms had no influence upon the essential healthfulness of the environment.... In 1913 the New York State Commission on Ventilation was organized to determine the merits of open window versus mechanical ventilation, but Society engineers did not have to wait until the final report in 1925 to realize that this body would throw the full weight of experimental science against the interests of mechanical ventilation," said historian Cooper.

These two issues in addition to the uncertainty of engineering data, which was particularly acute in the air-conditioning industry, created complex problems. These problems were illustrated at the 1917 Annual Meeting, in which the meeting organizers had difficulty arranging for technical papers to be presented at a session on unusual air-conditioning and drying installations in factories.

In his Presidential Report in 1917, Harry M. Hart expressed his frustration: "...a seeming reluctance by some of our members to present papers of this character would indicate a lack of accurate data or a mistaken idea that the giving out of such data would result in the loss of some advantage presumably over competitors...this subtle reticence, that seems to grip so many of our members has been one of the greatest drawbacks to the advancement of the science of heating and ventilation."

Organizational Meetings and Events

During the Fall of 1916, the Society's Michigan Chapter held a meeting at the University of Michigan, during which the question of establishing a fellowship at some university by the Society was discussed. In January 1917, the matter was presented to the Society.

At the 1917 Annual Meeting, President-elect J. Irvine Lyle, one of the most influential members in the shaping of the Research Bureau, strongly favored the Society supporting research, by saying:

"I do not think we can ever have too much research. Every one in the industry and in the country will benefit by it. I think the economic position of this country depends upon the research that is made along the line of arts and manufacture that is to be developed in this country.

J. Irvine Lyle
Chairman of the Committee on the Research Bureau during the Bureau's first year of operation, 1919 to 1920, and president of The A.S.H.V.E. in 1917-18. He oversaw the committee's work to negotiate an agreement for space at the U.S. Bureau of Mines for the Research Bureau and to raise funds to support the Research Bureau's work.

"During the last two and one-half years, we have heard a great deal about Germany's preparedness. To my mind their economic and business preparedness is a higher aim than their military preparedness, although that was the finest in the world. It is well known that Germany was conquering the markets of the world, and was doing it scientifically by discovering economic ways of manufacture and business.... There are many problems to be solved through the use of the research laboratory that no experience would exactly duplicate."

President Hart said: "Arthur K. Ohmes presented a paper at a recent [Society] Annual Meeting on an institution in Germany for the advancement of heating and ventilating art, and at that time a motion was made that a committee be appointed to look into the possibility of the establishment of a school of research. The Council did not feel that the Society was in shape to establish such a school....But, at a recent meeting, the matter came up again in view of some investigations that had been made on the possibility of the establishment of a fellowship chair, and the Council voted to have the matter brought up at this meeting for discussion and possibly for action."

The members debated the idea of establishing a Society research laboratory, including an extensive discussion on funding. They agreed that such a laboratory must be independent but disagreed on whether allowing corporate contributions would compromise the work of the laboratory. They further discussed the possibility of endowing a chair of heating and ventilating at a university or technical school, thus cutting the size of their program to better fit their finances. They also considered participating in cooperative research projects with universities and other institutions, obtaining government support and soliciting funds from the membership.

The discussions resulted in a motion to appoint a committee to investigate the feasibility of establishing a research laboratory. Those appointed included: George W. Barr, chairman; J.M. Hart; W.W. Macon; J.D. Hoffman; James W.H. Myrick; William F. McDonald; and Perry West.

Because Mr. Barr currently was serving in the military, Perry West acted as temporary chairman and presented the committee's report at the January 1918 Meeting. In part, Mr. West reported, "There is no question that the industry is greatly in need of specific determinations bearing upon the co-ordination and standardization of the practices of this art, and THE AMERICAN SOCIETY OF HEATING AND VENTILATING ENGINEERS is the proper organization, not only to perform some of this work, but to assume the direction and encouragement of such of this work as should be properly done by others.

"That there is no greater work before the Heating and Ventilating Engineers than, 1st—a determination of the standards and practices which will turn to best economic account the various apparatus which are available for use in connection with this work; 2nd—the co-operation with, and direction of, manufacturers in the determination of reliable data as to the performance of their apparatus and the further development of this apparatus to best meet requirements, and 3rd—the education of the consumer and others with whom we come into business contact along the lines of better co-operation and as to what we are attempting to do."

On August 1, 1919 the Research Bureau was officially opened and began to function. It was formally dedicated on September 29, 1919 for the use of research and experimentation. The building itself was completed in the Fall 1917, but dedication ceremonies were postponed on account of World War I. The building's laboratories were built at a cost of over one million dollars. The A.S.H.V.E. Research Bureau occupied rooms 279, 281, and 283 along with a room in the basement.

An aerial view of the Pittsburgh Experiment Station, U.S. Bureau of Mines where the A.S.H.V.E. Research Bureau was located from 1919 to 1944 when it was moved to Cleveland, Ohio.

View in the mechanical laboratory at the U.S. Bureau of Mines.

Research Bureau office staff at work. Top —Director John R. Allen; lower left—Elinor E. Mellon; and lower right—Otto W. Armspach.

The building at the U.S. Bureau of Mines where the Research Bureau was located.

Boiler testing laboratory used by the Research Bureau at the U.S. Bureau of Mines in Pittsburgh, Pennsylvania (1919).

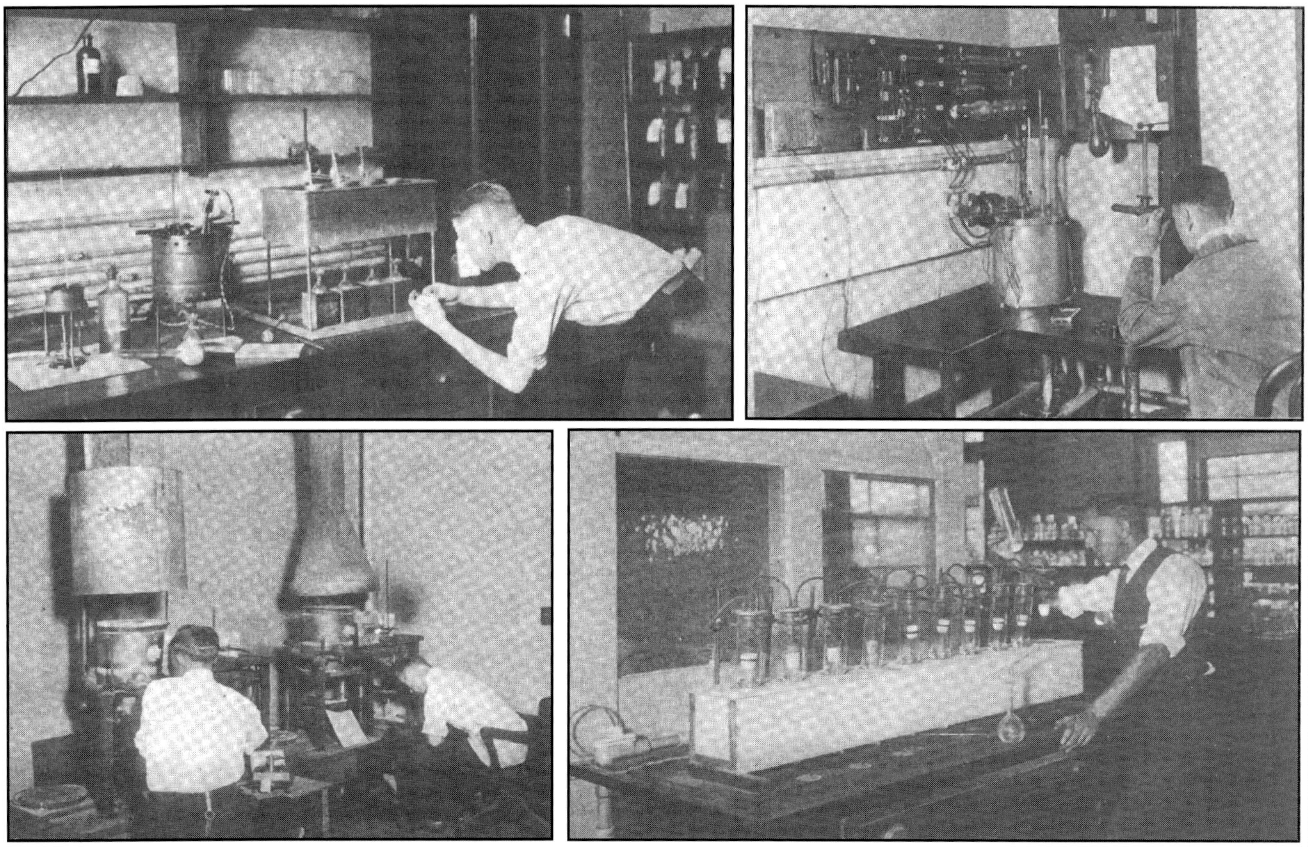

Typical views in the Research Bureau at the U.S. Bureau of Mines (1922).

As a result of this report, the proposal to establish the Research Bureau was referred to the Society's Council for action. According to Mr. Lyle, "At a Council meeting of March 6, 1918, the matter was referred to a Committee consisting of all the members of the previous Committee with the exception that Mr. J.I. Lyle was appointed to the Committee as Chairman. The Committee undertook to investigate the institutions which might be utilized in establishing the Bureau of Research, and was greatly pleased to receive a letter from Mr. O.R. Hood, chief engineer of the Bureau of Mines, U.S. Dept, of the Interior, suggesting that we investigate the facilities of the Bureau of Mines. This was done by the Chairman of the Committee who made a progress report to the Society at the Buffalo Semi-Annual Meeting in June 1918. The report of the committee was received and approved. Messrs. Hoffman, West, Hart and the Chairman of the Committee went from Buffalo, after the Meeting, to Pittsburgh to investigate the facilities further."

Engineers to Convention
On October 18, 1926, the Research Bureau held its first open house for Society members. Pictured are back row, left to right—C.F. Zobel; L.A. Harding; C.V. Haynes; A.E. Stacey, Jr.; H.P. Gant, chairman of the Committee of Research; A.J. Wood; F.B. Rowley; and F.C. Houghton, director of the Research Bureau. Bottom row, left to right—E.W. Stitt; William G. Boales; J.A. Donnelly; E.C. Lathrop; Percy Nicholls; Thomas M. Dugan; Samuel R. Lewis; and R.V. Frost. In the lower picture are Helen Cochran, secretary of the Research Bureau, and Margaret Ingels, mechanical engineer and research head of the Bureau.

The new Bureau of Mines Experiment Station had enough space, and the director of the Bureau of Mines, Vann H. Manning, considered it advantageous to have the Society's laboratory in this building since both organizations had similar interests.

The Society's research laboratory would have a director of research with a staff of two or three, and the Bureau of Mines would furnish a senior engineer to work with this group. Also, the Society agreed to spend at least $15,000 a year on the Research Bureau, and the Bureau of Mines agreed to furnish space, heat, light, and power and other assistance as was possible.

With enough funds and pledges raised from the membership to support the laboratory for five years, The Research Bureau of The American Society of Heating and Ventilating Engineers officially opened on August 1, 1919 in rooms 279, 281, and 283 of the U.S. Bureau of Mines Experiment Station, 4800 Forbes Street, Pittsburgh, Pennsylvania. Dean John R. Allen, of the University of Minnesota, assumed his position as director. To introduce members to the Research Bureau, the Society held its Semi-Annual Meeting in Pittsburgh that year, with the technical sessions held at the Experiment Station.

During the 1920 Annual Meeting, Research Bureau Director Allen reported, "These rooms are well

John R. Allen
Dean of engineering at University of Minnesota, served as director of the Research Bureau from the time it opened in 1919 until his death in 1921.

suited for the purpose and are in every way satisfactory. The Bureau has also secured a room in the basement of the building for a constant temperature room. This room is without windows and has adjoining it, a room in which all of the necessary apparatus for a constant temperature room can be located.

"The Bureau has not as yet been able to do any research work in its own laboratories. It has not been in existence long enough to build up the necessary apparatus and instruments to conduct any extensive series of tests."

Sub-committees of the Committee on Research Bureau

In its report to the Society's Annual Meeting in 1919, the Committee on Research Bureau recommended that a 15-member committee be appointed to investigate the needs for research, oversee research that is conducted, negotiate cooperative agreements with other institutions, and to report all conclusive data to the next regular meeting of the Society.

The committee also recommended that sub-committees be formed as many as may be found desirable, to properly carry on the research activities of the Society. These sub-committees were the forerunners of today's technical committees. As a result, the research results accrued on several fronts, in the Research Bureau, in university and industrial laboratories, and in field installations.

Meeting of the senior members of the Research Bureau staff with the Technical Advisory Committee on Cooling Load, in 1947.

Cooperative Research Activity

When establishing the Research Bureau, the members agreed that from a practical standpoint it was advantageous to work with other institutions on cooperative research projects in addition to conducting their own studies at the Bureau. These institutions, primarily universities, had excellent facilities, and under the direction of the Bureau, the cooperative research projects minimized duplication of equipment and personnel. These projects also gave student engineers instructive opportunities they might not otherwise had received.

Taken in the late 1940s, ASHVE Research Bureau technical staff meet to discuss the projects currently in progress at that time.

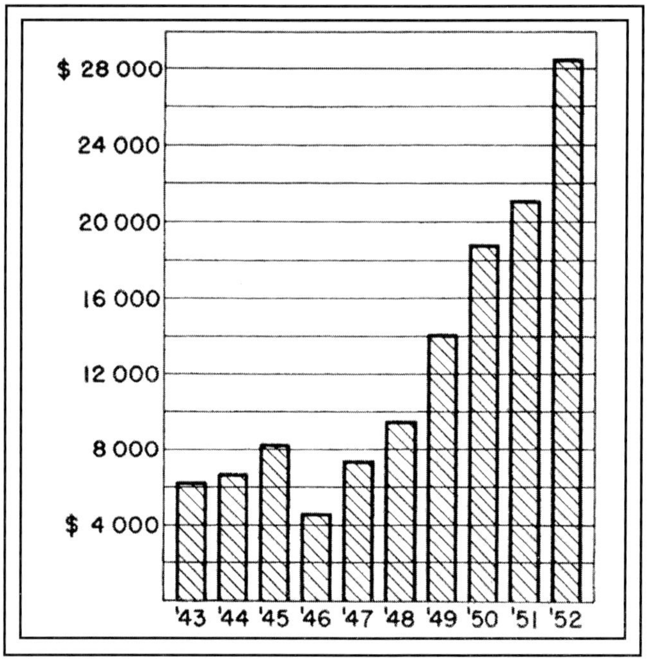

ASHVE Direct Grants to Cooperating Colleges, 1943-1952
This chart shows the growth in the Society's support of research at cooperating colleges and universities through direct grants from 1943 to 1952.

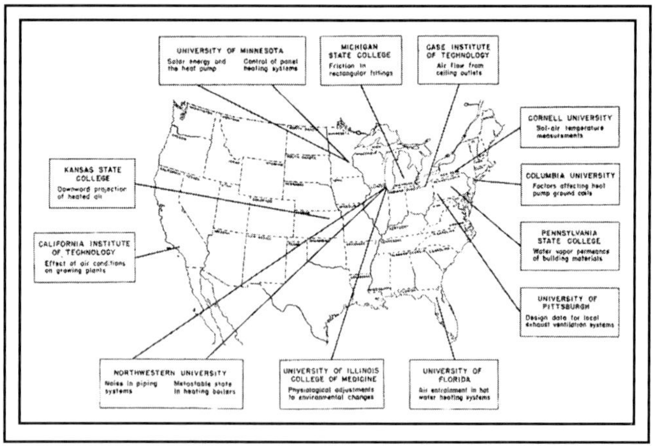

ASHVE Cooperative Research, 1952
This map demonstrates the cooperative projects sponsored by ASHVE in 1952.

Former Research Bureau Director Jennings recalled, "The store of knowledge received by the Society through such cooperative research ventures was of inestimable value."

Society worked closely with the University of Illinois, University of Minnesota, University of Wisconsin, Texas Agricultural and Mechanical College, University of Pennsylvania, University of California at Berkeley, and Harvard. From 1941 until the Bureau closed in 1961, the most active schools in these ventures were the University of California at Los Angeles, Cornell University, Lehigh University, Northwestern University, Kansas State University, University of Michigan, Michigan State, University of Iowa, Columbia University, Pennsylvania State University, Case Institute of Technology, University of Florida, Ohio State University, University of Arizona, and Purdue University.

E Paul Anderson
A.S.H.V.E. president in 1927 and an A.S.H.V.E. laboratory director from 1921 to 1925, he served as dean of engineering in what is now the University of Kentucky for 43 years until his death in 1934. During his tenure as director of the Research Bureau, 62 scientific papers were published, the most important of which concerned the development of the comfort zone of atmosphere. The Society's F. Paul Anderson medal is named after Dean Anderson, who in the words of 1930-31 A.S.H.V.E. President Thornton Lewis, "had directed the education of more engineers engaged in heating and ventilating profession than any other man in the world."

Margaret Ingels
One of the first women in the world to earn a degree in mechanical engineering; awarded in 1916 by the University of Kentucky. She became one of the first female members of The A.S.H.V.E. and joined the staff at the Research Bureau in 1922.

Move to Cleveland

In 1944, when a war-time emergency made it necessary for the Bureau of Mines to employ all of its space for military research, the Society decided to move the Research Bureau to a new location. A committee consisting of C.M. Ashley, chairman of the Committee on Research; J.F. Collins, Jr., chairman of the Finance Committee; E.N. McDonnell, an Executive Committee member; and Society President S.H. Downs investigated 12 proposals. They unanimously selected the former Western Reserve Historical Society Building at 7218 Euclid Avenue.

"The Cleveland Laboratory was exceptionally well suited for research, containing some 18,000 sq. ft. of working area, with 13,000 used for active research projects and the remaining 5,000 used for offices and meeting rooms," according to Mr. Jennings.

Temporary Facility
In March 1944, the Society moved the Research Bureau to Cleveland, Ohio. The Bureau had been located for the past 25 years at the U.S. Bureau of Mines in Pittsburgh, Pennsylvania. The Society first leased this temporary facility, located at the corner of East 107th Street and Euclid Avenue, and later moved into a Society-owned permanent facility, also located on Euclid Avenue.

A.S.H.V.E.-owned Facility
The Society purchased this site at 7218 Euclid Avenue in Cleveland, Ohio in July 1946. The Research Bureau operated in this facility until the Bureau was closed 1961. This location was exceptionally well suited for research, containing some 18,000 sq. ft. of working area, with 13,000 sq. ft. used for active research projects and the remaining area used for offices and meeting rooms.

Aerial View of A.S.H.V.E.-owned Facility
Aerial view of the Society-owned Research Bureau facility. The Committee on Research and Bureau staff hosted an open house on January 27, 1947, during the week of the Society's 53rd Annual Meeting. Members toured the facility and learned first hand the status of the projects then in progress. The facility was also dedicated that day.

F.C. Houghten
Director of the Research Bureau (standing) with staff members.

Because the building required renovations, the Bureau was first housed in a temporary location at 10700 Euclid Avenue, then in 1946, it moved into the 7218 Euclid Avenue building. Society members were cordially invited to attend an open house at the new location during the 1947 Annual Meeting, which was held in Cleveland.

Significant Contributions

The Research Bureau became a showcase for HVAC technology and was the source of many significant contributions to the heating, ventilating, and air-conditioning industries. During the development of the Bureau, Chairman of the Committee on Research Lyle requested the ideas of committee members on the direction of the Bureau. Their responses reflected the diversity of concerns within the Society. Presidential Member Fred R. Still, who was employed by a large manufacturer, American Blower Corporation in Detroit, Michigan, provided a list of technical problems, including complete determinations of the conductivity of various building materials, methods of distributing fresh air, the most economical water temperature for hot water heating plants, and the most effective air velocity in ducts and flues for mechanical ventilation.

In a February 28, 1918 letter to Mr. Lyle, Mr. West, a consulting engineer in New York, wrote, "the first and foremost work of this laboratory would be to dispel some of the doubts and misgivings which are in the minds of the public generally regarding the value of modern heating and ventilating and air conditioning.

According to historian Cooper, "As it took shape, the laboratory did indeed perform both functions, to suggest answers to technical problems and to supply the Society and its members with experimental data to defend modern heating, ventilating, and air-conditioning systems against the attacks of other professionals and government critics."

The most significant accomplishment during the early years of the Research Bureau was the study of the human response to environmental conditions, which was based on physiologic reactions to temperature, humidity, and air movement. These studies gave engineers an authoritative opinion in the legislative battles over ventilation standards.

One journal, *The Weather Vein,* commented in 1923 on the type of research conducted at the Research Bureau: "One of the Engineer's most effective safeguards against loss of public confidence is the development of fixed, rational standards and the determination of precise finite values that he may express himself with an exactness which ensures understanding."

Other areas investigated at the Bureau were fundamental fluid flow of air; steam and water through ducts and pipes; air distribution from jets; design of steam and hot water systems; computation of heating loads; heat transmission; cooling loads; solar effect of walls, roofs, and glass; the measurement of ground temperatures and resistance equivalence in round and square metal air ducts and fittings in addition to the measurement of odors and their control; the performance of controls; problems in combustion; sound and vibration analysis; and coordination of weather data.

In 1944, for the 50th Anniversary of the Society, Chairman of the Committee on Research A.E. Stacey, wrote:

"The Research Laboratory and its cooperative institutions over the last 32 years have presented to the Society a great volume of engineering information on many subjects. There have been over 100 papers on Engineering Fundamentals, such as physical properties of material, heat transfer, solar radiation, aeration of buildings and fluid flow. There are several papers on air pollution and climatic variables; many on the combustion and utilization of fuels; over 50 papers on physiological reactions and comfort sensations as to temperature and relative humidity. There are several papers on environmental control, such as steam heating and convected heat; also several on artificial cooling; and naturally many papers on ventilation and air purification. In all, there are over 250, certainly a

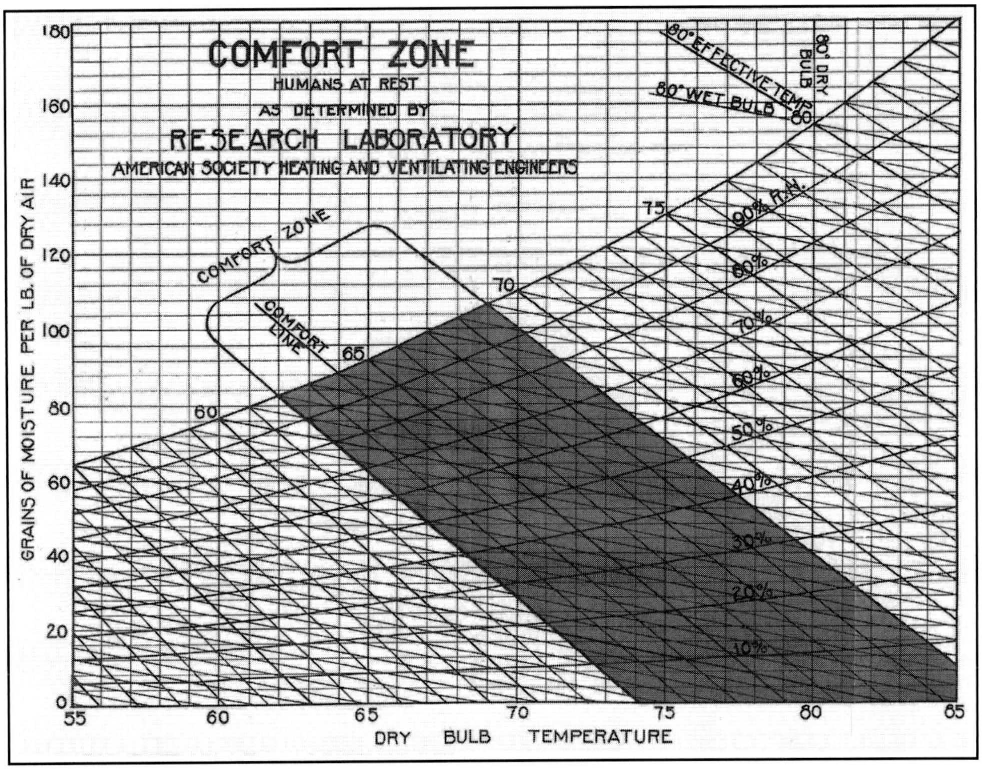

Comfort Zone Chart
Established in 1922 by A.S.H.V.E. in cooperation with the U.S. Public Health Service and the U.S. Bureau of Mines after studying physiological reactions to temperature, humidity, and air movement. The Comfort Zone chart, published in 1924, is superimposed upon the effective temperature chart and can be used to determine the relative comfort of ordinary indoor conditions from the dry- and wet-bulb temperatures of the air. According to historian Gail Cooper, "In this one piece of research, we can see the role of the Research Bureau in both enhancing professional expertise and solving technical problems in a profession which was in transition."

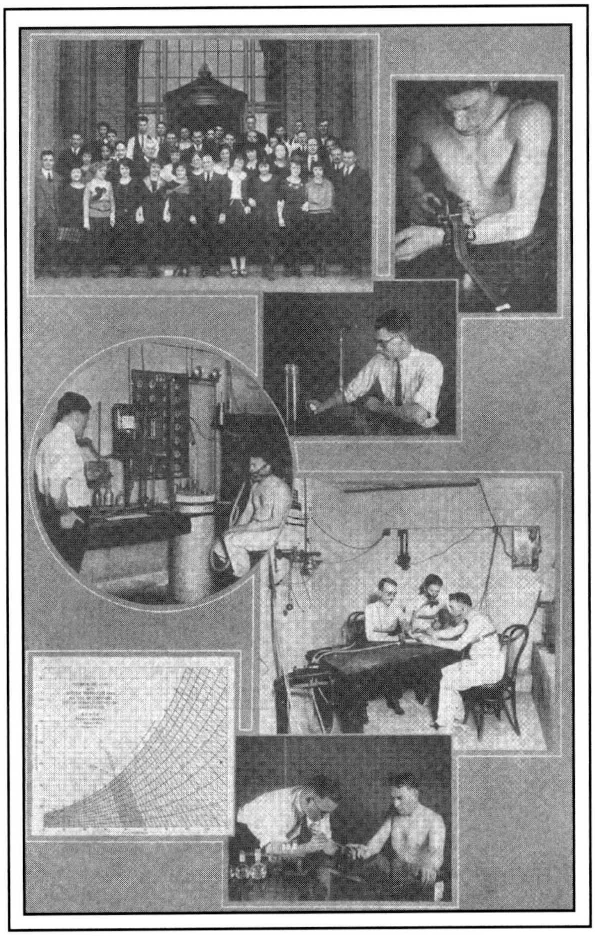

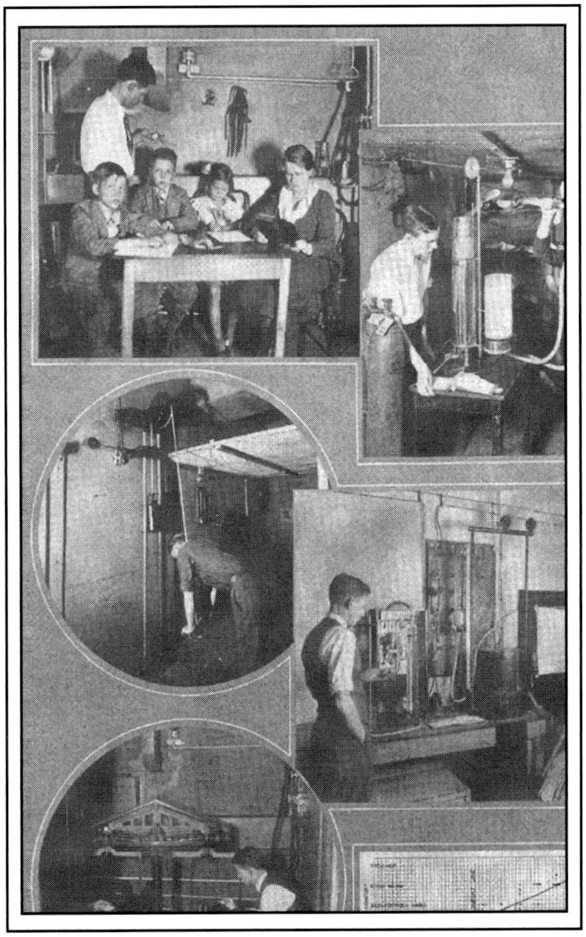

Comfort Zone Studies
Views showing studies of physiological reactions to temperature, humidity, and air movement. Heat and moisture losses and human efficiency of children and adults also were studied under various conditions of temperature and humidity at the A.S.H.V.E. Research Bureau (1931).

Calorimeter Apparatus
Later studies of solar heating effect and heat flow through building materials. This view is of a calorimeter apparatus in position for tests to determine transmission of solar energy through a glass block panel (1951).

Solar Heating
Early studies at the Research Bureau of solar heating effect and heat flow through building materials (1931).

Environmental Laboratory
A general view of the exterior of the Environment Laboratory at the ASHVE Research Bureau in Cleveland. It was substantially completed in 1951 and included a calorimeter room, with a ceiling adjustable to heights up to 12 ft. and auxiliary equipment consisting of compressors, a silica gel humidifier and heat exchangers. When the Research Bureau closed in 1961, the Environment Laboratory was given to Kansas State University. Under the direction of Dr. Ralph Nivens, a building was constructed to house the environmental chamber and it was made operational on the Kansas State campus (1951).

Forced Convection Heat Transfer
This special equipment, designed by the Research Bureau staff, was used for the study of forced convection heat transfer by smooth surfaces. Results obtained in these studies provided data for better estimating of convected heat transfer through windows (1947).

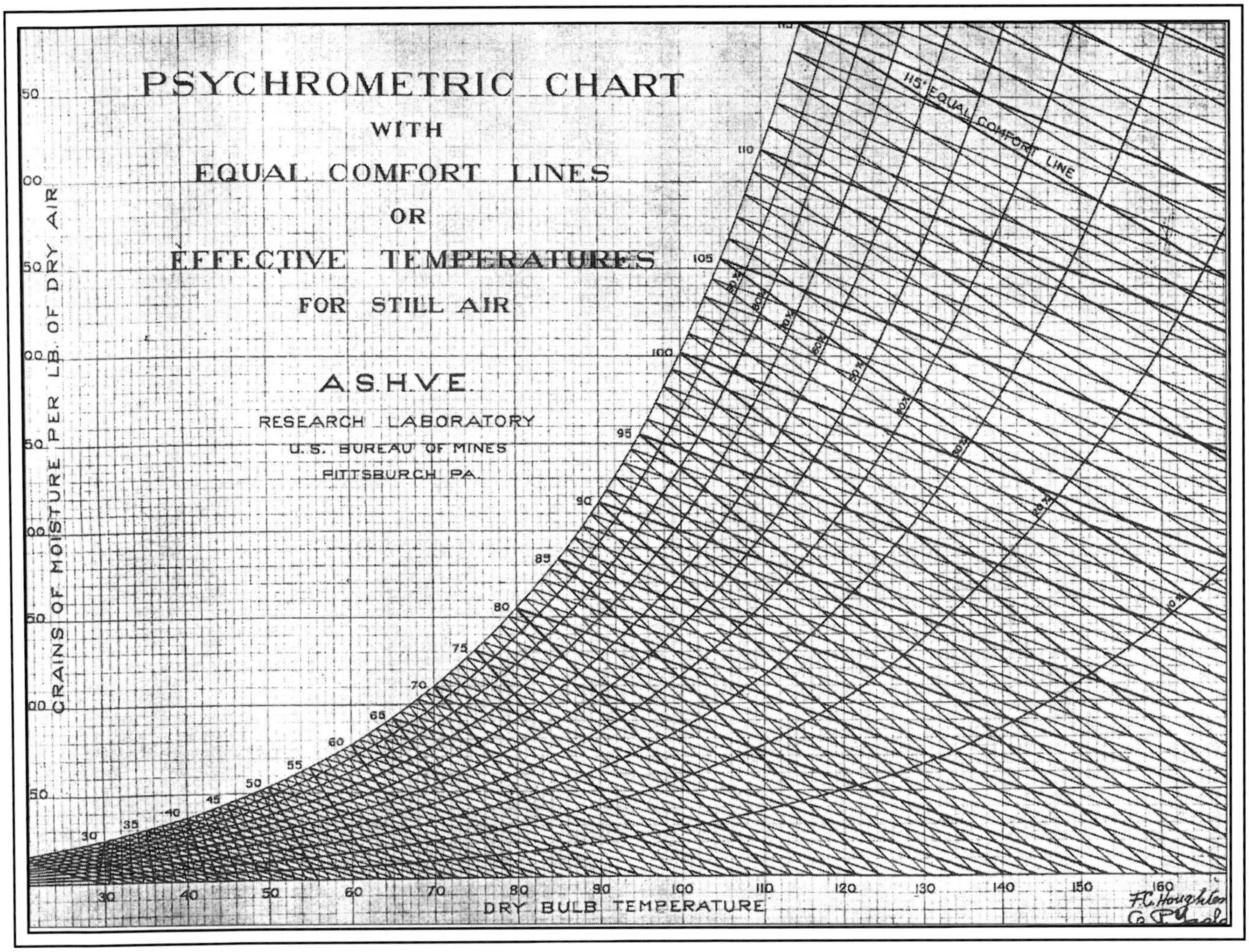

Psychrometric Chart
The Psychrometric Chart was calculated by Dr. Willis H. Carrier and published in his paper "Rational Psychrometric Formulae" which was presented in 1911. The chart details the relationship between dew point and temperature.

tremendous storehouse of information for the Heating and Ventilating Engineer."

The Research Bureau, in 1961, developed a new psychrometric chart, which was the result of 50 years of analysis and study. This new chart showed the complete properties of moist or dry air, requiring for its use only wet- and dry-bulb temperature readings. Basically an enthalpy-humidity ratio chart, it showed such factors as dry bulb, wet bulb, dew point, enthalpy, humidity ratio, and volume information.

Funding and Financial Growth of the Research Bureau

Throughout its tenure, the Research Bureau received its support from the Society in three principal ways:

- Since 1925, forty percent of all member dues was dedicated to supporting the research program.
- Contributions toward research were received from the income from the International Heating and Air-Conditioning Exposition.
- Contributions to the Research Bureau by industrial firms and individuals were given for general use or for restricted support of a specific research area.

The first year, the total budget was $20,000. Committee on Research Bureau Chairman Lyle announced in his report to the Society at the 1920 Annual Meeting a plan to initiate an annual drive to raise $25,000. For the fiscal year just prior to the merger of the American Society of Heating and Air-Conditioning Engineers and the American Society of Refrigerating Engineers that would create ASHRAE in 1959, and two years before the Society closed the Research Bureau, the Research Bureau's budget was $234,000.

Salary of Director and assistants		$11,000
Office supplies		500
Traveling expense		1,000
For supplies needed for investigation of heat	$1,500	
For ventilation	4,500	
For subsidizing work in other institutions	1,500	7,500
Total		$20,000

First Budget, 1919
The Research Executive Committee and the Director of Research John R. Allen met to determine the Research Bureau budget for the first year. The total budget was $20,000, beginning on August 1, 1919 when the Bureau actually was put into operation.

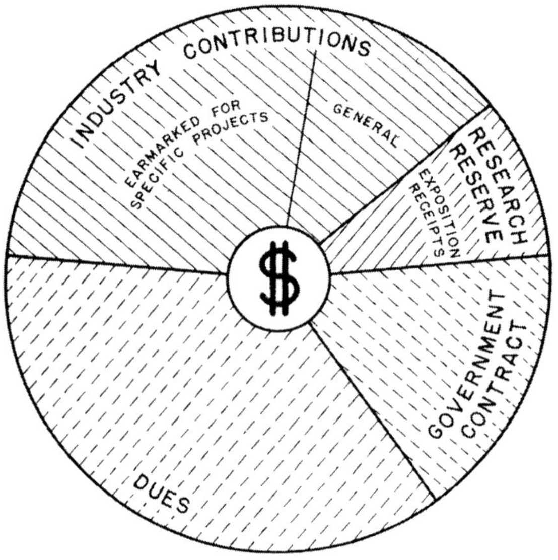

Dues	$ 59 915
Contributions	
Earmarked	42 972
General	19 273
Government Contract	27 062
Research Reserve	15 642
	$ 164 864

Society Research Pie Chart
This chart illustrates how the sources of funds for Society research were expended in 1952. Also listed are dollar amounts from each source totaling $164,864.

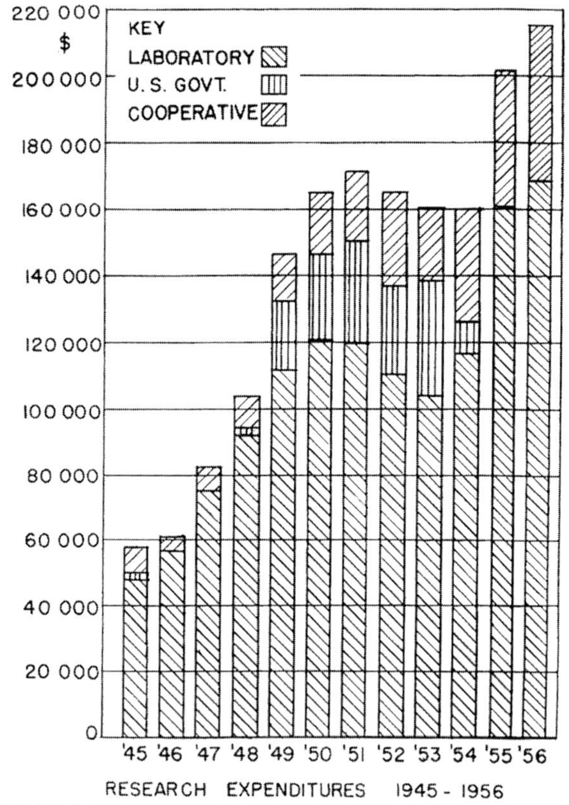

10-Year Research Expenditures Chart, 1945 to 1956
This chart shows the growth of the Society's research program following World War II, from the years 1945 to 1956.

Closing of the Research Bureau — When Time Ran Out

Although the Society's Research Bureau continued to grow and its work was highly respected, the Bureau experienced financial difficulties, especially in the early 1930s due to the Depression and again during the years of World War II. By the mid 1950s, according to Mr. Jennings, "with Federal and state governments pouring millions of dollars into research in their own laboratories and in the laboratories of many universities, the competitive position of a restricted-area laboratory to obtain financial support and to hold quality staff had become very difficult."

By the late 1950s and early 1960s, Mr. Jennings recalled that "the need for fundamental data had largely been satisfied by intensive research programs and the large amount of knowledge produced in four decades of work minimized the pressing need of the Society to have a laboratory of its own...the costs of necessary modern research tools...could hardly be justified unless the cost of such equipment could be shared through usage in numerous research areas as is the case in commercial and service laboratories." The Society, because of its charter and character, "could not change its laboratory into a broad-based commercial enterprise."

The Society's Long-Range Planning Committee in 1961 regretfully recommended that the Research Bureau be closed. The committee also recommended that at the same time other aspects of the research program be expanded.

Presidential Member John Everetts, Jr., in his President's Message in the 1960-61 Annual Report, explained the decision to the membership: "Probably the most critical issue of the year was the decision by the Board of Directors to expand the ASHRAE re-

Research Exhibit

A working example of the ASHVE cooperative research study at the University of Illinois drew crowds during the 1953 International Heating and Ventilating Exposition, held in conjunction with the Society's annual meeting in Chicago, Illinois. The display featured two booths, each 4 ft. × 4 ft. with transparent walls. Conditions simulating those of a hot, humid street in the summer were maintained in one booth, while conditions simulating those in an air-conditioned home, store, or office were maintained in the other. A model wearing summer attire and fitted with thermocouples attached to a indicator-recorder, vividly demonstrated the effects of sudden change of temperature and humidity on the skin and body temperature. Pictured are Dr. Raymond Hussey, scientific director, Council on Industrial Health, American Medical Association; Reg F. Taylor, president, ASHVE; and Dr. Robert W. Keeton, professor of medicine emeritus, and a member of the ASHVE Committee on Research.

Dedication ceremonies at the Laboratories.

Alfred J. Offner
President

L. P. Saunders
Chairman of Committee

AN INVITATION TO MEMBERS OF ASHVE

You are cordially invited to visit your Laboratory located at 7218 Euclid Ave., East, Cleveland, Ohio, where Open House will be held during the week of the 53rd Annual Meeting, January 27, 1947. This is your opportunity to meet the Staff and inspect the Laboratory, and to learn at first hand the progress of the projects upon which the Staff is now engaged. The Society is unique in having been helpful to industry and thus to have enhanced the prestige of the Society. The members of the Committee on Research with the Laboratory Staff, will do everything possible to make your visit to the Laboratory a memorable one.

search program by grants-in-aid to colleges and private laboratories and to close our laboratory in Cleveland. In existence since 1919, the laboratory had an impressive record of accomplishment and was regarded with pride and affection by many of our members. However, the high overhead, the scarcity of skilled research personnel and the inflexibility of our program made its closing advisable and inevitable. We are confident that our new program will be successful."

E.P. Palmatier, chairman of the ASHRAE Research and Technical Committee, wrote about the closing for the April 1961 *ASHRAE Journal's* Research Page:

"It was our [ASHRAE Research and Technical Committee] hope that through the preparation of a sound prospectus in each project area, enthusiastic support would be found from Society membership and from the industries which ASHRAE port might take the form of substantial financial contributions made in the interest of achieving the proposed objectives.

"But time ran out. On December 9 [1961], the Board of Directors deliberated and accepted the recommendations of the Long Range Planning Committee report, which advised closing down and liquidating the facilities of the Society's Research Laboratory at Cleveland and substantial expansion of our research programs in cooperating institutions."

The Research and Technical Committee worked diligently to see that the work in progress at the Bureau was concluded and that the equipment was relocated to institutions that would have the most use for it and would carry on the Society's work. The physiological research chambers, for example, were given to Kansas State University and the solar calorimeter was given to the University of Florida.

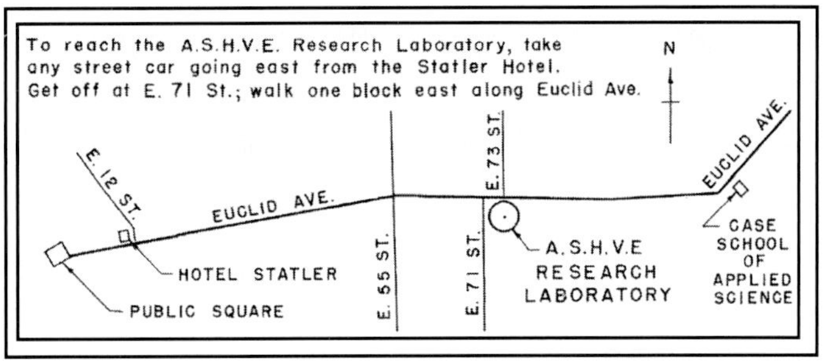

A S H V E

Research Laboratory

7218 Euclid Avenue

Cleveland, Ohio

This Laboratory was dedicated to the service of the membership and the heating, ventilating, and air conditioning industry

on January 27, 1947

on the occasion of the 53rd Annual Meeting of the Society

by

Dr. Arthur Cutts Willard

in the presence of the Society officers, members, and guests.

A. C. Willard

President

First Vice-President

Second Vice-President

Treasurer

Secretary

Technical Secretary

The drafting room at the Laboratory (1947).

Air Volume Studies
Measurement of air volume flowing from registers, grilles, and unit ventilation made at the Armour Institute of Technology by Professor L.E. Davies, under cooperative agreement with the Research Bureau (1931).

Critical Velocities of Steam Flow
Critical velocities of steam flow and data for standard piping systems for steam heating were established by the Research Bureau in cooperation with Carnegie Institute of Technology. Research on this subject extended over eight years, and a final paper was presented in 1931.

Industrial Ventilation
Equipment used at the Research Bureau for the study of air flow into suction openings (1947).

Research Brochures
Examples of covers of research brochures, published annually by the Society, detailing the activities of the Research Bureau.

Measuring Balancing Torque of Barometric Dampers
This special equipment, designed by the Research Bureau staff, measured balancing torque of barometric dampers (1947).

A. & M. College of Texas, College Station

University of Minnesota, Minneapolis

University of California, Berkeley

University of Wisconsin, Madison

From the inception of the Research Bureau, the Committee on Research sponsored cooperative investigations with colleges, universities, institutions and government agencies. In 1940, the Research Bureau sponsored research at fifteen institutions, four of which are pictured here.

1945 Committee on Research

The Committee on Research was responsible for administering the research program and the Research Bureau's budget. This committee approved a program that included studies at the Bureau on heat transfer coefficients for parallel flow past flat surfaces, solar radiation transmission through glass, automatic (barometric) dampers, heat transfer through finned tube services, air friction in ducts and fittings, and the building of new psychrometric rooms. Pictured is the Committee on Research, taken at their meeting at the Research Bureau October 6, 1945. Front Row – Dr. A.C. Fieldner; L.P. Saunders; Dr. C-E.A. Winslow, Society president; Professor G.L. Tuve, chairman; and C. M. Ashley. Back Row – W.E. Zieber; F.C. McIntosh; John James; Captain A.E. Stacey, Jr.; R.M. Conner, Professor Francis W. Hutchinson; and R.K. Thulman.

Air Duct Friction

Air-duct friction set-up showing metering box and nozzle from 1947 brochure. This large room, 50 ft. × 90 ft., was ideal for fluid flow and air distribution studies. The equipment was used to determine friction variations in equivalent round, square, and rectangular ducts.

Evolution from Conducting to Funding Research

By the time ASHRAE celebrated the Centennial of its founding in 1994, the Society was investing \$2.2 million on research projects annually, having grown from \$20,000 spent when the Research Bureau opened in 1919. Of the research investment, \$1.4 million was raised through efforts of ASHRAE volunteers working on grassroots committees. In 1993–94, more than 90 technical committees advised the Society on technical and research issues and guided 94 active projects, of which 20 were completed during the year.

As the Society took on the sole role of funding research rather than conducting research, ASHRAE never attempted to control the research. The focus became to identify research needs, establish qualified institutions and groups to conduct the research, monitor project progress, and approve reports of results. Research projects were initiated by Technical Committees, and usually by the specific efforts of one or more members engaged in industry or practice who saw a need.

J. Richard Wright, who was head of the Research & Technology Committee while at Tennessee Technical University before becoming ASHRAE Director of Technology in 1980, observed that much of the early research was in the areas of comfort and airflow and distribution. That shifted during his time from less hands-on research to more new areas that included techniques and methods unknown in earlier years.

A key driver in how ASHRAE's research program evolved after the millennium was the adoption of a proposal, dated June 11, 2002, for a Research Advisory Panel to develop five-year Research Strategic Plans. According to Bruce D. Hunn, who followed Wright as ASHRAE Director of Technology and who also was a former chair of R&T when he was with Texas A&M University, this changed the direction of the research program from strictly a bottom-up, tactical operation effort driven by Technical Committees to a strategic plan focused on longer-range goals. The new process provided avenues for input from the Society as a whole and from broad constituencies for ASHRAE research, including contractors, building owners, designers, researchers, and industry groups. New strategic plans were developed on a roughly five-year cycle.

Another element of the Research Strategic Plans was introducing into the planning process an explicit desire to include technology transfer (dissemination of research results) in potential research projects as part of the budget. Similarly, ASHRAE began including "high-risk" research set aside for potentially high-impact projects that often had a low probability of success.

ASHRAE's Research Journal

When Richard B. Hayter, a professor at Kansas State University, became president of ASHRAE in 1995, one initiative he had long championed was the creation of a publishing platform within ASHRAE for archival research. The intent was to keep academicians in the HVAC&R field active in ASHRAE for publication of their research, thereby keeping a direct link to students, and to provide a publication outlet for significant papers resulting from ASHRAE Research funding.

In 1994, approval was given to the Special Publications Committee of ASHRAE, chaired by Eugene Stamper, to launch a research journal in conjunction with the start of ASHRAE's second century. Ray Cohen from Purdue University was tapped to be the first editor.

Cohen's charge was to establish a quality journal for the HVAC&R research community that could stand comparison with

ASHRAE's Research Journal
Volume 1, Number 1 of *International Journal of Heating, Ventilating, Air-Conditioning and Refrigerating Research*, 1995, and Volume 25 of *Science and Technology for the Built Environment*, 2019.

any other publication in the field, with one measure being the journal's Impact Factor. The main objective was to establish a journal that adds to understanding of the scientific basis of HVAC&R, one that contained papers documenting fully referenced research of lasting value and reported in adequate detail to provide a basis for further research. Volume 1, Number 1 of the quarterly *International Journal of Heating, Ventilating, Air-Conditioning and Refrigerating Research* was published in January 1995. Within five years, more than 600 different authors from 30 different countries had contributed manuscripts.

From the start, the intent was to make the research journal a resource for researchers globally. An editorial board of associate editors was chosen to reflect a range of both research interests and geographic diversity. Following Cohen, John Mitchell from the University of Wisconsin and Reinhard Radermacher from the University of Maryland continued the tradition of ASHRAE publishing research of lasting value.

ASHRAE Expands Scope, Renames Research Journal

In recognition of the changing role of HVAC&R since it was first published 20 years ago, ASHRAE's *HVAC&R Research* has a new title, an expanded scope and an updated look.

As of this year, the journal will be known as *Science and Technology for the Built Environment*. All manuscripts in process now will be published in the journal under its new name.

"This new name reflects its expanded scope, which includes papers in many areas of science and technology for the built environment," said Reinhard Radermacher, editor. "In addition to traditional areas of research in HVAC&R, the Journal's papers now often cover topics that have come to be associated with the industry since the Journal was first published in 1995. These include smart buildings, thermal comfort, aircraft ventilation and automotive climate technology. *Science and Technology for the Built Environment* will offer comprehensive reporting of original research in science and technology related to the stationary and mobile built environment."

Future article topics include:

- Indoor environmental quality, occupant health, comfort and productivity;
- HVAC&R and related technologies;
- Thermodynamic and energy system dynamics, controls, optimization, fault detection and diagnosis, smart systems and building demand-side management;
- Experiments and analysis related to material properties, underlying thermodynamics, refrigerants, fluid dynamics, airflow, and heat and mass transfer;
- Renewable and traditional energy systems and related processes and concepts Integrated built environmental system design approaches and tools;
- Novel simulation approaches and algorithms and validated simulations;
- Building enclosure materials, assemblies, and systems for minimizing and/or regulating space heating and cooling modes; and
- Review articles that critically assess existing literature and point out future research directions.

Just as before, *Science and Technology for the Built Environment* will accept for publication only works reporting on research that is original and of lasting value. The journal will continue to be published by Taylor & Francis Group for ASHRAE and be included in the Web of Science and Current Contents Connect databases.

Learn more at www.ashrae.org/stbe.

In 2015, the name of the journal was changed to *Science and Technology for the Built Environment* to make clear the scope of the journal related to the broad field of stationary and mobile built environments, including indoor environmental quality (IEQ), thermodynamic and energy system dynamics, refrigerants, renewable and traditional energy systems, integrated design approaches and tools, and building enclosure assemblies. This reflected ASHRAE's rebranding to show the total scope of environmental design and impacts. Jeffrey D. Spitler from the University of Oklahoma became the editor in 2019.

Research Needs in ASHRAE's Second Century

A review of ASHRAE research funding from 1995 to 2019 serves as a road map for shifts in the needs of ASHRAE members. Hunn cites more stringent energy efficiency, improved building performance, sustainable building design, refrigerants development aligned with international regulation, understanding infectious airborne diseases, and the impact of computing.

One of ASHRAE's major milestones since 1995 was the launch of the Advanced Energy Design Guide (AEDG) series in collaboration with The American Institute of Architects (AIA), Illuminating Engineering Society of North America (IESNA), U.S. Green Building Council (USGBC), and the U.S. Department of Energy (DOE).

Donald G. Colliver, 2002–2003 ASHRAE President

During his presidential year in 2002–2003, Donald G. Colliver called for the development of a series of guides to exceed the energy requirements of existing energy standards. The effort started with 30% AEDGs that offered a 30% energy savings compared to buildings that met the minimum energy requirements of ANSI/ASHRAE/IES Standard 90.1-1999. Next was a series of 50% AEDGs that offered designers and contractors the tools needed for achieving a 50% energy savings compared to buildings that met the minimum requirements of Standard 90.1-2004. From there, ASHRAE moved to Zero Energy guides. ASHRAE's research program has provided valuable information for the development of the AEDGs in many direct and indirect ways. To date, nearly 700,000 copies of the guides have been put into circulation.

A new direction to focus on building performance metrics emerged beginning around 2000. This was driven by the need to quantify and validate claims of

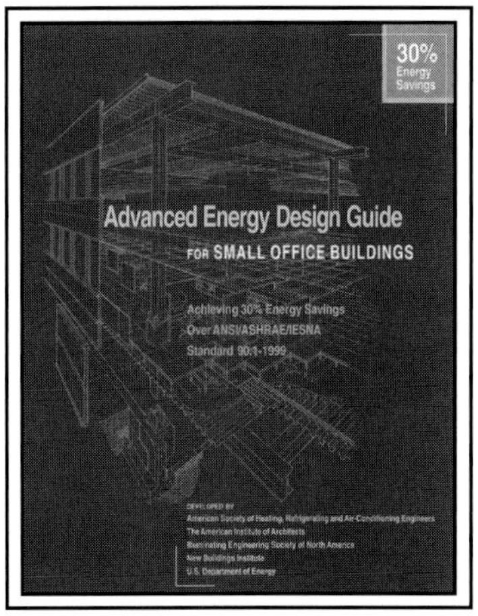

The cover of the first AEDG, 2004.

improved energy efficiency and overall building performance. This included emphasis on quantifying building environmental quality and understanding its impacts, principally indoor air quality (IAQ) and thermal comfort. ASHRAE research gathered baseline data and identified metrics for existing buildings. Also related to performance, building commissioning and fault detection and diagnostics reflect a focus on existing buildings. All were and are driven by the need to improve the energy and IEQ performance of existing buildings.

Control of moisture and mold, mixed-mode ventilation, underfloor air distribution, and integrated design concepts and tools were all advanced by ASHRAE research in the years following the turn of the century, driven by the need to promote sustainable design concepts.

In 2015, ASHRAE moved the AEDGs to provide design guidance for net zero energy buildings (NZEBs). This will likely be the focus of ASHRAE research for the rest of the decade. This latest series of AEDGs cover designs achieving zero-energy buildings with emphasis on stringent energy efficiency coupled with on-site renewables.

Another shift in research funding over the years was to support projects for investigating development and use of alternative and natural refrigerants. This was driven by the Montreal Protocol on Substances that Deplete the Ozone Layer, which was finalized in 1987, and the subsequent international policy regulations on chemicals that can cause atmospheric and global climate change.

Lastly, in the area of design of new buildings, building information modeling (BIM) has received considerable research emphasis in the past ten years, driven by the need for more comprehensive, automated design processes.

Eight for 2020

Michael Vaughn has managed the ASHRAE research program since 2001. With ASHRAE celebrating its 125th anniversary milestone, he sees eight major areas of HVAC study being shaped by ASHRAE Research.

Occupant Behavior. Occupant behavior in buildings refers to occupants' comfort preferences, presence and movement, and interactions with building systems (thermal, visual, acoustic, and IAQ) that have an impact on building performance. The interactions include adjusting the thermostat settings, opening or closing windows, dimming lights or turning them on or off, pulling window blinds up or down, switching plug loads on or off, and consuming domestic hot water. ASHRAE Research facilitates development of data, tools, technologies, and guidelines enabling integration of occupant behavior in the design, operation, and retrofit of new and existing commercial and residential buildings. The intent is that these products, focusing on the human dimension, may be used in the life cycle of buildings and potentially contribute to ASHRAE's energy-saving targets by demonstrations of behavior-driven passive and active building designs and identification of energy-saving opportunities from behavior measures. (For reference, see ASHRAE Research Projects [RPs] 1859, 1861, 1870, 1815, and 1883.)

Low Global Warming Potential (GWP) and Flammable Refrigerants and Safety. This is one of ASHRAE's most important research segments due to the safety implications and the impact on many codes when use of new refrigerants demanded by international regulation are implemented. Such changes not only impact the built environment but also transport regulations, firefighting safety, and servicing after installation. (For reference, see RPs 1580, 1583, 1584, 1717, 1806, 1807, 1808, and 1855.)

Energy Storage. Energy storage is a key component in the ability of engineers to design NZEBs. ASHRAE RPs advancing applications of thermal storage have laid the foundation for the industry's ability to develop NZEBs and will continue to be of paramount importance into the next decade. (For reference, see RPs 707, 1387, 1252, and 1719.)

Sustainable Refrigeration Facilities and Systems. One ASHRAE RP on the topic of sustainable refrigeration facilities and systems has benefits for application globally, especially in developing countries. The project cost approximately half a million dollars to complete. It is leading to additional derivative projects and programs for the Society that will advance technical capabilities needed for the cold chain in agricultural, marine, and medical applications. (For reference, see RP 1634. One of the products of this RP included the publication *ASHRAE Guide for Sustainable Refrigerated Facilities and Refrigeration Systems*.)

ASHRAE Guide for Sustainable Refrigerated Facilities and Refrigeration Systems, 2018.

Residential Indoor Air Quality Guide, published in 2018.

Residential Sector. From 1960 to 1995, ASHRAE had only completed a total of 9 projects on the residential sector and instead focused mostly on commercial buildings. Since 1999, ASHRAE has completed a total of 17 projects on the residential sector, including a residential IAQ guide that was completed in 2017. (For reference, see RP 1663, 1691.)

Infectious Diseases. For as long there has been ASHRAE Research, the Society has supported understanding how to control the spread of airborne infectious diseases. With the first recognized cases of Legionnaires' disease occurring in 1976 in Philadelphia, the topic became a major public health issue. ASHRAE publications serve as the industry's primary source of guidance. The recommendations presented in ASHRAE Guideline 12 and ANSI/ASHRAE Standard 188 result from information gathered from ASHRAE Research. (For reference, see RPs 610, 954, 1307, and 1361.)

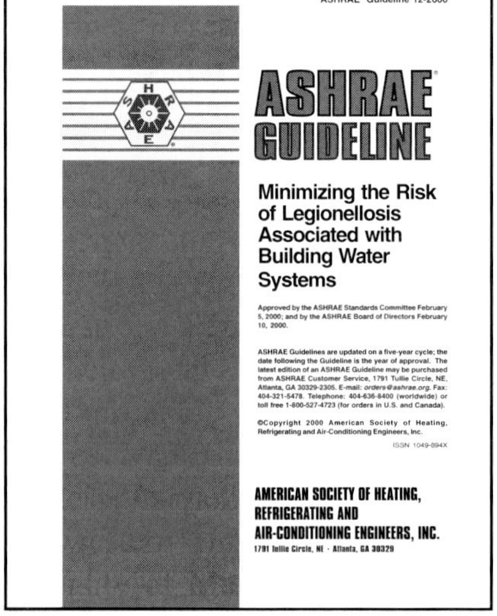

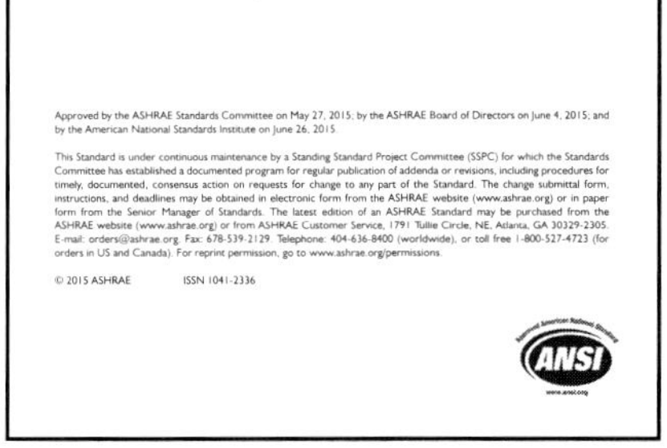

Big Data. Prediction models and data sets from a variety of sources are coming together online to streamline and integrate information flow and decisions for all industries, including the built environment. ASHRAE Research is now moving to crowd sourcing to identify the most accurate prediction models for whole-building energy meters, using the largest data set ever assembled for such a task. Also, in the past five years ASHRAE added data center energy use to the research agenda, driven by the explosion of cloud computing and ubiquitous computer use. (For reference, see RPs 1354, 1468, 1609, and 1633 and ASHRAE Great Energy Predictor Shootout 2019.)

Design Guides. Since 1974, ASHRAE has developed through the Research Program 41 different design guides on a variety of topics. ASHRAE's Research Administration Committee (RAC) is now working with ASHRAE's Publications Committee to develop a formal process within the Society for the review of technology-transfer-related projects so that some of the previous guides can be updated, if justified, and new ones can be created that have a strong demand. The new process will allocate up to 10% of the annual research budget for this purpose. The key difference with this new process is that RAC and Publications Committee will work closely together to identify projects that have good chances of recouping the costs of the new guides over time. (For reference, see RPs 143, 471, 526, 530, 592, 735, 737, 738, 741, 773, 786, 812, 849, 902, 920, 949, 969, 1047, 1058, 1064, 1065, 1133, 1180, 1214, 1217, 1228, 1254, 1261, 1384, 1565, 1581, 1592, 1627, 1634, 1663, 1673, 1674, 1675, 1712, 1719, 1762, 1807, and 1821.)

ASHRAE Commits $1 Million for Advanced Concepts Research in Emerging Technology

By William W. Seaton
Manager of Research

At the ASHRAE Winter Meeting in San Francisco, the Research Administration Committee (RAC) voted to strengthen the Society's commitment to more research in the areas of "emerging technologies" and "high risk" by establishing a classification of research entitled, "Advanced Concepts Research." This new classification is backed with a funding commitment of $1,000,000 for projects of this classification at any given time. The RAC also formally established two other classifications of research entitled "Basic and Applied Research" and "Research related to Technology Transfer".

Most of ASHRAE's past research projects have been of the basic and applied variety and these will continue. RAC also recognized that conducting research is of little value if the results can not be easily found and used by practicing engineers and designers. Therefore, they established the third classification, "Research related to Technology Transfer", to provide the means to present past, current and future research results in a more easily usable manner. Such things as design guides, toolkits, manuals and other special publications will be prepared for release for publication through projects in this classification.

Another major step was taken to advance ASHRAE's thinking in the area of Advanced Concepts through the establishment of a *Research Advisory Panel*. In the past, the majority of research projects have been initiated by the Society's 90 Technical Committees and Task Groups (TC/TGs), whose members are active in industry and academia and whose focus is on specific topics. Most of the resulting projects are of the Basic and Applied classification. The new Research Advisory Panel will be composed of individuals selected for their forward thinking and more general areas of interests. They will be selected from the new College of Fellows, from the research departments of Golden Circle corporate contributors and from academia. They will be charged with recommending those emerging technology, high risk, advanced concept type projects which ASHRAE has previously missed. Once identified, these projects will involve RAC and the Technical Committees and Task Groups for their initiation, monitoring and administration.

It is also anticipated that the encouragement of Unsolicited Research Proposals (URPs) will be another avenue for initiating Advanced Concept projects. URPs fitting this description will be reviewed first by RAC, and those recommended for approval will be forwarded to the TC/TGs for technical evaluation and monitoring.

Over the past several years, the ASHRAE Research Program has undergone several significant changes. The Research and Technical (R&T) Committee which has guided the program for years, and which was also responsible for the administration of the TC/TGs, was divided into two committees; the Research Administration Committee (RAC) and Technical Activities Committee (TAC). Now, TAC is responsible for the administration of the TC/TGs, in addition to other matters. This allows RAC to concentrate its time and resources totally on research matters. This division has gone quite smoothly and has resulted in the TC/TGs being better served and by the research effort being strengthened as evidenced by the accelerated production of Work Statements.

Another addition to the research program has been the establishment of the *New Investigator Award*. This program recognizes the fact that it is often difficult for junior faculty members to attract funding for their research work. The New Investigator program is a grant of $15,000 to a faculty member in the first five years of his/her research career. If the awardee can procure funding from industry for the project, an additional maximum of $15,000 in matching funds is available from ASHRAE. A final grant of another $15,000 may be requested if needed to complete the project and if the work is going satisfactorily. Only one of these awards is made each year and the winner is selected on a competitive basis. Normally, seven or eight applicants compete for the award annually.

In an effort to encourage more HVAC&R research by institutions outside of North America, the *International Cooperative Research Program* was established. This program allocates a maximum of $100,000 per year for projects which are to be conducted overseas and which are jointly funded by an organization, similar to ASHRAE, from within the researcher's country. The proposed project must be of value to ASHRAE as well as have a cosponsor. To date, only one such project has been funded under this program; a jointly-funded project with CIBSE and conducted at Loughbrough University in the United Kingdom.

1998

Golden Circle Investors Recognized

During the President's Luncheon at the ASHRAE Winter Meeting in Dallas, the following companies and their representatives were recognized for their support of ASHRAE Research at the Golden Circle investor level. Front row: (left to right) Bill Walter, manager, industry relations, Carrier Corporation; George Phelps, director of government and industrial affairs, NAIMA; James Bullock Jr., president, Environmental Air Systems; Mark Fly, director of Engineering - Governair Corp, CES Group; Glenn Hourahan, vice president, ARTI; Steven Blanc, Sr. research associate, Pacific Gas & Electric; Jay Jayaraman, Sr., energy management consultant, Enbridge Consumers Gas; Bill Denney, vice president of distribution, Automated Logic. Back row: (left to right) Mary Williams, secretary, Verle A. Williams & Associates and Verle A. Williams, president, Verle A. Williams & Associates; Clair Jenkins, president, Alerton Technologies; Clay Nesler, director of product development, Johnson Controls; James Domholt, marketing manager, McQuay International; Eli Howard, group director - technical resources, SMACNA; Norm Mattson, engineering manager, Commercial HVAC&R Division, Modine Manufacturing; Mike Ireland, executive vice president, NEBB; Kent Anderson, president, IIAR; Tom Mikulina, vice president - industry relations, The Trane Co.; Lee Burgett, vice president - New Ventures, The Trane Co.; Chris Candler, president, Invensys Building Systems and David Lewis, vice president - government affairs - Lennox International, Lennox Industries.

2000

Golden Circle Investors Honored

NEW YORK—Representatives of 24 Golden Circle investor companies and organizations gather during the President's Luncheon at the 2008 ASHRAE Winter Meeting. First Row (l–r): Pantelis Hatzikazakis and Denise Ernst, Lennox International; Maury Wawryk, Venmar CES; Boggarm Setty, Barthy Setty, and Raj Setty, Setty and Associates; Daniel Ellis, ClimateMaster; Karim Amrane, AHRI & ARTI; Mike Beda, MCA—Eastern Oklahoma. Second row: John Conover and Jeff Moe, Trane; Stuart Donaldson, Alerton; Mark Fly, AAON; Barb Popoli, Alerton; Frank Shadpour, The HVAC Exchange; Hugh Crowther, McQuay International; Paul Pieper, Venmar CES. Third row: Dave Knebel, AAON; Bruce Badger, IIAR; Rob Woodward, Carrier Corporation; Chris Taber and Brian Lynch, Big Ass Fans; Eli Howard, SMACNA; Manfred Gerber, Venmar CES; Brian Reynolds, Trane. Fourth row: Stefan Surdu and Terry Whitehead, Enbridge Gas Distribution; Anthony Picarazzi and John Hamilton, NEMI/ TABB; Jerry Bavers and Michael Dolim, NEBB; Bruce Anderson, CES Group. Other Golden Circle Investors include Applied Dehumidification Inc. (ADI); Chimney Design Solutions; Gray Metal Products; Siemens Building Technology; SMACNA Bay Area. The Golden Circle consists of investors who contributed $10,000 or more to the Society. Golden Circle investors contributed more than 10% of the total amount of funds collected for research.

2008

Chapter 4

Performing as Guaranteed

"The importance of standardization had been impressed upon my mind at every step in my experience, and now the necessity of getting away from the go-as-you-please method, which up to this time [1903] was the rule, became imperative, for at this time there were no standards."

John E. Starr
1924

At the time ASHRAE's predecessor societies were founded, a great deal of confusion and wild claims abounded in the heating, ventilating and refrigerating industries. The charter members of both societies realized that the growth of their respective industries depended on clarifying the confusion and confronting the wild claims by establishing reliable, fundamental data on which to base standards.

Dispelling Mysteries and Telling Secrets

The refrigeration industry made its first attempts at standardization in 1888 and 1889. In his address to The American Society of Refrigerating Engineers' 1924 Annual Meeting, titled "Twenty Years Ago," Thomas Shipley, president in 1912, reviewed the beginnings of this effort, and clearly stated the need for standards in the refrigerating industry at the turn of the century:

"It was necessary to arrive at some general agreement as to the condition under which it was proper to base guaranteed [dimensions and] capacities of [refrigerating and ice-making] plants. It was also necessary to publish and make generally known this information...that it would prevent the continuance of the practice, then in vogue, of making statements...that the industry was surrounded by mysteries and secrets, known only to the person spreading the propaganda or to the company he represented — which was an effort to obtain business by fear and intimidation, instead of merit. What was needed was an admission by men having proper authority from leading Companies engaged in the Industry — 'that each could produce a plant that would perform as guaranteed.'"

With this objective in mind, refrigerating and ice-making manufacturers in the United States founded the Ice Machine Builders Association of the United States in 1903, which was the forerunner of the Refrigerating Machinery Association (RMA), the Air-Conditioning & Refrigerating Machinery Association (ACRMA), and the Air-Conditioning & Refrigeration Institute (ARI). The first standard establish-ed by this association was the

Thomas Shipley
President of the American Society of Refrigerating Engineers in 1912-13, he was instrumental in starting the work on establishing standards in the refrigerating industry.

SPECIFICATIONS

OF

STANDARD ICE CANS

ADOPTED BY

THE ICE MACHINE BUILDERS' ASSOCIATION

OF THE UNITED STATES

Fifty pound can; 8 by 8 inches top; 7½ by 7½ inches bottom; 31 inches inside depth; 32 inches outside depth; band, 1½ inches by ¼ inch.

One hundred pound can; 8 by 16 inches top; 7¼ by 15¼ inches bottom; 31 inches inside depth; 32 inches outside depth; band, 1½ inches by ¼ inch.

Two hundred pound can; 11½ by 22½ inches top; 10½ by 21½ inches bottom; 31 inches inside depth; 32 inches outside depth; band, 2 inches by ¼ inch.

Three hundred pound can; 11½ by 22½ inches top; 10½ by 21½ inches bottom; 44 inches inside depth; 45 inches outside depth; band, 2 inches by ¼ inch.

Four hundred pound can; 11½ by 22½ inches top; 10½ by 21½ inches bottom; 57 inches inside depth; 58 inches outside depth; band, 2 inches by ¼ inch.

Fifty pound, one hundred pound, two hundred pound and three hundred pound cans to be made of heavily galvanized No. 16 steel, U. S. Gauge.

Four hundred pound cans to be made of heavily galvanized No. 14 steel, U. S. Guage.

All cans made of No. 16 material to have sides turned over top and bottom.

All cans made of No. 14 material to have sides flush at top and bottom.

All Cans to have one inch inverted bottom.

All bands to be punched ⅝ inch; bottom of hole to be $1\frac{5}{16}$ inches from the top of band.

All bands to be welded and galvanized.

This specification represents the refrigerating and ice-manufacturing industry's first attempt at standardization.

dimensions for 50-, 100-, 200-, 400-, and 500-lb ice cans. The next effort was the conditions under which a standard – or a unit – ton of refrigeration would be calculated.

With the founding of The American Society of Refrigerating Engineers in 1904, the effort to develop standards split into two distinct areas. As a technical society, the refrigerating engineers assumed the work from the Ice Machine Builders Association to establish the necessary technical standards for such items as test methods, instruments, and accuracy, by which testing is accomplished, and to define and list the terms used and data to be recorded. These standards are referred to by trade associations in their standards.

The Ice Machine Builders Association, as a trade association, focused on establishing standards that specified what constitutes good practice and what parts should be included, such as standard ratings, testing, design and construction, safety devices, air or water quantities, and velocities. These standards also stated what the industry voluntarily agreed was the minimum equipment and basis of performance for a unit or system.

Among the first areas addressed by The A.S.R.E. was determining standards for ammonia fittings and for measuring instruments, such as thermometers, hydrometers, hygrometers, and anemometers. The Society also took an active role in securing financial support for research on ammonia and worked jointly with the American Society of Mechanical Engineers (ASME) on defining a standard unit ton of refrigeration.

Ventilation Comes Next to Godliness

This phrase, proclaimed by the first president of The American Society of Heating and Ventilating Engineers, Edward R. Bates, during his presidential address at the Society's 1895 Annual Meeting, underscored the commitment of the charter members to establish a minimum standard of ventilation for all classes of buildings.

Mr. Bates also stated that "Every family has the right to have an abundance of good, fresh air, even if it is not aware of its rights. I hereby suggest that this be one the first problems which we handle."

The members concurred and a Committee on Standards was appointed. The committee's report at the 1896 Annual Meeting emphasized the scope of the task ahead: "A very little work sufficed to show the committee that there was a wide divergence of opinion among authorities as to the proper amount of air to be supplied per minute per person to crowded rooms."

1. That for all buildings, such as schools and asylums occupied almost entirely by children and youths under fifteen years of age, the minimum amount of air for ventilation shall be 1,800 cubic feet per hour per person.
2. That for all buildings occupied by persons over fifteen years of age the minimum amount of air for ventilation shall be 2,000 cubic feet per hour per person.
3. That for buildings lighted in part or wholly by gas the minimum amount of air supplied for each gas light shall be 3,000 cubic feet per hour.

Three-part Standard of Ventilation

Committee on Standards' Recommendation for Standard of Ventilation represents the first effort to establish a clearly defined minimum standard of ventilation by The American Society of Heating and Ventilating Engineers.

As a starting point for future study and discussion, committee members Professor John H. Kinealy, chairman, Hugh J. Barron, and William McMannis recommended a three-part standard of ventilation.

The question of what constitutes adequate ventilation was discussed by J.J. Blackmore in his paper,

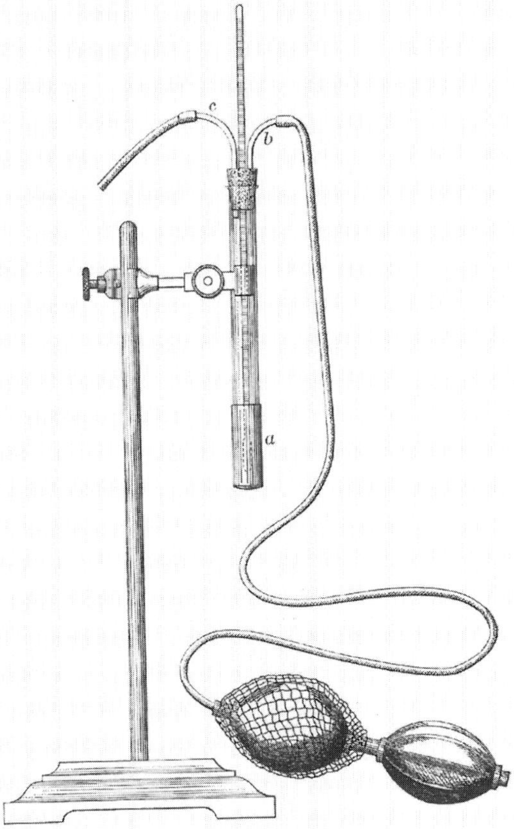

Dew-Point Apparatus

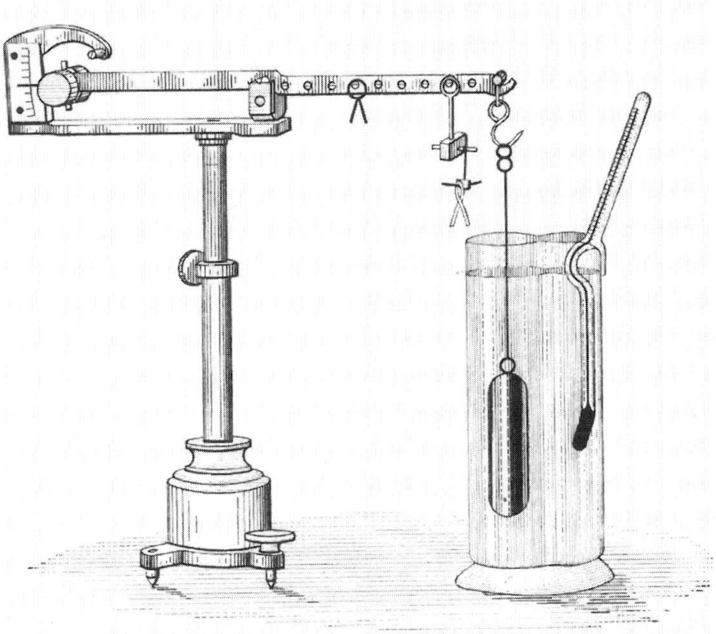

Westphal's Original Pattern Specific Gravity Balance for Liquids

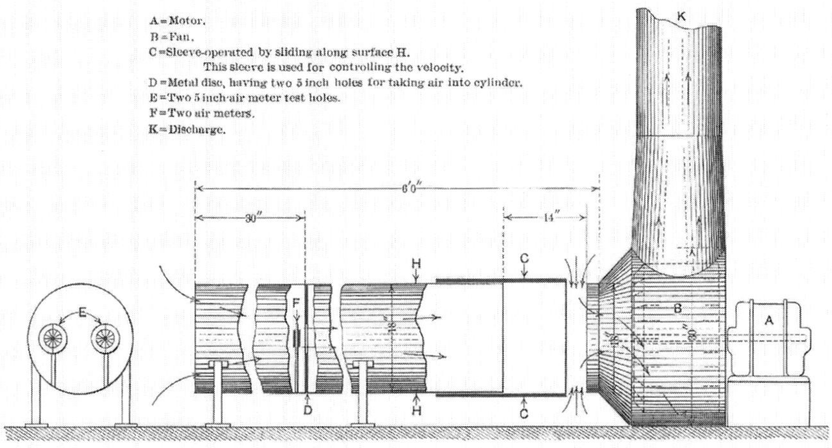

Anemometer

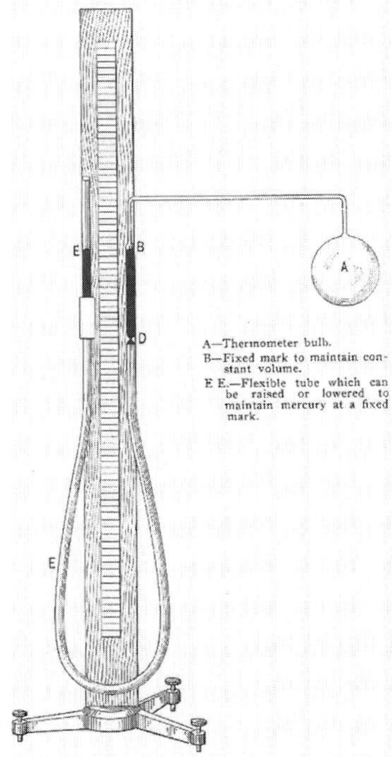

Simple Form of Gas Thermometer, Showing How Constant Volume May be Maintained by Raising or Lowering Tube

One of the first areas addressed by The A.S.R.E. in establishing standards was standardizing measuring instruments.

J.J. Blackmore

"Can We Standardize the Requirements for Ventilation?" He presented the paper at the 1916 Annual Meeting.

"There are so many factors to be considered and there has been so much opposition to some forms of artificial ventilation that it is not surprising that the engineer has some doubts as to the accuracy of our present understanding of the subject," said Mr. Blackmore.

He further stated that "the art of ventilation calls for several operations beyond that of conveying into a building a quantity of fresh air and the removal of a similar quantity of (so-called) foul air from the same building.... The other operations necessary for good ventilation may be designated as follows: Air cleansing, relative humidity, temperature, air movement, and odor removal."

TABLE 1. PRESSURE AND WEIGHT OF VAPOR AND DRY AIR IN A CUBIC FOOT OF ATMOSPHERE AT A PRESSURE OF 30 LB. WHEN SATURATED, AT VARYING TEMPERATURES.

Temp. deg. F.	Vapor Pressure	Dry Air Pressure	Vapor weight in gr. per cu. ft.	Dry air weight gr. per cu. ft.	Total weight of saturated air gr. per cu. ft.
0	0.038	29.962	0.48	605.32	605.80
10	0.063	29.937	0.78	591.93	592.71
20	0.103	29.879	1.24	578.79	580.03
30	0.164	29.836	1.94	565.79	567.73
40	0.247	29.753	2.85	552.89	555.74
50	0.360	29.640	4.08	539.93	544.01
60	0.517	29.483	5.74	526.75	532.49
70	0.732	29.268	7.98	513.00	520.98
80	1.022	28.978	10.93	598.48	509.41
90	1.408	28.592	14.79	482.65	597.64
100	1.916	28.084	19.77	465.77	485.54

In his discussion of what constitutes adequate ventilation at the 1916 Annual Meeting, J.J. Blackmore began by "describing the properties in the air as found in the open country and contrast them with the conditions as found in our cities and as they are known to exist in the buildings." This table "shows how rapidly the capacity of the air for moisture increases with the rise in temperature."

Areas addressed by the Society during the early years included establishing standards for heating and ventilating schools, sizes of steam and return mains, house-heating boilers, and a code for testing direct radiation heating plants to determine their efficiencies.

Just What Is a Standard?

During the 1909 Annual Meeting of The American Society of Heating and Ventilating Engineers, while considering a proposed standard for rating steam and house-heating boilers, the members debated how the term "standard" should be interpreted and used. Two reports were issued by the committee appointed to do the work because the members differed on how to interpret the resolution establishing the committee. Was the committee to determine a standard for rating or a standard rating for steam and hot-water heating boilers?

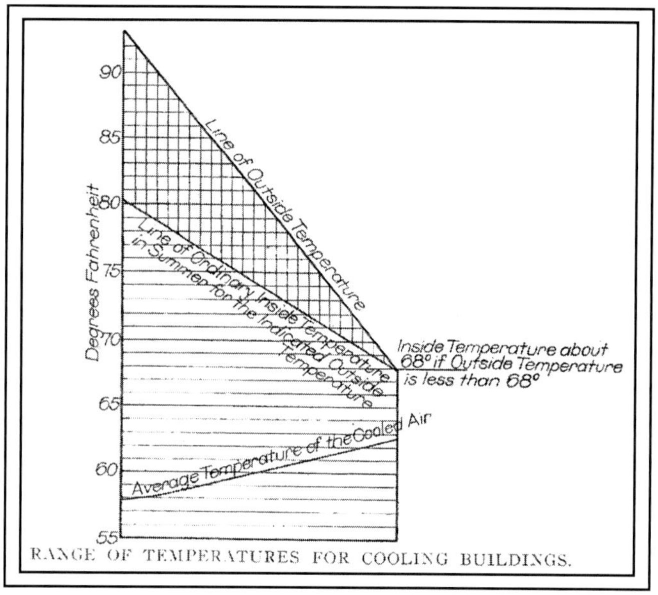

Range of Temperatures for Cooling Buildings

This chart from J.J. Blackmore's 1916 paper shows how the inside temperatures varied with outside differences at the New York Stock Exchange, which "is supplied with cooling apparatus to reduce the temperature of its room when the heat or humidity outside becomes excessive."

This debate established the precedent for how the Society would approach the writing of its standards, including the importance of achieving a consensus. Percival H. Seward, chairman of the Joint Committee on Standards and House-Heating Boilers, clarified the interpretation he used in writing the minority report:

"Now this minority report of mine is nothing more nor less than a series of recommendations or conditions that go to make up a method of rating, which, if accepted by the Society could become a standard method of rating. There is nothing compulsory about it. There is no legislation embodied or suggested. I do not believe this Society has any right to legislate. I think that all it can do is to recommend that certain conditions be accepted as standard, and then it is the privilege of anybody in the business to accept those recommendations or not as they see fit." At the close of the debate, the members agreed that further study was needed before the Society could take final action to recommend a basis or standard.

Ammonia Tables

At the time The American Society of Refrigerating Engineers was founded in 1904, there were several ammonia tables in use; no two of which were in agreement. The Society worked intermittently in this area until 1912 when the Society's members agreed that because of the discrepancies in the tables and the resultant difficulty in verifying data, assistance was needed to determine once and for all exact physical constants for refrigeration.

Members of the Society's Physical Constants Committee met with Dr. S.W. Stratton, chief of the U.S. Bureau of Standards, in Washington, D.C., about having the Bureau review the data on physical constants used in refrigeration.

Dr. Stratton said that "he was very glad to do the work, but he had neither the men nor the complete equipment nor an appropriation to do it. He suggested, however, that if [the Society] could induce Congress to make an appropriation to cover this proposed work, he would be very glad to take the matter up promptly."

TABLE XVIII—BUREAU OF STANDARDS TABLES OF THE PROPERTIES OF AMMONIA—(Continued).

Temp. Fahr.	Pres. Lbs. per Sq. In.	Spec. Vol. Cu. Ft. per Lb.		Total Heat of Liquid	Latent Heat of Evap.	Total Heat of Vapor	Entropy		
		Liquid	Vapor				Liquid	Evap.	Vapor
70	128.8	.02632	2.314	120.5	508.9	629.4	.254	.961	1.215
71	131.1	.02635	2.275	121.7	508.0	629.7	.256	.957	1.213
72	133.4	.02639	2.236	122.8	507.0	629.8	.258	.954	1.212
73	135.7	.02643	2.199	123.9	506.0	629.9	.260	.950	1.210
74	138.1	.02646	2.162	125.1	505.0	630.1	.262	.946	1.208
75	140.5	.02650	2.126	126.2	504.1	630.3	.264	.943	1.207
76	143.0	.02653	2.091	127.4	503.1	630.5	.266	.939	1.205
77	145.4	.02657	2.056	128.5	502.1	630.6	.268	.936	1.204
78	147.9	.02661	2.022	129.7	501.1	630.8	.271	.932	1.203
79	150.5	.02664	1.989	130.8	500.1	630.9	.273	.929	1.202
80	153.1	.02668	1.956	132.0	499.1	631.1	.275	.925	1.200
81	155.7	.02672	1.924	133.1	498.1	631.2	.277	.921	1.198
82	158.3	.02675	1.893	134.3	497.0	631.3	.279	.918	1.197
83	161.0	.02679	1.862	135.4	496.0	631.4	.281	.914	1.195
84	163.7	.02684	1.832	136.6	495.0	631.6	.283	.911	1.194
85	166.4	.02687	1.803	137.7	494.0	631.7	.285	.907	1.192
86	169.2	.02691	1.774	138.9	493.0	631.9	.287	.904	1.191
87	172.0	.02695	1.745	140.0	491.9	631.9	.289	.900	1.189
88	174.8	.02699	1.717	141.2	490.9	632.1	.292	.896	1.188
89	177.7	.02703	1.690	142.3	489.8	632.1	.294	.893	1.187
90	180.7	.02707	1.663	143.5	488.8	632.3	.296	.889	1.185
91	183.6	.02711	1.637	144.7	487.7	632.4	.298	.886	1.184
92	186.6	.02715	1.611	145.8	486.7	632.5	.300	.882	1.182
93	189.6	.02719	1.585	147.0	485.6	632.6	.302	.879	1.181
94	192.7	.02723	1.560	148.2	484.6	632.8	.304	.875	1.179
95	195.8	.02727	1.536	149.3	483.5	632.8	.306	.872	1.178
96	198.9	.02731	1.511	150.5	482.4	632.9	.308	.868	1.176
97	202.1	.02735	1.488	151.7	481.3	633.0	.310	.865	1.175
98	205.3	.02739	1.464	152.8	480.2	633.0	.312	.861	1.173
99	208.6	.02743	1.442	154.0	479.1	633.1	.314	.858	1.172
100	211.9	.02747	1.419	155.2	478.0	633.2	.316	.854	1.170
101	215.2	.02752	1.398	156.4	476.9	633.3	.319	.851	1.170
102	218.6	.02756	1.376	157.5	475.8	633.3	.321	.847	1.168
103	222.0	.02760	1.355	158.7	474.7	633.4	.323	.844	1.167
104	225.4	.02764	1.334	159.9	473.6	633.5	.325	.840	1.165
105	228.9	.02769	1.314	161.1	472.5	633.6	.327	.837	1.164
106	232.5	.02773	1.294	162.2	471.4	633.6	.329	.833	1.162
107	236.0	.02777	1.274	163.4	470.2	633.6	.331	.830	1.161
108	239.7	.02782	1.255	164.6	469.0	633.6	.333	.826	1.159
109	243.3	.02786	1.236	165.8	467.9	633.7	.335	.823	1.158
110	247.0	.02790	1.217	167.0	466.7	633.7	.337	.819	1.156
111	250.8	.02795	1.199	168.2	465.6	633.8	.339	.816	1.155
112	254.5	.02799	1.181	169.4	464.4	633.8	.341	.813	1.154
113	258.4	.02804	1.163	170.5	463.3	633.8	.343	.809	1.152
114	262.2	.02808	1.146	171.8	462.1	633.9	.345	.806	1.151
115	266.1	.02813	1.129	173.0	460.9	633.9	.347	.802	1.149
116	270.1	.02817	1.112	174.2	459.7	633.9	.349	.799	1.148
117	274.1	.02822	1.095	175.4	458.5	633.9	.351	.795	1.146
118	278.2	.02827	1.079	176.6	457.3	633.9	.353	.792	1.145
119	282.3	.02832	1.063	177.8	456.1	633.9	.355	.788	1.143
120	286.4	.02836	1.048	179.0	454.9	633.9	.358	.785	1.143

Tables of the Properties of Ammonia

The Society, with the cooperation of nearly all the organizations interested in refrigeration at that time, successfully campaigned members of both houses of the U.S. Congress. An initial appropriation of $15,000 was awarded to the Bureau of Standards, and research began in 1915. Additional appropriations of $20,000 each year for the next two years were considered to be necessary.

When Congress refused the appropriation for the second year, the Society raised the necessary funds from industry to retain the Bureau of Standards research staff, and the work continued.

The result was one reliable ammonia table in universal use throughout the world.

Standard Tonnage Basis of Refrigeration

Since 1893, ASME had been working on the issues of latent heat of fusion ice, establishing a standard tonnage basis of refrigeration, and preparing a set of rules for conducting tests of refrigerating machines. In 1908, The A.S.R.E. appointed a committee to work jointly with the ASME committee.

The work was undertaken under two heads: (a) The selection of units to measure the cooling effect of refrigeration produced and (b) the selection of a standard set of conditions under which a refrigerating machine, no matter what its type, shall be run in determining what is described as its commercial tonnage capacity. Until the correct value was established, engineers used the value of 142 Btu per pound as the latent heat of ice, and 284,000 Btu was used as the ton of refrigeration. The U.S. Bureau of Standards greatly assisted in resolving this question by establishing the value of 143.4 Btu as the latent heat of ice.

In 1920, after years of discussion in committee, The A.S.R.E. adopted the following values as its standard, thus settling this controversial subject:

- Standard ton of refrigeration — 288,000 Btu per day
- Standard commercial ton of refrigeration — 200 Btu per minute
- Condensing temperature — 86°F (30°C)
- Evaporating temperature — 5°F (–15°C)
- Standard rating of a refrigerating machine, using liquefiable vapor—the number of standard commercial tons of refrigeration it performs under adopted refrigerant pressures.

Safety Code for Mechanical Refrigeration

The first efforts to establish a safety code for refrigeration date back to 1914 when an ASRE committee working with fire department officials in New York City proposed regulations for refrigerating plants in the City. The regulations became law in 1915. The committee also worked with the state of Massachusetts on a more comprehensive law during this same year.

Harry D. Edwards

From this experience, The A.S.R.E. recognized the need for cities and states to enact safety regulations and for the Society to assist by preparing a code, which could be used as a model.

In response to this need, The A.S.R.E. Council in 1915 ap-pointed the Committee on Municipal and State Regulations for Refrigerating Plants and Refrigerants, chaired by W.E. Parsons. This committee proposed a tentative Refrigerant Safety Code in 1919. The second draft was presented at the 1922 Annual Meeting by F.E. Matthews, chairman of the renamed Mechanical Refrigeration Safety Code Committee.

H.D. Edwards, in 1934, wrote a paper reviewing the first two decades of the Refrigeration Safety Code, which appeared in the May 1934 issue of *Refrigerating Engineering*. In part, he said:

"The year 1922 marks also the first formulation of definite rules of procedure, and the adoption of a plan for balancing the personnel of the committee [to represent every conceivable interest]. For procedure, two sets of rules were involved—first, those drawn up by The A.S.R.E. Council at the suggestion of Mr. Matthews, and second, the rules of the national standardizing agency of that time, the American Engineering Standards Committee.

"The adopted procedures called for the use of Sectional Committees [the forerunners of today's Standards Project Committees] for principal standardizing activities, for periodical revision of all committee work such as codes and standards, for the use of small standing committees on temporary rulings and exceptions, and for presenta-

F.E. Matthews
F.E. Matthews was a staunch pillar of ASRE from the beginning and served as president of the Society in 1920. His writings, books and articles made his name well known for many years. He was a pioneer for the safety movement, and for 15 years, he was the chairman of the committee charged with developing the safety code.

PERSONNEL OF SECTIONAL COMMITTEE ASA-B9
Safety Code for Mechanical Refrigeration

Organization	*Representative*	
American Society of Refrigerating Engineers	George B. Bright, Detroit, Mich.	(E)
American Society of Refrigerating Engineers	Glenn Muffly, Springfield, Ohio.	(E)
American Society of Refrigerating Engineers	Van R. H. Greene, New York, N. Y.	(E)
American Society of Refrigerating Engineers	D. R. Harper, Pittsburgh, Pa.	(E)
American Society of Refrigerating Engineers	F. E. Mathews Leonia, N. J.	(E)
American Chemical Society	F. G. Keyes, Cambridge, Mass.	(E)
American Gas Association	N. T. Sellman, New York, N. Y.	(B)
American Institute of Electrical Engineers	H. P. Hill, New York, N. Y.	(E)
American Institute of Refrigeration	Fred Ophuls, New York, N. Y.	(E)
American Society of Civil Engineers	A. B. Heiser, New York, N. Y.	(E)
American Society of Heating and Ventilating Engineers	Lee Nusbaum, Philadelphia, Pa.	(B)
American Society of Mechanical Engineers	B. H. Coffey, Elizabeth, N. J.	(E)
American Society of Mechanical Engineers	Louis Doelling, Hoboken, N. J.	(F)
American Society of Mechanical Engineers	Walter F. Jones, New York, N. Y.	(A)
American Society of Mechanical Engineers	Chas. R. Neeson, York, Pa.	(A)
American Society of Mechanical Engineers	C. C. Spreen, Birmingham, Mich.	(E)
American Warehousemen's Association	Geo. A. Horne, New York, N. Y.	(B)
Asso. of Governmental Officials in Industry	M. H. Christopherson, New York, N. Y.	(D)
Bur. of Safe Transportation of Explosives	G. E. Carleton, New York, N. Y.	(D)
Compressed Gas Manufacturers' Association	F. R. Featherston, New York, N. Y.	(A)
Edison Institute	C. K. Nichols, New York, N. Y.	(B)
International Acetylene Association	H. D. Edwards, *(Chairman)* New York, N. Y.	(A)
International Asso. of Industrial Accident Boards	Jos. F. Scott, Trenton, N. J.	(D)
Manufacturing Chemists' Association	H. L. Miner, Wilmington, Del.	(A)
National Asso. of Ice Industries	George Lange, New York, N. Y.	(B)
National Asso. of Practical Refrigerating Engineers	M. Van der Veer. New Haven, Conn.	(C)
National Bureau of Casualty and Surety Underwriters	D. L. Royer, New York, N. Y.	(F)
National Electrical Manufacturers Asso.	J. W. Higham, Detroit, Mich.	(A)
National Electrical Manufacturers Asso.	E. B. Newell, Dayton, Ohio.	(A)
National Electrical Manufacturers Asso.	J. H. Ashbaugh, Springfield, Mass.	(A)
National Electrical Manufacturers Asso.	E. T. Williams, New York, N. Y.	(A)
National Fire Protection Association	H. E. Newell, New York, N. Y.	(F)
National Safety Council	David S. Beyer Boston, Mass.	(E)
New York Board of Fire Underwriters	Wm. B. White, New York, N. Y.	(F)
New York City Bureau of Fire Prevention	C. K. Michaels, New York, N. Y.	(D)
Refrigerating Machinery Association	A. H. Baer, Waynesboro, Pa.	(A) (A)
Refrigerating Machinery Association	W. H. Carrier, Newark, N. J.	(A)
Refrigerating Machinery Association	L. S. Morse, York, Pa.	(A)
Refrigerating Machinery Association	W. S. Kremer, Milwaukee, Wis.	(A)
Underwriters' Laboratories	S. V. James, Chicago, Ill.	(F)
U. S. Bureau of Standards	C. S. Cragoe, Washington, D. C.	(D)
U. S. Department of Labor	J. F. Dalton, Brooklyn, N. Y.	(C)

In 1922, The A.S.R.E. set up rules to guide the standards writing process. The Mechanical Refrigerating Safety Code Committee, chaired by F.E. Matthews, was expanded under these rules to include representatives from other associations, manufacturers, employers (users), employees, governmental agencies, insurance companies and consulting engineers who were interested in this area. This chart shows the membership scheme as of 1934 which illustrates the diversity of the committee.

tion of work in final form to the AESC after certain steps in the committee and The A.S.R.E."

Mr. Matthews' committee became the Sectional Committee for The A.S.R.E. Safety Code for Mechanical Refrigeration, and its membership was expanded to include representatives from 23 other associations and government bureaus with an interest in this area.

C.K. Michaels

According to Presidential Member Frank H. Faust, P.E., in his article, "80 Years of History of the Development of ASHRAE Standard 15, Safety Code for Mechanical Refrigeration," published in the November 1994 issue of *ASHRAE Journal:*

"The 1924 edition of the Safety Code was a refinement of the 1922 Code, but differed significantly in that it included provisions for new refrigerants methylchloride and the hydrocarbon refrigerants. It was primarily designed for industrial applications, with

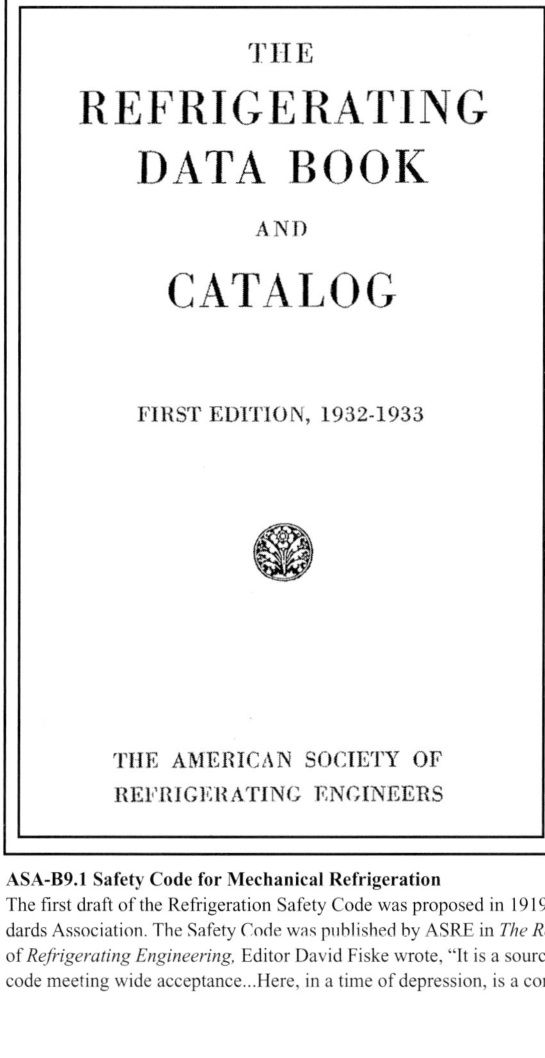

THE

REFRIGERATING DATA BOOK

AND

CATALOG

FIRST EDITION, 1932-1933

THE AMERICAN SOCIETY OF REFRIGERATING ENGINEERS

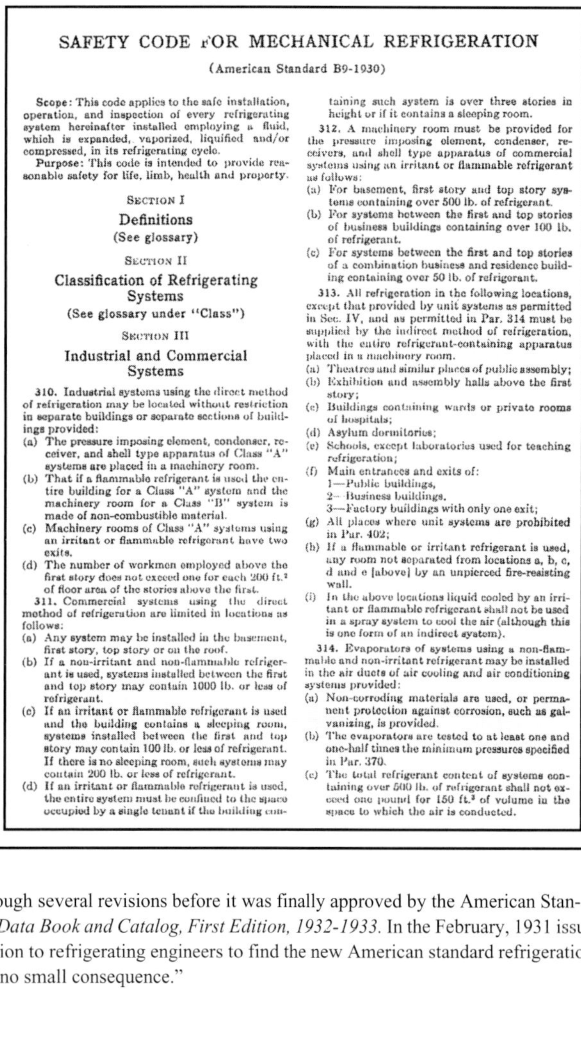

SAFETY CODE FOR MECHANICAL REFRIGERATION

(American Standard B9-1930)

Scope: This code applies to the safe installation, operation, and inspection of every refrigerating system hereinafter installed employing a fluid, which is expanded, vaporized, liquified and/or compressed, in its refrigerating cycle.

Purpose: This code is intended to provide reasonable safety for life, limb, health and property.

SECTION I

Definitions

(See glossary)

SECTION II

Classification of Refrigerating Systems

(See glossary under "Class")

SECTION III

Industrial and Commercial Systems

310. Industrial systems using the direct method of refrigeration may be located without restriction in separate buildings or separate sections of buildings provided:

(a) The pressure imposing element, condenser, receiver, and shell type apparatus of Class "A" systems are placed in a machinery room.
(b) That if a flammable refrigerant is used the entire building for a Class "A" system and the machinery room for a Class "B" system is made of non-combustible material.
(c) Machinery rooms of Class "A" systems using an irritant or flammable refrigerant have two exits.
(d) The number of workmen employed above the first story does not exceed one for each 200 ft.² of floor area of the stories above the first.

311. Commercial systems using the direct method of refrigeration are limited in locations as follows:

(a) Any system may be installed in the basement, first story, top story or on the roof.
(b) If a non-irritant and non-flammable refrigerant is used, systems installed between the first and top story may contain 1000 lb. or less of refrigerant.
(c) If an irritant or flammable refrigerant is used and the building contains a sleeping room, systems installed between the first and top story may contain 100 lb. or less of refrigerant. If there is no sleeping room, such systems may contain 200 lb. or less of refrigerant.
(d) If an irritant or flammable refrigerant is used, the entire system must be confined to the space occupied by a single tenant if the building containing such system is over three stories in height or if it contains a sleeping room.

312. A machinery room must be provided for the pressure imposing element, condenser, receivers, and shell type apparatus of commercial systems using an irritant or flammable refrigerant as follows:

(a) For basement, first story and top story systems containing over 500 lb. of refrigerant.
(b) For systems between the first and top stories of business buildings containing over 100 lb. of refrigerant.
(c) For systems between the first and top stories of a combination business and residence building containing over 50 lb. of refrigerant.

313. All refrigeration in the following locations, except that provided by unit systems as permitted in Sec. IV, and as permitted in Par. 314 must be supplied by the indirect method of refrigeration, with the entire refrigerant-containing apparatus placed in a machinery room.

(a) Theatres and similar places of public assembly;
(b) Exhibition and assembly halls above the first story;
(c) Buildings containing wards or private rooms of hospitals;
(d) Asylum dormitories;
(e) Schools, except laboratories used for teaching refrigeration;
(f) Main entrances and exits of:
1—Public buildings,
2—Business buildings.
3—Factory buildings with only one exit;
(g) All places where unit systems are prohibited in Par. 402;
(h) If a flammable or irritant refrigerant is used, any room not separated from locations a, b, c, d and e [above] by an unpierced fire-resisting wall.
(i) In the above locations liquid cooled by an irritant or flammable refrigerant shall not be used in a spray system to cool the air (although this is one form of an indirect system).

314. Evaporators of systems using a non-flammable and non-irritant refrigerant may be installed in the air ducts of air cooling and air conditioning systems provided:

(a) Non-corroding materials are used, or permanent protection against corrosion, such as galvanizing, is provided.
(b) The evaporators are tested to at least one and one-half times the minimum pressures specified in Par. 370.
(c) The total refrigerant content of systems containing over 500 lb. of refrigerant shall not exceed one pound for 150 ft.³ of volume in the space to which the air is conducted.

ASA-B9.1 Safety Code for Mechanical Refrigeration

The first draft of the Refrigeration Safety Code was proposed in 1919. It went through several revisions before it was finally approved by the American Standards Association. The Safety Code was published by ASRE in *The Refrigerating Data Book and Catalog, First Edition, 1932-1933.* In the February, 1931 issue of *Refrigerating Engineering,* Editor David Fiske wrote, "It is a source of satisfaction to refrigerating engineers to find the new American standard refrigeration code meeting wide acceptance...Here, in a time of depression, is a contribution of no small consequence."

little said about small systems, brine systems and direct expansion systems.

Frank H. Faust

"The 1928 edition was influenced by new revisions of the New York City law, under consideration in 1926 and 1927, and was passed in the form proposed by the Bureau of Fire Prevention under the direction of the fire commissioner, C.K. Michaels. It proved quite controversial, especially with respect to restrictions on direct systems of refrigeration."

The A.S.R.E. Council approved this edition on September 13, 1928. It was submitted to the American Engineering Standards Committee, but it was not approved. The next year, the American Engineering Standards Committee was replaced by the American Standards Association (ASA).

After further modification, the Safety Code was resubmitted in 1929. The American Standards Association approved it in 1932 and designated it ASA-B9, thus becoming the first American Standard Safety Code sponsored by The A.S.R.E. The Safety Code was published in the first edition of *The Refrigerating Data Book and Catalog.*

The 1939 edition is the first revision of the Safety Code in accordance with rules and regulations of the ASA. Mr. Faust recalls:

"The primary basis of classification was revised to building occupancy, replacing weight of refrigerant. The classifications became institutional, public assembly, residential, commercial, industrial, and mixed occupancy.

"This was a great improvement, because it simplified the writing of the code and enhanced its understanding. It is more nearly rational and logical, because type of occupancy is more nearly related to type of system, to refrigerant used, and installation requirement. The 1939 code edition introduced a classification of refrigerants based on their relative safety and it allowed new refrigerants to be added simply by assigning them to groups 1, 2 and 3."

Between 1939 and 1959, the Safety Code continued to be refined, and was designated as ASA-B9.1. During this period, the ASA was succeeded by the American National Standards Institute (ANSI). Following merger of ASRE and ASHAE in 1959, ASHRAE took over the sponsorship of the Safety Code. Subsequent editions appeared as ASA B9.1-1964, ANSI B9.1-1971, ANSI/ASHRAE 15-1978,

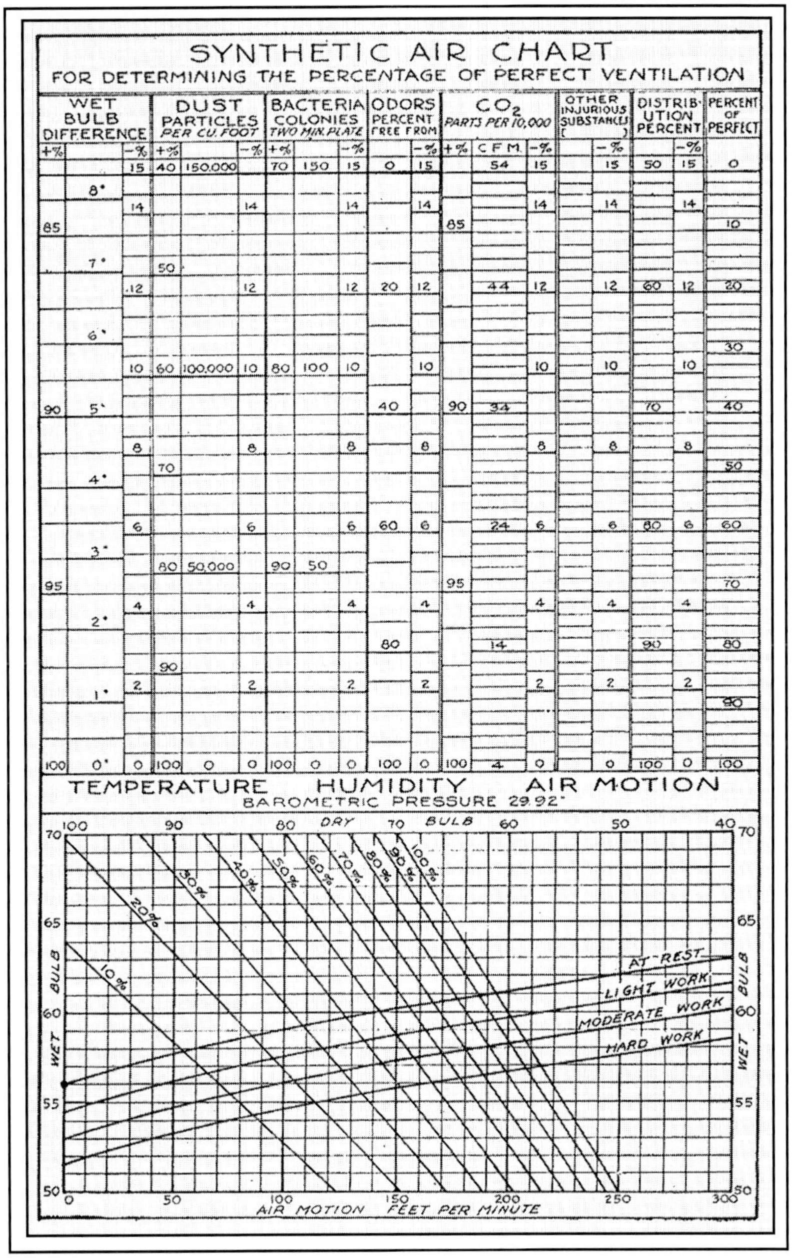

One of the first attempts to catalog and understand the importance of several physical and chemical properties of man's atmospheric environment was the development and presentation of the Synthetic Air Chart by Dr. E. Vernon Hill. The chart offered a means of determining the percentage of perfect ventilation by considering all the known factors that make up the air conditions in a room.

ANSI/ASHRAE 15-1989 and ANSI/ASHRAE 15-1992, and ANSI/ASHRAE 15-1994.

The foreword of the 1992 edition noted: "The industry response to the [chlorofluorocarbon] CFC issue has accelerated the introduction of alternative refrigerants. The entry of new refrigerants and blends in the market and the introduction of new safety classifications prompted the early revision of this standard." A short publishing history of this standard also appears in thc foreword.

Comfort Air Conditioning

Ferry C. Houghten observed in 1945 that "the history of the early development of standards for comfort air conditioning, like the history of the beginning of comfort air conditioning itself, is not clearly recorded in our annals."

One of the first attempts to catalog and understand the importance of human response to atmospheric conditions was the development and presentation of Dr. E. Vernon Hill's synthetic air chart in 1920. The chart served to center attention on the lack of accepted quantitative data and on the wide difference of opinion on the effect of a person's "feeling of warmth of such physical conditions of the atmosphere as its dry-bulb temperature, moisture content, and motion," according to Mr. Houghten.

These controversies and discussions, which at times became acrimonious, were instrumental in clarifying the need for laboratory research in this area and eventually to the organization of The A.S.H.V.E. Research Bureau. In fact, one of the primary goals of the Bureau was to develop standards of atmospheric conditions for the comfort of man. The continuing debate in this area was the source of twenty years of prolific research for the Society.

With the growing application of air conditioning and summer cooling in the late 1920s and early 1930s, some confusion and controversy developed about the conditions to be maintained. The early attempts were to use the same standards for summer comfort as were used for winter. The Society's research proved vital in resolving these questions through definitive studies on heat dissipation to the atmosphere and acclimatization.

Glenn Muffly

During the early to middle 1930s the focus shifted somewhat to applying air conditioning to alleviating unbearable conditions in industry. Worker efficiency and labor laws were the major incentives. Consequently, standards needed to be developed.

In 1938, the Society published a "Code for Minimum Requirements for Comfort Air Conditioning." It was developed by a joint A.S.H.V.E. and A.S.R.E. committee, with both societies approving the standard in 1938. The committee members were: L.A. Harding, chairman; Glenn Muffly, vice-chairman; representing ASHVE, D.E. French, John Howatt, A.R Kratz, and C.W. Walton, Jr.; and representing ASRE, W.L. Fleisher, L.A. Phillipp, H.J. Macintire, and W.E. Zieber.

This standard was revised and replaced by ASHRAE Standard 55-66, Thermal Comfort Conditions in 1966. It specified the environmental conditions that will provide year-round thermal comfort for most people, normally clothed, engaged in sedentary or near sedentary activities. It was again revised in 1974.

The development of Standard 55 from the 1920s to the 1970s was dictated in part by the abundance and low cost of energy. During this period, the preferred amount of clothing worn by building occupants decreased and correspondingly the preferred temperatures increased from about 20°C (68°F) for winter to the year round range of 22°C – 25.5°C (72°F – 78°F).

In response to the higher cost of energy and the increased emphasis on energy conservation, the 1981 revision included adjustments that can be made for clothing, activity, air movement and temperature drifts, which give greater flexibility and often have energy saving potential. Standard 55 was revised again in 1992.

ASHRAE's Early Participation in ISO

International standardization started in the electrotechnical field in 1906. While some attempts were made in the 1930s in other technical fields, it was not until the International Organization for Standardization (ISO) was created in 1947 that an international standards organization devoted to standardization of all fields, except electrotechnical, came into existence.

The object of ISO is to facilitate the international coordination and unification of industrial standards. The organization brings together the interests of producers, users (including consumers), governments and the scientific community in preparing international standards. Its scope covers all fields except electrical and electronic engineering standards, which are the responsibility of the International Electrotechnical Commission. The technical work of ISO is carried out by technical committees (TC).

When ASHRAE celebrated its Centennial in 1995, the United States through ANSI held secretariats of twenty-three technical committees and eighty-five sub-committees or sixteen percent of all technical committees. Other major national representations were Germany with seventeen percent, France with twelve percent and the United Kingdom also with twelve percent.

The Society's involvement in the ISO began in 1957 when ISO/TC 86, Refrigeration, was formed. In 1958, the Technical Advisory Group (TAG) Administrator role for ISO/TC 86 was transferred to ASRE, and in 1976, ASHRAE assumed the Secretariat of Sub-Committee 1, Safety, following Germany's resignation.

In 1991, ASHRAE assumed the Secretariat of ISO/TC 180/SC 4, Solar Energy Systems — Thermal Performance, Reliability and Durability. Also, ASHRAE was approved as Administrator of the U.S. TAG to TC 180. The ISO authorized ASHRAE, as Secretariat, to revitalize SC 2, Terminology.

In 1992, ASHRAE received formal approval from the ISO to serve as secretariat of a new ISO technical committee called, ISO/TC 205, Building Environment Design. This committee was charged to work on developing international standards on thermal and visual comfort, ventilation for acceptable indoor air quality, and energy conservation, design and retrofit. The intent was to base the TC's work on ANSI/ASHRAE 62-1989; Standard 55-1992; ASHRAE/IES Standard 90.1-1989, Energy Efficient Design of New Buildings Except Low-Rise Residential Buildings; and ASHRAE Standard 90.2-1993, Energy Efficient Design of New Low-Rise Residential Buildings.

Standards as Codes

Historically, ASHRAE had developed standards for voluntary acceptance, guiding or advising the user on actions. The U.S. energy crisis in the 1970s changed that. Through the insightful leadership of 1973–74 President Roderick R. Kirkwood and others, ASHRAE, with the Illuminating Engineering Society

Roderick R. Kirkwood, 1976–1974 ASHRAE President

of North America (IESNA), developed the first energy standard for new building design. It was a decision that put ASHRAE in the public spotlight and made ASHRAE a focal point of building industry interaction. That extraordinary broad impact would result in ASHRAE rethinking how it develops standards. First the energy crisis and later the drive for sustainability forced ASHRAE to act for the public's benefit, and the Society was never the same, as Kirkwood would later say reflecting on the birth of Standard 90.

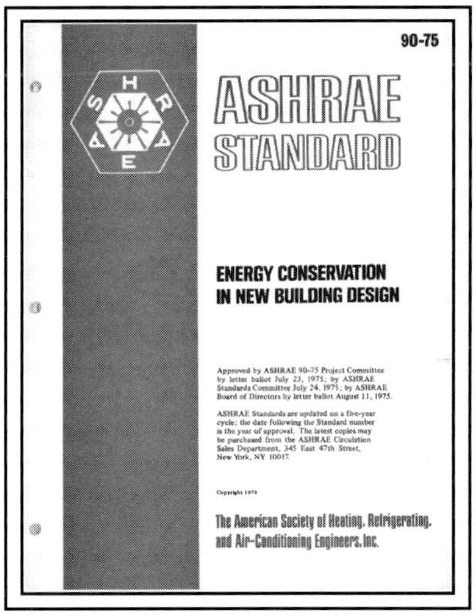
90-75

ASHRAE STANDARD

ENERGY CONSERVATION IN NEW BUILDING DESIGN

Approved by ASHRAE 90-75 Project Committee by letter ballot July 23, 1975; by ASHRAE Standards Committee July 24, 1975; by ASHRAE Board of Directors by letter ballot August 11, 1975.

ASHRAE Standards are updated on a five-year cycle; the date following the Standard number is the year of approval. The latest copies may be purchased from the ASHRAE Circulation Sales Department, 345 East 47th Street, New York, NY 10017.

The American Society of Heating, Refrigerating, and Air-Conditioning Engineers, Inc.

The first edition of Standard 90

Beginning in the 1990s, ASHRAE took further initiatives to promote acceptance of its standards throughout the world. In response to expressed needs by federal, state, and local governments, ASHRAE began writing some of its standards in code language to facilitate their adoption into building codes. The goal was to decrease the number of discrepancies between standards and model codes, thereby insuring that what is ultimately required by regulatory agencies mirrors the provisions developed through ASHRAE's standards-writing consensus process.

The first code-compatible language version of an ASHRAE standard was ASHRAE's *Safety Code for Mechanical Refrigeration*. It was approved as ASHRAE/ANSI Standard 15-1994 by ASHRAE's Board of Directors on June 30, 1994, and by ANSI on August 23, 1994. Next, ASHRAE Standards 55 and 62 were written in enforceable code language. By the 1990s, ASHRAE had entered the arena of codes, encouraging its standards to be adopted or referenced in codes as documents that were written to require actions of the user.

Continuous Maintenance of Standards

James E. Hill, 1996–1997 ASHRAE President

An initiative to handle the consequences of developing standards with greater industry impact was launched by James E. Hill, ASHRAE President in 1996–97. Hill wrote at the time, "Standards development is one of the most valuable services that we can provide to our members and the HVAC industry. They contribute significantly to the day-to-day commerce and business of this industry, the performance of buildings that are conditioned by our equipment, and the well-being of the general public that occupy these buildings."

By the mid-1990s, ASHRAE's leadership struggled with allocating the volunteer and staff resources to support standards referenced by or incorporated into codes. When ASHRAE's energy standard, Standard 90, was first developed, volunteers met every weekend for three months at their own or their employers' expense. The Society only paid for the meeting rooms and provided limited staff support. Two decades later, Standard 90 had been adopted or used in all 50 U.S. states. Standard 62, ASHRAE's ventilation standard, also required more resources. There were concerns about excessive energy use due to outdoor ventilation rates and at the same time growing awareness of poor indoor air quality due to a lowering of ventilation rates. *Sick building syndrome* was introduced into the technical language of the time. Both standards underwent extensive revisions in the 1980s, and Standard 90 was broken into two separate parts to address commercial and residential buildings.

In 1996 Hill wrote, "I am overwhelmed by the efforts of our members.We have had the brightest minds working on these standards for the past two decades. However, I've increasingly heard two concerns. First, these standards have gotten so complex many of our practitioners have found them difficult to understand and apply them and building code officials will not enforce them. Second, the resources of our members and staff are being drained by the enormous efforts needed to handle massive public reviews and the increasing numbers of appeals after the standards are published." Hill appointed a six-member committee to seek recommendations from all interested parties both within and outside ASHRAE for reducing the complexities of these types of multidisciplinary performance standards and to resolve conflicts much earlier in the development process.

A solution came in 1998. ASHRAE's so-called "high-profile standards" were placed under continuous maintenance. The intent was to keep ASHRAE standards viable by responding to requests for interpretation and to update them in the form of addenda to reflect new information, changing technology, or the need for clarification. Standards 15, 34, 62, 90.1, 90.2, and 135 were selected for the new process instead of the five-year revision cycle, the traditional "periodic maintenance" schedule that ASHRAE followed. A new type of committee was formed for each continuous maintenance standard, a Standing Standards Project Committee (SSPC), to reflect the ongoing nature of these standards' development.

With continuous maintenance, designers, building officials, producers, and others who develop new information or discover problems in applying one of these standards were encouraged to submit changes for prompt committee decisions. The entire standard no longer needed to be revised nor submitted to public review at a single time. Only those parts of the standard for which changes were proposed were able to open for public review, although the option to submit the full standard for public review remained.

BACnet—A Global Standard

H. Michael Newman, the first chair of the committee that developed BACnet, writes in his book *BACnet—The Global Standard for Building Automation and Control Networks* that the concept of what would become BACnet started with the arrival of the first microprocessor-based direct digital control (DDC) systems.

Cornell University, where Newman worked, had installed a diskless minicomputer in the mid-1970s that was interfaced to a manual control system through a series of binary outputs and relays. It allowed the operator to start and stop remote fans and pumps, pull up a 35 mm slide of the selected system, and even listen to the audio from an intercom system in the remote mechanical room. Later, computerless field equipment was possible via serial communications link. Then, around 1980, manufacturers introduced digital system controllers. The Cornell team was able to obtain the protocol specification that allowed communication with the new digital system controllers directly from a minicomputer. According to Newman, it turned out to be nontrivial to turn the protocol spec into viable software on the minicomputer, but after about a year or so they ended up with one central computer and three different types of field equipment. They wanted an integrated user interface and that is exactly what they ended up with.

H. Michael Newman

It became clear that the lack of a standard would ultimately present a huge impediment to the widespread adoption of DDC technology. Who would want to invest in DDC equipment knowing that their system could only be expanded with equipment from a single supplier? Newman asked Cornell's Facilities Engineering Director William Albern what organization might have interest in such a standard. Albern suggested Newman see what ASHRAE was doing about it.

So began ASHRAE development of BACnet, with Newman and Steven T. Bushby from National Institute of Standards and Technology (NIST) becoming the volunteers who provided early and ongoing leadership. Six years later, the ASHRAE Standards Committee approved the formation of Standard Project Committee (SPC) 135P, the "P" signifying that a new standard was being proposed.

News spread quickly. The editor of *Energy User News*, Rick Mullin, invited a group a controls and facilities folks to his office to discuss the new development. While most of those present hailed that ASHRAE had decided to take on the task of developing a standard, there was also a bit of skepticism. The one comment Newman will never forget was from a facilities manager who said, "We've got ASCII and RS-232, what do we need a standard for? You guys are wasting your time!" To Newman, that was like saying, "We have an alphabet and writing paper, why do we need the English language?"

The plan to develop BACnet was divided into three discrete parts. The first part was to figure out how to represent the functioning of a digital controller in a way that could be applied to any controller, regardless of manufacturer. The second part was to decide what messages should be exchanged between devices to allow them to communicate about their operation. The third and final part was to define how the various data elements would be represented as zeros and ones.

BACnet Gets its Name. The name assigned to the standard development project was "Energy Monitoring Control Systems Message Protocol." Even the engineers working on the standard knew a catchier name was needed to impact the market. Proposed were "ASHRAE Networking Protocol (ASHnet)," "ASHRAE Digital Open Building Environment (ADOBE)," "ASHRAE Facilities Automation Protocol (AFAP)," "ASHRAE Protocol for Building Control (APBC)," and "BACtalk," Eventually, Building Automation and Control Networks, BACnet, was selected.

Global Recognition. BACnet's timing was perfect. The global building automation and control system (BACS) industry had become aware of the problems posed by the lack of an interoperable data communication standard and everyone was looking for a solution. Moreover, no single multinational supplier had a majority or controlling position in the marketplace. This meant that a well-crafted, vendor-neutral standard could be accepted world-wide.

In addition to being recognized as an ANSI standard and as an ISO standard, BACnet has been adopted as a national standard by at least 30 other countries, including all those of the European Union, Korea, Japan, and Russia. It is also under consideration in some other major countries, including China.

European enthusiasm for BACnet was immediately apparent. Newman attributes this to the fact that there are a multiplicity of countries in a relatively small geographic area. That has led to acceptance of standards being seen as a key to successful commerce within the European Union. And, like the users of building automation everywhere, the Europeans were aware of the problems associated with proprietary protocols that effectively prevent interoperability.

Moreover, the Europeans had great experience with setting up user groups to support various technologies. It was therefore not surprising that in 1998 SSPC 135 was approached to form a BACnet Users Group in Europe. The committee welcomed the news. From the very beginning, all who had been working on BACnet knew that it would take support from the manufacturers for BACnet to make the transition from being a "paper tiger" to being a viable commercial reality. After suggesting that BACnet Interest Group would be generate a better acronym than "BUG," the first BIG met in May 1998 in Frankfurt, Germany. Since then, a number of BIGs have been added in the United States, AustralAsia, China, Finland, France, Italy, Middle East, Poland, Russia, and Sweden. Some are predominantly run by manufacturers. Others are more the creation of users. Some are partnerships. Around this same time, the BACnet Manufacturers' Association and BACnet International were formed.

Standards Globalization

At the time of ASHRAE's 125th anniversary, the Society is secretariat for ISO/TC 86, Refrigerating and Air Conditioning; ISO/TC 86/SC1, Safety and Environment; ISO/TC 86/SC8, Refrigerants and Refrigerant Lubricants; and ISO/TC 205 Building Environment Design. ASHRAE is also Technical Advisory Group (TAG) administrator for ISO/TC 86 and all its subcommittees (1, 4, 6, 7, and 8); for ISO/TC 59/SC13, ISO TC 205, the JWG 4 for TC 163, TC 205, and TC 163 (and three subcommittees). ISO/TC 59 is Buildings and Civil Engineering Works, and TC 163 is Thermal Performance and Energy Use in the Built Environment.

But since 2000, there are many stories of ASHRAE standards having global impact.

Among the examples of ASHRAE standards being adopted by a national body are Standard 90.1 by Kuwait and Saudi Arabia. In both cases the challenge was to adapt an existing ASHRAE standard to the needs of another country by reflecting that country's culture, climatic conditions, and building practices into the standard without changing the technical requirements.

BACnet began as ANSI/ASHRAE Standard 135-1995 and was adopted, following years of promotional efforts, by the ISO as ISO 16484-5 in 2003. ANSI/ASHRAE Standard 135.1-2003, a companion standard for testing conformance to BACnet was adopted as ISO 16484-6 in 2005.

International adoption of ASHRAE/NEMA Standard 201, *Facility Smart Grid Information Model*, is an example of how the international relationships established by the successful adoption of one ASHRAE standard can facilitate the adoption of

Delegation Travels to Russia to discuss BACnet, 2004. (From left) Mike Newman, past chair of Standard 135 committee; Mohsen Aboulnaga, vice president of ASHRAE-EFC; Jim Lee, president of BMA; Bassam Elassaad, president of ASHRAE-EFC; Steve Bushby, past chair of Standard 135 committee; and Girish Hira, treasurer of ASHRAE-EFC.

related standards. Standard 201 defines an information model that is intended to be used by groups who maintain standards for control technologies used in homes, commercial and institutional buildings, and industrial or manufacturing operations. It serves as a guide for how the control technologies need to evolve in order to enable the integration of those facilities with the smart grid.

BACnet is one of the control technologies that is a target beneficiary of Standard 201. Because of the previously established relationship with ISO/TC 205, Building Environment Design, the ISO home of the BACnet standard, TC 205 was informed about the plans for Standard 201 at the very beginning. International experts were invited to participate in the process, and regular progress reports were made along the way.

ASHRAE also has been successful in adopting ISO standards as American National Standards. ASHRAE agreed to jointly adopt and sponsor the

BACnet® Features Result of International Efforts

HONOLULU — A spirit of international cooperation was evident at the BACnet® meetings at the 2002 ASHRAE Annual Meeting held here June 22-26, with participants from Canada, Japan, Korea, Switzerland and the United States.

ANSI/ASHRAE Standard 135-2001, *BACnet—A Data Communication Protocol for Building Automation and Control Networks,* is the only open, consensus-developed standard in the building controls industry.

Foremost on the agenda were proposals to accommodate specific national and regional requirements in BACnet, resulting in two requirements proposed for a future addendum.

The BACnet committee also voted to recommend publication of addendum *b* to the 2001 version of the standard, said Steven Bushby, committee chair. This addendum will provide enhanced trending capabilities, which were limited to a single point. The addendum would allow multiple points to be collected in the same trend.

The committee also recommended addendum *a* for second public review. The addendum will provide advanced scheduling capabilities and several other features. BACnet schedule objects can represent even very complicated overlapping schedules, Bushby said. Currently, when there is more than one exception to the normal schedule, they are combined into a single, day-based exception schedule. This can cause a problem when a workstation from one manufacturer reads the schedule from a controller made by a different company.

Although the overall result is plainly visible, it is not possible to determine the individual components that went into making the exception schedule. The changes to the standard will make the individual components of the exception schedule network visible, thereby improving the interoperability of workstations and controllers made by different companies, Bushby said.

In other news, the BACnet Testing Laboratories (BTL) working group reported that an organization in Wuhan, China, is now under contract to further develop the Visual Test Shell (VTS) tool used to test devices for conformance to the BACnet standard.

The BTL provides independent testing and listing of BACnet products. It currently is testing application-specific controllers. Testing of other types of controllers is expected to begin this fall. More information about the BTL and product listings is available on www.bacnetassociation.org.

The BTL testing is based on proposed ASHRAE Standard 135.1P, *Method of Test for Conformance to BACnet.* While ASHRAE oversees the standards, the testing, certification and listing are done by BTL, which is an independent organization of manufacturers.

The BACnet Interest Group — Europe (BIG-EU), with 42 member organizations, also has allocated funds for VTS development to speed up conformance testing in Europe. An increasing number, perhaps as many as 50% of new projects, are specifying BACnet, according to BIG-EU.

In the U.S., the BACnet Manufacturers Association (BMA) and the BACnet Interest Group — North America (BIG-NA) will cosponsor a conference titled BACnet-CONNECTED! Sept. 22-24, 2002, in Columbus, Ohio.

More information about BACnet can be found at www.BACnet.org.

2002

following ISO standards: ISO 13256-1, *Water-source heat pumps - Testing and rating for performance Part 1: Water-to-air and brine-to-air heat pumps*, and ISO 13256-2, *Water-source heat pumps - Testing and rating for performance Part 2: Water-to-water and brine-to-water heat pumps*, as American National Standards. These standards were part of the work program for ISO/TC 86/SC 6, of which Air-Conditioning, Heating, and Refrigeration Institute (AHRI) is the secretariat.

At the time this was originally proposed, these standards related to ANSI/ASHRAE Standard 37, *Methods of Testing for Rating Electrically Driven Unitary Air-Conditioning and Heat-Pump Equipment*, and ANSI/ASHRAE 116, *Methods of Testing for Rating Seasonal Efficiency of Unitary Air Conditioners and Heat Pumps*. The rating standards were similar to, but not technically equivalent to, ANSI/ARI 320-93, *Water-Source Heat Pumps*, ANSI/ARI 325-93, *Ground Water-Source Heat Pumps*, and ANSI/ARI 330-93, *Ground Source Closed-Loop Heat Pumps*.

When the recommendation was made, ASHRAE was part of a joint committee with AHRI that proposed adopting these ISO standards as American National Standards. The joint committee considered input from U.S. experts as well as from those outside the U.S. in making this decision. The committee was also free to propose changes to ISO/TC 86. The process followed in approving and reaffirming these documents is the AHRI ANSI-approved process, which is a canvas ballot method. These standards continue to be American National Standards and were recently reaffirmed in 2012.

A reference to the ISO standard for ground-source heat pumps (13256 Parts 1 and 2) was included in Standard 90.1 since it was the only industry accepted standard for this product. There are also four Canadian Standards Association standards referenced in Standard 90.1. In the 2016 edition of the standard, two new additional ISO standards were included (ISO 9050 and ISO 25745).

90.1 in NFPA Consensus-Based Codes

Energy standards from ASHRAE will be included in the first full set of safety codes being developed through a consensus-based process accredited by the American National Standards Institute (ANSI).

The National Fire Protection Association (NFPA), overseeing the codes' development, recently approved publication of a key element, the NFPA 5000™, Building Construction and Safety Code™. The NFPA 5000 is part of a full set of codes being developed along with ASHRAE and other partners.

The full set of codes will contain ASHRAE's energy standards, Standard 90.1, *Energy Standard for Buildings Except Low-Rise Residential Buildings*, and Standard 90.2, *Energy Efficient Design of New Low-Rise Residential Buildings*.

The codes, known as the Comprehensive Consensus Codes™ (C3), represent the first full set of codes ever developed through a consensus-based process accredited by ANSI. They are expected to be published in April 2003.

"This full set of safety codes and standards through an ANSI-accredited process will provide states and municipalities with the option of using an integrated set of safety requirements developed in conjunction with experts throughout a variety of specialty areas," said ASHRAE President Donald Colliver, Ph.D., P.E. "We look forward to ASHRAE's energy standards immediately being part of that package. This is part of our continuing effort to promote the use and

See Codes, Page 2

2002

Test Method Established

New Energy Modeling Standard

Programs used to model the energy performance of buildings are complex, often containing 10,000 to more than 100,000 lines of computer language. A single typo, error or bug in any one of those lines can have devastating consequences on the accuracy of the program.

A new ASHRAE standard provides a standardized procedure to ensure that such simulation programs are accurate.

ANSI/ASHRAE Standard 140-2001, *Standard Method of Test for the Evaluation of Building Energy Analysis Computer Programs*, specifies test procedures for evaluating the technical capabilities and ranges of applicability of computer programs that calculate the thermal performance of buildings and their HVAC systems.

"Until development of Standard 140, there was no standardized procedure for ensuring any given computer program was accurate and appropriate for any given building energy modeling problems," Ron Judkoff, chairman of the standard committee, said. "Engineers and architects would simply have to take the word of the software vendor on faith."

Programs covered by the method of testing are used by engineers and architects to model the energy performance of buildings. Such programs can be used in the design of new buildings to make them more energy efficient and in the retrofit of existing buildings to determine what energy related improvements will deliver the "most bang for the buck," Judkoff said.

The standard provides a framework for adding all elements of an overall

See Energy, Page 2

2002

Chapter 5

The Opportunity to Congregate

"I have been a chapter man all of my life and closely identified as such in Philadelphia. I look forward to the opportunity each month of getting together with our group, sitting across the table from one another as we are tonight, and knowing them as individuals; even meeting your competitor and knowing him better and realizing that he is a very human individual just the same as you are, has the same problems, and is always willing to meet you half-way. It's these intangible things that mean the most in an organization like this."

Merrill F. Blankin
1943

On Thursday, July 18, 1907, at the Hotel Pfister in Milwaukee, John F. Hale of Chicago addressed the Semi-Annual Meeting of The American Society of Heating and Ventilating Engineers to report activities of the Illinois Chapter. Delegates, in attendance from as far away as New York, New Jersey, Pennsylvania and Massachusetts, anxiously awaited a description of just what a chapter was.

"The Chapter holds monthly meetings from October to May," Hale said. "Arrangements have been made for the use of the Meeting Rooms of the Western Society of Engineers in the Monadnock Block, Chicago. We have the use of the extensive library and reading-room, as well as the meeting room once a month. They also place at our disposal a lantern for reproducing views of buildings, apparatus or drawings for the purpose of illustrating any papers that may be read from time to time."

John F. Hale
First secretary of the Illinois Chapter and Society President 1913-1914.

Mr. Hale said of the forty-three Society members resident in the State of Illinois, twenty-three have identified themselves with the Chapter, and, he said, "we have expression from most of the others to the effect that they will join us in the Fall."

The First Chapter

The story of ASHRAE chapters begins when a group of members residing in Illinois formed a committee to entertain the Society at the 1905 Summer Meeting to be held in Chicago. This meeting was judged by all to be a resounding success, and as a result, the Society accepted the invitation of the Chicago members to return for its 1906 Summer Meeting.

To begin preparations for this second summer meeting, the Illinois members arranged a dinner, and rather spontaneously the idea of forming a permanent Chicago organization developed. Investigation of the governing constitution of the Society disclosed that there was no provision for chapters, so it was decided to petition the Society.

On July 19, during the afternoon session of the 1906 Summer Meeting, Society Secretary William M. Mackay read the following letter:

The A.S.H.V.E. Summer Meeting held at the Auditorium Hotel, Chicago, Illinois, July 19 & 20, 1906 was the first held in air-conditioned quarters. The hotel had just installed a carbon dioxide vapor refrigeration plant to comfort cool two dining rooms and a banquet hall.

"To the Board of Governors of the American Society of Heating and Ventilating Engineers.

Gentlemen: We, the undersigned, Illinois Members of the American Society of Heating and Ventilating Engineers, do herewith make application to form a Local Chapter of the Society, headquarters of which should be located at Chicago. Said Chapter to be governed by its local officers in conjunction with the By-laws of the American Society of Heating and Ventilating Engineers and under the supervision of its Board of Governors and such local by-laws as may be found necessary, approved by the parent body. All applicants for membership in the Chapter shall first be members of the American Society of Heating and Ventilating Engineers.

Yours respectfully,

TJ. Waters,	Jas. Mackay,
Aug. Kehm,	E.F. Capron,
J.M. Stannard,	Geo. Mehring,
John F. Hale,	John K. Allen,
R.A. Widdicombe,	Sam'l G. Neiler,
N.L. Patterson,	W.B. Graves,
S.R. Lewis,	John Boylston"

Following Mr. Mackay's reading of the letter, a motion carried to take a mail ballot on amending the by-laws to permit chapters. A second motion carried authorizing the establishment of the Illinois Chapter should the by-laws be amended.

Samuel R. Lewis
"We inaugurated the Illinois Chapter as a result of the social pleasure and professional benefit which were derived from the closer acquaintance engendered in the Society."

A vote on the amendment was sent out October 30, and 103 votes were cast, 91 being in favor and 12 against. The amendment read, "Local Chapters of the Society may be formed upon application of ten members in any State or Territory or in any political division of any other Country, if the organization of such local chapter will, in the judgment of the Board of Governors of this Society, advance the Society's interests." The amendment stipulated, "The membership of such chapter shall comprise only members of the different grades in good standing in this Society; any member of any local chapter who shall cease to be a member of this Society shall thereby forfeit all right to membership in such local chapter."

Programs and Committees

The following is a synopsis of the programs for the various 1911-1912 meetings of the Illinois Chapter and a list of the committees in charge of the programs for the various meetings:

OCTOBER.

Election of officers, installation of new officers and organization.

NOVEMBER.

Heating and Ventilating Practice in Europe by Augu... Kehm has recently ... an extended tour d... attended a meeting ... gineers, and inspect... ical equipment of a ... buildings. His addr... trated with mirrors...

DECEMB...

Hot water heatin... pliances—Committee... Joannis, Chairman, ... Geo. J. Phillips, F... This will include ...

6

special devices for forced or induced circulation of hot water, regulation insulation, valves, heaters, etc., and description of unusual or remarkable installations.

JANUARY.

The work of the Chicago Ventilation Commission—this Commission consists of three members of the Chapter: Dr. Young, Commissioner of Health of Chicago; Dr. Evans, Ex-Commissioner of Health; Dr. Tonney in charge of the municipal laboratories and Prof. Shepherd, representing the Chicago Board of Education. The Commis... ...n the results of two ...nd will outline the ...ived from the oper... ...st plant in the Chi... ...chool.

...BRUARY.

... Humidity on Heat... ...tion and the Elimi... from Heating Sys... ...tee: W. L. Bro... ...n; H. W. Ellis; J. ... Soule. The rela... ...ity to temperature,

7

YEAR BOOK
1911 - 1912

ILLINOIS
CHAPTER

The American Society
of Heating and Ventilating
Engineers

the experien... School and devices ... jection and contro... cussed. Devices fo... and methods of ins... automatically care ... tion will be conside...

MARC...

Special Test Com... Hogan, Chairman; ... W. A. Green, R. B. ... have been invited ... large plants, one i... cluding a theatre. ... bers has designed ... another has installed. Tests and studies of the operation of such plants will be presented, as well as the plans and specifications of the same, with criticisms and recommendations by the committee.

APRIL.

The Heating and Ventilating Plant at Northwestern University at Evanston, Ill. Committee: J. M. Stannard, Chairman; E. F. Capron; C. F. Newport; R. A. Widdicombe. A test of part of this plant was made some time since. The

8

... test, further tests ... description, illus... ...ns and photographs ...ant will be at hand.

...MAY.

...eting is the last of ... the past, it has ... to make the May ... a social nature. It ...at some unforseen ...y arise which will ...able to have one ...igned until later. Ample notice will be given of the program for the May meeting.

MEMBERSHIP.

Members of the American Society of Heating and Ventilating Engineers, residents of Illinois and in good standing are eligible to membership in the Illinois Chapter. Application blanks may be had upon request of the secretary.

9

The Illinois Chapter Yearbook of 1911-1912 included the synopsis of the programs for the various meetings and a list of the committees in charge of the programs.

With approval of the parent body now in hand, nine members of the Society, residents in Chicago, met on December 3 and formed the Illinois Chapter. The officers for the year 1907, elected at that meeting, were:

President:	T. J. Waters
Vice President:	James Mackay
Secretary:	John F. Hale
Treasurer:	August Kehm
Directors:	George Mehring, Edmund F. Capron, Samuel R. Lewis.

The Chapter was incorporated on March 5, 1907, and although other members of the Society were entitled to become charter members of the Chapter, only seventeen responded to the call by July.

Like the parent body, the Illinois Chapter formed a Committee on Compulsory Legislation, and its members made a number of trips to Springfield proposing laws to require the proper ventilation of all public buildings.

Interest in New York

Soon members in New York City also began to show interest in a chapter. In 1908 at the Society's 14th Annual Meeting, D.M. Quay, Society President in 1900, and Thomas Barwick spoke in favor of a New York Chapter. Calling it "purely a local matter," Society President James Mackay advised "the way to get at that is for twelve New York members to make application to the Board." Not until 1911, however, would New York members begin to organize.

On the evening of October 10, a number of New York members met at the Society's offices just recently situated at the Engineering Societies Building, 29 West Thirty-ninth Street. At this meeting it was voted that the Chapter be formed and the dues should be $5.00 per annum for Members and Associates and $3.00 for Junior members. The Chapter's Constitution and By-laws were submitted to the Society's Board of Governors and approved by mail ballot to the membership. The Chapter was formally recognized at the Board meeting of January 3, 1912.

James Mackay
Society President 1908-1909 who called organization of a Chapter in New York City a "local matter."

Monthly meetings had been initiated in November 1911, and soon the Chapter had appointed its first committee: three members who would prepare recommendations in regard to the ventilation of "moving picture show places." Within two months, the Chapter had sixty-four members.

The Engineering Societies Building where New York City area members gathered in 1911 to contemplate forming a chapter.

Of Benefit to the Public

Chapters enabled Society members through local committees to assist municipal and state governments in the legislation, regulation and enforcement of measures promoting healthful ventilation. In an era when travel over great distances was difficult, locally organized committees allowed the Society to be active in the city halls of Chicago, New York, Boston, Philadelphia and other urban centers and in their governing statehouses.

Fred R. Still, 1918
"To me it has such an important bearing on the future success of the Society, especially in the remote sections of this country, that I feel warranted in recommending that it be incumbent upon at least one of the future Officers to visit each Chapter once every year and that the expense so incurred be hereafter provided for in the budget for conducting the affairs of the Society."

In 1911, for example, the Illinois Chapter was instrumental in the City of Chicago creating a department for the inspection of heating and ventilating plants as a part of the city's Department of Health. "It is the duty of the engineer to pass on all plans and specifications, and it is necessary to obtain his [inspector's] approval before a building permit can be issued in the city of Chicago," reported Chapter secretary W.L. Bronaugh. The Chapter helped to establish the ordinances that guided the inspector. "These ordinances, while not perfect, are probably the strongest in existence, and now with the proper department for enforcing them we feel that we have accomplished a great deal," Mr. Bronaugh said at the 1912 Annual Meeting.

New York Chapter of the A.S.H.V.E.

Organized Oct. 24 1911.

"Breathe into a man an earnest purpose and you awaken in him a new power."

THE truth of these words has been amply demonstrated, for this earnest purpose of a number of public spirited members of the American Society of Heating and Ventilating Engineers has awakened a new power in the formation of

The New York Chapter of the American Society of Heating and Ventilating Engineers

A resourceful organization devoted to the extension of the benefits attending good Heating and Ventilating Work sprang into immediate active life on the gathering of the factors in response to a call that made a latent desire a live force.

The singleness of purpose to advance is reflected in the large membership actively and in unison engaged in utilizing the talent of all for the common good.

But three monthly meetings have demonstrated its value: in increasing the membership of the parent body, in helping to make the annual meeting of the Society a success, in recommendations of a Committee for public good and in the eagerness with which topics are presented for discussion and are discussed.

The future of the Chapter is best indicated by this brief past.

Participation in its work is invited from all.

W. M. MACKAY, *Prest.*, 113 Beekman St. JOSEPH GRAHAM, *Sec'y.*, 154 Nassau St.

AT the psychological moment, a new expression of the desire to provide for meetings of the heating and ventilating engineers in the vicinity of New York City met with an effective response, and resulted in the formation of the New York Chapter of the American Society of Heating and Ventilating Engineers, which was organized October 24, 1911, with a membership of forty-one members, which has since been increased to sixty-four.

The Parent Society having been organized in New York City some eighteen years ago, there is naturally a larger percentage of membership in New York State and vicinity. Owing to this fact, it was felt that a local Chapter, composed of the large membership of the Society in this section, would stimulate thought and action along engineering lines, and redound to the benefit not only of the Society, but to the entire profession.

As an engineering body the Chapter extends a cordial invitation to those who have ambition and courage to investigate engineering problems of mutual interest, and to participate in the formulation of plans for general advancement and the achievement of them.

Subjects for consideration, papers for presentation and suggestions for work will be gladly received by the Secretary, so that they may be made a part of the plans of the Chapter to utilize the time at the meetings to the best advantage.

"The Chapter has manifested an intention to work and to work intelligently along broad lines. It recognizes that a great deal of valuable experience, information and data is in possession of local men in its field and its primary intention is to afford an opportunity for the presentation and preservation of this material. While it hopes for a liberal support through membership, it invites co-operation, and a welcome will be given to those who desire to contribute something of value in an address or paper, and provision will be made for such co-operation upon the receipt of a request.

"Its purpose is not only to be useful to its members, but to render a wider service to the public, and nothing in its field that is of public interest or inimical to public interest will be neglected." (New York Chapter of The A.S.H.V.E. brochure, 1911)

By the Society's 19th Annual Meeting in New York, 1913, chapters had been formed in Chicago, New York and Boston and another was organizing in Philadelphia.

Members of the New York Chapter thought the practice of good ventilation would be greatly advanced by bringing the matter before the public in the shape of lectures. D.D. Kimball addressed the YMCA, Harlem Branch, City of New York on April 11 at a ventilation lecture which was well attended.

Of course, the social aspects of chapter affiliation were not neglected. In May 1911, Illinois Chapter members attended a performance of "Will-o'-the-Wisp" at the Studebaker theater, and afterwards adjourned to the Annex for an after-theater dinner and "love feast."

By the time the Society met for its 19th Annual Meeting in 1913, chapters had been formed in Chicago, New York and Boston and another was organizing in Philadelphia. The Board of Governors reported it is "altogether in order to express a word of encouragement toward the establishment of chapters, which have proved advantageous to a local group through the opportunity to congregate periodically, and to exchange information more or less informally."

The Sections of ASRE

The American Society of Refrigerating Engineers also organized local groups soon after its founding.

Four groups, some of which had already functioned independently, were granted charters by The A.S.R.E. on April 28, 1917—New York, St. Louis, Milwaukee and Chicago. New York might lay claim to being the oldest section since its organization meeting preceded those of the other three cities by about a month.

The 1917 amendment to The A.S.R.E.'s Constitution which provided for the creation of local organizations called the groups "Branch Associations." A 1931 amendment officially changed the reference to "Sections," although the term "Section" was already in popular use as early as 1918 when the Society established a Committee on Sections.

One responsibility of ASRE sections was to encourage the presentation of papers at national meetings. ASRE presented an annual award of merit to the section contributing the most valuable papers during the year. The first award was given in 1934 to the New York Section for the papers "Engineering and the Milk Industry" and "Details and Operation of a New Plant."

In the early years there was considerable discussion about section autonomy, and if, for example, the national organization should pass on new section members. Some sections had the three grades of national membership (Member, Associate member, and Junior member) and an affiliate member grade for those who were section members only. When a 1928 amendment to the national constitution stopped the practice of allowing sectional membership only, national membership increased by almost 30%. At one time only 35 of the 185 members of one section were national members.

Local Sections of the ASRE

Section	Charter Granted	Section	Charter Granted
New York	April 28, 1917	New Orleans	Dec. 11, 1944
St. Louis	April 28, 1917	Pacific Northwest	Dec. 11, 1944
Milwaukee	April 28, 1917	Connecticut Valley	June 12, 1945
Chicago	April 28, 1917	Erie	Dec. 16, 1946
Detroit	April 14, 1927	Buffalo	Dec. 16, 1946
Philadelphia	May 10, 1929	Dallas-Fort Worth	Dec. 16, 1946
Boston	Dec. 4, 1929	Georgia	Dec. 16, 1946
Los Angeles	May 9, 1931	Ontario	June 4, 1947
Baltimore-Washington	May 23, 1939	Evansville	Dec. 7, 1947
Richmond	June 9, 1940	Western Michigan	June 2, 1948
Pittsburgh	June 9, 1940	Carolina	June 2, 1948
Cincinnati	June 9, 1940	Indianapolis	May 27, 1951
Kansas City	March 10, 1941	Western Canada	Dec. 2, 1951
Cleveland	March 10, 1941	Houston	Nov. 30, 1952
Central New York	May 29, 1941	Dayton	July 1, 1953
San Francisco	May 10, 1944	Louisville	July 1, 1953
Twin City	June 4, 1944	Memphis	June 28, 1953
Northern New Jersey	Sept. 24, 1944	Colorado	July 11, 1954

Charter dates for ASRE Sections (Reprinted from 'The First Fifty Years, 1904-1954').

General Committees

Admission and Advancement: Roswell Farnham, *Chairman* (*one year*); C. S. Koehler (*two years*); P. R. Achenbach (*three years*).

Publication: J. W. May, *Chairman* (*one year*); H. M. Hendrickson (*two years*); W. L. Ross (*three years*).

Charter and By-Laws: J. C. Fitts, *Chairman* (*one year*); J. S. Locke (*two years*); G. B. Supple (*three years*).

F. Paul Anderson (Honors and Awards): A. J. Hess, *Chairman*; John W. James, C. H. Pesterfield, N. H. Peterson, R. A. Sherman, E. F. Snyder, Jr. (*Ex Officio*).

Guide: H. W. Alyea, *Chairman*; W. P. Chapman, R. C. Chewning, J. R. Duncan, R. A. Gonzalez, N. B. Hutcheon, M. W. Keyes, R. L. Maher, D. W. Nelson, E. F. Snyder, Jr. (*Ex Officio*).

Chapters Regional Committees

Region 1—Regional Director: F. H. Faust

Regional Areas	*Chapter*	*Member*	*Alternate*
Conn.	Connecticut (New Haven)	Walter Heywood, Jr.	J. D. Pierce
Del., Maine			
Mass.	Massachusetts (Boston)	E. L. Blair	R. F. Curry
Mass.	Western Massachusetts (Springfield)	F. A. Ferraro	C. R. Munn
N. H.			
N. J.	North Jersey (Newark)	S. H. Nitzberg	L. G. Huggins
N. Y.	Central New York (Syracuse)	L. A. Childs	S. F. Gilman
N. Y.	Empire State Capital (Albany)	H. F. Kruger	R. B. Taylor
N. Y.	Long Island	H. J. Campbell, Jr.	C. M. Alston
N. Y.	New York	J. B. Hewett	C. R. Hiers
N. Y.	Western New York (Buffalo)	C. W. Stone	J. P. Guerra
Pa.	Philadelphia	E. K. Wagner	C. J. Forve
Pa.	Pittsburgh	E. H. Riesmeyer, Jr.	E. J. Busch
Pa.	Johnstown	K. O. Schlentner	J. K. Thornton
R. I., Vt.			

Region 2—Regional Director: P. J. Marschall

Regional Areas	*Chapter*	*Member*	*Alternate*
Ill.	Illinois (Chicago)	H. E. Anderson	Herbert Kreisman
Ind.	Indiana (Indianapolis)	A. O. Roche, Jr.	G. W. Vogel
Mich.	Michigan (Detroit)	D. S. Falk	K. J. Wagoner
Mich.	Western Michigan (Grand Rapids)	B. J. Walter	R. J. Wantkes
Ohio	Central Ohio (Columbus)	W. A. Schoonover	T. R. Walker
Ohio	Cincinnati	T. D. Reiley	C. P. Krantz
Ohio	Miami Valley (Dayton)	L. P. Brehm	R. B. Walcott
Ohio	Northern Ohio (Cleveland)	J. L. Frissee	R. A. Urban
Ohio	Toledo	J. F. Guest	Robert Greenwald
Wis.	Wisconsin (Milwaukee)	R. D. Rodwell	A. A. Stutheit

Region 3—Regional Director: Fred Janssen

Regional Areas	*Chapter*	*Member*	*Alternate*
Colo.	Rocky Mountain (Denver)	A. S. Widdowfield	D. D. Pearsall
Iowa	Iowa (Des Moines)	R. S. Stover	R. T. Howard, Jr.
Iowa	Illinois-Iowa (Moline, Ill.)	W. W. Dodge	D. H. Ninow
Kan.	Kansas (Wichita)	T. L. Roberts	R. F. Jamison
Minn.	Minnesota (Minneapolis)	F. G. Vogt	J. H. Jester
Mo	Kansas City	J. C. Fasnacht	L. A. Heaven
Mo.	St. Louis	J. J. Blackmore	N. J. Hubbuch
Mont.			
Neb.	Nebraska (Omaha)	E. N. Seiler	F. P. Manchester, Jr
N. D., S. D., Wyo.			

Region 4—Regional Director: W. O. Stewart

Regional Areas	*Chapter*	*Member*	*Alternate*
Ariz.	Arizona (Phoenix)	E. P. Boothroyd	F. W. Gabbard
Calif.	Golden Gate (San Francisco)	Herb Duncan	J. I. Sprott
Calif.	Sacramento Valley (Sacramento)	M. J. Delavan	J. A. White
Calif.	Southern California (Los Angeles)	W. J. Biggar	A. Z. Levine
Idaho, Nev.			
Ore.	Oregon (Portland)	Keith Kruchbeck	W. B. Hayes
Utah	Utah (Salt Lake City)	L. K. Irvine	C. E. Ferguson
Wash.	Puget Sound (Seattle)	M. W. McKinstry	H. M. Hendrickson
Wash.	Inland Empire (Spokane)	R. D. Nevers	J. A. Doyle

vi

General Committees—1958 (*Continued*)

Region 5—Regional Director: J. W. May

Regional Areas	*Chapter*	*Member*	*Alternate*
Ala.			
Fla.	Jacksonville	W. H. Dowling, Jr.	H. A. Holborn
Ga.	Atlanta	J. S. Edgar	W. P. West
Ga.	Savannah	R. L. Reilley	S. H. Ball
Ky.	Bluegrass (Louisville)	O. J. Hill	H. L. Carr
La.	Delta (New Orleans)	J. H. Maloney	W. B. Moses
La.	Baton Rouge	A. W. Holland	W. J. Le Blanc
Md.	Baltimore	R. E. Dressell	F. M. Hewitt
Miss.	Mississippi (Jackson)	L. H. Smith	R. E. Vernon
N. C.	Northern Piedmont (Greensboro)	J. F. Hart	G. B. Rottman
N. C.	Southern Piedmont (Charlotte)	W. P. Wells	J. R. Clark
S. C.	South Carolina (Columbia)	B. A. Leppard	H. J. Haar, Jr.
Tenn.	Memphis	G. B. Ramsey, Jr.	J. G. Coleman
Va.	Virginia (Norfolk)	D. L. Gusler	J. A. Hoffman
D. C.	Washington, D. C.	H. W. Rush	J. W. Morgan
W. Va.			

Region 6—Regional Director: P. N. Vinther

Regional Areas	*Chapter*	*Member*	*Alternate*
Ark.	Arkansas (Little Rock)	J. W. Thompson	W. A. Bullard
La.	Shreveport	J. S. Malahy, Jr.	F. H. Spaulding, Jr.
N. Mex.	New Mexico (Albuquerque)	F. H. Bridgers	E. T. Krytko
Okla.	Northeastern Oklahoma (Tulsa)	J. E. Tumilty	G. A. McCune
Okla.	Oklahoma (Oklahoma City)	F. R. Denham	W. R. Johnson
Texas	Austin	J. L. Rea, Jr.	W. H. Luedecke
Texas	El Paso	G. H. Jackson	F. A. Hucnet, Jr.
Texas	North Texas (Dallas)	G. H. Meffert	O. H. Meil
Texas	South Texas (Houston)	H. D. McMillan	E. B. Appling
Texas	Southwest Texas (San Antonio)	F. S. Dalton	D. T. Kern
Texas	West Texas (Lubbock)	L. F. Davidson	R. A. Mixon
Texas	Fort Worth	T. B. Romine, Jr.	J. K. Mattox, Jr.

Region 7—Regional Director: W. G. Hole

Regional Areas	*Chapter*	*Member*	*Alternate*
B. C.	British Columbia (Vancouver)	S. W. Welsh	A. C. Martin
Man.	Manitoba (Winnipeg)	H. F. Randall	[illegible]
Que.	Montreal	D. J. McIntyre	Arthur de Breyne
Que.	Châpitre de la Ville de Québec	Jean Veilleux	P. [illegible] Lamarche
Que.	Ontario (Toronto)	John Thompson	R. A. Ritchie
Ont.	Ottawa Valley (Ottawa)	Jacob Klassen	A. H. Hargreaves
Ont.	Northern Alberta (Edmonton)	R. G. Proudfoot	G. N. Campbell
Alta.	Southern Alberta (Calgary)	H. W. Klassen	L. D. Ontonio

Committee on Research—1958

ASHAE Research Laboratory, 7218 Euclid Ave., Cleveland 3, Ohio
(Tel.: UTab 1-6161)

E. F. SNYDER, JR., *Chairman* — R. C. JORDAN, *Vice Chairman*
B. H. JENNINGS, *Director of Research* — C. M. HUMPHREYS, *Assistant Director*

Three Years	*Two Years*	*One Year*
P. R. ACHENBACH	D. D'EUSTACHIO	F. K. HICK, M.D.
S. F. GILMAN	E. S. HOWARTH	R. C. JORDAN
N. B. HUTCHEON	H. R. LIMBACHER	H. A. LOCKHART
R. M. STERN	E. F. SNYDER, JR.	ARTHUR NUTTING
H. E. ZIEL	J. I. TRIMBLE	

Research Executive: E. F. Snyder, Jr., *Chairman*; R. C. Jordan, *Vice Chairman*, D. D'Eustachio, N. B. Hutcheon, H. L. Lockhart.

Long-Range Research Program: R. C. Jordan, *Chairman*; H. A. Lockhart, *Vice Chairman*; N. B. Hutcheon, Arthur Nutting, J. I. Trimble.

Technical Advisory Committees—1958

Air Cleaning: W. C. L. Hemeon, *Chairman*; Arthur Nutting*, *Vice Chairman*; P. R. Achenbach, C. W. Coblentz, S. F. Duncan, O. C. Eliason, P. E. Engle, B. L. Evans, M. W. Keyes, R. C. Lower, C. H. Meyer, C. S. Stephens, J. R. Swanton, Jr.

* Member of Committee on Research.

vii

A list of ASHAE chapters in 1958.

Chapter and National Relationship

The American Society of Heating and Ventilating Engineers also debated the issue of chapter membership and its relation to Society membership.

In 1943 the matter was scientifically addressed through the preparation of a questionnaire sent to every member. The survey asked if members were in favor of a chapter subsidy to be added to national dues or for an allocation of national dues to be assigned to local chapters. Questionnaires were returned by 1,533 persons (50% of the membership). It was said to represent the greatest participation by the membership in any Society activity.

The results were two to one opposed to increasing dues for chapter support and six to one opposed to curtailing national services. The conclusion of the Chapter Development Committee was that "nearly half of the membership wanted something done about the Chapter-Society relationship, but more than two thirds did not wish to increase dues to obtain it and more than four fifths did not want to curtail any present Society services to obtain it."

Out of the 512 non-chapter members replying to the survey, 241 stated it is possible for them to belong to a chapter. The reasons they are not now members are (1) they have not been asked; (2) they do not feel the meetings are sufficiently informative and interesting to justify belonging; (3) they have not felt they had the time.

Regions

The first regional structure within ASHRAE came into existence at the 62nd Annual Meeting of the American Society of Heating and Air-Conditioning Engineers in 1956 where the membership approved revisions of the By-Laws for a plan of operating the chapters on a regional basis.

Then president John W. James explained, "The idea for this plan, which is primarily intended to strengthen the ties between the chapters and the Society, was developed during years of study by several committees assigned the responsibility for planning the growth and progress of the Society and its chapters. The gradual increase in the membership rolls and in the number of chapters emphasized the advantages that could accrue from operating the chapters on a regional basis. In the 20 years immediately preceding the adoption of the plan, the rapid Society growth included an increase in membership from approximately 1,800 to over 10,000 and an increase in the number of chapters from 20 to 61."

John W. James
President of ASHAE in 1956, he oversaw implementation of a plan to operate chapters on a regional basis

Prior to adoption of a regional structure, integration of chapters into the overall operation of the Society was accomplished through the headquarters office, various Society committees, the Nominating Committee and by visits of Society officers to each chapter. The approved plan called for the creation of regional boundaries, election of seven regional directors, and the creation of Chapters Regional Committees, composed of designated members from each chapter. The Chapters Regional Committees were authorized to meet annually.

ASRE also adopted a regional structure in the 1950s, a move made necessary by the fact that the ASRE Council consisted of a representative from each section along with Society officers, past presidents and directors-at-large.

In the December 1952 issue of *Refrigerating Engineering,* Secretary M.C. Turpin wrote, "Appreciative of the fact that the membership of our governing body has grown to a number considerably larger than is permitted by our Charter and of other comparable societies, ASRE Council decided last year to take steps to reduce its number of members. Accordingly, President Simons appointed a committee to study the need and feasibility of installing a Regional Director Plan."

A new plan was developed and accepted, with ASRE's 31 sections in existence in 1952 grouped into 15 regions, with each region having a director to represent it on the Council. Mr. Turpin summarized, "It is felt by the Committee that a Regional Director will accomplish much to strengthen the regions and their representation on Council and should do much to help solve problems of Section operation."

From time to time, the regional structure was altered to meet the needs of a growing Society, and in 1979, the regional structure underwent the most recent significant boundary change, increasing from ten to twelve regions.

Region No.	Regional Director	Location & Date Chapters Reg. Com. Mtg.	Area In Region
1	John Everetts, Jr.	Hartford, Conn. May (date to be announced)	Maine, New Hampshire, Vermont, Massachusetts, Rhode Island, Connecticut, New York, Pennsylvania, New Jersey, and Delaware
2	C. H. Pesterfield	Toledo, Ohio April 2, 1956	Ohio, Indiana, Illinois, Michigan, and Wisconsin
3	John E. Haines	Omaha, Neb. May 8, 1956	Minnesota, North Dakota, South Dakota, Montana, Wyoming, Colorado, Nebraska, Kansas, Iowa, and Missouri
4	A. J. Hess	Portland, Ore. February 17-18, 1956	Idaho, Washington, Oregon, California, Nevada, Utah, and Arizona
5	C. B. Gamble	Atlanta, Ga. March 12, 1956	Maryland, District of Columbia, Virginia, West Virginia, Kentucky, Tennessee, North Carolina, South Carolina, Georgia, Florida, Alabama, Mississippi, Louisiana (except Shreveport)
6	D. M. Mills	Dallas, Tex. March 19, 1956	Arkansas, Oklahoma, New Mexico, Texas, and Shreveport, La.
7	J. H. Fox	Toronto, Canada April 9, 1956	The Provinces of Canada

At ASHAE's January 1956 meeting, the Council appointed regional directors, fixed regional boundaries and selected locations and dates for the spring meetings of the Chapters Regional Committees.

Table 1. Transition Timetable

	1952	*1953*	*1954*	*1955*
Officers	4	4	4	4
Past Presidents..	5	3	3	3
Directors-at-Large	15	14	13	12
Section Directors	31	22	10	0
Regional Directors	0	5	10	15
Total	55	48	40	34

Transition timetable for ASRE to shift from Section Director to Regional Director plan.

The first Student Branch of A.S.H.V.E. was formed at New York University in 1932. Professor R.D. Morrill was Faculty Advisor. In the 1933 A.S.H.V.E. *Transactions*, the Branch was no longer listed.

ASRE elects first director under regional plan. Newly elected Regional Director Carl R. Fagerstrom (center) receives congratulations.

Table 2. Regions Under New Plan

Region	*Section and year present director retires*		*Additional areas in region*
1	New York	1953	
	Northern N. J.	1954	
2	Balt.-Wash.	1955	
	Philadelphia	1953	
3	Boston	1953	Maine, Vt., N. H., R. I.
	Conn. Valley	1954	
4	Ontario	1953	Eastern Can.
	Central N. Y.	1955	
	Buffalo	1954	
5	Erie	1954	W. Va.
	Cleveland	1955	
	Pittsburgh	1955	
6	Richmond	1955	S. Car.
	Carolina	1955	
7	Detroit	1953	
	West. Mich.	1954	
8	Evansville	1955	Ky.
	Indianapolis	1954	
	Cincinnati	1955	
9	Kansas City	1955	Kans., Nebr., Colo., So. Ill.
	St. Louis	1953	
10	Chicago	1954	S. Dak., Manitoba, N. Dak., Ia.
	Milwaukee	1953	
	Twin City	1953	
11	Georgia	1954	Fla., Ala., Eastern Tenn.
12	New Orleans	1954	Ark., Miss., Western Tenn.
13	Dallas-Ft. Worth	1954	Texas, Okla., N. Mex.
14	San Francisco	1955	Nev., Ariz., Utah
	Los Angeles	1953	
15	Pacific N.W.	1954	Idaho, Mont., Oreg., Wyo., Western Can.
	West. Canada	1955	

Organization of ASRE Sections under its new Regional Director plan approved in 1952.

CHAPTER AND SECTION DATES*

Chapter/Section	Mar.	Apr.	May
Atlanta (H)	9	13	11
Austin (H)	19	16	21
Arizona (H)	2	6	4
Arkansas (H)	19	21	19
Baltimore (H)	18	15	20
Baltimore (R)	10	2	7
Baton Rouge (H)	18	15	20
Birmingham (R)	18	18	14
Bluegrass (H)	9	13	11
British Columbia (H)	11	8	13
Boston (R)	3	7	5
Buffalo (R)	5	—	7
Carolina (R)	13	10	8
Central Michigan (R)	19	16	21

* Pending establishment of unified ASHRAE chapters, meetings of former ASHAE Chapters (H) and former ASRE Sections (R) are proposed upon the basis indicated above for early months.

Chapter/Section	Mar.	Apr.	May
Central New York (H)	18	15	20
Central New York (R)	18	15	13
Central Ohio (H)	16	20	18
Central Pennsylvania (R)	10	8	6
Chicago (R)	12	9	14
Cincinnati (H)	3	7	5
Cincinnati (R)	16	20	—
Cleveland (R)	2	4	2
Colorado (R)	9	13	11
Columbus (R)	23	27	25
Connecticut (H)	19	16	21
Connecticut Valley (R)	12	9	14
Dallas-Fort Worth (R)	9	13	11
Dayton (R)	10	14	23
Delta (H)	17	21	19
Detroit (R)	9	6	4
El Paso (H)	16	20	18
Empire State Capital (H)	11	8	13
Erie (R)	—	14	10
Evansville (R)	3	7	5

Chapter/Section	Mar.	Apr.	May
Florida West Coast (R)	—	—	—
Fort Worth (H)	18	15	20
Georgia (R)	9	13	11
Golden Gate (H)	5	2	7
Hudson-Mohawk (R)	16	20	18
Houston (R)	3	7	5
Illinois (H)	9	13	11
Illinois-Iowa (H)	16	20	18
Indiana (H)	24	28	26
Indianapolis (R)	18	15	20
Inland Empire (H)	2	6	4
Iowa (H)	10	14	11
Jacksonville (H)	3	7	5
Johnstown (H)	—	—	—
Kansas (H)	3	7	5
Kansas City (H)	2	6	4
Kansas City (R)	16	20	18
Long Island (H)	9	13	11
Los Angeles (R)	—	—	—
Louisville (R)	23	27	25
Manitoba (H)	26	23	28
Massachusetts (H)	17	21	19
Memphis (H)	16	20	18

Chapter/Section	Mar.	Apr.	May
Miami Valley (H)	4	1	6
Michigan (H)	16	13	11
Mid South (R)	9	13	11
Milwaukee (R)	3	7	5
Minnesota (H)	2	6	4
Mississippi (H)	23	27	25
Mobile (R)	23	27	25
Montreal (H)	16	20	18
Montreal (R)	9	13	11
National Capital (R)	10	7	8
Nebraska (H)	10	14	12
New Mexico (H)	17	21	19
New Orleans (R)	10	6	4
New York (H)	16	20	18
New York (R)	2	6	4
Northeastern Oklahoma (H)	10	14	12
Northern Alberta (H)	18	15	20
Northern New Jersey (R)	—	—	—
Northern Ohio (H)	9	13	11
Northern Piedmont (H)	—	—	—
North Jersey (H)	10	14	12
North Texas (H)	16	20	18
Oklahoma (H)	9	13	11

Chapter/Section	Mar.	Apr.	May
Ontario (H)	2	6	4
Ontario (R)	6	3	1
Oregon (H)	3	9	7
Oregon (R)	—	—	—
Ottawa Valley (H)	17	21	19
Pacific-Northwest (R)	—	—	—
Panama Canal Zone (R)	17	15	20
Philadelphia (H)	12	9	14
Philadelphia (R)	6	3	8
Pittsburgh (H)	16	20	18
Pittsburgh (R)	9	4	—
Puget Sound (H)	10	14	12
La Ville de Quebec (H)	—	—	—
Richmond (R)	2	6	4
Rochester (R)	4	4	—
Rocky Mountain (H)	4	1	6
Sacramento Valley (H)	4	1	6
San Antonio (R)	10	14	12
San Francisco (R)	19	23	21
San Joaquin (R)	17	21	19
Savannah (H)	—	—	—
Shreveport (H)	19	16	21
South Carolina (H)	16	20	18

Chapter/Section	Mar.	Apr.	May
Southern Alberta (H)	—	—	—
Southern California (H)	3	7	4
Southern Connecticut (R)	17	21	19
Southern Piedmont (H)	10	27	25
South Florida (R)	10	14	12
South Texas (H)	20	17	15
Southwest Texas (H)	17	21	19
St. Louis (H)	11	8	13
St. Louis (R)	16	20	18
Switzerland (H)	—	—	—
Toledo (H)	2	6	4
Twin City (R)	9	13	11
Utah (H)	19	16	21
Virginia (H)	18	15	20
Washington, D. C. (H)	11	8	13
Western Canada (R)	23	27	25
Western Massachusetts (H)	—	—	—
Western Michigan (H)	9	13	11
Western Michigan (R)	4	1	6
Western New York (H)	9	13	11
West Texas (H)	3	7	5
Wichita (R)	17	21	19
Wisconsin (H)	16	20	18

After the merger. Pending establishment of unified ASHRAE chapters, meetings of former ASHAE chapters (H) and former ASRE sections (R) were proposed upon the basis indicated above for early months.

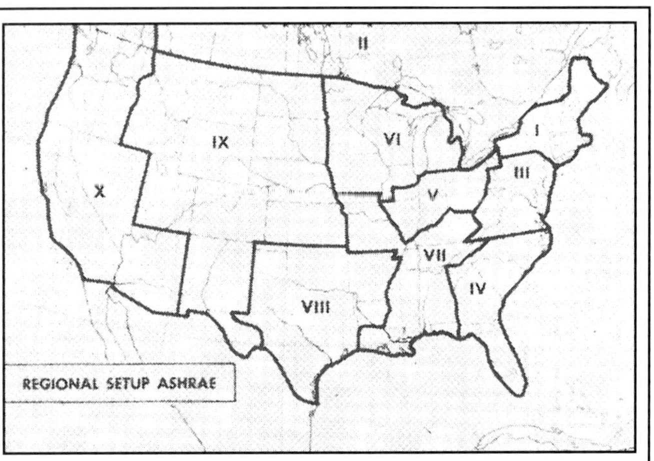

"Regional organization of our Society has played an important part in the handling of the recent merger at the Chapter level. The excellent manner in which this was accomplished was due in no small part to the activities of the Regional Directors and others concerned with the regional setup. This same regional organization can be expected to facilitate the future health and growth of the Society." (1959)

THE RADIATOR (RED HOT)

St. Louis Chapter, American Society Heating and Ventilating Engineers

No. 4 — ST. LOUIS, MO., JULY 20, 1923 — Subscription $1.00 per Year

THE RADIATOR

A DISCERNING SPIDER

THE INCONSISTENT ARCHITECT

STAY IN YOUR OWN FIELD

The July Meeting of the St. Louis Chapter will be held later in the month. Due notice of place and date will be given by the Chapter Secretary.

CERTIFIED HEATING

Installed from plans reviewed and certified correct by this Association's Engineer.
Costs less in the end than an uncertified job.
Ask for our bulletin.

The Heating and Piping Contractor's St. Louis Association

325 Odd Fellows Building — Olive 8632

ASHRAE CHAPTER AND REGIONAL BOUNDARIES

REGION I

CHAPTER	LOCATION
1. Boston	Boston, Mass.
2. Western Massachusetts	Springfield, Mass.
3. Rhode Island	Providence, R. I.
4. Northern Connecticut	Hartford, Conn.
5. Southern Connecticut	New Haven, Conn.
6. Long Island	Garden City, L. I., N. Y.
7. North Jersey	Newark, N. J.
8. New York	New York, N. Y.
9. Northeastern New York	Albany, N. Y.
10. Central New York	Syracuse, N. Y.
11. Rochester	Rochester, N. Y.
12. Niagara Frontier	Buffalo, N. Y.

REGION II Canada

CHAPTER	LOCATION
13. Chapitre de la Ville de Quebec	Quebec City, Que.
14. Montreal	Montreal, Ont.
15. Ottawa Valley	Ottawa, Ont.
16. Ontario	Toronto, Ont.
17. Manitoba	Winnipeg, Man.
18. Southern Alberta	Calgary, Alta.
19. Northern Alberta	Edmonton, Alta.
37. Niagara Peninsula	Hamilton, Ont.

REGION III

CHAPTER	LOCATION
21. Philadelphia	Philadelphia, Pa.
22. Central Pennsylvania	Harrisburg, Pa.
23. Johnstown	Johnstown, Pa.
24. Pittsburgh	Pittsburgh, Pa.
25. Baltimore	Baltimore, Md.
26. National Capital	Washington, D. C.
27. Hampton-Roads	Norfolk, Va.
28. Richmond	Richmond, Va.

REGION IV

CHAPTER	LOCATION
29. North Piedmont	Greensboro, N. C.
30. South Piedmont	Charlotte, N. C.
31. South Carolina	Columbia, N. C.
32. Atlanta	Atlanta, Ga.
33. Savannah	Savannah, Ga.
34. Jacksonville	Jacksonville, Fla.
35. Florida West Coast	Tampa, Fla.
36. South Florida	Miami, Fla.

REGION V

CHAPTER	LOCATION
38. Cleveland	Cleveland, Ohio
39. Columbus	Columbus, Ohio
40. Cincinnati	Cincinnati, Ohio
41. Dayton	Dayton, Ohio
42. Toledo	Toledo, Ohio
43. Central Indiana	Indianapolis, Ind.
44. Evansville	Evansville, Ind.

REGION VI

CHAPTER	LOCATION
45. Michigan	Detroit, Mich.
46. Central Michigan	Battle Creek, Mich.
47. Western Michigan	Grand Rapids, Mich.
48. Wisconsin	Milwaukee, Wis.
49. Illinois	Chicago, Ill.
50. Illinois-Iowa	Moline, Ill.
51. Iowa	Des Moines, Iowa
52. Minnesota	Minneapolis, Minn.

REGION VII

CHAPTER	LOCATION
53. Kansas City	Kansas City, Mo.
54. St. Louis	St. Louis, Mo.
55. Louisville	Louisville, Ky.
56. Memphis	Memphis, Tenn.
57. North Alabama	Birmingham, Ala.
58. Mobile	Mobile, Ala.
59. New Orleans	New Orleans, La.
60. Baton Rouge	Baton Rouge, La.
61. Mississippi	Jackson, Miss.
88. Middle Tennessee	Nashville, Tenn.

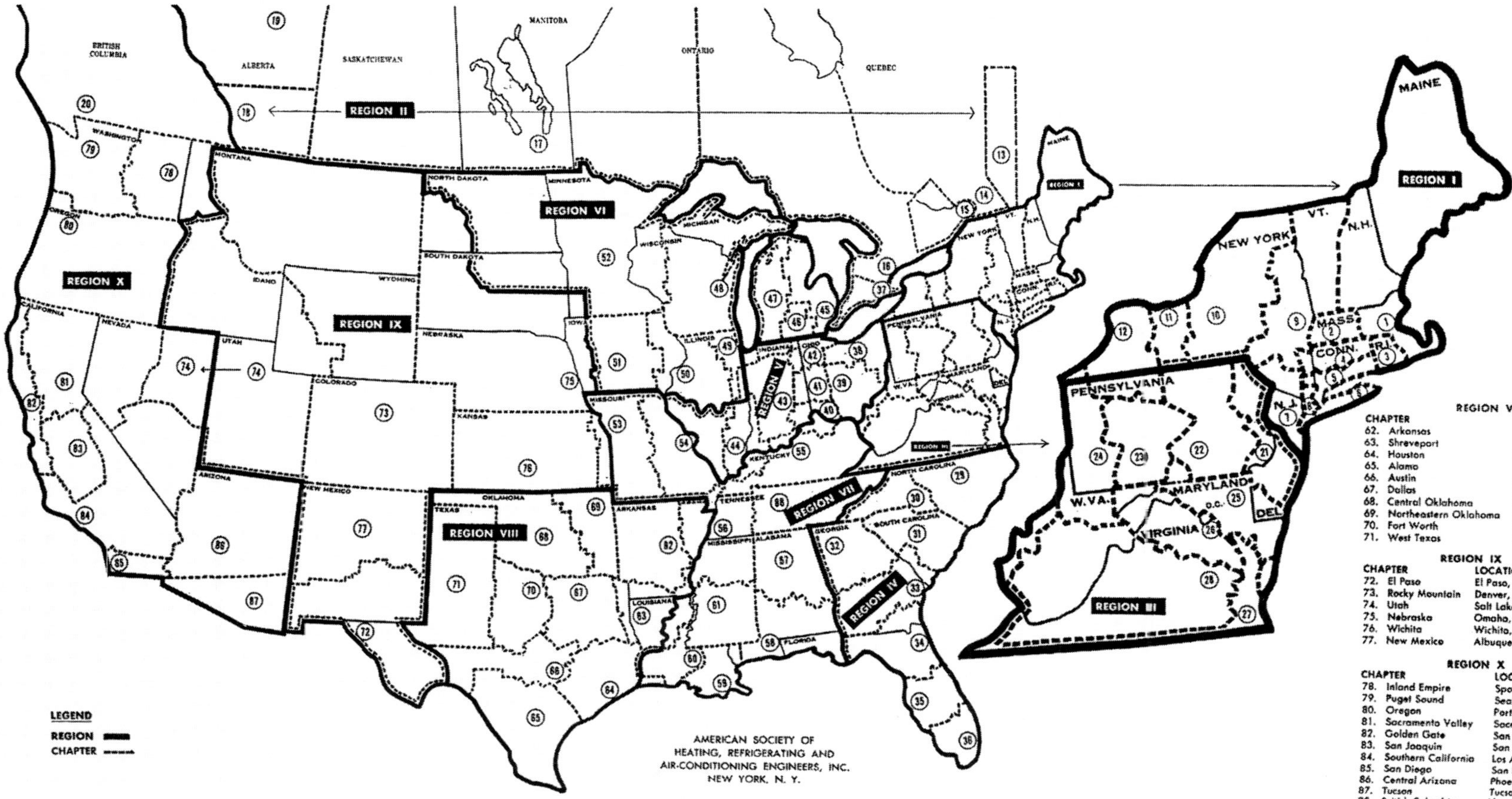

REGION VIII

CHAPTER	LOCATION
62. Arkansas	Little Rock, Ark.
63. Shreveport	Shreveport, La.
64. Houston	Houston, Tex.
65. Alamo	San Antonio, Tex.
66. Austin	Austin, Tex.
67. Dallas	Dallas, Tex.
68. Central Oklahoma	Oklahoma City, Okla.
69. Northeastern Oklahoma	Tulsa, Okla.
70. Fort Worth	Fort Worth, Tex.
71. West Texas	Lubbock, Tex.

REGION IX

CHAPTER	LOCATION
72. El Paso	El Paso, Tex.
73. Rocky Mountain	Denver, Colo.
74. Utah	Salt Lake City, Utah
75. Nebraska	Omaha, Neb.
76. Wichita	Wichita, Kans.
77. New Mexico	Albuquerque, N Mex.

REGION X

CHAPTER	LOCATION
78. Inland Empire	Spokane, Wash.
79. Puget Sound	Seattle, Wash.
80. Oregon	Portland, Oreg.
81. Sacramento Valley	Sacramento, Calif.
82. Golden Gate	San Francisco, Calif.
83. San Joaquin	San Joaquin, Calif.
84. Southern California	Los Angeles, Calif
85. San Diego	San Diego, Calif.
86. Central Arizona	Phoenix, Ariz.
87. Tucson	Tucson, Ariz.
20. British Columbia	Vancouver, B C., Can

In 1979, during the presidency of Morris Backer, the regional structure underwent a significant boundary change, increasing from 10 to 12 regions.

Ode to the Chapter
New York City

Words by
New York Chapter
A.S.H.V.E.

Music by
Gus Edwards

Arrangement by
P. Mathis

For the first anniversary meeting of the New York Chapter a souvenir handbook was published telling about how it was formed and listing all officers and members. It also contained a special Ode to the Chapter entitled "N.Y.C." and sung to the tune of "Tammany." It was actually issued at the May meeting in 1912.

Global Communities Spring from Singapore

ASHRAE's global regional structure sprang from a seed planted in Singapore.

ASHRAE's first member in Singapore joined in 1955. In December 1980, a survey among the ASHRAE members in Singapore was conducted to establish whether there was any interest in the formation of a local organization. Encouraged by the response, a meeting of ASHRAE members was held on April 9, 1981, laying the foundation for the creation of the Singapore Association of ASHRAE Members (SAAM). The first Annual General Meeting was held on March 13, 1982, when the membership was 46 strong. William C. Sundberg was elected the first SAAM President.

On July 1, 1983, Richard P. Perry became ASHRAE president, with a theme of Growth and Improved Technology Through International Cooperation. The activities of SAAM and the vision of Perry and President-Elect Robert O. McDonald led to the presentation of a chapter charter on January 30, 1984, to Sundberg, George Lim, and P.S. Loh at ASHRAE's Winter Meeting in Atlanta. Singapore became ASHRAE's 142nd chapter and its first international chapter. A chapter in Hong Kong, nurtured by McDonald, became the second chapter operating outside North America.

By 1991, ASHRAE members had formed chapters in India, Malaysia, and Taiwan.How would these new chapters, and more to come, be integrated into the Society's regional structure?

"Chapters at Large"

In conjunction with the ASHRAE Far East Conference in November 1991 in Hong Kong, ASHRAE President-Elect Richard A. Charles led a mini chapter regional committee (CRC) meeting for the five Asian chapters. There, the Singapore Chapter presented a motion to establish a new region for these so-called "chapters at large." The motion passed unanimously and was forwarded to Regions Council at the 1992 ASHRAE Winter Meeting in Anaheim. The outcome was not to form a new region but instead to assign the chapters at large to ASHRAE Region X.

Richard A. Charles, 1992–1993 ASHRAE President

Suddenly Region X had grown by five additional chapters and extended its western boundary from the Hawaii Chapter to the Far East and South Asia. Formation of a chapter in Saudi Arabia was also on the horizon. John Sosoka, the outgoing Director and Regional Chair (DRC), and Sukhdev Mathoudhu, the incoming DRC, had their hands full. The immediate task was to help the chapters understand the Society and regional structures and to explain how the CRC provides a major link between the Society and its members by allowing broad participation in the nominating of Society and regional officers and bringing forward motions for improved service and direction.

The ASHRAE membership outside of North America was growing at a considerably faster rate than membership was growing within traditional geographies. In 1993, the membership outside North America was 6,169. By May 1998, it was 8,579. More and more members and various countries were inquiring about forming chapters.

Billy R. Manning, 1994–1995 ASHRAE President

In 1993, ASHRAE President Billy R. Manning chartered the Cairo Chapter in Egypt. In March 1995, a student branch was chartered in Delhi, India. In October 1995, President Richard B. Hayter launched the Lebanese Chapter and student branches at the American University in Beirut, Lebanon, and Cairo, Egypt. In March 1996, chapters were chartered in Kuwait and Western India. ASHRAE was global, not just in individual membership but in operations.

The continued assignment of all these chapters to Region X was a solution that many of the overseas chapters preferred, but both these chapters and the Society realized that having a region so large and diverse was not practical.

Richard B. Hayter, 1995–1996 ASHRAE President

In October 1995, ASHRAE surveyed eight non–North American chapters at the time (prior to Kuwait and Western India, which were chartered in 1996) regarding the formation of a new region. In November, in-depth discussions were held in Hong Kong. Among the options were remaining within a restructured Region

X, creating a new region with all chapters, dividing chapters among the other North American regions, and creating a new region for the chapters that wanted to form a region and assigning the others to one or more existing regions.

Consensus among the chapters was that they wanted two regions—one with the Far East chapters and one with the others. But this group of new chapters was not quite ready to evolve into one or two stand-alone regions.There was yet another step in the evolution.

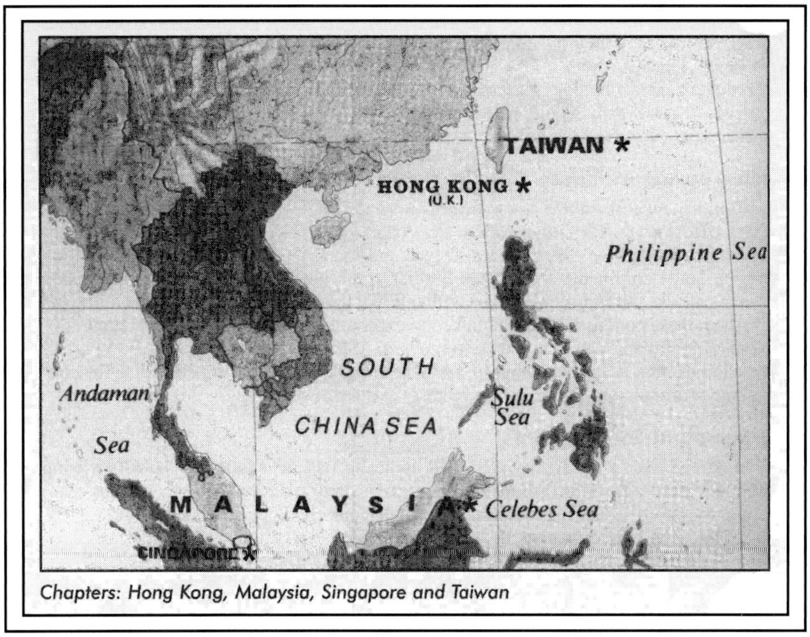

Map of Region XIII when it was first formed, 1998.

A New Region—In Asia

ASHRAE's international activities were coordinated in that period by the International Relations Committee. The September 1962 *ASHRAE Journal* featured this new international role of the Society. Over time the International Relations Committee evolved into the ASHRAE International Committee, and the ASHRAE Affiliate Societies, with few exceptions, became known as Associate Societies. The International Committee oversaw the applications of overseas Societies for Associate Society status and administered the ASHRAE Libraries provided to these overseas Societies.

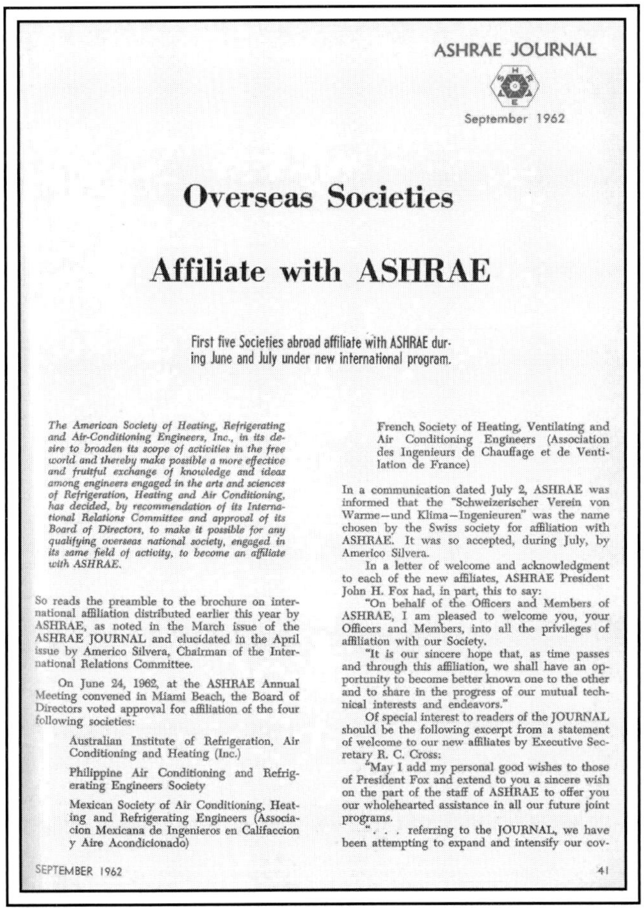

ASHRAE JOURNAL

September 1962

Overseas Societies

Affiliate with ASHRAE

First five Societies abroad affiliate with ASHRAE during June and July under new international program.

The American Society of Heating, Refrigerating and Air-Conditioning Engineers, Inc., in its desire to broaden its scope of activities in the free world and thereby make possible a more effective and fruitful exchange of knowledge and ideas among engineers engaged in the arts and sciences of Refrigeration, Heating and Air Conditioning, has decided, by recommendation of its International Relations Committee and approval of its Board of Directors, to make it possible for any qualifying overseas national society, engaged in its same field of activity, to become an affiliate with ASHRAE.

So reads the preamble to the brochure on international affiliation distributed earlier this year by ASHRAE, as noted in the March issue of the ASHRAE JOURNAL and elucidated in the April issue by Americo Silvera, Chairman of the International Relations Committee.

On June 24, 1962, at the ASHRAE Annual Meeting convened in Miami Beach, the Board of Directors voted approval for affiliation of the four following societies:

Australian Institute of Refrigeration, Air Conditioning and Heating (Inc.)

Philippine Air Conditioning and Refrigerating Engineers Society

Mexican Society of Air Conditioning, Heating and Refrigerating Engineers (Associacion Mexicana de Ingenieros en Califaccion y Aire Acondicionado)

French Society of Heating, Ventilating and Air Conditioning Engineers (Association des Ingenieurs de Chauffage et de Ventilation de France)

In a communication dated July 2, ASHRAE was informed that the "Schweizerischer Verein von Warme—und Klima—Ingenieuren" was the name chosen by the Swiss society for affiliation with ASHRAE. It was so accepted, during July, by Americo Silvera.

In a letter of welcome and acknowledgment to each of the new affiliates, ASHRAE President John H. Fox had, in part, this to say:

"On behalf of the Officers and Members of ASHRAE, I am pleased to welcome you, your Officers and Members, into all the privileges of affiliation with our Society.

"It is our sincere hope that, as time passes and through this affiliation, we shall have an opportunity to become better known one to the other and to share in the progress of our mutual technical interests and endeavors."

Of special interest to readers of the JOURNAL should be the following excerpt from a statement of welcome to our new affiliates by Executive Secretary R. C. Cross:

"May I add my personal good wishes to those of President Fox and extend to you a sincere wish on the part of the staff of ASHRAE to offer you our wholehearted assistance in all our future joint programs.

". . . referring to the JOURNAL, we have been attempting to expand and intensify our cov-

SEPTEMBER 1962 41

ASHRAE had an International Relations Committee dating to the 1950s. In the 1960s its focus changed to managing the process by which ASHRAE affiliated with national organizations, administering ASHRAE Libraries established with these Associate Societies, and identifying non–North American activities in which ASHRAE should engage. Membership consisted of active members from outside the United States and Canada, including ASHRAE members who also belonged to ASHRAE Associate Societies, and members from the United States and Canada active in overseas work.

At the 1996 Annual Meeting in San Antonio, the Society voted to restructure the International Committee, charging it to consider how to best serve members outside North America, especially through chapters. On the newly constituted International Committee were members from North America, various other geographical areas, and each chapter outside North America. Under the new International Committee, chapters wishing to form a region were free to do so by submitting a petition to the International Committee and, if approved, to the Regions Council and Board of Directors.

Soon after the first meeting of the new International Committee at the 1997 Winter Meeting in Philadelphia, chapters from Hong Kong, Malaysia,

Singapore, and Taiwan proposed the creation of a new region effective July 1998. The proposal received all the necessary approvals.

Vincent Tse

Region XIII was born when Vincent Tse of Hong Kong was installed as DRC of the first region outside of North America at the 1998 ASHRAE Annual Meeting.

Region-at-Large

Creation of Region XIII was only one step in the global structuring of ASHRAE. How would the other overseas chapters be serviced and nurtured moving forward, especially as their numbers grew? Most thought one or more regions would follow Region XIII, but when and where?

The story of what followed would become the Region-at-Large, a path similar to that of Region XIII.

A seed was planted in India. Four ASHRAE members formed the Indian Society of Heating, Refrigerating and Air-Conditioning Engineers (ISHRAE) in 1980. In 1987, the members of ISHRAE applied to form an ASHRAE chapter. Twenty-five ASHRAE members signed a petition for presentation to the Society at the ASHRAE Far East Conference in Hong Kong in 1987. They were disappointed to learn new rules required a minimum of 50 member signatures. Two years later a new petition was submitted at ASHRAE's Far East Conference in Kuala Lumpur. It was approved, and ASHRAE President David S. Butler, Sr., officially chartered the India Chapter on March 29, 1990, at the Hyatt Regency Delhi. Saudi Arabia formed in 1993. Cairo and Lebanon followed in 1995 and Western India and Kuwait in 1996.

After Region XIII was formed in 1997, the remaining overseas chapters were left to be supported by the International Committee. It was soon apparent that this was not an adequate long-term solution because there was no provision for conducting CRCs, business sessions, and chapter training, thus not providing a mechanism to develop an effective regional leadership.

The International Committee was also placed in a challenging position because it was also responsible for relations with ASHRAE Associate Societies, some of whom saw the potential competition from ASHRAE chapters being formed in their countries. A short-term solution was to create the Overseas Regional Group.

In 1999 representatives of all the overseas chapters were invited to the Region XIII CRC in Hong Kong where special training programs were launched. Some chapters began to feel they were ready for their own region, and the push began at the 2000 ASHRAE Winter Meeting in Dallas to create Region XIV. By now, a seventh chapter, Bangalore, and eighth, Hellenic, reported to the International Committee.

After more discussion—and more committees—a new region was approved at the 2001 Annual Meeting in Cincinnati. The region included all chapters formerly reporting to the International Committee. Due to its wide geographic range, however, it was not called Region XIV but Region-at-Large (RAL). The

Among the people present at the chartering of the Cairo Chapter were the following chapter and Society officers (left to right) Emad Mokhtar (chapter board of governors [BOG]), Hani Olama (BOG), Ahmed Medhat (BOG), Sukhdev Mathaudhu (Society Director and Regional Chairman, Region X); ASHRAE President Billy R. Manning, Mohamed Salem (Chapter President), Ahmed Abdel Ghani (President Elect), Mohamed Farag Ahmed (Secretary) and Ali Shamah (Treasurer).

1995

Region XII says "Hola" CRC to its first CRC outside North America. From left: Bill Malphus, Ross Montgomery, Roberto Aguiló.

first RAL Planning Committee meeting was held in Taipei, Taiwan, at the Region XIII CRC in September, and RAL regional officers were elected. The U.K.'s David Arnold served as the first director and RAL chair from 2002–2005.

South America and Mexico

In 1979 ASHRAE created Region XII by splitting the Florida chapters from Region IV. In 2002, Region XII evolved in a different way. As the result of strong ASHRAE leadership concentrated in the Florida West Coast Chapter, Tampa's role as an international port, and the high Latino population, existing business relationships were easy to expand into the growing of ASHRAE in South America. The Florida West Coast Chapter first sponsored members in Brazil as a section, and on March 22, 2002, Brazil became the tenth chapter in Region XII. Three years later the Florida West Coast Chapter sponsored a section in Argentina that rapidly became a chapter. Argentina hosted the first Region XII CRC held outside of North America in Buenos Aires in August 2008. South and Central American chapters and sections now are active participants in Region XII activities.

Members in Mexico found their home in Region VIII with the formation of the Mexico City Chapter in 1997. The Monterrey Chapter followed.

With Region XIII in the Far East, Region-at-Large, and assignment of Mexican Chapters to Region VIII and Latin American chapters to Region XII, the globe was embraced by ASHRAE's regional structure.

Extending in Europe

In 2014 ASHRAE approved its sixth Strategic Plan. Bjarne W. Olesen referred to it in his presidential address at the 2017 Annual Conference in Long Beach, California. The Dane was the second ASHRAE president to be from outside the U.S. and Canada, following Richard H. Rooley from the United Kingdom, president 2003–04. Said Olesen, "Like the two presidents before me, I plan to focus on specific aspects of our strategic plan. President David Underwood focused on Connect, and President Tim Wentz focused on Adapt… We must connect with other societies or individually with other people. We must adapt to new technologies and

Bjarne W. Olesen, 2017–2018 ASHRAE President

Monterrey Hosts Student Branch

TAMAULIPAS, Mexico—The Monterrey Chapter recently sponsored its third student branch at *Instituto Tecnológico de Ciudad Madero* Student Branch, in Tamaulipas, Mexico. Shown at the chartering are (from left) Eduardo Vega, branch advisor, Donald Hay, chapter president, Hugh McMillan, director and regional chair Region VIII, Pedro Garza, member of the board of governors, Felix Rodriguez, student chair, Ricardo Arellano, president-elect, and Gregorio Hernandez, branch professor. McMillan also gave a speech at the chapter's monthly meeting.

2004

different ways of doing things. Only then can we EXTEND, which brings me to my theme: Extending Our Community.”

By 2017, 42 of the 44 chapters formed since 1990 were outside of North America. But in Europe most of the 1,800 members did not enjoy the benefits of a local chapter. One reason, Olesen said, was that the roles of national societies often overlap the traditional role of ASHRAE chapters. In Europe national HVAC&R societies have about 100,000 members.

The Sri Lankan Chapter was formed at a meeting held at the Organization of Professional Associations Auditorium in Colombo, Sri Lanka. Those elected as officers include (from left) J.O. Yatawara, president elect; M.S.M.Y. Marikkar, president; C. Dalugoda, secretary; and P. Amarasinghe, vice president.

To better serve ASHRAE European members and to improve the influence of ASHRAE members in Europe, Region XIV began operation in 2017 with the intent to improve member representation and to identify ways to engage members not served by a chapter. Because the new region added a European member to the Board, its creation also enabled the Board to think more globally. The region was formed with chapters in Greece, Spain, Danube, Portugal, Cyprus, and UK Midlands. Constantinos A. Balaras from Greece was the first director and regional chair.

Constantinos A. Balaras

Olesen said history has proven that the impact of creating a new region can be very significant, citing Region XIII in South Asia, which when it started had four chapters. By 2017, there were 10. With the new Region XIV came a new chapter in Ireland. London and South East Chapter followed in 2018 and Israel in 2019.

Citing the global impact of creating Region XIV, Olesen also noted there are HVAC engineers in parts of the world where ASHRAE does not have a strong presence. Creating a European region, he said, will allow the RAL to focus on growth in areas that may now be underserved by ASHRAE, such as in Africa.

“Although ASHRAE’s global presence has grown, we as a Society need to be more strategic as a leader, in some cases as a partner, and in other cases as both,” Olesen said. “Why should we be more global? How do members here in the U.S. and around the world benefit from a more global Society? The answers to these questions should serve as the foundation of a new global strategy that addresses challenges facing the global building industry today. Is it possible to be global without speaking the same language and without using the same units of measure? The answer is YES! The world is getting smaller, and ASHRAE is getting bigger.”

Members of the new Central Pakistan Chapter and two new local student branches gather at the recent chartering ceremony.

2011

Chapters and Organizational Dates

Year	Society	Chapter/Section
1906	ASHVE	Illinois
1911	ASHVE	New York
1912	ASHVE	Massachusetts (now Boston)
1916	ASHVE	Michigan (now Detroit)
		Northern Ohio (now Cleveland)
		Philadelphia
1917	ASHVE	Kansas City
1917	ASRE	New York
		St. Louis
		Milwaukee
		Chicago
1918	ASHVE	Minnesota
1919	ASHVE	Western New York (now Niagara Frontier)
		Pittsburgh
1922	ASHVE	Ontario (now Toronto)
		Wisconsin
1927	ASRE	Detroit
1928	ASHVE	St. Louis
		Pacific Northwest (now Puget Sound)
1929	ASRE	Philadelphia
		Boston
1930	ASHVE	Southern California
1931	ASHVE	Western Michigan
1931	ASRE	Los Angeles
1932	ASHVE	Cincinnati, Ohio
1935	ASHVE	Manitoba
		Oklahoma (now Central Oklahoma)
		Washington (now National Capital)
1936	ASHVE	Montreal
1937	ASHVE	Atlanta
		Golden Gate
1938	ASHVE	North Texas (now Dallas)
		South Texas (now Houston)
1939	ASHVE	Delta (now New Orleans)
		North Carolina
		Oregon
1939	ASRE	Baltimore/Washington
1940	ASHVE	Connecticut
		Iowa
		Nebraska
1940	ASRE	Richmond
		Pittsburgh
		Cincinnati
1941	ASRE	Kansas City
		Cleveland
		Central New York
1943	ASHVE	Indiana (now Central Indiana)
1944	ASHVE	Central New York
		Central Ohio (now Columbus)
		Memphis
		Rocky Mountain
		Utah
1944	ASRE	San Francisco
		Twin Cities
		Northern New Jersey
		New Orleans
		Pacific Northwest

Year	Society	Chapter/Section
1945	ASRE	Connecticut Valley
1946	ASHVE	Virginia (now Hampton Roads)
		Southwest Texas (now Alamo)
1946	ASRE	Erie
		Buffalo
		Dallas-Fort Worth
		Georgia
1947	ASRE	Ontario
		Evansville
1948	ASHVE	Shreveport (dissolved 2019)
		Northeastern Oklahoma
1948	ASRE	Western Michigan
		Carolina
1950	ASHVE	Miami Valley (now Dayton)
		Inland Empire
1951	ASHVE	Empire State Capital (now Northeast)
		Kansas (now Wichita)
1951	ASRE	Indianapolis
		Western Canada
1952	ASHVE	North Jersey
		Ottawa Valley
		British Columbia
		Northern Piedmont (now North Piedmont)
		Southern Piedmont
		Arkansas
		Sacramento Valley
1952	ASRE	Houston
1953	ASHVE	Mississippi
		West Texas
		Arizona (now Central Arizona)
1953	ASRE	Dayton
		Louisville

Year	Society	Chapter/Section
1954	ASHVE	South Carolina
		Toledo
		Bluegrass (now Louisville)
		New Mexico
1954	ASRE	Colorado
1955	ASHAE	Baton Rouge
		Western Massachusetts (dissolved 1989)
1955	ASRE	San Joaquin
		South Florida (now Miami)
1956	ASHAE	Austin
		El Paso
		Illinois-Iowa (now Central Illinois)
		Northern Alberta
		Quebec, La Ville de
1956	ASRE	Central Pennsylvania
		Florida West Coast
		Rochester
1957	ASHAE	Long Island
		Southern Alberta
		Johnstown
		Jacksonville
		Fort Worth
1957	ASRE	Mobile
1958	ASHAE	Savannah (dissolved 1989)
1958	ASRE	Central Michigan (dissolved 1997)
1959	ASHRAE	Middle Tennessee (now Nashville)
		Rhode Island
		Niagara Peninsula (now Hamilton)
		North Alabama (now Birmingham)
		San Diego
		Tucson

Year	Society	Chapter/Section
1961	ASHRAE	Chicago (merged with Illinois)
		Akron/Canton
		East Texas
		South Dakota
1962	ASHRAE	Southern Nevada
		Central Florida
		Madison
1963	ASHRAE	Saskatchewan (now Regina)
		Greenville
1964	ASHRAE	Lehigh Valley
		East Tennessee
1965	ASHRAE	Halifax
		San Jose
1966	ASHRAE	Saskatoon
		Northern Indiana
1967	ASHRAE	Gold Coast
1968	ASHRAE	Orange Empire
		Triangle
1969	ASHRAE	Northeast Wisconsin
1970	ASHRAE	Hawaii
		Puerto Rico
		Champlain Valley
		Delaware (dissolved 2012)
1971	ASHRAE	Charleston
		Tennessee Valley
1972	ASHRAE	La Crosse Area
		London, Canada
		New Brunswick
		Maine
1973	ASHRAE	Rockford (dissolved 2010)
1974	ASHRAE	Fort Wayne
		Eastern Michigan (dissolved 2014)
		Alaska
		Mississippi Valley
		Montgomery (dissolved 2002)
1975	ASHRAE	Roanoke
		Northern Nevada
1976	ASHRAE	Southwest Georgia (dissolved 1990)
		Black Hills Area
1977	ASHRAE	Central Kentucky (now Bluegrass)
		Twin Tiers
1978	ASHRAE	Northwest Florida
		Big Sky
1979	ASHRAE	Gulfstream (dissolved 2010)
		North Alabama
1980	ASHRAE	Anthracite
		Idaho
1981	ASHRAE	Spacecoast
		Mid-Columbia (dissolved 2018)
1982	ASHRAE	East Central Illinois (dissolved 1998)
		Tri-Cities (dissolved 1986)
1983	ASHRAE	Southwest Florida
		Saguenay-Lac St. Jean (dissolved 1995)
		Windsor
1984	ASHRAE	Singapore
		Hong Kong
		Sierra Delta
1985	ASHRAE	Vancouver Island
		Bi-State
		United Arab Emirates (dissolved 1990)
1986	ASHRAE	Pikes Peak
		Malaysia
		Ozarks

Year	Society	Chapter/Section
1987	ASHRAE	Tombigee (dissolved 2002)
		Granite State
		Mississauga (dissolved 1992)
		South Texas
1988	ASHRAE	Tri-County
1989	ASHRAE	Mountaineer (dissolved 2006)
		Taiwan
1990	ASHRAE	India
1992	ASHRAE	Cedar Valley
1993	ASHRAE	Saudi Arabia
1995	ASHRAE	Cairo
	ASHRAE	Lebanese
1996	ASHRAE	Manual de Anda (now Mexico City)
	ASHRAE	Kuwait
	ASHRAE	Western India
1999	ASHRAE	Monterrey
	ASHRAE	Philippines
	ASHRAE	ASHRAE Bangalore
2000	ASHRAE	Thailand
	ASHRAE	Hellenic
2002	ASHRAE	Guadalajara
	ASHRAE	Brasil
	ASHRAE	Sri Lankan
2003	ASHRAE	Emirates Falcon (now ASHRAE Falcon)
	ASHRAE	Pakistan
2005	ASHRAE	Argentina
	ASHRAE	Danube
	ASHRAE	Portugal
2006	ASHRAE	Bahrain
	ASHRAE	Northern Pakistan
	ASHRAE	Polonia (dissolved 2012)
2007	ASHRAE	Indonesia
	ASHRAE	Spain
2008	ASHRAE	Qatar Oryx
2009	ASHRAE	ASHRAE Nigeria
	ASHRAE	Chennai
	ASHRAE	Pune
2010	ASHRAE	Colombia Chapter
	ASHRAE	ASHRAE Mumbai
	ASHRAE	Central Pakistan
2011	ASHRAE	ASHRAE Deccan
2013	ASHRAE	West Virginia
2014	ASHRAE	Japan
	ASHRAE	South Korea
	ASHRAE	Turkish
2015	ASHRAE	Chile
	ASHRAE	Bangladesh
2016	ASHRAE	Ecuador
	ASHRAE	Macao
2017	ASHRAE	Paraguay
	ASHRAE	Cyprus
	ASHRAE	Ireland
	ASHRAE	UK Midlands
	ASHRAE	UK London and South-East
	ASHRAE	South Africa
2018	ASHRAE	Northwest Arkansas
	ASHRAE	ASHRAE Caricom
	ASHRAE	Faisalabad
	ASHRAE	Jordan
	ASHRAE	Pyramids
2019	ASHRAE	South Brazil
	ASHRAE	Israeli
	ASHRAE	East India
	ASHRAE	Rajasthan
	ASHRAE	Chandigarh

Chapter 6

Becoming One

"Prestige is itself difficult to evaluate, but a combined society with a broader scope and an increased membership can be expected to be looked on with greater respect by other professional groups as well as by its own members. The merged society should be better able to sustain full and unquestioned leadership in covering professional engineering in matters in Refrigeration, Heating, Air Conditioning and Ventilation."

E.R. Queer
1958

In the first decade of the 20th century, The American Society of Heating and Ventilating Engineers had little in common with the newly formed American Society of Refrigerating Engineers. This soon began to change, however, as heating and ventilating engineers learned to control humidity by using mechanical refrigeration equipment to cool the air. Willis Carrier's epic paper on rational psychrometric formulae published in 1911 established the scientific basis that he and others would use to promote the concept of conditioning the air.

In the 1920s, this new field of air conditioning was further advanced by exploding technological accomplishments in the household refrigeration industry. Made possible by the entry into the industry of manufacturers with mass market production ability and the capital necessary to finance new technology, these new developments included direct expansion systems, extended surface condensers and evaporators, thermostatic valves and hermetically sealed compressors.

The overall significance of these events was that air conditioning became a field of interest to both the members of the heating and ventilating engineer's society and to the refrigerating engineers.

As heating systems evolved from steam and hot water to forced warm air systems, combining the heating and air-conditioning functions, the American Society of Heating and Ventilating Engineers in 1954 changed its name to the American Society of Heating and Air-Conditioning Engineers. That same year, the Refrigerating Engineers mailed proxy ballots to its membership proposing to add Air Conditioning to its name, but too few votes (both pro and con) were received and the proposal was lost.

By the 1950s, there was significant overlap in the research programs and in the meeting sessions of the two societies. There was a large cross-over membership as well, with many members of the two societies, particularly the leadership, attending annual, semi-annual and regional meetings of both organizations.

Much of this chapter is drawn from "The Merger of ASHAE and ASRE" written by Presidential Member Frank H. Faust, which appeared in the May 1992 issue of *ASHRAE Insights*.

Consolidation of the two societies had been considered as early as the 1920s. Willis Carrier, president of ASRE in 1927 and ASHVE in 1931, was an early proponent. A plan for consolidation had been defeated in 1937, and in 1941, a joint committee operated to review the ASHVE and ASRE relationship. Joint meetings of the two organizations were held in Cleveland (1932), Buck Hill Falls, Pennsylvania (1936), and New York City (1938).

Willis Carrier
An early proponent of consolidation, he campaigned for the term "thermal engineers."

By 1954, with talk of overlapping interests greater than ever before, it was clear to the leaders of both societies that closer cooperation was required. To achieve this, a joint Committee on Cooperation was formed.

When first appointed, the objective of the committee was to determine how the societies could cooperate without consolidating. As the committee's work progressed, however, the idea of merger gained wider acceptance. In 1956, two ASHAE regions put forward suggestions for merger. By 1958, about 1,000 people belonged to both ASHAE and to ASRE. ASHAE's membership total was 11,700 and ASRE's was 7,000. About 60% of activity in each society was devoted to air conditioning.

The principal problem facing a merger was opposition by individuals interested in only limited segments of the industry.

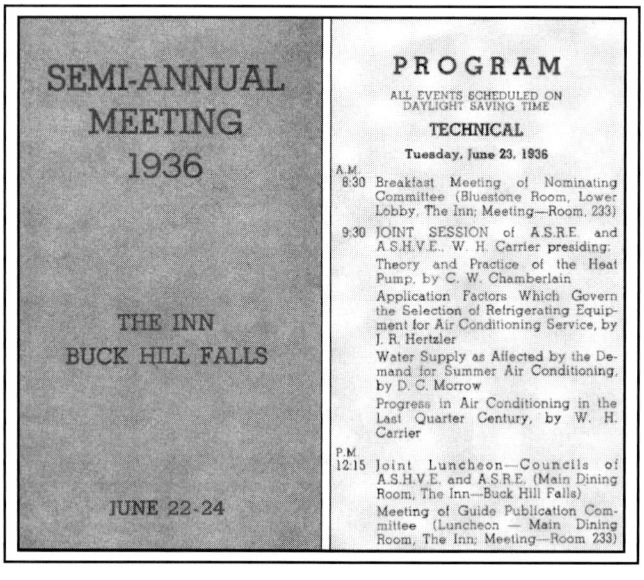

SEMI-ANNUAL MEETING 1936

THE INN BUCK HILL FALLS

JUNE 22-24

PROGRAM

ALL EVENTS SCHEDULED ON DAYLIGHT SAVING TIME

TECHNICAL

Tuesday, June 23, 1936

A.M.
8:30 Breakfast Meeting of Nominating Committee (Bluestone Room, Lower Lobby, The Inn; Meeting—Room, 233)

9:30 JOINT SESSION of A.S.R.E. and A.S.H.V.E., W. H. Carrier presiding:
Theory and Practice of the Heat Pump, by C. W. Chamberlain
Application Factors Which Govern the Selection of Refrigerating Equipment for Air Conditioning Service, by J. R. Hertzler
Water Supply as Affected by the Demand for Summer Air Conditioning, by D. C. Morrow
Progress in Air Conditioning in the Last Quarter Century, by W. H. Carrier

P.M.
12:15 Joint Luncheon—Councils of A.S.H.V.E. and A.S.R.E. (Main Dining Room, The Inn—Buck Hill Falls)
Meeting of Guide Publication Committee (Luncheon — Main Dining Room, The Inn; Meeting—Room 233)

These people included the ice and cold storage industry, domestic refrigeration industry, the steam and hot water heating industry and the ventilation and exhaust-air industry.

H.F. Spoehrer
ASRE President in 1958 said, "We cannot ignore the repeated requests from many members who have an interest in air conditioning and who would welcome a merger."

In June, 1958, the councils of each society approved the Proposed Merger Plan drafted by the Committee on Cooperation. The plan next would be mailed to ASHAE chapter presidents and ASRE section presidents to stimulate discussion at the local level.

E.R. Queer
ASHAE President in 1958 said, "The Merger Plan is expected to permit increased services to each member, and also provide a sufficiently broad and varied program to insure something for every member. There should be no neglected minority groups."

ASHAE President Elmer Queer outlined the premises for the merger. "An extensive research program similar to that now conducted ASHAE would be carried out by the merged Society.... The Society would continue to conduct a comprehensive program in the development of codes and standards, as now carried out by ASRE. The merged Society would furnish financial support to local groups, similar to the present practice of ASRE, and so established as not to interfere with the current practice of having local group dues as now done by ASHAE...."

There was much debate, especially within ASRE. C.F. Holske, ASRE President in 1948, wrote, "As to common interests in air conditioning, competitive operations generally produce more and better results than unilateral opera-

C.F. Holske
ASRE president in 1948 urged a "NO" vote to the merger.

tions.... I suggest you vote NO to the merger proposal."

Cecil Boling, president of ASRE, crossed the country, explaining details of the plan. "Personally, I have no feelings except for the preservation of the hard-won standing of ASRE and for the welfare of the interests represented by its members and its programs. However, it is my earnest conviction that the march of time, the inevitable shifts of technology, the present and undoubtedly to-be-continued emphasis upon newer factors within what was once a predominantly refrigeration situation, lead to the conclusion that what is best for ASRE is a merger which will permit broader coordinated development in two closely allied fields where the common problems are the transfer of heat and the circulation of air....Today it is really not a question of whether ASRE and ASHAE should merge but of when."

Cecil Boling
"As President of ASRE, I am truly neutral as to the possible merger; as an individual member I have my opinion and vote."

As required by the Membership Corporations Law of New York State, the Plan for Merger was submitted to the memberships of ASHAE and ASRE. To become effective, the plan would require the approval of each society by two-thirds of those voting, either by proxy or in person.

At a special meeting held in Chicago on December 1,1958 in the Conrad Hilton, ASHAE members overwhelmingly approved the plan, with 5,307 voting in person or by proxy in favor and only 405 against.

ASRE's vote was held at the opening session of its Annual Meeting in New Orleans on December 1. Crosby Field, ASRE president in 1938 and a staunch opponent of the merger, was next to President Boling until 4:40 in the morning as the proxies were counted.

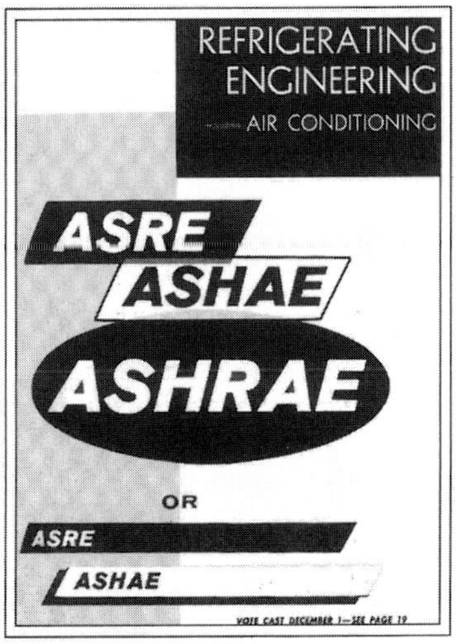

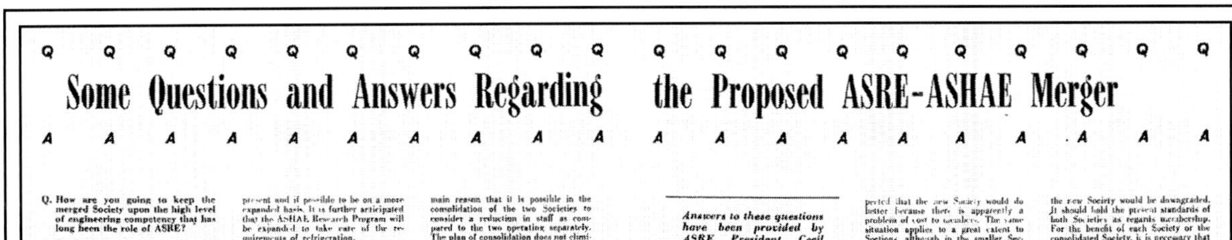

Q Q Q Q Q Q Q Q Q Q Q Q Q Q Q Q Q Q Q Q

Some Questions and Answers Regarding the Proposed ASRE-ASHAE Merger

A A A A A A A A A A A A A A A A A A A A

Answers to these questions have been provided by ASRE President Cecil Boling

Q. How are you going to keep the merged Society upon the high level of engineering competency that has long been the role of ASRE?

A. The level of engineering competency of any Society will depend upon the interest and activity of the individual members. Any worthwhile plan would have to anticipate this and provide the framework within which it might be effective.

Q. Why wasn't a vote taken among the members of both Societies first to determine whether they want a merger, and then have a plan developed afterwards if the vote indicated that a merger was desirable rather than in the reverse order?

A. Your governing body, the Council, felt that it was desirable to have a plan for the merger of the two Societies to submit to the membership for vote so that they would have a clear picture of what would happen should the two Societies be consolidated. If members were asked to vote without a merger plan how could they anticipate that specific problems could or would be handled?

Q. What is there in common between the interests and problems of refrigerated warehouse builders and operators and the corresponding activities of those who work with industrial blowers and space heaters?

A. The answer to this question is naturally that the common bond is the transfer of heat and movement of air. It was because of this particular question that the plan as set up provides for operation of a divisional basis of heating, refrigeration, air conditioning and ventilating.

Q. ASRE has a Standards Program. ASHAE has a Research Program. Will these be maintained separately, or will there be an overall Standards as well as an overall Research activity?

A. The plan anticipates the maintenance of a Standards Program comparable to that being carried on by ASRE at present and if possible to be on a more expanded basis. It is further anticipated that the ASHAE Research Program will be expanded to take care of the requirements of refrigeration.

Q. If progress requires that ASHAE and ASRE merge what assurance do we have that there will result a more dynamic, effective Society rather than just a larger one? Does this not call for an extension of purpose and program beyond the relatively narrow limits of engineering only?

A. The plan as drawn anticipates that the new Society would provide additional research for the benefit of present ASRE members, a better overall monthly publication, more stress on membership activities particularly the encouraging of better section meetings and programs. However, it must be remembered that it is still up to the members to see that this will be so and the plan can only provide the framework for such accomplishment. It does not seem logical that the new Society would have to go beyond the relatively narrow limits of engineering as after all, engineering is its foundation as it is with the two Societies today.

Q. Why shouldn't the members be given a longer time to study the proposed merger plan and give it consideration before being asked to vote? The time between now and December is too short.

A. This is answered, I believe, in detail in the President's Page in this issue.

Q. If there are 16 employees too many in the present two-Society arrangement and the merger will enable the equivalent results with reduced manpower, there must be too many now. What specific things are we going to eliminate in terms of services and functions?

A. In any organization where volume is increased, you do not have to increase your personnel proportionately from an administrative standpoint. This is the main reason that it is possible in the consolidation of the two Societies to consider a reduction in staff as compared to the two operating separately. The plan of consolidation does not eliminate service to the members and from the study made, it was felt that the organization outlined could handle the work. Naturally it might be that some additional assistance may be necessary in certain categories although it was felt that the entire plan was set up conservatively.

Q. Who profits (benefits) by the merger?

A. Unless the members of both Societies benefit from the merger, the idea of the merger is not sound. This is a basic question each member must answer for himself before he votes for or against the merger in December. No particular individual or group will make any money out of this consolidation.

Q. Who is going to pay for all this? It is stated that ASHAE will lose substantial income in the shift in the publishing of its Journal Section. How will this be offset?

A. It is expected that we would have a greatly stepped up advertising sales organization and promotional program to accomplish the sale of the required additional advertising. Increased circulation would tend to create a more attractive advertising medium. Any losses would naturally come out of the surpluses of the combined Societies.

Q. If the merger is approved in December, why must it be put into effect immediately? Why should it not be made effective a year, or a year and a half from December in order to give further time for study?

A. After a merger is voted, the new Society takes over just as soon as the papers are legally cleared by the State of New York except for any interim steps as may be outlined in the plan for merger. There no doubt would be operating details that could take a year or two to straighten out but the operation must be legally under the new Society.

Members who have their own questions are invited to submit them for answers in later issues of REFRIGERATING ENGINEERING. Within the limits of subject duplications and available space, an endeavor will be made to provide factual replies to all such requests for information. See President's Page this issue.

Q. There seems to be a vague element in the combining of Guide and Data Books. Why should there be so many? Why not consolidate, combine and replan for not more than two different volumes?

A. Under the present plan, as regards the Guide and Data Books, the plan for the transition period was worked out by the Publications Committees of both ASRE and ASHAE. There is considerable sentiment that the transition period is taking too long and is too cumbersome and it appears that the two committees or the Publications Committee of the new Society, if the merger is voted, should go to work on this and see if they can simplify the program.

Q. How large a publication will the new Society sponsor? Twice as many editorial pages calls for corresponding printing costs. Can the new paper double the advertising that appears in REFRIGERATING ENGINEERING? How soon?

A. It has not been decided how large the new monthly publication would be; however, it was expected that we would get at least 50% more advertising which would certainly permit the new magazine to handle 50% or more additional editorial pages, initially. Membership circulation would double upon merger and provide a more attractive advertising base. Non-member circulation would be expected to increase also.

Q. Seldom, if ever, does 10% of the ASRE membership attend a National Meeting. What about Section Meetings, under merger? Most Sections tend to develop around local activities, interests and companies with specialized emphases. So do the Chapters of ASHAE. Is it not true that there is less community of interest between local Sections (ASRE) and Chapters (ASHAE) than there is at the national level? How can this be unified?

A. It is true that seldom does 10% of the ASRE membership attend a national meeting and this applies to ASHAE meetings too, except the annual meeting at its show time. It would not be expected that the new Society would do better because there is apparently a problem of cost to members. The same situation applies to a great extent to Sections, although in the smaller Sections, it is possible under the new plan that they would be able to have better programs and better meetings. In certain areas, there is considerable community of interest between the local Sections of ASRE and ASHAE but in the more metropolitan areas, there is not much community of interest. It is quite possible that in the larger metropolitan areas there would be a continuance of separate meetings along divisional lines but this would not be true in the less metropolitan areas where even today ASRE and ASHAE local Sections are cooperating and meeting together with frequency. Regional technical meetings would have an important part in this.

Q. Is this merger being proposed because of any problems financial or otherwise within ASRE, or is there some other reason?

A. There is no financial problem in ASRE and, therefore, this has in no way been any point for consideration as regards the merger. The only reason for consideration of this merger derives from the suggestions of a large number of our members and relates to the community of interest within the two Societies.

Q. Our nominal three-day national meetings actually occupy almost five days for active members with committee duties. How long a meeting would combined activities call for?

A. The question of the length of the national meetings has not been settled but it is understood that they would be so set up as to cover the necessary technical programs, conferences, forums and the like and that might mean some extension in time. It was felt that by the use of concurrent programs and careful timing of committee meetings and the like that there would be no need to extend the meetings at least not more than another day.

Q. Presently, new ASRE members tend to be more numerous in the Associate and Affiliate grades than in full Membership. Will our pattern be upgraded or downgraded in a merger? If further downgrading occurs what will we have to offer the top engineering and science men?

A. We see no reason under the plan that the new Society would be downgraded. It should hold the present standards of both Societies as regards membership. For the benefit of each Society or the consolidated Society, it is necessary that there be a continued and constant effort to upgrade more to full membership.

Q. ASRE is committed to an "interest" in participating in the new Engineering Center in New York and to go along with other National Societies in this program. Is ASHAE so committed and would the merged Society maintain that plan as a longer-time objective?

A. It is anticipated that the new Society would have its headquarters at the Engineering Center in New York as would ASRE and ASHAE operating separately.

Q. Sections and Section Meetings are the base upon which such a Society as ASRE rests; much the same can be said of ASHAE, in its Chapters. There are many members who have never attended a National Meeting —perhaps never will. Their participation is less for technical reasons than those of acquaintanceship and fellowship. How are you going to make them care about individuals and groups with wholly different interests and with whom they consider they have nothing in common?

A. As pointed out in a previous question in certain areas, there is already considerable community of interest between Sections of ASRE and the Chapters of ASHAE. However, the plan visualizes these problems and it is expected that in certain areas, the local Sections will operate on a divisional basis or as will be explained in the Plan, there will be various alternative methods for the local Sections to operate depending upon what seems best for the area. Regional meetings would be an additional constructive factor. They are an integral part of the Plan and should accomplish much toward this end.

Q. Because ASHAE has more members than ASRE, will ASHAE in effect absorb ASRE and will it dominate the activities of the merged Societies?

A. This plan is specifically set up so that there is no basis for feeling that ASHAE is absorbing ASRE. In fact, every effort has been made in the plan to set up the new Society on an equal basis.

46 Refrigerating Engineering August 1958 47

When all votes were tabulated, 86% of ASRE's members had voted with 3,516 in favor and 1,293 against.

Milton Garland, an ASRE member at the time, remembers of the merger, "I was against it, but, of course, I stayed with the Society because if that's what the majority wanted, that's the way we should have gone. But I know quite a few of the refrigeration people dropped out at the time. It was obvious that the refrigeration people were going to lose control simply because there are far more people in the heating and ventilating business, and there always will be."

Cecil Boling recalled discussion about what the new organization should be named. Among the suggestions was the Society of Environmental Engineers. Ultimately, Boling said, "We decided to stick with history." This satisfied many ASRE members who wished to make sure that "refrigerating" would not disappear from the name of their new society.

The approved plan called for elected officers of ASHAE and ASRE to serve alternating six-month terms. Cecil Boling served as the first president of ASHRAE from January 1959 to June, followed by Arthur J. Hess, the last president of ASHAE. Mr. Hess had been sworn in as ASHAE president on the evening of January 28, 1959, and served until the next day when the consolidation became effective. John Everetts, Jr., served the first full-year term as president of ASHRAE, June 1961 to June 1962.

On the morning of January 29,1959, the needed documents were filed in the office of the Secretary of State in Albany, New York. Thus in its 55th year, the

SOME FACTS AND FIGURES ABOUT ASRE, ASHAE AND PROPOSED ASHRAE

All data herein quoted have been taken from the official Plan of Merger as submitted to Councils and available in complete form upon request of members.

	ASRE	ASHAE	ASHRAE
Date of incorporation	ASRE 1905	ASHAE 1895	
Total number of members	ASRE 7000 (app)	ASHAE 11,800 (app)	ASHRAE 17,800 (est)
Local Sections or Chapters	ASRE 52	ASHAE 72	ASHRAE 84
Geographical Regions	ASRE 9	ASHAE 7	ASHRAE 10
Membership corporation—State of New York	ASRE Yes	ASHAE Yes	ASHRAE (prop)
Council or Board of Directors Members	ASRE 20	ASHAE 17	ASHRAE 24
Standing, Council or General Committees	ASRE 20	ASHAE 14	ASHRAE 25 (tent)
Full Member dues	ASRE $25.	ASHAE $25.	ASHRAE $25.
Staff members	ASRE 24	ASHAE 46 (includes laboratory staff)	ASHRAE 54
Member of Engineers Joint Council?	ASRE Yes	ASHAE Yes	ASHRAE (planned)

Annual budget data	ASRE	ASHAE	Combined	ASHRAE
income	$417,207.	761,095.	1,178,302.	1,137,000.
expenses	$427,540.	642,231.	1,069,771.	1,113,500.

Invested funds	ASRE	ASHAE	Combined
	$147,507.	190,202.	337,709.

Publications	Magazine	Transactions	Journal	Standards
ASRE	Yes	No	No	Yes
ASHAE	No	Yes	*	No
ASHRAE	Yes	Yes	**	Yes

	Research Reports	Meetings Preprints	Article Reprints	Roster
ASRE	No	Yes	Yes	Yes
ASHAE	Yes	No	Yes	Yes
ASHRAE	Yes	Yes	Yes	Yes

*Published as a Section of Heating, Piping and Air Conditioning
**Becomes part of ASHRAE Magazine

American Society of Refrigerating Engineers ceased its corporate existence, and in its 65th year the charter of the American Society of Heating and Air-Conditioning Engineers was amended to bring into corporate existence the consolidated American Society of Heating, Refrigerating and Air-Conditioning Engineers.

Operation of ASHRAE began with a meeting of its executive committee at 10:30 a.m. at the Bellevue Stratford Hotel in Philadelphia on January 29, 1959.

Elmer Queer wrote in that month's *Refrigerating Engineering* magazine, "An opportunity presents itself for real membership activity in the work to be done at the local level. The basic planning merely sets up guide lines with the chapters having virtual autonomy in organizing to fit local needs. The Regional Directors will provide guidance in solving problems and serve as liaison with the national organization and with the Board of Directors."

Cecil Boling's prediction was "a future of even greater proportions." He said, "True, numbers alone do not make a great organization. But the give and take of the past few months offers convincing evidence that the members of ASRE and ASHAE have the highest of professional standards, clear-cut objectives for further accomplishments and the sustained ability and willingness to see things through to rewarding ends. ASHRAE will greatly strengthen our profession."

Officers and Board of Directors

January 1959 to June 1959

President	Cecil Boling	4th Vice President	Robert H. Tull
1st Vice President	Arthur J. Hess	5th Vice President	ASHAE
2nd Vice President	Daniel D. Wile	1st Treasurer	ASHAE
3rd Vice President	Walter A. Grant	2nd Treasurer	Franklyn Y. Carter

***Hermann F. Spoehrer	**ASHAE	*Willis R. Woolrich
***Elmer R. Queer	ASHAE	*Charles L. Hall
***Carlyle M. Ashley	ASHAE	*William F. Wischmeyer
***Leon Buehler, Jr.	John Engalitcheff, Jr.	*Thomas J. Phillips
**William G. Hole	Charles T. Hamilton	*John W. Chandler
**Peter J. Marschall	Everett P. Palmatier	*Russell A. Baker
**Weslev O. Stewart	Robert G. Werden	*ASRE (1)
**Percy N. Vinther	Carl R. Fagerstrom	*James P. McShane
**Frank H. Faust	Ralph A. Gonzalez	*Charles C. E. Harris
Fred Janssen	James W. Snyder	*Thomas G. Crider
**James W. May	John E. Dube	*William E. Fontaine
Gayle B. Priester	Harold M. Hendrickson	*J. Guy Woodroof
**ASHAE	Si J. Williams, Jr.	*George B. Rottman

Total 47

*ASRE Regional Director. **ASHAE Regional Director. (1) Replacement for T. J. Ammel (resigned)
***These individuals plus all elected officers constitute the Executive Committee.

ASHRAE Transactions

Officers and Board of Directors

June 1959 to January 1960

President .... Arthur J. Hess

1st Vice President	Daniel D. Wile	4th Vice President	ASHAE
2nd Vice President	Walter A. Grant	1st Treasurer	Franklyn Y. Carter
3rd Vice President	Robert H. Tull	2nd Treasurer	ASHAE

***Cecil Boling	**ASHAE	*Willis R. Woolrich
***Hermann F. Spoehrer	ASHAE	*Charles L. Hall
***Elmer R. Queer	ASHAE	*William F. Wischmeyer
***Carlyle M. Ashley	Carl R. Fagerstrom	*Charles C. E. Harris
**Frank H. Faust	Ralph A. Gonzalez	*Thomas G. Crider
Fred Janssen	James W. Snyder	*William E. Fontaine
**James W. May	John E. Dube	*J. Guy Woodroof
Gayle B. Priester	Harold M. Hendrickson	*Thomas J. Phillips
**ASHAE	Si J. Williams, Jr.	*George B. Rottman

Total 34

In January 1959, the Executive Committee of the Consolidated Society designated elected officials from ASHAE and ASRE to fill posts in the merged Society.

Officers and Board of Directors

January 1960 to June 1960

President..........Daniel D. Wile

1st Vice President...........Walter A. Grant
2nd Vice President...........Robert H. Tull
3rd Vice President..................ASHAE
Treasurer

***Arthur J. Hess
***Cecil Boling
***Hermann F. Spoehrer
***Elmer R. Queer
**ASHAE
**ASHAE
ASHAE
ASHAE
Harold M. Hendrickson
Si J. Williams, Jr.
*Willis R. Woolrich
*Charles L. Hall
*William F. Wischmeyer
10 new members

Total 28

Officers and Board of Directors

June 1960 to January 1961

President.....................Walter A. Grant
1st Vice President..........Robert H. Tull
2nd Vice President..................ASHAE
Treasurer

***Daniel D. Wile
***Arthur J. Hess
***Cecil Boling
***Hermann F. Spoehrer
***Elmer R. Queer
10 Members from period January 1960 to June 1960
9 New members

Total 28

Officers and Board of Directors

January 1961 to June 1961

President—Robert H. Tull
1st Vice President—ASHAE
2nd Vice President
Treasurer

***Walter A. Grant
***Daniel D. Wile
***Arthur J. Hess
***Cecil Boling
10 Members from period January 1960 to June 1960
9 Members from period June 1960 to January 1961

Total 27

*ASRE Regional Director.
**ASHAE Regional Director
***These individuals plus all elected officers constitute the Executive Committee

Consolidation Documents

Officers and Board of Directors

June 1961 to June 1962

President—ASHAE
1st Vice President
2nd Vice President
Treasurer

***Robert H. Tull
***Daniel D. Wile
6 Members from period January 1960 to June 1960
4 New members
9 Members from period June 1960 to January 1961
3 New members

Total 28

*** These individuals plus all elected officers constitute the Executive Committee.

The first ASHRAE chapter formed after the ASHAE and ASRE merger was organized in Nashville, Tennessee. Its first meeting was in September 1959. Elections included: I.C. Thomasson, President; Roy L. King, Vice President; Theodore Moats, Secretary; James R. Potter, Treasurer; and Edward Kennedy, Robert Bibb and Farrell Hickerson, Board of Governors.

OFFICIAL PUBLICATION

ASHRAE JOURNAL

Heating • Refrigerating • Air Conditioning • Ventilating

AMERICAN SOCIETY OF HEATING, REFRIGERATING AND AIR-CONDITIONING ENGINEERS

Successor to both REFRIGERATING ENGINEERING including Air Conditioning, and the *ASHAE Journal*, the ASHRAE JOURNAL becomes the official publication of the consolidated American Society of Heating, Refrigerating and Air-Conditioning Engineers.

The consolidated Society (1959) has been formed of the merger of the American Society of Heating and Air Conditioning Engineers (1894) and The American Society of Refrigerating Engineers (1905).

There will result new unity and concentrated efforts upon the solution of engineering, research, design, development, installation, application and operation problems of members.

Your ASHRAE JOURNAL will be your foremost guide to news of professional engineering, progress and people in these dynamic fields.

formerly REFRIGERATING ENGINEERING INCLUDING AIR CONDITIONING AND THE ASHAE JOURNAL

MARCH 1959

At the first Annual Meeting of ASHRAE, Lake Placid, New York, 1959 16 past presidents of either ASHRAE or ASRE, or both, received acclaim at the Annual Banquet. Shown above: A.J. Hess, E.R. Queer, J.E. Haines, L.N. Hunter, L.E. Seeley, A.E. Stacey, G.L. Tuve, M.F. Blankin, Cecil Boling, Henry Torrance, Jr., Below: Crosby Field, B.H. Jennings, J.G. Bergdoll, Jr., L. Buehler, Jr., C.M. Ashley, H.F. Spoehrer.

1959 ANNUAL BANQUET

A
S
H
R
A
E

TUESDAY, JUNE 23, 1959

Lake Placid Club
In the Adirondacks

Program

ANNUAL BANQUET ASHRAE
June 23, 1959

INVOCATION

INTRODUCTIONS

PRESENTATIONS
By President A. J. Hess
To Past President Cecil Boling

KLIXON AWARD
To: Dr. H. O. Spauschus
R. S. Olsen

WOLVERINE AWARD
To: Professor H. M. Hendrickson

DANCING
Agora Auditorium

Music by Paul Jouard
and his
Lake Placid Club Orchestra

Menu

Shrimp Cocktail

Assorted Relishes

Broiled Prime Tenderloin, Bercy

Oven Roast Potato French Style Green Beans

Princess Salad, French Dressing

Dinner Rolls

Lake Placid Club Ice Cream Pie
Wild Mountain Blackberry Sauce

Tea Coffee Sanka Postum Buttermilk Milk Skim milk

Chapter 7

New Horizons

"And so we look forward to new horizons for ASHRAE in the year ahead... to expand our borders in an effort to infuse worldwide technology into the most important literature in our industry—the ASHRAE Handbooks, Journal, Transactions *and* Standards... *to create an atmosphere for worldwide research activities, standards preparation, and cooperation in exchange of knowledge."*

David Rickelton
1974

The charter members of The American Society of Heating and Ventilating Engineers were keenly aware of the international aspects of their profession and of their industry. In fact, the impetus for forming the organization came from the inadequate attention given by the National Association of Master Steam and Hot Water Fitters to a paper presented by a London engineer on the heating of English school houses.

While only people from the United States attended the charter meeting of the organization on September 10, 1894, in New York City, the list of prominent engineers to whom invitations were sent included names from outside the country. Likely the state of communication and transportation in the late 19th century contributed to the fact that the charter members traveling the furthest distance to the organizational meeting were from Chicago; Saginaw, Michigan; and Chattanooga, Tennessee.

The first non-U.S. engineer elected to membership was Henry S. Downe, Paris, France, in 1895. He was followed by David M. Nesbitt, the London engineer treated rudely by the Master Steam Fitters; Andres Borch Reck from Copenhagen, Denmark; and Robert Ernest Atkinson from Leicester, England. As a point of interest, the first member from California, Charles Fox Tay, was not elected until 1896.

President William M. Mackay spoke with considerable pride when he proclaimed in 1897 that The American Society of Heating and Ventilating Engineers embraces the leading men in the United States and in Europe. By 1900, of 119 members, seven were from England, one from France, one from Denmark, and one from Ireland.

In 1934, the *A.S.H.V.E. Journal* profiled the ten then-current members holding the longest terms of membership in their respective countries. Representing England was J.N. Russell, of London, a past president of Britain's Institution of Heating and Ventilating

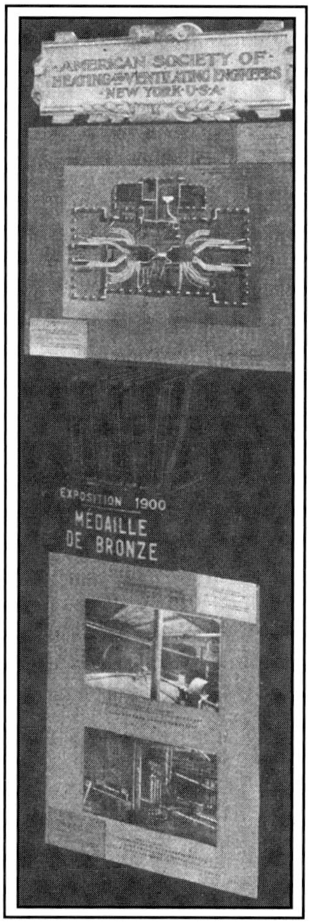

At the Paris Exposition of 1900, the United States exhibit included two complete copies of the Society's proceedings, which were awarded a bronze medal.

H.S. Downe
President, Cie Nationale des Radiateurs
Paris, France

J.N. Russell
Managing Director, Rosser & Russell, Ltd.
London, England

Hugo Theorell
Consulting Engineer, Hugo Theorells, Ingeniorsbyra
Stockholm, Sweden

Kunisuke Sekido
Consulting Engineer
Tokyo, Japan

Walter Leek
President Managing Director, Leek & Co. Ltd.
Vancouver, B.C., Canada

Alf Tjersland
Director, E. Sunde & Co., Ltd., Oslo, Norway

H.W. Hart-Baker
Director, Merritt Limited
Shanghai, China

P.I. Barry
Managing Director, M. Barry Lrd., Cork, Ireland

Dr. Albert Klein
Managing Director, Carrier Lufttechnische Gesellschaft
Stuttgart, Germany

M.L. Sakouta
Consulting Engineer, Leningrad, U.S.S.R.

Engineers, elected in 1899. Hugo Theorell of Stockholm, Sweden joined in 1902. Kunisuke Sekido, Tokyo, Japan and Walter Leek, Vancouver, B.C., Canada were elected in 1903. Alf Tjersland of Oslo, a 1920 meeting attendee, represented Norway. Henry W. Hart-Baker was an Englishman, but by 1918 he was a member of the Society and a practicing engineer residing in China. For Ireland, the person with the most membership years was Patrick I. Barry, the sole proprietor of his father's business in Cork. In Germany, it was Dr. Albert Klein who spent nearly 15 years with construction and manufacturing firms in the U.S. and then became managing director of Carrier Lufttechnische Gesellschaft. Mathieu L. Sakouta, the first A.S.H.V.E. member in the U.S.S.R., was elected in 1924. A consulting engineer since 1906, Mr. Sakouta wrote to the Society saying he finds "pleasure in his membership because of the valuable research reports and data which appear in the official publications."

International Cooperation

In 1902, as the Society began preparations for its 10th Anniversary meeting, the suggestion was made to convene the meeting at the St. Louis World's Fair of 1904 and to organize there an engineering congress of all the different branches of engineering, including the "Society of Heating and Ventilating Engineers." The committee, headed by Andrew Harvey, discussed inviting the heating and ventilating associations in England, Germany and France. Still another thought was to hold an American meeting in Europe during 1904 to better advertise the work of the Society.

By 1903, less ambitious plans were pursued. It was suggested to invite the president of the British Institution of Heating and Ventilating Engineers to the anniversary meeting and possibly to invite the members of the German society of the heating and ventilating trades.

When the 1904 meeting was finally convened, either the earlier plans for European involvement were forgotten or invitations were not accepted, but there is no mention of the other societies' participation in the minutes.

The first formal contact between the Society and Britain's Institution, founded in 1897, appears to be a cablegram read at two o'clock p.m., Friday, July 7, 1905, at the semiannual meeting of the Society in Chicago: "It is from 'The Heating and Ventilating Society of Great

Britain,'" announced Secretary William M. Mackay. "Hope you decide to hold united meeting in England next year. Haden." Haden was William Nelson Haden, a member of The A.S.H.V.E. from Trowbridge, England. The next morning a detailed letter arrived from George Crispin, president of The Institution of Heating and Ventilating Engineers, proposing a joint summer meeting in England for 1906.

Secretary Mackay who read a cablegram from William Haden proposing a meeting in England in 1906.

The following January, it was decided to hold the summer meeting in Chicago and to decline the invitation of The Institution. Secretary Mackay noted there are "some thirty odd members over there, twice a quorum," but President William Kent concluded, "We would like to be present with the British engineers in London, in July, but I do not think, we are ready yet to hold our meeting in London." It would not be until 1981 that such a meeting would take place.

In 1929, however, The A.S.H.V.E. did meet on British soil when the Ontario chapter hosted the Semi-Annual Meeting at the Bigwin Inn, Lake-of Bays, Canada. In what certainly was one of the most entertaining of Society meetings, travelers from various cities were welcomed in Toronto to board a special eight-car train on the Canadian National Railway for the trip to Bigwin Inn. A special luncheon was served in the two dining cars.

In 1981, ASHRAE held its first meeting outside of North America, a joint meeting with CIBS in London. ASHRAE President Charles E. Sepsy (left) and his CIBS counterpart Peter Coles exchanged gifts to commemorate the occasion.

During the first morning of the meeting, the ladies walked Bigwin Island and climbed to the observation tower. In the afternoon, a steamer left the dock for a three-hour sail. The men played a qualifying round in preparation for the Research Cup golf tournament, which was held on Thursday afternoon. The ladies golf tournament was held that morning.

The Rotunda of Bigwin Inn offered a scenic view of the lake, where in 1929, the International Bang and Go Back Motor Boat Race took place. Each chapter attending the meeting was given a boat to race.

Other activities included dancing in the pavilion, theatrical entertainment, an international polo match between the Canadians and the Americans, a chariot race, the introduction of the world's strongest man and others of unusual physical and mental attainments, a masquerade party with prizes, a tennis tournament, lawn bowling, ladies bridge and tea, badminton, swimming, a log rolling contest by local talent, and the highlight of meeting the international bang and go back motor boat race. Technical sessions and committee meetings also took place.

The A.S.R.E.

Among the charter members of The American Society of Refrigerating Engineers was Frank H. White of the Nonpareil Cork Works, 521 Coristine Building, Montreal, Canada. Within a year, Mr. White was joined by foreign members Cecil H.G. Croll of Wellington, New Zealand; Edgar W. Thompson of Boyd's Ice Factory in Bombay, India; and Arthur R.T. Woods of Liverpool, England.

In 1906, three engineers from Buenos Aires, Argentina were elected Members (Carlos Maschwitz, Charles E.G. McReddie and Jose Santiago Rey y Basadre). Four non-U.S. Associates were elected

To the Institute of Heating and Ventilating Engineers

Whereas:

The American Society of Heating and Ventilating Engineers

is assembled in its 35th Semi Annual Meeting, and

Whereas:

For the first time in its history, the Society is meeting outside the limits of the United States, and

Whereas:

This most successful and delightful event is being held under the auspices of the Ontario Chapter and within the confines of the British Empire; therefore, be it

Resolved:

That the greetings of this Society be extended to the members of the

Institution of Heating and Ventilating Engineers of Great Britain;

and be it further

Resolved:

That as an additional mark of our esteem these Greetings be personally conveyed and delivered to the President of the British Institution of Heating and Ventilating Engineers by the President of this Society, Mr. Thornton Lewis.

June 26, 1929

Thornton Lewis President

A. V. Hutchinson Secretary

(W.D. Ashton Bost of Paisley, Scotland; O.M. Gould of Montreal, Canada, the only non-U.S. attendee at the first Society meeting; Charles A.L. Loney of Sydney, Australia; and John A. Ruddick of Ottawa, Canada). One non- U.S. Junior was elected (Alexander S. Mitchell of Wellington, New Zealand).

Recognizing the value of international participation from its inception, the Refrigerating Engineers' original constitution and bylaws allowed applicants who were not residents in the United States and Canada to be exempted from submitting recommendations for membership from four Members or Associates. Instead, such members could be "recommended for ballot by four members of the Council, after sufficient evidence had been secured to show that in their opinion the applicant was worthy of admission to the grade which he seeks."

International Congresses of Refrigeration

The international character of the refrigerating industry was in no greater evidence than at the First International Congress of the Refrigerating Industries in 1908 at Paris, France. More than thirty nations had official delegations. The Society was represented in the American delegation, and considerable time was spent at the following Society meeting sharing what was learned.

J.F. Nickerson
Headed American delegations to five International Congresses of Refrigeration abroad and to one in his native Chicago.

J.F. Nickerson, a charter member of The Society and publisher of the trade journal Ice and Refrigeration, reported "The American delegation received much attention from the officials of the Congress as well as from the delegations of the various countries represented....It seemed to be quite generally recognized that America led in the practical application of the principle of mechanical refrigeration.... It also became evident at the Congress that America led in the scientific and practical investigations in the influence of low temperatures upon perishable produce."

In 1909, Mr. Nickerson participated in the organization of the American Association of Refrigeration. This organization, later known as the American Institute of Refrigeration, arranged for American participation in the International Refrigeration Congresses, including the hosting in Chicago of the third Congress in 1913. Following the end of World War I, the International Institute of Refrigeration, an association of countries, was formed as a result of discussions at the previous Congresses.

Dr. Mary E. Pennington
The first female member of the Society, she served as Chief of the Food Research Laboratory of the Bureau of Chemistry in the Department of Agriculture before becoming a consultant to organizations interested in the proper development of ice usage, cold storage, and allied subjects. Dr. Pennington was regarded as the foremost American authority on home refrigeration and the many problems connected with the proper use of ice in the home. Her paper on the influence of low temperatures upon perishable produce was received with marked attention and the deepest interest at the First International Congress of the Refrigerating Industries in 1908 at Paris.

The International Congresses of Refrigeration were The A.S.R.E.'s most important opportunity for international exchange. In 1934, for example, a delegation traveled to The Hague in The Netherlands to attend the Seventh Congress. Secretary of The A.S.R.E. David L. Fiske commented on refrigerating practice of the time. "The main field where the Europeans excel and where we in time are likely to follow them more closely is in the field of food technology at large," Mr. Fiske wrote. "The difference lies in the food situation, in the constant attention those countries have to give to food supply and the conservation of foodstuffs which is more nature to their region than to ours."

In Germany, Mr. Fiske visited Karlsruhe's new laboratory of the Kaeltechnische Institute. In Britain, it was the Low Temperature Research Station in Cambridge. Much of Mr. Fiske's time during the visit was spent with German engineer and researcher Dr. Rudolph Plank, who later would serve as a foreign editor of Refrigerating Engineering.

In 1937, when the International Institute of Refrigeration created the Associate Member grade to accompany its country memberships, The A.S.R.E. became a member.

Growth in Canada

The first non-U.S. chapter of The A.S.H.V.E. was organized in Toronto, on September 15, 1922. Called the Ontario Chapter of the Canadian Division of the

On tour with the Deutsch Kalte-Verein—Mr. Fiske, Dr. Rudolph Plank, and Dr. E.C. Smith of the British Low Temperature Research Station.

E. Holt Gurney

"It seems to me that the selection of Council men each year should always keep a fair distribution as between the three great classes that make up our Society. I refer to the executive business man in engineering work, the professional engineer, and the academic man. These three groups intermingle in our Society in a way that gives so much of our strength." (1939)

Society, Society Secretary C.W. Obert predicted that with assistance from the new chapter, the Canadian Division would soon grow from more than thirty members to fifty.

E. Holt Gurney, an engineer and industrialist, served as the first Canadian president of The

"Old Timer's Night" was featured at the February 1952 meeting of the ASRE Ontario Section. A panel of five member reminisced on early cooling coils and their improvement and modernization. "Old Timers" Victor Pope, Gordon Tendall, and Harry Parish get ready for business.

A.S.H.V.E. Born in Toronto, Mr. Gurney joined the Society in 1929. The year of his presidency, 1938, was marked by the adoption of resolutions to improve procedures for the election of Society officials and by increased support of the "speakers bureau."

Mr. Gurney, perhaps drawing on his own chapter experience, believed the "far-away" chapters would benefit greatly from the Society financing several outstanding technical speakers to travel coast to coast for the purpose of addressing chapter members. Mr. Gurney also fought to change the process of nominating Society officers, recognizing that members not affiliated with a chapter were inadequately represented in the nomination process. At the time of the Gurney administration, nearly fifty percent of Society members had no chapter affiliation, many because of the geography of the situation.

The first Canadian Chapter of ASRE was founded in Ontario in 1947.

The First Special Branch

In 1952 members of ASHVE residing in Switzerland petitioned the Society's Council for a local organization. Their request was approved, and during a two-day excursion in the Swiss Alps, September 5-6,1952, the Switzerland Special Branch received its

Marking the years 1947 to 1957, the past chairmen (from left to right) of the ASRE Ontario Section: R.H. Lock, R.A. Stencel, J.G. McMillen, E.N. Yungbluth, H.S. Parish, W.W. Miller, W.J. Marshall, J.M.K. Harvie, W.J. Bright, and I.M. Bodine.

charter, becoming the first local ASHVE organization outside of North America.

The ASHVE Journal reported, "Over 20 members of the Society, prominent in their profession and residing in various industrial centers, now comprise the group that petitioned the Council of the Society for a local organization. Favorable action on their request to organize a special branch is creating a great deal of interest among the members in Switzerland. They now have an opportunity to meet as an organization where formerly no group relations existed for discussion of professional problems and exchange of ideas."

Leo F. Debruyn
President of the Switzerland Special Branch, the Society's first Special Branch.

A tradition within the Society prior to World War II was for the youngest chapter to present a gift, an object representative of its local area, to the next group receiving a chapter charter. Records show that the Oregon Chapter presented a myrtlewood gavel at the inauguration of the Delta Chapter in New Orleans. Subsequently, the Delta Chapter presented a gavel of sycamore to the Connecticut Chapter, which presented one of sturdy New England oak to the Iowa Chapter which followed.

Then came the war years, after which it is uncertain if the practice continued. But on receiving word that the first foreign branch would be formed in Switzerland, then Oregon Chapter President Ken Hansen wrote to Swiss President Leo DeBruyn sending felicitations and a myrtlewood gavel. In appreciation, the Swiss group sent a polished Swiss bell, forging a unique tie between the Oregon Chapter and the first foreign branch.

In 1960, a second overseas branch was organized, Gruppo Italiano ASHRAE, in Milan, Italy.

Charter Meeting of Swiss Special Branch held September 5, 1952 with Past President and Mrs. Alfred J. Offner (standing in center) as honored guests.

ASRE had a unique local group of its own as well. In January 1959, with Canal Zone Lt. Governor John D. McElheny presenting the charter and the Minister of Public Works of the Republic of Panama installing the officers, the Panama-Canal Zone Section of ASRE was born. The group continued as a "special branch" of ASHRAE after the merger but was disbanded shortly after.

Gruppo Italiano under the leadership of its president Gian Felice Bertolini convened its second exhibition of Heating, Air Conditioning, Refrigeration and Hydrosanitation with its second Air Conditioning Meeting in 1961. There were 85 exhibitors. Today, the show "Mostra Convegro" has grown into one of the most important in Europe.

Affiliation with ASHRAE

In 1961 the Society embarked on a new program to increase its international effectiveness.

"ASHRAE, in its desire to broaden its scope of activities in the free world and thereby make possible a more effective and fruitful exchange of knowledge and ideas among engineers engaged in the arts and sciences of Refrigeration, Heating and Air Conditioning, has decided, by recommendation of its International Relations Committee and approval of its Board of Directors,

John H. Fox (right) launched a program to recognize national engineering organizations as affiliates of ASHRAE. He is shown here with E.K. Stevens (left), manager of the ASHRAE membership-sponsored International Heating and Air Conditioning Exposition. The 1963 show covered four full floors in the New York Coliseum.

to make it possible for any qualifying overseas national society, engaged in its same field of activity, to become an affiliate with ASHRAE."

So read the preamble to a brochure on international affiliation distributed by ASHRAE in 1961.

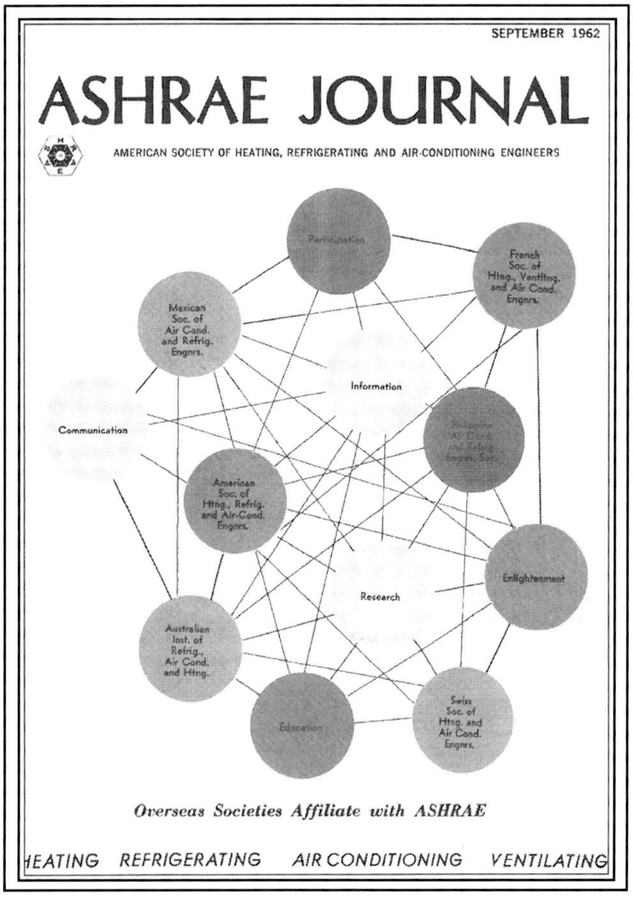

In June, 1962, the Board of Directors voted approval for affiliation of societies in Australia, The Philippines, Mexico and France. Marking ASHRAE's desire to encourage the formation of national societies in countries where such societies do not exist, the Board also voted to end recognition of overseas branches. Consequently, the local ASHRAE organizations in Switzerland and in Italy reorganized as national societies, and each was given affiliate status by ASHRAE.

In a letter of welcome and acknowledgment to each of the new affiliates, ASHRAE President John H. Fox, had, in part, this to say: "It is our sincere hope that, as time passes and through this affiliation, we shall have an opportunity to become better known one to the other and to share in the progress of our mutual technical interests and endeavors."

First Steps to a New Vision

Beginning in the 1950s, U.S. participation in the International Institute of Refrigeration (IIR) was organized by a U.S. National Committee, the secretariat of which was organized by the Divisions of Engineering, Biology and Agriculture, Physical Sciences and Chemistry of the National Academy of Sciences–National Research Council.

In the 1970s, it became apparent that U.S. efforts in the IIR tended to concentrate on the engineering

Dr. Richard C. Jordan was instrumental in involving the National Academy of Sciences—National Research Council to allow formal participation of the U.S. in the IIR, an association of countries. The U.S. State Department had long objected to the U.S. becoming a country member. Mr. Jordan (left) received congratulations from Edward Simons (right on becoming 1953 ASRE president. J.R. Hornady, 1953 program chairman, watches the ceremony.

aspects of refrigeration rather than on the scientific understanding and agricultural applications. To continue U.S. participation in the Institute, ASHRAE was asked to assume the role of secretariat in 1976. This participation, coupled with ASHRAE's work in the International Organization of Standardization, substantially increased recognition of ASHRAE as an international organization.

A pivotal Society year was 1983–84, when ASHRAE President Richard P. Perry declared it an international year of cooperation.

By 1984, ASHRAE membership outside of the United States and Canada had grown to more than 5,500 persons. With it, there was increased interest in forming local ASHRAE chapters, especially in the rapidly growing commercial centers of the Pacific rim.

The year saw ASHRAE organize a three-week technical exchange visit to China under the auspices of People to People International. Through seminars and meetings in a number of Chinese cities, the delegation, headed by 1984-85 President Robert O. McDonald, examined China's needs in HVAC&R technology, particularly in areas concerning environmental control, energy conservation, food storage and transportation.

Also in 1984, ASHRAE's first chapter outside of North America was formed, the Singapore Association of ASHRAE Members. More than 550 people welcomed Society President Perry at their first official meeting. In June, a second chapter-at-large was approved in Hong Kong. Of those in attendance when 1984–85 President Robert O. McDonald presented the chapter with its charter, 370 were ASHRAE members.

In 1985, ASHRAE co-sponsored CLIMA 2000 in Copenhagen, Denmark, the first world congress for HVAC&R. Organized as in previous years by REHVA, the Federation of European Heating and Ventilating Associations, the involvement of ASHRAE made CLIMA 2000 a true global forum and cemented

Refrigerated transport of perishable foodstuffs was one of the topics at the 10th International Congress of Refrigeration held at Copenhagen in 1959.

ASHRAE's posture as not only an organization of individuals from many nations but also as an international organization.

When ASHRAE celebrated its 125th Anniversary in 2019–20, ASHRAE had three regions consisting entirely of chapters outside the U.S. and Canada, and Regions VIII and XII operated with U.S. chapters and chapters in Mexico and South America, respectively. ASHRAE standards development had also broadened and been influenced by international adoptions.

Adapting to a Global Membership and Technology

By the time ASHRAE began its 101st year in July 1995, the world was getting smaller and ASHRAE, as 2017–18 President Bjarne W. Olesen would later say, was getting bigger. The need for ASHRAE to understand the strategic implications of its emerging global growth had become apparent.

ASHRAE's Strategic Plan approved by the Board of Directors in 2006 set as one of four directions for ASHRAE to be a global leader in the HVAC&R community. The rationale was recognition that the world had evolved from independent national economies to an interdependent global economy. The world was flat, as Thomas Friedman wrote, using a metaphor to describe how the global playing field was being leveled. The same influences Friedman saw applied to ASHRAE as it competed for the time of volunteers and industry resources. Significant growth opportunities were present in developing countries, and technologies being developed outside North America could enhance ASHRAE's knowledge base. But ASHRAE needed to be prepared.

In 2007 the Board approved 14 strategies to act in the flat world:

1. While ASHRAE's chapter and regional structure shall be the backbone of ASHRAE's structure globally, it shall be flexibly applied to serve our membership.
2. ASHRAE will cooperate with organizations with shared objectives and strengthen the ASHRAE Associate Societies Alliance.
3. The cost of annual membership dues will be balanced with the cost of providing membership benefits and services in different geographic regions.
4. Publications and educational products will be priced so they are within reach of ASHRAE's

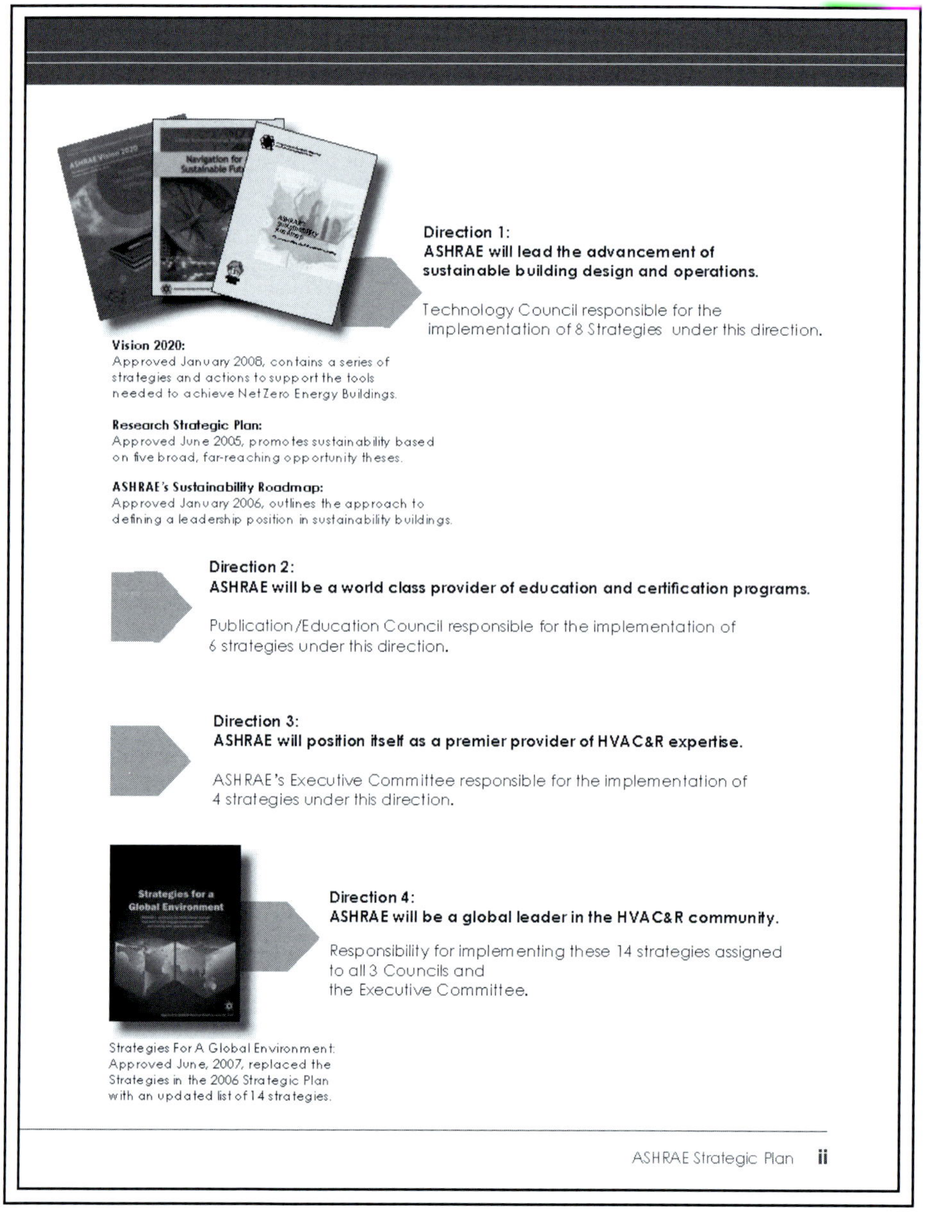

Direction 1:
ASHRAE will lead the advancement of sustainable building design and operations.

Technology Council responsible for the implementation of 8 Strategies under this direction.

Vision 2020:
Approved January 2008, contains a series of strategies and actions to support the tools needed to achieve Net Zero Energy Buildings.

Research Strategic Plan:
Approved June 2005, promotes sustainability based on five broad, far-reaching opportunity theses.

ASHRAE's Sustainability Roadmap:
Approved January 2006, outlines the approach to defining a leadership position in sustainability buildings.

Direction 2:
ASHRAE will be a world class provider of education and certification programs.

Publication/Education Council responsible for the implementation of 6 strategies under this direction.

Direction 3:
ASHRAE will position itself as a premier provider of HVAC&R expertise.

ASHRAE's Executive Committee responsible for the implementation of 4 strategies under this direction.

Direction 4:
ASHRAE will be a global leader in the HVAC&R community.

Responsibility for implementing these 14 strategies assigned to all 3 Councils and the Executive Committee.

Strategies For A Global Environment: Approved June, 2007, replaced the Strategies in the 2006 Strategic Plan with an updated list of 14 strategies.

ASHRAE Strategic Plan ii

2006 Strategic Plan at a glance.

ASHRAE Helps Developing Nations

New Membership Option Available

To encourage membership outside North America, ASHRAE has launched a program that provides a decreased dues structure option for individuals residing in countries categorized as developing countries by the World Bank List of Economies Statistics.

The program opens June 1 for new members qualifying for Member or Associate Member grades. Current members who are eligible can apply on their membership renewal date for 2009 memberships effective July 1.

The program is applicable to more than 100 countries defined by the World Bank as low-income or lower-middle-income.

"By offering more affordable dues to members in developing countries, ASHRAE is expanding its reach into countries that can contribute to and benefit from the technology and information sharing in the Society," said ASHRAE president Kent Peterson. "This will help in creating a worldwide best practices databank of innovative and successful technologies that can serve the HVAC&R community."

The cost of the new program is $90 (USD) per year with benefits to include electronic-only monthly access to ASHRAE Journal and *ASHRAE Insights*, and the annual ASHRAE Handbook in CD format. Members in eligible countries also can pay the full membership price of $165 (USD) and receive full benefits (with print versions of publications).

The program is part of ASHRAE's strategic plan, which calls for reaching global goals through increased membership. This reduced fee structure ensures that ASHRAE membership is fiscally feasible for potential members worldwide. A shift in membership benefits for this dues structure enables ASHRAE to offer this program while allowing the Society to remain financially healthy, ensuring many years of continued service to its diverse membership worldwide, according to Peterson.

For more information, visit www.ashrae.org/membership.

2008

global membership but will not be priced at less than the cost of providing them.

5. ASHRAE will develop its expertise in HVAC&R technologies to embrace whole-building sustainable design and be one of the most valuable global resources for publications and educational products related to sustainable HVAC&R technology.
6. ASHRAE will pursue opportunities and processes along with translations to publish its literature in various languages.
7. Volunteer participation obstacles will be overcome through meeting planning and organization that is sensitive to global participation and that benefits from electronic communication technologies.
8. ASHRAE will support, in cooperation with national associations, a uniform, international standard for credentialing in the disciplines and practices of HVAC&R.
9. ASHRAE will actively support and participate in international standard development activities.
10. ASHRAE will actively protect its intellectual property rights.
11. ASHRAE will provide enhanced staff support outside of the United States.
12. ASHRAE will align its business practices to better serve members globally.
13. ASHRAE, in cooperation with national societies or independently, will pursue conferences and exhibitions outside North America.
14. The ASHRAE brand will be strengthened to reflect a global strategy that serves the needs of all members.

Progress on all the strategies was made in the following years.

Red Ocean, Blue Ocean

ASHRAE's next strategic plan, approved in 2014, also had a global focus. Its Initiative 4 noted that while ASHRAE has already had significant impact in many countries around the world, there was more that could be done.

After extensive research into past business performance in international markets and anticipated demand, ASHRAE chose to expand activities in "Red Ocean" (mature market) and "Blue Ocean" (emerging market) communities. The experience would give ASHRAE operating experience for developing a comprehensive global business model and support structure.

At the time, ASHRAE had a total of 10,323 international members, of which 8,023 were industry members (Member, Associate, and Affiliate) located in 126 countries. Just 26 countries had more than 100 members and together represented 81% (6,587) of the total. The remaining 100 countries had between 1 and 99 members. ASHRAE had an additional 2,240 Student Members in 64 countries, of which just 6 countries had more than 100 members. The countries with the most student members were located in emerging economies (rather than in the mature markets of Europe).

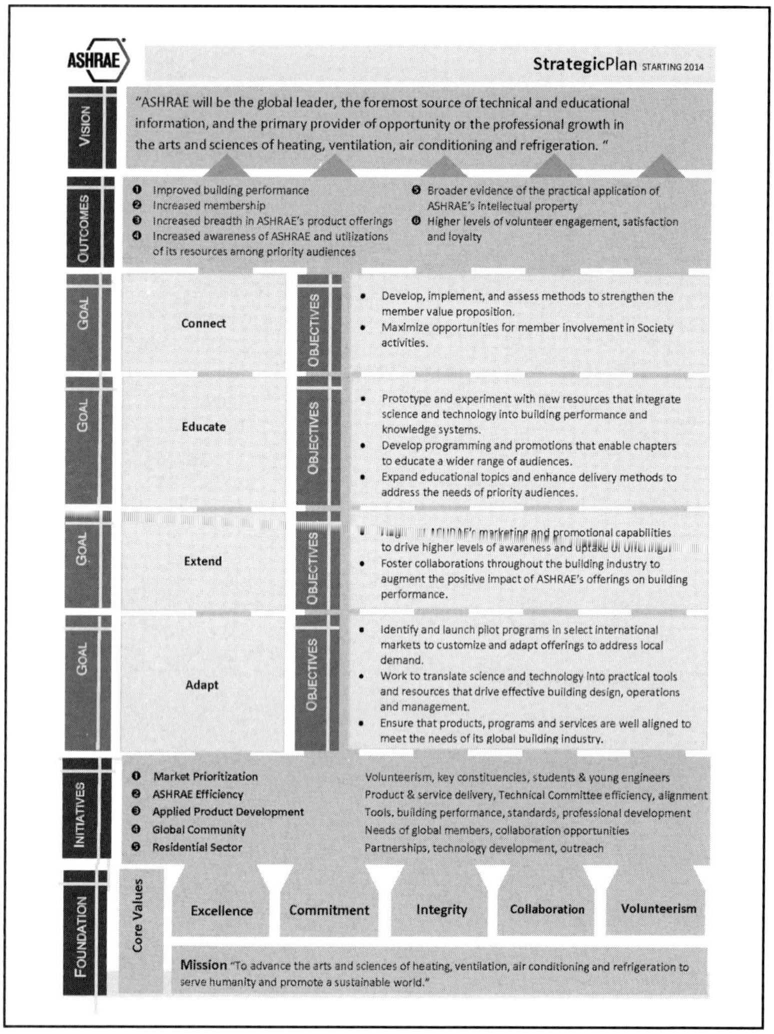

2014 Strategic Plan at a glance.

When taken as a whole, some 70% of ASHRAE's international membership resided in Middle East, Asia and Africa, with growth driven by rapid development of infrastructure, need for standards, desire to fast-track knowledge, and the influence and penetration of U.S. companies who rely on ASHRAE documents. But the research also revealed that while membership is growing in emerging markets, Europe had a higher renewal tendency.

Dubai and Brussels

Establishing a training center in Dubai that focused on delivering ASHRAE learning products was selected as the Blue Ocean market experience. In July 2017, the center began operation with the delivery of training customized for the climate, design and construction practices, standards, and culture of the Middle East, along with the use of regionally based instructors. The inaugural instructor team was Walid Chakroun, Samir Traboulsi, Hesham Safwat, and Hassan Younes. Ayah Said became a new hire from the Middle East to coordinate training in the center, reaching out to chapters, government agencies, associations, and companies in the Middle East, North Africa, and West Asia.

In July 2018 ASHRAE began to lease space in the European Union District in Brussels, Belgium, to support activities of members in Region XIV and to interact with the European institutions with which many European ASHRAE members interact.

The Red Ocean experience began in 2018 with the opening of an office in Brussels. The office's immediate charge was supporting chapters in the newly formed Region XIV through delivery of HVAC&R training to their memberships and building the ASHRAE community through outreach to members not belonging to chapters and through collaboration with European-based associations. The ultimate goal was to make the Society more accessible to members and to other engineers in Europe and to

ASHRAE opened its first global training center in Dubai in 2017. Walid Chakroun, Ahmed Alaa Eldin, Ayah Said, Hassan Younes, Hesham Safwat, and Samir Traboulsi visit the new office.

AASA meeting in 2018 at ASHRAE Winter Conference, Chicago.

promote European member engagement, thereby enriching ASHRAE's body of knowledge and fostering volunteer spirit. W. Stephen Comstock transitioned from ASHRAE's Director of Publishing and Education to head the office.

ASHRAE Associate Society Alliance

In 1962, ASHRAE opened the possibility for national associations to be affiliated with the Society. By the 1970s they were referred to as Associate Societies. The International Relations Committee was renamed the International Committee, and it managed those relationships, reviewed applications for societies to be recognized, and administered Associate Society ASHRAE Libraries.

In the 1990s, the International Committee took on a new role, assuming responsibility for ASHRAE chapters established in overseas countries where sufficient interest and viability were demonstrated by a nucleus of ASHRAE members. The committee provided support for the overseas chapters who had not petitioned to form a region.

Some Associate Societies saw the overseas ASHRAE chapter initiative as competitive with their own interests, and it became clear that a different structure for management of relationships with the overseas Societies and chapters would be beneficial. Initially, a new dual structure was established as a transitional step. This involved coordination of Associate Society relationships by the International Committee and an Overseas Regional Group that coordinated relationships with the overseas chapters. By the mid-1990s the number of overseas chapters had grown substantially, and it was decided to form a new overseas region (the Region-at-Large) to administer chapters consistent with ASHRAE's North American chapter and region organization.

In order to not diminish the importance of Associate Societies in ASHRAE's international activities, the ASHRAE Board of Directors established, in 1997, a new structure called the ASHRAE Associate Society Alliance, which would include ASHRAE and all recognized Associate Societies as members. The purpose of this Alliance remains true to the objectives of the original ASHRAE Affiliate Society program: to enable ASHRAE to participate collaboratively in the advancement of the arts and sciences of air conditioning, heating, ventilating, and refrigerating technologies and to foster effective and fruitful exchanges of ideas and information between participants.

Today, there are 65 societies in the ASHRAE Associate Society Alliance representing an estimated 300,000 total engineers and specialists.

The following roster of Associate Societies incorporates overseas national societies engaged in the same or similar fields of technical and scientific endeavor as ASHRAE. To be accepted as Associate Societies, the societies must have been in existence a minimum of three consecutive years, have no fewer than 100 members, and have requirements for membership equal to the minimum requirements in ASHRAE.

Country	Associate Society	Date approved by BOD	Date rescinded by BOD
Australia	Australian Institute of Refrigeration ("Air-Conditioning and Heating" added in 1974) (AIRAH)	1962	
Philippine	Philippine Air Conditioning and Refrigerating Engineers Society	1982	1986
Mexico	Mexican Society of Air Conditioning, Heating and Refrigerating Engineers	1962	1983
France	French Association of Heating and Ventilation Engineers (AICVF)	1962	
Switzerland	Swiss Society of Heating & A/C Engineers (SWKI)	1962	
Argentina	Asociacion Argentina del Frio (AAF)	1962	1973 (reinstated 1974)
New Zealand	New Zealand Institute of Refrigeration ("and Air-Conditioning" added in 1979) Engineers, Inc.	1962	1989
Italy	Italian Society of A/C, Heating, Refrigeration (AICARR)	1963	
Japan	Society of Htg A/C & Sanitary Engrs of Japan (SHASE)	1963	
Netherlands	Dutch Society for Building Services (TVVL)	1963	
United Kingdom	The Institute of Refrigeration (IOR)	1964	
Sweden	Swedish Society of Htg A/C Engineers (SWEDVAC)	1964	
Brazil	Brazilian Assoc of Refrig A/C Ventilation & Htg (ABRAVA)	1966	
Belgium	Royal Assoc Htg Ventilation A/C & Related Sys (ATIC)	1967	
Finland	Society of Bldg Svcs and Engy Engrs (LIVI)	1967	
Norway	Norwegian Engineering Society	1967	1984
India	Indian Society of Refrigerating Engineers	1967	1979
Germany	Deutscher Kaelte-und Klimatechnischer Verein e.V. (DKV)	1968	
New Zealand	The New Zealand Institute of Engineers, Inc. (Building Services Group	1973	1989
Norway	Association of Heating and Ventilating Engineers (NORSK VVS)	1974	
Spain	Spanish Tech Assoc A/C & Refrigeration (ATECYR)	1975	
Israel	Israel Society of Heating Refrigerating & A/C Engineers (ISHRACE)	1976	1976 (reinstated 1978)
Denmark	Danisk Society of Heating, Ventilation and Air Conditioning Engineers (DANVAK)	1976	
South Africa	South African Institute of Refrigeration & Air Conditioning (SAIRAC)	1976	
Japan	Japan Society of Refrigerating & A/C Engineers (JSRAE) (formerly The Japanese Association of Refrigeration, JAR)	1978	
Netherlands	Royal Dutch Association of Refrigeration (KNVVK)	1978	
New Zealand	New Zealand Institute of Heating and Ventilating Engineers	1979	1989
Taiwan	Taiwan Refrigerating and Air-Conditioning Engineering Association	1980	1984
Colombia	Asociacion Colombiana del Acondicionamiento de Aire y de la Refrigeracion (ACAIRE)	1983	
Mexico	Mexican Assoc Co Indus Bldg Installation (AMERIC)	1983	
South Korea	Society of Air Conditioning and Refrigerating Engineers of Korea (SAREK)	1985	
Egypt	Egyptian Society of Mechanical Engineers (ESME)	1985	
Serbia	Serbian Society of HVAC&R-KGH (KGH) (formerly Klimatizacija, Grejanje Hladjenje, JUKO-KGH)	1985	
Philippines	Philippine Society of Ventilating, Air Conditioning and Refrigerating Engineers (PSVARE)	1986	
China	Chinese Association of Refrigeration (CAR)	1987	

Country	Associate Society	Date approved by BOD	Date rescinded by BOD
China	China Committee of Heating, Ventilating and Air Conditioning (CCHVAC)	1988	1988 (reinstated 1998)
New Zealand	Institute of Refrigeration, Heating and Air Conditioning Engineers of New Zealand, Inc. (IRHACE)	1989	
Poland	Polish Association of Sanitary Engineers & Technicians (PZITS)	1990	
Russia	Russian Association of Engineers for HVAC Heat Supply & Building Thermal Physics (ABOK)	1991	
Spain	Catalan Association of Technicians in Energy Air Conditioning and Refrigeration (ACTECIR)	1992	
Chile	Cooling and Air Conditioning Technical Division of Chile (DITAR)	1993	
Turkey	Turkish Society of Heating, Ventilation, Air Conditioning and Sanitary Engineers (TTMD)	1993	
Latvia	Association of Heat, Gas and Water Technology Engineers (AHGWTEL)	1994	
Portugal	Associacao Portuguesa dos Engenheiros de Frio Industrial e de Ar Condicionado (EFRIARC)	1994	
Romania	Romanian General Association of Refrigeration (AGFR)	1994	
India	Indian Society of Heating, Refrigerating and Air Conditioning Engineers (ISHRAE)	1994	
Slovenia	Slovenian Society of Refrigerating, Heating and Air Conditioning Engineerrs (SITHOK)	1994	
Venezuela	Associacion Nacional Capitulo Technico ASOFRIO (TECFRIO)	1994	1994
Hungary	Epitestudomanyi Egyesulet (ETE)	1995	
Iceland	The Icelandic Heating, Ventilating and Sanitary Association (ICEVAC)	1995	
Lithuania	Lithuanian Thermotechnical Engineers Society (LITES)	1995	
Finland	Finnish Association of HVAC Societies (FINVAC)	1996	
Pakistan	Pakistan HVACR Society (PHVACR)	1997	
Czech Republic	Society of Environmental Engineering (STP)	2005	
Slovakia	Slovak Society of Environmental Technology (SSTP)	2005	
Lebanon	Order of Engineers & Architects Beirut (OEAB)	2006	
Austria	Oesterreichischer Kaelte-und Klimatechnischer Verein (OEKKV)	2006	
Brazil	Associacao Sul Brasileira de Refrigeracao Ar Condicionado Ventilacao e Aquecimento (ASBRAV)	2009	
Ecuador	Asociacion Tecnica Ecatoriana de Aire Acondicionado y Refrigeracion (ATEAAR)	2009	
Lebanon	Order of Engineers and Architects Tripoli (OEAT)	2010	
Greece	Technical Chamber of Greece (TEE)	2011	
Uruguay	Asociacion Uruguaya de Refrigeracion, Ventilacion, Aire Acondicionado y Calefaccion (ASURVAC)	2011	2011
Peru	Asociación Peruana de Ventilación, Aire Acondicionado, Refrigeración y Calefacción (APVARC)	2011	
Brazil	Sociedade Brasileira De Controle de Contaminacao (SBCC)	2012	
Iran	Iranian Society of Heating, Refrigeration and Air Conditioning Engineers (IRSHRAE)	2012	
Philippines	Philippine Society of Mechanical Engineers, Inc. (PSME)	2013	
Denmark	Danish Refrigeration Association (DRA)	2014	
Philippines	Philippine Green Building Initiative (PGBI)	2014	
Georgia	Georgian Association of Refrigerating, Cryogenic & Air Conditioning Engineers NGO (GARCAE-NGO)	2015	
Bahrain	Bahrain Society of Engineers (BSE)	2015	
Chile	Camara Chilena de Refrigeracion y Climatization A.G. (CCHRYC)	2016	
Brazil	Associacao Brasileira de Facilities (ABRAFAC)	2017	

Partnering with UNEP

In 2007, ASHRAE and the United Nations Environment Programme (UNEP) entered into a partnership agreement aimed at promoting state-of-the-art technologies and practices that can support developing countries to move towards non–ozone depleting substances (ODSs) and lower global warming potential (GWP) technologies as well as promote best practices and techniques that support eliminating emissions of refrigerants during servicing of refrigeration and air-conditioning applications.

Working with the OzonAction division within UNEP to implement the Montreal Protocol on Substances that Deplete the Ozone Layer, ASHRAE provides technical guidance that assists the Protocol's Article 5 countries to simultaneously implement the timely phase-out of their remaining hydrochlorofluorocarbon (HCFC) consumption while at the same time preparing for the phase-down of hydrofluorocarbons (HFCs). Countries need to ensure legal preparedness by adjusting laws and regulations and adopt energy-efficient and climate-friendly technologies that are good for the environment and their industry's bottom line.

The partnership agreement enables UNEP to access industry experts and have access to have training products based on ASHRAE standards, research, and other ASHRAE resources. Another contribution offered by ASHRAE is its presence through members, chapters, and associate societies covering more than 130 nations, which provides a multinational platform, especially in developing countries, for development of locally relevant technical guidance.

In 2017 ASHRAE received the Partnership Award from UNEP's Ozone Secretariat for its extraordinary commitment and contribution to the progress and achievements of the Montreal Protocol on Substances that Deplete the Ozone Layer on the occasion of the Protocol's 30th anniversary. Said ASHRAE President Bjarne W. Olesen, "We are proud to be a part of this initiative and look forward to continuing our partnership with UN Environment as we work toward a more sustainable built environment." Estonia's Deputy Environment Minister Meelis Munt (right) presented the award to Olesen (left).

In return, government officials and end-user industries in developing countries are made aware of the local ASHRAE chapters and membership interests. ASHRAE and UNEP eLearning courses on refrigerants knowledge and practices were jointly developed and made available to National Ozone Units (NOUs) in multiple languages in developing countries as well as to all ASHRAE members globally.

ASHRAE participated in a 2018 UNEP-organized Refrigeration Service Sector workshop in order to identify resources, gaps, and overlaps in training for refrigeration and air-conditioning sector technicians.

The A.S.H.V.E. Research Laboratory was modeled after the Testing Institute of Heating and Ventilation Appliances at the Berlin University in Germany. Arthur K. Ohmes wrote in the 1916 Transactions: "Our country, so much advanced in many ways, possesses nothing of the kind. Many of our institutions of higher education do not consider the subject of heating and ventilation of enough importance to warrant such an institution, but Germany appears to be fully alive to the importance of the subject and considers that accurate knowledge of the art vitally concerns the physical as well as the commercial welfare of the people....I would like a thorough discussion in the merits of such a similar institution for our country....An active campaign extending over several years should be started at once for the purpose of collecting a large sum of money for the building and endowment of such an institution. The large corporations should contribute, because they all have the heating and ventilating plants and appliances to operate and maintain and they are interested in having the art advance."

"Growth and Improve Technology through International Cooperation" was the focus of the 1983–84 term of President Richard P. Perry. Mr. and Mrs. Perry were greeted in Japan by Mr. and Mrs. Sachio Hotani representing the Japanese Association of Refrigeration.

ASHRAE 1984–85 President Robert O. McDonald (third from left) led an ASHRAE-organized People-to-People delegation to China with Andrew T. Boggs (second from right) in 1984.

CLIMA 2000, the first world congress for HVAC&R

Donald R. Bahnfleth, 1985–86 ASHRAE President, and Walter H. Knoll, president of REHVA, wait to speak at opening ceremonies for CLIMA 2000 in 1985.

1984–85 President Robert O. McDonald presents material for the ASHRAE library to Alan Thompson, member of the Board of Governors, Hong Kong Chapter. Also pictured are Hong Kong Chapter President Sammy Wong (far left) and ASHRAE Affiliate Richard Yuen.

Conference attendees gather in the lecture hall at Dublin's Trinity College, founded in 1952 by Queen Elizabeth II, to hear opening speeches.

ASHRAE, REHVA, and ATECYR sponsored Solar 83 in Mallorca, Spain. From right, Mario Constantino represented REHVA, Richard P. Perry, ASHRAE, and Gabriel Barcello Rico-Avello, ATECYR.

ASHRAE President Frederick H. Kohloss (left) and CIBSE President and ASHRAE member Eoin Kenny (center) welcome President of Ireland Dr. Patrick J. Hillery. In 1986, ASHRAE and CIBSE sponsored "The Engineered Environment" in Dublin.

In 1991, ASHRAE President Damon Gowan (right) represented ASHRAE at the first annual meeting of ABOK in the U.S.S.R. Yuri A. Tabunschikov accepted a certificate of association from Mr. Gowan.

In 1962, representatives of ISO/TC 86 met in London. At the chairman's table are Professor Geneve, representative of the British Standards Institution, A.T. Boggs, and F.J. Reed (standing). At the meeting, ASHRAE Standard 16 on rating room air conditioners and ASHRAE Standard 34 on designation of refrigerants were submitted as the basis of International Standards.

At his visit to the British Industries Fair at London in 1950, ASHVE President John W. James had the honor of being among those presented to Her Majesty The Queen and H.R.H. The Duke of Edinburgh.

CIBSE/ASHRAE '86 delegates meet outside the dining hall at Trinity College.

ASHRAE 1992-93 President Richard A. Charles meets winners of the AIRAH Work Skills competition for young refrigeration and air conditioning tradesmen. Awards were presented at the 1993 Annual Conference of the Australian Institute of Refrigeration, Air Conditioning and Heating.

VIEWPOINT

GLOBAL ISSUES

Billy R Manning, president elect of the American Society of Heating, Refrigeration and Air Conditioning Engineers (ASHRAE), offered the US view on current environmental concerns in the course of an official visit to the CLIMA 2000 international conference held in London this month.

LET me begin by emphasising the fact that the need to think internationally has never been greater than it is now.

"Environmental" is a hot button in the USA, as I know it is over here, and there is growing acceptance by world leaders that limitations must be placed on human activity that destroys the environment if the earth as we know it is to survive.

Two words can sum up how environmental awareness can turn an industry upside down: ozone depletion.

The Montreal Protocol and the Copenhagen Accord which strengthened it are unprecedented examples of international co-operation. While the ozone depletion caused by the CFCs used in our industry accounts for only 2 to 5 per cent of the total depletion which is occurring, we still have a responsibility to reduce it. New refrigerants such as R123 and R134a have been developed to replace R11 and R12, and these nearly solve the ozone depletion challenge.

> **The earth's rosources are not infinite**

But one thing that must be kept in mind is that the ideal refrigerant must have little or no ozone depletion potential, must be efficient, and must have low global warming potential. And, of course, the ideal refrigerant must also be non-flammable and non-toxic. No refrigerant that exists today perfectly meets all these criteria, and the search for the perfect refrigerant will continue throughout the 1990s.

ASHRAE will help in this search, through its support of research. For one of the fundamental strengths of ASHRAE is its commitment to research as a building block of hvacr technology. Its research program now operates on a $2m annual budget and typically supports about 70 projects worth more than $6m at any given time. Currently, the society is sponsoring eight projects that are CFC-related.

We are also promoting the use of existing alternative refrigerants and the use of all refrigerants wisely, and ASHRAE Guideline 3 explains to our industry how to prevent the inadvertent escape of refrigerants through design, installation and service.

ASHRAE Standard 15 describes precautions that must be in place for the safe use of refrigerants in different types of equipment. And ASHRAE Standard 34 classifies refrigerants by toxicity and flammability, and standardises refrigerant nomenclature.

Another area of international concern is energy, and three aspects drive this issue: finite energy resources; impact on the environment; and the limitations of electrical generation and distribution.

The earth's resources are not infinite. Decades ago, an eminent geologist by the name of King Hubbard graphically expressed the fact of our diminishing resources in what has been called the Hubbard Pimple. He explained that we are using energy resources faster than we are discovering new ones — a situation that cannot continue unchecked if we are to sustain our present standard of living.

The second aspect of the energy problem lies in the fact that, the more hydrocarbons that are burned, the greater the global warming or greenhouse effect. So, not only must we reduce consumption of our energy resources simply to preserve them, but we must also minimise their global warming impact.

Manning: "The search will continue for the perfect refrigerant."

Finally, there is the problem of electrical generation and distribution.

The USA is already a net importer of electrical energy. Our electricity generation capacity cannot keep up with our consumption, and we are therefore purchasing an increasing percentage of our power each year from Canada. The lead time today on fossil fuel plant is approximately five years. On nuclear plant, it is usually between ten and 15 years. Beyond this, the electricity generation plants that are currently on the boards will not keep up with our currently increasing rate of electrical consumption.

In the USA, power companies have adopted rate structures that encourage efficiency, peak shaving and thermal storage. In fact, some of the rebates now offered by utilities for thermal storage systems actually pay for the installed first cost.

Of course, there are some things that our industry can feel proud of.

For instance, the comfort system in a typical US office building today consumes less than half the energy per square foot consumed by the system in a typical office building in 1970. Our industry has achieved this through more efficient equipment, more efficient systems and better building design.

However, we will need to do even more in the future as the National Energy Policy Act of 1992 mandates that each state in the USA should have an energy code in place by October 1994 that meets or exceeds efficiencies of the current version of the ASHRAE/IES Standard 90.

Indoor air quality is another major concern for the US industry, as it is in Europe. For it is estimated that over half of commercial buildings today have an indoor air quality problem to some degree — and a more serious condition known as "building-related illness" and the litigation resulting from it may very well make the indoor air quality issue rival asbestos in terms of its impact on the building owner's bottom line.

How will indoor air quality impact on our industry?

The answer is pretty straightforward. The US National Institute of Safety and Health recently carried out a study of 432 buildings that had indoor air quality problems — and the primary cause in 52 per cent of cases involved inadequate ventilation.

There are three important aspects of the indoor air quality issue — health, comfort and productivity.

The health issue is obvious, but it is important to note that a building can meet the health criteria and still not be comfortable...and comfort is important because it relates directly to productivity.

> **Indoor air quality may rival asbestos**

I should like to give an example that emphasises the importance of the comfort-producing capabilities of hvac systems to a building's overall economic viability.

Let's take a typical office building, and let's assume that the average person who works in that building, when you take into account his or her salary and fringe benefits, costs $30,000 a year. And let's assume that the average person occupies 150sq ft, or 14 sq m, of space. The people cost of that office building is therefore $200 per sq ft, or $2,200 per sq m.

Now let's assume that, because of an inadequately designed hvac system, the people in the building are not as comfortable as they ought to be. According to a study recently carried out by the Building Owners and Managers Association, the impact of comfort on productivity can range from 2 to 18 per cent. So, taking the most conservative estimate, a 2 per cent impact on productivity costs $4 per sq ft (or $43 per sq m) per year.

The energy bill for the building will only be about $2 per sq ft ($22 per sq m) per year. And when you consider that the installed cost of the entire comfort system was probably $5 to $10 per sq ft ($50 to $100 per sq m), and that another 50 cents to $2 per sq ft ($5 to $20 per sq m) could have made the difference between a poor comfort system and an excellent comfort system, I am left totally baffled as to why we as an industry have not done a better job of selling our value to the building owner.

> **We spend our efforts cheapening systems**

We all seem to have a cost-cutting mentality. Instead of selling a better system with smaller control zones and building automation, we spend our efforts cheapening systems and undercutting each other. The increased emphasis on indoor air quality therefore provides us with an outstanding opportunity to get healthy economically.

Total building design — for energy efficiency, for indoor air quality and for comfort — has become the standard by which all buildings are measured, and this will soon have additional impact through international standards.

Last year, ASHRAE was appointed the secretariat for TC 205, a new ISO technical committee which has been given the task of writing ISO standards covering total building environment design.

It is ASHRAE's objective to incorporate into this standard technologies from around the world which provide for the most energy-efficient, comfortable and healthful environment which our industry can offer. We hope through our work for ISO to give our industry a worldwide indoor environment standard to design for, to build for, and to maintain.

But ASHRAE's work in the area of alternative refrigerants and total building environments will not succeed unless we incorporate knowledge from all corners of the world.

ASHVE President Seeley and Vice Pres. Szekely welcome French Delegation visiting U.S. under Marshall Plan auspices at 58th Annual Meeting in 1952.

ASHRAE Historical Committee member Paul Yunni (left), ASHRAE Executive Vice President Frank Coda (center), and ASHRAE President Don Holtz share a lighter moment at CLIMA 2000 in Brussels in 1997.

ASHRAE President Bill Goodman attended FEBRAVA 99, a trade show held Aug.3-6 in Sao Paulo, Brazil. Sponsored by the Brazilian Congress on Refrigeration, Ventilation and Air Conditioning (CONBRAVA), the show attracted some 20,000 buyers and traders and 300 companies from 25 countries. Pictured, left to right, are ABRAVA Vice President Joao Hamilton; Roberto Aguilo; Goodman; ABRAVA President Ceslo Simoes Alexandre; Air Conditioning and Refrigeration Institute President Ted Rees; and Sindratar Vice President Pedro Evangelinos.

1999

ASHRAE/AICARR Meeting Reaffirms Close Relationship

By Cesare Maria Joppolo
Vice President AICARR
Member ASHRAE

Presidential Member Harley W. Goodman, Jr., P.E. (right), is shown here following a presentation at the ASHRAE/AICARR meeting. Also shown from left to right: Cesare M. Joppolo, AICARR Vice President and Renato G. Merati, AICARR President.

The annual meeting of the Italian members of ASHRAE was a special one this year. The joint meeting of the ASHRAE/AICARR members began five years ago and is an annual affair. The meeting this year was held at the little parliament of Palazzo Giureconsulti (the old law courts of Spanish age in downtown Milan).

The Italian group of ASHRAE members discussed and approved statutes and bylaws. Assisting in this process were Renato G. Merati, AICARR President and Cesare M. Joppolo, AICARR Vice President.

Special guests included ASHRAE Presidential Member Harley W. Goodman, Jr., P.E. and ASHRAE Executive Vice President Frank Coda. Goodman addressed the group and explained his presidential theme "ASHRAE in the New Millennium's Global Community." He also recommended an increase in commitment of Italian experts and engineers within ASHRAE technical committees.

The ASHRAE/AICARR group should play a prominent role in the dissemination of the HVAC&R technical culture through seminars and meetings organized within the two associations. A five member executive committee will be elected soon with one member to be named "ex-officio" and will be the AICARR representative to the ASHRAE Associate Societies alliance.

2000

ASHRAE Helps Put on Workshops At India Trade Fair

Host organizer V. Krishnan (left) accepts an ASHRAE publication from ALI instructor Lew Harriman.

MUMBAI, India—ASHRAE and its Associate Society in India, ISHRAE, teamed to present a three-day series of educational workshops in conjunction with the Indian trade fair, ACREX. ACREX is the largest international HVAC&R exposition in India.

In all, 17 half-day sessions were organized, drawing from ASHRAE Learning Institute programs on humidity control, Standard 90.1, Standard 189.1, chilled beams, thermal storage, and health care facility design.

2010

In 2018 ASHRAE participated in hands-on workshops for energy and environment officials from developing countries to improve regulations and training related to refrigerant management and energy efficiency in air conditioning in refrigeration.

CIBSE and ASHRAE sign historic joint agreement

Organisations mark 40th anniversary by agreeing greater collaboration

Posted in October 2016

CIBSE and the American Society of Heating, Refrigerating and Air-Conditioning Engineers (ASHRAE) have signed a partnership agreement to mark the 40th anniversary of their relationship.

The organisations met in London to implement a range of initiatives, including: working together strategically on projects in each other's regions; creating a staff-exchange programme; encouraging collaboration between regions, groups and chapters; and mutually promoting the publication of new codes and standards.

CIBSE and ASHRAE have worked closely together for four decades, but this is the first time they have committed to a joint approach to promoting their mutual global interests, and agreed to a range of activities and goals to promote a more sustainable world.

As well as a commitment to improve knowledge sharing – including jointly presenting work to industry, members and legislators – the organisations have agreed to work at a grass-roots level. This includes encouraging cooperation between ASHRAE chapters and CIBSE regions, coordinating the programmes of similar groups – such as Women in Building Services Engineering (WiBSE) and Women in ASHRAE (WIA) – aligning activity for young engineers, and working together on topics such as Legionella, resilience and cyber security.

John Field, CIBSE President (pictured, right), said: 'This is an unprecedented opportunity to spread the benefits of our work together, through every level of our organisations.'

Tim Wentz, ASHRAE president (pictured, left), added: 'Collaboration and sharing of knowledge are key to advancing the built environment industry.'

Falcon Chapter Signs MOU on UAE Codes

Ahmed Alaa Eldin Mohamed (left) and H.E. Abdulla Al Maeeni sign the memorandum of understanding.

DUBAI, United Arab Emirates—The ASHRAE Falcon Chapter and the Emirates Authority for Standardization and Metrology (ESMA) recently signed a memorandum of understanding (MOU) to advance the mutual interest of their respective members and collaborate in energy codes, standards, communication and research. ESMA is the national standards body in the UAE, responsible for issuing standards and technical regulations that serve quality, health, safety and the environment.

The signing took place at the 4th Symposium for Alternative Refrigerants for High Ambient Countries, which was organized in part by ESMA and the Falcon Chapter, along with several other international and regional associations and organizations.

H.E. Abdulla Al Maeeni, ESMA director general, signed the MOU with Ahmed Alaa Eldin Mohamed, regional vice chair of Grassroots Government activities for the ASHRAE Region-At-Large. The MOU ensures the collaboration between the chapter and ESMA on common public affairs goals and ideologies. During annual liaison meetings, public affairs strategies will be discussed and common goals identified. Numerous collaborative opportunities to be considered include:

- Joint promotion of codes and standards at the local, state and national levels in the fields of HVAC&R equipment and systems and building performance;
- Promotion of mutually beneficial positions during the development and passage of municipal and national legislation;
- Education of legislators on issues important to the members of each organization; and
- Creation of a national system of measurement and calibration.

2014

The China Committee of Heating, Ventilation, and Air-Conditioning (CCHVAC) visited the ASHRAE Headquarters in 2010.

Chapter 8

The Use and Abuse of Fuel

"Overshadowing everything else is the question of conservation of natural resources. For how much longer may we waste stored heat resources to save first-cost only of buildings? Our instinct is so to live as to make living for our descendants a better proposition. How are we intelligently following the instinct?... We refine the artificial heating plant, spend time and dollars and skill and genius in elaborating the heat transmitting appliances and the consuming devices with no more than cursory investigation of the type of construction of the building, and with no effort to influence it so as to reduce the heat losses. Many of us, I believe, stand convicted of crime in this regard against future generations."

S.R. Lewis
1914

While S.R. Lewis chided his contemporaries for not doing enough to conserve the natural resources used to maintain comfort in buildings, he cited the work of his organization, The American Society of Heating and Ventilating Engineers, to improve the practice of heating efficiently. He told of an effort by one of the Society's committees: "Imagine for a minute that instead of trying to heat the inside of a building against the cold outside that we were trying to cool the-inside of the building with ice against the heat outside; would we put the ice against the outside wall, the hottest surface available? I doubt it. I think we would put the ice at some point where it would absorb heat from the contents of the room rather than from the hot outside walls. We would not expose one half of each ice cake to the direct heat from the walls, in such a way as to limit its cooling influence on the room.

"In the past although we know that less radiation was required if we didn't put radiators up against the cold walls our custom has been nevertheless to set the radiator against the cold walls. We [The A.S.H.V.E.] have a committee now working on the best and most economical place in a room to set a radiator."

It seems members of The American Society of Heating and Ventilating Engineers and their refrigerating counterparts had always realized that good design and practice required attention to fuel conservation. Would we expect anything else from the members of these organizations, the leading professionals of their time? For example:

- In the 1920s, the laboratory of The American Society of Heating and Ventilating Engineers exhibited measurements of air leakage through windows.
- At the turn of the century, it was reported at ASHVE meetings that heating engineers should consider the addition of insulation in building design, taking ideas that were practiced in the refrigeration field.
- In the '30s, fuel savings from use of storm windows and doors were investigated and reported.
- Automatic temperature regulation to achieve efficiency was a topic of ASHVE discussion in the 1890s.
- To meet the power restrictions of World War II, ASRE promoted shifting air-conditioning loads to off-peak hours using refrigeration storage devices.
- In 1909, Louis Block in his ASRE presidential address pointed out that the coal pile, the fireman, the furnace, the boiler and the refrigerating machine all are intimately related, and only by

good engineering and intelligent management and operation of the whole can refrigerating engineers obtain that economy "for which we are all so earnestly striving."

Exterior of single-glazed test house studied by The A.S.H.V.E. in 1939.

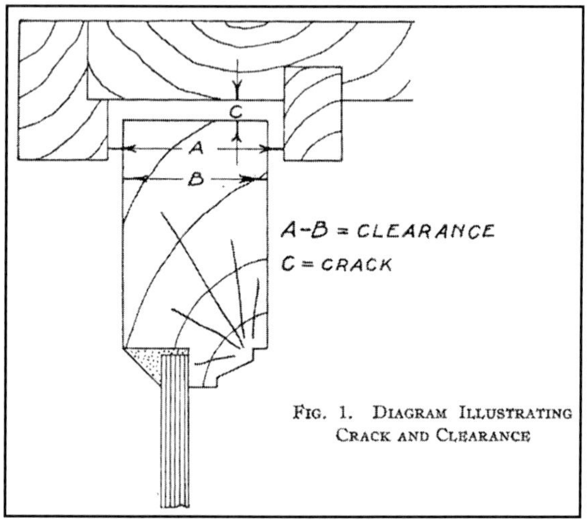

Diagram illustrating crack and clearance for a study of air leakage around window openings, reported in the 1924 *Transactions* of A.S.H.V.E.

American Society of Heating and Ventilating Engineers' President Reginald Pelham Bolton in his paper "Use and Abuse of Fuel" spoke of conservation in 1912: "The subject of fuel is of fundamental importance to the heating engineer, and the economic utilization of available materials constitutes a most important part of the service of our profession, not only to our own clients, but to the community.... A special obligation lies upon our Society, as representing engineers engaged in the art of heating, to impress upon the public and in particular, upon the users of fuel, a better understanding of these fundamental facts and principles."

Reginald Pelham Bolton
"The subject of fuel is of fundamental importance." (1912)

Predictions of Energy Shortages

In 1951, the American Society of Heating and Ventilating Engineers published "Energy—Choose It Wisely Today for Safety Tomorrow." It summarized the essential objective of reducing dependence upon depleting energy resources with documented geological and consumption data. The author, G.W. Gleeson, dean of engineering at Oregon State College, drew these conclusions:

Dean G. W. Gleeson
Stressed the fact that our present sources of energy are exhaustible.

- With the exception of hydro-electric power, our energy comes from discontinuous sources, the fuels of which are finite in amount.
- Our economy is expanding in proportion to our energy use, and we can expect greater demands upon our energy sources.
- In the interest of future generations as well as in the interest of true conservation, we should hoard our fossil fuels wherever possible, particularly petroleum.
- Energy sources, limitations and locations may well influence our living patterns through changes in architectural design, industrial locations, comparative price of fuels, and the development of more integrated energy systems.
- In addition to development of new sources of energy, we have much to accomplish by way of improvement in use of currently developed sources through higher efficiencies.
- We should be willing to pay a premium now in terms of research and development to effect conservation of our least adequate in amount, but most useful in form sources of energy.
- We should direct conservation effort preferentially to areas of largest consumption.

Standard 90

Not until 1973, however, would the world awake to the dangers of energy dependency. Soon,

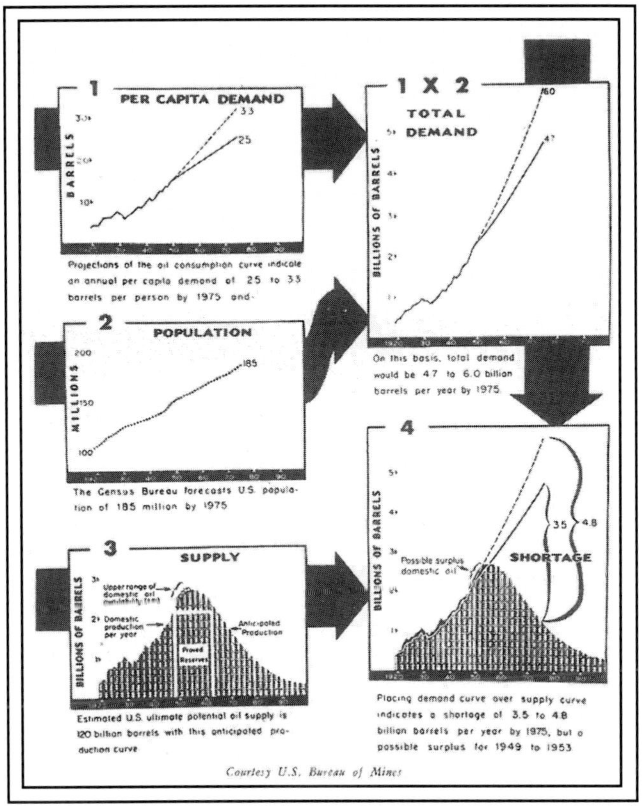

Oil problem in the United States (1951).

Roderick R. Kirkwood
Warned against standards that could end up as straight-jackets.

Frank M. Coda
In 1975, Frank Coda was executive director of the Illuminating Engineering Society. He served as chairman of the Standard 90-75 panel on the lighting power budget determination procedure and as a member of the Standard's Coordinating Committee.

ASHRAE would embark on an activity that would bring it national and international attention in the effort to conserve energy.

The world was in the throes of the first of several disruptions in energy supply, disruptions that would send shock waves through national economies. "Various levels of government may establish consensus standards to legislate control of building design, as well as design of heating, ventilating and air-conditioning systems and commercial plants," predicted ASHRAE 1973-74 President Roderick R. Kirkwood. "These standards, if prepared by people with little real experience, could end up as a straight-jacket that will prevent innovation and growth in our industry for years to come."

In response, ASHRAE's Standards Committee voted in June 1973 to form a committee to develop a standard for energy conservation in new buildings. To begin its work, the committee obtained a draft building energy document prepared by the U.S. Government's National Bureau of Standards (NBS). NBS had initiated the work at the request of the National Conference of States on Building Codes and Standards (NCSBCS).

In February, 1974 at its Semi-Annual Meeting, ASHRAE determined that it would base its standard on the NBS document, and NCSBCS formally asked that ASHRAE assume responsibility for the work begun by NBS. Noting that several states were preparing legislation on energy conservation, NCSBCS asked ASHRAE to reduce to a minimum the time required to write such a standard. NBS supported ASHRAE's involvement because of the Society's ability to constantly update the document after its publication.

To gain comment, ASHRAE distributed some 1,500 copies of the NBS document to ASHRAE technical committee and task group members and to ASHRAE chapters. In addition, copies were distributed to the Illuminating Engineering Society (IES) and to the Electric Energy Association. IES would become a co-sponsor of the standard. Through an accelerated development schedule, a public review draft of ASHRAE Standard 90P "Design and Evaluation Criteria for Energy Conservation in Buildings" was released in July 1974.

According to Jack E. Tumilty, chairman of the 90P Committee, the intent of Standard 90 was to provide a method of designing the energy consuming systems in a building and to evaluate these systems so that the overall energy consumption could be reduced to a minimum while still maintaining occupant comfort.

ASHRAE 90P was a complete rewrite of the NBS document. Among its innovations:

- The chapter on building envelopes described state of the art heat transfer factors, utilizing a degree-day method of determining U-values for roofs and ceilings, for walls, and for wall areas.
- Air leakage allowances were reduced from then current standards based on the fact that improved products were becoming rapidly available in the marketplace.
- The chapter on power distribution considered the type of voltage distribution within the building as well as the inefficiencies of the building's electrical equipment. The chapter recommended use of high distribution voltages in order to minimize distribution losses and recognized that inefficient motors with lower factors should have power factor correction equipment installed.
- Energy efficiency ratios (EER) and seasonal performance factors (SPF) were used to allow designers to determine the relative amount of energy required by different equipment.
- The chapter on building systems recognized the need for multi-zone systems and suggested utilizing electric heat as a terminal re-heat device, because "the state-of-the-art of air-conditioning systems today does not yet provide a method of completely capturing all of the waste heat from buildings and economically redistributing it in those areas where heating may be needed."
- The chapter on lighting was based on using illumination levels for work areas different from illumination levels for other areas. Background or surrounding lighting was designed "to provide adequate contrast so the worker will not experience visual fatigue."

In August 1975, after two public reviews, ASHRAE published Standard 90-75 "Energy Conservation in New Building Design." Soon it became the basis of model energy conservation codes, and many states enacted energy regulations based on it. ASHRAE 1974-75 President David R. Rickelton announced the standard would be available "just in time to permit fulfillment of [U.S.] President Ford's promise for legislation to make thermal efficiency standards mandatory."

Major revisions to the standard were made in 1980.

ASHRAE/IES Standard 90A-1980 provided a more precise method for evaluating compliance of the roof/ceiling combination through the use of overall thermal

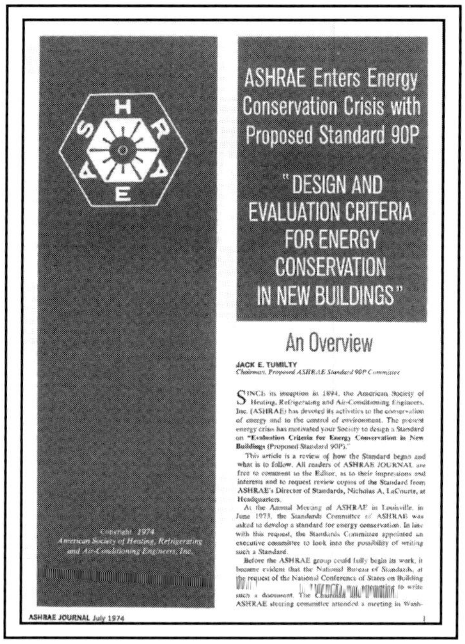

ASHRAE Enters Energy Conservation Crisis with Proposed Standard 90P

"DESIGN AND EVALUATION CRITERIA FOR ENERGY CONSERVATION IN NEW BUILDINGS"

An Overview

JACK E. TUMILTY
Chairman, Proposed ASHRAE Standard 90P Committee

SINCE its inception in 1894, the American Society of Heating, Refrigerating and Air-Conditioning Engineers, Inc. (ASHRAE) has devoted its activities to the conservation of energy and to the control of environment. The present energy crisis has motivated your Society to design a Standard on **"Evaluation Criteria for Energy Conservation in New Buildings** (Proposed Standard 90P)."

This article is a review of how the Standard began and what is to follow. All readers of ASHRAE JOURNAL are free to comment to the Editor, as to their impressions and interests and to request review copies of the Standard from ASHRAE's Director of Standards, Nicholas A. LaCourte, at Headquarters.

At the Annual Meeting of ASHRAE in Louisville, in June 1973, the Standards Committee of ASHRAE was asked to develop a standard for energy conservation. In line with this request, the Standards Committee appointed an executive committee to look into the possibility of writing such a Standard.

Before the ASHRAE group could fully begin its work, it became evident that the National Bureau of Standards, at the request of the National Conference of States on Building [illegible] to write such a document. The [illegible] ASHRAE steering committee attended a meeting in Wash-

Copyright 1974
American Society of Heating, Refrigerating and Air-Conditioning Engineers, Inc.

ASHRAE JOURNAL July 1974 1

David R. Rickelton
"In time to permit fulfillment of President Ford's promise."

transfer values, required more efficient air-moving systems through a change in the value of the air transport factor, included improved energy efficiency ratios which were required to be posted on equipment, and added a new provision to promote the capture and reuse of condenser heat, other waste heat and solar energy in the production of domestic hot water.

The April 1980 issue of *ASHRAE Journal* reported ASHRAE's response to proposed Building Energy Performance Standards. "Standard 90 is saving energy right now," Hugh D. McMillan said in his State of the Society report.

ASHRAE 1980-81 President Charles F. Sepsy declared, "Publication of 90A is an important event, particularly in light of the decision of Congress to postpone publication of the Department of Energy's Building Energy Performance Standards."

Standard 90 would go through a third major revision as 90.1-1989. Research conducted by an ASHRAE Technical Evaluation Committee under contract with the U.S. Department of Energy (Special Project 41) formed a basis of this revision. Much more was understood about building dynamics. To allow the designer flexibility, the new standard included a system performance method and a building energy cost budget method, the latter relying on the consumer using cost of energy to equate tradeoffs in various energy forms and usages.

In 1993, ASHRAE published an energy conservation standard for new residential buildings to complement Standard 90.1 which had been restricted to commercial buildings.

EBTR

The U.S. Federal Government's Emergency Building Temperature Restrictions Program (EBTR) was launched in 1979 to reduce energy use through imposing temperature limits in buildings. At all the early hearings on EBTR, ASHRAE expressed its reservations about the proposed program. "EBTR may be self-defeating," ASHRAE 1979-80 President Hugh D. McMillan told government officials. "In the long term, giving building owners and operators incentives to upgrade their buildings by installing modern, energy-efficient heating, ventilating and air-conditioning systems could save as much as 20, 30, even 40% per building and keep people happy." Mr. McMillan cited worker productivity fall off and higher incidence of on-the-job accidents. The original EBTR proposal was for all commercial and industrial buildings to be maintained at no more than 65°F during the heating season and no less than 80°F during the cooling season. Largely due to input by ASHRAE, the Department of Energy (DOE) eventually modified the restrictions to 65°F and 78°F and excluded additional building types.

Indigestion

On August 1, 1979, Mr. McMillan urged that the program not be made permanent, but he concluded, "ASHRAE's role today, like any other citizen's now

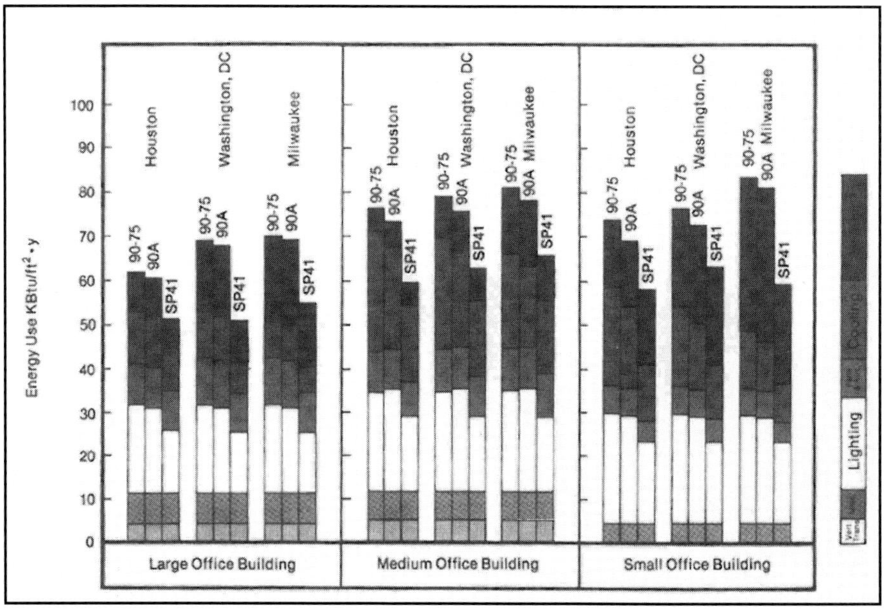

Comparison of energy use of three office buildings which comply with Standards 90-75 and 90A-1980 and with the Special Project 41 recommendations.

that EBTR is the law of the land, is to assist DOE in effectively implementing the regulations. To this end, ASHRAE has mobilized its technical and professional resources to develop a seminar program to provide technical understanding of the regulations and

Donald. R. Bahnfleth
1985-1986 President, who in 1979 headed the ASHRAE Committee which developed training materials to implement the EBTR program.

operational strategies that will produce compliance with the least expense and disruption and general guidance for compliance inspections."

Donald R. Bahnfleth chaired the ASHRAE committee that launched the training program. Six other ASHRAE members joined him on a coordinating committee to develop educational materials and to organize the training of ASHRAE chapter members so they in turn could conduct programs on a local level. Hundreds

"Henry – it's the thermostat police!"

In 1979, ASHRAE organized seminars to explain EBTR. At the ASHRAE/DOE seminar held in New York City, Al Greenberg (left) and Eugene Stamper (center) reviewed the regulations with Marriott Corporation's John Siepp (right). "The rules of reason apply," said Mr. Stamper, one of the ASHRAE-trained presenters.

of ASHRAE volunteers successfully implemented EBTR from start to finish in a matter of months.

"A major spinoff of the EBTR program," Mr. Bahnfleth said, "will be a broadened and sharpened awareness that energy shortages are real and that energy conservation is an ongoing necessity even in the 'land

Jack Bronson, DOE's Regional Program Manager in New York, displays the Certificate of Building Compliance at the New York City seminar in 1979. The Certificate is to be shown in all buildings that are subject to the regulation.

of plenty.' Renewed interest in energy conserving techniques embodied in ASHRAE/IES Standard 90-75 for new buildings, and the soon to be issued 100 Series for existing buildings is anticipated, making possible greater reductions in energy consumption while maintaining thermal environments which promote productivity and minimize thermal stress."

"ASHRAE Needs Visibility"

With the energy crisis, a fundamental change occurred in the way ASHRAE perceived its role in the world. "We must move out into the glare of public view and not withdraw to the quiet of just talking to

ourselves," Mr. Kirkwood challenged members. "We need visibility so that the message of optimum energy utilization through technology can be received by all segments of our economy."

Mr. Kirkwood appointed a Task Force on Energy Conservation during his 1973-74 presidency. "We are now in a time of great change and we must live up to this evolutionary period or be buried. No one can just stand aside and watch the world go by," he said.

Mr. Rickelton, his successor, put the problem in perspective: "It is time that governing bodies and businessmen in general stop asking 'ASHTRAY?' - 'What is ASHTRAY?' We can no longer sit in our ivory tower of engineering competence while those of lesser capability legislate us into a Pandora's box."

A few years earlier, in 1970, ASHRAE created a Presidential Committee on Technical and Financial Outreach charged with planning and promoting Society research in the public interest in cooperation with industry and government.

Presidential Member Frank H. Faust was the first committee chairman, and for many years after served as a consultant to continue the initiative. With the advent of the energy crisis, the U.S. government began funding more programs than ever before in ASHRAE's field of interest. Mr. Faust's efforts facilitated ASHRAE-government cooperation so that the ASHRAE research program had access to additional financial resources and government had access to ASHRAE member expertise.

Frank H. Faust
Retired as consultant for special projects in 1983.

But while awareness of ASHRAE within government had increased as a result of this work, much broader recognition was required to influence the major energy initiatives which were being debated beginning in 1973. Said Mr. Kirkwood, "Government agencies and the general public must be informed about ASHRAE, what kind of capability there is available in ASHRAE, and how we can help them." Kirkwood urged every chapter to establish a Chapter Energy Committee to obtain publicity at the local level and to broadcast that "ASHRAE is a group of experts who have technological knowledge." He appointed regional committeemen responsible for energy conservation efforts in each region. "We must have greater visibility as a Society. This is our goal: to convince public agencies to call upon ASHRAE in their plans relating to buildings and energy conservation."

SHRAE energy standard ears final approval

ASHRAE develops continuing education program for professional development

For graduate students

ASHRAE establishes energy research award

ergy awareness main thrust ASHRAE research, education

• Refrigerating Equipment covers condensers, evaporators, metering devices, accessories, absorption chillers, heat pumps and compressors.

• Fluid-Handling Equipment covers pumps, fans, and testing, adjusting and balancing.

• Systems covers airs conditioning and heating ventilation, refrigeration and heat recovery.

The modules were developed by a

Establish Energy Research Award

GRADUATE student research o[n] renewable energy sources o[r] energy conservation applied t[o] heating, refrigeration, air condi[-]tioning, or ventilation will b[e] recognized by an annual awar[d] recently established by th[e] American Society of Heating, Re[-]frigerating and air conditionin[g] Engineers

World energy consumption must be curbed say ASHRAE officials

Dr R P Perry, new ASHRAE president

AT THE recent AGM in Washington of ASHRAE, Dr Albert A Bartlett, Professor of physics at the University of Colorado at Boulder, said "Even with enormous discoveries of new energy

ASHRAE sets up research award

ATLANTA, GA — Graduate student research on renewable energy sources or energy conservation applied to heating, refrigeration, air conditioning, or ventilation will be recognized by an annual award recently established by ASHRAE.

tificate and $800 honorarium and will be presented for the first time at the 1983 ASHRAE Annual Meeting in Washington, D.C. on June 26-29.

Nominations for the award will be accepted only from faculty members. Nominees must be graduate students or

September 1982

es Gov't To Take urching Indoor Control

door air quality standard into state and local codes without delay.

The private sector, including technical societies like ASHRAE, should be involved in "improving products,

Summer 1983

Energy

ASHRAE Unveils Stan[dard]

ASHRAE speakers

Third of e[nergy c]ould be saved

By JOHN LECKIE

TORONTO (DCN) — There

Easy Ways to Save

Here are some no-cost and low-cost savings tips and a rough idea of how much money they'll save from the American Society of Heating, Refrigerating and Air-Conditioning Engineers, a to[...] members:

• Reduce your hot-water [...] if you have a dishwasher; oth[...] ings run from $10 to $90 a y[ear] of the temperature reduction, type of heater.

• Avoid partial washer [...] use a warm wash, cold rins[e] from $20 to $65, depending o[n] and the cost of energy.

• Take a quick shower, r[...] $20 to $100. Baths consume [...]

• Close drapes and shad[es] during the need for air co[...] many variables to give an [...] this simple task can cut heat[...]

• Fix leaky hot-water fi[xtures...] is a new washer, the cost is

ASHRAE Advocates Research In Indoor Air Quality By Gov't

The American Society of Heating, Refrigerating and Air-Con[ditioning Engineers]

Energy conservation in existing build[ings] is focus of ASHRAE 100 Series stan[dards]

ATLANTA, Ga. — The American Society of Heating, Refrigerating and Air-Conditioning Engineers (ASHRAE) has announced publication of three standards for energy conservation in existing buildings.

The newly published standards, all part of the ASHRAE 100 Series, "Energy Conservation in Existing Buildings," provide requirements and criteria

components; and providing procedures and programs essential to energy-conserving operation, maintenance, and monitoring of existing structures.

In addition to the specific energy-efficiency options set forth in the standards, an alternative is provided to allow for innovative procedures. This alternative involves determining the performance of, and upgrad-

Within a year, ASHRAE chapters were sponsoring a wide range of activities to promote energy efficiency and to promote ASHRAE. This evolved into the Energy Management Committee which initiated ASHRAE Energy Awards to recognize demonstrated success in the conservation and management of energy.

In 1974-75, President Rickelton appointed a Government Affairs Committee. "The members of this committee are highly qualified to offer advice in the

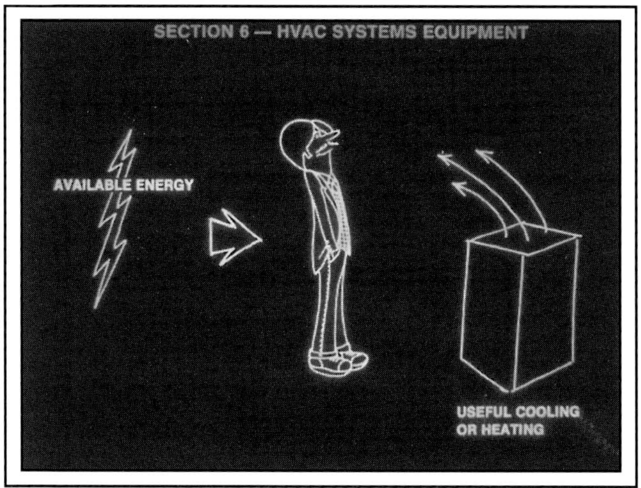

An ASHRAE-developed slide show was distributed to chapters to explain the provisions of Standard 90-75.

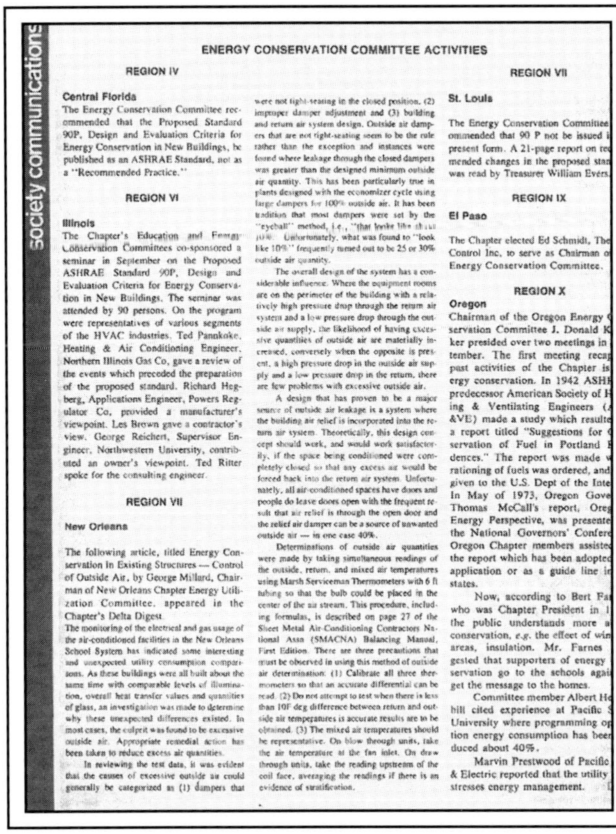

society communications

ENERGY CONSERVATION COMMITTEE ACTIVITIES

REGION IV

Central Florida

The Energy Conservation Committee recommended that the Proposed Standard 90P, Design and Evaluation Criteria for Energy Conservation in New Buildings, be published as an ASHRAE Standard, not as a "Recommended Practice."

REGION VI

Illinois

The Chapter's Education and Energy Conservation Committees co-sponsored a seminar in September on the Proposed ASHRAE Standard 90P, Design and Evaluation Criteria for Energy Conservation in New Buildings. The seminar was attended by 90 persons. On the program were representatives of various segments of the HVAC industries. Ted Pannkoke, Heating & Air Conditioning Engineer, Northern Illinois Gas Co, gave a review of the events which preceded the preparation of the proposed standard. Richard Hegberg, Applications Engineer, Powers Regulator Co, provided a manufacturer's viewpoint. Les Brown gave a contractor's view. George Reichert, Supervisor Engineer, Northwestern University, contributed an owner's viewpoint. Ted Ritter spoke for the consulting engineer.

REGION VII

New Orleans

The following article, titled Energy Conservation in Existing Structures — Control of Outside Air, by George Millard, Chairman of New Orleans Chapter Energy Utilization Committee, appeared in the Chapter's Delta Digest.

The monitoring of the electrical and gas usage of the air-conditioned facilities in the New Orleans School System has indicated some interesting and unexpected utility consumption comparisons. As these buildings were all built about the same time with comparable levels of illumination, overall heat transfer values and quantities of glass, an investigation was made to determine why these unexpected differences existed. In most cases, the culprit was found to be excessive outside air. Appropriate remedial action has been taken to reduce excess air quantities.

In reviewing the test data, it was evident that the causes of excessive outside air could generally be categorized as (1) dampers that were not tight-seating in the closed position, (2) improper damper adjustment and (3) building and return air system design. Outside air dampers that are not tight-seating seem to be the rule rather than the exception and instances were found where leakage through the closed dampers was greater than the designed minimum outside air quantity. This has been particularly true in plants designed with the economizer cycle using large dampers for 100% outside air. It has been tradition that most dampers were set by the "eyeball" method, i.e., "that looks like about 10%." Unfortunately, what was found to "look like 10%" frequently turned out to be 25 or 30% outside air quantity.

The overall design of the system has a considerable influence. Where the equipment rooms are on the perimeter of the building with a relatively high pressure drop through the return air system and a low pressure drop through the outside air supply, the likelihood of having excessive quantities of outside air are materially increased, conversely when the opposite is present, a high pressure drop in the outside air supply and a low pressure drop in the return, there are few problems with excessive outside air.

A design that has proven to be a major source of outside air leakage is a system where the building air relief is incorporated into the return air system. Theoretically, this design concept should work, and would work satisfactorily, if the space being conditioned were completely closed so that any excess air would be forced back into the return air system. Unfortunately, all air-conditioned spaces have doors and people do leave doors open with the frequent result that air relief is through the open door and the relief air damper can be a source of unwanted outside air — in one case 40%.

Determinations of outside air quantities were made by taking simultaneous readings of the outside, return, and mixed air temperatures using Marsh Serviceman Thermometers with 6 ft tubing so that the bulb could be placed in the center of the air stream. This procedure, including formulas, is described on page 27 of the Sheet Metal Air-Conditioning Contractors National Assn (SMACNA) Balancing Manual, First Edition. There are three precautions that must be observed in using this method of outside air determination: (1) Calibrate all three thermometers so that an accurate differential can be read. (2) Do not attempt to test when there is less than 10F deg difference between return and outside air temperatures is accurate results are to be obtained. (3) The mixed air temperatures should be representative. On blow through units, take the air temperature at the fan inlet. On draw through units, take the reading upstream of the coil face, averaging the readings if there is an evidence of stratification.

REGION VII

St. Louis

The Energy Conservation Committee
ommended that 90 P not be issued i
present form. A 21-page report on re
mended changes in the proposed sta
was read by Treasurer William Evers.

REGION IX

El Paso

The Chapter elected Ed Schmidt, The
Control Inc, to serve as Chairman o
Energy Conservation Committee.

REGION X

Oregon

Chairman of the Oregon Energy
servation Committee J. Donald K
ker presided over two meetings in
tember. The first meeting reca
past activities of the Chapter is
ergy conservation. In 1942 ASH
predecessor American Society of H
ing & Ventilating Engineers (
&VE) made a study which result
a report titled "Suggestions for
servation of Fuel in Portland
dences." The report was made
rationing of fuels was ordered, and
given to the U.S. Dept of the Inte
In May of 1973, Oregon Gove
Thomas McCall's report, Ore
Energy Perspective, was present
the National Governors' Confer
Oregon Chapter members assiste
the report which has been adopte
application or as a guide line i
states.

Now, according to Bert Fa
who was Chapter President in
the public understands more
conservation, *e.g.* the effect of wi
areas, insulation. Mr. Farnes
gested that supporters of energy
servation go to the schools aga
get the message to the homes.

Committee member Albert H
hill cited experience at Pacific
University where programming o
tion energy consumption has bee
duced about 40%.

Marvin Prestwood of Pacific
& Electric reported that the utility
stresses energy management.

Chapter energy activities underway in 1975.

inter-relation between our technology and government requirements...for assistance in technical and legislative matters," announced Mr. Rickelton. With Standard 90-75 published, Mr. Rickelton inaugurated another crash program to assist governmental bodies. He appointed a committee to develop standards for energy use in existing buildings. The 100 Series Standards as they became to be known appeared on the scene in the early 1980s.

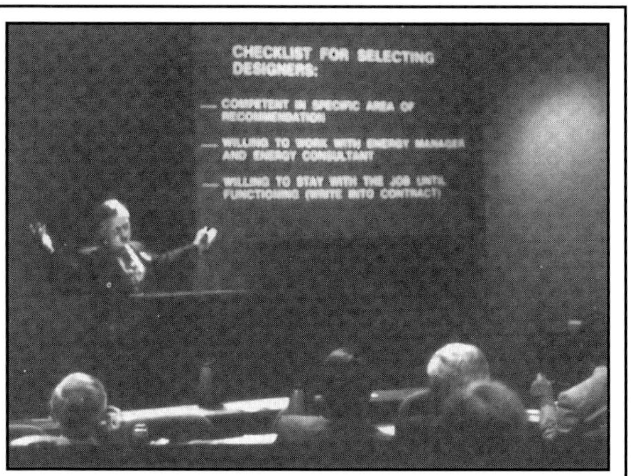

In 1983 ASHRAE organized seminars on energy management for corporate decision makers. The intent was to demonstrate how energy savings could be achieved and how energy management could be implemented at an organizational level.

Appearing on the "Today" show in 1977, President Bruno Morabito explained the various types of and the importance of insulation to Jane Pauley of NBC.

Washington Office

By 1980, ASHRAE's need for timely and effective interaction with all branches of the Federal government was greater than ever. The dramatic increase in the number of appearances and testimony by ASHRAE officers in matters relating to legislation further identified the need for continuous representation.

ASHRAE 1979-80 President Hugh D. McMillan appointed a subcommittee to recommend establishment of a means for ASHRAE representation in the

First Annual
ASHRAE Energy Awards

FIRST PLACE
Institutional/Commercial
New Construction

Data processing equipment waste heat recovered for heating use is the [illegible] this project First Place in the Institutional/Commercial catagory for New Construction. [illegible] Inc. of Bloomington, MN were the project engineers.

Energy management measures at the Printpak Inc. facilities include a move to high pressure sodium lighting in a new warehouse addition and an emphasis on insulation. A heat pipe recovery system was chosen for estimated savings of $5000 per year from this feature alone.

FIRST PLACE Industrial Buildings

Savings of over $30,000 a year due to an energy conservation program highlighted combined efforts of Printpack Inc. management and Georgia Power Company engineers who worked on this First Place winning project in the industrial catagory.

Retrofit of the old Honeywell building in Minneapolis for the new owners, Zielinski & Wolff, C.P.A., was conducted by Climate Engineering Corporation. The project was a First Place winner in the Existing Structures category for Institutional/Commercial buildings.

FIRST PLACE
Institutional/Commercial
Existing Structures

January 1981.

1977-78 President Bruno Morabito (center) and 1976-77 President William P. Chapman were ASHRAE representatives at a U.S. Government-sponsored conference in Washington, DC in 1977. It brought together those technical and professional organizations most involved in building energy standards. At right is David Pellish, a representative of the Energy Research and Development Administration.

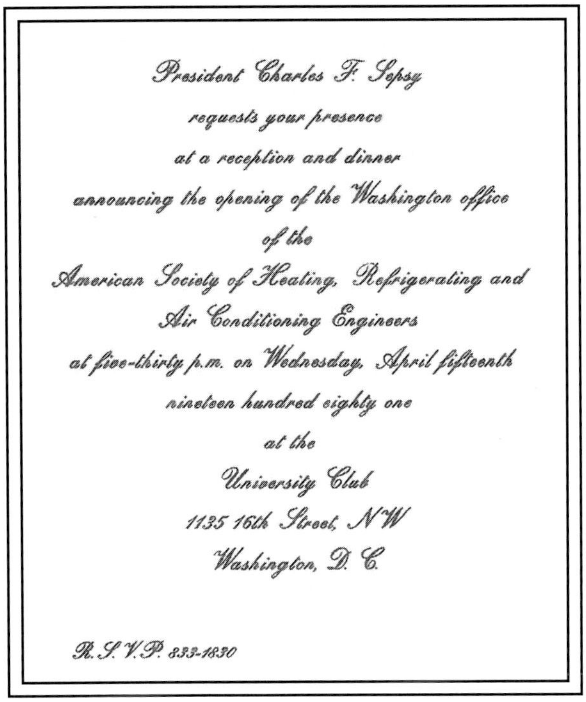

President Charles F. Sepsy
requests your presence
at a reception and dinner
announcing the opening of the Washington office
of the
American Society of Heating, Refrigerating and
Air Conditioning Engineers
at five-thirty p.m. on Wednesday, April fifteenth
nineteen hundred eighty one
at the
University Club
1135 16th Street, NW
Washington, D. C.

R. S. V. P. 833-1830

national capital. The subcommittee, chaired by Clinton W. Phillips, concluded that ASHRAE open a Washington office to function in an "engineering support" mode to government. Dr. J.E. Cox was retained as ASHRAE's Washington Representative. In April 1981, ASHRAE President Charles F. Sepsy announced the office's official opening, then situated in the headquarters building of the National Society of Professional Engineers. Building Energy Performance Standards, EBTR, efforts to curtail voluntary consensus standards in favor of Federally mandated standards, and the emerging chlorofluorocarbon/ozone depletion issue occupied the new Washington office in the early 1980s.

The Energy Code

The U.S. Energy Policy Act of 1992 required states to revise building codes by October 1994 to meet or exceed ASHRAE/IES Standard 90.1-1989. To help states comply with these requirements, ASHRAE published a code version of its standard. Said ASHRAE President Neil R. Patterson in December 1993, "Rather than have multiple states develop multiple code versions of Standard 90.1 and risk having some of the technical provisions in the Standard modified or deleted, ASHRAE decided to codify it. With this code language version, state officials will be able to add the required technical provisions cited in the Standard into their building codes quickly and easily." The principal difference in the code and the 90.1 Standard is that the code is written in enforceable language, with many of the recommended or unenforceable provisions of the Standard deleted.

Neil R. Patterson
Warned against the risk of multiple states with multiple code versions of Standard 90.1

The energy code was one of several activities undertaken by ASHRAE in the 1990s to transfer its

A team of ASHRAE members, which included Jordan Heiman, briefed government officials on ASHRAE standards in the mid 80s at a number of Washington forums.

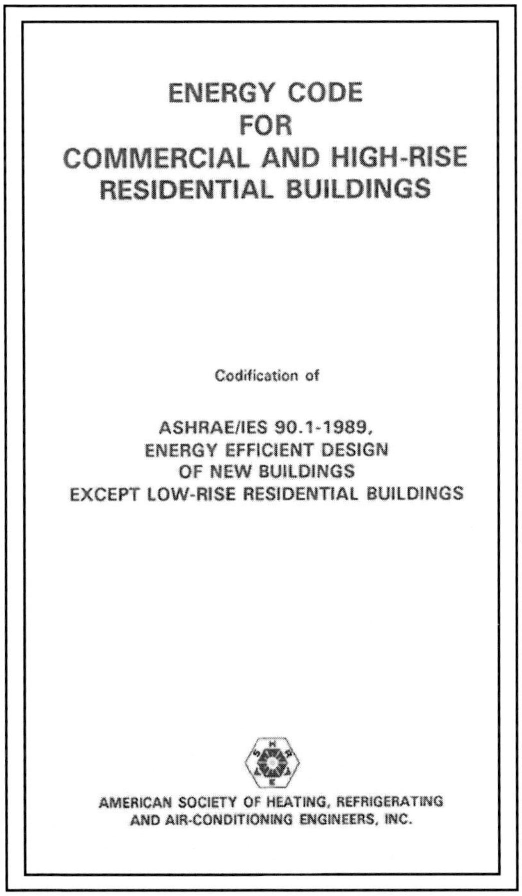

ENERGY CODE
FOR
COMMERCIAL AND HIGH-RISE
RESIDENTIAL BUILDINGS

Codification of

ASHRAE/IES 90.1-1989,
ENERGY EFFICIENT DESIGN
OF NEW BUILDINGS
EXCEPT LOW-RISE RESIDENTIAL BUILDINGS

AMERICAN SOCIETY OF HEATING, REFRIGERATING
AND AIR-CONDITIONING ENGINEERS, INC.

standards technology and technical expertise to those who develop model codes and other similar voluntary sector documents. In general, the Society became more involved in responding to the expressed needs of those who adopt, administer and enforce building design and construction regulations. As ASHRAE Member and consultant to the 90.1 Codification Panel David R. Conover wrote in 1993, "Adoption and implementation are fundamental to achieving the purposes addressed by ASHRAE standards because until a standard is formally codified and adopted, it is voluntary and has no major bearing on technology or construction practice." As they are written, ASHRAE standards typically are not enforceable. How, Mr. Conover asked, could anyone determine compliance with a provision that suggests but does not require assessment of some alternative technical design strategy?

ASHRAE took two steps. First, ASHRAE standards intended for use in building regulations would now be written in enforceable code language. Second, ASHRAE would become more involved with organizations that write and publish model codes. This involvement recognized that model code publishers do not seek out and incorporate standards and other provisions in their codes. Instead, they rely on suggested revisions to their codes that are submitted annually by any interested party and considered at open public hearings. The objective, Mr. Conover explained, was that more standards technology would be transferred to model codes, thus decreasing the number of discrepancies between ASHRAE standards and related codes and ensuring that what is ultimately required by regulatory agencies mirrors provisions developed in the consensus process by industry.

Concern with energy changed the Society in a fundamental way. The process by which ASHRAE members shared information and by which ASHRAE, through research and standards, generated information, was taxed as never before. But more importantly, concern with energy altered the Society's relationship with other organizations, governments and the public.

In 1973 as ASHRAE President Walter Spiegel concluded his term in office, he predicted what the future would hold. "It is increasingly obvious that in spite of whatever temporary reprieve from the energy crunch may become available, it will be necessary to analyze seriously the problem of energy conservation and the related ecological and social aspects at all levels of decision making. As enlightened citizens, we must utilize our franchise to insist that decisions of national and international impact be made on a careful and objective basis, considering all pertinent factors. Ultimately, it is for society to express through the laws it passes what constraints it wants to put on the energy consumption decisions of the executives of its industry....The time that remains before the energy crisis becomes a permanent way of life must be used wisely."

ASHRAE ADOPTS ENERGY POLICY

The ASHRAE Board of Directors adopted an energy policy at its 1980 Semiannual Meeting in Los Angeles which calls for a wide variety of measures to make use of existing supplies of energy more efficiently and to develop new sources of power.

Commenting on the newly adopted policy, ASHRAE President Hugh D. McMillan, Jr., said, "For several years ASHRAE has been in need of an energy policy upon which the Society could base its actions regarding energy in all its aspects."

"This policy is a result of a tremendous amount of work on the part of the Society's Energy Council and other interested ASHRAE members," he continued.

The full text of the ASHRAE Energy Policy is printed on page 28.

Hugh D. McMillan, Jr.

Energy Council Chairman William J. Collins, Jr.

Energy Policy

of the
American Society
of Heating, Refrigerating and
Air-Conditioning Engineers

Adopted by the Board of Directors
February 6, 1980

As stated in its Bylaws the American Society of Heating, Refrigerating and Air-Conditioning Engineers, Inc. (ASHRAE) is organized and operated for the exclusive purpose of advancing the arts and sciences of heating, refrigeration, air conditioning and ventilation, the allied arts and sciences, and related human factors for the benefit of the general public; and to fulfill its role, the Society shall recognize the effect of its technology on the environment and natural resources to protect the welfare of posterity.

Never before have so many people depended upon a single class of resource for their welfare and survival as we depend upon depletable energy resources. And because of the complexity of this problem, ASHRAE finds it necessary to state specifically the policy of the Society regarding energy resources to carry out the mandate of its Bylaws.

Energy resources are a fundamental ingredient of all economic systems. They are essential to the defense of nations, necessary to feed the world's populace, and vital for our protection from the elements. The conversion of these resources from their natural states to end-use energy forms is a science known and practiced by the engineering profession. For this reason, ASHRAE will expend every possible effort to develop the knowledge necessary to address the energy problem, to disseminate this knowledge, and to assume a leadership role in these efforts.

Recognizing that the world's energy goals can be reached only through aggressive and unrelenting cooperative effort involving all segments of society, and consistent with the needs, aims, and aspirations of the international community, ASHRAE, aware of its mounting responsibilities, has adopted the following energy policy:

The ASHRAE Energy Policy is to utilize existing and new energy resources efficiently and economically to satisfy human needs in heating, ventilation, air conditioning and refrigeration, with judicious regard for human comfort, preservation of environmental quality, and conservation of all types of resources.

Methods utilized in the implementation of this policy shall include, but not be limited to, publications, educational activities, standards, research, position statements on all significant energy issues, and pertinent involvement in public service.

In the implementation of this policy, the Society will:

1. Place emphasis on the efficient utilization of energy in facilities and systems and the development of energy-efficient equipment and systems;
2. Promote and conduct research and develop methods and techniques for the production and efficient and effective utilization of all forms of energy;
3. Encourage continued development of nuclear technology, improved construction techniques in power generation and industrial processes, and energy reclamation from waste materials;
4. Promote the utilization of heat-reclaiming-and-recovery systems;
5. Support protection of the environment while eliminating unreasonable environmental restraints;
6. Encourage aggressive development of the practical applications of solar heating and cooling of buildings and other solar energy utilization;
7. Provide leadership in the development of new standards and improvement of existing standards for energy conservation;
8. Participate in the formulation of reasonable energy-related policies, laws and regulations of governments and keep environmental and health concerns in balance, while recognizing the need to maintain an economically sound and productive society;
9. Encourage consideration of the effects of price controls on all aspects of energy-resource production and utilization;
10. Encourage effective development of energy resources on public lands with reasonable environmental constraints.

28 ASHRAE JOURNAL April 1980

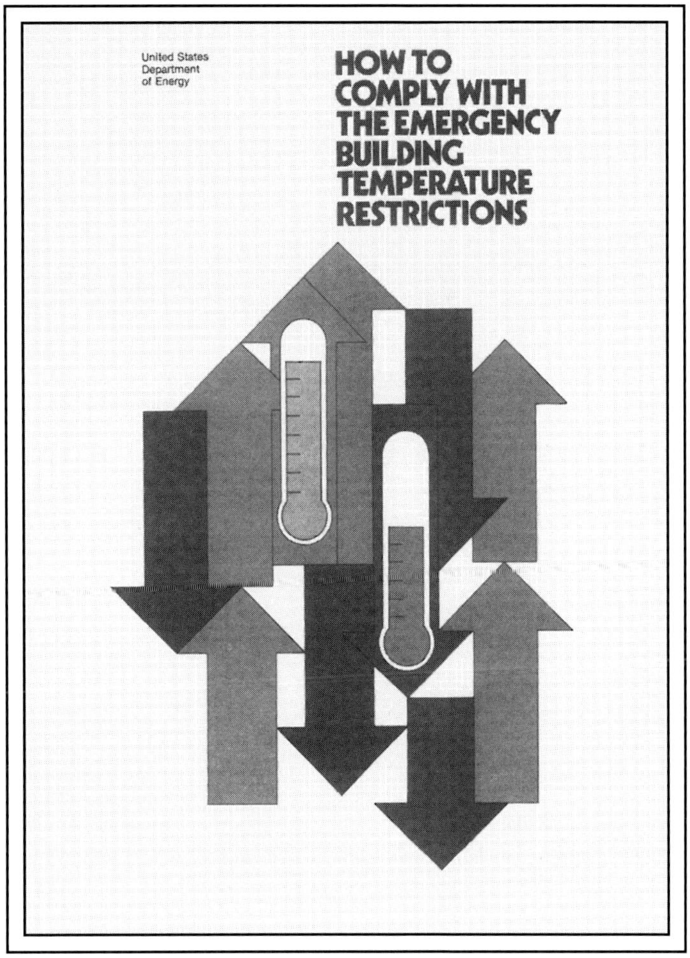
United States Department of Energy

HOW TO COMPLY WITH THE EMERGENCY BUILDING TEMPERATURE RESTRICTIONS

CS-198 Form Approved OMB No. 038-S79046

EMERGENCY BUILDING TEMPERATURE RESTRICTIONS
CERTIFICATE OF BUILDING COMPLIANCE

Building Name

Address

Telephone | No. of Stories | No. of Square Ft.

This is to certify that the undersigned is in compliance with the Emergency Building Temperature Restrictions Plan. Accordingly, the cooling, heating, and hot water temperatures of these premises have been adjusted in an attempt to achieve the reductions in energy consumption contemplated under the emergency measures.

(Check Appropriate Category)

☐ Full Compliance

☐ Exempted Compliance *(See Building Manager for Exemption Details)*

☐ Excepted From Compliance *(See Building Manager for Exception Application)*

Building Owner or Operator (Signature) | Date

ASHRAE
HEATING, REFRIGERATING
AND AIR-CONDITIONING
JOURNAL
WHAT N
February 1974
American Society of Heating, Refrigerating and Air-Conditioning Engineers, Inc.

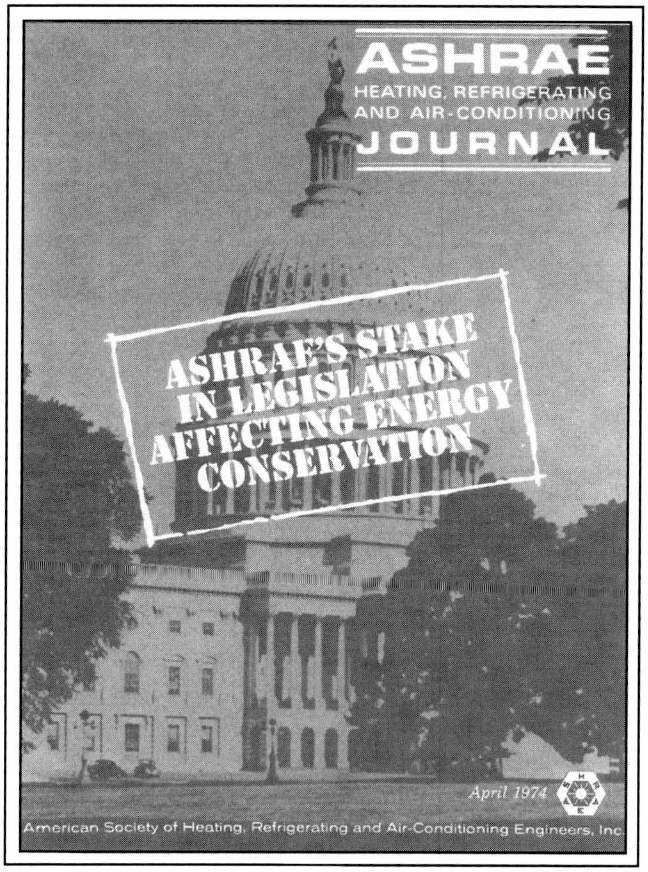
ASHRAE
HEATING, REFRIGERATING
AND AIR-CONDITIONING
JOURNAL
ASHRAE'S STAKE
IN LEGISLATION
AFFECTING ENERGY
CONSERVATION
April 1974
American Society of Heating, Refrigerating and Air-Conditioning Engineers, Inc.

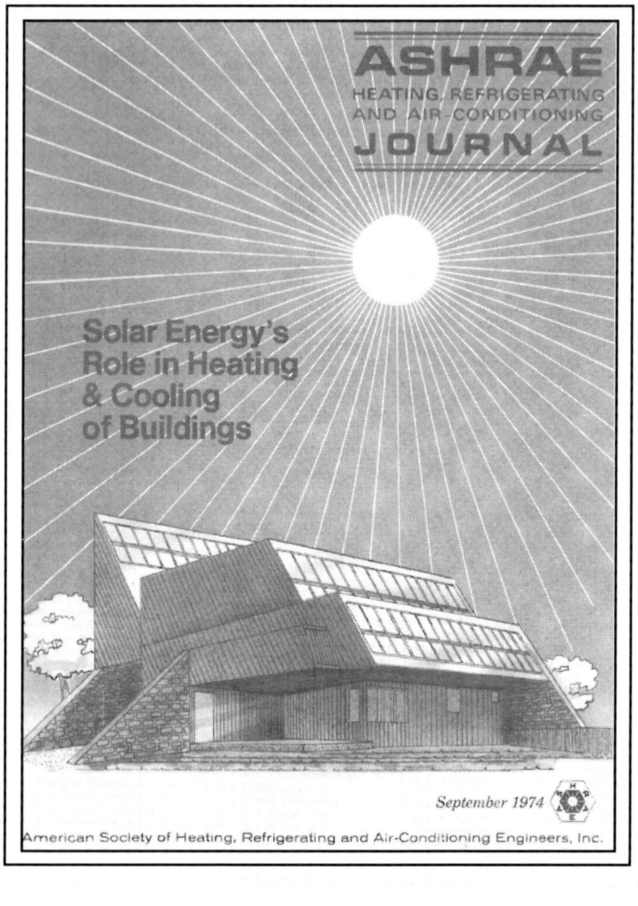
ASHRAE
HEATING, REFRIGERATING
AND AIR-CONDITIONING
JOURNAL
Solar Energy's
Role in Heating
& Cooling
of Buildings
September 1974
American Society of Heating, Refrigerating and Air-Conditioning Engineers, Inc.

ASHRAE
Journal
Denver
Annual Meeting
Registration
Form p.33
INSULATION
for Energy
Conservation

The First U.S. State Energy Regulations

In 1974, California became the first U.S. state to implement minimum energy-efficiency standards. It was also the first to establish an energy regulation commission—the California Energy Commission. And in 1978, California created Title 24. The intent of this regulation, still in place today, is to achieve higher energy efficiency, preserve environmental quality, and create minimum energy-efficiency levels for new residential and nonresidential buildings.

But how did all this activity begin? What was the foundation for the state's requirements for energy calculations?

Thomas A. Gilbertson, ASHRAE's Golden Gate Chapter Historian, remembers from where all that regulation came. "You can blame the Golden Gate Chapter of ASHRAE," he says.

As late as 1973 there existed no regulation of energy use within buildings. There was no statutory requirement for "energy consumption" in buildings. No building code of any state had any requirements to regulate energy consumption as a design-consideration of buildings.

Several ASHRAE Golden Gate Chapter members at the time had the drive, resources, and connections to get things done. They included Tom Campbell, Owen-Corning Fiberglass Corp.'s Manager of Engineering Standards for Public Safety; Tom Simonson, G.M. & T.R. Simonson Consulting Engineers; and Bob Voelz, Skidmore Owings & Merrill Director of Mechanical & Electrical Engineering, San Francisco.

California State Senator Alfred E. Alquist, whose district included Santa Clara and who was one of the state's most respected senators, made the chapter aware that the State of California's Public Utility Commission (OUC) had identified California's electrical consumption as growing in excess of 8% per year and that the state legislature was issuing the PUC's list of possible "mandates" to address the "energy growth problem."

PUC Mandate Number 1 was an extensive directive to "Develop guidelines to streamline the siting of new nuclear generation plants…." That wouldn't do much in the short term. But PUC Mandate Number 3 was three short lines that said something vague about energy conservation. Opportunity knocked.

The state established an Energy Commission, funding it with a $0.00002 surcharge on each kilowatt of electricity that was sold in California, and issued a directive that five "eminently qualified individuals should be retained to develop energy conservation directives for buildings that were to be constructed in the State."

Tom Campbell and ASHRAE Golden Gate Chapter President Lou Pollack lobbied the state to appoint Tom Simonson to the committee to prepare the "energy directives." Simonson was qualified to say the least. He held a Bachelor of Science degree and a PhD in physical chemistry from the University of California was a licensed professional engineer in both mechanical and electrical engineering, and was partner in his consulting engineering firm.

Simonson was appointed by the state, and he engaged Bob Voelz. Voelz held a degree from Purdue University, was a professional engineer, had experience as the site engineer on the U.S. Air Force Academy in Colorado Springs, and was Director of Engineering at Skidmore, Owings & Merrill's San Francisco Office. Simonson's and Voelz's challenge was "how to establish a method to restrict energy consumption in buildings." They did just that, Gilbertson recalls.

"Think this over a bit… There are no rules… no starting-point on tonnage requirements or cfm, or heating use… let alone 'energy' to provide buildings' requirements. So it is decided that to design a building, a primary basis for heat gain and loss, must be established," says Gilbertson.

Simonson and Voelz decided that the basis for heat gain and loss must be "standardized and required," Gilbertson says, and they decided that "U-Factors must be specified." The rest is history. California accepts the concept, and in a few years the state issues these "Golden Gate Member design concepts" as law. The state now had what became Title 24.

Members of ASHRAE's Golden Gate Chapter brought about the first energy consumption regulations in the U.S. But how did we get to where we are today with the increasingly expanded regulations?

Gilbertson is philosophical. "As the saying goes… If you give a mouse a cookie… he's going to want some milk. The regulations just kept on growing."

Is Minimum Good Enough?

In 2002, Donald G. Colliver became ASHRAE president. While ANSI/ASHRAE/IESNA Standard 90.1 had become the basis for building codes and the standard for building design and construction throughout the U.S., Colliver saw a new challenge. "For too long we have emphasized setting minimum requirements. While these are extremely important, we need to get back to what brought us excellence and look toward energy-efficient design," he said. "We have found that a single document cannot effectively be used for multiple objectives. To maintain our status, I propose simplification and increased usability by creating within the next three to five years a suite of four types of documents related to energy efficiency."

Colliver proposed the first set of documents provide minimums suitable for use in building codes. A second set of documents would be called "good practice," outlining ways to increase the energy conservation of new buildings so that they use only 70% of the energy used by buildings built to the 2001 edition of Standard 90.1. A third set would identify "excellent practice"—what should be considered if the design goal is 50% of the energy used by buildings built to Standard 90.1-2001. The last set of documents would include "futuristic" practices for designers who want off-site energy usage of 25% of buildings built 30 years ago. Colliver said, "They would represent the latest research on innovative practices and renewable energy sources. They would be the focal point for advanced practices—not only for developed countries but for developing countries as well."

Donald G. Colliver, 2002–2003 ASHRAE President

The vision was in place for what would become the Advanced Energy Design Guide (AEDG) series.

AEDG Series

By 2004, the first AEDG for 30% energy savings in small office building design was ready. It was a collaboration among ASHRAE, The American Institute of Architects (AIA), Illuminating Engineering Society of North America (IESNA), and U.S. Green Building Council (USGBC), with support from the U.S. Department of Energy (DOE). Like the guides that would follow, it provided recommendations and user-friendly design guidance, including prescriptive packages of recommendations presented by climate zone that covered enhanced envelope technologies, lighting and daylighting technologies, and HVAC and service water heating technologies. Thirty percent AEDGs for five other building types followed, and 50% AEDGs for five different building types were published next.

By 2020, ASHRAE had published zero energy AEDGs for two building types and was writing the guide for a third. A zero energy building is defined as a building that, on an annual basis, draws from outside resources equal or less energy than it provides using on-site, renewable energy sources. The AEDGs offer contractors and designers the tools, including recommendations for practical products and off-the-shelf technology, needed for achieving a zero energy building. The collaboration with AIA, IES, USGBC, and DOE has continued.

Since 2004, nearly 700,000 copies of the guides in the series have been distributed.

Maintain to Sustain

By the mid-2000s, ASHRAE leaders shifted to emphasizing building performance rather than energy efficiency. The driver was the added concern for sustainability and the realization that too many green buildings were turning gray after only a few years of operation or were never achieving the performance targets envisioned in the design.

Kent Peterson, 2007–2008 ASHRAE President

In 2007–08, ASHRAE President Kent Peterson called for development of better building performance metrics and the need for ASHRAE to continue to provide commissioning guidance to ensure buildings perform as intended. In 2008–09, President William A. Harrison said delivering ASHRAE's sustainability promise means that ASHRAE members need to work more closely with others in the buildings business. A collaborative or integrated design process is essential if a building is to be designed and operated as a high-performing building. Collaborative, integrated design processes must go beyond a building's initial energy performance and must consider the effect building design will have on energy over the building's entire life.

William A. Harrison, 2008–2009 ASHRAE President

30%
Advanced Energy Design Guide for Small Office Buildings
Achieving 30% Energy Savings Toward a Net Zero Energy Building
30%
Advanced Energy Design Guide for Small Retail Buildings
Achieving 30% Energy Savings Toward a Net Zero Energy Building
30%
Advanced Energy Design Guide for Small Warehouses and Self-Storage Buildings
Achieving 30% Energy Savings Toward a Net Zero Energy Building
30%
Advanced Energy Design Guide for K-12 School Buildings
Achieving 30% Energy Savings Toward a Net Zero Energy Building
30%
Advanced Energy Design Guide for Highway Lodging
Achieving 30% Energy Savings Toward a Net Zero Energy Building
30%
Advanced Energy Design Guide for Small Hospitals and Healthcare Facilities
Achieving 30% Energy Savings Toward a Net Zero Energy Building
50%
Advanced Energy Design Guide for Small to Medium Office Buildings
Achieving 50% Energy Savings Toward a Net Zero Energy Building
50%
Advanced Energy Design Guide for K–12 School Buildings
Achieving 50% Energy Savings Toward a Net Zero Energy Building
50%
Advanced Energy Design Guide for Medium to Big Box Retail Buildings
Achieving 50% Energy Savings Toward a Net Zero Energy Building
50%
Advanced Energy Design Guide for Large Hospitals
Achieving 50% Energy Savings Toward a Net Zero Energy Building
50%
Advanced Energy Design Guide for Grocery Stores
Achieving 50% Energy Savings Toward a Net Zero Energy Building
ZERO ENERGY
ACHIEVING ZERO ENERGY
Advanced Energy Design Guide for K–12 School Buildings
ZERO ENERGY
ACHIEVING ZERO ENERGY
Advanced Energy Design Guide for Small to Medium Office Buildings

Gordon Holness, the next ASHRAE President, called for determining the right building performance metrics to help consumers understand and support sustainability efforts. We must provide the training that is required for building operators to manage the buildings we design, he said. "This is not a challenge that we can undertake on our own. We need to work with owners' organizations as well as with building service organizations to develop educational programs."

Gordon V.R. Holness, 2009–2010 ASHRAE President

Building Energy Quotient

Management thinker Peter Drucker believed you cannot manage what you cannot measure. To provide a tool that assisted engineers and owners in determining building performance, ASHRAE launched Building Energy Quotient (bEQ at the time, now Building EQ) in 2010, a voluntary energy rating label that gave facility managers a detailed overview of their efficiency standing. Building EQ was more than a performance score—the process also included an ASHRAE Level 1 audit plus a list of improvement recommendations. Only by verifying where inefficiencies exist can a designer, owner, or operator prioritize meaningful energy-saving projects. Building EQ let owners benchmark their energy use, disclose the rating to the public, and receive professional guidance on how to improve building operations.

A key feature of Building EQ was that it offered two rating labels that qualify energy performance: In Operation and As Designed. The In Operation rating focused on a property's actual energy use for the preceding 12 to 18 months, based on concrete operating data supplied from utility bills. This lets owners and operators see how their energy usage compared to the energy usage of a median baseline property and highlights the potential for energy performance improvement. Using the As Designed rating, owners could evaluate a building's performance potential by stripping away occupant and operational factors.

Real Buildings/Real Data

If the Building EQ tool was one leg of a three-legged stool launched by ASHRAE to support improved building performance, the second was education, and its focal point was ASHRAE's *High Performing Buildings* magazine (HPB). Launched in 2007, its dual objectives were to educate designers on successful applications and demonstrate to building owners that new building technologies improve occupant satisfaction and make for good financial investments.

Front cover of the first issue of *High-Performing Buildings Magazine*, 2008.

As its editorial mission, HPB described measured performance of practices and technologies to promote better buildings, presenting case studies that featured integrated building design practices and improved operations and maintenance techniques.

The magazine's case studies included measured performance data and lessons learned through design, construction, and operation, making it unique among building technology publications.

Professional Certification

The third leg of ASHRAE's sustainable buildings plan was assurance that those responsible for how a building performed had adequate understanding of

Learning Institute to Offer Certification

CINCINNATI — A certification plan that would test understanding of the nine-course *Fundamentals of HVAC&R* series is tentatively scheduled to begin in September 2004. The Board of Directors approved the proposal at the 2001 Annual Meeting.

"ASHRAE is responding to the requests of its members by making a commitment of close to $800,000 to develop the material and set up a certification system," William "Joe" Buck, chair of the ASHRAE Learning Institute, said. "Employers and the public can be assured that certified individuals have studied the material necessary to attain competency in the fundamentals of HVAC&R design."

Currently, students are considered to have successfully completed a course in series if they answer all exercises and problems. However, students are not tested on their knowledge of course material. Students who complete all of the exercises and problems receive a certificate of completion.

Information from the Learning Institute shows that a low percentage of students who purchase a course complete it. The Institute feels that an incentive, such as a test leading to certification, is needed beyond the completion certificate.

"Certification provides a reward for those who expend the effort to complete the self-directed learning courses," Buck said. "Certified individuals will have stronger credentials when seeking employment."

The certification proposal calls for students to complete four mandatory courses and two other courses selected by students. Mandatory courses are *Fundamentals of HVAC Systems, Fundamentals of Thermodynamics, Fundamentals of Psychometrics* and *Fundamentals of Heating and Cooling Loads*. Student-selected courses are *Fundamentals of HVAC Control Systems,*

See Certification, Page 2

the relevant knowledge base needed to apply new technologies and assess building performance. ASHRAE would begin a professional certification program.

The first certification, Healthcare Facility Design Professional (HFDP), launched in 2007 to meet a need identified by the American Society for Health Care Engineering (ASHE). The High-Performance Building Deign Professional (HBDP) certification followed in 2008.

Building Commissioning Professional (BCXP) certification launched in 2009. "ASHRAE's certification program recognizes that people who manage the commissioning process need to have people- and project-management skills in addition to a level of understanding of building design, construction, operations and maintenance," President Harrison said. "This is what distinguishes the commissioning program from other HVAC commissioning certifications."

Also in 2009, ASHRAE offered Operations and Performance Management Professional (OPMP) certification, aimed at helping building owners know they are hiring and retaining employees and consultants who know how facility operations and maintenance impact HVAC&R systems' performance. According to a study by the Energy Systems Laboratory (ESL) at Texas A&M University released at the time, energy use in buildings can be reduced 10% to 40% by improving building operational strategies. "Every building, new or old, must be operated at its own optimum level," Harrison said. "To do so, we must apply advanced knowledge and skills to building operations. ASHRAE's OPMP certification helps professionals attest that they are well prepared to manage and maintain buildings to fully achieve reliability and their potential energy savings."

To ensure that professionals modeling a building's energy use have the skills necessary to produce an accurate model, ASHRAE launched the Building Energy Modeling Professional (BEMP) certification in 2010.

"Energy modeling is one of the most effective ways to achieve energy efficiency when designing sustainable buildings," said President Holness. "Since energy modeling is only as good as the consultant who uses it, ASHRAE's newest certification program strives to ensure that engineers and architects achieve the highest possible standards when it comes to sustainable design." Those who passed the exam demonstrated their ability to evaluate, choose, use, calibrate, and interpret the results of energy modeling software, as well as confirm their competence to model new and existing buildings and systems with their full range of physics.

The certification would be an essential element for guaranteeing the quality of ASHRAE's soon-to-be launched Building EQ program by ensuring that there is a competent pool of building energy modelers. ASHRAE built Building EQ to rely heavily on energy modeling in its As Designed component, which could compare predicted energy performance to the In Operation component, actual energy use.

Thomas H. Phoenix, 2014–2015 ASHRAE President

The companion certification program for Building EQ, Building Energy Assessment Professional (BEAP), followed in 2011. "We can't manage what we can't measure," said Thomas H. Phoenix, chair of the committee that developed the BEAP certification and ASHRAE President in 2014–15. "Providing reliable energy analysis means we are holding ourselves more accountable for the energy our buildings use. The results of an analysis can tell us which systems are working efficiently and which systems provide opportunities for improvement." BEAP certified an individuals' ability to determine project scope, collect data, analyze building performance, interpret results, evaluate alternatives, submit recommendations for energy conservation measures, and assist with the implementation of the resulting recommendations.

Better Buildings Workforce

In 2011, impacted by the same trends that prompted ASHRAE to focus on building performance and integrated building design, DOE launched the Better Buildings Initiative. One of the key elements was the Better Buildings Workforce.

Recognizing like ASHRAE that improving buildings' operational performance requires highly skilled and qualified workers, particularly as building technologies become more advanced, DOE worked with National Institute of Building Sciences (NIBS), ASHRAE, and other groups to develop the Better Buildings Workforce Guidelines, voluntary national guidelines to improve the quality and consistency of commercial building workforce credentials for four key energy-related jobs: Building Energy Auditor, Building Commissioning Professional, Building Operations Professional, and Energy Manager.

The two ASHRAE certifications relevant to the Better Buildings Workforce scope achieved DOE recognition in the initiative: Building Energy Assessment Professional (BEAP) and Building Commissioning Professional (BCXP).

In order to gain the recognition, ASHRAE received accreditation from American National Standards Institute (ANSI) under ISO/IEC 17024 (#1139) for the two certifications along with submitting and receiving accreditation for Building Energy Modeling Professional (BEMP) and High-Performance Building Design Professional (HBDP).

Building EQ Toolkit Helps Promote Label

The Building Energy Quotient pilot is due to premiere soon, and ASHRAE chapters and individual members will play a vital role in ensuring that state and local governments understand the value of implementing a building energy disclosure program. To help ASHRAE members inform their local policymakers, the Washington, D.C., office has created an advocacy toolkit to be used by chapters and individuals in an effort to raise awareness to the importance of Building EQ.

The toolkit is, according to Ryan Colker, ASHRAE manager of government affairs, a "mechanism of implementation" and includes a number of helpful, easy to use resources. For example, a template letter for addressing local governments concerning the labeling program only requires members to fill in the blanks with their pertinent information. PowerPoint slides are provided for members to use at town hall meetings or during face-to-face meetings with city or county council members or mayors. Even model legislation has been included for easy, early adoption.

"The presentation is targeted at state and local policymakers with justification of why a mandatory program referencing BEQ should be adopted," said Colker.

Due to the fact that the program will initially be voluntary, it is essential that ASHRAE members lead the way in urging policymakers and governments to adopt Building EQ into the legislation of their

See Building EQ, Page 5

Building EQ, From Page 1

cities and states. As the Building EQ program gains participants across the country, ASHRAE members will increasingly be looked to by governments and building owners to provide the expertise to obtain a building energy label and ensure that buildings are designed and operated to use energy efficiently.

The Building Energy Disclosure Program advocacy packet and other tools on how chapters and individual members can engage in public policy activities can be found by visiting www.ashrae.org/advocacy and selecting "Advocacy Toolkit."

Additional advocacy packets are available in the toolkit including commercial building energy codes, state use of voluntary consensus standards and licensure requirements for engineers.

Contact your representative/senator and urge them to adopt ASHRAE's building labeling program. It is important to be familiar with your topic, in this case the building labeling program.

Information is available at www.buildingeq.com.

Chapter 9

Ventilation Comes Next to Godliness

"There is still another side to the work of this society which should be constantly borne in mind, and that is the physical good that is being done for humanity by good warming and ventilating and its effect on the comfort and health of the people. Most, if not all, of our states have laws governing house drainage, safe construction of houses, and fire protection. Why not, therefore, reasonable warmth and good air, both of which our Creator provided the means of obtaining....It is just as essential in these days in this climate to warm and ventilate a dwelling as to properly build or drain it."

Stewart A. Jellett
1896

Proper ventilation, and in effect indoor air quality, was a subject of critical importance to Society members from the time of the founding of The American Society of Heating and Ventilating Engineers. "Ventilation comes next to Godliness," said Edward P. Bates, the first president of the Society in 1894. Not only did concern about proper ventilation reflect members' more humanitarian concerns, some popular views of the time threatened the professional standing of these early heating and ventilating engineers. "Old fogyism," J.H. Kinealy, 1901 President, called it.

J.H. Kinealy
Decried "old fogyism."

"The heating engineer must have to a certain degree, that kind of knowledge which a physician has, in order to enable him to determine what are the effects of too high or too low a temperature upon the human body, what are the effects of too great or too small an amount of moisture in the air breathed by human beings, and what are the effects of impure air upon the health and well being of the occupants of rooms," Mr. Kinealy said. "There are today, many physicians who either through old fogyism or lack of broad training do not know what they should, or at least do not advocate what should be advocated for the proper ventilating and heating of schools, hospitals and other buildings in which large numbers of people are to be congregated for a considerable period of time....Heating engineers must be able to convince the physician that he knows what he is talking about and is right in what he says, or he must be able to convince those who have the deciding voice in the question of how a building shall be heated and ventilated."

What concerned Mr. Kinealy and his colleagues was the view of some turn-of-the-century physicians that mechanical ventilation was unhealthy, contributing to the spread of such diseases as tuberculosis.

Adoption of a Minimum Ventilation Rate

At the first organizational meeting of the Society on September 10, 1894, eight "objects" for the new organization were decided: Among them, "To establish a clearly defined minimum standard of heating and ventilation for all classes of buildings" and "To favor legislation compelling the ventilation of all public buildings in accordance with the standard of this society." In 1895, the Society adopted a minimum ventilation rate of 30 cfm per occupant, the same as had been in Massachusetts state law since the 1880s.

Telephone booths at South Station, Boston, Massachusetts, equipped with ventilating apparatus (1912).

Reginald P. Bolton
American Society of Heating, Ventilating and Hygiene Engineers.

In 1911, President Reginald P. Bolton went so far as to conclude that the Society's name should include "hygiene," since, he said, "we can lead on problems of prolonging life and solving the spread of tuberculosis."

For several centuries there had been two schools of thought concerning ventilation. Architects and engineers were concerned with providing comfort and freedom from noxious odors and the debilitating effects of oxygen depletion and or carbon dioxide accumulation. Physicians, on the other hand, were concerned with minimizing the spread of disease. Dr. J.S. Billings, a physician and the time's leading authority on ventilation and its effect on health, recommended 60 cfm of ventilating air per person to minimize the spread of disease while he believed 30 cfm was adequate for comfort. Not eligible for membership because he was not a heating and ventilating engineer, Dr. Billings was elected as the first Honorary Member of the Society in 1896. He was the librarian of what was called the finest medical library in the world at the time.

Dr. J.S. Billings
Not eligible for membership because he was not a heating and ventilating engineer, Dr. Billings was elected as the first Honorary Member of the Society in 1896. He was the librarian of what was called the finest medical library in the world at the time.

The Society's Model Code

In 1910, the Chicago Department of Health appointed a commission which included representatives of the Illinois Chapter of The American Society of Heating and Ventilating Engineers and the Chicago Public School System to study ventilation of school buildings. The commission's report concluded that

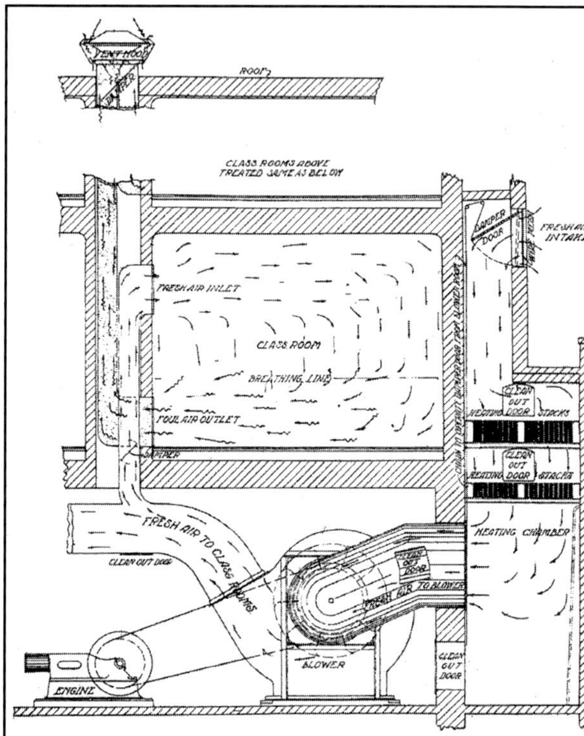

General scheme of plenum system of ventilating public school buildings (1908).

carbon dioxide was "not the harmful agent of major importance in expired air or air otherwise contaminated."

The report also concluded that the temperature of 68°F (20°C) with proper humidity control is desired in living rooms that are artificially heated; the then-current state of knowledge was insufficient to designate all harmful factors; and, "that from the standpoint of health, relative humidity is one of the important factors in ventilation."

The American Society of Heating and Ventilating Engineers went on to write a model code in 1914 with a minimum ventilating rate of 30 cfm (14 L/s) per occupant of outdoor air. By 1925, twenty-two states had regulations requiring a minimum of 30 cfm per occupant of outdoor air.

CCCXXXI

REPORT ON WORK OF VENTILATION DIVISION OF THE CHICAGO HEALTH DEPARTMENT FOR 1913

BY E. VERNON HILL, M.D.

A brief summary of work done by the Ventilation Division of the Chicago Health Department, for the past year, is shown in the accompanying Chart 1.

The heading "plans examined" refers to the total number submitted to the Division during the year, of which 473 were approved as complying with the requirements of the ordinance.

The total number of installations inspected comprises ventilating equipments of every kind, from an exhaust fan in the alley wall of a restaurant kitchen to the complete installation in a large theatre.

Of the various classes of buildings inspected, including theatres, lodge halls, schools, etc., some are equipped with mechanical ventilating devices and some are not; in each instance, however, a record is made, with a scale drawing of the building or room, with the proper notations as to the number of occupants, temperature, relative humidity, etc., and also the results of air analyses and bacterial counts.

License applications inspected and approved cover new buildings or those that were remodeled or converted into theatres or halls where an amusement license is required.

Complaints received refer mostly to letters received by the Department complaining of the poor ventilation of theatres and street cars.

Street car test runs refer to tests made on 16 street cars which were equipped with various natural or mechanical systems of ventilation. These test runs occupy usually from 4 to 7 or 8 hours, and require two or sometimes three men. Anemometer readings are taken at the outlets or inlets, as the case may be, to determine the amount of air actually supplied to the passengers. Dust counts and culture determinations are also made, and observations of temperature, relative humidity, etc.

The New York Study of Schools

The New York State Commission on Ventilation conducted various research studies on ventilation in school rooms beginning in 1913 through the 1920s. The Commission found that window-related rooms at a temperature from 59° to 67°F (15° to 19°C) had the lowest rate of respiratory illness. Fan ventilation with a temperature of 70°F (21°C) had 18% more absences and 70% more respiratory illnesses.

It was postulated that the more uniform air conditions (better mixing) with fan-inducted circulation increased the rate of spread of airborne disease. It was believed that 68°F (20°C) was an ideal temperature for comfort and minimizing the spread of disease. But an important result of the research was that with proper temperature control, the ventilating rate could be reduced below 30 cfm (14 L/s) of outdoor air per occupant.

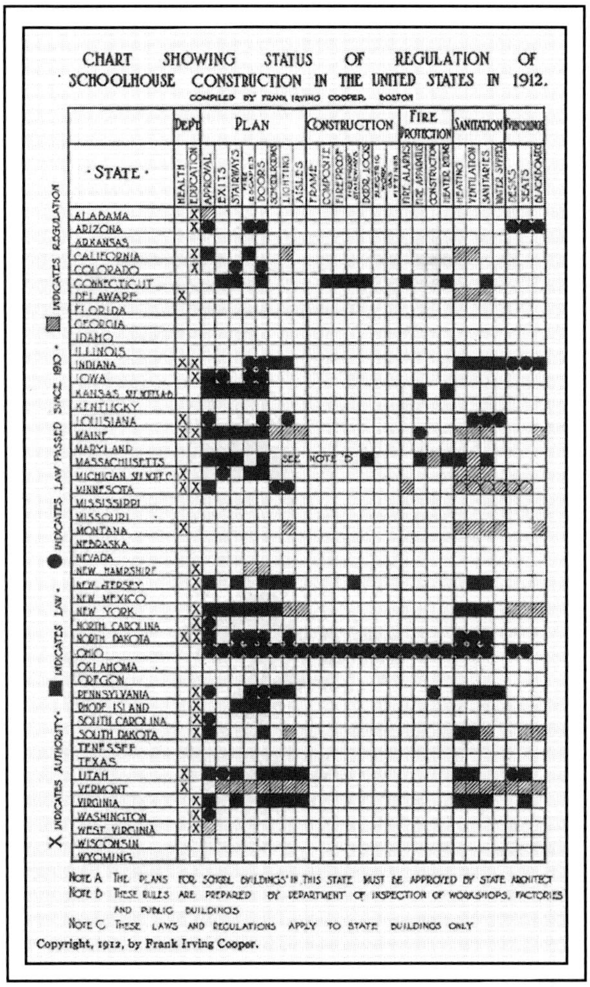

Copyright, 1912, by Frank Irving Cooper.

Society Research

The next important development occurred in 1934. Under contract from the Society, W.H. Lehmberg and his associates at Harvard University measured, in a laboratory environment, the minimum ventilation requirement using the human nose as the sensor. The olfactory nerves of the nose are exceedingly sensitive. Their paper was published in The A.S.H.V.E. Transactions of 1935.

A total of 10 subjects and 15 trained judges performed experiments at ventilating rates ranging from 1 to 50 cfm (0.5 to 24 L/s) per occupant. They found the odor to be acceptable (index number two) at 65°

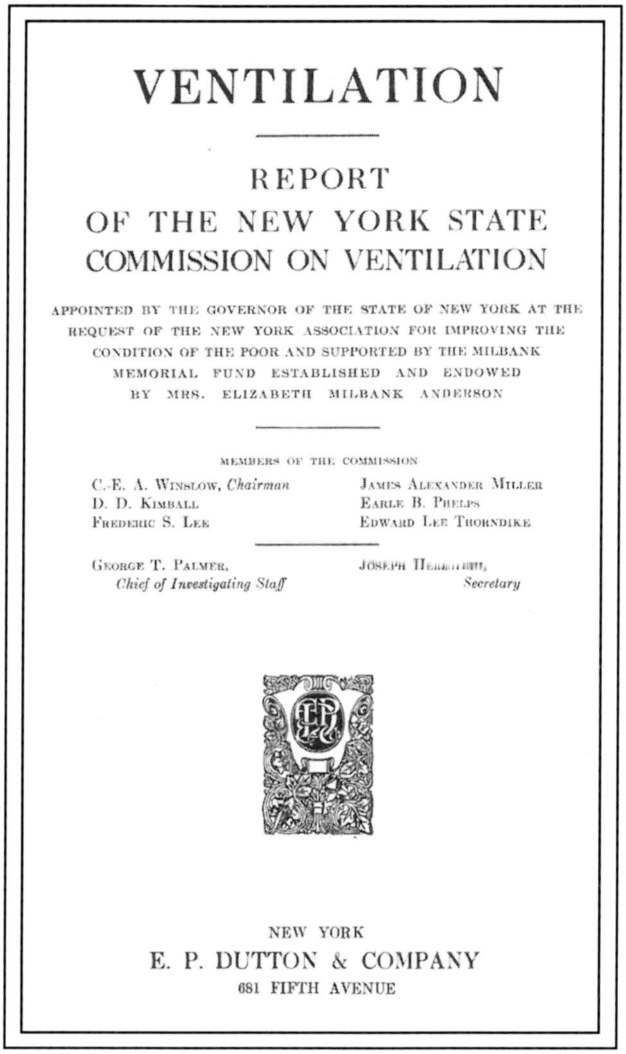

VENTILATION

REPORT
OF THE NEW YORK STATE
COMMISSION ON VENTILATION

APPOINTED BY THE GOVERNOR OF THE STATE OF NEW YORK AT THE REQUEST OF THE NEW YORK ASSOCIATION FOR IMPROVING THE CONDITION OF THE POOR AND SUPPORTED BY THE MILBANK MEMORIAL FUND ESTABLISHED AND ENDOWED BY MRS. ELIZABETH MILBANK ANDERSON

MEMBERS OF THE COMMISSION

C.-E. A. WINSLOW, *Chairman*
D. D. KIMBALL
FREDERIC S. LEE
JAMES ALEXANDER MILLER
EARLE B. PHELPS
EDWARD LEE THORNDIKE

GEORGE T. PALMER,
Chief of Investigating Staff

JOSEPH [illegible],
Secretary

NEW YORK
E. P. DUTTON & COMPANY
681 FIFTH AVENUE

On the desk tops, under metal cones, are lighted candles which produce the same amount of heat as a classroom of children would emit. (New York State Commission on Ventilation, G. T. Palmer 1915).

The air thermometer, devised to record minor air-movements, consists of a glass tube covered by a piece of moistened muslin and connected in a closed circuit with a sensitive rubber tambour.

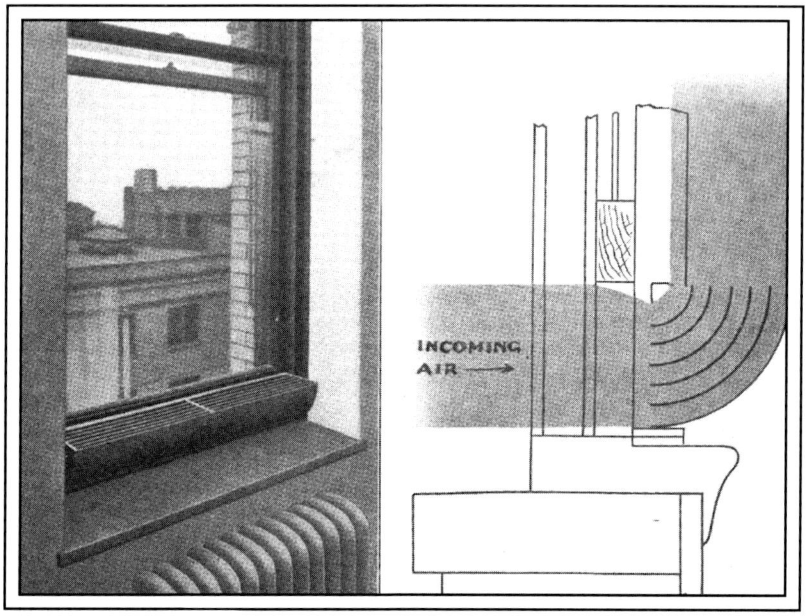

The Type A deflector (with view and cross-section) is a metal box with closed ends and with a series of parallel curved plates leading from the side exposed to the outer air to the room. This deflector is set just inside the sash so that as the sash is raised more of the air channels between the vanes are brought into use in proportion to the size of the sash opening. The curvature of the plates is designed to divert the incoming air from its entering horizontal direction to its departing vertical direction with a minimum of resistance.

to 72°F (18° to 22°C) and 20 cfm (9 L/s) per person. When the temperature was raised to 79° to 86°F (26° to 30°C), the ventilation had to be increased to 30 cfm (14 L/s).

Constantin Yaglou, E.C. Riley and D.I. Cogins continued this work in a more exhaustive study also at Harvard and also under A.S.H.V.E. sponsorship. They found a strong correlation between the required outdoor ventilating rate and the net air space per occupant. For example, at 150 ft^3 (4 m^3) per person, 20 cfm (9 L/s) of outdoor was needed to control the perceived body odor to an acceptable level of 2 on Lehmberg's scale. If the occupant density was reduced to the equivalent of an air space of 300 ft^3 (8 m^3) per occupant, ventilation was reduced to 12 cfm (6 L/s) per occupant for sedentary adults.

TABLE 1. SENSORY INTENSITY SCALE OF BODY ODOR

Odor Intensity Index	Characteristic Term	Qualification
0	None	No perceptible odor.
½	Threshold	Very faint, barely detectable by trained judges; usually imperceptible to untrained persons.
1	Definite	Readily detectable by all normal persons but not objectionable.
2	Moderate	Neither pleasant nor disagreeable. Little or no objection. Allowable limit in rooms.
3	Strong	Objectionable. Air regarded with disfavor.
4	Very strong	Forcible, disagreeable.
5	Overpowering	Nauseating.

A sensory intensity scale of body odor used by W. H. Lehmberg in his 1935 paper.

TABLE 2. INFLUENCE OF HUMIDITY ON ODOR INTENSITY (JUDGES' IMPRESSIONS)

Outdoor Air Supply CFM per Person	Average Box Temperature											
	65–72 F				72–79 F				79–86 F			
	R. H. Under 40%		R. H. Over 40%		R. H. Under 40%		R. H. Over 40%		R. H. Under 40%		R. H. Over 40%	
	No. of Observations	Odor Intensity	No. of Observations	Odor Intensity	No. of Observations	Odor Intensity	No. of Observations	Odor Intensity	No. of Observations	Odor Intensity	No. of Observations	Odor Intensity
Under 5	2	3.9	3	3.6	2	3.5	7	3.6	2	4.0	4	4.4
5–15	5	2.6	7	2.3	8	2.8	11	2.3	5	2.8	2	3.4
15–25	4	1.8	3	2.4	4	1.9	4	3.0	1	2.4	4	2.5
25–35	2	1.7	5	1.3	2	1.6	3	1.7	4	2.3	3	1.6
All air flows	13	2.4	18	2.3	16	2.5	25	2.7	12	2.8	13	3.0

TABLE 3. SUBJECTIVE IMPRESSIONS OF AIR QUALITY IN RELATION TO AIR SUPPLY

(Under comfortable conditions of temperature and humidity)

Outdoor Air Supply CFM per Person	Number of Subjects Recording					Consensus
	Excellent	Good	Fair	Poor	Bad	
1–2	..	..	..	..	2	Bad
4–5	..	1	1	4	..	Poor
6–8	..	2	2	..	..	Fair to good
9–11	2	3	5	1	..	Fair to good
12–16	1	3	1	..	..	Good
17–20	5	2	..	..	..	Excellent
21–35	..	4	1	..	..	Good
36–50	1	1	9	..	..	Fair

Influence of humidity on odor intensity (judges' impression) from W. H. Lehmberg's 1935 paper.

Constantin P. Yaglou

Interestingly, grade school children required more ventilation: 25 cfm (12 L/s) per child at 150 ft^3 (4 m^3) per child and 17 cfm (8 L/s) per child at 300 ft^3 (8 m^3) per child. Fifty percent more ventilation was required if children had gone 6.5 days without a bath and change of underwear than if they had bathed and changed underwear within 0.5 days. Only 33% increase in ventilation was required for adults one week after a bath.

Untreated recirculated air was found to have no effect on odor density, but washing, humidifying, cooling and dehumidifying recirculated air were all

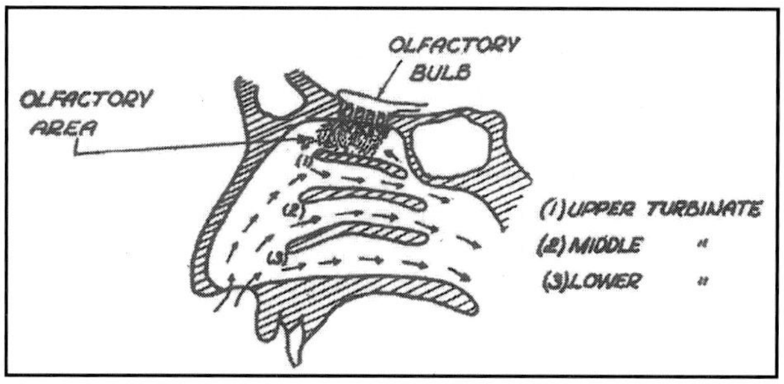

Section through right nasal cavity showing olfactory region and direction of air currents during inspiration from C.P. Yaglou's 1935 paper.

TABLE 3. SOCIO-ECONOMIC STATUS, BATHS, ODOR INTENSITY, AND VENTILATION REQUIREMENTS

Experiments with Simple Ventilation

Type of Subjects	Total Number of Subjects	Air Space per Person Cu Ft	Outdoor Air Supply per Person Cfm	Average Odor Intensity	Computed Ventilation Requirements Cfm per Person	Last Bath Average Number of Days
Laborers	7	200	7.3	3.29	24	7.2
Laborers	7	200	14.4	2.40	22	7.4
Average for Laborers	...	...	...	...	23	7.3
Medical Students	7	200	7.5	2.60	15	1.3
Medical Students	7	200	14.5	2.11	16	1.2
Average for Medical Students	...	...	...	...	15.5	1.25
Average Sedentary Adult Subject (See Fig. 2)	..	200	...	...	16	2.2
Grade School Children of Poorest Class	7	200	22.0	2.83	38	8.0
Grade School Children of "Better Class"	14	200	20.9	1.87	18	3.0
Average Grade School Child (See Fig. 3)	..	200	...	...	21	4.2
Grade School Children of Best Class	14	100	16.4	2.34	22	0.8
Average Grade School Child (See Fig. 5)	..	100	...	...	29	4.9

Socio-economic status, baths, odor intensity and ventilation requirements in C.P. Yaglou's 1935 paper.

found beneficial in reducing the outdoor air requirement. Twelve cfm (6 L/s) of outdoor air in the total supply of 30 cfm (14 L/s) was found acceptable for sedentary adults if there was at least 200 ft^3 (6 m^3) of air space per person. There were significant differences due to children versus adults, socioeconomic class, and air space per occupant.

ASA Lighting Standard

Air conditioning of buildings began to be used in the 1920s with increasing frequency. In the late 1930s, a practice began of taking room exhaust air out through the lighting fixtures to minimize this load during cooling operation.

Consequently, when in 1946 the American Standards Association promulgated a new lighting standard, The A.S.H.V.E. was invited to participate. The resulting standard, A53.1 "Light and Ventilation," established a specification of 10 cfm (5 L/s) per person of exhaust for ventilation and removal of heat.

In 1966, responsibility for the mechanical ventilation section of A53.1 was assigned to ASHRAE which appointed a standards project committee to carry out the revision. In 1973, their work was published.

ASHRAE Standard 62-73

Yaglou had concluded from his experiments that variations in demand made it impossible to set one outdoor air ventilating rate for all applications. It was not until about 1970 that ASHRAE started writing a detailed standard for ventilation. This standard was published in 1973, just before the first oil embargo.

ASHRAE Standard 62-73 was based on Yaglou's work and the experience of practicing engineers. Two hundred sixty-nine separate applications were identified. Both a recommended range of ventilating rates and a minimum rate for each application were presented. The range of ventilation specified was intended to give designers latitude in meeting a desired environmental quality in any one application. The minimum rate of 5 cfm (2.5 L/s) of outdoor air per occupant was not to be violated.

For example, school classrooms had a recommended rate of 10 to 15 cfm (5 to 7 L/s) per student with a minimum specified rate of 10 cfm (5 L/ s). Office spaces had a recommended range of 15 to 25 cfm (7 to 12 L/s) per occupant with a minimum of 15 cfm (7 L/s). These specified flow rates were all for 100% outdoor air.

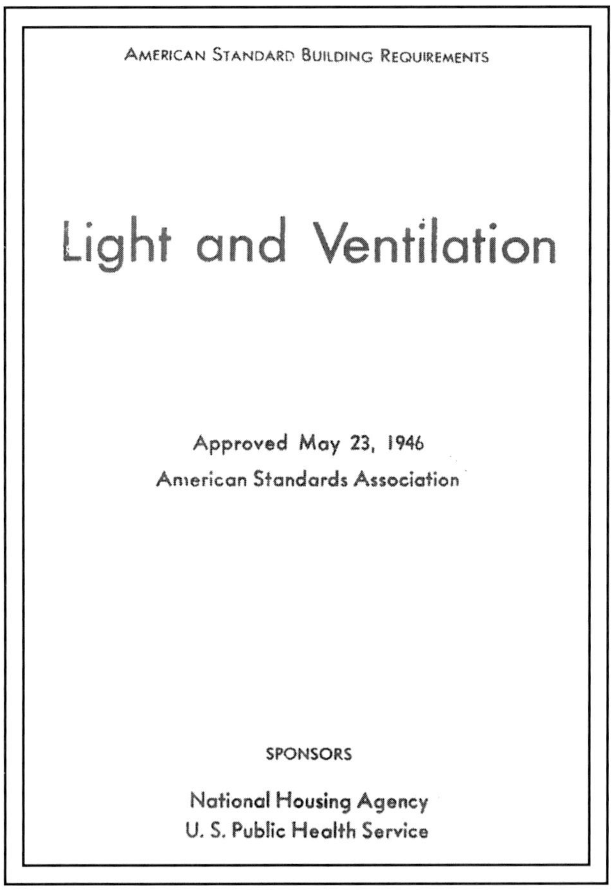

AMERICAN STANDARD BUILDING REQUIREMENTS

Light and Ventilation

Approved May 23, 1946
American Standards Association

SPONSORS

National Housing Agency
U. S. Public Health Service

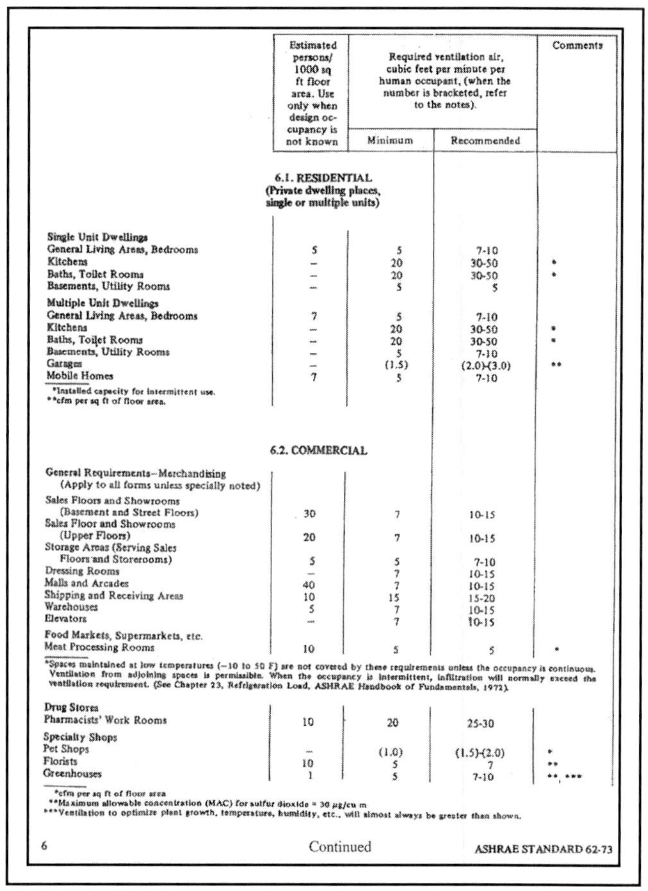

	Estimated persons/ 1000 sq ft floor area. Use only when design occupancy is not known	Required ventilation air, cubic feet per minute per human occupant, (when the number is bracketed, refer to the notes).		Comments
		Minimum	Recommended	
6.1. RESIDENTIAL (Private dwelling places, single or multiple units)				
Single Unit Dwellings				
General Living Areas, Bedrooms	5	5	7-10	
Kitchens	–	20	30-50	*
Baths, Toilet Rooms	–	20	30-50	*
Basements, Utility Rooms	–	5	5	
Multiple Unit Dwellings				
General Living Areas, Bedrooms	7	5	7-10	
Kitchens	–	20	30-50	*
Baths, Toilet Rooms	–	20	30-50	*
Basements, Utility Rooms	–	5	7-10	
Garages	–	(1.5)	(2.0)-(3.0)	**
Mobile Homes	7	5	7-10	

*Installed capacity for intermittent use.
**cfm per sq ft of floor area.

6.2. COMMERCIAL				
General Requirements—Merchandising (Apply to all forms unless specially noted)				
Sales Floors and Showrooms (Basement and Street Floors)	30	7	10-15	
Sales Floor and Showrooms (Upper Floors)	20	7	10-15	
Storage Areas (Serving Sales Floors and Storerooms)	5	5	7-10	
Dressing Rooms	–	7	10-15	
Malls and Arcades	40	7	10-15	
Shipping and Receiving Areas	10	15	15-20	
Warehouses	5	7	10-15	
Elevators	–	7	10-15	
Food Markets, Supermarkets, etc.				
Meat Processing Rooms	10	5	5	*

*Spaces maintained at low temperatures (−10 to 50 F) are not covered by these requirements unless the occupancy is continuous. Ventilation from adjoining spaces is permissible. When the occupancy is intermittent, infiltration will normally exceed the ventilation requirement. (See Chapter 23, Refrigeration Load, ASHRAE Handbook of Fundamentals, 1972).

Drug Stores				
Pharmacists' Work Rooms	10	20	25-30	
Specialty Shops				
Pet Shops	–	(1.0)	(1.5)-(2.0)	*
Florists	10	5	7	**
Greenhouses	1	5	7-10	**, ***

*cfm per sq ft of floor area
**Maximum allowable concentration (MAC) for sulfur dioxide = 30 μg/cu m
***Ventilation to optimize plant growth, temperature, humidity, etc., will almost always be greater than shown.

6 Continued ASHRAE STANDARD 62-73

The standard did permit a reduction to one-third of the recommended rate when recirculation was used. If the recirculated air was properly filtered, the outdoor air flow rate could be reduced to 15% of the recommended rate provided there was at least 5 cfm (2 L/s) per occupant of outdoor air in the supply.

When energy suddenly became a serious concern following the Arab oil embargo, ASHRAE promulgated ASHRAE Standard 90-75 Energy Conservation in New Building Design. This standard specified the use of the minimum ventilating rates in Standard 62-73. Thus, ventilation was reduced to 5 cfm (2 L/s) of outdoor air per person.

12 Portland, Maine, Press Herald, Tuesday, March 16, 1982

Indoor air pollution plagues 'tight' homes

By BOB CUMMINGS
Staff Writer

LEWISTON — Federal and state air pollution laws regulate "ambient" air — the pollution of the outdoor air from giant industries.

But the really serious air pollution may be the air inside modern energy-efficient homes, especially homes where residents use super-efficient kerosene heaters, smoke cigarettes and burn bottled or natural gas, says William Turner of the Harvard School of Public Health.

Turner spoke at the annual tech-

Energy efficiency can poison you

By Pam Armstrong-Hunt

ASHRAE Standard 62-1981

In 1978, ASHRAE began to review Standard 62-73 for revision. The over-riding objective was to determine if the 5 cfm (2 L/s) per person rate was justified. The committee determined at once that 5 cfm (2 L/s) of outdoor air was insufficient to control tobacco smoke. Formaldehyde had also become a key contaminant because of poorly executed efforts at energy conservation.

The revised Standard 62-1981, Ventilation for Control of Indoor Air Quality, was a double standard. No adequate justification could be found for not permitting a minimum of 5 cfm (2 L/s) per occupant in "clean" environments when smoking was prohibited, but three to five times more outdoor air was required when smoking was allowed.

The Formaldehyde Institute objected to the recommended limit on formaldehyde and the Tobacco Institute objected to the separate requirements when smoking was permitted. Consequently, ASHRAE Standard 62-1981 was not endorsed by the American National Standards Institute as Standard 62-73 had been endorsed.

Many state and city building codes had adopted Standard 62-73 in whole or in part. But, the lack of ANSI endorsement prevented Standard 62-1981 from being adopted in building codes. Also, many applications listed in Standard 62-73 were deleted from Standard 62-1981 because they were for industrial applications. OSHA had assumed responsibility for these.

ANSI/ASHRAE Standard 62-1989

By the end of the decade, W.S. Cain and R.O. Fanger had published results of new laboratory studies that generally confirmed Yaglou's early results. Cain working at Yale University and Fanger at the Technical University of Denmark both agreed that 15 cfm (7 L/s) of outdoor air was needed to dilute occupant odors to a concentration acceptable to 80% of the "visitors" entering an occupied space. However, these new data did not confirm Yaglou's dependence on air space. Thus, Standard 62-1989 adopted 15 cfm (7 L/s) per occupant of outdoor air as the minimum.

John Janssen, chair of the ASHRAE Standards Project Committee revising the standard, found, based on work by B.P. Leaderer and Cain and W.W. Thayer, that 15 cfm (7 L/s) of outdoor air per occu-

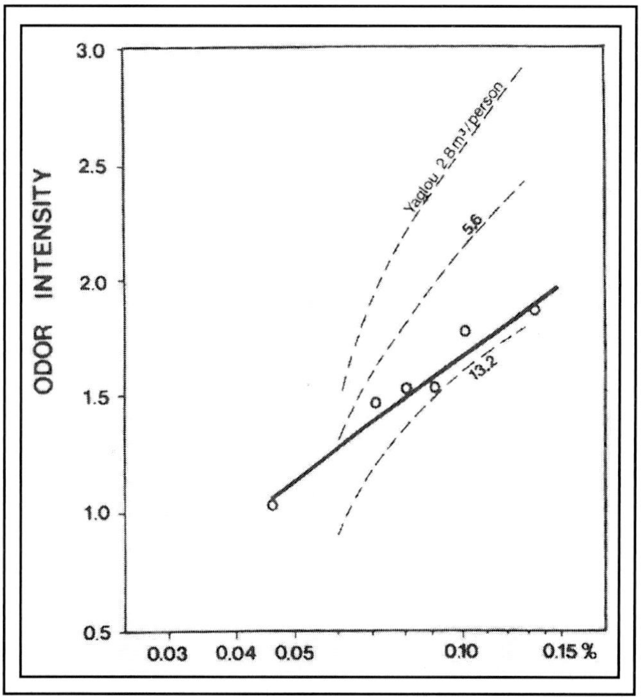

In his 1983 paper, Dr. P.O. Fanger showed odor intensity as a function of the carbon dioxide concentration. For comparison, predictions of body odor from a reanalysis of Yaglou's data with estimated CO_2 concentrations are shown. The present experiments showed no significant effect of space volume per person, while Yaglou claimed a strong effect of this factor as indicated by the three dotted curves.

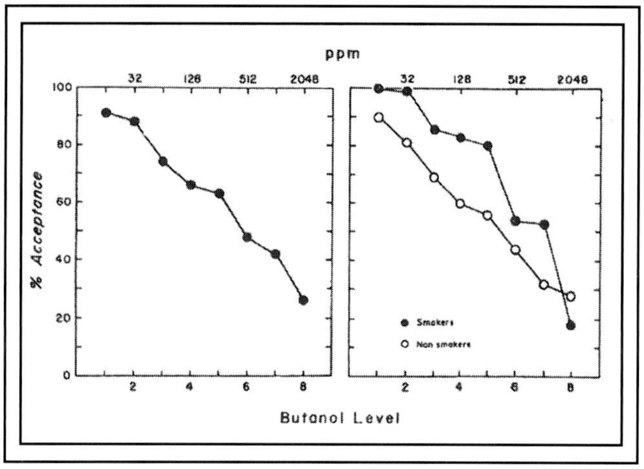

In his 1983 paper, W.S. Cain showed on left the relation between acceptance and intensity of tobacco smoke odor, expressed as butanol equivalent (butanol level on bottom abscissa, ppm on top abscissa). The data comprise the impressions of all visitors in all experiments and show results for more than 2300 participant-hours. The right shows the relation between acceptance and odor intensity for smokers and nonsmokers separately.

pant was sufficient to reduce the concentration of tobacco smoke to a level acceptable to 80% of the population at today's reduced smoking rate. Thus, Standard 62-1989 did not discriminate between smoking allowed and smoking prohibited. However, the new standard did require more ventilation for applications such as bars, cocktail lounges and smoking lounges where smoking activity is expected to produce higher levels of tobacco smoke.

IAQ in 1995

In 1904, Andrew Harvey assumed the presidency of the American Society of Heating and Ventilating Engineers. "I trust that within the next ten years, the people of every state of the Union will have become so well informed of the necessity for properly ventilated schools and public buildings that it will be con-

TABLE 2
OUTDOOR AIR REQUIREMENTS FOR VENTILATION*
2.1 COMMERCIAL FACILITIES (offices, stores, shops, hotels, sports facilities)

Application	Estimated Maximum** Occupancy P/1000 ft² or 100 m²	Outdoor Air Requirements cfm/ person	L/s· person	cfm/ft²	L/s·m²	Comments
Dry Cleaners, Laundries						Dry-cleaning processes may require more air.
Commercial laundry	10	25	13			
Commercial dry cleaner	30	30	15			
Storage, pick up	30	35	18			
Coin-operated laundries	20	15	8			
Coin-operated dry cleaner	20	15	8			
Food and Beverage Service						
Dining rooms	70	20	10			
Cafeteria, fast food	100	20	10			
Bars, cocktail lounges	100	30	15			Supplementary smoke-removal equipment may be required.
Kitchens (cooking)	20	15	8			Makeup air for hood exhaust may require more ventilating air. The sum of the outdoor air and transfer air of acceptable quality from adjacent spaces shall be sufficient to provide an exhaust rate of not less than 1.5 cfm/ft² (7.5 L/s·m²).
Garages, Repair, Service Stations						
Enclosed parking garage				1.50	7.5	Distribution among people must consider worker location and concentration of running engines; stands where engines are run must incorporate systems for positive engine exhaust withdrawal. Contaminant sensors may be used to control ventilation.
Auto repair rooms				1.50	7.5	
Hotels, Motels, Resorts, Dormitories						
				cfm/room	L/s·room	Independent of room size.
Bedrooms				30	15	
Living rooms				30	15	
Baths				35	18	Installed capacity for intermittent use.
Lobbies	30	15	8			
Conference rooms	50	20	10			
Assembly rooms	120	15	8			
Dormitory sleeping areas	20	15	8			See also food and beverage services, merchandising, barber and beauty shops, garages.
Gambling casinos	120	30	15			Supplementary smoke-removal equipment may be required.
Offices						
Office space	7	20	10			Some office equipment may require local exhaust.
Reception areas	60	15	8			
Telecommunication centers and data entry areas	60	20	10			
Conference rooms	50	20	10			Supplementary smoke-removal equipment may be required.
Public Spaces				cfm/ft²	L/s·m²	
Corridors and utilities				0.05	0.25	
Public restrooms, cfm/wc or cfm/urinal		50	25			Normally supplied by transfer air. Local mechanical exhaust with no recirculation recommended.
Locker and dressing rooms				0.5	2.5	
Smoking lounge	70	60	30			
Elevators				1.00	5.0	Normally supplied by transfer air.

Continued

sidered as great a crime to construct these buildings without providing for sufficient and proper ventilation as it would be to erect a building without a proper foundation."

As ASHRAE's 1994-95 President Billy R. Manning stated in his inaugural address, ASHRAE and the engineering community still have an obligation to better inform the public about the means of achieving indoor air quality (IAQ). There is also much the engineering community needs to learn about applications of technologies that impact and control indoor air quality. ASHRAE meetings, such as the annual IAQ symposia, help engineers and other professionals interested in the indoor environment meet these challenges.

The addition of outdoor air to recirculated air—providing ventilation for diluting odors, carbon dioxide and other contaminants—was and is the norm. The question has always been: How much outdoor air is needed? There has been an inevitable trade-off between the goals of energy conservation and acceptable indoor environments.

IEQ and Sustainability

Towards the end of the twentieth century, building design moved from a focus on reduced energy use to sustainability, defined by the United States Environmental Protection Agency (EPA) as the practice of creating structures and using processes that are environmentally responsible and resource-efficient throughout a building's life cycle from siting to design, construction, operation, maintenance, renovation, and deconstruction.

Similarly, the concern about IAQ shifted to indoor environmental quality (IEQ) with emphasis on the quality of a building's environment in relation to the health and well-being of those who occupy the space according to the National Institute for Occupational Safety and Health (NIOSH).

Both trends reflected a broader understanding of the complex relationships found in building design and operation. And both found their way into new standards and guidance from ASHRAE.

Lee Burgett, 2005–2006 ASHRAE President

In 2005, an ad hoc committee appointed by ASHRAE President Lee Burgett prepared a report approved by the ASHRAE Board of Directors that stated "ASHRAE activities and publications including but not limited to position documents, handbooks, special publications, standards and guidelines, and technical and education programs and conferences shall consider health and safety impacts where appropriate." In the 1980s and 1990s there had been discussion about whether ASHRAE should provide guidance on creating conditions for occupant health rather than only establishing ventilation rates. The committee's report affirmed the position that ASHRAE should not put health considerations aside in its building environment work.

After the turn of the twenty-first century, ASHRAE adopted position documents addressing health-related issues including airborne infectious diseases, environmental tobacco smoke, legionellosis and mold growth, moisture management of buildings, and indoor air quality. In 2011 ASHRAE published Guideline 10, *Interactions Affecting the Achievement of Acceptable Indoor Environments*.

ASHRAE, EPA Team to Produce IAQ Guide

Throughout ASHRAE's first 100 years, IAQ was traditionally addressed through minimum ventilation requirements in building codes. In the 1970s, these were based on industry consensus standards, namely ASHRAE Standard 62.

In 1997, ASHRAE's Standard 62.1 committee was directed by the ASHRAE Board to write the standard in mandatory and enforceable language to facilitate its adoption and reference by building codes. That direction implied the standard would contain only minimum requirements. Plus, as a standard, it could not contain a wide range of potentially useful material such as case studies and discussions of design approaches and technologies that could improve IAQ.

To provide adequate background information to support Standard 62.1 and other IAQ documents, ASHRAE entered into a cooperative agreement with the EPA in 2006 to develop a comprehensive publication and educational program to assist building professionals in designing and constructing buildings with improved IAQ.

Building on the positive experience with the Advanced Energy Design Guide (AEDG) series, ASHRAE sought to bring other key organizations in the building community into the IAQ effort, developing collaborative agreements with The American Institute of Architects (AIA), Building Owners and

ASHRAE JOURNAL
September 1991
The magazine of the American Society of Heating, Refrigerating and Air-Conditioning Engineers, Inc.
Microbial Growth (in humidifiers, spray coil units, and cooling coils, & air washers
Lead (water coolers)
Organic Materials (wet-copy machines)
Ozone (from photocopiers)
Cleaning Liquids
Ammonia (blue print machine)
Poor Cleaning Practices (allows bacteria to grow)
Formaldehyde
Outdoor Air (micro-organisms, ozone, carbon monoxide, nitrogen dioxide/carbon monoxide particles)
Body Contaminants Pesticides
Poor Maintenance Practices (floor waxes)
Tobacco Smoke
Rate of Outgassing (Soil gases (e.g. Radon)
INDOOR AIR QUALITY
VALVES
1991 SOFTWARE DIRECTORY

Boston, Mass., August 18, 1887

Gentlemen,

Your system of Ventilation as introduced into our Dairy Lunch Rooms, No. 6 Exchange Place, and 1 and 3 Spring Lane, answers the purpose called for, and gives perfect satisfaction, and we cheerfully recommend it. It has added greatly to the comfort of our patrons.

Yours truly,
OAK GROVE FARM CO.

NO. 4. LUNCH COUNTER

An old-time moving picture theater without mechanical equipment but having "deodorizers" hung on the walls. (1919)

An up-to-date moving picture theater showing sidewall introduction of air. (1919)

A "freak" ventilating system, introducing air through pipes suspended from ceiling and having perforated spheres at ends. (1919)

A poor installation, showing large intake duct to the right leading to enclosed coils; the top of fan housing is shown back of coils and the outlet of fan and right angle delivery at rear and to the left. Motor not visible because of motion picture machine in foreground. (1919)

Managers Association (BOMA), Sheet Metal and Air Conditioning Contractors' National Association (SMACNA), and U.S. Green Building Council (USGBC) in addition to EPA.

A group started meeting in spring 2007 and worked for more than two years to complete a guidance document. Two focus groups of architects, engineers, building owners, and sustainable building specialists reviewed early outlines and provided input on what they found most useful in other design guides. Two peer reviews of drafts of the guide also generated input that helped to shape the final publication.

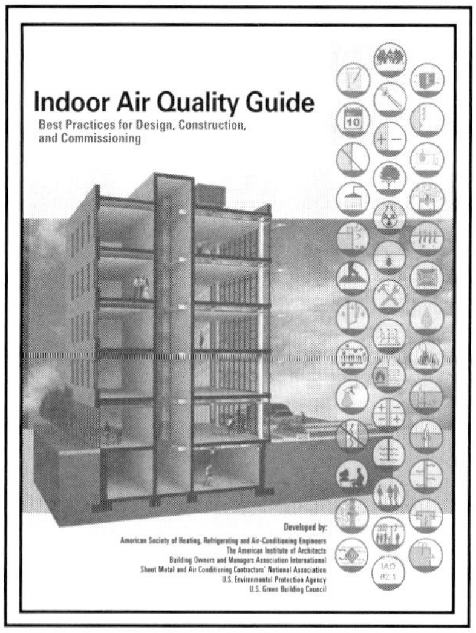

Indoor Air Quality Guide, 2009

In 2010 the new *Indoor Air Quality Guide* was published, representing a major step forward in achieving good IAQ by presenting comprehensive and practical guidance for building professionals. Recognizing the financial support from EPA, ASHRAE made the publication available for download for free, like it had the AEDGs.

Two contributors to the guide, Andrew K. Persily and Martha J. Hewett, wrote in *ASHRAE Journal* at the time, "Many IAQ problems occur because IAQ was not considered at the beginning of the design process. Basic design decisions related to site selection, building orientation, location of outdoor air intakes and how the building will be heated, cooled and ventilated are critical to good IAQ. Efforts to achieve high levels of building performance without diligent consideration of IAQ at the beginning of the design process can lead to IAQ problems and represent missed opportunities to ensure good IAQ."

The guide noted that while building codes and standards have addressed outdoor air ventilation for decades, many buildings and spaces are poorly ventilated, which increases the likelihood of IAQ problems. The reasons for inadequate ventilation could be lack of compliance with applicable codes and standards, installation or maintenance problems that lead to the design ventilation rate not being achieved in practice, and space use changes without an assessment of the need to modify ventilation rates. Even if system-level outdoor air intake rates are adequate, air distribution problems can lead to certain areas in the building being poorly ventilated.

Based on these common categories of IAQ problems and proven approaches to avoid them, the guide was organized around eight objectives:

1. Manage the Design and Construction Process to Achieve Good IAQ
2. Control Moisture in Building Assemblies
3. Limit Entry of Outdoor Contaminants
4. Control Moisture and Contaminants Related to Mechanical Systems
5. Limit Contaminants from Indoor Sources
6. Capture and Exhaust Contaminants from Building Equipment and Activities
7. Reduce Contaminant Concentrations through Ventilation, Filtration, and Air Cleaning
8. Apply More Advanced Ventilation Approaches

Mold and Dampness

In the last decades of the twentieth century, the public press began reporting how mold was moving from the kitchen and bathroom to the courtroom—not literally, but figuratively. *American Banker* reported that in Texas toxic mold insurance claims went from 228 in 2000 to 1,188 in the first half of 2001, and one U.S. law journal reported that toxic mold insurance claims increased five- to ten-fold across the country from 2001 to 2002.

To help engineers, the public, and governments better understand how to minimize indoor mold problems, ASHRAE issued its first position document on the subject in 2005. It was revised in 2010, and a landmark revision was issued in 2012. It reported conclusions by public health researchers on how building designers, contractors, and operators take actions to avoid and fix problems that lead to persistent indoor dampness, and it also helped to limit the unnecessary pushing of the "panic button."

When humidity and moisture are not effectively controlled, persistent dampness can lead to material damage, corrosion, structure decay, and microbial growth, including mold. The position document stated that because heath authorities have established an association between damp buildings and the increased potential for adverse health effects, all who can act should act to avoid and fix problems that lead

Lewis G. Harriman III

to persistent dampness. This represented a major change from previous ASHRAE positions.

Lewis G. Harriman III, the chair of the committee, wrote in *ASHRAE Journal* that ASHRAE members had accused previous ASHRAE positions on mold as being unhelpfully vague. "The new document describes observations of real-world investigations," Harriman wrote. "One of the key messages is that the microbial growth and other moisture problems are rarely caused by a single action taken by a single person. More commonly, the big problems occur when several less than prudent decisions are made by different professionals that affect the same building."

Small amounts of wetting and drying in buildings and in HVAC systems are normal and represent no long risk for durability, increased energy consumption, or mold growth, the article concluded. "The committee believed that too often, building occupants, building professionals and their attorneys have hit the panic button when things get wet or when small amounts of mold are found in buildings," Harriman wrote. "ASHRAE should help building professionals find the off switch for needless panic about occasional coffee spills on carpets or mold on a grimy layer of a dirty bathtub."

The position document noted that in buildings shown to have health risk, three problems are often present at the same time:

1. moldy or earthy odors,
2. mold growth visible to the unaided eye, and
3. visually apparent evidence of water damage (stains, buckled wall covering, crumbling wall board, sagging ceiling tiles, etc.) and/or enough moisture in materials or furnishings to be perceptible to the touch as being damp

Because this three-part trigger for concern is not useful to help avoid problems before there is a significant increase in risk, the position document recommended new ASHRAE research to develop a practical and repeatable inspection and measurement protocol for buildings suspected of being "too damp."

IAQ APPLICATIONS

2012 ASHRAE Position Document

Mold and Dampness

By Lew Harriman, Fellow ASHRAE

The ASHRAE Board of Directors approved in June a major revision to the Society's position document "Limiting Indoor Mold and Dampness in Buildings." In summary, ASHRAE takes the positions that:

1. When humidity and moisture are not effectively controlled, persistent dampness can lead to material damage, corrosion, structural decay and microbial growth, including mold. Cognizant health authorities have established an association between damp buildings and the increased potential for adverse health effects. ASHRAE believes that the potential for these problems can and should be reduced by limiting the buildup of indoor moisture through the decisions and actions taken by designers, contractors, owners and occupants of buildings.

2. Small amounts of wetting and drying in buildings and in HVAC systems are normal and represent no long-term risk for durability, increased energy consumption or mold growth. Occasional wetting is not usually a problem provided that wetting is followed promptly by drying. Problems occur when the dampness becomes persistent. To limit the potential for problems, professionals and the general public should be aware there are risks associated with prolonged dampness and should take action to prevent and correct such conditions.

3. Currently, no quantitative, health-based exposure guideline or thresholds can be recommended for acceptable levels of contamination by microorganisms. While associations between persistent dampness and adverse health effects have been observed, relationships between persistent dampness, microbial exposure and health effects cannot be quantified precisely at this time. In light of this information, ASHRAE believes the most effective course is to limit the potential for microbial growth indoors by reducing the causes of persistent dampness.

Changes in ASHRAE Positions

Observant readers will note that ASHRAE's first position recognizes the association between damp buildings and the potential for adverse health effects. This recognition by ASHRAE is a major change, and one that did not occur without considerable debate.

ASHRAE is not a health authority. But cognizant health authorities have recognized health risks associated with building dampness. And building dampness can be affected by decisions made by building professionals. Therefore, the revised position document notes the association between dampness and health effects, to alert our members, our fellow professionals and those who make public policy. According to public health researchers, the risk is real. Therefore, ASHRAE takes the position that all those who *can* take action *should* take action to avoid and fix problems that lead to persistent indoor dampness.

At the same time, the second position reflects the belief held by most of our committee members that too often, building occupants, building professionals and their attorneys have "hit the panic button" when things get wet, or when small amounts of mold are found in buildings. Committee members believed ASHRAE should help building professionals "find the off switch" for needless panic about occasional coffee spills on carpets or mold on the grimy layer of a dirty bathtub.

The third position alerts the professions and the public that ASHRAE has not been able to find measurements that reliably quantify the relationships between dampness, microbial growth and increased heath risk. Reliable and achievable measurements of risk, the committee firmly believed, are urgent needs. More about this need later. But until that relationship is known and quantifiable, all those who *can* take action *should* take action to eliminate any causes of persistent dampness.

Risk Factors

The 2012 position document is quite lengthy. It describes both the positions taken by the Society and the reasons for those positions in a total of 11 pages of text. The revision includes 40 references that support statements made in the document.

Many of our committee members believed that often, the Society's past positions on mold have been unhelpfully vague and indirect, or so general as to be obvious. For example, suggestions regarding HVAC and building design that end with "...factors that should be considered..." are especially annoying and counterproductive. Such statements warn the reader of a decision with important consequences, yet these words fail to provide either the dimension of the potential problem or useful guidance with which to "consider" the factors. One needs to know "...considered with respect to what metrics?" and "...considered with respect to what consequences or what mitigation strategies?"

Therefore, the current document is longer than in the past, because most members of the committee believed we needed to describe observations from the real world of field investigations to support the Society's positions. The document includes separate sections to help each different professional group as well as sections for policy makers, occupants and homeowners.

One of the key messages of the document is that microbial growth and other moisture problems are rarely caused by a single action taken by a single person. More commonly, the big problems occur when several less-than-prudent decisions made by different professionals affect the same building.

Increased Health Risks

The position document notes that public health investigations by cognizant authorities have found that in buildings shown to have an increased health risk, three problems are often present *at the same time*:

1. Moldy or "earthy" odors;
2. Mold growth visible to the unaided eye; and
3. Visually apparent evidence of water damage (stains, buckled wall covering, crumbling wall board, sagging ceiling tiles, etc) and/or enough moisture in materials or furnishings to be perceptible to the touch as being damp.

This not to say that these are the only circumstances where increased health risks have been found. Nor does this observation mean that increased health risks have been found in every building where these three factors are present.

But to most of the members of our committee, it seemed useful to provide this observation to the membership and to the public to serve as a warning of increased risk. None of those three conditions is desirable or useful. And when they all occur simultaneously, it should be a cause for concern and action. The attachment to the position document provides more than 60 observations that can help professionals understand and fix such problems.

Yet this three-part trigger for concern is not useful to help avoid problems *before* there is a significant increase in risk. So the position document strongly recommends new ASHRAE research to develop a practical and repeatable inspection and measurement protocol for buildings suspected of being "too damp."

Inspectable Definition for Buildings

ASHRAE is an engineering society. As technical professionals, we measure important variables in order to design, build and operate buildings that achieve desirable and repeatable results. Most of us are uncomfortable with warnings that our actions can affect health risk without any guidance from health authorities that would allow us to reliably measure and reduce that risk.

This strong discomfort led to the document's principal recommendation: that the building professions need a quantitative definition of a building that is dry enough to limit health risks, along with an inspection and measurement protocol that is relevant, repeatable and economical enough for everyday use by building investigators and building managers. ASHRAE alone does not have the public heath expertise necessary for such health-coupled research. But our Society's technical committees can and must be involved in such research to ensure the practicality, both economic and physical, of the eventual inspection protocol.

Indoor mold: a cause for concern and action, but not panic.

Step in the Right Direction

Until that research is funded and completed, and the protocol exists, the National Institute of Occupational Safety and Health (NIOSH), one of the U.S. Centers for Disease Control and Prevention, has offered to share the forms they have used in the past to assess moisture and mold in schools and other buildings during their workplace health hazard evaluations.

The completed forms—one per room—provide the foundation for a simple yet quantitative inspection. In past NIOSH investigations, higher numbers have been correlated with increased risk. Software is also in development to assist field inspection by recording room observations on portable devices instead of on the manual forms. (Progress on this project is posted regularly at www.cdc.gov/niosh/topics/indoorenv/mold.html.)

Note that these numbers still indicate *relative* risk. An exact correlation has not been established yet between specific values and the percentage increase in health risk those values represent. But still, this protocol is a big step in the right direction. As more building owners and investigators use this NIOSH protocol to assess relative risk, one can imagine that over time a more quantitative relationship will become apparent between health risks and easily observable symptoms of building dampness.

At that point perhaps the ASHRAE position document can be revised once again to more helpfully quantify exactly "how dry is dry enough" to avoid problems in buildings and their furnishings.

The 11-page document is available at www.ashrae.com/about-ashrae/position-documents.

Lew Harriman is a building science consultant and director of research at Mason-Grant Consulting in Portsmouth, N.H. He is chair of ASHRAE TC 1.12, Moisture Management in Buildings) and served as chair of the Document Revision Committee for the 2012 ASHRAE Position Document "Limiting Indoor Mold and Dampness in Buildings." ■

132 ASHRAE Journal ashrae.org December 2012 | December 2012 ASHRAE Journal 133

A Global Alliance for IEQ

When William P. Bahnfleth became ASHRAE President in 2013, he called for ASHRAE members to restore a proper emphasis on indoor environmental quality (IEQ) and become leaders again for the good of humanity. "We can be a leader again by doing what ASHRAE does best: connecting science to practice," he said. "We can take the results of research and use them to create real change applications. We can educate and equip the industry in the principles and practice of indoor environmental quality as we have done in others."

Bahnfleth sought to fulfill that objective by creating a global alliance among the engineering and scientific groups that shared common IEQ interests. He appointed an ASHRAE ad hoc committee chaired by Bjarne W. Olesen, ASHRAE treasurer and indoor environment researcher, to take on the task of exploring ways in which industry groups could work together to create a global source for information, guidance, and knowledge on IEQ.

William P. Bahnfleth, 2013–2014 ASHRAE President

In June 2014, during ASHRAE's 2014 Annual Conference in Seattle, a memorandum of understanding to create the alliance was agreed to by ASHRAE, Air & Waste Management Association (A&WMA), Indoor Air Quality Association (IAQA), American Industrial Hygiene Association (AIHA), Air Infiltration and Ventilation Centre (AIVC), and REHVA. The alliance was incorporated in 2019 with the Italian association AiCARR and the Indian association ISHRAE also joining as founding members.

The IEQ Global Alliance began its life committed to promote education, research, and knowledge exchange at a global scale; to develop standards, codes, and guidelines; and to encourage advocacy among the general public in indoor environments around the world.

"An important attribute of IEQ-GA is that it is a non-industrial alliance among societies representing members that promote IEQ," said Olsen at IEQ-GA's launching. "The intent of IEQ-GA is to work with all partners of the value chain for indoor environmental quality including building research, comfort and health research, building design, installation, commissioning, operation and occupant behavior."

Bahnfleth noted that ASHRAE is on a long road when it comes to IAQ. "The first ASHRAE IAQ conference in 1986 was held to review the latest research in indoor air pollution and provide missing current data for Standard 62 with the understanding that the indoor environment should minimize any impact on health and should be free of any impact on comfort, and control should minimize the use of energy. Implicit in this statement is the belief that the performance measures needed to realize this goal could be defined in practical terms," he said, speaking at ASHRAE's 18th IAQ Conference in 2016. "After three decades we have come back to the point where we began, recognizing the need to deal with indoor environmental impacts and energy in an integrated way. It's an important step in the right direction."

Founding member representatives (from left) Atze Boerstra, Luca Alberto Piterá, Bjarne Olesen, Darryl K. Boyce, Don Weeks, and Peter Wouters receive IEQ-GA's certificate of incorporation.

Chapter 10

People Pollution

"Unfortunately, the inter-relationship among the social costs, ecological costs, occupational health costs and energy costs is extremely complex. The champions of each of these areas scream out in righteous indignation for their cause. The biggest headlines are generally awarded to the party who most flagrantly abuses the statistics. The real problems are much less dramatic and much more challenging. The excruciatingly difficult tradeoffs must be carefully examined."

Walter F. Spiegel
1973

As ASHRAE celebrated the 75th anniversary of its founding in 1969, members considered the effect of pollution as one of the driving forces which would shape the Society as it approached the twenty-first century. Presidential Member William L. McGrath termed it "people pollution." "Air pollution, water pollution, noise pollution, thermal pollution and waste pollution...Most of these areas either do relate or could well relate to the broad scope of technology embraced by engineers who are members of ASHRAE," said Mr. McGrath. He echoed U.S. President Richard M. Nixon, who in his 1969 inaugural address cited preservation of the environment as a national objective.

In was when Mr. Nixon was vice president that ASHRAE began sponsoring sessions on air pollution. Future ASHRAE President James W. May, said in 1956 that development and installation of dust control equipment by the ASHVE membership would undoubtedly be important in improving the outdoor environment.

By 1969, the ASHRAE leadership envisioned a larger role for the Society as the world struggled with answers to "people pollution." One of those leaders was Fellow ASHRAE Paul Reece Achenbach.

William L. McGrath
"People pollution."

In a symposium on the urban environment, he cited ASHRAE's heritage of interdisciplinary involvement in challenging the Society to broaden its perspective. "Enter the 1970s with a research effort and a mission that is responsible to the national need for environmental control," he said. Develop a sound foundation of knowledge on the relation of outdoor and indoor air pollution; examine the social, psychological and comfort effects of spatial allocation in cities and buildings; study the effects of urban development on the microclimates

The Metropolitan Transit Authority's 63rd Street Tunnel in New York City, under construction in 1969, was the subject of an ASHRAE symposium "Your Stake in the Urban Environment." It was a time when ASHRAE members were urged to expand their discipline to impact improvement of social and natural environments as well as the indoor environment.

ASHRAE Executive Director Andrew T. Boggs meeting President Richard M. Nixon. Mr. Nixon had called on the nation to preserve the environment.

of cities; analyze urban design to improve the purging of pollutants from cities; discover methods to minimize thermal pollution of air and water resources; and examine the effectiveness and economy of enclosing cities, he urged.

ASHRAE formed new Task Groups in the 1960s: Air Pollution; Energy Requirements for Buildings; Urban Environment; and Human Factors in Air-Conditioned Buildings.

In 1972, ASHRAE President Stanley F. Gilman cited United Nations' studies which projected that world population would reach seven billion by the year 2000. "It is perfectly obvious that just generating more energy and further depleting our resources is

not the long range answer....Energy conservation is a brand new field before us," he said. Dr. Gilman appointed a Task Group on Energy Conservation to lay the groundwork for a chapter on energy conservation principles and practices in the ASHRAE Handbook. The chapter on owning and operating costs was to be expanded to include a thorough treatment of building life-cycle costs.

Stanley F. Gilman
"Energy conservation is a brand new field before us."

In this time before energy shortages, restrictions and regulations, ASHRAE Fellow Alwin B. Newton would write, "Throughout all of our ASHRAE research, there seems to be increasing awareness of the need not only to improve the human, plant and animal environment, but also to minimize other environmental impacts of operating air-conditioning and refrigeration equipment. These are areas of greatest interest to our TG on Urban Environment as well as other TCs and TGs concerned with design of more efficient systems and their proper utilization. Activities of such

TCs as 3.7, Fuels & Combustion; 4.6, Owning & Operating Costs; 5.5, Air to Air Heat Recovery; 6.7, Solar Energy Utilization; and the TG on Energy Requirements for Heating and Cooling are all obvious examples of ASHRAE concern for better and more efficient systems."

In 1973, the Society amended its Bylaws to add, "To fulfill its role, the Society shall assume its responsibility for the effect of its technology on the environment and natural resources to protect the welfare of posterity."

Then the oil stopped flowing.

The Energy Crisis

The first disruption in the supply of energy resources elicited from ASHRAE a call to increase its visibility among government officials, business leaders, and the public. The Society had much to accomplish.

But from an engineering perspective, ASHRAE moved swiftly and effectively. It initiated work on a standard governments could use for energy conservation in new building design. Its publications and meeting programs were filled to the brim with studies, reports and case histories on how to save energy. Soon ASHRAE would move beyond simple solutions, and it would focus attention on a larger aspect of the energy issue: Environmental warming.

Mr. Newton in 1974 warned that heat was the ultimate pollutant. "The vast amount of energy utilized in large cities was already resulting in an increase in ambient temperature," Mr. Newton said. "In effect, we are creating heat islands, and the control of inside conditions is likely to produce even more heat. The ultimate disaster may be gross thermal pollution."

At ASHRAE's 1974 Semi-Annual Meeting, Robert T. Jaskee predicted that the energy pinch may be blessing in disguise. "Hopefully, it will last long enough for technology to overcome the influence of traditional economics and the inability to evaluate

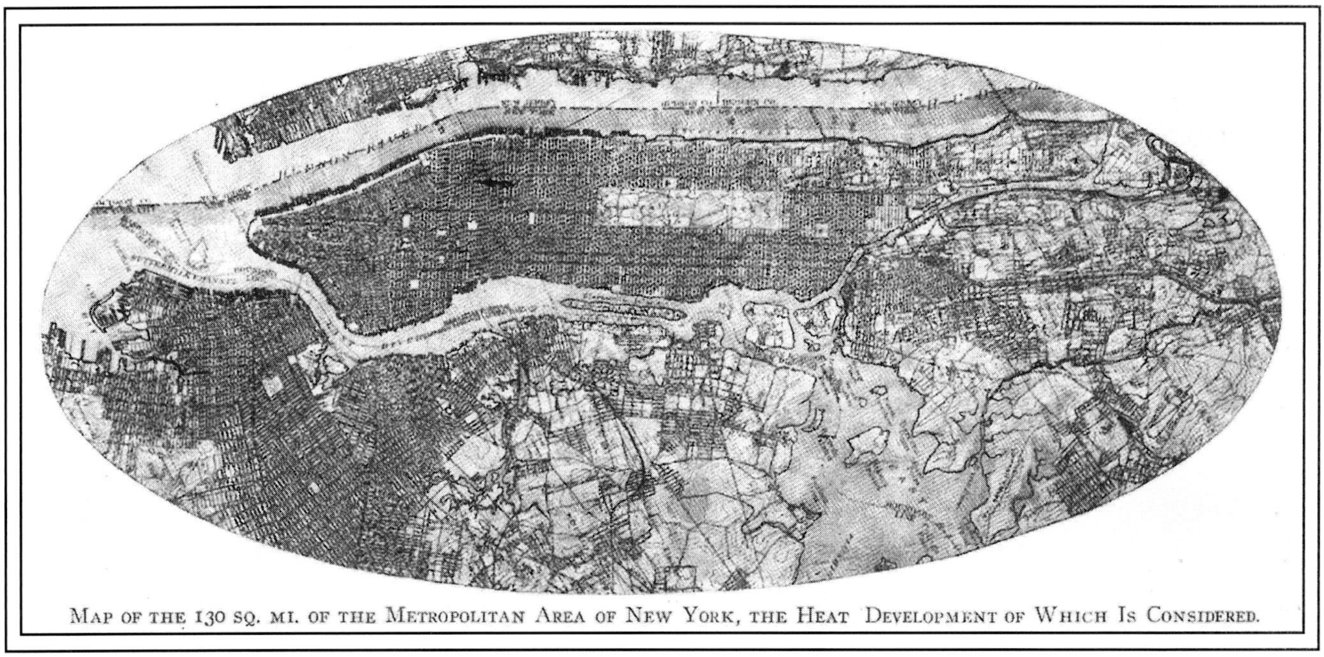

A heat-developed map of New York City produced from a set of statistics released in 1911 and published in ASHVE *Transactions,* which documented that in 1900 New York City had a total equivalent coal consumption of 18,950,000 tons raising the atmospheric temperature 3 1/2° for a 1/2 mi. height and an area of 130 sq. miles.

Advertisement

ENERGY UTILIZATION AND THE DESIGN PROFESSIONAL

An Approach to the Present
and Future Impact of the
Energy Crisis on the
Professional Engineer

This Special Bulletin contains the proceedings of a conference entitled "Energy Utilization and the Design Professional," which was held in Atlanta, Georgia, March 3-6, 1974, and was co-sponsored by Professional Engineers in Private Practice (PEPP), a division of the National Society of Professional Engineers (NSPE), and by the American Society of Heating, Refrigerating and Air-Conditioning Engineers, Inc. (ASHRAE).

Covering topics from solar energy utilization to the economic forecast of the construction industry, this Special Bulletin offers twenty-one perspectives on how the present crisis is affecting **and will continue to affect** the professional engineer.

The authors, each closely involved with some facet of the current problem, represent a variety of private and public interests: the result is an objective overview of the professional engineer's potential influence on the energy crisis, from both an applications and a legislative viewpoint.

Featured are discussions on electric, solar, geothermal, nuclear, and solid waste power sources; building codes at the Federal, state, and local levels; and environmental and economic ramifications, as seen by the industry.

Now available, this Bulletin may be purchased from ASHRAE Publications Sales Dept., 345 East 47th Street, New York, N.Y. 10017, at a cost of $6.00, plus $1.00 for postage and handling. Full remittance in U.S. funds must accompany orders.

resources beyond the short-term worth accorded them by a fluid market system."

Mr. Jaskee based his analysis on conclusions drawn by the chief economist of the U.S. Chamber of Commerce Carl H. Madden. Mr. Madden concluded we were on the threshold of a great new energy age, an age which will rely on sophisticated technology to manage and distribute resources on the basis of applied knowledge rather than politics. "A great threat, besides war, to machine civilization is to be buried by its own problems. We are now dealing with vast, interlocking and complex systems, seeing the world as a whole; water systems, urban systems; health delivery systems; and the like. They give us more tools to cope with our problems; what we need now is determination to do so."

To some, solar heating and cooling was the answer. "One of the nice things about solar energy is the absence of thermal pollution," said Mr. Newton. Among other champions of the "non-polluting" energy source during the 1960s and early '70s were ASHRAE members John Yellott, J.L. Threlkeld, George Lof and Richard Jordan.

Ozone Depletion

As was typical of ASHRAE meetings during the 1970s, energy-related topics dominated the technical program at the 1976 Winter Meeting in Dallas, Texas. Dr. Jerold Jones spoke about residential energy requirements and opportunities for conservation. Clark Pennington and Clayton Morrison told about improved fenestration for energy savings. Eugene Drucker described solar assisted heat pump systems. Richard J. Pearson spoke about energy recovery for hospitals and schools. James E. Woods addressed the impact of ASHRAE Ventilation Standard 62-73 on energy use. And at 9:00 a.m. on Tuesday, February 3, Stewart L. Segerstrom opened an ASHRAE/ARI seminar on fluorocarbon/ozone impact on air conditioning and refrigeration.

In 1974, the ozone depletion hypothesis had first been published. Scientists began theorizing that the upward diffusion of chlorofluorocarbons into the stratosphere could initiate a sequence of reactions with ozone, resulting in the depletion of the ozone layer. Mr. Segerstrom asked the audience, "What are our possible alternatives to present fluorocarbon refrigerants? We need to answer this challenge with facts, not emotions."

ASHRAE Position Statements

The feature section of the August 1976 *ASHRAE Journal* reported on the growing debate in a series of articles entitled "ASHRAE and the Ozone/Fluorocarbon Issue." Fellow ASHRAE Hans O. Spauschus emphasized these points in his introduction:

- All refrigerant and air-conditioning products operating on the vapor compression principle have been designed to function with specified working fluids which are carefully selected for optimum performance based on their engineering properties and safety considerations.
- Unavailability of any of the common halocarbon refrigerants will require new hardware designs, major modifications, manufacturing facilities and policy decisions regarding the servicing and maintenance of installed equipment using banned refrigerants.

Said the ASHRAE Board of Directors on February 5, 1976, in its first position statement issued on the subject, "Prior to any legislation of the ozone-fluorocarbon issue, a thorough technology assessment be required, including a constructive dialogue between Government and industry, thereby assuring that any changes deemed necessary are achievable without undue harmful effects."

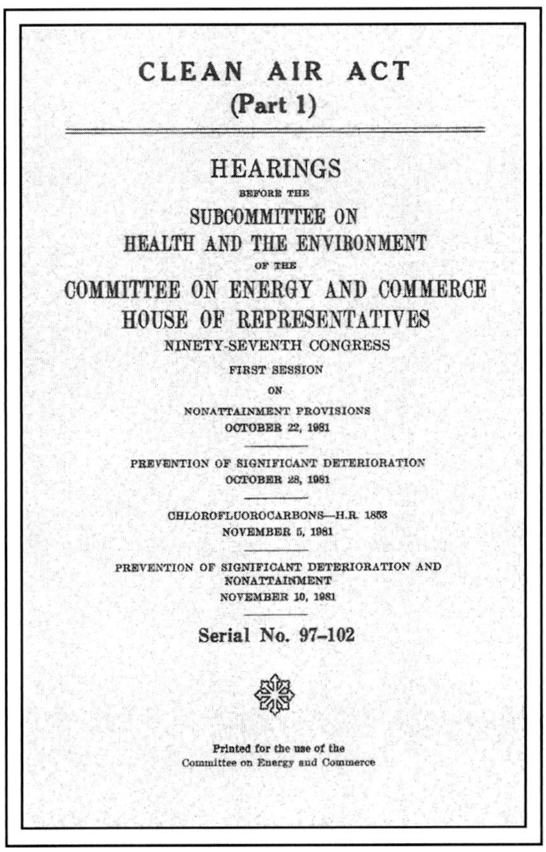

CLEAN AIR ACT
(Part 1)

HEARINGS
BEFORE THE
SUBCOMMITTEE ON
HEALTH AND THE ENVIRONMENT
OF THE
COMMITTEE ON ENERGY AND COMMERCE
HOUSE OF REPRESENTATIVES
NINETY-SEVENTH CONGRESS
FIRST SESSION
ON
NONATTAINMENT PROVISIONS
OCTOBER 22, 1981

PREVENTION OF SIGNIFICANT DETERIORATION
OCTOBER 28, 1981

CHLOROFLUOROCARBONS—H.R. 1853
NOVEMBER 5, 1981

PREVENTION OF SIGNIFICANT DETERIORATION AND NONATTAINMENT
NOVEMBER 10, 1981

Serial No. 97–102

Printed for the use of the
Committee on Energy and Commerce

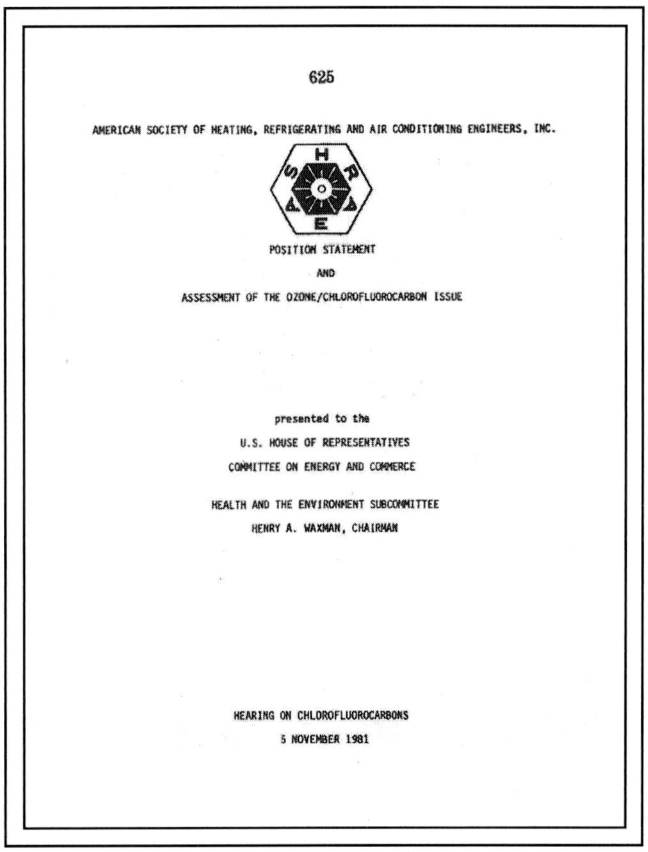

625

AMERICAN SOCIETY OF HEATING, REFRIGERATING AND AIR CONDITIONING ENGINEERS, INC.

POSITION STATEMENT
AND
ASSESSMENT OF THE OZONE/CHLOROFLUOROCARBON ISSUE

presented to the
U.S. HOUSE OF REPRESENTATIVES
COMMITTEE ON ENERGY AND COMMERCE

HEALTH AND THE ENVIRONMENT SUBCOMMITTEE
HENRY A. WAXMAN, CHAIRMAN

HEARING ON CHLOROFLUOROCARBONS
5 NOVEMBER 1981

In 1982 ASHRAE provided testimony before the U.S. House of Representatives on assessment of the ozone/chlorofluorocarbon issue. At the time, ASHRAE stated that Federal regulations were not warranted until further research was conducted to validate the depletion theory and until a plan to address the issue globally was in place.

Progress is steady on finding alternatives to CFCs, but the meter is running

by Thomas A. Mahoney

ASHRAE approves CFC research

At the 1989 winter meeting of the ... the impact of chlorofluorocarbons on the ozone layer.

According to Dr. Wilber F.

CFC Legislation "Unstoppable" Says ASHRAE's Cox

The momentum for phasing out CFC's is "almost out of control" on the state and local level, according to ASHRAE legislative affairs aide J.E. Cox. Cox noted at an association meeting in Atlanta (GA) in February that 102 CFC-related bills have been introduced in 21 states, and at least 27 local bills to control CFC's have been proposed. States that have been most active in developing CFC control legislation include those in the Northeast, Upper Midwest, and Pacific Coast. The international Montreal Protocol is expected to be amended at a London meeting in June, probably resulting in a call for total CFC phaseout by 2000, says Cox.

ASHRAE warns of bans on CFC compounds

Refrigerants widely used in air-conditioning systems are suspected of breaking down the earth's ozone layer

The issue of reducing chlorofluorocarbons (CFCs) to help preserve earth's ozone layer was one of the main subjects addressed at the annual meeting of the American Society of Heating, Refrigerating and Air-Conditioning Engineers (ASHRAE) June 27-July 1 in Nashville.

CFCs are used extensively in many ...

HCR NEWS SECTION

DU PONT AWARDED PATENT ON CFC BLENDS

ASHRAE TRIES TO BRING ORDER TO CFC RESEARCH

ASHRAE Publishes Guideline to Control CFC Emissions

ATLANTA—The American Society of Heating, Refrigerating and Air-Conditioning Engineers, Inc., has published a guideline for controlling the release of chlorofluorocarbons (CFCs) from air-conditioning and refrigerating systems. Scientists believe that CFCs ...

ASHRAE guidelines identify a possible approach to the design, testing and application or evaluation of a specific product, concept or practice. In writing the guideline, the project committee attempts to achieve consensus in resolving comments received during public review, but consensus is not mandatory as it is for an ASHRAE standard.

ASHRAE Approves Revised Position Paper On Environmental Effects Of CFC's

The American Society of Heating, Refrigerating & Air-Conditioning Engineers (ASHRAE) approved a revised position paper at its recent annual meeting dealing with the environmental effects of chlorofluorocarbons (CFS's), set priorities for CFC related projects and approved research for the investigation of refrigerants.

In the revised paper entitled, "Implications of the Environmental Effects of CFC's," the society endorsed wordwide consensus that unrestricted use of fully-halogenated CFC's provides an unacceptable risk for environmental damage. ASHRAE urged prudent steps in replacing CFC's, including:

- Phasing out of CFC refrigerants at the earliest possible date, with consideration of available alternatives
- Accepting hydrogen containing CFC's as an alternate to CFC's
- Adopting stringent practices to minimize emissions of all refrigerants and recover from equipment, as outlined in ASHRAE Guideline 3-1990
- Supporting developing countries' ... need to encourage worldwide compliance with the Montreal Protocol

CFC research projects will receive 2... the society's 1990-91 research budget of ... million. Among the projects approved ... ASHRAE was the study of the thermodynamic properties of refrigerants 125 and 141b at the Texas Engineering Experiment Station.

BUILDING SERVICES & ENVIRONMENTAL ENGINEER DECEMBER 1989

US REPORT

ASHRAE warns on c.f.c.s

Ozone Depletion Focus Of ASHRAE Slide Show

The impact of the Montreal Protocol on ozone-depleting substances and development of new refrigerants are covered in a new slide/sound presentation produced by the American Society of Heating, Refrigerating and Air-Conditioning Engineers (ASHRAE).

"Ozone Depletion and CFS—A Technological Challenge" reviews the environment consequences of using fully halogenated chlorofluorocarbons (CFCs). The slide show provides an overview of the CFC issue by discussing the restrictions of the Montreal Protocol, by identifying CFCs with low ozone depletion factors as alternatives to current refrigerants, by reviewing research now underway to find new, safer refrigerants, and by explaining how to minimize inadvertent CFC losses.

Since major changes in the air-conditioning and refrigeration industry can be expected in the next decade, the intent of the CFC show is to provide information and to review the ozone depletion issue in a format beneficial to those in the air-conditioning and refrigeration industry as well as the general public.

The 25-minute slide show consists of 79 slides, audio cassette, and script. "Ozone Depletion and CFCs — A Technological Challenge" is available for $65 (ASHRAE member price, $44). To order, send payment in U.S. funds to ASHRAE Publication Sales, 1791 Tullie Circle, N.E., Atlanta, Georgia 30329.

ASHRAE Urges Steps To Control CFC Use; Will Issue Guidelines

The American Society of Heating, Refrigerating and Air-Conditioning Engineers (ASHRAE) has urged that "prudent steps" be taken to control the worldwide growth of emissions of those chlorofluorocarbons (CFCs) considered to exert the most adverse effects on the environment.

A CFC position statement approved by the Atlanta-based association's board at its semi-annual meeting in January committed ASHRAE to do the following:

- Develop voluntary and workable guidelines to minimize inadvertent losses of CFCs during manufacture, installation, service and disposal of end products which utilize CFCs.
- Actively encourage research, including allocation of ASHRAE research funds, on CFC alternatives or alternative technologies, and on methods of CFC reclamation from CFC-using products

(Continued on page 52)

Colder future for refrigerants

The Montreal Protocol on substances that deplete the ozone layer is expected to be strengthened this year to call for a complete phaseout of CFCs such as R11 and R12 by the year 2000. The current requirement is for a 50% cut in use by 1998. Ozone friendlier substances such as HCFC-22, now exempt from the protocol, are also expected to be affected.

Participants to a roundtable discussion sponsored by the American Society of Heating, Refrigerating & Air Conditioning Engineers and the Air-Conditioning & Refrigeration Institute believe that calls for the ...

ASHRAE president David Butler is concerned that changes to the Montreal Protocol will shorten the life of existing equipment.

David Didion of the National Institute of Standards & Technology

Position on CFCs Approved

At its recent annual meeting in St Louis MO, the American Society of Heating, Refrigerating and Air-Conditioning Engineers Inc (ASHRAE) approved a revised position paper on environmental effects of chlorofluorocarbons (CFCs), set priorities for CFC-related projects, and approved research for the investigation of refrigerants.

The group also approved other research totaling more than $500,000, increased international standard activity, and installed new officers.

In a revised position paper entitled "Implications of the Environmental Effects of CFCs," the society endorsed the worldwide consensus that unrestricted use of fully halogenated CFCs poses an unacceptable risk of environmental damage. ASHRAE urged prudent steps in replacing CFCs, including:

—Phasing out CFC refrigerants at the earliest possible date, with consideration for available alternatives.

—Accepting hydrogen-containing CFCs as an alternative to CFCs.

—Adopting stringent practices to minimize emissions of all refrigerants and recover them from equipment.

CFC research projects will receive 20% of the society's 1990-91 research budget of $1.4 million. Among the projects ASHRAE approved at the meeting was one to study the thermodynamic properties of refrigerants 125 and 141b at the Texas Engineering Experiment Station.

Trailer/Body Builders

ASHRAE Slide Show Focuses on Montreal Protocol, Ozone Depletion

Atlanta—The impact of the Montreal Protocol on ozone-depleting substances and development of new refrigerants are the subject of a new slide/-sound presentation produced by the American Society of Heating, Refrigerating and Air-Conditioning Engineers (ASHRAE).

Ozone Depletion and CFCs—A Technological Challenge reviews the environment ...

... the general public.

The 25-minute slide show consists of 79 slides, audio cassette, and script. *Ozone Depletion and CFCs—A Technological Challenge* is available to ASHRAE members for $44, and to nonmembers for $65.

To order, send payment to ASHRAE Publication Sales, 1791 Tullie Circle, N.E., Atlanta, GA 30329. VISA, Mastercard, and American Express card orders, (404) 636-8400 or by mail. Include credit card number and expiration date.

Encouraging Progress in CFC Phaseout

At the ASHRAE (American Society of Heating, Refrigeration and Air Conditioning Engineers) meeting in Chicago recently, Du Pont made a series of announcements in connection with the worldwide effort to reduce the release of fully halogenated chlorofluorocarbons (CFCs). Based on strong evidence that CFCs in the atmosphere are a factor in the depletion of stratospheric ozone, the company had announced plans earlier to end production of the compounds by the turn of the century at the latest.

The Chicago announcements were: 1) availability of refrigerant blend candidates ... announcement, can help provide immediate reduction in CFC emissions in the transition period until replacements can be put into full use. Du Pont's program, which was developed for internal use, is being made available in the interest of achieving immediate reductions. The program focuses on three main areas: emission reduction, on-site recovery and bulk recycling. Beginning this spring a training program that will focus on locating and eliminating emission sources in refrigeration machines will be available.

To promote on-site recovery, Du Pont will work with refrigeration users and analysis laboratories to determine levels of contamination. The analyses will help the user decide between reuse as is or cleanup to return to acceptable specifications. The company will also introduce a bulk recycling service to Freon customers with quantities of 10,000 pounds or more of CFCs 11, 12 or 113. The bulk recycling program will be monitored to assess feasibility of expanding the service to include smaller quantity users.

The Montreal Protocol

A Briefing Book

Alliance For Responsible CFC Policy
December 1987

But it was not until 1985, when scientists issued dramatic reports of seasonal thinning of the ozone layer over the Antarctic region, that public attention—and proposed governmental action—became focused on the air-conditioning and refrigeration industry. The "Arctic Hole" findings, as they came to be known, prompted ASHRAE to issue a second position statement and position paper in 1987 and 1988, respectively. In them, ASHRAE pledged support of the United Nations Environment Programme of September 1987 (known as the Montreal Protocol) as the basis for controlling world-wide CFC emissions.

> Ozone Agreement Is Hailed As a First Step in Cooperation
>
> The New York Times, May 5, 1987

The CFC Roundtable

In 1988, ASHRAE, along with the Air-Conditioning and Refrigeration Institute, began its series of CFC Roundtables for the refrigeration and

air conditioning industry. Some fifty persons representing 23 associations and refrigerant suppliers attended the first session, where much of the discussion focused on response to the Montreal Protocol and its mandates for international action and CFC phase-out schedules.

"We are in a position to manage our destiny," said ASHRAE 1987-88 President H.E. "Barney" Bur-

CFC Roundtable attended by some 50 persons representing various associations and companies.

CFC Roundtable Co-Chairmen H.E. Burroughs (right) and Richard W. Snyder, chairman of ARI.

Flagg speaking
At the 1989 ASHRAE-ARICFC Roundtable, ASHRAE President Louis F. Flagg reported, "Currently, ASHRAE is funding seven CFC research projects. Another seventeen are under consideration.

roughs. "The industry agrees on where it is now and where it needs to go. The issue discussed at the roundtable was what is necessary to allow for a smooth transition and how that is best managed so the customer and the public are best served." Mr. Burroughs reported widespread support for the provisions of the Montreal Protocol among participants.

"An important accomplishment of the Roundtable was to bring the air-conditioning and refrigerating industry together. Today, we not only recognize the need to communicate with each other, we are exploring ways to make technological information more widely available, more rapidly available and available through joint educational programs.

ASHRAE at 100: Ozone Depletion Activities

The Society's activities related to the ozone depletion issue have four dimensions: (1) policy; (2) guidelines and standards; (3) research; and (4) technology transfer.

ASHRAE has prepared several position statements and papers on the relationship of air conditioning and refrigeration to the ozone depletion theory. The most current was approved by the Board of Directors on July 2, 1992. It calls for a careful evaluation of the issue and an orderly transition in replaced substances scheduled for phase out.

ASHRAE Guideline 3 for reducing emissions of fully halogenated chlorofluorocarbon refrigerants addresses various aspects of refrigerant use from the design of products to installation and service. ASHRAE Standard 34 "Number Designation and Safety Classification of Refrigerants" and Standard 15 "Safety Code for Mechanical Refrigeration" are under continuous review and are updated as replacement refrigerants are introduced to the marketplace.

In research, ASHRAE is expending approximately 15% of its research budget to identify and characterize alternative refrigerants and to reduce emissions from refrigerants. In addition, ASHRAE spends 15% of its research budget on energy conservation projects.

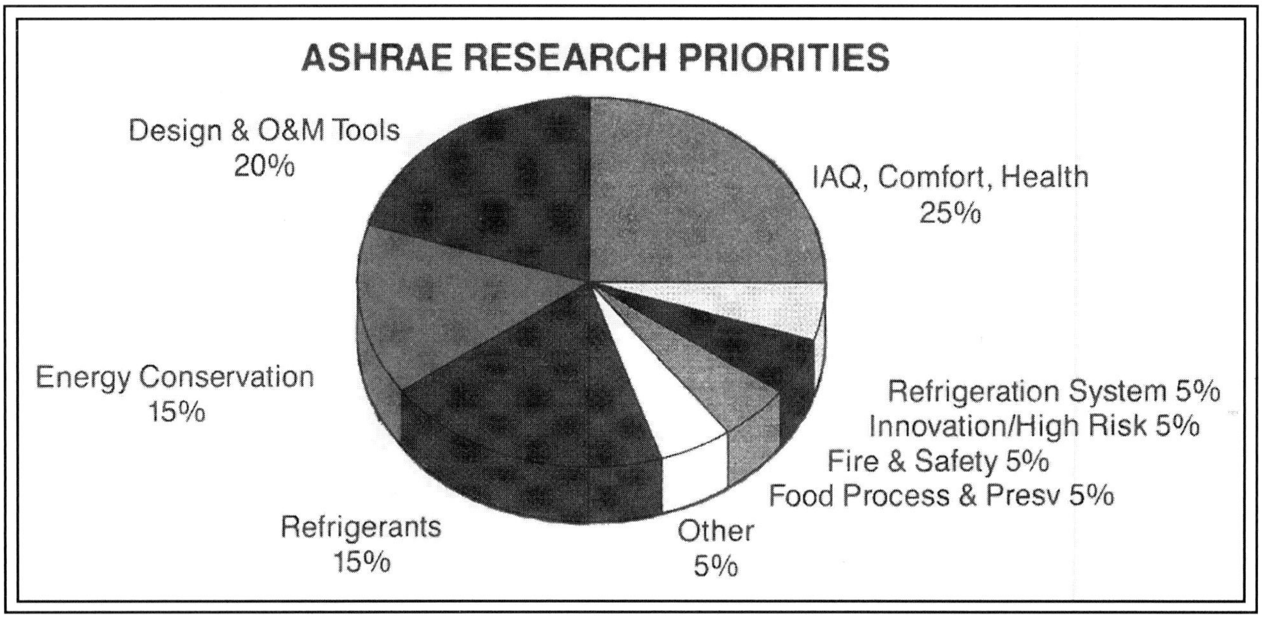

1994-95 Strategic Plan

It is in the area of technology transfer and education that ASHRAE may make its greatest contribution. Emerging technology, including results of ASHRAE sponsored research, is described in technical programs at the Society's semi-annual meetings and is made available in ASHRAE publications. In addition, the Society sponsors specialized conferences on alternative refrigerants.

Not Easy Being Green

When Donald E. Holte told fellow members his presidential theme for 1997–98 would be "The Greening of ASHRAE," what he said he heard was a resounding "NO." "Yes," Holte told them, "I am one of those. I am very concerned about what we are doing to our global environment."

Holte explained that being green requires a sustainable approach to designing and building buildings and managing our natural resources. By "green" or "sustainable" he meant that we must design and build buildings that do not deplete the earth's natural resources nor harm our global environment nor jeopardize the ability of future generations to meet their needs. Over the next year, almost all within ASHRAE were one of "them."

Donald E. Holte, 1997–1998 ASHRAE President

Holte authorized ASHRAE sponsorship of the Green Building Challenge, a two-year process culminating in 14 countries presenting examples of work in the field of green, sustainable buildings, and he added Presidential Activity to the Presidential Award of Excellence that rewarded chapters for organizing meetings on the impact of energy consumption on the global environment, meetings with the architectural community, and meetings on new technologies for a truly sustainable building.

A green path had been set to achieving building sustainability.

ASHRAE's Sustainability Road Map

In August 2005, ASHRAE President Lee Burgett appointed a Sustainability Roadmap Ad Hoc Committee. Burgett said, "The issue of sustainability is broad, and ASHRAE is deep and strong in some aspects such as energy conservation. The thrust is to identify new areas of involvement, including relationships with other organizations."

The committee began its work by examining the Society's Position Statement on Sustainability.

Cover of the first edition of *ASHRAE GreenGuide*, 2003. The book has been updated several times since the first edition.

Approved in June 2002, it pledged the Society's support of building sustainability to provide a safe, healthy, comfortable indoor environment while simultaneously limiting the impact on the earth's natural resources. ASHRAE broadened standards, guidelines, and the ASHRAE Handbook to consider the wide range of factors that influence building performance. ASHRAE partnered with U.S. Green Building Council (USGBC), The American Institute of Architects (AIA), and Building Owners and Managers Association (BOMA). And ASHRAE made educational programs available on lighting, building envelope, and other disciplines that interacted with HVAC design.

Providing further thrust to the initiative, ASHRAE completed a broad-based market research study of members and potential members in 2005. The primary objective was to examine growth opportunities and to identify how ASHRAE can make its business practices more customer and member focused. The research indicated strong desire among members and nonmembers of all ages for products and services on green-building topics. Based on this opportunity, the Board of Directors endorsed "Engineering for Sustainability" as a Society priority.

ASHRAE Engineering for Sustainability

In January 2006, the ASHRAE Sustainability Roadmap was approved. "The intent of this roadmap is to guide ASHRAE to achievement of a leadership position in sustainability," said Ron Jarnagin, who chaired the ad hoc. "The roadmap will stimulate and guide the process of doing things differently within ASHRAE. The result will be an ASHRAE, which by responding to its membership, better enables its members to make a profound impact on what it means to design, build and operate sustainable buildings. If implementation of this roadmap is successful, buildings employing sustainable technologies will be in greater demand, the critical need for contributions by ASHRAE members will be better understood, and the quality of life will be enhanced in the present and long into the future."

The road map called for ASHRAE to lead the march to give substance to the charge of "Engineering for Sustainability." Among its goals were for ASHRAE to conduct its own affairs in a sustainable manner, integrate building sustainability principles into all appropriate ASHRAE resources, partner with appropriate sustainability advocacy organizations, and develop programs related to sustainability to educate and inspire the current and next generation of members.

"We need to aggressively market ASHRAE's sustainability profile in the industry and 'walk the talk' by practicing what we preach," said Jarnagin.

Metrics: Keeping the Promise of a Sustainable Future

By the time Terry Townsend became president in 2006, ASHRAE had its sustainability roadmap and a new strategic plan, whose first stated direction was for ASHRAE to lead the advancement of sustainable building design and operations.

To keep the promise of a sustainable future that Townsend articulated, there was a challenge. "You can take three engineers and have them look at any facility," Townsend said, "and I guarantee you would

Terry Townsend, 2006–2007 ASHRAE President

have five opinions about how well a building performs relative to energy, water consumption, indoor air quality and comfort." Townsend called for ASHRAE to develop metrics to produce results that are repeatable, verifiable, and can be used anywhere on the planet.

Although many buildings claim to be "green," "low energy," or "high performance," it is rarely clear on what evidence or data these claims are based. If claims of high performance are to be credible, it is essential that a common set of measurements be used, and the results reported against meaningful and consistent benchmarks. Such protocols are also needed to give usable feedback to building designers and operators when measured performance does not match design intent and expectations.

Tools to Measure Sustainability

In 2010, ASHRAE published *Performance Measurement Protocols for Commercial Buildings*. This book provided a standardized set of protocols over a range of accuracies and costs that could be applied consistently to the assessment of building performance. The protocols identified what to measure, how to measure it, and how often it is to be measured for inclusion in the building's operation and maintenance plan. And reflecting the integrated design approach being championed by ASHRAE, the book presented protocols at three levels for each of six performance categories: energy, water, thermal comfort, indoor air quality, lighting, and acoustics.

In 2012 ASHRAE launched a voluntary building labeling program designed to rate commercial buildings according to their in-operation energy use. It also provided owners with suggested measures to improve energy efficiency. ASHRAE's Building Energy Quotient (Building EQ) assigned buildings an energy-use quotient based on completion of an In Operation assessment that included an energy audit. The audit served as the standard for determining a building's energy use and producing an actionable plan to improve performance.

What had not yet launched as a component of the program was an As Designed label that rates the building's potential energy use under standardized conditions—independent of the building's occupancy and usage.

Modeling a Sustainable World

During ASHRAE's first century, designers constructed physical models of projects to illustrate their concept of a building's form and appearance. By 2010, when Lynn G. Bellenger became ASHRAE's president, engineers had long had the tools to create a virtual model that can be completed more quickly and can be modified easily to consider options in size, shape, and appearance. But more than just a visual representation, these new models could simulate energy performance, assess daylighting options, and predict thermal comfort. And they were getting more sophisticated.

Lynn G. Bellenger, 2010–2011 ASHRAE President

Bellenger highlighted the role ASHRAE members play as leaders in sustainable design by focusing on the tools available to them. "In energy simulation, daylight analysis, computational fluid dynamics and building information modeling software, we have powerful modeling tools that enable us to create and refine our vision of a building: its appearance, systems, operation and performance," Bellenger said. "Those resources, used effectively in an integrated design process for new buildings and in analyzing retrofit opportunities in existing buildings, will help us guide building owners, architects, developers and contractors in building orientation, shading and shape and in selecting materials, windows, equipment and systems that optimize building performance."

To exploit the full capability of modeling tools, ASHRAE led the way toward transforming the design approach from a sequential process—where one discipline completes its work and hands off the design to the next—to a collaborative process—where all of the disciplines involved in the building design and construction work as a team from the beginning to evaluate options and optimize the design.

"Our biggest challenge is implementing integrated design in daily practice," Bellenger said. "The traditional approach, where the architect designs the building shape, orientation and envelope and then transmits the drawings to the mechanical and electrical engineers for their design, is a sequential approach that misses the rich opportunities for optimizing building performance through a collaborative approach throughout the design process. It is going to require a cultural shift in our industry to transform the design process, and it's a shift that must occur if we are going to reach our goal of net zero energy buildings."

In 2013, the As Designed label was added to Building EQ. It rated the building's potential energy use under standardized conditions—independent of the building's occupancy and usage.

Standard 189.1: The First Green Building Standard

A significant accomplishment driven by ASHRAE's Engineering for Sustainability charge occurred in 2006, when ASHRAE announced it would team with U.S. Green Building Council (USGBC) and Illuminating Engineering Society (IES) to develop a new standard for high-performance green buildings.

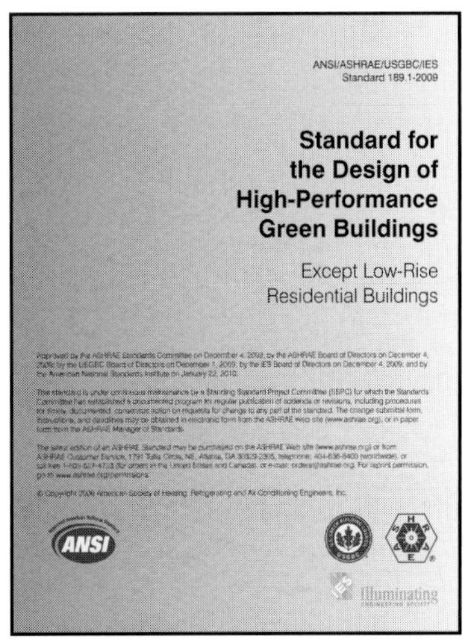

The first edition of ANSI/ASHRAE/USGBC/IES 189.1 was published in 2009.

Proposed Standard 189, *Standard for the Design of High-Performance Green Buildings Except Low-Rise Residential*

Buildings, aimed to provide minimum requirements for the design of sustainable buildings to balance environmental responsibility, resource efficiency, occupant comfort and well-being, and community sensitivity. Using USGBC's Leadership in Energy and Environmental Design® (LEED®) Green Building Rating System as a key resource, Standard 189P was intended to provide a baseline that would drive green building into the mainstream by making it a prerequisite under LEED. During development, it gained the designation of 189.1 to differentiate it from 189.2, for high-performance health-care facilities.

"The greening of building codes is the next natural progression in the evolution of standards for building design, allowing us to weigh system solutions against their impact on the environment, while ensuring that buildings meet the needs of those who work or live in them," said Kent Peterson, chair of the Standard Project Committee (SPC). The standard provided a "total building sustainability package" for those who design, build, and operate green buildings. From site location to energy use to recycling, the standard set the foundation for green buildings through its adoption into local codes.

What made ANSI/ASHRAE/USGBC/IES Standard 189.1 different from existing voluntary green building rating programs? Programs like USGBC's LEED had become the fundamental catalyst for how the industry designs and constructs buildings to be more sustainable. However, when striving to set the minimum mandatory requirements for green building projects, these systems contained few mandatory provisions that could be incorporated into green building codes. As an ANSI standard developed in model code language, Standard 189.1 set minimum requirements for high-performance buildings and was designed to complement the other voluntary rating systems.

The standard followed in the footsteps of earlier game changers, Standard 90 and California's Title 24, both of which were released in 1975. Prior to that, the United States had no requirements regarding energy-efficient buildings. But Standard 189.1 was more stringent than Standard 90.1-2007, and the standard's mandatory provisions included improved source contaminant control, ventilation rates per ANSI/ASHRAE Standard 62.1, elimination of air bypass around filters, and outdoor air delivery monitoring. The standard also had requirements for acoustical control, daylighting by toplighting, and isolation of the building from pollutants in soil.

"The far-reaching influence of the built environment necessitates action to reduce its impact," said Gordon Holness, ASHRAE president when the standard was published. "Provisions in the standard can reduce negative environmental impacts through high-performance building design, construction and operations practices.

189.1's Path to Becoming a Code

The International Code Council (ICC) introduced its *International Green Construction Code*® (IgCC®) in 2009 with its partners, AIA and ASTM International. The industry now had 189.1, a standard written in code language, and a model code, the IgCC, from which to choose.

Against that backdrop of construction choices, Dominic Sims, ICC Chief Executive Officer, and Jeff H. Littleton, ASHRAE Executive Vice President, signed an agreement in 2010 that would allow for the inclusion of 189.1 within the 2012 IgCC as an alter-

ASHRAE, ICC Link Standard 189.1, IgCC

In a deal nearly two years in the making, the International Code Council (ICC) and ASHRAE have signed the final agreement that outlines each organization's role in the development and maintenance of the new version of the International Green Construction Code (IgCC) sponsored by the American Institute of Architects (AIA), ASHRAE, ICC, the Illuminating Engineering Society (IES) and the U.S. Green Building Council (USGBC). The code, scheduled to be released in 2018, will be powered by ANSI/ASHRAE/ICC/IES/USGBC Standard 189.1, Standard for the Design of High-Performance, Green Buildings Except Low-Rise Residential Buildings developed using the American National Standards Institute (ANSI) approved ASHRAE consensus process. The joint Standing Standards Project Committee 189.1 (SSPC) will serve as the consensus body that will work to ensure the standard is consistent and coordinated with the ICC Family of Codes.

The ICC will be responsible for Chapter 1, Scope and Administration. For the 2018 IgCC, ICC will coordinate the technical provisions developed by ASHRAE with the provisions in Chapter 1 of the 2015 IgCC. As a result, the 2016 Group B Cycle will not include Chapter 1 of the IgCC for code changes.

Standard 189.1 provides total building sustainability guidance for designing, building, and operating high-performance green buildings.

With ASHRAE developing technical provisions, ICC's 2017 Group C cycle to develop the 2018 IgCC has been cancelled. Part of the development process for the 2018 technical provisions will include the SSPC review of the 2015 IgCC and consideration of content for inclusion in 189.1-2017 along with changes generated by the committee and proposals submitted by stakeholders. Following the completion of the 2018 IgCC, Chapter 1 of the IgCC will be developed by ICC using its consensus code development process.

"Our goal in this partnership all along has been to share resources to increase use of the IgCC and make it simpler for code officials, designers and contractors to build environmentally efficient structures that will lessen energy and water consumption and reduce the carbon footprint," said ICC Board President Guy Tomberlin, CBO. "We are now situated to do just that. We thank our partners, ICC Members and all who will contribute to the development of the IgCC powered by 189.1."

The Executive Steering Committee for the effort to align 189.1, the IgCC and LEED consists of representatives of ICC, ASHRAE, USGBC, AIA and IES, and the SSPC Chair.

"The full integration of Standard 189.1 to serve as the technical content of the IgCC will leverage ASHRAE's techni-

See IgCC Powered by 189, Page 2

cal expertise and increase the standard's influence on sustainable buildings," noted ASHRAE President David Underwood. "We look forward to continuing to engage a broad spectrum of stakeholders in development of Standard 189.1 following the ANSI consensus standards development process. The result will be a comprehensive compliance tool that can be used by jurisdictions worldwide that are committed to a more sustainable built environment."

The new publication also will align the Leadership in Energy & Environmental Design (LEED) rating system program to ensure a streamlined, effective set of regulatory and above-code options. The green building certification program recognizes best-in-class building strategies and practices. To receive LEED certification, building projects satisfy prerequisites and earn points to achieve different levels of certification.

"This joint initiative will forge the fundamental regulatory building blocks of green construction on which future green building leadership initiatives can grow," said Brendan Owens, chief of engineering at USGBC. "It takes courage to think differently and to commit to a new model, and for that we thank the leadership of the partner organizations behind the IgCC powered by 189.1."

SAFE & SUSTAINABLE BY THE BOOK

"IgCC Powered by 189.1" will provide the design and construction industry with the single most-effective way to deliver sustainable, resilient, high-performance buildings.

"Our combined membership, consisting of practicing design professionals, code officials, and the building industry representatives, supports the development of codes and standards that protect the health, safety and welfare of the public at large," said AIA CEO Robert Ivy, FAIA. "Through this significant agreement, both the AIA and the ICC agree to work more closely to achieve our common goals."

In 2010, ASHRAE and ICC joined forces by making 189.1 an alternative compliance path for the IgCC. The new agreement between ASHRAE and ICC furthers the effort these organizations initiated in 2010 by providing the market with a single code that is coordinated with the International Family of Codes.

"IES looks forward to continuing to partner with ASHRAE in developing technical content for Standard 189.1," said Rita Harrold, IES representative, "and to participating with the other organizations in this unique collaborative opportunity to satisfy the goals for the new version of IgCC."

The agreement creates a comprehensive framework for jurisdictions looking to implement and adopt green building regulations and codes. The unprecedented collaboration leverages the unique organizational expertise of the partners participating in this evolution of green building codes and brings AIA, ASHRAE, ICC, IES and USGBC into strategic and tactical alignment on the relationship between 189.1 and the IgCC.

Other organizations that support this vision and would like to join the effort are invited to contact ICC CEO Dominic Sims at DSims@IccSafe.org or ASHRAE executive vice president Jeff Littleton at JLittleton@ashrae.org.

native compliance. This enabled IgCC to provide multiple solutions to satisfy demand when design of high-performance buildings is required. And it exposed the IgCC network of 50 states and more than 22,000 local jurisdictions to the ASHRAE standard.

In 2015, the collaboration moved even closer. ICC and ASHRAE announced that an agreement had been reached for the new edition of the IgCC, scheduled to be released in 2018, that would be "Powered by ASHRAE Standard 189.1 for the Design of High-Performance Green Buildings." ASHRAE, ICC, ASHRAE, AIA, IES, and USGBC were now all partners on a single document.

The ICC would be responsible for IgCC's Chapter 1, Scope and Administration, so the green code would continue to be integrated into the ICC construction codes. ASHRAE would develop all the technical provisions of the IgCC. The collaboration created a comprehensive framework for jurisdictions looking to implement green building regulation or provide incentives for voluntary leadership programs like LEED. The 2018 IgCC would also now align with LEED to provide "a streamlined, effective set of regulatory and above-code options."

"The full integration of Standard 189.1 to serve as the technical content of the IgCC will leverage ASHRAE's technical expertise and increase the standard's influence on sustainable buildings," ASHRAE 2015–2016 President T. David Underwood said. "We look forward to continuing to engage a broad spectrum of stakeholders in development of Standard 189.1 following the ANSI consensus standards-development process. The result will be a comprehensive compliance tool that can be used by jurisdictions worldwide that are committed to a more sustainable built environment."

ICC Board President Guy Tomberlin said, "Our goal in this partnership all along has been to share resources to increase use of the IgCC and make it simpler for code officials, designers, and contractors to build environmentally efficient structures that will lessen energy and water consumption and reduce the carbon footprint. We are now situated to do just that."

From Ozone Layer to Climate Change

When ASHRAE celebrated its centennial in 1994–95, the chlorofluorocarbon (CFC) refrigerant phase-out was in full swing as required by the Montreal Pro-

Global Warming Expert Addresses Human Caused Climate Change

ATLANTA—Over the next century, significant climate change is inevitable, according to Jerry D. Mahlman, Ph.D., former director of the National Oceanographic and Atmospheric Administration (NOAA) Geophysical Fluid Dynamics Laboratory.

Dr. Jerry D. Mahlman discusses climate change during the President's Luncheon held at the Atlanta meeting.

As a result, society must decide whether to reduce the use of fossil fuels or adapt to substantial changes in Earth's climate to limit the severity of consequences.

Mahlman, who serves on national and international committees addressing global warming and climate change, presented a keynote address at the President's Luncheon at the Winter Meeting. He spoke on "Human-Caused Climate Warming: Implications for Practically Everything."

His presentation focused on how broadly the impacts of global warming will reach. He discussed the impacts and responses of global warming, lessons contained in observations of climate change over the past century and the expected climate change over the next several centuries.

Mahlman quoted a primary finding of the 1995 assessment by Intergovernmental Panel on Climate Change (IPCC) that "the balance of evidence suggests a discernible human influence on global climate." He noted that the revision approved just days before the Atlanta meeting for the next IPCC assessment states "there is new and stronger evidence that most of the warming of the last 50 years is due to human activities."

Potential impacts of climate change include decreases in agricultural productivity, changes in forest resources, increased flooding in coastal areas and along waterways, increased dry-area droughts, loss of water resources and unmanaged ecosystems. He showed plots suggesting changes to both average temperatures and more pronounced rises in heat indexes in mid-latitude locations, such as the United States. He also noted that some of these changes could foster increased occurrence of a number of diseases. Mahlman noted that many of the potential impacts remain poorly quantified but that significant impacts already are unavoidable.

2001

tocol on Substances that Deplete the Ozone Layer. In the 2000s, the hydrochlorofluorocarbon (HCFC) refrigerant phase-out began.

Both CFCs and HCFCs had contributed to depletion of the ozone layer. In 2017, atmospheric measurements showed that actions taken under the Montreal Protocol had led to decreases in the atmospheric abundance of controlled ozone-depleting substances (ODSs). Measurements also showed the size of the ozone hole was the smallest since its discovery in 1982.

But there was another problem: climate change.

Another group of substances, hydrofluorocarbons (HFCs), were introduced as non-ozone-depleting alternatives to support the timely phase-out of CFCs and HCFCs. While HFCs do not deplete the stratospheric ozone layer, some of them have high global warming potential (GWP), ranging from 12 to 14,000. In 2016, their emissions were growing at a rate of 8% per year. Uncontrolled growth in HFC emissions would challenge efforts to keep global temperature rise at or below 2°C this century.

During the 28th Meeting of the Parties to the Montreal Protocol in Kigali, Rwanda, in 2016, more than 170 countries agreed to amend the Protocol. The Kigali Amendment, entered into force on January 1, 2019, aims for the phase-down of HFCs by cutting their production and consumption.

ASHRAE had a new challenge.

ASHRAE's Refrigerant Position and UNEP

In 2018, ASHRAE published the latest version of its Position Document on Refrigerants and Their Responsible Use. ASHRAE stated its belief that selection of refrigerants and their systems must be based on a holistic analysis including energy efficiency and performance attributes, environmental impacts, employee and public safety, and economic considerations. A refrigerant should not be selected based on any one single factor such as GWP, operating pressure, flammability, etc. The wide range of HVAC&R applications and their requirements throughout the world necessitate a variety of refrigerants to meet these needs.

ASHRAE also voiced its support of ongoing efforts to develop new refrigerants and improve the application of existing refrigerants to meet these criteria. This included balancing the safety, energy efficiency, cost, and environmental impacts of refrigerants using a consistent and comprehensive methodology across all

UNEP Programme Officer Ayman Eltalouny and 2018-2019 ASHRAE President Sheila J. Hayter after signing the UNEP ASHRAE 2019-2020 Work Plan.

refrigerants and system types using benchmarks such as total life cycle climate performance (LCCP) or total equivalent warming impact (TEWI).

There were many other recommendations, such as calling for the introduction and management of onsite emission prevention measures including improved system tightness for leak prevention, good commissioning and installation practices, regular leak checking, monitoring, labeling, and record keeping. These elements can be incorporated as part of a comprehensive refrigerant management program.

The position document also called for ASHRAE to introduce procedures and guidelines working with the United Nations Environment Programme (UNEP) and other organizations and regulatory bodies to enable sustainable procurement policies that promote the deployment of lower total system GWP refrigerants and their responsible use. Training programs about lower-GWP refrigerants and their responsible use for different stakeholders would be critical.

ASHRAE's path to cooperate with UNEP was outlined in a cooperative agreement singed in 2007. A key element of that agreement was for ASHRAE and UNEP to implement biennial work plans which outline joint development of various educational tools and products that the Society makes available to its members, UNEP clients, and OzonAction network officials. Among them is a Guide for Refrigeration and Air-Conditioning Plant Assessment that will serve as an international reference for the safe and sustainable operation and maintenance of air-conditioning and refrigeration plants, with special focus on developing markets. Compliance to the practices it

Projects selected for 2019 ASHRAE-UNEP OzonAction Lower-GWP Refrigeration and Air-Conditioning Innovation Awards were recognized at an ASHRAE-UNEP side event held during the Meeting of the Parties to the Montreal Protocol in Rome. Members of the judging committee present for award presentations were (back row left to right) Stephen Gill (UK), Jim Curlin (UNEP OzonAction), Jim Wolf (US), and Roberto Peixoto (Brazil). Certificates were accepted on behalf of winning project teams by National Ozone Unit representatives from regions where projects were implemented.

describes will be verified through a point-based qualification scheme.

ASHRAE and UNEP also created an award, presented for the first time in 2019, recognizing teams of researchers, engineers, and technicians who have implemented innovative lower-refrigeration-and-air-conditioning (lower-RAC) applications using lower-GWP refrigerants in countries defined by the Montreal Protocol as being Article 5.

A2L Refrigerant Research

Like those on other subjects, the ASHRAE Position Document on Refrigerants and Their Responsible Use called for engagement of ASHRAE Research resources.

In anticipation of a global plan to phase down high-GWP refrigerants, the industry began researching potential alternatives as early as 2010. Through that effort, several promising refrigerants were identified, many of which were low toxicity but classified, according to ASHRAE Standard 34, as mildly flammable or flammable or A2L. If these new refrigerants are to be used, safety standards will need to be reassessed and updated and extensive training will need to be made available.

In 2016, ASHRAE Research initiated a major program. With ASHRAE contributing $1.2 million, Air-Conditioning, Heating, and Refrigeration Institute (AHRI) contributing $1 million, and U.S. Department of Energy (DOE) contributing $3 million, a $5.2 million research effort was launched to discover technical knowledge needed to phase down the use of high-GWP refrigerants and identify appropriate climate-friendly alternatives.

The effort is a valuable recognition of the growing importance that A2L fluids will play in meeting targets for adoption of low-GWP refrigerants.

The results of this research will immediately be transmitted to the committees responsible for ANSI/ASHRAE Standard 15, *Safety Standard for Refrigeration Systems*, and ANSI/ASHRAE Standard 34, *Designation and Safety Classification of Refrigerants*, with a goal of using the results to update the standards as soon as possible, subject to full compliance with the American National Standards Institute (ANSI) consensus process. The ICC has also stated that these revised ASHRAE standards will be eligible to be fast-tracked into the international codes, in accordance with ICC procedures.

"ASHRAE has a strong history and commitment to refrigerants, having written our first standard on the topic in 1919," said Underwood in 2016. "We have continued our work in this area since that time, publishing the industry's leading standards on refrigerants (Standards 15 and 34) as well as conducting hundreds of research projects on the topic. As such, ASHRAE is fully committed to this project. In fact, the funds we are using for our share represent the largest transfer from our Research Reserve Fund in our 122-year history."

Appendix A

Headquarters

ASHVE Offices

1894	146 World Building, New York City
1897	Post Office Box 1818, New York City
1912	Engineering Societies Building, 29 West 39th Street, New York City*
1930	New York Life Insurance Building, 51 Madison Avenue, New York City
1951	62 Worth Street, New York City

ASRE Offices

1905	258 Broadway Street, New York City
1907	154 Nassau Street, New York City*
1923	35 Warren Street, New York City
1927	Engineering Societies Building, 37 West 39th Street, New York City
1941	50 West 40th Street, New York City
1944	American Radiator Building, 40 West 40th Street, New York City
1954	234 Fifth Avenue, New York City

ASHRAE Offices

1959	234 Fifth Avenue and 62 Worth Street, New York City
1961	United Engineering Center, 345 East 47th Street, New York City
1981	ASHRAE International Headquarters, 1791 Tullie Circle, Atlanta

**First dedicated headquarters offices.*

ASHVE Secretaries

1894–97	L.H. Hart
1897–98	H.M. Swetland
1898–99	Stewart A. Jellett
1899–1911	William M. Mackay
1911–13	W. W. Macon
1913–14	E. A. Scott
1914–16	J. J. Blackmore
1916–24	Casin W. Obert
1924–26	Ferry C. Houghten
1926–58	A. V. Hutchinson

ASRE Secretaries

1904–27	William H. Ross
1927–47	David L. Fiske
1947–54	M. C. Turpin
1954–58	Robert C. Cross

ASHRAE Secretaries

1958–59	A. V. Hutchinson
1959–67	Robert C. Cross
1967–84	Andrew T. Boggs, III
1984–2004	Frank M. Coda
2004–	Jeff H. Littleton

This silver loving cup was presented to W.M. Mackay by the members of The American Society of Heating and Ventilating Engineers at their Tenth Anniversary Dinner in 1904 to recognize his five years' service as secretary.

(Left to Right): Carl H. Flink, Technical Secretary; Walter L. Fleisher, President—1941; Mr. Hutchinson; Pres. Alfred J. Offner; R. H. Carpenter, Council 1930-35; Harold J. Ryan, President, New York Chapter

On June 5, 1946, A.S.H.V.E. President Alfred J. Offner presented a silver platter to Secretary A.B. Hutchinson at the headquarters office. The inscription read, "Presented to A.V. Hutchinson, January 1946, by the members of the A.S.H.V.E. in appreciation of his twenty years National Secretary."

FEBRUARY, 1942 103

Left—50 West 40 St., New York City, home of the new A.S.R.E. headquarters. Above—North view from the new Society offices—through the right window one sees the RCA tower in Rockefeller Center, tops in interest to sightseers.

A.S.R.E. Headquarters Now at 50 West 40th, New York City

The attractive building and offices illustrated on this page are the new national headquarters of the A.S.R.E., to which the headquarters staff moved on November 1. The new offices are at 50 West 40th St., in New York City, in an annex to the American Radiator Company, similar in architecture to the familiar black-and-gold skyscraper designed by the late Raymond Hood.

The new suite is characterized by a modern entrance and elevators and a splendid view of Bryant Park, located at the rear of the 42nd St. Public Library. Other buildings in the same block are occupied by the Engineers' Club, the National Republican Club and the Scientific American.

While the floor space is no greater than the quarters previously occupied at 37 West 39th St., a better arrangement makes the general effect more spacious. The suite includes a reception room and library, two private offices, and a large general office space affording ample room for records and publication stocks. Headquarters staff employees are enthusiastic about displaying the new offices to members from all parts of the country.

The Society last moved on February 1, 1927, from 35 Warren St., in downtown New York, to 37 West 39th St., next door the Engineering Societies Building. Long-time members will recall that the Warren Street offices were in an ancient and run-down building, and that the move represented real progress. In 1927 the Society's membership totalled approximately 600, and its financial affairs were unsatisfactory, there being a deficit of thousands. In the intervening 15 years, the membership has grown to 1800, the financial status has improved to include a sizeable reserve, and the annual business operations of the A.S.R.E. have more than tripled in size. This period of growth coincides with the administration of David L. Fiske, executive secretary, who joined the Society in January, 1927.

Below—A.S.R.E. reception-room library. Right—A corner of the general office. Mathilde Johnsen is at the files, Betty Foye wears the broad smile, in the background is Anna M. Koons, in charge of membership and financial records, and standing is Julia I. Szabo, circulation manager. (The phone call was authentic, a coincidence which pleased the photographer.)

1941

1956

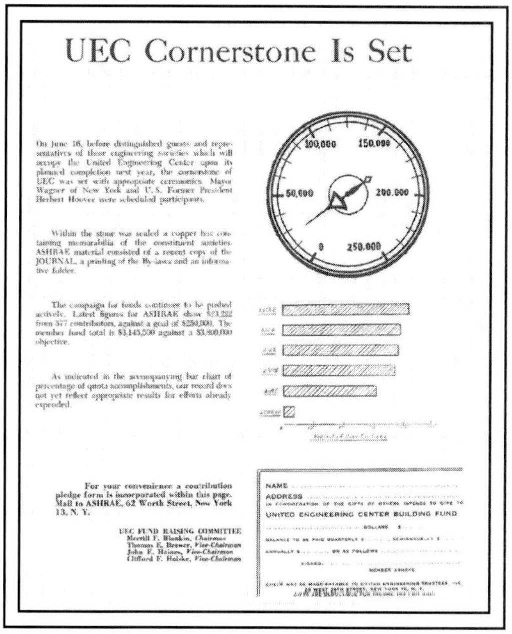

UEC Cornerstone Is Set

On June 16, before distinguished guests and representatives of those engineering societies which will occupy the United Engineering Center upon its planned completion next year, the cornerstone of UEC was set with appropriate ceremonies. Mayor Wagner of New York and U. S. Former President Herbert Hoover were scheduled participants.

Within the stone was sealed a copper box containing memorabilia of the constituent societies. ASHRAE material consisted of a recent copy of the JOURNAL, a printing of the By-laws and an informative folder.

The campaign for funds continues to be pushed actively. Latest figures for ASHRAE show $23,222 from 577 contributors, against a goal of $250,000. The member fund total is $3,145,500 against a $3,800,000 objective.

As indicated in the accompanying bar chart of percentage of quota accomplishments, our record does not yet reflect appropriate results for efforts already expended.

For your convenience a contribution pledge form is incorporated within this page. Mail to ASHRAE, 62 Worth Street, New York 13, N. Y.

UEC FUND RAISING COMMITTEE
Merrill F. Blankin, *Chairman*
Thomas E. Brewer, *Vice-Chairman*
John E. Haines, *Vice-Chairman*
Clifford F. Holske, *Vice-Chairman*

NAME
ADDRESS
IN CONSIDERATION OF THE GIFTS OF OTHERS INTENDS TO GIVE TO
UNITED ENGINEERING CENTER BUILDING FUND
DOLLARS $
BALANCE TO BE PAID QUARTERLY $ SEMIANNUALLY $
ANNUALLY $ OR AS FOLLOWS
SIGNED
MEMBER ASHRAE

July, 1960

Former U.S. President Herbert Hoover speaks at the dedication ceremonies for the United Engineering Center at New York, November 1961.

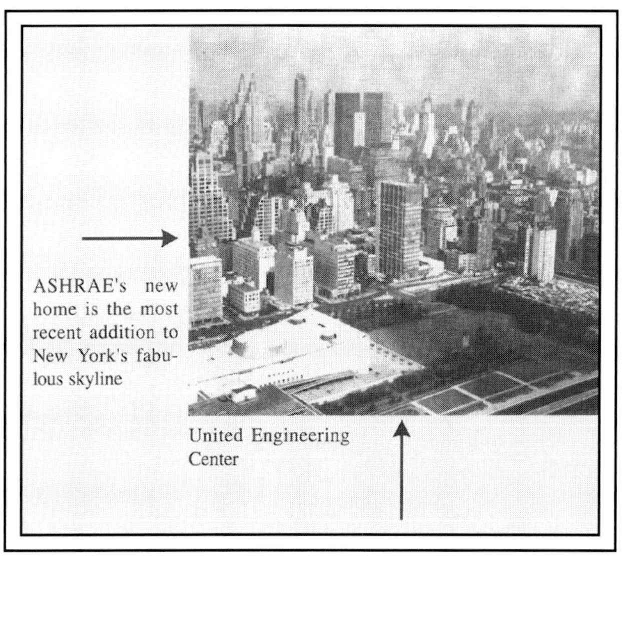

From the ASHRAE entrance, United Engineering Center. Office at the far right, far end of hall is that of the Executive Secretary.

At Headquarters

LUNCHEON FOR CARL FLINK

Marking the retirement of Carl Flink as Editor of the ASHRAE GUIDE AND DATA BOOK at the end of June (page 77, July JOURNAL), a luncheon was tendered him by his Staff fellow members.

Carl Flink delightedly examines fishing equipment presented to him by the staff. C. W. MacPhee looks on.

Among those present were: Irene Eggeling, JOURNAL Production Manager; H. P. Tinning, Technical Secretary; R. C. Cross, Executive Secretary; Carl Flink; C. W. MacPhee, new GUIDE AND DATA BOOK Editor; J. H. Cansdale, Assistant Secretary Public Relations; A. T. Boggs, III, Associate Secretary.

Marking the retirement of Carl Flink as Editor of *ASHRAE Guide and Data Book* at the end of June 1962, a luncheon was tendered him by his Staff fellow members.

In 1967, Andrew T. Boggs, Executive Director, presents a gift to Robert C. Cross, Consulting Director of Publications, at a party given in his honor by the ASHRAE Staff, shortly before his retirement. Mr. Cross had served as Executive Secretary for 13 years.

ASHRAE STAFF HONORS OLDEST EMPLOYEE — WORLEY GIERHART

Each year, just before Christmas, all of us at ASHRAE headquarters look forward to the birthday of "Gary," a staff employee since 1953. This past Christmas we helped him celebrate his 85th birthday.

Gary's career began when, as a close friend and classmate of General Hershey, he graduated from Tri-State College, Angola, Indiana in 1913 with a BS in math and science. Immediately after graduation he went to the Philippines where he worked in the school system. He served in the Army during World War I, spending most of his time in France. After his discharge in 1919, he went back to the Philippines for another two years. The next twelve years Gary spent in Panama with the United Fruit Company; from there he went to British Guiana to work for a construction company, and to Nicaragua and Columbia to try his hand at gold mining. Not one to stand still for long, Gary worked at Oak Ridge, Tennessee when the Atom bomb was being developed, and, still yearning for distant places, spent a year in Korea as a civilian with the Army.

After retirement he considered buying an orange grove in Florida, but looked for a temporary job until the final arrangements could be completed. That was in 1953, when he came to ASRE to work in the mailroom. He was then 63 years "young," and handled this assignment by himself until the merger with ASHAE in 1959.

Gary is still very much on the job. He is usually the first to arrive in the office, the last to leave, and he has a near-perfect attendance record. Never seen without a cigar or cigarette (unlit), Gary is a great favorite among the staff employees, and he still has an eye for pretty girls. This past Christmas we celebrated with Gary 22 years on the job. We hope he will be with us for many years to come. □ □

1975

The first Board of Directors-Headquarters Gold Tournament was held during the 1968 Annual Meeting at Lake Placid, New York. After 18 holes of play, the trophy – the Peanut Bowl, donated by Presidential Member P.N. Vinther, was won by the Headquarters team. ASHRAE Treasurer Dr. Stanley F. Gilman (at left), representing the Board of Directors, presents the trophy to Executive Secretary Boggs with the comment, "We'll get you next year," – to which Mr. Boggs replied, "We are going to weld the trophy to its place of honor."

In November 1926 Julia I. Szabo began employment with The A.S.R.E. as a "probationary stenographer." Forty-nine years later she retired, completing an ASHRAE career which included managing editor, circulation manager, office manager, and from 1959 until her 1975 retirement, meetings secretary.

Combining 130 years of ASHRAE service (l. to r.) at the staff's 1980 Christmas Party, the last in New York City: Isabel Sullivan (28 years), Irene Eggeling (25 years), Andy Boggs (25 years), and Doris Flandorffer (25 years).

The above photograph shows Mr. Boggs with a 25-year service gift from President Charles F. Sepsy.

ASHRAE Will Move to Atlanta

Meeting at ASHRAE's 1980 Semiannual Meeting, the Society's Board of Directors has unanimously decided to move its headquarters from New York to Atlanta. The ASHRAE office has been in New York since the Society's founding eighty-five years ago.

President Hugh D. McMillan, Jr., said the move was dictated by a variety of reasons, including the need for moderately priced office space and meeting rooms. "Over the long run there will be a number of advantages, including financial ones," he said. Twenty-eight cities were studied before the selection of Atlanta.

To make sure that ASHRAE's sixty-five employees are treated fairly, the Society has retained the services of The Fantus Co., the nation's leading consultant on relocation problems.

Washington Presence Established

The Board also voted to approve in next year's budget funding for the establishment of a Washington, DC, presence.

When announcing the decision, Mr. McMillan said, "This will help us to do some of the things we are doing now in a more efficient manner and will help us to coordinate our activities with other societies in the Washington area."

In recent years, ASHRAE has dramatically increased its involvement with the United States Government. These activities have included cooperative research projects, the use of ASHRAE consultants by government agencies, testimony before government bodies and agencies, and responses to government actions and policies.

Exec. V.P. Andrew T. Boggs (above) starts unveiling of ASHRAE pylon. Ribbon cutting and dedication was completed by (left to right): Bruno P. Morabito, Hugh D. McMillan, Jr., and Morris Backer.

ASHRAE International Headquarters Dedicated in Atlanta Ceremony

Andrew T. Boggs, Executive Vice President emeritus, received congratulations on his retirement from Frank M. Codea in 1985. Mr. Coda succeeded Mr. Boggs as Society Secretary a year earlier.

Jim Cox Named Washington Representative

ASHRAE Creates New Staff Positions

Frank M. Coda Named Executive Director

Associate Editor of ASHRAE JOURNAL

W. Edmond Gutman has joined the headquarters staff as Associate Editor of ASHRAE JOURNAL. Born in Paris, France, he is a graduate of the Faculty of Journalism, School of High Social Studies and International Affairs, Paris, and has a Master's degree in Journalism.

Before joining ASHRAE, he was Managing Editor of Building Systems Design and has had some 13 years of experience as a writer/editor/reporter for such construction- and HVAC-related publications as Southwest Builder & Contractor and Mechanical Contractor.

Technical Secretary Is Named by ASRE

Andrew T. Boggs III was named to the post of Technical Secretary of ASRE as of Oct. 1. He succeeds Gurdon R. Munger, who is now associated with ...

GEORGE GRAY ADVANCES TO CIRCULATION MANAGER

GEORGE GRAY

JULY 1962

J. F. Cuba Appointed Assistant Director of Research

D. A. Goebel Joins RE

Robert C. Blatt, Director of Publications and Editor has named Dolores A. Goebel as an Editorial Assistant of REFRIGERATING ENGINEERING.

Before coming to RE Miss Goebel was associated with *Electrical World*, a McGraw-Hill weekly trade publication.

Edward R. Searles Appointed New RE Editor

Stewart Named ASHRAE Director of Member and Chapter Services

Director of Communications Named

W. Stephen Comstock has been named director of communications, a newly created staff position which reflects the growing diversity of ASHRAE activity.

J. Richard Wright Named Director of Technology

... members appointed by ASHRAE

ASHRAE RESEARCH AND TECHNICAL STAFF RESTRUCTURED

MADELEINE CALDWELL

ROYAL S. BUCHANAN

NICHOLAS A. LA COURTE

J. H. CANSDALE SUCCEEDS R. J. ANTHONY AS JOURNAL EDITOR

ASHRAE Appoints New Staff Members

WALTER A. GLASSER BECOMES ASHRAE CONTROLLER

Effective April 3, Walter A. Glasser was appointed Controller of ASHRAE. In this newly-created position, he will be responsible for staff administration of financial activities. Mr. Glasser will also function as Director of Membership Services, including Membership and Meetings Arrangements.

A graduate of New York University with a Bachelor of Science degree in Accounting, Mr. Glasser also has a degree in Hotel Administration from the State University of New York and has attended courses on computer applications conducted by International Business Machines Corporation.

Before joining ASHRAE, Mr. Glasser was Senior Staff Assistant to the Comptroller at the American Broadcasting Corporation in New York City and, from 1956 to 1963, was Assistant Controller at Stahl-Meyer, Inc, meat packers.

Mr. Glasser has recently been elected a member of the National Assn of Accountants.

Gloria Cofer Selected Employee of the Year

Gloria Cofer, selected the 1994 ASHRAE Employee of the Year, displays an inscribed plaque presented to her by ASHRAE Executive Director Frank M. Coda. The award is presented in recognition of excellence in the performance of duties. Gloria is the Assistant to the Board of Directors and is the staff liaison to the Long Range Planning Committee, the President-Elect Advisory Committee and the Nominating Committee. Gloria began her career at ASHRAE in 1981.

1994

Tony Giometti Selected ASHRAE Employee of the Quarter

Tony Giometti (left), public relations manager, received ASHRAE's Fourth Quarterly Employee Award of Excellence for 1994 from Frank Coda, executive director. The award is presented quarterly to an ASHRAE staff member in recognition of excellence in the performance of their duties. Tony's duties include providing information about ASHRAE to the trade press covering the HVAC&R industry, and he is the editor of ASHRAE Insights. The Employee of the Year will be announced in next month's issue.

1995

Pat Mathis Selected ASHRAE Employee of the Quarter

Pat Mathis, administrative assistant to the director of communications and publications, received ASHRAE's Second Quarterly Employee Award of Excellence from Frank Coda, ASHRAE executive director. The award is presented quarterly to an ASHRAE staff member in recognition of excellence in performance of their duties. Pat began working at ASHRAE in 1992. She provides administrative support to the Publishing Council and has also provided assistance to the Centennial and other special committees.

1995

ASHRAE Staff Employee of the Quarter

Judy Marshall receives the Employee of the Quarter Award (Second Quarter) from ASHRAE's Executive Vice President Frank Coda. Judy joined ASHRAE in 1986. She serves as Manager of Meetings and Conferences. She was recognized with the Second Quarter Award of Excellence in recognition of award service to the membership and the ASHRAE staff. Her hard work and dedication have resulted in increased attendance through the years at ASHRAE's Winter and Annual Meetings. The award is presented quarterly to an ASHRAE staff member in recognition of excellence in the performance of their duties.

1996

ASHRAE Librarian Emily Walker receives her employee Quarterly Award of Excellence from Executive Vice President Frank M. Coda for her work with outside vendors for the ASHRAE Home Page.

ASHRAE Librarian Emily Walker receives Quarterly Award of Excellence from EVP Frank M. Coda, 1997.

Jim Heldenbrand, (left), Manager of Standareds is shown here with Bruce Hunn, Director of Technology after receiving a Certificate of Appreciation at the ASHRAE Winter Meeting in San Francisco. Secretary and Executive Vice President, Frank Coda noted in his Plenary remarks that Jim Heldenbrand's wise counsel greatly assisted the volunteers and staff in the development, promulgation and evolution of ASHRAE Standards.

1998

Five Staff Members Receive Quarterly Awards of Excellence

Five ASHRAE employees received Second Quarter Awards of Excellence during the month of September. The employee award program recognizes employees who, in the course of their work, perform some special task or project that is unusual, or is in addition to their normal work load.

The awards presented were for the second quarter of 1998 and exemplify the teamwork aspect of the awards program as well as individual effort. (Bottom photo) Pearl Silveira, Beverly Fulks, Lavice Shank, and Angela McFarland from ASHRAE's Standards group were recognized for their work in logging over 50,000 comments received during the last public review of ASHRAE's Standard 90.1. The group developed special procedures for handling the comments while dealing with power outages from tornadoes and manually stamped the 50,000 comments and managed to meet the deadlines required in spite of all of the obstacles.

(Photo right) Nancy Thysell of the Publications group was recognized by Executive Vice President, Frank Coda, for her quality work which resulted in getting the most recent edition of ASHRAE's Handbook published on time and also contributed to the publication of ASHRAE's Publications Catalog and ASHRAE *Insights*. During the same period of time she also managed to contribute to the publication of ASHRAE's *International Journal of Heating, Ventilating, Air-Conditioning and Refrigerating Research*.

1998

ASHRAE Award of Excellence Presented for E-Conference Paper Preparation

From left to right: Tiffany DeLoach, Executive Vice President Frank Coda, Melanie Brooks, and Michshell Phillips following the awards ceremony.

Melanie Brooks, Tiffany DeLoach, and Michshell Phillips received the ASHRAE 2nd Quarter Award of Excellence for their work on a special ASHRAE conference that took place in Dublin Ireland in September. The conference was jointly organized by ASHRAE and The Chartered Institution of Building Services Engineers (CIBSE).

ASHRAE's job was to solicit, review and submit completed electronic manuscripts from ASHRAE members in North America. Brooks coordinated manuscript acceptance by the committee and final submission to CIBSE. DeLoach was responsible for the completion of the review process, and Phillips was responsible for providing reviewer comments to authors and receiving the revised manuscripts. The project completed by the three helped to move ASHRAE's conference publishing process further toward a totally electronic system.

Brooks was recently promoted to administrator of intellectual property. DeLoach is the secretary in the communications and programs section and Phillips is the secretary in the special publications section.

2000

Frank Coda, ASHRAE's executive vice president, congratulates Micki Geshwiler and Nancy Thysell for receiving ASHRAE's Award of Excellence.

2001

New Technical Services Manager Named

The engineer responsible for the design and installation of the "World's Longest Gondola System" is now an ASHRAE employee.

Michael Vaughn has been named manager of technical services for ASHRAE. He will answer written and telephone inquiries and coordinate technical committees as well as serve as liaison to the Technical Activities Committee and the Environmental Health Committee.

Vaughn

Previously, Vaughn served as project engineer/manager for Premiere Engineering Corp. in Atlanta.

Among his major projects, Vaughn counts the design and installation of an eight-passenger, high-speed, detachable gondola (ski lift) system for a winter/summer resort in the panhandle of Idaho. The system, billed as the "world's longest," is 3.1 miles in length.

"To avoid obsolescence and boredom, I have always strived in my career to develop a broad base of mechanical engineering experience," Vaughn said. "My current position at ASHRAE allows me to utilize that experience, while at the same time gaining knowledge in new areas such as indoor air quality, and alternate energy source powered equipment."

Other projects include design and construction of the maintenance and control facility, guideway switches and maintenance/recovery vehicle for a monorail people-mover system at Newark, N.J., International Airport; a 20-passenger, funicular system at a resort hotel in Alaska; and refrigerated boxcars for use by Amtrak.

His overall experience includes design and refurbishment of transportation air-conditioning and refrigeration equipment, including refrigerated boxcars for AMTRAK and air-conditioned funicular, peoplemover, transit and commuter rail vehicles. He also has worked extensively with architects and mechanical design firms to develop HVAC requirements for station and maintenance/control facility buildings used in the transportation system.

2001

Meetings Coordinator Jan Young receives a 20-year anniversary award from EVP Frank M. Coda, 2004.

Seaton Receives Service to ASHRAE Research Award

Bill Seaton (standing), retired ASHRAE manager of research, is the recipient of the first Service to ASHRAE Research Award. The award, sponsored by the Research Administration Committee and Technology Council, recognizes committed and long-standing contributions to ASHRAE research. The award was presented on April 22 by ASHRAE director of technology Bruce Hunn (seated) in Atlanta.

Seaton was recognized for his 21 years of service to ASHRAE research.

2003

Mark Owen New Editor Of Handbook

Mark Owen has been named as the editor of the ASHRAE Handbook series. He also will serve as a technical editor on ASHRAE's other publications.

Owen

Owen will work with staff and volunteers in the planning and scheduling of ASHRAE Handbook production in both print and electronic formats. The ASHRAE Handbook, distributed annually to all ASHRAE members in good standing, is the most widely used reference book in the HVAC&R industry for system design, application and equipment operation and maintenance.

Previously, Owen was vice president of production at William E. Owen and Associates in Marietta, Ga. He designed commercial, industrial and residential HVAC systems and managed engineering projects through construction coordination phase. Prior to that, he was a technical sales representative for Enplas (USA) Inc., a custom plastic injection-molding firm, where he specialized in automotive and medical markets.

"The ASHRAE Handbook represents the voluntary contributions of more than 2,000 ASHRAE members who serve on the Society's 90-plus technical committees," W. Stephen Comstock, ASHRAE's publisher, said. "Mark Owen's technical background will ensure that the Handbook's high level of technical accuracy continues, and his experience in project planning will guide the Handbook as it evolves into a fully electronic as well as print product."

The Handbook is available in one-volume CDs and as a four-volume CD.

2001

Irene Eggeling Celebrates 50 Years at ASHRAE

In 1955, Irene Eggeling was mulling two job offers — one with a medical company and the other with The American Society of Refrigerating Engineers (ASRE).

The medical company paid more and the commute was shorter. But in the end, she chose ASRE. And doing so, set out on the path to make history for ASHRAE. On Nov. 21, 2005, Eggeling marked her 50th anniversary with ASHRAE, making her the employee with the longest career with the Society.

"I chose ASRE because of the people," she said. "I felt comfortable with the people."

An anniversary luncheon was held for Eggeling at ASHRAE Headquarters, attended by ASHRAE staff and retirees.

Eggeling started in 1955 as an editorial assistant. Through the years, she became more involved in advertising production. Her adeptness at learning and diversified skills earned her titles leading up to advertising production manager, the position she currently holds. She works with advertisers to compile and process their ads for printing in ASHRAE's monthly publication, *ASHRAE Journal*, ensuring the ads run correctly and on schedule each month.

When ASHRAE moved its headquarters from New York in 1981, Eggeling was one of 12 staff members who came along.

During the luncheon, Eggeling was presented with a special issue of *ASHRAE Journal* marking her anniversary. Jeff Littleton, ASHRAE executive vice president, also told her that a flagpole from which the American flag will be flown will be erected outside ASHRAE headquarters in honor of her anniversary. Eggeling had lobbied Littleton for a flagpole since he came to work at ASHRAE in 2003.

Jeff Littleton, ASHRAE executive vice president, presents Irene Eggeling with a plaque representing a flagpole in honor of her 50 years as an ASHRAE employee.

She also took the opportunity to give staff a pep talk.

"Everything we do here is important, but it's not just important to ASHRAE," she said. "Whether you work in accounting or in standards, everything we do makes life better for people around the world. That's amazing."

Outside of work, Eggeling enjoys sports, including bowling and golf (she was a badminton champion in the 1970s in New Jersey), travel and her pets.

ASHRAE members who would like to congratulate Eggeling can do so at the ASHRAE Booth at the AHR Expo in Chicago. She has attended the last 40+ shows.

2005

ASHRAE Employees Earn Awards of Excellence

Two ASHRAE employees have received awards for excellence for their efforts in a standards-related audit and on the ASHRAE Handbook.

Rosy Douglas, procedures administrator in the standards section, and Heather Kennedy, associate editor of the ASHRAE Handbook, received their awards in August. The award recognizes employees who perform some special task or project that is unusual or is in addition to their normal workload.

Douglas has worked at ASHRAE since June 2000. She is staff liaison to Standing Standards Project Committee 62, and the Planning, Policy and Interpretations Subcommittee, and recording secretary to the Appeals Panel.

She was the lead person in preparing ASHRAE's standards section for the American National Standards Institute (ANSI) audit. The audit is required by ANSI for ASHRAE to maintain its accreditation. Douglas spent many hours working with other staff in reviewing all of the standards files. She established a checklist used in reviewing the files, along with sample documentation. She also conducted a training class for staff. Prior to the auditor arriving on site, Douglas again reviewed the files being audited and organized them along with summaries.

The auditor noted that of the 300 audits he had done, this was the easiest due to Douglas' organizational work.

Kennedy has worked at ASHRAE since July 2001. Her efforts enabled the Handbook to return to its normal publication schedule — early June — in both print and CD formats. She introduced innovative ideas to speed the publication process, including introduction of a new, all-electronic author proofing process in which highlighted portable document format files were sent to authors instead of paper proofs.

Rosy Douglas (left) and Heather Kennedy (right) received their awards from Frank Coda, ASHRAE's executive vice president.

This was accomplished while learning a new job and helping the Handbook section to catch up with other tasks, including production of a textbook and two issues of the *International Journal of HVAC&R Research*.

She also kept a positive attitude when difficulties arose, such as being called for jury duty and working through font problems.

2002

ASHRAE's renovated headquarters building provides a living lab with sensing and monitoring capabilities that can be used for research.

ASHRAE's Living Lab

By **Ronald E. Jarnagin,** Member ASHRAE; and **Michael R. Brambley, Ph.D.,** Member ASHRAE

ASHRAE recently completed a comprehensive renovation of its headquarters building in Atlanta. Although the renovation was driven by the need to renew a number of the building systems to address performance issues, the Headquarters Renovation Committee decided to use this opportunity to make a broader statement with the renovation.

The priorities for the renovation effort were to create a safe, healthy, productive environment for staff, demonstrate a commitment to the ASHRAE Strategic Plan for Sustainability, and create a living lab to provide enduring value to ASHRAE members.

While each of these priorities is important, this article will focus on the living lab by discussing the need for the capability, taking a brief look at the building systems being monitored as part of the lab, discussing the capabilities and system architecture of the lab as well as suggesting some potential projects that might be used to exploit its capabilities.

About the Authors

Ronald E. Jarnagin, is staff scientist/program manager and **Michael R. Brambley, Ph.D.,** is staff scientist at Pacific Northwest Laboratory, Richland, Wash. Jarnagin is chair and Brambley is a member of the technical advisory committee for the renovation.

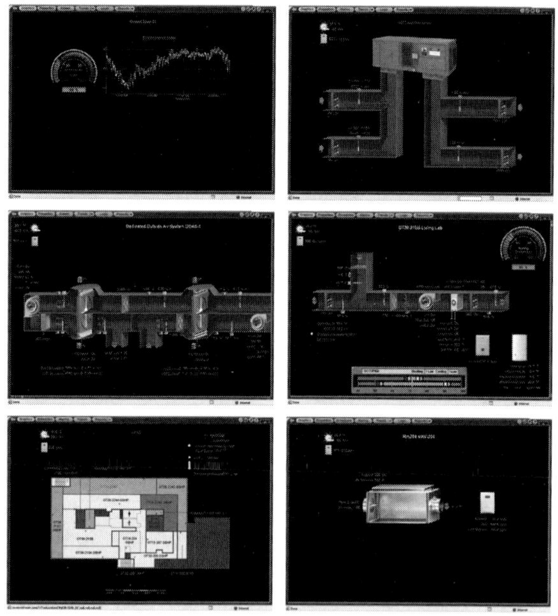

ASHRAE's building management system has a variety of views into building conditions and systems operations.

The living lab provides sensing and monitoring capabilities that go well beyond the needs for operating the building efficiently. In recognizing the need for these capabilities, ASHRAE's Research Administration Committee (RAC) made a generous commitment of funds to greatly enhance the usability of the living lab for research projects. In addition, a number of vendors contributed to the capabilities of the living lab through their donations of equipment and resources.

This support has allowed the living lab to be developed as a true laboratory that can be used for experimentation, research and testing. A range of uses are possible including the development of new control algorithms, evaluation of new sensors and controllers and the assessment of building faults through the

ASHRAE has reduced its estimated annual energy use by more than 31.5% through enhancements to the building envelope and use of dedicated outdoor air system with energy recovery, ground-source heat pumps, and variable refrigerant flow (VRF) systems with heat recovery.

ability to selectively disable building systems. These capabilities will be managed through the ASHRAE research program.

The Need for the Living Lab

With 40% of the energy use in the U.S. being attributable to buildings, it should be no surprise that the greatest potential for improvement in energy use comes from the construction and operation of buildings. For ASHRAE to contribute significantly to reducing energy use in buildings, continuing research and efforts to improve educational materials on energy-efficient building construction and operations are needed. Research and development using the living lab can contribute significantly to the body of knowledge in this field.

Since relatively few of ASHRAE's 50,000 members actually have the opportunity to visit the headquarters building in Atlanta, the living lab also serves as a medium to allow all members to participate in and benefit from the improvements in the building and its systems. Effectively, the building now can serve as a "laboratory without walls," extending its capability and information reach to a worldwide audience. Much can be learned about the real-world issues and benefits of operating the ASHRAE headquarters building more efficiently in the future, with all members sharing in that experience.

The Headquarters Renovation Committee decided to pursue a LEED-NC[1] Gold rating as well as a LEED-EB[2] Gold rating from the U.S. Green Buildings Council for the headquarters building. The LEED-NC rating is being pursued initially and the living lab contributes to earning that rating. For the NC rating, the living lab helps to gain LEED points for EA5-Measurement and Verification as well as EQ1-Outdoor Air Delivery Monitoring. In addition, flat screen displays of building performance address the need for educational requirements of the LEED rating.

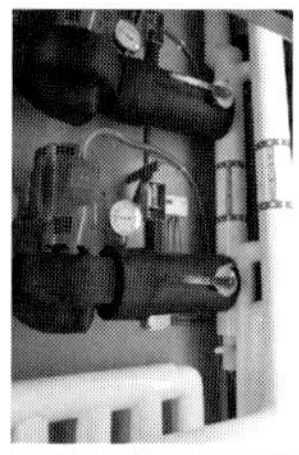

Ground-source heat pumps operate with a geothermal field of 12 wells that are 400 ft (122 m) deep and a closed loop piping system.

Overview of Headquarters Building Systems

One of the distinguishing characteristics of the newly renovated headquarters building is the number of energy systems serving the building. A diverse set of systems provides a rich opportunity for data collection and analysis that will ultimately exercise the living lab to its fullest while delivering greater value to the ASHRAE membership.

A separate dedicated outdoor air system (DOAS) provides tempered and dehumidified ventilation air for the building. The DOAS system includes dual desiccant energy recovery wheels, direct expansion (DX) cooling coils and variable frequency drive (VFD) controllers for supply and exhaust fans. The first floor of the building is heated and cooled by variable refrigerant flow (VRF) heat pumps operating in a heat recovery mode supplied by inverter-driven DX condensing units. The second floor of the building is heated and cooled by two-stage ground source heat pumps using variable speed fans and pumps.

The headquarters building produces on-site renewable energy through a roof-mounted photovoltaic (PV) array. Additional systems control the daylighting in the building, as well as the security, phones, and white noise generators for conversation masking. Monitoring equipment is provided for refrigerant leak detection as well as indoor air quality (IAQ) sensing.

Living Lab Capabilities

The renovated headquarters building provides sensing, data collection and data storage capabilities sufficient to support a broad range of HVAC&R research and development on buildings, the building environment, building systems, subsystems, equipment, and controls. This required installing sensors and data acquisition capabilities beyond those of most ordinary small office buildings. The building includes sensors to support monitoring the energy performance of the whole building but also its major systems—the dedicated outdoor air system, the ground source heat pump system providing space conditioning to the second floor and the variable refrigerant flow system providing cooling for the first floor.

Energy System Measurement capabilities include:

- Energy use and electric power demand of the whole building, major systems, subsystems, and individual system components/equipment segregated by energy type;
- Conditions, such as on/off status, operation mode, temperature, humidity, pressure, and flow rate, at numerous points in the various systems and equipment;
- The values of all control points can be monitored and recorded;
- Indoor environmental conditions, such as air temperature, humidity, CO_2 concentration, concentration of other air pollutants, airflow rates, lighting levels, and daylight availability;
- Water consumption by the whole-building and targeted end uses; and
- Outdoor weather conditions including total and diffuse solar radiation and air quality.

A weather station (left) monitors outdoor weather conditions. Building systems (right) provide independent monitoring of ambient conditions.

A detailed list of measured points is shown in *Table 1*. All data will be stored at five-minute or 15-minute intervals, but the capability exists to adjust the collection interval for select sets of data for specific studies to one-minute interval or less.

The data collected will be sufficient, for example, for monitoring and studying the indoor environmental quality, the energy use of the building and individual systems, equipment performance (efficiency, reliability, degradation, fault occurrence) in the short term and over its lifetime, control system performance, benchmarking, and investigation of new techniques and technology such as automated fault detection and diagnostics, advanced controls, ventilation strategies, energy conservation strategies, maintenance practices, etc.

The laboratory is envisioned to include occupant satisfaction survey capability, although this is not yet implemented. Occupant surveys will not be implemented on the building control system. They will be administered via the building business computer network.

Several large flat screen monitors have been installed at strategic locations in the building to provide on-site displays for viewing by ASHRAE staff and visitors. The display interface will also be viewable via the worldwide web for all ASHRAE members. The specific information to be displayed and its presentation format have not yet been decided, but it will include graphical display of significant indicators of building performance (such as electric power demand and consumption, and indicators of indoor conditions).

Two conference rooms will be available for dedicated research space suitable for a wide range of real-world investigations of interest to ASHRAE technical committees and other organizations working on ASHRAE research. These spaces have been outfitted with unused sensor inputs on controllers to enable the installation of additional sensors specific to the research conducted in the space. Such research is expected to be conducted in the presence of occupants, thus not interfering in any substantial way with the normal use of the rooms.

System Architecture and Data Access

A high-level schematic of the overall living lab data acquisition, storage and access system is shown in *Figure 1*. The diagram shows the relationship between the building control system and additional components for the living lab. Living lab components (e.g., additional sensors) that are not part of the control system are shown outside the dashed boundary of the control system. All sensor data are gathered and communicated back to the living lab server by the control system.

The system provides the capability to effectively manage the data collected from the building with a minimum of active human involvement (i.e., labor). This will include the capability to collect the data, store it in a suitable database, ensure adequate secure backups, and provide access to all ASHRAE members and performers of ASHRAE research via the Internet and World Wide Web. On-site and off-site backup of data to ensure its safety will be provided as part of the overall ASHRAE IT system, which protects all ASHRAE computer data in a similar manner protecting it from loss as a result of a system crash or other unfortunate occurrence (e.g., a fire).

Web access to the data will be provided to members and research project contractors by secure access through a firewall. The Web server will initially be provided by the control system but may later be transitioned to another computer on which the living lab data base resides. In addition, the new headquarters building's controls system provides 24-hour data storage in field panels, which provides backup in the event of power outages. Users generally will have read-only access to the data and no access directly into the control system, unless arranged specifically in advance (e.g., for specifically approved purposes on a limited time basis as part of a research project).

Electrical panels provide monitoring of power and power factor for their circuits.

Potential Projects Using the Living Lab

While ASHRAE members anywhere in the world will be able to access detailed data on the operations of the headquarters building, it will likely take some specific projects to help fully use the capabilities of the facility. Members of the Technical Advisory Committee for the headquarters renovation project have been working to identify potential projects that might be launched in cooperation with the ASHRAE technical committees and the RAC. These projects represent only a starting point for ideas from the members.

Contest to remotely detect and diagnose operational faults with the building systems. Members would compete to develop software and algorithms for fault detection and diagnosis that could be trained on data from the operating building. Then, under controlled circumstances, known faults would be induced in the system at planned points in time and member's algorithms would attempt to detect and correctly diagnose the faults. Winners of the competition would be declared based on a scoring system that rewards both speed and accuracy of the diagnostic process.

Contest to predict the second year's energy performance given the first year's energy performance. Members would compete to develop software and algorithms for predicting energy performance based on previous years' measured data. Contestants would be provided with detailed operational data for use in training algorithms and tools. These algorithms and tools would then be used to predict a subsequent year's performance. Winners would be declared based on a scoring system that rewards accuracy of the prediction process. This contest would be similar in nature to the previous Great Energy Predictor Shootout[3] conducted by ASHRAE technical committees. The enhancement in this contest compared to the previous contest would be the ability to predict the performance of specific energy end uses.

Table 1: ASHRAE's Living Lab Sensor Points

Dedicated Outdoor Air System		
Supply fan speed Exhaust fan speed Supply duct static pressure Return duct static pressure Static pressure setpoints Outdoor air damper position signal Exhaust air damper position signal Static pressures in zones Outdoor air temperature	Outdoor air humidity Outdoor airflow rate Exhaust air temperature Exhaust air humidity Exhaust airflow rate Supply air temperature (discharge from cooling unit) Supply air humidity (discharge from cooling unit) Supply air temperature upstream of heat wheel Supply air humidity upstream of heat wheel	Supply air temperature downstream of heat wheel Supply air humidity downstream of heat wheel Exhaust air temperature upstream of heat wheel Exhaust air humidity upstream of heat wheel Exhaust air temperature downstream of heat wheel Exhaust air humidity downstream of heat wheel Electric energy use of DOAS unit
Dedicated Outdoor Air Supply VAV Units		
Outdoor airflow rate; Outdoor air temperature; Corresponding zone carbon dioxide concentration		
VRF System		
Total electric power use Air-conditioning mode for each unit Heater status	Temperature into each indoor unit Temperature of air leaving each indoor unit Airflow rate for each room unit	Air temperature of each zone Humidity of each zone Indoor fan operation status for each indoor unit
Ground Loop Heat Pump System		
System electricity use Water-side: Ground loop water supply temperature Ground loop water return temperature Ground loop water flow rate Air-side: Zone air temperature Zone air humidity Zone air carbon dioxide concentration Zone air temperature setpoint Zone air temperature humidity setpoint	Discharge air temperature Discharge air humidity Return air temperature Return air humidity Mixed air temperature Mixed air humidity Fan status Operation mode (cooling, heating, or fan only) Compressor status Additional sensing for two of the twelve heat pumps: Heating/cooling mode Water flow rate	Water entering temperature Water leaving temperature Water leaving temperature setpoint Electric power use Discharge air temperature Discharge air humidity Discharge airflow rate Return air temperature Return air humidity Return airflow rate Mixed air temperature Mixed air humidity
Lighting and Plug Loads		
Lighting and plug-load electricity use monitoring separately for: First floor (not including learning center) Second floor Exterior lighting	Ambient illumination levels measured on each side of the building on each floor in the exterior zones and in a few representative core zones First floor plug loads	Second floor plug loads Domestic water heater and pump Total building electricity
Zone Monitoring		
At least five stations in different zones distributed across the first floor/learning center and second floor shall measure and report: Space air temperature; Space air humidity; Space air carbon dioxide concentration; Occupancy (occupied/unoccupied)		
Indoor Air Quality Measurement System		
Dry-bulb temperature Dew-point temperature (Relative humidity)	Fine particulates less than or equal to 2.5 microns (PM 2.5) Enthalpy	Carbon dioxide Total volatile organic compounds (TVOC)
Photovoltaic Array		
Electricity generated (kWh)		
Building Water Usage		
Flow meter		
Weather Station (Outdoor Conditions)		
Outdoor air temperature: 10-minute minimum based on 1-minute samples 10-minute maximum based on 1-minute samples Instantaneous every 10 minutes Outdoor air humidity Dew point Relative humidity Air pressure Measured barometric pressure QFF (mean sea level pressure, which is the station pressure adjusted to sea level assuming an isothermal layer) QFE (field evaluation, which is the barometric altimeter setting that will cause an altimeter at the building location to read zero)	QNH (nautical height, which is the barometric altimeter setting that will cause an altimeter at the building location to read the elevation of the building above sea level) Wind direction Instantaneous 10-minute average Wind speed Instantaneous 10-minute average Wind gusts Magnitude and direction Solar radiation Total solar radiation Diffuse (net) solar radiation Hours of sunlight	Outdoor air carbon dioxide concentration Data from Peachtree-Dekalb Weather Station Wind direction and speed Visibility Sky conditions Weather Temperature Dew point Relative humidity Barometric pressure Maximum and minimum temperatures for past six hours Maximum and minimum temperatures for past 24 hours 24-hour summary

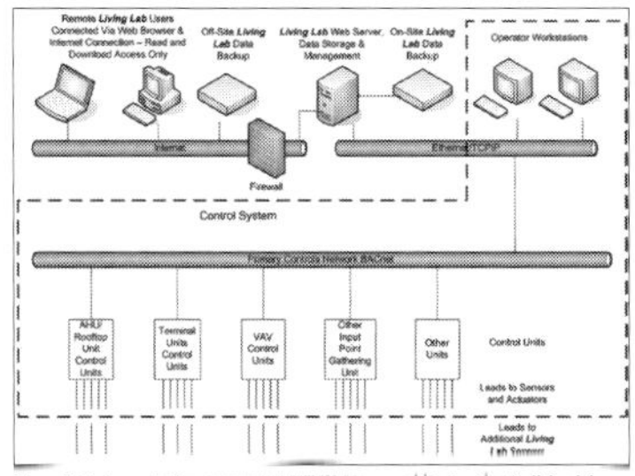

Figure 1: Data acquisition, storage and remote access architecture for the living lab.

Contest to develop the most interesting, informative user interface for presenting monitored data from the living lab. Members would compete to design innovative user interfaces for video displays of energy use and building performance. These displays ultimately would be implemented in the control software for the headquarters building. Winning interfaces would provide a higher degree of clarity and communication to users than interfaces currently available. Emphasis would be placed on clarity and the educational value of the interface that could be licensed to private sector vendors.

Contest by joint student branch and ASHRAE chapter to predict energy use in the headquarters building using modeling software. Members of local ASHRAE Chapters would team with student branch members to develop building simulation models that can be used to predict energy use in the headquarters building. This would serve as a training opportunity for the student members and a mentoring opportunity for local ASHRAE chapter members. Students would be presented not only with an additional learning opportunity but also an opportunity to work side by side with ASHRAE members in solving relevant HVAC problems. This project could be conducted in concert with the ASHRAE Student Activities Committee as well as with the local chapters.

A roof-mounted 20 kW photovoltaic electrical power generating array provides power back to the grid.

Develop performance models for VRF HVAC equipment. The ASHRAE headquarters uses a VRF system for serving the first floor of the building. Systems of this type are very common in other parts of the world, but are less common in the U.S. As a result, few of the building simulation tools contain adequate models for expressing the performance of these systems, thus limiting the ability of ASHRAE practitioners to effectively model them for their clients. Detailed performance data from the ASHRAE headquarters could be used by technical committees and researchers to improve the modeling capability of the simulation tools and help equip ASHRAE practitioners to better serve their clients.

Evaluate performance characteristics of a DOAS in conjunction with mechanical heating and cooling systems. The ASHRAE headquarters uses a DOAS system to provide pre-conditioned outside air for the building mechanical heating and cooling systems. Experiments could be conducted to evaluate the performance of the DOAS without preconditioning vs. the DOAS data acquisition, storage remote access architecture for the living lab. preconditioning in conjunction with the mechanical heating and cooling systems under real-world building operations. This research could firmly establish the value of DOAS systems for commercial applications.

Summary

ASHRAE has created a new living lab as part of its building renovation project. This living lab is intended to provide ongoing value to ASHRAE members by allowing for evaluation of the ongoing energy and operational performance of the building at a level that is unprecedented in current commercial buildings. Every ASHRAE member with an interest in energy efficiency and operational performance should take advantage of the opportunity presented by the living lab. Make sure to check the ASHRAE Web site at www.ashrae.org for updates on availability of data on the headquarters building.

References

1. U.S. Green Building Council. 2005. *LEED for New Construction & Major Renovations*, Version 2.2.

2. U.S. Green Building Council. 2005. *Green Building Rating System for Existing Buildings, Upgrades, Operations and Maintenance*, Version 2.

3. Haberl, J.S., J.F. Kreider. 1994. "Instructions for 'The Great Energy Predictor Shootout II: Measuring Retrofit Energy Savings.'" Energy Systems Laboratory Texas A&M University, Department of Mechanical Engineering, Texas A&M University.●

ASHRAE President Bill Harrison (third, l.) is joined by the Building Renovation Committee: (l.-r.) Ron Jarnagin, Darryl Boyce, Gordon V.R. Holness, Damon Gowan, and Mike Vaughn, in cutting the ribbon to "reopen" the Society's Atlanta Headquarters.

200-Plus Tour 'Sustainability Showcase'

The ribbon is cut, the donors have been honored, and ASHRAE's newly renovated sustainability showcase is officially open for business.

Some 200 people gathered Thursday, Oct. 23, for the Headquarters dedication ceremony in Atlanta. The guests included industry partners who donated nearly $1.65 million in equipment and services for the $7.65 million renovation.

"None of this would have been possible without the hard work and commitment from many volunteers and staff involved in the renewal for the last three years," said Bill Harrison, ASHRAE president. "More importantly, generous donations by companies and firms have ensured that not only our building will be here for a long time to come but that ASHRAE can continue to provide the sustainable building technology guidance that we are known for."

"Not only is the renovation a technology and productivity showcase, it also exemplifies the incredible potential of determined ASHRAE members and the greater ASHRAE community working toward a common goal," said Jeff Littleton, ASHRAE executive vice president. "This renovation represents the largest capital investment in ASHRAE history at $7.65 million."

Major contributors to the Headquarters project include the ASHRAE Foundation, Carrier Corp., Automated Logic Corp./Automated Logic Georgia, ClimateMaster Inc., Daikin Industries Ltd., Southern Company/Georgia Power Company, and Trane.

Partners also include Aircuity Inc. and Interface FLOR. Also donating are Allsteel®/Ivan Allen; Mark H. Brandli, design principal for Richard Wittschiebe Hand; CxGBS; Dynamic Air Quality Solutions; EBTRON Inc.; GE Power; Bill and Margaret Harrison; Bruce Hunn; ITT/Bell & Gossett/James M. Pleasants Co.; NorthWrite Inc.; PolyCon Manufacturing; Thermal Gas Systems Inc.; U.S. Green Building Council; and VFA Inc.

2008

HQ Earns ENERGY STAR® Label

ASHRAE has earned the U.S. Environmental Protection Agency's (EPA) ENERGY STAR label, the national symbol for protecting the environment through superior energy efficiency, for its renovated Headquarters in Atlanta.

This signifies that the building performs in the top 25% of similar facilities nationwide for energy efficiency.

Jean Lupinacci, chief of the ENERGY STAR Commercial & Industrial Branch, presented the award during ASHRAE's 2010 Annual Conference. Lupinacci spoke during the Presidential Luncheon and presented an ENERGY STAR plaque to 2009–10 ASHRAE President Gordon Holness.

Jean Lupinacci of ENERGY STAR presents a plaque to 2009 – 10 President Gordon Holness, P.E.

"Improving the energy efficiency of our nation's buildings is critical to protecting our environment," Lupinacci said. "From the boiler room to the boardroom, organizations are leading the way by making their buildings more efficient and earning EPA's ENERGY STAR."

"In deciding to renovate our existing Headquarters building, ASHRAE followed its mission of 'promoting a sustainable world'," said Holness. "The renovation gave us the opportunity to demonstrate

See ENERGY STAR, Page 2

that existing buildings can be upgraded to provide equal or better than new building performance. We are delighted to have achieved the ENERGY STAR rating as further indication of successful implementation and real-world performance."

Commercial buildings that earn the ENERGY STAR use an average of 35% less energy than typical buildings and also release 35% less carbon dioxide into the atmosphere. ASHRAE improved its energy performance by managing energy strategically across the entire organization and by making cost-effective improvements to its building. ASHRAE has prevented greenhouse gas emissions equal to the electricity use from nearly 22 households for a year.

The national average site energy use index (EUI) is 68 and average source EUI is 228. ASHRAE's site energy intensity is 49 and source is 162.

The building received an A– rating "As Designed" in the new building energy labeling program launched by ASHRAE. The Building Energy Quotient™ (Building EQ) program will include both asset and operational ratings for all building types, except residential.

The renovation also earned LEED Platinum Certification in the New Construction 2.2 rating system from the U.S. Green Building Council. It is one of only six buildings in the state of Georgia to receive a LEED Platinum rating, the highest certification the program offers.

ENERGY STAR was introduced by EPA in 1992 as a voluntary, market-based partnership to reduce greenhouse gas emissions through energy efficiency. Today, the ENERGY STAR label can be found on more than 60 different kinds of products, new homes and commercial and industrial buildings. Products and buildings that have earned the ENERGY STAR prevent greenhouse gas emissions by meeting strict energy-efficiency specifications set by the government.

To Earn ENERGY STAR, ASHRAE:

- Reduced its estimated annual energy usage by more than 32.5% through enhancements to the building envelope and use of the following systems: Dedicated outside air system with energy recovery, ground-source heat pumps and mini-split systems with heat recovery.
- Used an extensive permanent air quality monitoring system to help sustain occupant comfort and well-being in the renovated building.
- Used a 6,000 cfm (2831 L/s) dedicated outside air system for the building that can provide ventilation rates to each space that are 30% higher than Standard 62.1-2004.
- Reduced IAQ problems resulting from the construction/renovation process in order to help sustain the comfort and well-being of construction workers and building occupants by developing and following a construction IAQ management plan.
- Provided a comfortable thermal environment that supports the productivity and well-being of all building occupants by adhering to the requirements of ASHRAE Standard 55 and by surveying their occupants for feedback on a regular basis.
- Demonstrated how PV arrays can be used to generate clean power by taking advantage of under-used space on the building roof. It is estimated that the installed array will provide more than 8% of the building's total annual energy cost in the form of renewable energy (in addition to the energy savings measures taken).

For a complete list of sustainability measures undertaken by ASHRAE, visit www.ashrae.org/building.

2010

Appendix B

The Show

In 1922, the International Exposition Company organized the National Exposition of Power and Mechanical Engineering, an outgrowth of the Exposition of Chemical Industries formed in 1915. A portion of the Power Show was devoted to heating and ventilating equipment, which, over the years, grew in size and importance. Post-show editorial coverage on the sixth Power Show which was held in 1927 indicated that of 450 displays, 225 included some phase of heating, refrigeration or air conditioning.

Some of the heating and ventilating exhibitors at the 1927 Power Show.

By 1927, the Heating and Ventilating Section of the Power Show had grown to such size—and the industry to such strength and importance—that officials of the International Exposition Company turned their thoughts to the establishment of an exposition devoted solely to heating and ventilation.

During this same period, The A.S.H.V.E. considered initiating its own annual exposition to present its members' information concerning the latest mechanical equipment to the industry and to the public. In 1927, The A.S.H.V.E. Council appointed a special committee headed by Thornton Lewis to investigate the possibility of having a heating and ventilating exposition.

So it was that late that same year International Exposition Company Vice President Charles Roth wrote to The A.S.H.V.E. asking for its opinion on organizing an exposition. In a period of enlightened self-interest, the company and The A.S.H.V.E. entered into a cooperative effort to stage biennial product expositions. The first International Heating and Ventilating Exposition opened January 27, 1930 at Philadelphia's Commercial Museum under "the auspices of The American Society of Heating and Ventilating Engineers."

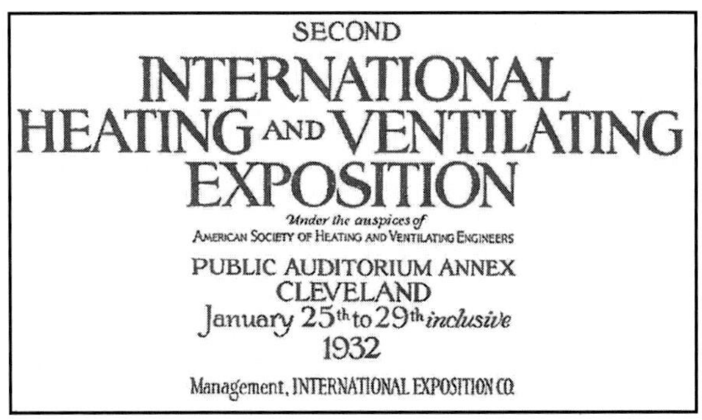

In 1947, the seventh exposition was staged. It proved so popular that ASHVE voted to hold the show annually through 1950. In making this decision, the ASHVE Council noted that through the annual combination of physical exhibits, technical papers and general discussions, the Society was

---

Much of this appendix is drawn from "The Expo" by Andrew T. Boggs which appeared in the June 1985 issue of *ASHRAE Journal*.

able to best transfer and exchange information to its members and to the industry. It was with the idea of broadening avenues of information that ASHVE decided to hold the annual exposition with concurrent sessions of the Society meeting.

Following the 1950 exposition in Dallas, Texas, ASHVE decided to hold international expositions only in major cities (Chicago, Philadelphia, New York) and only in the odd-numbered years.

Refrigeration Shows

The International Refrigeration Exposition Association was incorporated October 2, 1912 for purposes of obtaining the best solutions to scientific, technical and industrial questions concerning refrigeration and the transportation of perishable products, for considering laws and regulations governing the transport of perishables, and for holding conventions and exhibitions so that anyone interested in the topic could participate.

The first exhibition was held less than twelve months later, September 17 to October 1, 1913, at Chicago in conjunction with the third International Congress of Refrigeration. The show designated special days for everyone from meat packers to ice men, from housewives to technical college students, from children to butchers. Displays and demonstrations, including a variety of special foods, highlighted the art of refrigeration.

For all of its promise, the International Refrigeration Exposition was not as successful as its organizers had hoped, and in 1914, the shareholders voted to dissolve the corporation. The only refrigeration exhibitions held for a number of years were small, local affairs.

In 1939, the Refrigeration Supplies and Parts Association sponsored its first exposition devoted to products utilized in commercial and industrial refrigeration. Named the All-Industry Exposition, it took place in January 1939 in Chicago at the Stevens Hotel. There were 97 exhibitors and the total attendance was 6,274.

In 1940, the association changed its name to the Refrigeration Equipment Manufacturers Association, which in 1953 through merger became the Air-Conditioning and Refrigeration Institute (ARI). Its biennial show continued throughout these years, becoming known in 1955 as the National Exposition.

The ASRE's 1954 Research Exhibit held at its 50th Anniversary Meeting included seventeen displays and "drew hundreds." Carrier Corporation showed the electronic fan. Left to right: M. Eisenstein & R.K. Chapman, Carrier; F. Saver, Emerson; C.A. Hathaway, Torrington; and L. Schneider, Emerson.

In 1951, The ASRE initiated the Research Exhibit Program at its annual meetings to stimulate creative thinking by demonstrating research in progress. Said The ASRE, "This program is not a duplication of any existing exhibit and should not be confused with any commercial trade shows."

Officials on hand at the opening of the 16th National Air Conditioning & Refrigeration Institute's Exposition in Cleveland in 1970 represented SMACCNA, NHAW, NESCA, ASHRAE, ARW, RETA and RSES. ARI Managing Director L.N. Hunter cut the ribbon.

The ASHRAE-ARI Exposition

In 1970, ARI voted to combine its show with the ASHRAE-sponsored show in order to maximize the marketing potential that a single, industry-wide show would provide. The first combined show was held in 1972 at New Orleans.

It was agreed that both sponsors shared responsibility for providing enough frequency of exposure to make the joint exposition an effective marketing

tool. Thus, the show would be held every year. Similarly, it was decided to rotate the show to sites other than Chicago and New York so that population shifts would be accounted for and a broadened marketing base would be established.

A.T. Boggs, executive director of ASHRAE, and L.N. Hunter, managing director of ARI, issued a joint statement: "The decision to hold shows in large centers on alternate years, and in certain specified major areas on a planned schedule of rotation in other years, will offer a market place for all types of exhibiting companies—those who believe that an all-industry show should be taken to different areas of the country, and those who believe that their best interests lie in exhibiting in the large metropolitan areas of the East and Mid-West.

"Bringing together these two national shows under a unified direction will permit long-range scheduling of the new annual show, and thus be of value to exhibitors who want to make long-range plans for their participation in expositions."

At left, Andrew T. Boggs, Executive Director of ASHRAE, and L.N. Hunter, Managing Director of ARI, announced the first joint show would be held in 1972.

1932

1932

1936

ASHVE Exhibit Gets Crowds

Working example of cooperative research study at the University of Illinois plays to good audiences at recent exposition

1953

Gathering at the 1955 ASHRAE booth are G.B. Boone of Tecumseh, C.M. Ashley of Carrier, John Engalitcheff, Jr., of Baltimore Air Coil, Wesley L. Guiles of Flexible Tubing.

1957

1961

1987

Exhibitor
REGISTRATION
EXHIBITS
ASHRAE BOOKSTORE
ASHRAE

1987

1994

Bring Home the Gold in '96...

Exhibit at the AHR Expo

INTERNATIONAL
AIR-CONDITIONING
HEATING
REFRIGERATING
EXPOSITION

FEBRUARY 19-21, 1996
GEORGIA WORLD CONGRESS CENTER
ATLANTA, GA

Co-sponsors:

First Atlanta Show in 6 years...

Who Attends the AHR Expo*?

Attendee Job Titles

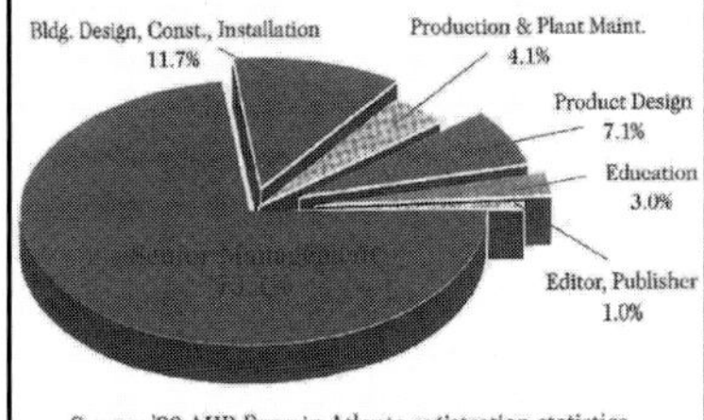

Source: '90 AHR Expo in Atlanta registration statistics based on 100% of assigned categories.

- **84% have purchase authority.** Of these, 35% make the final purchasing decision.
- **70% will buy one or more products** as a direct consequence of seeing them at the show.
- **43% are first-time attendees,** so you penetrate markets you may miss through other sales channels.
- **1 out of 3 is an engineer or architect** – more than any other HVAC&R show.
- **More than a third are top management:** presidents, owners, partners and vice presidents.

* Independent attendance survey conducted by Exhibit Surveys for '92 AHR Expo in Anaheim.

Classification by Industry	Percent
Contracting	27.9%
Distribution	26.6%
Engineering & Construction	9.7%
Facility Management	2.0%
Industrial Plant Operation	1.7%
Public Utilities	1.9%
Manufacturers of HVAC, Refrig. and Allied Equipment & Components	13.0%
Government Departments	1.1%
Publishing	.6%
Education	3.0%
Others	12.5%

Source: '90 AHR Expo in Atlanta registration statistics.

Note: The AHR Expo reaches into many areas where visitors cannot be placed in traditional categories – thus the "Other" designation where new opportunities for your product may be hidden.

Atlanta from 1978 to Present: Enormous Growth!

Year in Atlanta	Attendance	Exhibitors	Square Footage
1996	25,000+*	900+*	265,000+*
1990	23,677	800	249,686
1984	15,813	577	185,655
1978	10,878	322	103,283

* Projected

AHR Expo Preview

75 Years of Innovation

A view of the Emerson Electrical Manufacturing booth at the inaugural International Heating and Ventilating Exposition, held in the Commercial Museum, Philadelphia, Jan. 27–31, 1930.

The HVAC&R industry has changed dramatically in the last 75 years and it's a safe bet that every advance has been showcased at the Air-Conditioning, Heating and Refrigeration Exposition (AHR Expo).

This year's show marks the 75th year of the Show, and continues that trend. It also continues a partnership with ASHRAE and the International Exposition Company that started with the first Show on Jan. 27–31, 1930 at the Commercial Museum in Philadelphia. At that time, air-conditioning was just emerging as a technology and the Show was known as the International Heating and Ventilating Exposition, and ASHRAE was the American Society Heating and Ventilating Engineers.

What follows here are excerpts from a history of the Show from Proclaiming the Truth, a book published by ASHRAE in 1995.

Reprinted from ASHRAE's *Proclaiming the Truth*

In 1922, the International Exposition Co. (IEC) organized the National Exposition of Power and Mechanical Engineering, an outgrowth of the Exposition of Chemical Industries, which was formed in 1915. A portion of the show was devoted to heating and ventilating equipment, which, over the years, grew in size and importance. Post-show editorial coverage on the sixth show held in 1927 indicated that of 450 displays, 225 included some phase of heating, refrigeration or air conditioning.

By 1927, the heating and ventilating section of the show had grown to such size — and the industry to such strength and importance — that officials of IEC turned their thoughts to the establishment of an exposition devoted solely to heating and ventilation.

During this same period, the American Society of Heating and Ventilating Engineers (ASHVE) considered initiating its own annual exposition to present to its members information concerning the latest mechanical equipment to the industry and to the public. In 1927, the ASHVE Council appointed a special committee headed by Thornton Lewis to investigate the possibility of having a heating and ventilating exposition.

So it was that late that same year IEC vice president Charles Roth wrote ASHVE asking for its opinion on organizing an exposition. In a period of enlightened self-interest, the company and ASHVE entered into a cooperative effort to stage biennial product expositions. The first International Heating and Ventilating Exposition opened Jan. 27, 1930, at Philadelphia's Commercial Museum under "the auspices of The American Society of Heating and Ventilating Engineers."

In 1947, the seventh exposition was staged. It proved so popular that ASHVE voted to hold the show annually through 1950 with concurrent sessions of the Society meeting.

Following the 1950 exposition in Dallas, Texas, ASHVE decided to hold international expositions only in major cities (Chicago, Philadelphia, New York) and only in the odd-numbered years.

Refrigeration Shows

The International Refrigeration Exposition Association was incorporated Oct. 2, 1912, and the first exhibition was held less than 12 months later, Sept. 17 to Oct. 1, 1913, in Chicago in conjunction with the third International Congress of Refrigeration. The show designated special days for everyone from meat packers to ice men, from housewives to technical college students, from children to butchers. For all of its promise, the International Refrigeration Exposition was not successful as its organizers had hoped, and in 1914, the shareholders voted to dissolve the corporation. The only refrigeration exhibitions held for a number of years were small, local affairs.

In 1939, the Refrigeration Supplies and Parts Association sponsored its first exposition devoted to products utilized in commercial and industrial refrigeration. Named the All-Industry Exposition, it took place in January 1939 in Chicago at the Stevens Hotel. There were 97 exhibitors and the total attendance was 6,274.

In 1940, the association changed its name to the Refrigeration Equipment Manufacturers Association, which in 1953 through merger became the Air-Conditioning and Refrigeration Institute (ARI). Its biennial show continued throughout these years, becoming known in 1955 as the National Exposition.

ASHRAE-ARI Exposition

In 1970, ARI voted to combine its show with the ASHRAE-sponsored show in order to maximize the marketing potential that a single, industry-wide show would provide. The first combined show was held in 1972 at New Orleans.

It was agreed that both sponsors shared responsibility for providing enough frequency of exposure to make the joint exposition an effective marketing tool. Thus, the show would be held every year. Similarly, it was decided to rotate the show to sites other than Chicago and New York so that population shifts would be accounted for and a broadened marketing base would be established.

Innovations on Display for 2005

Eighty-four products were entered in the 2005 AHR Expo Innovation Awards, created to recognize the most innovative HVAC&R products showcased at the International Air-Conditioning, Heating, Refrigerating Exposition. The competition, sponsored by ASHRAE, the International Exposition Co. (IEC), and the Air-Conditioning and Refrigeration Institute (ARI), is intended to encourage innovation and provide vocational school scholarships for HVAC&R students.

The awards were open to all products exhibited at the 2005 AHR Expo except those that won Innovation Awards in 2004 or 2003.

"In 1929, the chair of the Society's increase the membership committee encouraged members to attend the first-ever Expo with this message: 'In this simple way you can do your part to build up your industry and make your Society of greater influence and usefulness,'" said ASHRAE President Ron Vallort, P.E. "I echo his sentiments. Attending the Expo lets you see first-hand how the technology developed by our members is put to practical use. In return, you may take away ideas on how to further improve technology. The Innovation Awards recognize the best of this technology, and I encourage ASHRAE members to take time to visit the Expo to see these products."

Products were judged by a panel selected by ASHRAE Journal based on application, innovation, value, and market impact. Descriptions of the 84 entries follow.

Location

The 2005 AHR Expo will be held in the North/South Building, South Concourse Entrance of the Orange County Convention Center.

Show Hours

Mon., Feb. 7 10 a.m. – 6:00 p.m.
Tues., Feb. 8 10 a.m. – 6:00 p.m.
Wed., Feb. 9 10 a.m. – 4:00 p.m.

AHR Expo, Feb. 7–9, 2005, Orlando, Fla.

2004

An Investment in the Future

ASHRAE Research & AHR Expo

The AHR Expo has not only showcased the latest in technology over the past 75 years, it has allowed ASHRAE to further technology through its research program.

Income from the Expo is used to match contributions to ASHRAE's research program from members and their companies. These funds allow ASHRAE to fund some $2 million of research each year.

Since its research program was started in 1919, the Society has funded thousands of projects addressing such topics as sound, duct design, the effect of oil in refrigerants, load calculations, thermal conductivity, simplified energy analysis procedures, weather data, refrigerant property data, fire and smoke control and solar design.

"The most significant ASHRAE research has been in the areas of human comfort and the properties of materials and systems used in buildings and refrigeration systems," said Larry Spielvogel, P.E., a director-at-large and former chair of ASHRAE's energy conservation committee. "Only an organization such as ASHRAE has the continuity, the ability to generate research funding, and is able to attract researchers from disparate backgrounds and institutions, and provide a forum to integrate their knowledge to advance the science of HVAC&R engineering and the art of human comfort."

Significant projects in the early years of the Society's research program include creation of a comfort zone chart in 1922; studies of thermal comfort, many of which were conducted by F.C. Houghten and C.P. Yaglou; Margaret Ingles' development of the "effective temperature" scale to incorporate humidity and air movement in the equation for human comfort; and creation of a new psychrometric chart in 1961.

Since the late 1960s, when the Society began keeping detailed records, ASHRAE has funded more than 1,300 projects, including:

- RP-43, *ASHRAE Environmental Studies*, Frederick Rohles, Preston McNall and Ralph Nevins, Kansas State University
- RP-66, *Load Profiles and Energy Requirements for Heating and Cooling Buildings*, C.F. Sepsy, Ohio State University
- RP-102, *Measurement of Thermal Characteristics and Response Factors of Walls and Roofs*, C.O. Pedersen and W. F. Stoecker, University of Illinois
- RP-118, *Thermal Requirements for Human Comfort*, Nevins and Rohles, Kansas State University
- RP-158, *Development of a Heating and Cooling Load Calculation Manual*, William Rudoy, University of Pittsburgh
- RP-185, *Line Sizing with Refrigerants 717, 12, 22 and 502*, D.D. Wile, consulting engineer
- RP-198, *Optimizing Thermal Transients for Comfort and Energy Use*, Rohles, Kansas State University
- RP-202, *Ventilation Requirements in Operating Rooms*, J.E. Woods, Iowa State University
- RP-207, *Pressurization and Smoke Shaft Concept*, Integrated Systems and National Bureau of Standards
- RP-251, *Degree Days Method for Simplified Energy Analysis*, R.D. Fishcher, Battelle Columbus Laboratories
- RP-309, *Dynamic and Seasonal Performance of Central Forced Warm Air Heating Systems Installed in Residences*, D. Locklin and R. Fischer, Battelle Columbus Laboratories
- RP-462, *A Study to Establish a Database on Existing Thermal Environments in Office Buildings*, A. Arens, University of California, Berkeley.
- RP-548, *Determining the Solar-Optical and Solar Heat Gain Properties of Fenestration Systems*, S. Selkowitz, Lawrence Berkeley Labs
- RP-577, *Attic Radiant Barrier Systems*, Byron Jones, Kansas State University
- RP-610, *Control of Legionella Strains in Non-Cooling Tower Reservoirs*, Victor L. Yu, University of Pittsburgh
- RP-626, *Upgrade of GRP-158, Cooling and Heating Load Calculation Manual*, Faye McQuiston, Oklahoma State University, and Edward Sowell, Ayres Sowell Associates

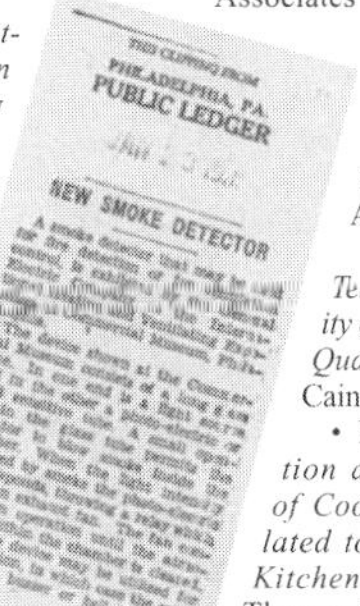

THIS CLIPPING FROM PHILADELPHIA, PA. PUBLIC LEDGER

NEW SMOKE DETECTOR

- RP-641, *Duct Design Using the T-Method with Duct Leakage Incorporated*, Robert Tsal, Netsal and Associates
- RP-695, *Effects of Temperature and Humidity on Perceived Indoor Air Quality, Phase I*, William Cain, J.D. Pierce FND.
- RP-745, *Identification and Characterization of Cooling Effluents as Related to Optimum Design of Kitchen Ventilation Systems*, Thomas Kuehn, University of Minnesota
- RP-777, *Computer Algorithms for Moisture Loss and Latent Heat Loads in Bulk Storage of Fruits and Vegetables*, Bryan Becker, University of Missouri
- RP-785, *Building Insulation System Thermal Anomalies*, Alex McGowan, Enermodal Eng.
- RP-843, *Human Response to Air Movement: Part 1: Preference and Draft Discomfort*, P.O. Fanger, Technical University of Denmark
- RP-864, *Controlling Moisture in Walls Exposed to Hot and Humid Climates*, M.H. Hosni, Kansas State University
- RP-890, *Updating the Tables of Design Weather Conditions in the* ASHRAE Handbook –Fundamentals, Don Colliver, University of Kentucky
- RP-903, *Experimental Validation of Multizone Models for Predicting Air Contaminant Transport in High-Rise Buildings*, G.K. Yuill, Pennsylvania State University
- RP-942, *Comparison of Load Calculation Procedures*, Philip Haves and Jeff Spitler, Loughborough University
- RP-957, *Relate Air Quality and Other Factors to Symptoms Reported by Passengers and Crew on Commercial Aircraft*, J.N. Janczewski, Consolidated Safety Serv.
- RP-959, *Determine Air Contaminants in the Engine Bleed-Air Supply on Commercial Aircraft*, Niren Nagda, Energen Consulting
- RP-969, *Laboratory Design Guide*, Charles Dorgan, Dorgan Associates
- RP-987, *Preparation of a Toolkit for Building Load Calculations*, Curt Pedersen, University of Illinois
- RP-1047, *Development of a Design Guide for Humidity Control*, Lew Harriman, Mason Grant
- RP-1161, *The Effect of Personal Control and Thermal Variability on Comfort and Acceptability*, Gail Brager, University of California-Berkeley
- RP-1257, *Indoor Environmental Effects on Performance of School Work by Children*, David Wyon and Pawel Wargocki, Technical University of Denmark
- RP-1261, An *HVAC Design Guide for Tall Buildings*, Donald Ross, Donald E. Ross.
- RP-1262, *Relate Air Quality and Other Factors to Comfort and Health-Related Symptoms Reported by Passengers and Crew on Commercial Transport Aircraft*, Chet Spicer, Battelle Mem. Inst.

LENOX® LENOX® *Gold*™ features a new patented tooth design and specially formulated titanium nitride (TiN) coating that works together to make it the longest-lasting reciprocating saw blade ever and the fastest cutting blade on the market.

Midwest Tool and Cutlery Co. Upright Snips™. The patent pending 90° blade-to-handle design ergonomically improves cutting motion. Use push or pull cutting motion; snip turns in hand while cutting; creates ergonomic wrist posture that improves wrist range motion.

PROMAX ProVax is a unique portable machine that uses a combined motor, oil-less compressor and vacuum pump, which enables technicians to recover and evacuate HVAC&R systems with a single tool.

Spectronics OPTIMAX™, uses super-high-flux LED technology to deliver 10 times brighter fluorescent light than regular LED lights. Its power equals that of 100 W lamps plugged into an ac power source.

SUPCO SmarTester. This hand-held instrument can test circuits simultaneously. It pinpoints current and voltage problems and intermittent problems without having to strip any wires or analyze equipment diagrams. It replaces the need for several test instruments.

Veris Industries Hawkeye smart fan/pump switch. This microcontroller-based current switch utilizes unique algorithms, enabling this product to self-calibrate at the push of a button, "learning" conditions of load and setting trip points accordingly.

Victaulic Co. Vic-300 MasterSeal butterfly valve, features a patent-pending, pressure responsive seat design that yields continuous 360° seat seal equally on both sides of disc when fully closed and minimizes long-term wear, resulting in a higher life cycle.

Vulcain Inc. VA30IEM expansion module. Designed with dual-beam, electronic self-calibrating IR sensor technology, it monitors up to four remote sensors and includes built-in features and programming to meet mechanical code standards.

WIKA Instrument Corp. OT-1. The OT-1's thin film sensor technology enables pressure measurement in very low ranges. Never before has high performance been associated with economical sensor technology.

Ventilation

A.J. Manufacturing, Inc. pressure/vacuum relief door. A non-mechanical infinitely variable adjustment latch mechanism combined with an insulated door and unique seal provide industry leading reductions in leakage of the system's processed air, while simultaneously maintaining precise release performance.

BIG ASS FANS Powerfoil fan. The unique foil design produces more cfm/watt than any fan offered. It costs 50% less to operate in the winter than the company's Wickerbill fan. At maximum speed, the fan can produce up to 332,000 cfm (157 000 L/s) for cooling.

Broan-NuTone, Recessed Fan/Light. This one-of-a-kind product is a fan and recessed light all in one unit, making for easier, quicker installation. The product also is inconspicuous, stylish and quieter than traditional house fans.

Dais Analytic Corp., ConsERV, utilizes proton exchange membrane material providing highly efficient recovery of both sensible and latent heat. It has the performance of ERV wheels with no moving parts and zero leakage.

Hardcast, FLEX-GRIP 550. Hardcast is the first to offer a spray-grade, water-based duct sealant. This innovative system eliminates the inconvenient bottleneck caused by sealing ductwork manually with labor-intensive bucket and brush applications.

The Dryer Box's The Dryerbox will influence the architectural layout of the laundry room, reduce the number of dryer-related house fires and provide for better dryer exhaust efficiency by eliminating some of the restrictive bends.

Jackson Systems, LLC Comfort System™ VAV diffuser is designed to maintain draft-free discharge air along the ceiling, providing sustained discharge velocity throughout the volume range. The diffuser includes a room thermostat enabling users to adjust temperature.

At the Exposition, 100-year-old stoves were exhibited.

METU Meinig AG LX access door. A set of levers fitted with security devices against accidental opening allow fast installation and access door operation. Additionally, smoother inner surface, elegant design, no protruding bolts and duct opening rubber-edge molding for additional security.

Moffitt Corp., hurricane wind driven turbine vent, enables engineers to lower customers' energy consumption while providing environmentally friendly designs. It uses recycled content and can be recycled, con serves energy using wind power, generates no emissions or noise, reduces construction materials traditionally required and contributes to a healthy indoor environment.

Titus TFS Fantom IQ incorporates an optional but integral patent-pending slide-out attenuator. This device provides for sound levels that are among the quietest in the industry. The integral feature eliminates field labor costs for installation.

AHR Mexico

In 1997 the AHR Expo added a new market, Mexico. More than 250 companies exhibited at the first Mexico show at the Cintermax Convention Center in Monterrey. Almost 6,000 visitors viewed the products, including large chillers and cooling towers, and saw live demonstrations of operating machinery.

ASHRAE and ARI sponsored the expo, and ASHRAE organized a full slate of training courses, some of which were co-organized with the Refrigeration Service Engineers Society (RSES).

The show alternated between Monterrey and Mexico City since that first show and in 2015 was held for the first time in Guadalajara, an important manufacturing center in Mexico. As the show grew, the host, the ASHRAE Mexico Chapter, organized the accompanying educational program.

In anticipation of the 2020 show in Monterrey, the organizers expect 80,000 ft^2 of exhibits, 11,000 visitors, 400 exhibitin companies, and 30 specialized educational events given by the ASHRAE Monterrey Chapter.

MEXICO CITY—ASHRAE President William J. Coad (left) is shown with Xochitl Galvaz and Jose Luis Trillo, P.E., Member ASHRAE, at the 2001 AHR Expo-Mexico held here Sept. 25-27. Galvaz is an energy specialist in Mexico. She also is a popular government official, serving in the cabinet-level position that represents Mexico's 13 million indigenous people. Trillo is president of the ASHRAE chapter in Mexico City. More than 6,500 people and 260 companies participated in AHR Expo-Mexico. First held in 1997, the event is sponsored by ASHRAE and the Air-Conditioning and Refrigeration Institute (ARI).

2001

AHR Showcase for Innovation

In 2003, AHR Expo launched an awards program to recognize products judges considered the most innovative in different award categories. *ASHRAE Journal* organized the competition. Since then the awards program has come to becrecognized as one of the industry's most prestigious. The 2003 winners of the AHR Expo Innovation Awards were:

- Heating: York International UPG, Stealth Hot Heat Pump
- Cooling: Baltimore Aircoil Co., HXV-Hybrid FXV
- Refrigeration: Copeland Corp., Digital Scroll
- Ventilation: Control Resources, Inc., SmartFan Nimbus AC Fan Speed Control
- Indoor Air Quality: PureChoice, Inc., PureTrac Air Monitoring System

ASHRAE In Mexico

Manuel de Anda Chapter Chartered, Society to Co-sponsor AHR Expo-Mexico

ATLANTA – ASHRAE has chartered the Manuel de Anda Chapter in Mexico during a special chartering ceremony held November 12, 1996 in Mexico City, Mexico. The Society also announced that it will co-sponsor the first Air-Conditioning, Heating, Refrigeration Exposition (AHR Expo-Mexico) to be held in Monterry, Mexico on September 10-12, 1997.

"The chartering of the Manuel de Anda chapter underscores ASHRAE's dedication to serving our members around the world, especially those living and working outside the U.S. and Canada. As the fastest growing segment of the Society's membership, their participation, enthusiasm and work on behalf of ASHRAE is integral to the Society's ability to achieve its mission of advancing the arts and sciences of HVAC&R technology around the world," said ASHRAE President James E. Hill, Ph.D.

"The Manuel de Anda Chapter becomes the 165th chapter to be chartered since the Society was founded more than 100 years ago and the 11th chapter to be chartered outside the U.S. and Canada. It also is the first ASHRAE chapter to be named after a person," he said.

Manuel de Anda, 1906-1989, was a well-respected consulting engineer, researcher and teacher in Mexico, specializing in air conditioning, hydraulics, electrical installations and fire protection. He taught for many years at the University of Mexico's School of Engineering and Architecture and at the National Polytecnic of Mexico. He also founded and served as president of the Asociacion Mexicana de Empresas del Ramo de Instalaciones para la Construccion, an ASHRAE Associate Society, said Hill.

De Anda's numerous contributions included designing HVAC&R systems for more than 3,000 buildings and power plants. His research focused on measuring solar impingement on windows and developing formulas to calculate the amount of heat gain at different hours throughout the year, said Hill. For more than 40 years (1941-88), he collected climatological data in 840 Mexican cities, which were published by the AMICA and approved by the International Civil Aviation Organization and the United Nations.

ASHRAE and the Air-Conditioning and Refrigeration Institute have agreed to co-sponsor the first AHR Exposition - Mexico, said Hill. The goal of this new exposition is to further advance HVAC&R technology and to provide a way for manufacturers of HVAC&R products to identify new customers, agents and distributors in the Mexican and Central American markets, he said.

"The AHR Expo-Mexico is patterned after the very successful ASHRAE-ARI co-sponsored AHR Exposition held annually in conjunction with ASHRAE's Winter Meeting. We expect this first exposition to attract more than 4000 contractors, engineers, wholesalers, representatives, agents, facilities managers and equipment manufacturers, and to feature state-of-the-art in HVAC&R systems, equipment and components," he said.

For more information about AHR Expo-Mexico contact the International Exposition Company, 15 Franklin Street, Westport, CT 06880, Tel: 203-221-9232, Fax: 203-221-9260 in the U.S., and in Mexico contact ISOA International c/o Cintermex, Local 33, primer Nivel, Av. Parque Fundidora #501, Col. Obrera 64010, Monterrey, N.L. Mexico, Tel: 011-52-8-369-6627, Fax: 011-52-8-369-6628.

1996

The first presentation of AHR Expo Innovation Awards took place in 2003. The award recipients are shown here with Donald Colliver, 2002–2003 ASHRAE President (back row, third from left); Thomas Bettcher, AHRI chairman (back row, fourth from left); and Hank Stevens, president of International Exposition Company.

- Energy: Turbocor Inc., TT 300 Centrifugal Refrigerant Compressor
- Instruments, Tools and Software: Honeywell Intl., Burner & Boiler Controls, HVAC Service Assistant

AHR Expo in 2020

By the time ASHRAE turned 125, the AHR Expo had become the world's largest HVAC&R event, attracting the most comprehensive gathering of industry professionals from around the globe each year.

The AHR Expo continues to provide a unique forum where manufacturers of all sizes and specialties, whether major industry brands or innovative start-ups, can come together to share ideas and showcase the future of HVAC&R technology under one roof. Since 1930, the AHR Expo has remained the industry's best place for original equipment manufacturers, engineers, contractors, facility operators, architects, educators, and other industry professionals to explore the latest trends and applications and to cultivate mutually beneficial business relationships.

Within the 2020 show will be product showcases. The Building Automation & Control Showcase features building automation, energy, and facility management systems; climate controls; monitoring systems; networked building systems such as lighting, security, and fire alarms; and wireless/cloud-based technologies. In the Software Center a visitor can find both off-the-shelf and customized solutions for project and field service management, including estimating; inventory control; GPS tracking; systems design, specification, and analysis; remote-based and cloud-based software; and more. Hundreds of seminars and demonstrations on the exhibit floor and in the classroom are presented.

There will be a new Product & Technology Theater, certifications, and other exams, and for the first time, a Podcast Pavilion where podcasts will be recorded live, sharing content with guests from the show floor and answering visitors' questions.

The annual AHR Expo Innovation Awards competition continues to honor the most inventive and original products, systems, and technologies showcased at each year's AHR Expo. The 2020 categories are building automation; cooling; green building; heating; indoor air quality; plumbing; refrigeration; software; tools and instruments; and ventilation. The *ASHRAE Journal* judges evaluate all award entries based on innovative design, creativity, application, value, and market impact.

AHR Mexico 2010

AHR Mexico 2010

AHR Mexico 2012

AHR Expo 2013

AHR Mexico 2015

AHR Mexico 2015

2003

2008

2009

2013

AHR EXPO Atlanta JAN 14-16 · 2019 — **ATTENDANCE REPORT**

STATISTICAL OVERVIEW

NEW FOR 2019: ATTENDANCE DATA VERIFIED USING RFID TECHNOLOGY learn more at ahrexpo.com/rfid

Verified Visitor Attendance	**27,047**
Verified Exhibitor Personnel	**18,031**
Total Verified Attendance	**45,078**
International Visitors	**4,868**
Countries Represented	**112**
First-time Visitors	**11,269**

Net Sq. Ft. of Exhibit Space	**493,120**
Exhibiting Companies	**1,824**
International Exhibitors	**495**
Countries Represented	**32**
Sponsors & Endorsing Associations	**34**

GEOGRAPHIC BREAKDOWN

ALL 50 STATES AND 112 COUNTRIES REPRESENTED

UNITED STATES

West Coast	**1,552**
Mountain	**887**
North Central	**3,129**
South Central	**3,579**
New England	**887**
Mid Atlantic	**3,105**
South Atlantic	**8,871**
Puerto Rico & US Territories	**169**

TOTAL 22,179

INTERNATIONAL

Canada	**1,509**
Europe	**535**
Mexico	**488**
South/Central America/Caribbean	**876**
Middle East	**341**
Asia/Pacific Rim/Australia	**1,002**
Africa/All other regions	**117**

TOTAL 4,868

TYPE OF BUSINESS

42% RESIDENTIAL; 80% COMMERCIAL; 54% INDUSTRIAL; 33% INSTITUTIONAL

Contractors/Dealers	**5,950**
Engineering, Design & Construction	**2,705**
Distribution	**8,903**
Manufacturers of HVACR and Allied Equipment & Components	**5,309**
Facility/Building/Plant Mgt. & Operations	**811**
Public Utilities	**371**
Education	**623**
Publishing/Press	**87**
Allied to the Field/Other	**2,288**

JOB FUNCTION

72% HAVE A ROLE IN PURCHASING

Senior Management	**10,548**
Engineer/Architect	**3,832**
Operations/Maintenance	**871**
Technician	**1,182**
Purchasing	**751**
Research/Product Design & Dev.	**766**
Marketing/Sales	**6,762**
Consultant/Allied to the Field	**1,032**
Publishing/Education	**491**
Not given/Other	**812**

International Expositions Sponsored/Cosponsored by ASHRAE

Show #	Year	City	NSF	# of Exhibitors	Attendance
1	1930	Philadelphia	46,650	273	842
2	1932	Cleveland	37,400	242	7900
3	1934	New York	23,203.5	148	15,256
4	1936	Chicago	46,195.5	298	27,743
5	1938	New York	61,647	327	40,057
6	1940	Cleveland	67,658	303	24,614
7	1941	San Francisco	12,973	73	3606
8	1947	Cleveland	80,158.5	305	30,516
9	1948	New York	75,660	335	36,446
10	1949	Chicago	87,240.32	305	24,440
11	1950	Dallas	50,934	213	8320
12	1951	Philadelphia	94,436	345	17,821
13	1953	Chicago	120,005	429	29,549
14	1955	Philadelphia	133,162	472	21,162
IS	1957	Chicago	171,374.5	532	23,442
16	1959	Philadelphia	152,245.62	489	20,699
17	1960	Dallas	59,676	221	7135
18	1961	Chicago	177,122.2	529	21,627
19	1963	New York	150,110.45	504	29,633
20	1965	Chicago	179,136	527	20,506
21	1967	Detroit	172,752.5	513	18,815
22	1969	Chicago	181,078.5	518	28,152
23	1971	Philadelphia	162,396.55	468	21,740
24	1972	New Orleans	82,136.25	281	8923
25	1973	Chicago	182,315	493	24,413
26	1974	Los Angeles	97,731	282	10,336
27	1975	Atlantic City	152,448	440	16,214
28	1976	Dallas	90,197.25	263	8993
29	1977	Chicago	184,016	522	25,316
30	1978	Atlanta	103,283.2	322	10,878
31	1979	Philadelphia	186,855.13	491	22,701
32	1980	Los Angeles	126,303.6	410	12,224
33	1981	Chicago	224,059	666	26,060
34	1982	Houston	154,779.3	537	12,585
35	1983	Atlantic City	221,656	636	25,505
36	1984	Atlanta	185,654.65	577	15,813
37	1985	Chicago	268,767	794	26,569
38	1986	San Francisco	167,009	501	14,364
39	1987	New York	293,972.30	836	29,082
40	1988	Dallas	203,424.30	601	15,813
41	1989	Chicago	311,725	945	30,288
42	1990	Atlanta	249,980.56	852	23,677
43	1991	New York	268,116.96	837	26,481

International Expositions Sponsored/Cosponsored by ASHRAE

Show #	Year	City	NSF	# of Exhibitors	Attendance
44	1992	Anaheim	239,220	833	17,583
45	1993	Chicago	306,236.5	1001	34,060
46	1994	New Orleans	255,975.12	930	18,095
47	1995	Chicago	336,326	1089	36,881*
48	1996	Atlanta	316,748	1083	23,838
49	1997	Philadelphia	315,427	1020	33,439
50	1998	San Francisco	301,463	1034	20,431
51	1999	Chicago	399,927	1299	33,367
52	2000	Dallas	315,021	1312	25,401
53	2001	Atlanta	385,745	1292	27,012
54	2002	Atlantic City	299,403	1143	28,062
55	2003	Chicago	400,416	1408	38,224
56	2004	Anaheim	324,590	1214	21,751
57	2005	Orlando	372,955	1378	26,849
58	2006	Chicago	410,415	1432	37,292
59	2007	Dallas	347,000	1224	28,170
60	2008	New York	363,405	1884	38,534
61	2009	Chicago	396,048	1911	34,799
62	2010	Orlando	354,864	1825	28,114
63	2011	Las Vegas	379,450	1937	33,612
64	2012	Chicago	428,645	1966	39,557
65	2013	Dallas	397,000	1951	33,778
66	2014	New York	385,000	1942	42,893
67	2015	Chicago	486,600	2118	42,344
68	2016	Orlando	469,540	2063	42,396
69	2017	Las Vegas	500,159	1968	48,568
70	2018	Chicago	534,080	2155	49,995
71	2019	Atlanta	493,120	1824	27,047**

* Visitor attendance
** Audited visitor attendance

Appendix C

Presidential Award of Excellence

Frank H. Bridgers initiated the Presidential Award of Excellence during his presidential term, 1970–71. Said Mr. Bridgers as he concluded his year:

"I proposed an 'Award of Excellence for Improvement of Chapter Operations' which sets forth simple measurable criteria for judging three aspects of chapter operations: (1) a 10% increase in membership, (2) a 10% increase in average attendance, (3) the equivalent of $10 per member contributed to the ASHRAE Research Fund by local businesses in the Chapter area.

"It appears that 20 to 25% of our chapters will earn this 'Award of Excellence' which will be presented at the Annual Meeting in Washington [1971]. In a year that has been classified as a recession, I am perfectly aware that some chapters may actually deserve more credit for 'holding their own' than those that will receive the 'Award of Excellence.' To those who tried but did not qualify due to economic conditions, I want to express my sincere gratitude for their efforts. I am very much aware that some of the chapters in Canada fall in this category.

"I would be remiss if I did not mention the Central Oklahoma Chapter (Oklahoma City area) which not only met the criteria, but more than doubled its performance in all requirements."

PAOE has evolved over the years, but it has remained a motivator of chapter performance. In 2000, ASHRAE President James E. Wolf assigned much of the reporting responsibility to chapters and regions, giving them greater ownership of the PAOE process. And all ASHRAE presidents in recent years have used PAOE to emphasize the pursuit of Society initiatives at the local level such as sustainability and young engineer development.

To recognize Presidential Award of Excellence winners in 1978-79 and in succeeding years, a mahogany plaque was designed for display at Society Headquarters.

1993-94 Results

Presidential Award of Excellence Measures Chapters' Achievements

The Presidential Award of Excellence (PAOE) measures chapter performance based on the following criteria: membership promotion; chapter history; chapter meeting attendance; CRC attendance; research promotion; educational activities; technical, energy and government activities; chapter program activities; and refrigeration. The following listing summarizes chapters' achievements in the PAOE program during the presidential year of Neil R. Patterson.

KEY

PAOE—(Regular) Chapters that meet the minimum requirements in eight of nine categories, with a minimum of 2,900 total points.
Star Award (*)—Chapters earning the PAOE and reaching par in all categories.
Special Citation (SC)—Chapters earning the PAOE and obtaining 4,400 or more total points.
Honor Roll (HR)—(Silver Emblem) Chapters that have earned the PAOE for at least four consecutive years.
High Honor Roll (HHR)—(Blue Emblem) Chapters that have earned the Star Award for at least four consecutive years.
Premier (PR)—(Gold Emblem) Chapters that have earned the PAOE every year since the award was originated, or the Chapter's inception (since 1970), with a minimum of four years; except that a chapter shall remain eligible for the Premier award if the PAOE is not achieved during the first year.

Region I

- Bi-State ... PAOE
- Boston ... SC,PAOE
- Central New York ... SC,PAOE
- Champlain Valley ... SC,HR
- Connecticut ... SC,HR
- Granite State ... SC,PR
- Long Island ... SC,HR
- New York ... SC,HR
- Niagara Frontier ... HR
- North Jersey ... SC,HR
- Northeast ... SC,HR
- Rochester ... SC,HR
- Twin Tiers ... *,SC,PR

Region II

- La Ville de Quebec ... SC,HR
- London ... PAOE
- Montreal ... SC,PAOE
- Ottawa Valley ... *,SC,HR
- Windsor ... SC,PAOE

Region III

- Anthracite ... *,PR
- Baltimore ... *,SC,HR
- Central Pennsylvania ... SC,HR
- Delaware ... HR
- Hampton Roads ... SC,PAOE
- Johnstown ... SC,HR
- National Capital ... SC,HR
- Philadelphia ... SC,HR
- Pittsburgh ... SC,HR
- Richmond ... HR
- Roanoke ... PR

Region IV

- Atlanta ... *,SC,HR
- Charleston ... *,SC,HR
- Greenville ... *,SC,HR
- North Piedmont ... *,SC,HR
- South Carolina ... *,HR
- Southern Piedmont ... *,SC,HHR
- Triangle ... *,SC,HR

Region V

- Cincinnati ... *,SC,HR
- Cleveland ... SC,HR
- Columbus ... SC,PAOE
- Detroit ... SC,HR
- Eastern Michigan ... HR
- Fort Wayne ... HR
- Toledo ... PAOE
- Western Michigan ... HR

Region VI

- Cedar Valley ... PAOE
- Central Illinois ... SC,HR
- Illinois ... SC,HR
- La Crosse Area ... SC,PR
- Madison ... HR
- Minnesota ... SC,HR
- Mississippi Valley ... PR
- Rockford ... SC,HR
- St. Louis ... SC,HR

Region VII

- Birmingham ... *,SC,HR
- East Tennessee ... *,SC,PAOE
- Louisville ... SC,HR
- Memphis ... HR
- Mississippi ... SC,HR
- Mobile ... SC,HR
- Nashville ... SC,PAOE
- New Orleans ... SC,PAOE
- North Alabama ... SC,PAOE
- Northwest Florida ... PAOE
- Tennessee Valley ... SC,PAOE

Region VIII

- Alamo ... *,SC,HR
- Arkansas ... SC,PAOE
- Central Oklahoma*,SC,HHR,PR
- Dallas ... HR
- East Texas ... HR
- Ft. Worth ... SC,HR
- Houston ... SC,HR
- Northeastern Oklahoma *,SC,PR
- West Texas ... SC,PAOE

Region IX

- Idaho ... SC,PAOE
- Kansas City ... SC,HR
- Nebraska ... *,SC,HHR
- New Mexico ... *,SC,HR
- Pikes Peak ... PAOE
- Rocky Mountain ... SC,HR
- South Dakota ... PR
- Utah ... SC,HR
- Wichita ... PAOE

Region X

- Central Arizona ... PAOE
- Golden Gate ... PAOE
- Hawaii ... SC,HR
- Northern Nevada ... PAOE
- Orange Empire ... SC,PAOE
- Sacramento Valley ... PAOE
- San Jose ... PAOE
- San Diego ... *,SC,PAOE
- Southern California ... SC,PAOE
- Tri-County ... PAOE

Region XI

- Alaska ... HR
- British Columbia ... HR
- Manitoba ... PAOE
- Oregon ... HR
- Puget Sound ... PAOE
- Southern Alberta ... HR

Region XII

- Central Florida ... *,SC,HR
- Florida West Coast ... *,SC,HHR
- Gold Coast ... SC,HR
- Gulfstream ... SC,HR
- Jacksonville ... *,SC,HHR
- Southwest Florida ... SC,HR
- Spacecoast ... SC,PAOE

PRESIDENTIAL AWARD OF EXCELLENCE

SCORING SYSTEM FOR 1976-77

William P. Chapman
President ASHRAE

Since its initiation by President Bridgers in July 1970, the Presidential Award of Excellence has become a valuable tool for ASHRAE. It is popular, useful, and an excellent means of inspiring chapters to work on issues of current importance. Hopefully, through continual changes and updating, it will remain popular and useful.

This year, the Award will be based on the principles that chapter performance should be related to a predetermined par, and all factors are of approximately equal importance.

In previous years, awards often were based on improvement. This meant that a chapter with a poor performance in the previous year could earn a large number of points by improving to a performance level that was average for the Society as a whole. This year, absolute performance will be the criterion.

In an effort to develop equality of opportunity for all chapters, I analyzed the performance for 1974-75. I found that chapter size has a significant influence on the awards for membership growth and chapter meeting attendance. Therefore, those awards should have a factor related to chapter size. The three other awards, research promotion, CRC conference attendance, and educational activities, are not affected by chapter size, providing of course that research promotion is stated in terms of dollars per member.

Statistical analysis indicates that three factors – growth, attendance, and research promotion – can be expressed algebraically as:

$$P_x = f(X/N)^b$$

where N is the par performance, and f is a factor related to chapter size in the cases of chapter growth and attendance. It is sufficiently accurate to simplify the general expression so that b = 1 or 0.5. Also, the factor f can be published for each chapter once for a given year, as soon as the membership, as of July 1, can be determined.

The par performance for each award factor is based on the performances for all the chapters in the last year for which we have full records; namely 1974-75. Par is approximately the median performance or that level exceeded by about half the chapters. For example, as of June 30, 1975, we had research contributions from 121 chapters. Sixty chapters had contributions of $10.07 per member or less; 60 had $10.33 per member or more; and one chapter had $10.18; therefore, the median was $10.18 per member. I have chosen $10.00 per member as par.

To make the factors of equal importance, I have selected 250 points as the award for a par performance. Again, using the expression for research contributions as an example:

$P_c = 250$, when c = 10, N =10, b =1/2

$$P_c = f\,(C/N)^{1/2}$$

$$250 = f(10/10)^{1/2}$$

so f=250

then $P_c = 250\ (c/10)^{1/2} = 79.057\sqrt{c}$

GENERAL CONDITIONS

The award will be based on performance in five separate and independent sections; namely:

- Membership Growth.
- Chapter Meeting Attendance.
- Research Promotion.
- CRC Conference Attendance.
- Educational Activities.

A total of 1,200 points is required to win the award. Special recognition will be given to those chapters that receive 2,400 or more points. An appropriate certificate and a streamer for the chapter banner will be awarded to each chapter winning the award. The streamers are color coded as follows:

1st year of award, streamer is RED.
2nd " " " " " GREEN.
3rd " " " " " BROWN.
4th " " " " " BLUE.
5th " " " " " PURPLE.
6th " " " " " WHITE.
7th year of award, streamer will be GOLD.

The Society year, 1976-77, will be the seventh year of the Presidential Award of Excellence.

The CRC conference attendance award is limited to a maximum of 250 points, and the educational activities award is limited to 525 points. The other three awards have no limit on the number of points that can be earned.

The reference to chapter membership is based on the Society records for the chapter area as of July 1, 1976, except that Life, Retired, and Student members are excluded.

MEMBERSHIP GROWTH

Previously we had the Blue Ribbon Award for growth and the Award of Excellence for "Applications received at Headquarters." This should be reversed

W.P. Chapman is Vice President Operations, Johnson Controls, Inc., Milwaukee, WI.

with the Blue Ribbon Award given for new members, and the Award of Excellence for growth.

It takes a chapter effort to have an increase in membership. Also, it is membership that counts, not applications, nor percentage growth. A new member is as important to the Society in one chapter as in another, and a drop-out is as harmful in one chapter as another. By basing the award on real growth, chapters are induced to assign someone, or a committee, the responsibility of retaining existing members. Headquarters has been instructed to make appropriate allowances for members that transfer.

The expression for evaluating the award, $P_g = f_g \sqrt{g}$ allows for chapter size. The reporting format simplifies the calculation. For example, Table 1 is the format that will be used; it will be sent to all chapters and Regional Chairmen and will have the exact values for g and a for each chapter. The complete tabulation will appear in the next Society Newsletter.

The expression for f_g is based on a statistical analysis of actual performance. This analysis determined that the normal, or par, performance is:

$$N_g = 0.05M\,(1-0.001\,M)$$

where M is chapter membership.

The general expression is:

$$P = a\,(g/N_g)^{1/2}$$

and when $g=N_g$, P=250 so

$$a = 250.$$

Substituting N_g in the general expression yields:

$$f_g = \frac{35355}{\sqrt{M\,(1000-M)}}$$

MEETING ATTENDANCE

An analysis of actual performance for 1974-75 indicates that a par performance is related to chapter size, and good accuracy results from using the expression for par,

$$N_a = 3.75\ .$$

Since the general expression is:

$$P_a = a(A/N_a) \text{ and } a = 250,$$

then substituting N_a yields

$$P_a = 200A/3\sqrt{M} \text{ with } f_a = 200/3\sqrt{M}$$

we can say $P_a = f_a A$.

f_a will be published for each chapter using chapter membership, M, as of 7-1-76 (see format in the section of Membership Growth).

•RESEARCH PROMOTION

This award is expressed by:

$$P_c = a\sqrt{c} = 250\sqrt{c/10}$$

$$= 79.057\sqrt{c}$$

where c = contributions, $/member, and a par performance is $101 member.

•CRC ATTENDANCE

In previous years, the requirements to earn points for CRC conference attendance were too severe. As a result, only 6 chapters that were not hosts for CRC conferences won 250 points in the year 1974-75. This year, the points will be as shown in Table 2. If the two delegates and four committee chairmen attend the CRC conference, the chapter will earn 250 points. The par performance and the maximum award is 250 points.

•EDUCATIONAL ACTIVITIES

The Education Committee has reviewed the previous requirements for earning award points, and has suggested fewer factors. Previously these were ten factors; now there will be four. The new calculation forms have been sent to the Regional Education Committeemen, but Table 3 illustrates the new scoring system.

Chapter sponsored seminars include energy conservation seminars and training courses. This means that credit will be given for work in energy conservation, such as Standard 90-75 seminars, through the educational activity section of the Award of Excellence.

The par performance earns 245 points, and is based on 10 seminar hours (175 points) and one faculty liaison (70 points). The maximum educational award is 525 points.

Table 1 – Typical Status Report Format

Chapter	Members as of 7-1-76	Factors f_a	Factors f_g	Objectives* Attendance Ave. per Meeting	Objectives* Growth, Members
A	50	9.428	162.22	26.517	3
B	100	6.667	117.580	37.500	5
C	200	4.714	88.387	53.033	8
D	500	2.981	70.710	83.853	13
E	900	2.222	117.850	112.5	5

* Objective is to earn 250 points

Table 2 – CRC Attendance Points

Attendees	Points/Ea.
Chapter delegate & altrenate	25
Chapter Officers & board of governors (member other than delegate or alternate)	50
Chapter Education Committee Chairman	50
Chapter Membership Committee Chairman	50
Chapter Research Promotion CommitteeChairman	50
Chapter Energy Conservation Committee Chairman	50
All other chapter members	25
If delegate or alternate misses any caucus or CRC session	0

Note: Max award is 250 points

Table 3 – Educational Activities Points

Factor		Maximum Points
Faculty Liaison[1]	$\frac{\text{Faculty Liaison Members}}{\text{Total available institutions}} \times 70$	140
Student Incentive[2]	$\frac{\text{Awards Conferred}}{\text{Total available institutions}} \times 70$	140
Student Membership[3]	$\frac{\text{New student members}}{\text{Total available students}} \times 700$	70
Chapter Sponsored Seminars[4]	Seminar Hours x 17.5	175
	MAXIMUM ALLOWABLE =	525

1 "Faculty" refers to both University and Technical school faculties in the chapter area.
2 "Student" refers to students enrolled in the universities and technical schools in the chapter area.
3 The coefficient 700 is derived from 70 x 10 and the coefficient 17.50 is derived from 70 ÷ 4.
All factors are based on 70 points per unit.

ASHRAE

2019-2020 PRESIDENTIAL NEWSLETTER

DATE: July 2019

TO: Chapter Presidents
ASHRAE Membership Promotion Committee
ASHRAE Student Activities Committee
ASHRAE Research Promotion Committee
ASHRAE Chapter Technology Transfer Committee
ASHRAE Government Affairs Committee
ASHRAE Young Engineers in ASHRAE Committee
Regional Communications Chairs (formerly RECC)
Regional Historians
Region Members Council Representatives
ASHRAE Board of Directors

FROM: Darryl K. Boyce

SUBJECT: PRESIDENTIAL AWARD OF EXCELLENCE (PAOE)

ASHRAE members and their chapters are the backbone of our Society and play a vital role in achieving its goals and mission. Through their collective efforts, ASHRAE chapters are the global driver of volunteer activity as we strive to meet our goal of shaping tomorrow's built environment.

Our theme for 2019 – 2020, 'Building for People & Performance-Achieving Operational Excellence,' focuses on adapting ASHRAE's resources, investments and technology to energize our membership and empower our chapters. Through the theme's initiatives, ASHRAE will continue to build a worldwide network of innovative people and successful technologies to transform building operations and the indoor environment. ASHRAE members have a tremendous passion for our mission, which this year's theme builds upon to assist building owners and operators to improve the operation of their buildings to meet the design intent and the operators expectations. Our ability to shape tomorrow is borne by our willingness to adapt today, which is the driving force behind our theme and is incorporated into this year's PAOE program.

The PAOE for the coming year reflects the following points of emphasis.

See Chapter Operations:

- For each chapter member that submits a building assessment for a Building EQ rating (either in Operation or As Designed)
- For each chapter member promoting or presenting on Building EQ to an outside organization, building owner, facility manager, building operator or tenant
- For a chapter presentation by the Chapter President on the new strategic plan by November 30
- For holding an Effective Building Operations (topic) Chapter Meeting
- For each Professional Development Hour (PDH) earned by a chapter member on a building science topic other than HVAC&R (e.g. fenestration, insulation, lighting, indoor air quality)
- For a chapter creating a grassroots program specific to the needs of the local community. To qualify, the chapter program must include similar breadth and scope as President Boyce's concept of supporting Effective Building Operations (ex: working with local utility and institutional organization, provide training for improvements to building operations while improving the indoor environment and wellness in the buildings in the community)

See Chapter Technology Transfer:

- For each chapter program or chapter sponsored educational seminar with a clearly defined sustainability theme (e.g. energy efficiency, indoor air quality, high-performance buildings)
- For a chapter program if the technical topic is a panel discussion about effective building operations, including representatives from the local building owner/operators, researchers undertaking studies on smart buildings, controls service providers, or other specialists relevant to the topic. The intent is to have the panel discuss the problems and opportunities related to effective building operations and the impact of technology in the chapter assigned area.
- For a chapter program if the technical topic is a panel discussion about building resilience, such as research undertaking studies on building resilience, controls service providers addressing how control strategies and resiliency are linked, cyber security challenges in the built environment, technical representatives from the local weather authority sharing insights about future weather patterns, utility representatives to discuss how buildings impact grid performance, or other specialists relevant to the topic. The intent is to have the panel discuss where the integration of resilience into new and existing buildings and how it might affect infrastructure in the Chapter assigned area.
- For each 3-hour seminar sponsored/hosted by the chapter on a building science topic other than HVAC&R

See Student Activities:

- For each Building EQ submittal where a student branch assists with the work as overseen by a chapter member(s)

The numbering system will continue to be added to the PAOE program to better identify PAOE line items. There are nine PAOE categories included this year: Chapter Operations, Chapter Technology Transfer, Government Affairs, Communications, Historical, Membership Promotion, Research Promotion, Student Activities and Young Engineers in ASHRAE.

To achieve PAOE, the chapter must earn the minimum points in six of the following seven categories: Chapter Operations, Chapter Technology Transfer, Government Affairs, Membership Promotion, Research Promotion, Student Activities and Young Engineers in ASHRAE. Please refer to the criteria specified in each of the categories for calculating the PAOE points. For additional information or clarification, consult the PAOE Frequently Asked Questions (FAQ) section on the ASHRAE website. Please note that appropriate documentation must be kept by the Chapter to support PAOE point input, and that "chair" is defined as the individual listed in the Chapter Information Questionnaire (CIQ) on file with Society.

I am excited that you will be part of our global society and I appreciate the dedication, enthusiasm and hard work you bring to ASHRAE each year. I look forward to working with you as we extend globalization and new energy in our future and our community.

ASHRAE

2019-20 PAOE AWARDS

Chapters must meet "minimum" by obtaining points in the PAOE categories, there are no maximum limits on points earned however some line items are capped.

PAOE**	Minimum in 6 of the following 7 categories: Chapter Operations, Chapter Technology Transfer, Government Affairs, Membership Promotion, RP, Student Activities and Young Engineers in ASHRAE
Special Citation	Minimum in 6 of the 7 categories, with a minimum of 5,800 points
STAR	PAR in all categories
Honor Roll	PAOE for at least four consecutive years
High Honor Roll	STAR for at least four consecutive years
Premier	PAOE every year since the chapter's inception or since 1970; minimum of four years; chapter's first year is excluded

Sustainability Activities Award: A Chapter Sustainability Award in the form of a certificate is available for each chapter that obtains a total of at least 200 points from the items listed under Sustainability Activities in the Chapter Operations category of PAOE. The Chapter with the highest PAOE Sustainability point total (excludes the Community Sustainability Project points), will receive a Regional award in the form of a plaque and a certificate. The line items for Sustainability Activities are located in the Chapter Operations section of PAOE.

Community Sustainability Project Award: 500 points are entered by the DRCs for chapters who participate in the Community Sustainability Project as outlined in the Chapter Operations section of the PAOE. An award will be presented to chapters who complete their community project during the 2019-2020 Society year. For more information, visit https://www.ashrae.org/communities/chapters/ashrae-chapters/ashrae-community-sustainability-projects to review the case studies, quick start guidelines and more.

ASHRAE

2019-2020 ASHRAE PAOE REPORTING

CHAPTER REPORTING

The Chapter President is responsible for reporting the points in the Chapter Operations category. Each Chapter Committee Chair is responsible for reporting the points for his/her respective category. The PAOE points are entered online by the Chapter President and Chapter Committee Chairs using their email address and password to login. The Chapter President and the Chapter Committee Chairs are responsible for ensuring that the data is entered and the final reporting is completed by July 15, 2020. The Director and Regional Chairs (DRCs) and Regional Vice Chairs (RVCs) may access the website to obtain information for chapters in their Region and to enter points as indicated below.

November	Reflects October 31 results
January	Reflects December 31 results
March	Reflects February 28 results
April	Reflects March 31 results
May	Reflects April 30 results
June	Reflects May 31 results
July 15	June 30 results (reflects all final PAOE entries for the Society year)

DRCs Assigns: Chapter Operations PAOE Points

RVCs Assigns Points in their respective PAOE category:
Chapter Technology Transfer
Government Affairs
Membership Promotion
RP (points assigned by ASHRAE staff)
Student Activities
Young Engineers in ASHRAE
Communications (points assigned by RCC)
Historical (points assigned by Regional Historian)

ASHRAE HEADQUARTERS REPORTING

Beginning July 1 of each Society year, PAOE is available in dual form; the current Society year and the previous Society year. Chapters are able to enter PAOE points for both years during the month of July until the deadline date of July 15. The PAOE Point Summary data can be obtained for each chapter in the Region from the PAOE website. RP points will be calculated and entered by Headquarters staff.

Appendix D

Financial Statements

Income and Expense—Society General Fund for the First Consolidated Fiscal Period January 29, 1959, through June 30, 1959

INCOME		
From		
Membership Dues	$152,228.71	
Admission Fees	6,244.00	
Exposition Balance	3,188.76	
Emblems	385.35	
Publications		
ASHRAE Journal	$ 81,324.28	
Data Book	12,412.56	
Guide	174,409.73	
Transactions	622.40	
Standards, Reprints, Charts, etc.	5,549.99	$ 436,365.78
EXPENSE		
Direction and Guidance Travel		
Board of Directors	3,708.54	
Committees		
Officers and Executive	2,367.23	
Chapter Regional	6,423.21	
Regional General	2,304.96	
Finance	11.39	
Long Range Planning	280.94	
Admissions and Advancement	247.30	
International Relations	135.88	
Program	229.03	
Publications	120.09	
Standards	327.97	
Public Relations	192.00	$ 16,348.54
Chapter Supplies and Allowances		9,642.15
Certificates		104.05
Emblems		668.36
Medals and Awards		24.91
Dues – E. J. C.		2,981.00
Memory Books		331.18
Consolidation – Moving, Printing, Mailing, etc.		1,822.10
Meetings		
Host Chapter Allowances	800.00	
Annual Meeting	10,035.70	10,835.70
Total Direction and Guidance Expense		42,759.99
Income available for Publications and Administration		393,605.79

Publications		
ASHRAE Journal	67,949.35	
Data Book	9,818.82	
Guide	136,873.76	
Transactions	201.1	
Standards, Reprints, Charts, etc.	3,805.02	218,647.96
Administration		
Salaries	127,014.29	
Payroll Taxes	3,501.38	
Public Relations	2,264.61	
Secretary and Staff Travel	5,518.85	
Rent and Electric	10,323.45	
Telephone	2,610.26	
Telegraph	274.04	
Postage	4,982.36	
Printing and Stationery	8,773.19	
Membership Tabulations	2,051.04	
Professional Services	1,925.00	
Bank Charges	13.54	
Insurance	735.26	
General Office Expenses	3,117.74	
Pension, Group Life Insurance and Service Fee	3,097.39	
Depreciation – Furniture and Fixtures	1,006.59	
Provision for Doubtful Dues	15,166.16	
	192,375.65	
Total Publications and Administrative Expense		411,023.61
Excess of Expense over Income		17,417.82
Less: Financial Income		
Distribution from Investments Account	2,737.17	
Interest on Savings Deposits	648.55	
Interest on Short-Term Notes	53.38	
Foreign Exchange Conversion	376.98	
Total Financial Income		3,816.08
Excess of Expense Charged to Fund Balance		$ 13,601.74

Consolidated Statements of Activities and Net Assets for the Years Ended June 30, 2019, and 2018

	2019	2018
NET ASSETS WITHOUT DONOR RESTRICTIONS		
REVENUES		
Membership dues	$ 7,779,880	$ 7,772,752
Publication sales	3,492,605	3,664,001
Advertising income	3,958,178	4,207,378
Meetings and seminars	3,456,568	3,728,027
Contributions	2,219,725	2,153,335
Exposition income	5,975,745	6,085,682
Special projects	74,340	62,905
Other income	603,928	614,481
Total revenues	27,560,969	28,288,561
NET ASSETS RELEASED FROM RESTRICTIONS	409,174	483,865
EXPENSES		
Salaries	9,720,861	9,730,380
Publications and promotion	3,230,012	3,428,756
Payroll taxes and benefits	2,636,853	2,875,332
Meetings and conferences	2,512,197	2,929,775
Outside services	2,357,507	2,069,630
Research projects and grants	2,226,590	2,941,451
Transportation expense	2,168,963	2,228,835
Office expenses	1,630,457	1,631,674
Miscellaneous	945,434	1,004,204
Occupancy and insurance	768,337	639,328
Awards, certificates and logo	443,927	353,685
Depreciation	379,131	556,931
Special projects	111,374	107,678
Total expenses	29,131,643	30,497,659

Appendix E

Going to War

(In this survey of progress in refrigerating engineering during the war years, Secretary of the A.S.R.E. David L. Fiske pointed out in a 1944 Refrigerating Engineering article that the war has been a great stimulus to engineering skills. The military situation, with innumerable new demands calling for new designs, compelled refrigerating engineers to accelerate their usual pace. The result was a vast number of new uses for refrigeration, many as yet unpublicized in 1944.)

Five years ago most foresighted people thought the United States would soon be at war. Among these same people, those who tried to foresee the economic conditions of the oncoming years agreed on one thing—that normal civilian production and consumption would have to be curtailed. Every previous war seemed to stand in proof that war meant privation on the home front.

But this proved to be in error. Things did not work out this way. Where the national income spent for consumption had in 1939 been on the order of 60 billions, this peak was exceeded in 1941 and again in the following year, arriving now at the undreamed-of total of about 90 billions. Practically all the economists in the country had guessed wrong. They had not realized the enormous productive capacity of American industry and the immense amounts of cash which were to find their way into the hands of the purchasing public.

The war years have been outstanding years of American prosperity. Refrigeration was one of her most promising prewar industries, and is regarded as even more promising for the future. Yet the war years have not been ones when this industry saw its greatest dollar income. Indeed, if we consider the income of that portion of the industry composed of the manufacture of refrigerators, commercial refrigeration, industrial refrigerating equipment and air conditioning, the volume of sales has been reduced to a point below that of any period in the past 15 years. In this case, the economists were right that the war would mean a reduction of civilian production. The elimination of household refrigerators, normally amounting to 200 or more millions annually at factory prices, brought down the total output to something like half the 1937 peak.

On the other hand, other phases of this manufacturing industry have been enormously stimulated by the war. Some of these are railway refrigerator cars, industrial or large-scale refrigerating compressors, air conditioning equipment for such uses as gun turrets and wind tunnels, and refrigeration for seagoing vessels, the last having "done more" in the past three years than in the previous twenty.

Moreover, the industries normally consuming refrigerating equipment have in general enjoyed the general prosperity—cold storage has been undergoing a boom, as has the manufacture of frozen and other foods. And of course all those forms of refrigeration demanded by the armed services have constituted a great activity. All in all, considered broadly, the refrigeration industry, like the whole country, has been undergoing a stimulus of new economic activity.

It is against this background of boom times, that one must study the war years of the refrigeration industry—which I have been invited to survey by your Editor. For a time, before the war, I prepared an annual review of progress. Now three years have to be reviewed, for American history from here on will, of course, date from December, 1941. What have we done that will remain of permanent importance in these years? Of course, the industry has contributed enormously to the favorable trend of the war—that is of the greatest permanent importance, but it is a story which will have to be told elsewhere. In this article, I am trying to look at the refrigeration industry through long-range glasses.

Boom Years Bring Technical Activity

There was another forecast of five years ago that went all wrong—it was foreseen that manufacturing firms would be driven out of their normal fields. It was supposed that these producers would tend to forget their normal peacetime identities to a much greater degree than actually proved to be the case. A very considerable portion of the producers of refrigerating machinery and equipment went into other lines of work, some of which was closely related, as for example equipment for high pressure gases, special compressors, and testing equipment. Other products, such as machine guns and airplane wings, were not related to refrigeration at all. But to a very marked degree these firms, and the engineering personnel attached to them, have continued to think of themselves as refrigeration folk. This has tended to add a glamorous touch to the industry.

Boom Stimulates Technique

Boom years are not necessarily good engineering years. During an inflation sellers have little incentive to improve their products. Contrariwise, the depression of ten years ago proved very stimulating toward improved engineering of most goods sold in this industry. It gave engineers time to become more inventive, and the buyers became far more particular.

This boom has been a very great stimulus to all our engineering skills. The pressure has been that of the military situation, with innumerable new demands calling for new designs. Some of these have no special value for peacetime production, while others, such as the use of new, lighter and stronger materials, will undoubtedly prove of lasting value. How this will affect the immediate future will remain to be seen. Certainly we shall see with the return of peace the return of many of the same old gadgets we have always found in the market, with a new coat of paint perhaps, but the same old thing none the less. Mixed with them will be many new ones. Certainly, too there will be many new faces. Moneys made in countless war industries will be ploughed into this field of ours, hopefully expected to bring forth lavish fruit. (The current fashion is to assume it will blossom forth the first season—but these are boom times. You could define boom times as those when business men can't see a cloud in the sky bigger than a man's hand.)

Complete answer to the questions I am addressing will not be available for years, because the war demand has resulted in new uses for refrigeration, new twists upon old methods, new tricks and inventions—these beyond all reckoning.

Most of this has not been publicized. I do hope that we will not go back to peace so quickly as to neglect study of the record in full. The most marked change will probably be from a period when heavy machinery predominated toward a period of activity in small units. This is akin to a shift from industrial markets to commercial ones. There will be a reduction in the demand for heavy ammonia or Freon compressors for cold storage plants, refrigerant production, oil refining, synthetic rubber, oxygen manufacture, and the like. There will be a renewed demand for commercial refrigerators, ice cream cabinets, water coolers and the like.

Maybe you do not agree with this. There are those who maintain that the war years have caused great wear and tear on the national refrigeration plant. There has been a hue and cry from industry about necessary maintenance which could not be financed because of the tax laws, nor permitted by the availability of priorities. Well, there is room for difference of opinion here. I am not inclined to think this demand is very great, but I have no way to prove it aside from the opinion of various informed people to whom I have talked. No doubt there will be some demand for new plants from meat packers, bakers, dairies and the like.

As to the demand for commercial and household units, there is considerably less argument., Certainly there will be a postwar boom in this direction. What may we expect in the way of new designs in the ice cream or frozen food cabinets of 1946? In the beverage coolers and dispensers? In the household refrigerators? My guess would certainly not be so good as that of those who have written about these matters in these years, in these pages..

We have had many new ideas presented—greater convenience, better streamlining of appearance, greater ease of cleaning, decrease in weight. Household refrigerators with quick ice cube service, more compact arrangement in the kitchen, and separation of compartments by temperature have been discussed.

Postwar Methods to be Improved

Forecasts of postwar refrigerators contemplate changes in the way of refinements, rather than revolutionary designs or wholly new applications. Moreover, as far as one can now foresee, the benefit of wartime invention and engineering will be in the infusion of ideas from rather remote fields rather than any immediate evolutionary changes in domestic or commercial refrigeration as practiced now. The same collection of compressors, motors, valves, heat exchangers and the like, are being employed now that were before. Indeed, the military does not buy novelties when "tried and true" equipment is available for a job. While large amounts of small-unit refrigeration have been bought for military purposes, I am not aware of any great departures in principle.

Yet there has been some excellent work by designers. A familiar example is the gasoline driven self-contained unit now purchased in quantity by the Corps of Engineers for the prefabricated sectional refrigerator. This unit is also used by the Navy, along with other portable refrigerators of what we would normally call commercial sizes. Still another development is the QMC refrigerated truck with separate engine drive. These units are suggestive of other possible advances in the way components of refrigerating systems can be assembled and housed.

Impact of New Techniques

Perhaps still greater stimuli to progress will come through seemingly remote fields. We may expect new ideas about say, commercial refrigeration, to come from air conditioning and quick freezing and from engineering wholly outside refrigeration. There have been many examples of this. Our ideas about refrigeration were greatly influenced by what we learned in the field of ventilation and heating. When we come to build a household storage locker, it is not unlikely that we can pick up ideas from penicillin production, fish freezing tunnels or aircraft heat exchangers.

It is in this spirit that we must review the progress of these three years. By way of summary, a number of general subjects may be mentioned. The following are items which have been under concentrated study during, and because of, the war. Undoubtedly I have not mentioned a number of vital developments which might be given attention in an analysis in terms of mechanical units. There has been much interest and improved understanding of refrigerants, substitute materials, and insulating materials, in liquid distribution within evaporators, intermittent movement of heat, and all sorts of work on controls, motors, cooling towers and other kinds of equipment. But for purposes of brief review, some of the highlights of technical progress may be summarized as follows:

1. Farm and Storage Lockers

Farmer locker plant construction has been sponsored by the agricultural agencies of the government in the last two years. Interest in lockers has been active, in various parts of the country, and much written about them in the refrigeration literature. Akin to this subject is the highly interesting topic of home lockers made especially popular by wartime home gardening.

2. Low Temperature Applications

Many uses of refrigeration at temperature levels far below the normal at prewar lows, have become important in the last three years. Some of these have amounted to previously known uses of dry ice, while some new ones have appeared, such as the cooling of welding electrodes. The cooling of airplane rivets to slow up the aging or setting process, has been another application depending upon dry ice.

Other uses include installations of tremendous magnitude. A number of testing plants have been built capable of accommodating devices as large as an entire tank. These installations may call for loads running into tonnages of three or four figures, while there are many smaller test cabinets for various laboratory uses such as the calibration of instruments, testing radio tubes, and the like.

Experience with low temperatures, as used especially for test rooms, will undoubtedly go far to educate engineers toward better designs for ordinary levels of refrigeration. If you know that a gadget failed in a certain way at a low temperature, you would have just that much of an edge on the man who would have to wait for the same event under less severe conditions. All this must have taught us something about coil ratings and the behavior of liquids in evaporation. Every Btu. extracted at –100° F. is worth ten that extracted at zero. Dealings with these high cost Btu. must have revealed some things we did not take too seriously in the cheaper ones of peacetime. And, of course, some, perhaps many, of these low temperatures will continue to be required in peace.

3. Medical Applications

The awareness of refrigeration gained by the medical profession in the past three years will probably prove fruitful of new applications in the future. Notable has been the preservation of blood plasma; certainly new uses of the principle of drying from freezing are possible. Penicillin production has been followed here with interest. Another remarkable development in which refrigeration technique, by fortunate accident, played a part was the insecticide work involving Freon. This has civilian applications of direct importance.

4. Portable Units

As noted, great importance has attached to portable compressor units, for use either with or without electric power. The military services have called for refrigeration from one end of the earth to another, for many purposes, particularly the cooling of hospital supplies and food for men in hospitals, as well as for field storage purposes in relation to troop feeding establishments. These have often amounted simply to an assemblage of existing parts, but what has been learned is of great importance and bears directly on unsolved peacetime problems such as the development of refrigerated truck bodies and refrigerator cars.

5. Refrigerated Foods

Much progress has been seen in the field of foods. Quick freezing for civilian consumption has not slackened but grown during these three years, and many new products have been heard from—such as frozen cooked foods, frozen dog food, and frozen bread. Dehydrated foods have had their greatest stimulus, and will undoubtedly stay with us in many new packages to appear on the civilian market once the demand for the military is removed. Probably the outstanding new product of the war is frozen boneless beef, a highly successful item of great demand in the army now. One of the main bottlenecks to the development of this food, shortage of skilled labor, has been broken and the packers will have every incentive to extend this practice after the war. This should contribute much to increase the declining consumption of meats, and in turn stimulate the need for refrigeration. Army experience has likewise contributed greatly to new ideas on packaging.

6. Ships' Refrigeration

This branch of refrigeration has been undergoing a boom which has attracted rather limited attention—a characteristic of the subject in former times as well. The number of refrigerated ships under U. S. registry has grown greatly, and there is a tendency also to supply more refrigeration for the crew and passengers' food storage.

7. Industrial Air Conditioning

While comfort air conditioning has been curtailed because of restrictions on materials, industrial air conditioning has found scores of new uses in connection with the production of precision instruments and many items of war material. The manufacture of special parts essential to ammunition (naval torpedo fuses, time train fuses, delays for armor piercing shells, and the like), the manufacture of smokeless powder—these are but a few of the many applications of air conditioning required to turn out satisfactory products in a minimum time. We will not be making war material after the Axis is defeated, it is assumed, but it is probable that the widespread use of air conditioning during the war years will lead to a broader industrial use of air conditioning in the postwar period.

Summary

The specific fields of refrigeration progress mentioned above are only an indication of the work that has been done in this industry in the war years. Space does not permit a more detailed discussion of other branches of refrigeration in which similar progress has been noted. The general conclusion is that refrigerating engineers, and the refrigeration industry, have made a vital contribution to the war, at the same time improving their own techniques. This advancement which has been thrust upon us will prove a distinct advantage in the further inevitable expansion of refrigeration in the postwar years.

The following letters are typical of the large number received at the headquarters office from members who were actively engaged in the war:

A.S.R.E.
Gentlemen:

Mrs. Iwashita has just forwarded me my membership card in the A.S.R.E. and you may be sure that I'm carrying it around with me as a prize possession. I appreciate the Courtesy you are extending to all members in the service, too. I'm enjoying the periodicals to say the least. They are being read at the oddest places, but you can't imagine how much we appreciate them.

This war can't last very much longer, so we will all be seeing each other soon-I hope. Refrigeration is surely doing a lot in this war-more than most people realize. I'm in the Infantry but my heart is still with Refrigeration.

Thanks again and please extend my regards to all members of the A.S.R.E. They're a great bunch.

Gratefully yours,
George K. Iwashita
Capt., Infantry

Somewhere in France

The American Society of Refrigerating Engineers
Dear Sirs:

Your September 1st letter advising me of dues cancellation while in the Army along with my 1944-45 membership card arrived today.

You are hereby advised of my up-to-date address, rank, and unit. Your publication is being read by several members of my unit and we look forward to future issues.

As you may guess from the name of my unit we are working with refrigeration, but hardly of the common conception of the word. Our process starts with the manufacture of liquid air and temperatures produced are lower than I came across in civilian life.

Again I thank you for taking care of my dues and chance to read what's new in the industry.

Very truly yours,
Thomas C. McKee, Jr.
1st Lt., C.E.

Mr. A.B. Stickney, President,
American Society of Refrigerating Engineers
Dear Mr. Stickney:

I am in receipt of your letter of September 1st advising me that in accordance with the policy of the Society I will continue to receive the publications during the time that I am in the Armed Services of the Country and that no dues will be assessed during such period. I wish to express my appreciation of this generous attitude toward members of the Service and you may rest assured that I will advise you when I am released from active duty so that you may indicate the change of status upon your records.

My address is correctly shown on your records, but my rank is now that of Lieutenant Colonel.

Sincerely yours,
Allen Rushton Lt.
Col., Ord. Dept.

A.S.R.E. Gentlemen:

Thank you for you letter informing me of being on the "Suspense List" of the Society. I did so wish to retain membership and am glad such a service has been voted on.

As for the *Refrigerating Engineering* magazine; if possible, I would like very much to have it, for now there is more time to read such literature and it is a good means to keep up with post-war equipment and methods, etc.

I shall keep the Society informed of the correct address whenever it is changed, for I expect to be moving soon. Once again, thank you for writing.

Very truly yours,
John B. O'Neill
Corporal

A.S.R.E. Gentlemen:

This is a rather late answer to your very welcome letter of August 15th. I forwarded the good news on to Mr. Gillis, who is somewhere in the Admiralties Islands, that his dues had been suspended for the duration and six months, with the privilege of full membership; asking him also whether it would be advisable to send Refrigerating Engineering to him while he is in the service.

I received a letter this past week from Mr. Gillis, who asked me to extend his sincere thanks and appreciation for the action you have taken. He is very proud of his membership in your society-and wants always to belong to your splendid group of refrigerating engineers. He has suggested that since he is not at a permanent station-and is subject to be moved from time to time-that you discontinue sending the magazine to him. As soon as he gets permanently located, and can give you a permanent address-I know he will do so at once since your monthly publication carries the up-to-the-minute news, and is so timely in the unsettled war time era.

Again, thanking you in his behalf, and lots of luck and success for the future of your society, and I can truthfully say he will be looking forward to the time when he can be on your regular monthly mailing list again permanently.

Very truly yours,
Mrs. H.W. Gillis, Jr.

What ASHVE Is Doing in Wartime

(Excerpts taken from Merrill F. Blankin's Presidential Speech to Chapters, 1943)

I am thinking of my travels around the country under wartime conditions; visits to the Arsenal of Democracy, particularly some of the large bomber plants, and possibly what I have seen at some of the flying fields. However, I think the most important thing that I can discuss with you tonight is the Society itself; its history; its present-day situation particularly with regards to Finances and Membership; and some thoughts on Research. In other words, try to give you enough information that will satisfy your own mind that the Society can easily weather the storm of war.

By 1930 our membership had increased to 1995 and in 1940 it was at a new high of 3147 members. Since then, however, I regret to say that our advance has stopped. Most everybody has been blaming it on the war, saying that it was natural to expect a loss of membership during wartime because so many would be changing their business affiliations and there would be migration of engineers all over the country....I feel that with what we have to offer, membership can be increased substantially in spite of wartime conditions, and I have asked the Membership Committee to attack this problem with the thought that it is possible to get 300 new members this year, and I am proud to say that we have already achieved that goal, and gone beyond it - so that now we are setting our sights at the possibility of 500 members.

In 1941 and 1942 we had very important Research Projects conducted in our own Laboratory direct for the U.S. Navy. There isn't much I am permitted to say about this, but it is known that it was in the field of physiological reaction, and we have been highly complimented by the Navy for the work that we have done and the results have been a direct contribution to the war effort, making it possible for our men in the South Pacific to better withstand the high temperatures and high humidity that prevails there. Anyone should be proud of the opportunity to make this small contribution through their dues to the marvelous Research work that we are doing.

Our Finance Committee was very pessimistic when they made up the Budget regarding income for this year, but with the splendid increase in membership and the fact that our income from the sale of the Guide is up and there is every indication that our income from advertising will be increased tremendously, limited only by the amount of paper that we can secure and in fact we will probably have to turn down ads, I would hazard a guess that the Net worth of the Society at the end of this year will be around $140,000.00. And they said it couldn't be done in wartime - but it can, particularly when you have the enthusiastic cooperation of the type of membership that we have.

I discussed with some of the members in Indianapolis the question of a Chapter there. They were afraid that it couldn't be done in wartime, what with everyone being so busy on war work, gas rationing, etc. However, early in September we had a meeting with as many members from Indiana as we could get together. After a thorough discussion they became enthusiastic over the prospects and 24 members signed a petition for a Chapter; an organization was perfected, and officers elected. The petition was represented to Council, who voted unanimously to grant the petition and establish a Chapter in Indiana. November 1st was set as the installation date and the Fall Meeting of the Council was called for October 31st in Indianapolis.

The question comes up as to what the Society is doing in wartime. Let me take time to tell you some of this story. We have 301 members and 31 foreign members in the Service, a total of 332. Some of our most prominent ones are Brigadier General W.A. Danielson who was Chairman of our Guide Publication Committee and was Chairman of the Research Committee for 2 years; and many others in the service of the Army. In the Navy there is Captain Ned Stacey, one of the first from the Naval Reserve Forces to be promoted to the rank of Captain, who is a member of Council, member of the Research Committee and Past-Chairman of the Research Committee; Commander T.H. Urdahl, a member of Council and a member of the Research Committee; who is chief of the Air Conditioning Section of the Bureau of Ships in Washington, D.C. When you go into his office it seems as if you are going into a meeting of the Society, as far as the personnel is concerned. Associated with him are Lt. Commander F.C. Houghten, for many years Director of our Research Laboratory; Lt. Commander Queer; Lt. Van Alsburg, past-member of the Research Committee; Lt. Jack Everett, and many others, both in uniform and in the civilian branch. One of our English members, Captain J.K.M. Pyrke was a prisoner of war in Germany, having been captured in the First African Campaign. We heard that he was in this camp and thought he would be interested in receiving the Guide if it could be gotten to him. It was sent by means of the International Red Cross. We heard from him saying that he received it and that he is conducting classes on heating, ventilating and air conditioning among the prisoners, and naturally, is using the Guide as a textbook.

Two of our members have already paid the supreme sacrifice; one is Flying Officer H.L. Temple of London, England, a member of the R.A.F. who was killed in a mission over enemy territory. The other I knew quite well, he was a member of the Manitoba Chapter in Canada, and known facetiously as "the flying plumber." He came from a gold mining town close by the Arctic Circle, with the mystic name of Flin Flon. He always attended the Annual Meetings and I never knew anyone who had so much enthusiasm and so much spirit and vitality.

The Society has been very active in the Fuel Rationing and Fuel Conservation Program. Last year there was created a War Service Committee which represented the Society in the Fuel Oil Rationing Program at Washington. We were not entirely in accord with the Program as adopted, but all of our members pitched in and helped make the Program work, many of them serving on rationing boards all over the country....70,000 copies of the now famous pamphlet "War on Fuel Waste, 10 Ways to Save Fuel" have been printed and distributed all over this country and in England, where they adopted many of the recommendations.

This year our War Service Committee consisted of John Howatt, Past-President, as Chairman; W.H. Driscoll, Past-President; E.N. McDonnell, member of Council; Dr. B.M. Woods, member of Council; and Prof. L.E. Seeley. Early in the year they sent out a questionnaire, and they represented the Society at the Fuel Oil Conference held in Washington by the O.P.A. on March 16th and 17th, 1943. At this meeting the ground work was laid for the Fuel Oil Rationing Program for the winter of 1943-44.

Keep up with our work in this war effort. There is much that we can do. We can buy Bonds. I told you the Society had purchased $54,000.00 worth. Well that wasn't all. This year we have bought in the Second War Loan Drive $18,000.00 worth more and we have also bought $8,000.00 worth of Canadian Victory Bonds. Have you as individuals bought your share? If not, go out tomorrow and buy another one. Don't say that you have made too much of a sacrifice already. Think of our two members who have made the supreme sacrifice, who have given their all. Let's do everything we can to get this great storm over so that it will not last a day, an hour, or a minute longer than necessary, and when it is finished we will not have too many of our brothers and sons with a gold star after their name, like Flying Officer Temple and Pilot Officer Phil Foster.

A Message From ASHRAE's President

On September 11, 2001, an almost incomprehensible act of terrorism was perpetrated against the people of the world community. On behalf of the 58,000 members of our great Society, ASHRAE, I express our sympathy and heartfelt condolences to all of those whose lives have been affected by this tragedy.

As a society of engineers, it is in our nature to build. To witness purposeful destruction of lives, machines and structures is repulsive to us not only as human beings but also as mankind's builders.

Ours is an international society and I would like to tell our members in the United States that we have received untold letters of sympathy, concern and encouragement from our fellow members, colleagues and friends throughout the world. This tragedy assuredly will bring the world community closer together than ever, to work as a single unit with the objective to rebuild what has been destroyed and to build a world where people of all nations will live in harmony and peace while realizing an ever-improving quality of life.

William J. Coad, P.E.
President, ASHRAE

Building Safety Report Issued

ATLANTIC CITY — Making sure buildings are working properly now will give owners and managers an edge if extraordinary incidents take place, according to a report issued to ASHRAE.

The report, *Risk Management Guidance for Health and Safety Under Extraordinary Incidents,* was delivered at the public session at ASHRAE's 2002 Winter Meeting. The report was written by the Society's Presidential Study Group on Health and Safety Under Extraordinary Incidents, which was appointed after the attacks of Sept. 11 and subsequent events.

"Most of the recommendations included in this report are common sense measures that owners and managers should already be following," said ASHRAE President William Coad, P.E. "Much of the guidance given by ASHRAE relating to acceptable indoor environments, human comfort and safety also serves to protect the health and safety of building occupants under extraordinary incidents."

A free copy of the complete report is available at www.ashrae.org.

The report included three overall recommendations that ASHRAE should take to continue its mission of advancing the arts and sciences of HVAC&R for the public's benefit. These include:

• That ASHRAE recognize increasing responsibilities of building owners, operators and maintenance providers.

"Building owners and occupants may now be willing to redirect resources to enhance building performance to further reduce occupant risk associated with extraordinary incidents, while continuing to provide acceptable indoor environments, with energy efficiency and cost effectiveness during normal conditions," said James Woods, Ph.D., P.E., chair of the study group.

See Safety, Page 2

2002

Making Buildings Safe Topic of Public Session

In light of the Sept. 11 attacks, the HVAC industry and the general public was inundated with information on how to protect buildings from bioterrorism.

Unfortunately, some of this information was incorrect or misleading, according to William Coad, P.E., ASHRAE president.

Taking specific actions, such as sealing off outdoor air intakes, without seeking professional advice can cause serious problems and exposure to liability, Coad said.

To clear up misconceptions and misinformation, ASHRAE will offer professional guidance on maintaining safe, healthy and comfortable indoor environments at the public session held at the 2002 Winter Meeting in Atlantic City, N.J.

The Aftermath of 9/11/01: Ensuring the Safety of America's Buildings will feature a report on the work of an ASHRAE Presidential Study Group on Health and Safety Under Extraordinary Incidents. This group, chaired by James E. Woods, Ph.D., P.E., chairman of ASHRAE's Environmental Health Committee, consists of a blue-ribbon panel of recognized experts in the fields of technology related to this topic. The session will take place from 3-5 p.m. Monday, Jan. 14, in room 302 at the Atlantic City Convention Center. Admission is free.

"ASHRAE's mission calls for us to be the foremost, authoritative, timely and responsive source of technical information," Coad said. "Much of our technology and knowledge developed for improved indoor air quality and fire safety can be applied to protecting building environments."

Scheduled speakers include Woods and other members of the study group whose expertise is reflected in the report.

The speakers are expected to address all aspects of health and safety, except structural integrity and security protection. These include materials, egress, chemical, biological and radiological protection, fire extinguishing, smoke removal or purging, filtration, maintenance of comfort and air quality, entrance paths for contaminants, building envelopes, water supplies and electrical reliability.

Specifically the speakers will discuss:

• Steps that managers of existing building facilities can take to improve the safety performance of their buildings.

• What ASHRAE can do to inform its members of the steps that can and should be taken to improve the health and safety of existing buildings through various system retrofit steps.

• What ASHRAE can encourage its membership to do in regard to the design of new facilities to provide enhanced safety inside buildings.

• Recommend action regarding the need for research, standards, codes, formation of technical committees or task groups and educational programs, or any other needs to address the subject matter.

• Identify ongoing work with other organizations that may be relevant.

2002

ASHRAE Hosts Meeting on Iraq

ASHRAE representatives and others discuss U.S. standards and building codes with four senior officials from the Iraqi Ministry of Construction and Housing.

WASHINGTON—As Iraqi engineers work to rebuild their country's roads, bridges, public buildings and houses, they are dependent upon technical information from 20 years ago.

To assist Iraq in obtaining the latest in technical information, including standards, ASHRAE recently hosted a meeting between four senior officials of the Iraq Ministry of Construction and Housing and representatives of major U.S. building codes and standards developing organizations and engineering societies. The meeting was arranged by the U.S. Commerce Department.

The meeting was held to provide the Ministry representatives with information about U.S. standards and for the participating organizations to learn how they might assist the Ministry in addressing its objectives in constructing and rehabilitating Iraq's roads, bridges, public buildings and houses.

"While the Iraqis' major focus was on civil engineering related standards and construction issues, they also talked about mechanical, electrical and plumbing standards," said Larry Spielvogel, who chaired the meeting. "Most of the standards they use are American along with some British. Due to the political situation there and the embargo for the past 15 years, the latest information they have is from the 1980s."

Spielvogel is chair of ASHRAE's Presidential Ad Hoc Committee on Homeland Security.

Most of the participating organizations offered to provide access to their publications and information and to invite Iraqi participation in their activities, including standards development.

"As you might expect, there are still many hurdles, and the U.S. State and Commerce Departments offered their assistance in improving communications and relations," said Spielvogel.

Organizations participating in the meeting include ASHRAE, the American Association of State Highway and Transportation Officials (AASHTO), the American Concrete Institute (ACI), the American National Standards Institute (ANSI), the American Society of Civil Engineers (ASCE), the American Society of Mechanical Engineers (ASME), the American Society for Testing and Materials (ASTM International), the International Association of Plumbing and Mechanical Officials (IAPMO), the International Code Council (ICC) and the National Fire Protection Association (NFPA).

2004

Appendix F

2018–19 ASHRAE Officers, Directors, Committee Members, and Staff

Executive Committee

OFFICERS

President
Sheila J. Hayter, PE

President-Elect
Darryl K. Boyce, PEng

Treasurer
Charles E. Gulledge III

Vice Presidents
Julia A. Keen, PhD, PE
Malcolm Dennis Knight, PE
Michael CA Schwedler, PE
Farooq Mehboob, PE

Secretary
Jeff H. Littleton

Board of Directors

DIRECTORS

July 2016–June 2019
George W. Austin, Jr. (IV)
Douglas D. Fick (V)
Benjamin A. Skelton (VI)
Daniel R. Rogers (XII)
Ng Yong Kong (XIII)
Essam E. Khalil*
Thomas M. Lawrence*
Lawrence C. Markel*

July 2017–June 2020
Michael P. Cooper (VII)
Jonathan I. Symko (VIII)
Trenton S. Hunt (IX)
Marites Dagulo Calad (X)
Constantinos A. Balaras (XIV)
Farooq Mehboob (RAL)
Van D. Baxter*
Donald L. Brandt*
Tim J. McGinn*

July 2018–June 2021
Christopher G. Phelan (I)
Jeff Clarke (II)
Dunstan Laurence Maculey III (III)
Russell J. Lavitt (XI)
Ahmed Alaa Eldin Mohamed (RAL)
Katherine G. Hammack*
Sarah E. Maston*
Chandra Sekhar*

**Directors-at-Large*

Staff

Executive Vice President **Jeff H. Littleton**
Manager, Board Services **Candace DeVaughn**
Business Manager, Europe, Middle East, Africa **W. Stephen Comstock**
Manager, Global Training Center, Dubai **Ayah Said**
Director of Government Affairs **Alice Yates**
Manager, Government Affairs–State & Local **Caroline Sevier**
Manager, Government Affairs–Federal **Jeremy Pollack**
Director of Finance and Administrative Services **Craig Wright**
Manager, Accounting **Annmarie S. Wilhoit**
Manager, Human Resources **Sharon L. Priebe, PHR**
Manager, Information Technology **Brian Unrein**
Manager–Accounting Systems Analyst **Candice Richards**
Director of Publications & Education **Mark S. Owen**
Editor, Special Publications **Cindy Michaels**
Editor, Handbook **Heather Kennedy**
Editor, ASHRAE Journal & HPB **Jay Scott**
Manager, Advertising Sales **Greg Martin**
Manager, Professional Development **Karen Murray**
Group Manager, Electronic Products and Publishing Services **David Soltis**
Manager, Inventory and Subscriptions **Kimberly Gates**
Manager, Certification **Timothy Kline**
Manager, eLearning **Eunice Njeru**
Director of Member Services **Joyce Abrams**
Sr. Manager, Conference Programs **Anthony Giometti**
Manager, Region Activities **Vickie Grant**
Manager, Membership **Daniel Gurley**
Manager, Conference Services **Lizzy Seymour**
Director of Technology **Stephanie C. Reiniche**
Sr. Manager, Research and Technical Services **Michael R. Vaughn, PE**
Manager, Research and Technical Services **Steven Hammerling**
Sr. Manager, Standards **Steve Ferguson**
Manager, Special Projects **Lilas Pratt**
Manager, Codes **Connor Barbaree**
Manager, American Standards **Mark Weber**
Chief Development Officer **Kim Mitchell**
Sr. Manager, Major & Planned Gifts **Nicole Blount**
Development Manager, Foundation **Margaret Smith**
Development Manager, RP **Julia Mumford**
Director of Marketing **Vanita Gupta**
Sr. Manager, Marketing Communications **Joslyn Ratcliff**
Marketing Manager **Anne Wilson**

ASHRAE ORGANIZATIONAL CHART

ASHRAE Membership

Board of Directors

Members Council
- Chapter Technology Transfer
- Conferences and Expositions
- Government Affairs
- Honors and Awards
- Membership Promotion
- Research Promotion
- Student Activities
- Young Engineers in ASHRAE

Technology Council
- Environmental Health
- Refrigeration
- Research Administration
- Residential Buildings
- Standards
- Technical Activities

Publishing and Education Council
- Certification
- Electronic Communications
- Handbook
- Historical
- Professional Development
- Publications

Committees not reporting to a council: Audit, Building EQ, Development, Finance, Nominating, Planning, President-Elect Advisory, and Society Rules.

2018–2019 COUNCILS AND COMMITTEES

(BOD ExO = ex officio Board of Directors, CO = coordinating officer, NVM = nonvoting member, MAL = member-at-large, RAL = region-at-large, DAL = director-at-large)

Audit
George W. Austin, Jr., *Chair*
Russell J. Lavitt
Michael P. Cooper
Craig Wright, *Staff Liaison*

Building Energy Quotient
William K. Klock, *Chair*
Douglas C. Cochrane, *Vice Chair*
K. William Dean, *Tech Council Mbr.*
Esteban Baccini Jauregui
Chris Balbach
John Constantinide
Hywel Davies
Charles N. Eley
Hugh F. Crowther, *Consultant*
Bruce D. Hunn, *Consultant*
Daniel J. Redmond, *Consultant*
Dennis Knight, *CO*
Lilas Pratt, *Staff Liasion*

Development
Erich Binder, *Chair*
Mark F. Miller, *Vice Chair*
Donald G. Colliver, *College of Fellows*
Derek A. Crowe, *Mbr/RP ExCom*
James R. Fields, *Mbr/Foundation ExCom*
William A. Harrison, *Mbr/Foundation ExCom*
Anthony Jonkov, *Mbr/RP ExCom*
Scott A. Martin, *Mbr/RP ExCom*
Tim McGinn, *Mbr/PLC Liaison*
Salih Zeki Poyraz, *Mbr-at-Large*
M. Ginger Scoggins, *Mbr-at-Large*
Jeff Gatlin, *Mbr/Scholarship Trustees*
Thomas E. Watson, *Mbr/Foundation ExCom*
Dennis J. Wessel
James E. Wolf
Charles E. Gulledge III, *Consultant*
Farooq Mehboob, *CO*
Kim Mitchell, *Staff Director*

Finance
Charles E. Gulledge III, *Chair/CO*
Jason Z. Alphonso
Blake E. Ellis
Arthur L. Giesler
Mick Schwedler, *Mbr, VP*
Julia Keen, *Mbr, VP*
M. Ginger Scoggins
Edward K.C. Tsui

Nominating
Timothy G. Wentz, *Chair*
Bjarne W. Olesen, *Vice Chair*

Selected by Region
Joseph L. Furman (I)
Nicolas Lemire (II)
Sherry Abbot-Adkins (III)
Andrew L. Cochrane (IV)
Filza H. Walters (V)
Tina Brueckner (VI)
Michael R. Bilderbeck (VII)
John C. Rhodes (VIII)
Blake E. Ellis (IX)
Devin A. Abellon (X)
Rob Craddock (XI)
William Malphus (XII)
Han Guan Den Low (XIII)
Eduardo Maldonado (XIV)
M. Bassel Anbari, *RAL*
Richard E. Vehlow (I), *Alternate*
Isabelle Lavoie (II), *Alternate*
James M. Grant (III), *Alternate*
Charlie D. Curlin (IV), *Alternate*
Richard A. Zbin (V), *Alternate*
Mark Hegberg (VI), *Alternatve*
Dustin Eric Jason Meredith (VII), *Alternate*
Nathan P. Hart (VIII), *Alternate*
Michelle L. Swanson (IX), *Alternate*
Tiffany Bates Abruzzo (X), *Alternate*
Jeffery D. Hurd (XI), *Alternate*
William B. Bradford (XII), *Alternate*
Dominador DeGuzman Castro, Jr. (XIII), *Alternate*
Ioanna Deligkiozi (XIV), *Alternate*
Krishnan Viswanath (RAL), *Alternate*

Elected by BOD
Erich Binder (XI)
Nohad I. Boudani (RAL)
Steven T. Bushby (III)
Jennifer Isenbeck (XII)
Walter W. Law Jr. (VII)
John H. Nix (XII)
T. David Underwood (II)
Thomas E. Watson (III)
Richard J. Bowman (IX), *Alternate*
Gary L. Cooper (IX), *Alternate*
Arthur D. Hallstrom (XII), *Alternate*
John L. Harrod (VIII), *Alternate*
Francis A. Mills (XIV), *Alternate*
John H. Nix II (XII), *Alternate*

Planning
William P. Bahnfleth, *Chair*
Thomas H. Phoenix, *Vice Chair*
Michael P. Cooper
Jennifer A. Isenbeck
M. Dennis Knight
Karine Leblanc
Sarah E. Maston
William F. McQuade
Rachel Romero, *YEA Rep.*
Bjarne W. Olesen
Hassan Ali Sultan
Timothy G. Wentz
Mark P. Modera, *Consultant*
Emilia Agata Targonska, *Consultant*
Jeff H. Littleton, *NVM/EVP*
George W. Austin, Jr., *NVM BOD Cons.*
Constantinos A. Balaras, *NVM BOD Cons.*
Marites Dagulo Calad, *NVM BOD Cons.*
Tim J. McGinn, *NVM BOD Cons.*
Daniel R. Rogers, *NVM BOD Cons.*
Vanita Gupta, *NVM/Staff Director*
Mick Schwedler, *CO*
Claire Neme, *Staff Liaison*

Society Rules
Donald L. Brandt, *Chair*
Lawrence C. Markel, *Vice Chair*
Kenneth M. Fulk
William K. Klock
Dunstan L. Macauley III
Trent Hunt
Arthur L. Giesler, *Consultant*
Leon Shapiro, *Consultant*
Julia A. Keen, *CO*
Claire Neme, *Staff Liaison*

MEMBERS COUNCIL

Darryl K. Boyce, *Chair/President Elect*
Charles E. Gulledge III, *Vice Chair/ Treasurer*
Erich Binder, *Mbr/Director*
Christopher G. Phelan, *Mbr/Director*
Essam E. Khalil, *Mbr/Director*
Jeff Clarke, *Mbr/Director*
Russell Lavitt, *Mbr/Director*
Dunstan Macauley, *Mbr/Director*
Daniel R. Rogers, *Mbr/Director*
William F. Walter, *RMCR (I)*
Ronald Gagnon, *RMCR (II)*

Mark Tome, *RMCR (III)*
Steven A. Marek, *RMCR (IV)*
Douglas F. Zentz, *RMCR (V)*
John A. Rieke, *RMCR (VI)*
Chris M. Gray, *RMCR (VII)*
Randy Schrecengost, *RMCR (VIII)*
Tyler Glesne, *RMCR (IX)*
Scott Wayland, *RMCR (X)*
N. Eileen Jensen, *RMCR (XI)*
Robin Bryant, *RMCR (XII)*
Cheng Wee Leong, *RMCR (XIII)*
Dimitris Charalambopoulos, *RMCR (XIV)*
Richie Mittal, *RMCR (RAL)*
Joyce Abrams, *Staff Liaison*

Chapter Technology Transfer

Farhan A. Mehboob, *Chair*

Nathan P. Hart, *Vice Chair*
Thursten D. Simonsen, *Vice Chair*
Charles J. Bertuch III (I)
Daniel Robert (II)
Tracey N. Jumper (III)
Christopher A. Adams (IV)
Carl Schultz (V)
Andrew Babler (VI)
David Ballard (VII)
Peter J. Sudbeck (VIII)
Russell C. Pratt (IX)
Kevin Blankemeier (X)
Heric D. Holmes (XI)
Walter R. Lenzi, Sr. (XII)
Bing-Chwen Yang (XIII)
Serafin Grana (XIV)
Mohammad H. Al Tassi (RAL)
Andrew Reilman, *Mbr/Chap. Progs. Coord.*
Stephen Piccolo, *Mbr/Web Broadcast Coord.*
Essam E. Khalil, *BOD ExO*
Darryl K. Boyce, *CO*
Candace DeVaughn, Staff Liaison

Conferences and Expositions

Kevin Marple, *Chair*

Michael M. Collarin, *Vice Chair*
Devin A. Abellon
Vikrant C. Aute
Robert A. Cox
Gary C. Debes
Melanie Derby
Joseph Firrantello
Ashu Gupta
Richard D. Hermans
Stephen A. Idem
Rupesh Iyengar
Nivedita Jadhav
Bing Liu
Ryan M. MacGillivray
Corey B. Metzger
Maggie M. Moninski
Carrie Anne Monplaisir
Leticia DeOliveira Neves
Kimberly Pierson
Sonya Pouncy
Ashish Rakheja
Chris Reinders-Caron
Lee Riback
Raul Simonetti
Marianna Vallejo
Daniel Rogers, *BOD ExO*
Darryl K. Boyce, *CO*
Tony Giometti, *Staff Liaison*

Government Affairs

T. David Underwood, *Chair*

Walid Chakroun, *Vice Chair*
Robin Bryant, *Members Council Rep.*
Mo Hosni, *PubEd Council Rep.*
Michael Bilderbeck, *Tech Council Rep.*
William F. McQuade
Terry Townsend
Andrew Manos (I)
Robert P. Hoadley (II)
Kinga Porst Hydras (III)
Roger T. Ashby (IV)
James Arnold (V)
Matthew S. Jesson (VI)
Ryan A. Williams (VII)
Chad D. Smith (VIII)
Jessica J. Errett (IX)
David A. Palty (X)
Jeffery D. Hurd (XI)
Eduardo Jose Conghos (XII)
Sam C. M. Hui (XIII)
Stephen Gill (XIV)
Maged Fouad Hashem (RAL)
Roger K. Jones, *Member/Comm.Coord.*
Dunstan L. Macauley III, *BOD ExO*
Charles E. Gulledge, *BOD ExO/Treas.*
Darryl K. Boyce, *CO*
Alice Yates, *Staff Liaison*
Jim Scarborough, *Staff Liaison*
Jeremy Pollack, *Staff Liaison*

Honors and Awards

Tiffany Bates Abruzzo, *Chair*

Paul E. Petrilli, *Vice Chair*
Sherry Abbott-Adkins
Donald Colliver
Rob Craddock
Stephen Duda
John L. Harrod
N. Eileen Jensen
Jake Kopocis
Isabelle Lavoie
Florentino Roson Rodriguez
Samir Traboulsi
Essam E. Khalil, *BOD ExO*
Darryl K. Boyce, *CO*
Candace Pettigrew, *Staff Liaison*

Membership Promotion

Michelle L. Swanson, *Chair*

Carrie Kelty, *Vice Chair*
Erik D. Sanchez, *Vice Chair*
Lee Feigenbaum (I)
Genevieve Lussier (II)
Patrick Marks (III)
Brian K. Justice (IV)
Adam Doubblestein (V)
Dan Chudecke (VI)
Casper Briggs (VII)
R. Alan Neely (VIII)
Jonathan R. Smith (IX)
Meg Gates (X)
Greg Fluter (XI)
Florentino Roson Rodriguez (XII)
Henry Seck Kan Yeo (XIII)
Monica Del Fresno (XIV)
Altayeb Ibrahim, *RAL*
Russell J. Lavitt, *BOD ExO*
Darryl K. Boyce, *CO*
Daniel Gurley, *Staff Liaison*

Research Promotion

Derek A. Crowe, *Chair*

Scott A. Martin, *Vice Chair*
Anthony Jonkov, *Vice Chair*
Tiffany Bates Abruzzo, *Vice Chair*
Thomas Zoller (I)
Mark Lawrence (II)
Chris Desoto (III)
Matt C. Rowe (IV)
Lane D. Snowberger (V)
Duane Rothstein (VI)
Scott B. Peach (VII)
Kimberly M. Thompson (VIII)
Megan L. Sterl (IX)
Heather R. Schopplein (X)
Lester J. Pereira (XI)
Jason Hardman (XII)

Ching Loon Ong (XIII)
Liviu Drughean (XIV)
Aakash Patel, *RAL*
Guy Perreault, *Consultant, ASHRAE Research Canada*
Jaideep S. Karnik, *International RP Consultant*
Christopher G. Phelan, *BOD ExO*
Darryl K. Boyce, *CO*
Julia Mumford, *Staff Liaison*

Student Activities
Adam Davis, *Chair*
Benjamin Oliver, *Vice Chair*
Steven C. Sill (I)
Mai Anh Dao (II)
James Piscopo (III)
Adam B. Parker (IV)
Jake Taylor (V)
Eric Sturm (VI)
Michael A. Kersanac (VII)
Christopher J. Ahne (VIII)
Kevin Amende (IX)
Burton Wright (X)
Jared R. Larson (XI)
Geraldo Alfonso (XII)
Manuel Belino (XIII)
Zoltan Magyar (XIV)
Michel D. Hayek, *RAL*
Michael Brandemuehl, *Accred. Rep/ ABET BOD*
S. David Cassel, *Accred. Rep/ABET EAC*
Mansour Zenouzi, *Accred. Rep/ABET TAC*
Megan Tosh, *Consultant*
William P. Simpson, *Consultant*
Russell J. Lavitt, *BOD ExO*
Darryl K. Boyce, *CO*
Katie Thomson, *Staff Liaison*

Young Engineers in ASHRAE
Stephanie Kunkel, *Chair*
Vanessa Freidberg, *Vice Chair*
Chonghui Liu (I)
Alexis Gagnon (II)
Lindsey King (III)
Jackson Willis (IV)
Matthew K. Colvin (V)
Shona O'Dea (VI)
Jac Cooper (VII)
Madison W. Schultz (VIII)
Rachel L. Romero (IX)
Alyse Falconer (X)
Branislav Cvijetinovic (XI)
Kathleen Simpson, *Region (XII) RVC*
Pang Ching Man Tracy, *Region (XIII) RVC*
Aleksandar Andjelkovic, *Region (XIV) RVC*
Muhammed Omer Khan, *RAL RVC*
Ashu Gupta
Carrie Anne Monplaisir
Carrie R. Kelty, *Liaison/MP*
Benjamin Oliver, *Liaison/SA*
Emilia A. Targonska, *Consultant/CIBSE*
Jake Kopocis, *Consultant*
Jeff Clarke, BOD ExO
Darryl K. Boyce, *CO*
Rhiannon Masterson, *Staff Liaison*

PUBLISHING AND EDUCATION COUNCIL

Julia Keen, *Chair, VP*
Farooq Mehboob, *Vice Chair, VC/VP*
George W. Austin, Jr., *Mbr/Director (19)*
Katherine G. Hammack, *Mbr/Director (21)*
Ahmed Alaa Eldin Mohammed, *Mbr/ Director (21)*
Chandra Sekhar, *Mbr/Director (21)*
Benjamin Skelton, *Mbr/Director (19)*
Cameron R. Labunski, *Mbr/ Past Certification (21)*
Heather L. Platt, *Mbr/Past ECC (19)*
Daniel J. Dettmers, *Mbr/Past Handbook (20)*
Larry J. Fisher, *Mbr/Past Prof. Development (21)**
Jin Jin Huang, *Mbr/Past Publications (20)*
Mohammad H. Hosni, *MAL (19)*
K. William Dean, *MAL*
Mark S. Owen, *Staff Liaison*

Certification
Eric M. Fullerton, *Chair*
Mark J. Bettin, *First Vice Chair*
D. Nirmal Ram, *Second Vice Chair*
Nicholas H. Armstrong
Kimberly R. Cowman
Mark W. Fly
Kurt Montiero
Daniel C. Pettway
Rachel C. Stuckey
Ashley Weekly
Kevin P. White
Chandra Sekhar, *BOD ExO*
Julia Keen, *CO*
Tim Kline, *Staff Liaison*

Electronic Communications
Megan Tosh, *Chair*
Gerardo Alfonso, *Vice Chair*
Cynthia A. Callaway
Kenneth Cooper
Pamela L. Duffy
Mark Hydeman
Karine Leblanc
Jessica Mangler
Nitin Naik
Justin D. Stonehocker
Benjamin Skelton, *BOD ExO*
Julia Keen, *CO*
Joslyn Ratcliff, *Staff Liaison*

Handbook
Donald L. Fenton, *Chair*
Suzanne LeViseur, *Vice Chair*
Katharine G. Hammack, *BOD ExO*
Julia Keen, *CO*
Heather Kennedy, *Staff Liaison*

Subcommittee for 2019 HVAC Applications Volume
Suzanne LeViseur, *Subcommittee Chair*
Bryan R. Becker
Narayanan S. Chandrasekar
Bryan M. Holcomb
Harris M. Sheinman
Lynn F. Werman

Subcommittee for 2020 Systems and Equipment Volume
Michael P. Patton, *Subcommittee Chair*
Caroline C. Calloway
Prakash R. Dhamshala
Nicolas Lemire
Florentino Roson Rodriguez, Sr.
Steven C. Sill

Subcommittee for 2021 Fundamentals Volume
Bass Abushakra, *Subcommittee Chair*
Jason A. Atkisson
Guy S. Frankenfield
Kevin B. Gallen
Javier Korenko
Stephanie J. Mages

Subcommittee for 2022 Refrigeration Handbook
David Scott Fisher, *Subcommittee Chair*
Frederick W. Betz
Carlos Alberto Brignone
Brian A. Fricke
Scott E. Seigel
Nicholas D. Shockley

Historical
Bruce L. Flaniken, *Chair*

Stanley Westhoff, *Vice Chair*
Ahmed Alaa Eldin Mohamed Mahmoud
Pamela M. Immekus
Lindsey King
Bernard Nagengast
Eric Sturm
Branislav Todorovic
Douglas Cochrane, *BOD ExO*
Julia Keen, *CO*
Emily Sigman, *Staff Liaison*

Regional Historians

Stanley Westhoff (I)
Robert T. Pollard (II)
Gary C. Debes (III)
Maurice Richard Harrison (IV)
Lane D. Snowberger (V)
Sherman M. Sweeney (VI)
Benjamin D. Godfrey (VII)
Dusty Stoabs (VIII)
Gary Cooper (IX)
Dean Borges (X)
Douglas B. LeCren (XI)
John Davant (XII)
Siew Meng Leong (XIII)
Triantafyllos A. Triantafyllopoulos (XIV)
Kadir Isa, *RAL*

Professional Development
Charles E. Henck, *Chair*

Fred W. Betz, *Vice Chair/Planning*
Jeremy T. Smith, *Vice Chair/Operations*
Timothy C. Dwyer
Jesse A. Fisher
Lindsey King
Walter W. Law, Jr.
Tyler Lewis
Askash A. Patel
Sarah Poursharafeddin
Keith H. Reihl
James K. Vallort
George W. Austin, Jr., *BOD ExO*
Julia Keen, *CO*
Karen M. Murray, *Staff Liaison*

Publications
Jose Luis Correa, *Chair*

Chee Sheng Ow, *Vice Chair*
Roberto R. Aguilo
Vinay Ananthachar
Jorge Eduardo Donoso
Jack Glass
Antonio Marquez
Norm Maxwell
Adeeba Mehboob
Hugh D. McMillan III
Vikram Murthy
Renison W. Tisdale, Jr.
Ronald P. Vallort
Benjamin Skelton, *BOD ExO*
Julia Keen, *CO*
Cindy Michaels, *Staff Liaison*

TECHNOLOGY COUNCIL

Mick Schwedler, *Chair/VP*

Dennis Knight, *Vice Chair/VP*
Van D. Baxter, *Mbr/Director*
Douglas D. Fick, *Mbr/Director*
Thomas M. Lawrence, *Mbr/Director*
Lawrence C. Markel, Mbr/Director
Sarah E. Maston, *Mbr/Director*
Steven J. Emmerich, *Mbr/Past Standards*
Arthur L. Giesler, *Mbr/Past RAC*
Kenneth M. Fulk, *Mbr/Past DRC*
Charles H. Culp III, *Member/Past TAC*
Michael Bilderbeck, *MAL*
Byron W. Jones, *MAL*
Kelley P. Cramm, *MAL*
Stephanie Reiniche, *Staff Liaison*

Environmental Health
W. Elliott Horner, *Chair*

Wade H. Conlan, *Vice Chair*
Peter F. Alspach, *Past Stds.*
Charlene W. Bayer, *Past TC Chair*
Hans Besselink
Hoy Bohanon
Nicholas Clements
Kishor K. Khankari, *Past RAC*
Luke C. H. Leung
Andrew K. Persily
Max H. Sherman
Erica Stewart, *Health Professional*
Wei Sun
Shin-ichi Tanabe
Wayne Thomann
Lain Chi Nguyen Weekes, *Consultant*
Thomas M. Lawrence, *BOD ExO*
Mick Schwedler, *CO*
Steve Hammerling, *Staff Liaison*

Refrigeration
Martin Dieryckx, *Chair*

Rajan Rajendran, *Vice Chair*
Walid Chakroun
Didier Coulomb
Ayman Taha Hussein Eltalouny
Stephen C. Gill
Charles C. Hon
Yunho Hwang
Dustin Lilya
Barbara Minor
William F. Walter
Tony Welter
Sarah E. Maston, *BOD ExO*
Mick Schwedler, *CO*
Steve Hammerling, *Staff Liaison*

Residential Buildings
Theresa A. Weston, *Chair*

Paul Francisco, *Vice Chair*
Pankaj Dharkar
Patricia T. Graef
Glenn C. Hourahan
Jeff Inks
Daniel Int-Hout
John Jones
Leslie A. Jonsson
Richard Karg
Neil P. Leslie
David J. Weishuhn
Van D. Baxter, *BOD ExO*
Mick Schwedler, *CO*
Lilas Pratt, *Staff Liaison*

Research Administration
John A. Shonder, *Chair*

David A. Yashar, *Vice Chair*
Chris K. Wilkins, *RAS Chair*
E. Curtis Eichelberger, Jr., *RPS Chair*
Omar A. Abdelaziz
Shinsuke Kato
H. Ezzat Khalifa
Stephen Kujak
Dennis L. Loveday
Michael A. Pouchak
Paolo M. Tronville
Pawel Wargocki
Xudong Wang, *Consultant/AHRI*
Hywel Davies, *Consultant/CIBSE*
Ian Cull, *Consultant/IAQA*
Douglas D. Fick, *BOD ExO*
Mick Schwedler, *CO*
Michael Vaughn, *Staff Liaison*

Standards
Donald M. Brundage, *Chair*

Wayne H. Stoppelmoor, Jr., *Vice Chair*
Els Baert
Charles S. Barnaby
Niels Bidstrup
Michael D. Corbat
Drury B. Crawley
Julie M. Ferguson
Michael W. Gallagher

Walter T. Grondzik
Susanna S. Hanson
Roger L. Hedrick
Rick M. Heiden
Jonathan Humble
Kwang Woo Kim
Larry Kouma
R. Lee Millies, Jr.
Karl L. Peterman
Erick A. Phelps
David Robin
Lawrence J. Schoen
Dennis A. Stanke
Richard T. Swierczyna
Rusty Tharp
Adrienne G. Thomle
Michael Woodford
Craig P. Wray
Lawrence C. Markel, *BOD ExO*
Mick Schwedler, *CO*
Steve Ferguson, *Staff Liaison*

Technical Activities

Thomas A. Justice, *Chair*
Jay A. Kohler, *Vice Chair*
Victor W. Goldschmidt
Carl F. Huber
Amir Jokar
Dawen Lu
Sarah Maston
Dustin E.J. Meredith
Criag S. Messmer
Barbara Minor
Vance Payne
Elbert G. Phillips
Larry A. Smith
James R. Tauby
Marija S. Todorovic
Dennis J. Wessel
Krishnan Gowri, *Cons.*
Thomas M. Lawrence, *BOD ExO*
Mick Schwedler, *CO*
Michael Vaughn, *Staff Liaison*

Appendix G

ASHRAE Honors and Awards

A full listing of ASHRAE Honors and Awards is published in Part 2 of every volume of *ASHRAE Transactions*. The listing published here includes selected awards focused on technology advancement in ASHRAE fields of interest that have been presented as of January 2020.

ASHRAE HALL OF FAME

Established in 1990, this award honors deceased members who have made milestone contributions to the growth of ASHRAE-related technology and/or the development of ASHRAE as a Society. Individuals inducted into the Hall of Fame must have been an ASHRAE member (any grade) or a member of a predecessor Society. The award consists of a plaque and crystal award for the family, including transportation and one night's lodging to the meeting where the award is presented.

	Year Inducted
F. Paul Anderson	1994
Willis Haviland Carrier	1994
Francis W. Hutchinson	1994
Carlyle Martin Ashley	1995
A. Pharo Gagge	1995
Gianfelice Bertolini	1996
John Engalitcheff, Jr.	1996
Margaret Ingels	1996
George Lewis Tuve	1996
Reuben N. Trane	1997
Charles S. Leopold	2000
Rudolf Plank	2001
Frank H. Faust	2003
Milton W. Garland	2003
Henry Galson	2005
Gardner Voorhees	2005
Jasper G. Woodroof	2006
Mary E. Pennington	2007
Frank J. Dean, Jr.	2008
P. Ole Fanger	2008
William J. Collins, Jr.	2010
J. Donald Kroeker	2010
Roderick R. Kirkwood	2012
Wilbert F. Stoecker	2013
Fred W. Wolf, Jr.	2014
Rolla Carpenter	2015
Robert Tamblyn	2015
Calvin D. MacCracken	2016
John Edwin Starr	2016
A. Damon Gowan	2018
George B. Hightower	2019

F. PAUL ANDERSON AWARD

Established in 1930 to honor the accomplishments of the late F. Paul Anderson, Past President of the Society, this award is presented annually for notable scientific achievement or outstanding services performed in the field of heating, ventilating, or air conditioning. The award consists of a medallion and plaque.

Willis H. Carrier	1932
Arthur C. Willard	1936
Frank B. Rowley	1939
Frederick E. Giesecke	1942
Ferry C. Houghten	1944
Alfred E. Stacey, Jr.	1946
James H. Walker	1947
Chas.-Edward A. Winslow	1950
Samuel R. Lewis	1951
Homer Addams	1952
Everett N. Mcdonnell	1953
Walter I. Fleisher, Sr.	1954
Charles S. Leopold	1955
Robert W. Keeton, MD	1956
M.F. Fahnestock	1957
George Lewis Tuve	1958
C.P. Yaglou	1959
Peter Ben Gordon	1960
J. Donald Kroeker	1961
C.M. Ashley	1962
Arthur J. Hess	1963
Axel B. Algren	1964
Louis N. Hunter	1965
Richard C. Jordan	1966
Walter A. Grant	1967
Crosby Field	1968
Dean W.R. Woolrich	1969
Glenn Muffly	1970
Donald K. Tressler	1971
Robert H. Tull	1972
Seichi Konzo	1973
William L. Mcgrath	1974
Neil B. Hutcheon	1975
Paul R. Achenbach	1976
Daniel D. Wile	1979
Herbert L. Laube	1980

Burgess H. Jennings 1981
John Engalitcheff, Jr. 1982
William P. Chapman 1983
Walter F. Spiegel 1985
A. Pharo Gagge 1986
Everett P. Palmatier 1987
Milton W. Garland 1988
George O.G. Löf 1989
Frank H. Bridgers 1990
William Goodman 1991
P. Ole Fanger 1992
Jack B. Chaddock 1993
Hans O. Spauschus 1994
Frank H. Faust 1995
William J. Coad 1996
Joseph B. Olivieri 1997
William J. Collins, Jr. 1998
Donald R. Bahnfleth 1999
Arthur E. Bergles 2000
Clark W. Bullard 2004
Gerald C. Groff 2010
Richard P. Perry 2011
Richard H. Rooley 2013
Kent W. Peterson 2014
A. Damon Gowan 2015
Thomas E. Watson 2016

LOUISE AND BILL HOLLADAY DISTINGUISHED FELLOW AWARD

Established in 1979, this award honors a Fellow of the Society for continuing preeminence in engineering or research work. The award consists of a medallion and plaque.

Carlyle M. Ashley 1979
John I. Yellott 1980
A. Pharo Gagge 1981
P. Ole Fanger 1982
Daniel D. Wile 1983
Frank H. Faust 1984
Alwin B. Newton 1985
John H. Fox 1986
Tamami Kusuda 1987
Donald G. Rich 1988
William J. Coad 1989
Frederick H. Rohles, Jr. 1990
Thomas B. Romine, Jr. 1991
Ralph F. Goldman 1992
Donald R. Bahnfleth 1993
Preston E. McNall 1994
Milton W. Garland 1995
Harold E. Straub 1996
Joseph B. Olivieri 1997
Frederick H. Kohloss 1998
Harry J. Sauer, Jr. 1999
George B. Hightower 2000
Arthur E. Bergles 2002
Olli A. Seppänen 2003
Prem C. Jain 2005
Max H. Sherman 2006
James E. Hill 2008
Byron W. Jones 2011
Stanley A. Mumma 2012
Kent W. Peterson 2014
Raymond Cohen 2015
Steven T. Taylor 2016
Zahid Ayub 2017
William P. Bahnfleth 2018
Predrag Pega Hrnjak 2019

ASHRAE FELLOWS

The grade of Fellow is conferred on Members who have attained distinction in the arts relating to the sciences of heating, refrigeration, air-conditioning, ventilation, or the allied arts and sciences. The award consists of a lapel pin and plaque.

Abedin, A 1998
Achenbach, P.R. 1959
Acorn, W. A. 2006
Adams, L. 1955
Advani, A. 1996
Aguilo, R.R. 2013
Akerman, J.R. 1981
Alderman, B., Jr. 1977
Altieri, J.L. 1986
Anderson, P.P., Jr. 1979
Angus, D.L. 1971
Armstrong, P.R. 2015
Armstrong, R.M. 1950
Armstrong, R.S. 1997
Arnold, D. 2001
Atwood, T. 1992
Ayub, Z. 2008
Azer, N.Z. 1992
Bahnfleth, W.P. 2005
Balaras, C. 2011
Bales, E.L. 1999
Bansal, P. 2008
Barkman, H.G. 1987
Barnaby, C. 2016
Basso, P.J. 1997
Bathgate, T.A. 1992
Bauman, F.S. 2018
Baxter, V. 2011
Bayer, C. 2016
Beaty, D.L. 2007
Becker, B. 2004
Becker, S. 2008
Belt, Jr., N.W. 1998
Bendelius, A.G. 1997
Berglund, B. 1992
Berglund, L.G. 1991
Bernier, M. 2016
Bertrand, L. 1998
Besant, R.W. 1993
Bhatti, M. 2004
Bilderbeck, M.R. 2005
Bisset, J.B. 1995
Blatt, M.H. 1999
Blossom, J.S. 1977
Boggs, A.T., III 1979
Bong, T.Y. 1990
Bosworth, C.M. 1971
Bottum, E.W. 1984
Bovay, H.E., Jr. 1981
Boyd, R.L. 1967
Boyce, D.K. 2009
Bradley, T.W. 1989
Brager, G.S. 2002
Brambley, M.R. 2009
Branson, D.J. 2013
Brandemuehl, M.J. 2009
Braun, J. 2005
Briede, J.D. 1994
Broadbent, C.R. 2015
Brown, C.R. 1991
Brown, J.S. 2013
Brown, L.N. 1977
Brown, M.R. 1993
Brundrett, G.W. 1998
Bruning, S.F. 1996
Bryant, D.C., Sr. 1981
Bullard, C.W. 2002
Bullock, C.E. 1996
Burch, R.M. 1995
Burdick, R.S. 1993
Burr, R.W. 1994
Burroughs, H.E. 1994
Bushby, S. 2008
Bushnell, J. 2016
Butcher, T.A. 2013
Butkus, A.S. 2018
Calm, J.M. 1997
Campbell, H.J., Jr. 1988
Capehart, B.L. 2012
Carter, D.E. 2012
Cavallini, A. 2007
Cawley, R.E. 2002
Chakroun, W. 2010
Chan, J.V., Jr. 2005

Charneux, R. 2005
Chee, Y.P. 2004
Chen, Q. 2005
Chen, T.L. 2004
Chiriac, F. 2006
Chongvatana, P. 2006
Chou, S.K. 2005
Chow, T. 2008
Chow, W.K. 2015
Chu, C.-Y. 2003
Chuah, Y.K. 2003
Claridge, D. 2007
Clark, E.M. 1999
Clark, K.M. 1994
Clements-Croome, D.J. 1998
Cleland, D.J. 2009
Cloke, T.H., Jr. 1974
Coggins, J.L. 1999
Cohen, R. 1977
Colborne, W.G. 1979
Colliver, D.G. 1995
Colvin, T. 2016
Cooper, K. 2005
Cooper, W.S. 1997
Copeland, C.C. 1991
Costa, A. 2014
Coward, C.W., Jr. 1996
Cox, J.E. 1993
Crawford, J.G. 2001
Crawley, D.B. 2009
Cromer, C.J. 2009
Crosland, R.B. 1983
Culp, C. 2005
Cummings, J.B. 2010
Cummings, S.D., Jr. 1994
Dale, K.W. 1984
Davidson, L.A. 2007
Deltz, P.N. 1994
Depew, C.A. 1995
DesChamps, N.H. 1999
Deshpande, S.D. 2015
Dharkar, P. 2014
Didion, D.A. 1991
Dillon, M.E. 1993
Domanski, P.A. 2007
Donoso, J.E. 2010
Dorgan, C.B. 2010
Dorgan, C.E. 1985
Downing, R.C. 1968
Driscoll, D.J. 1982
Duda, S.W. 2013
Dunlap, J. 2016
DuPernell, P.C. 1994
Durkin, T.H. 2012
Dussault, R.E. 1992
Dwyer, T. 2008
Dzelzitis, E. 2014
Eley, C. 2018
Elmahdy, A.H. 2009
Elovitz, K.M. 2019
Emery, A.F. 2007
Emmerich, S. 2016
Ensor, D. 2003
Evans, G.F. 1987
Evans, R.A. 1993
Ferdelman, T.J. 1998
Fernandes, E.O. 1997
Ferreira, F. 1993
Field, J. 2008
Fiorino, D.P. 2001
Fischer, H.C. 1979
Fisher, D. 2009
Fisk, W. 2005
Fitzner, K. 1999
Flaniken, B. 2014
Fleming, W.S. 1991
Fly, M.W. 2012
Fogelman, S.R. 1981
Fox, J.H. 1965
Francisco, P.W. 2018
Frankfurt, W.W. 1977
Freeman, G.A. 1983
Friedman, G. 2012
Gage, C. 2006
Galson, E.L. 1988
Ganta, R. 2014
Garbarino, A. 2005
Gardner, M.D. 1997
Gates, A.S., Jr. 1966
Gatley, D.P. 1984
Gendler, G.L. 1973
Gerstler, W.D. 2015
Gilbertson, T.A. 1991
Gilson, P.D. 1991
Glaser, D.L. 1995
Glicksman, L. 2008
Goldman, R.F. 1983
Goldschmidt, V.W. 1985
Gonzalez, R.R. 1994
Goswami, D.Y. 2013
Gowri, K. 2016
Graber, E. 1982
Graef, P.T. 2007
Graham, L. 1984
Grasso, M. 2007
Grimsrud, D. 2005
Groff, G.C. 2004
Groll, E.A. 2006
Grondzik, W.T. 2007
Grossman, G. 2010
Grumman, D.L. 1991
Guimaraes, E.T. 2013
Guinn, G.R. 1993
Guntermann, A.E. 1992
Gupta, V. 2003
Gupta, V.P. 2011
Guttman, K. 1981
Haberl, J. S. 2006
Haghighat, F. 2007
Hague, J.T. 1998
Hahn, W. 2008
Haines, R.W. 1974
Hallstrom, A.D. 2000
Halyard, P.J. 2000
Han, Hwataik 2018
Hanley, A.J. 1990
Hansen, C., III 1998
Hansen, E.G. 1993
Hargan, M.R. 1996
Harrison, W.D. 1982
Harriman, L.G. 2009
Harrod, J. 2016
Haves, P. 2003
Hay, D.J. 2014
Hayakawa, T.G. 1982
Hayes, H.P. 1962
Hayter, R.B. 1991
Hayter, S. 2008
Heinemeier, K. 2015
Henck, C.E. 1997
Hens, H.S.L.C. 2007
Hensen, J.L.M. 2007
Hill, J.E. 1992
Hiller, C. 2005
Hirsch, S.R. 1951
Hng, H.C. 1995
Hogeling, J.J. 2010
Holness, G.V.R. 1990
Hopper, R.E., Jr. 1993
Horstman, R.H. 2012
Hosni, M.H. 2005
Hourahan, G.C. 2009
Houston, S.H. 1998
Howell, R.H. 1986
Hrnjak, P.S. 2005
Hu, Y.R. 2005
Hubard, B. 1988
Huergo, J. 2016
Hughes, D. 2008
Hunn, B.D. 1994
Hunt, E. 1994
Hunton, R.O. 1993
Hwang, Y. 2018
Hydeman, M. 2006
Int-Hout, D. 2007
Irwin, A.A. 2018
Jackins, G.A. 1993
Jacobi, A.M. 2009
Jang, J.Y. 2006
Jarik, G.J. 1977
Jensen, R.E. 1993
Jensen, R.N. 1981
Jimenez-Segovia, M. 2015
Johnson, G.E. 1991
Jones, B.W. 2000
Jones, J.W. 1989
Jones, R.R. 1977
Jordan, C.H. 1984
Jordan, R.C. 1959
Jorgensen, R. 1977
Kamm, J. 2018
Kampmeyer, J.E. 1997
Kanan, K. S. 2006
Katipamula, S. 2009
Kato, S. 2007
Kavanaugh, S. 2003

Kazachki, G. 2003
Keeler, R.M. 2010
Keen, Julia 2016
Kelley, W. 2000
Kelly, E.E. 1981
Kelly, G.E. 1991
Kelso, R.M. 1992
Kelter, S.L. 1995
Kennedy, J.M. 1979
Kenny, E. 1987
Kerschbaumer, H.G. 1989
Khalifa, H.E. 2009
Khalil, E.E. 2009
Khankari, K. 2015
Khattar, M.K. 2009
Kilkis, B. 2004
Kim, K.W. 2015
Kimball, W.R. 1994
Kimura, K.I. 1987
Kittler, R. 2001
Klassen, J. 1982
Klein, S.A. 1998
Klote, J.H. 1993
Knebel, D.E. 1995
Knight, M.D. 2013
Knutson, G.W. 2013
Koch, P.H. 1977
Kohlenberger, C.R. 1996
Kohloss, F.H. 1973
Koptis, C.R. 1994
Krafthefer, B. 2004
Krapek, A. 1975
Kreisman, H. 1975
Kroll, M.N. 1996
Kruse, H.H. 1997
Kuehn, T. 2004
Kuehner, R.L. 1971
Kulkarni, R.S. 2010
Kwok Ping-Ki, A. 1991
Lagomarsino, W.L. 2014
Laksanakorn, W. 2008
Landman, W.J. 1989
Landsberg, D.R. 2015
Lawrence, T. 2016
Lawson, C.N. 2009
Lebrun, J. 2001
Lee, C.H. 1985
Lee, E.C. 2004
Lehr, V.A. 1988
Lesser, N.I. 1990
Levin, H. 2003
Lewis, R.H. 1996
Li, Y. 2006
Lim, C.L. 2010
Lin, C.H. 2013
Lindvall, T. 1995
Lipshultz, M. 1989
Listijono, J.B. 2009
Lizardos, E.J. 1989
Lord, R. 2013
Lorf, G.O.G. 1988
Lortie, R.P. 1993
Lotz, W.A. 1992
Lovvorn, N.C. 2005
Lstiburek, J. 2005
Lum, F.Y.S. 1991
Lumlertpongpana, A. 2010
Madison, R.D. 1960
Madsen, T.L. 1996
Magyar, Z. 2016
Manning, B.R. 1993
Markel, L.C. 2002
Markel, M.L. 1991
Marks, P.C. 2015
Marschall, P.J. 1960
Masters, R.E. 1985
Mathur, G.D. 2005
McCarry, B.T. 2002
McCloskey, W.D. 1997
McConahey, E. 2014
McCoy, J.D. 2002
McDonald, T.W. 1996
McFall, J.D. 1992
McGuire, A.B. 2000
McKew, H.J. 2007
McMillan, H.D. 2010
McNamara, T. 2008
McQuade, W.F. 2012
Mehboob, F. 2010
Meckler, M. 1986
Meitz, A.K. 1999
Melikov, A. 2003
Melton, B.J. 2012
Mendez, F.J. 1995
Mentzer, J.C. 2000
Meriwether, R.F. 1983
Miclea, P.C. 2013
Miller, R.D. 1998
Missimer, D.J. 1972
Mitchell, J.W. 1994
Moakes, R. 1992
Modera, M. 2011
Montgomery, R. 2012
Morris, D.J. 1991
Moses, W.G. 1983
Mumma, S.A. 1992
Murakami, S. 2001
Murphy, J.A. 2015
Murphy, W.E. 2004
Nall, D.H. 2014
Naman, I.A. 1977
Nellis, G.F. 2013
Newman, H.M. 2000
Ng, E.H. 2001
Nielsen, P.V. 2004
Niess, R.C. 1992
Nishi, Y. 1994
Niu, J. 2013
Norman, J.H. 2007
North, F.H. 1985
Nottage, H.B. 1960
Novak, P. 1999
Novakovic, V. 2005
Nutter, D.W. 2011
Nye, G. 2008
O'Dell, L.J. 1991
Ohadi, M. 2004
Olesen, B.W. 2001
Olsen, E.J. 1999
Olson, D. 2016
O'Neal, D.L. 1999
Opatrny, C.J. 1993
Ossi, F. 2000
Ostrander, W.S. 1983
Ow, C.S. 2002
Owen, K. 2018
Pahwa, D. 2005
Palmizi, F. 1990
Papar, R. 2015
Paranjpey, R. 2005
Pavlak, R. 2016
Pearson, A.B. 2015
Pearson, R.J. 1984
Penney, G.W. 1981
Perisic, Z.B. 1999
Perkins, C.S. 1968
Perlman, M. 1992
Persily, A.K. 2004
Petersen, K. 2006
Peterson, R. 2014
Petras, D. 2014
Pflug, I.J. 1975
Phaklides, W.J. 1982
Phetteplace, G. 2018
Phillips, E. 2018
Phillips, H. 1991
Phoenix, T.H. 2011
Pouchak, M.A. 2018
Powell, J.V., Jr. 1985
Procell, C.J. 1992
Punsalan, L. 2006
Punwani, D.V. 2018
Radermacher, K. 2006
Rákóczy, T. 1997
Ram, D.N. 2007
Ranade, M.S. 2015
Rands, G.F. 1988
Reddy, A. 2007
Reedy, W.R. 2005
Reig, J.A. 1996
Reindl, D. 2008
Reistad, G.M. 1992
Rengholt, U.N. 1993
Rich, D.G. 1979
Richards, W.V. 1985
Richardson, G. 2002
Ridenour, S.M. 1992
Rivers, R.D. 1993
Roberts, J.F., Sr. 1983
Robinson, K.E. 1972
Rock, B. 2005
Rodriquez, J.T. 1994
Rogers, B.T. 1988
Rohles, F.H., Jr. 1984
Rooley, R.H. 1986
Rose, W.B. 2012

Rosenberg, M. 2016
Ross, D.E. 1984
Roubal, J.P. 1996
Rountree, H.E. 1984
Rumsey, P. 2008
Salsburg, J.F. 1971
Sami, S.M. 2001
Sanchez, A.J. 1998
Sandfort, J.F. 1971
Sankaran, S. 2005
Sanvordenker, K.S. 1982
Schoen, L. 2005
Schreiner, J.R. 1975
Schuchart, O.W. 1994
Schulze, J.L. 1999
Schumacher, E.W. 1995
Schuyler, G. 2005
Schwedler, M. 2015
Schwenker, E.H. 1998
Scofield, C.M. 2002
Scoggins, M.G. 2018
Scott, N.R. 1997
Scriven, J.A. 1989
Sekhar, S.C. 2007
Seppänen, O.A. 1996
Sestak, G.J. 2001
Setty, B.S. 2002
Shadpour, F. 2005
Shah, M.M. 2000
Shavit, G. 1991
Shedd, T.A. 2016
Shefferman, S.M. 1994
Sheikh, A.S. 2011
Shelton, R.L. 2005
Shelton, S.V. 1988
Sherif, S.A. 2002
Sherman, M.H. 1995
Shitzer, A. 2005
Shiver, W.D. 1987
Simha, R.V. 1997
Simmonds, P. 2006
Simonson, C. 2016
Singh, H. 1994
Singh, J. 2008
Sirjord, A.B., Jr. 1996
Slayton, C. 2008
Smith, G.W. 1997
Smith, L.R. 1971
Somasundaram, S. 2006
Sosoka, J.R. 1989
Soumerai, H.P. 1969
Sowell, E.F. 1990
Spauschus, H.O. 1971
Speich, C.F. 1993
Spielvogel, L.G. 2000
Spitler, J.D. 2005
Stanke, D.A. 2007
Starner, K.E. 1998
Steimle, F.W. 1990
Strong, R.H. 2002
Sud, I. 2005
Suggs, R.M., III 1993
Sun, T.Y. 1984
Sundaresan, G. 2000
Surange, A. 2008
Synn, I.CO. 1996
Tabunschikov, Y.A. 2001
Tan, S.C.L 2001
Tanabe, S. 2006
Taneja, O. 2015
Tao, W.K. 1977
Taylor, S. 2004
Tauby, J.R. 2018
Taylor, W. 1975
Thirakomen, K. 2009
Thompson, C.A. 1989
Thornton, R.C. 1991
Todorovic, B.B. 1987
Todorovic, M. 2009
Toub, S.G. 2002
Towell, R. 2016
Townsend, T.E. 1997
Traboulsi, S. 2014
Trafton, P. 2016
Tree, D. 2005
Tse, V.K.C. 1996
Tully, R.E. 1980
Tumilty, J.E. 1983
Turaga, M. 1992
Underwood, T.D. 2007
Uselton, R.B. 2004
Utesch, A.L. 1986
Vaidyanathan,N. 2012
Vallort, J.K. 2013
Vallort, R.P. 1997
Vechaphutti, T. 2004
Vijayakumar, R. 2016
Vineyard, E.A. 2011
Vogel, C.T. 1990
Walker, I.S. 2011
Walkinshaw, D. 2008
Walton, G. 2005
Wang, C. 2005
Wang, D.W.P 2002
Wang, F. 2016
Warwicker, B. 2011
Waterfill, R.W. 1971
Watson, T. 2008
Watt, J.R. 1992
Webb, R.L. 1998
Webb, W.A. 2002
Weld, G.B. 1986
Wen, S.M. 1986
Wentz, T.G. 2005
Wepfer, W.J. 1996
Werden, R.G. 1965
Wessel, D.J. 1998
White, T.J. 1981
Whitescarver, C.K., Jr. 1982
Wildin, M.W. 1997
Williams, V.A. 1988
Willis, L.E. 1999
Wingfield, G. 2006
Winston, D. 2014
Wolfberg, H.A. 1984
Wong, S.P.W. 1988
Wong, Y.W. 2002
Woodroof, J.G. 1958
Woods, J.E. 1992
Woody, A.W. 2000
Worek, W.M. 2011
Wright, J.R. 1998
Yang, K. 2006
Yang, X. 2011
Yoshino, H. 2006
Yousoufian, H.H. 1997
Yu, P.C.H 2018
Yuill, G.K. 1990
Zhang, J. 2011
Zhang, Y. 2008

This listing does not include deceased members who had been awarded the membership grade of Fellow. List is current as of July 2019.

ASHRAE HONORARY MEMBERS

Honorary Members are elected by the Board of Directors and are defined as notable persons of preeminent professional distinction. The award consists of a medallion and plaque.

Allen V. Astin 1969
L.M.K. Boelter 1966
Andrew T. Boggs 1985
Milton S. Eisenhower 1956
Crosby Field 1951
A.C. Fieldner 1944
Henry V. Heuser 1995
Herbert C. Hoover 1956
F.G. Keyes 1936
W.H. McAdams 1963
Albert J. Nesbitt 1972
Stefano Marino 2015
Peter A. Hancock 2016
Terry M. Manon 2016
Stephen T. Ayers 2017
William Henry Gates, III 2019

HOMER ADDAMS AWARD

Established in 1956 to perpetuate the memory of Homer Addams, Charter Member and Past President of ASHVE, this award recognizes a graduate student who has been engaged in an ASHRAE research project. The award consists of a $1,500 honorarium, plaque, and lapel pin.

Paul M. Chun 1957
University of Minnesota

W.E. Springer 1958
University of Illinois

John Y. Payton 1959
University of California

Frank D. Farrington 1960
University of Arizona

Alan B. Wagner 1961
Case Institute of Technology

Albert C. Kent 1962
Kansas State University

John M. Craig 1963
University of Florida

Joseph R. Gartner 1964
University of Wisconsin

Isaiah Kopelman 1965
Michigan State University

Eugene R. Michaud 1966
Purdue University

Norman G. Ziesse 1967
Carnegie Institute of Technology

Jon M. Rueck 1968
Kansas State University

James E. Shahan 1969
University of Illinois

Raymond E. Knotts 1970
Ohio State University

Donald R. Witt 1971
Pennsylvania State University

Thomas E. Bursey 1972
University of Saskatoon

Edward C. Skuchas 1973
Duke University

Fernando Duran 1974
University of Pittsburgh

Douglas C. Hamilton 1975
Purdue University

Kevin F. O'Brien 1976
Oklahoma State University

Douglas R. Bryant 1977
University of Manitoba

Sriram Somasundaram 1978
Case Western Reserve University

Gary L. Reynolds 1979
Iowa State University

Joseph B. Olivieri 1980
Lawrence Institute of Technology

Charles F. Rhein 1981
University of Missouri–Rolla

Shimao Ni 1982
Concordia University

Mean Shang Chen 1983
Kansas State University

Michael S. Sherber 1984
Georgia Institute of Technology

Steven M. Harris 1985
Oklahoma State University

Polyvious Eleftheriou 1986
Tenn. Technological University

James J. Baustian 1987
Iowa State University

John S. Schliesing 1988
Texas A&M University

Marc E. Fountain 1989
University of California–Berkeley

Ralph M. Diguilio 1990
Georgia Institute of Technology

S. Imam Haider 1991
Pennsylvania State University

Ernesto Embriz-Santander 1992
University of Florida

Zhenhai Li 1993
University of Illinois

Brian A. Fricke 1994
University of Missouri

Marianna Luoma 1995
University of Michigan

Donald J. Wolfe 1996
University of Kansas

Jeanne M. De Greef 1997
Kansas State University

James E. Bryan 1998
Texas A&M University

Jafar Darabi 1999
University of Maryland

William D. Gerstler 2000
University of Minnesota

Jelena Srebric 2001
MIT

Marija Radosevic 2002
Danish Technological Institute

Shehab Ahmad 2004
Texas A&M University

Dongyi Xiao 2005
Oklahoma State University

Pankaj Hande 2006
University of Missouri–Rolla

Bereket Nigusse 2008
Oklahoma State University

Nathan Kotey 2010
University of Waterloo

Sebastian Herrman 2011
University of Rostock

Harrison M. Skye 2012
University of Wisconsin–Madison

Ricardo J. Da Silva 2013
Fédérale de Lausanne

Ryan Tanner
University of Colorado–Boulder 2014

Limin Zhou
University of Kentucky 2015

Parham Azimi 2017
Illinois Institute of Technology, Chicago

Alireza Behfar 2018
University of Nebraska-Lincoln

Omer Sarfraz 2019
Oklahoma State University

RALPH G. NEVINS PHYSIOLOGY AND HUMAN ENVIRONMENT AWARD

Established in 1978, this award is presented annually to a promising investigator for significant accomplishment in the general area of man's response to the environment, which may include thermal, moisture, visual, acoustical, toxic, allergic, olfactory, vibrational, and microbiological effects on man's health, comfort, and well-being. The award consists of a plaque and lapel pin.

James E. Woods 1978
Larry G. Berglund 1979
Yasunobi Nishi 1980
Donald A. McIntyre 1981
Bjarne W. Olesen 1982
Richard R. Gonzalez 1983
Deanna M. Munson 1984
Elizabeth McCullough 1985
Lars Molhave 1986
Richard B. Hayter 1987
Byron W. Jones 1988
Gail Ellen Schiller 1989
Shin-Ichi Tanabe 1990
Geo Henrik Clausen 1991
Kenneth C. Parsons 1992
Richard J. De Dear 1993
Amanda K. Meitz 1994
Marc E. Fountain 1995
William J. Fisk 1996
Clifford C. Federspiel 1997
Jorn Toftum 1999
Lei Fang 2000
Jerry M. Sipes 2001
Pawel Wargocki 2002
Yanzheng "Don" Guan 2003
Zhang Hui 2004
Christopher Chao 2005
Charlie Huizenga 2007
Henry C. Willem 2008
Gwelen Paliaga 2010
Jan Kaczmarczyk 2011
Lily M. Wang 2012
Stefano Schiavon 2013
Benjamin Yang Bin 2014
Zhecho Bolashikov 2015
Jovan Pantelic 2016
Dusan Licina 2018
Bin Cao 2019

CROSBY FIELD AWARD

Established in 1973, the Crosby Field Award was named for an ASHRAE President. This award is for the highest rated paper presented at a Technical Session, Symposium, or Poster Session for the year. The award consists of a $750 honorarium and plaque.

1974 Paul R. DeCicco and Robert J. Cresci —"Smoke and Fire Control in High-Rise Office Buildings"

1975 Herbert P. Becker—"Energy Conservation Characteristics of Various Pumping Systems Compared with Variable Speed Systems"

1976 J.E. Hill and T. Kusuda—"Dynamic Characteristics of Air Infiltration"

1977 Clayton A. Morrison, James M. Wheeler, Jr., and Erich A. Farber—"An Experimental Determination of Shading Coefficients for Selected Insulating Reflective Glasses and Draperies"

1978 William Rudoy and L.M. Robins—"Comparison of Cooling Load Calculation"

1979 Istvan L. Ver—"A Review of the Attenuation of Sound in Straight Lined and Unlined Ductwork of Rectangular Cross Section"

1980 George T. Tamura—"The Calculation of House Infiltration Rates"

1981 Lawrence G. Spielvogel—"The Solar Bottom Line"

1982 Warren E. Blazier, Jr.—"Revised Noise Criteria for Design and Rating of HVAC Systems"

1983 Robert D. Fischer, Lawrence J. Flanigan, Sherwood G. Talbert, and Daniel A. Jaffee—"Degree Days Method for Simplified Energy Analysis"

1984 Brian P. Leaderer and William S. Cain—"Air Quality in Buildings During Smoking and Nonsmoking Occupancy"

1985 D.W. DeWerth, S.G. Talbert, S.M. Sobieski, and D.D. Paul—"Vent Capacity Data for High Efficiency, Condensing-Type, Gas-Fired Appliances"

1986 William J. Coad—"Variable Flow in Hydronic Systems for Improved Stability, Simplicity and Energy Economics"

1987 Will K. Brown, Jr.—"Fundamental Clean Room Concepts"

1988 John P. Kettler—"Efficient Design and Control of Dual-Duct Variable-Volume Systems"

1989 Joseph H. Eto and Cecile Meyer—"The HVAC Costs of Increased Fresh Air Ventilation Rates in Office Buildings"

1990 Milton Meckle—"Computer Analysis of Smoke Transport During Hotel Fire"

1991 Emil E. Friberg—"Central Heating and Cooling Plant Economics for the College Campus"

1992 Eric D. Larson and Lars J. Nilsson—"Electricity Use and Efficiency in Pumping Air-Handling Systems"

1993 Nancy J. Banks—"Field Test of a Desiccant-Based HVAC System for Hotels"

1994 Dale T. Hitchings and Richard S. Shull—"Measuring and Calculating Laboratory Exhaust Diversity—Three Case Studies"

1995 Frederic B. Morris, James E. Braun, and Stephen J. Treado—"Experimental and Simulated Performance of Optimal Control of Building Thermal Storage"

1996 Paul C. Tseng, Robert Krout, Dale Stanton-Hoyle, and Steve Kimsey—"Energy Program of Requirements for a New Detention Center—Energy Design Criteria for Prisons"

1997 Robert H. Green and Linda Roberts—"The Effect of Air-Coil Design on the Performance of Heat Pumps and Air Conditioners"

1998 Shuzo Murakami, Shinsuke Kato, and Jie Zeng—"Flow and Temperature Fields Around Human Body with Various Room Distribution, Part 1—CFD Study on Computational Thermal Manikin"

1999 Richard J. deDear and Gail Schiller Brager—"Developing an Adaptive Model of Thermal Comfort and Preference"

2000 Melvin W. First, Edward A. Nardell, William Chaisson, and Richard Riley—"Guidelines for the Application of Upper-Room Ultraviolet Germicidal Irradiation for Preventing Transmission of Airborne Contagion—Part I"

2001 Steve Kavanaugh and Marita Allan—"Thermal Conductivity of Cementitious Grouts and Impact on Heat Exchanger Length Design for Ground Source Heat Pumps"

2002 Jim L. Heldenbrand—"NBS Research and ASHRAE's 90 Series Standards"

2003 Paul Riemer, John W. Mitchell, and William A. Beckman—"The Use of Time Series Analysis in Fault Detection and Diagnosis Methodologies"

2004 William J. Rahmeyer—"Pressure Loss for PVC Pipe Tees"

2005 Ali Jalalzadeh-Azar—"A Comparison of Electrical and Thermal-Load Following CHP Systems"

2006 Sang-Min Lee and Jin-Won Lee—"A New Local Ventilation System Using a Vortex Flow Generated with a Finned Rotating Annular Disk"

2007 Michael R. Collins and John L. Wright—"Calculating Center-Glass Performance Indices for Windows with a Diathermanous Layer"

2008 Francis M. Farrell, Thoms M. Fitch, and Michael J. Morgan—"Development and Performance of a Retrofittable, High-Efficiency Grease Filter System for Kitchen Hoods"

2008 Kee-Chiang Chung, Tsai Kuo-Pao, and You-Hsuan Wang—"Performance of Local Ventilated Hood 1: A General Ventilation Working Environment"

2009 Jelena Srebric and Paulo Cesar Taberes Velasco—"The Role of Plants in the Reduction of Heat Flux Through Green Roofs: Laboratory Experiments"

2010 Jeffrey D. Spitler and Bereket A. Nigusse—"Refinements and Improvements to the Radiant Time Series Method"

2011 Jacob L. Edmondson, Dennis L. O'Neal, John A. Bryant, and Michael A. Davis, —"Performance of Series Fan-Powered Terminal Units with Electronically Commutated Motors"

2012 John A. Bryant, Michael A. Davis, and Dennis L. O'Neal—"Modeling the Performance of ECM and SCR Parallel Fan-Powered Terminal UnitsinSingle-DuctVAVSystems"

2013 James W. VanGilder, Christopher M. Healey, Zachary M. Pardey, and Xuanhang Zhang—"A Compact Server Model for Transient Data Center Simulations"

2014 Didier Thevenard and Mark W. Shephard—"Temperature Trends for Locations Listed in the Tables of Climatic Design Conditions in the 2013 *ASHRAE Handbook—Fundamentals*"

2015 John A. Shonder; Cyrus Nasseri "Achieving Deeper Energy Savings in Federal Energy Performance Contracts"

2016 Stephen Kujak; Edward M. Hamilton—"Examination of the Reactions of R-40 with R-134a and POE Refrigeration System Materials"

2017 Michael Roth—"Updating the ASHRAE Climate Design Data for 2017"

2018 Amy Van Asselt, Douglas T. Reindl, and Gregory F. Nellis— "Strategies to Increase Deployment of Renewables Using Cool Thermal Energy Storage"

WILLIS H. CARRIER AWARD

Established in 1960, the Willis H. Carrier Award, sponsored by the Carrier Corporation, is awarded for the best published paper of outstanding quality presented at a Society meeting by a member of any grade who was 32 years of age or less at the time of presentation of the paper. The award consists of a $500 honorarium and plaque.

Aaron L. Brody....1959–60
Carl F. Speich....1960–61
J. Richard Wright....1961
Charles E. Bullock....1967
George D. Huffman....1968
Richard E. Barrett....1969
Yosunobu Nishi....1970
E. McDuffie, Jr.....1971
Stanley A. Mumma....1973
Douglas M. Burch....1975
Merle F. McBride....1976
Stephen M. Sessler....1977
A.F.M. Ali....1978
Sudhir K. Sastry....1979
Stephen E. Selkowitz....1980
Amir L. Ecker....1981
Francesco Pompei....1982
Van D. Baxter....1983
Nancy J. MacDonald Banks....1984
Frank E. Jakob....1985
Joseph E. Laviana....1986
Robert W. Rasmussen....1987
Alain P. Fobelets....1988
Joseph H. Eto....1989
Anil K. Trehan....1990
Andreas K. Athienitis and Jiangang Shou....1991
Lars J. Nilsson....1992
Nancy J. Banks....1993
Barbara A. Stefl....1994
Frederic B. Morris....1995
Chad B. Dorgan....1996
Shane A. Moeykens....1997
Steve P. Rottmayer....1998
Brian W. Lee....1999
Carey J. Simonson and Dustin L. Ciepliski....2000
Andrew Manning....2001
Xianghong Huang....2002
Dongyi Xiao....2003
Guan Yanzheng....2004
Nicholas Long....2005
Barbara H. McCrary....2007
Joseph Firrantello and Alexander P. Michaud....2008
Paulo Cesar Taberes Velasco....2009
Michael S. Waring....2010
Jacob L. Edmondson....2011
Daniel C. Gibbs....2012
Paul Glanville....2013
Morgan D. Hayes....2014
Dustin W. Demetriou and Hamza Salih Erden....2015
Carl L. Reid and Peng Ying....2016
Mohammad Rafati Nasr....2017
Carl Lewis Reid and Peng Yin....2018

JOURNAL PAPER AWARD

This award is presented to the author of the best article published in the *ASHRAE Journal* during the Society year. The award consists of a plaque and an honorarium in the amount of $500. (The dates listed reflect the date of the paper's publication.)

Bruce J. Novell 1983
Francis J. McCabe 1984
R.L. Webb
and A. Villacres 1985
Carl H. Jordan
and Makio Goto 1986
Clifford M. Scofield
and James R. Taylor 1987
Mark O. McLinden
and David A. Didion 1988
Carl H. Jordan 1989
Gershon Meckler 1990
William J. Coad 1991
Thomas B. Romine, Jr. 1992
F. Sherwood Rowland 1993
Martha J. Hewett, Mary Sue Lobenstein,
and Susan K. Nathan 1994
Bernard A. Nagengast 1995
Steven T. Taylor 1996
Lewis G. Harriman, III 1997
Gurvinder Singh
and John Mitchell 1998
Lewis G. Harriman, III, Donald G. Colliver,
and K. Quinn Hart 1999
Rudolph Stegmann 2000
Thomas B. Hartman 2001
John Frederick Straube 2002
Gordon V. R. Holness 2003
Joseph W. Lstiburek 2004
Dennis Stanke 2005
Michel Bernier 2006
Fredrick Rohles 2007
James Cummings
and Charles Withers, Jr. 2008
James Steven Brown 2009
Steven Taylor
and Hwakong Cheng 2010
John Murphy 2011
John Murphy 2012
Daniel Nall
and Robert Sedlack 2013
Paul Lindahl 2014
Philip Bartholomew 2015
Hugh Crowther
and Yi Teng Ma 2016
Omar John Hawit
and Trevor Jaffe 2017
Daniel Koenigshofer
and John W. Roberts 2018

SCIENCE AND TECHNOLOGY FOR THE BUILT ENVIRONMENT BEST PAPER AWARD

Established in 2013, this award recognizes the best referred paper published in the volume year of *Science and Technology for the Built Environment*, ASHRAE's research journal, preceding the ASHRAE Winter Conference. The name of the award was changed from HVAC&R Research Best Paper Award in June 2015. The form of the award is a plaque.

Bryan Rassmussen 2012
Arsen Melikov, Barbora Krejcirvova,
Jan Kaczmarcyzk, Marcin Duszyk,
and Tomonori Sakoi 2013
David Yashar, Piotr Domanski,
Hong Cho 2014
Sorin Bengea, Pengfei Li, Soumik Sarkar,
Sergey Vichik, Veronica Adetola,
Keunmo Kang, Teems Lovett,
Francesco Leonardi 2015
Nesreen Ghaddar, Bachir El Fil,
Kamel Ghali 2016
Daniel Bacellar, Vikrant C. Aute,
Zhiwei Huang,
Reinhard Radermacher 2017
Burak Gunay, Weiming Shen,
Chunsheng Yang 2018

TECHNOLOGY AWARD OF ENGINEERING EXCELLENCE

The Award of Engineering Excellence was created in 1989 to recognize a first place winner of the Society-level Technology Award Competition for an outstanding application of innovative design and effective energy utilization. It is awarded at the judges' discretion.

Douglas M. Brant 1992
Byron H. Bakenhus 2000
Frederic Genest 2004
Joe Tai 2013
Peter Rumsey 2014
Johnathan Rumohr,
Jesse Hendershot 2018

Appendix H

Meeting Dates and Places

	ASHVE			
	Annual		Semi-Annual and Fall	
1895	New York, NY	1/21-23	None	
1896	New York, NY	1/21-23	None	
1897	New York, NY	1/26-28	New York, NY	6/18
1898	New York, NY	1/25-27	Atlantic City, NJ	7/15
1899	New York, NY	1/24-26	Saratoga, NY	7/21-22
1900	New York, NY	1/23-25	None	
1901	New York, NY	1/22-24	Chicago, IL	7/12-13
1902	New York, NY	1/21-23	Atlantic City, NJ	6/16
1903	New York, NY	1/20-22	Niagara Falls, NY	7/17-18
1904	New York, NY	1/19-20	Detroit, MI	7/15-16
1905	New York, NY	1/17-19	Chicago, IL	7/7-8
1906	New York, NY	1/16-18	Chicago, IL	7/19-20
1907	New York, NY	1/22-24	Milwaukee, WI	7/18-19
1908	New York, NY	1/21-23	Niagara Falls, NY	7/24-25
1909	New York, NY	1/19-21	Indianapolis, IN	7/15-16
1910	New York, NY	1/18-20	St. Louis, MO	6/30-7/1
1911	New York, NY	1/24-26	Chicago, IL	7/6-8
1912	New York, NY	1/23-25	Detroit, MI	7/11-12
1913	New York, NY	1/21-23	Buffalo, NY	7/17-19
1914	New York, NY	1/20-23	Cleveland, OH	7/9-11
1915	New York, NY	1/20-22	Atlantic City, NJ	9/16-17
1916	New York, NY	1/18-20	Detroit, MI	7/19-21
1917	New York, NY	1/16-18	Chicago, IL	7/18-20
1918	New York, NY	1/22-24	Buffalo, NY	6/26-28
1919	New York, NY	1/28-30	Pittsburgh, PA	6/10-12
1920	New York, NY	1/27-29	St. Louis, MO	5/26-28
1921	Philadelphia, PA	1/26-28	Cleveland, OH	6/14-17
1922	New York, NY	1/24-26	Buffalo, NY	6/6-7
1923	New York, NY; Washington, DC	1/23-26	Detroit, MI; Chicago, IL	6/8-10; 5/21-23
1924	New York, NY	1/22-25	Kansas City, MO	6/19-22
1925	New York, NY; Boston, MA	1/27-30	Atlantic City, NJ	6/15-17
1926	New York, NY	1/28-30	Lexington, KY	5/26-28
1927	St. Louis, MO	1/26-28	White Sulphur Springs, WV	6/28-30
1928	New York, NY	1/23-25	West Baden, IN	6/26-29
1929	Chicago, IL	1/28-31	Bigwin Inn, ON,	6/26-28

	Annual		Semi-Annual and Fall	
1930	Philadelphia, PA	1/27-31	Minneapolis, MN	6/24-27
1931	Pittsburgh, PA	1/26-29	Swampscott, MA	6/22-25
1932	Cleveland, OH	1/25-29	Milwaukee, WI	6/27-29
1933	Cincinnati, OH	1/23-25	Detroit, MI	6/22-24
1934	New York, NY	2/5-9	Buck Hill Falls, PA	6/20-22
1935	Buffalo, NY	1/28-30	Toronto, ON	6/16-19
1936	Chicago, IL	1/27-30	Buck Hill Falls, PA	6/22-24

ASHAE

	Annual		Semi-Annual and Fall	
1955	Philadelphia, PA	1/24-27	San Francisco, CA	6/27-29
1956	Cincinnati, OH	1/23-25	Washington, DC	6/18-20
1957	Chicago, IL	2/25-28	Murray Bay, PQ	6/24-26
1958	Pittsburgh, PA	1/27-29	Minneapolis, MN	6/23-25

ASRE

	Annual		Semi-Annual, Spring or Western	
1905	New York, NY	12/4		
1906	New York, NY	12/3-4		
1907	New York, NY	12/2-3		
1908	New York, NY	11/30-12/1		
1909	New York, NY	12/6	Chicago, IL	10/18-19
1910	New York, NY	12/5-6		
1911	New York, NY	12/4	St. Louis, MO	10/2-3
1912	New York, NY	12/2-3		
1913	New York, NY	12/1-2	Chicago, IL	9/18
1914	New York, NY			
1915	New York, NY	12/6-8	San Francisco, CA	9/23-24
1916	New York, NY	12/4-6		
1917	New York, NY	12/3-5	Milwaukee, WI	6/7-9
1918	New York, NY	12/2-4		
1919	New York, NY	12/1-3	Cincinnati, OH	5/19-21
1920	New York, NY	12/6-8	St. Louis, MO	5/26-28
1921	New York, NY	12/5-7	Chicago, IL	5/25-27
1922	New York, NY	12/4-6	Detroit, MI	5/24-26
1923	New York, NY	12/3-5	St. Louis, MO	4/30-5/2
1924	New York, NY	12/1-3	Cleveland, OH	5/27-29
1925	New York, NY	11/30-12/2	Milwaukee, WI	5/20-22
1926	New York, NY	12/6-8	Chicago, IL	6/2-4
1927	New York, NY	12/5-7	White Sulfur Springs, WV	5/23-25
1928	New York, NY	12/5-8	Detroit, MI	6/4-7
1929	New York, NY	12/4-7	State College, PA	6/20-22
1930	New York, NY	12/3-6	Atlanta, GA	5/7-9
1931	Cleveland, OH	1/25-29/1932	Kansas City, MO	5/6-8
1932	New York, NY	12/7-9	Boston, MA	6/9-11
1933	New York, NY	12/6-8	Chicago, IL	6/26-28

	Annual		Semi-Annual, Spring or Western	
1934	New York, NY	12/5-7	Skytop Lodge, PA	6/20-22
1935	New York, NY	12/4-6	Detroit, MI	5/22-24
1936	New York, NY	12/2-4	Skytop Lodge, PA	6/22-24
1937	New York, NY	1/25-27/1938	French Lick Springs, IN	6/8-10
1938	New York, NY	12/6-8	State College, PA	6/19-24
1939	Chicago, IL	1/17-19/1940	Hershey, PA	5/21-23
1940	New York, NY	12/3-5	Skytop, PA	6/9-11
1941	St. Louis, MO	12/2-5	Cincinnati, OH	5/27-29
1942	New York, NY	12/1-2	Skytop, PA	6/7-9
1943	Philadelphia, PA	12/7-9	Cleveland, OH	6/1-3
1944	New York, NY	12/10-13	Pittsburgh, PA	6/5-7
1945	New York, NY	12/9-12		
1946	New York, NY	12/16-18	St. Paul, MN	6/3-5
1947	Atlantic City, NJ	12/7-10	Los Angeles, CA	6/8-11
1948	Washington, DC	12/5-8	Swampscott, MA	5/30-6/2
1949	Chicago, IL	12/4-7	St. Lawrence/Saguenay River Cruise	6/5-9
1950	New York, NY	12/3-6	Kansas City, MO	6/4-7
1951	New Orleans, LA	12/2-5	Detroit, MI	5/27-30
1952	New York, NY	11/30-12/3	Atlanta, GA	6/1-4
1953	Washington, DC	12/5-9	Lake Placid, NY	6/28-7/1
1954	Philadelphia, PA	11/28-12/1	Seattle, WA	7/10-14
1955	Atlantic City, NJ	12/1-3	Milwaukee, WI	6/12-15
1956	Cincinnati, OH	6/4-6	Boston, MA	11/25-28
1957	Miami Beach, FL	6/2-5	Chicago, IL	11/14-16
1958	Minneapolis, MN	6/23-25	New Orleans, LA	12/1-3

ASHRAE

Meeting	Date	Place
1959 Annual	June 22–24, 1959	Lake Placid, NY
Semiannual	February 1–4, 1960	Dallas, TX
1960 Annual	June 13–15, 1960	Vancouver, BC
Semiannual	February 13–16, 1961	Chicago, IL
1961 Annual	June 26–28, 1961	Denver, CO
Semiannual	January 28–February 1, 1962	St. Louis, MO
1962 Annual	June 25–27, 1962	Miami, FL
Semiannual	February 11–14, 1963	New York, NY
1963 Annual	June 24–26, 1963	Milwaukee, WI
Semiannual	January 27–29, 1964	New Orleans, LA
1964 Annual	June 29–July 1, 1964	Cleveland, OH
Semiannual	January 25–28, 1965	Chicago, IL
1965 Annual	July 5–7, 1965	Portland, OR
Semiannual	January 24–27, 1966	Houston, TX
1966 Annual	June 27–29, 1966	Toronto, ON
Semiannual	January 30–February 2, 1967	Detroit, MI
1967 Annual	June 26–28, 1967	Minneapolis, MN
Semiannual	February 5–8, 1968	Columbus, OH

Meeting	Date	Place
1968 Annual	June 24–26, 1968	Lake Placid, NY
Semiannual	January 27–30, 1969	Chicago, IL
1969 Annual	June 30–July 2, 1969	Denver, CO
Semiannual	January 19–22, 1970	San Francisco, CA
1970 Annual	June 28–July 1, 1970	Kansas City, MO
Semiannual	January 24–28, 1971	Philadelphia, PA
1971 Annual	August 22–25, 1971	Washington, DC
Semiannual	January 23–27, 1972	New Orleans, LA
1972 Annual	June 25–29, 1972	Nassau, Bahamas
Semiannual	January 28–February 1, 1973	Chicago, IL
1973 Annual	June 24–28, 1973	Louisville, KY
Semiannual	February 3–7, 1974	Los Angeles, CA
1974 Annual	June 23–27, 1974	Montreal, PQ
Semiannual	January 26–30, 1975	Atlantic City, NJ
1975 Annual	June 22–26, 1975	Boston, MA
Semiannual	February 1–5, 1976	Dallas, TX
1976 Annual	June 27–July 1, 1976	Seattle, WA
Semiannual	February 13–17, 1977	Chicago, IL
1977 Annual	June 26–30, 1977	Halifax, NS
Semiannual	January 29–February 2, 1978	Atlanta, GA
1978 Annual	June 25–29, 1978	Albuquerque, NM
Semiannual	January 28–February 1, 1979	Philadelphia, PA
1979 Annual	June 24–28, 1979	Detroit, MI
Semiannual	February 3–7, 1980	Los Angeles, CA
1980 Annual	June 22–26, 1980	Denver, CO
Semiannual	January 25–29, 1981	Chicago, IL
1981 Annual	June 28–July 2, 1981	Cincinnati, OH
Semiannual	January 24–28, 1982	Houston, TX
1982 Annual	June 27–30, 1982	Toronto, ON
1983 Winter	January 23–26, 1983	Atlantic City, NJ
1983 Annual	June 26–29, 1983	Washington, DC
1984 Winter	January 29–February 1, 1984	Atlanta, GA
1984 Annual	June 17–20, 1984	Kansas City, MO
1985 Winter	January 27–30, 1985	Chicago, IL
1985 Annual	June 23–26, 1985	Honolulu, HI
1986 Winter	January 19–22, 1986	San Francisco, CA
1986 Annual	June 22–25, 1986	Portland, OR
1987 Winter	January 18–21, 1987	New York, NY
1987 Annual	June 27–July 1, 1987	Nashville, TN
1988 Winter	January 31–February 3, 1988	Dallas, TX
1988 Annual	June 25–29, 1988	Ottawa, ON
1989 Winter	January 28–February 1, 1989	Chicago, IL
1989 Annual	June 24–28, 1989	Vancouver, BC
1990 Winter	February 10–14, 1990	Atlanta, GA
1990 Annual	June 9–13, 1990	St. Louis, MO

Meeting	Date	Place
1991 Winter	January 19–23, 1991	New York, NY
1991 Annual	June 22–26, 1991	Indianapolis, IN
1992 Winter	January 25–29, 1992	Anaheim, CA
1992 Annual	June 27–July 1, 1992	Baltimore, MD
1993 Winter	January 23–27, 1993	Chicago, IL
1993 Annual	June 26–30, 1993	Denver, CO
1994 Winter	January 23–27, 1994	New Orleans, LA
1994 Annual	June 25–29, 1994	Orlando, FL
1995 Winter	January 28–February 1, 1995	Chicago, IL
1995 Annual	June 24–28, 1995	San Diego, CA
1996 Winter	February 16–21, 1996	Atlanta, GA
1996 Annual	June 22–26, 1996	San Antonio, TX
1997 Winter	February 24–29, 1997	Philadelphia, PA
1997 Annual	June 28–July 2, 1997	Boston, MA
1998 Winter	January 17–21, 1998	San Francisco, CA
1998 Annual	June 19–24, 1998	Toronto, ON
1999 Winter	January 23–27, 1999	Chicago, IL
1999 Annual	June 18–23, 1999	Seattle, WA
2000 Winter	February 5–9, 2000	Dallas, TX
2000 Annual	June 24–28, 2000	Minneapolis, MN
2001 Winter	January 27–31, 2001	Atlanta, GA
2001 Annual	June 23–27, 2001	Cincinnati, OH
2002 Winter	January 12–16, 2002	Atlantic City, NJ
2002 Annual	June 22–26, 2002	Honolulu, HI
2003 Winter	January 25–29, 2003	Chicago, IL
2003 Annual	June 28–July 2, 2003	Kansas City, MO
2004 Winter	January 24–28, 2004	Anaheim, CA
2004 Annual	June 26–30, 2004	Nashville, TN
2005 Winter	February 5–9, 2005	Orlando, FL
2005 Annual	June 25–29, 2005	Denver, CO
2006 Winter	January 21–25, 2006	Chicago, IL
2006 Annual	June 24–28, 2006	Québec City, QC
2007 Winter	January 27–31, 2007	Dallas, TX
2007 Annual	June 23–27, 2007	Long Beach, CA
2008 Winter	January 19–23, 2008	New York, NY
2008 Annual	June 21–25, 2008	Salt Lake City, UT
2009 Winter	January 24–28, 2009	Chicago, IL
2009 Annual	June 20–24, 2009	Louisville, KY
2010 Winter	January 23–27, 2010	Orlando, FL
2010 Annual	June 26–30, 2010	Albuquerque, NM
2011 Winter	January 29–February 2, 2011	Las Vegas, NV
2011 Annual	June 25–29, 2011	Montreal, QC
2012 Winter	January 21–25, 2012	Chicago, IL
2012 Annual	June 23–27, 2012	San Antonio, TX

Meeting	Date	Place
2013 Winter	January 26–30, 2013	Dallas, TX
2013 Annual	June 22–26, 2013	Denver, CO
2014 Winter	January 18–22, 2014	New York, NY
2014 Annual	June 28–July 2, 2014	Seattle, WA
2015 Winter	January 24–28, 2015	Chicago, IL
2015 Annual	June 27–July 1, 2015	Atlanta, GA
2016 Winter	January 23–27, 2016	Orlando, FL
2016 Annual	June 25–39, 2016	St. Louis, MO
2017 Winter	January 28–February 1, 2017	Las Vegas, NV
2017 Annual	June 24–28, 2017	Long Beach, CA
2018 Winter	January 20–24, 2018	Chicago, IL
2018 Annual	June 23–27, 2018	Houston, TX
2019 Winter	January 12–16, 2019	Atlanta, GA
2019 Annual	June 22–26, 2019	Kansas City, MO

Appendix I

ASHRAE Membership Levels

Year Ending	Members ASHVE or ASHAE	Members ASRE	Aggregate Membership	Net Change over Previous Year	Percent Change over Previous Year
1894	75	....	75		
1895	88	—	88	+13	+17.3%
1896	109	—	109	+21	+23.9%
1897	129	—	129	+20	+18.3%
1898	153	—	153	+24	+18.6%
1899	121	—	121	–32	–20.9%
1900	126	—	126	+5	+4.1%
1901	137	—	137	+11	+8.7%
1902	158	—	158	+21	+15.3%
1903	198	—	198	+40	+25.3%
1904	211	—	211	+13	+6.6%
1905	231	118	349	+138	+65.4%
1906	261	144	405	+56	+16.0%
1907	301	186	487	+82	+20.2%
1908	335	185	520	+33	+6.8%
1909	357	256	613	+93	+17.9%
1910	377	257	634	+21	+3.4%
1911	405	256	661	+27	+4.3%
1912	437	268	705	+44	+6.7%
1913	455	274	729	+24	+3.4%
1914	485	280	765	+36	+4.9%
1915	571	283	854	+89	+11.6%
1916	683	337	1020	+166	+19.4%
1917	784	372	1156	+136	+13.3%
1918	839	378	1217	+61	+5.3%
1919	993	437	1430	+213	+17.5%
1920	1192	452	1644	+214	+15.0%
1921	1388	596	1984	+340	+20.7%
1922	1574	645	2219	+235	+11.8%
1923	1667	721	2388	+169	+7.6%
1924	1845	747	2592	+204	+8.5%
1925	1791	776	2567	–25	–1.0%
1926	1927	815	2742	+175	+6.8%
1927	1918	658	2576	–166	–6.1%
1928	1988	947	2935	+359	+13.9%

Year Ending	Members ASHVE or ASHAE	Members ASRE	Aggregate Membership	Net Change over Previous Year	Percent Change over Previous Year
1929	1961	970	2931	–4	–0.1%
1930	2234	990	3224	+293	+10.0%
1931	2256	1025	3281	+57	+1.8%
1932	2250	1046	3296	+15	+0.5%
1933	2069	1076	3145	–151	–4.6%
1934	1889	1105	2994	–151	–4.8%
1935	1850	918	2768	–226	–7.5%
1936	2044	1027	3071	+303	+10.9%
1937	2372	1032	3404	+333	+10.8%
1938	2712	1051	3763	+359	+10.5%
1939	3067	1110	4177	+414	+11.0%
1940	3147	1453	4600	+423	+10.1%
1941	3032	1724	4756	+156	+3.4%
1942	3132	1812	4944	+188	+3.9%
1943	3006	2172	5178	+234	+4.7%
1944	3344	3025	6369	+1191	+23.0%
1945	3929	3747	7676	+1307	+20.5%
1946	4506	4472	8978	+1302	+17.0%
1947	5284	5143	10427	+1449	+16.1%
1948	6063	5585	11648	+1221	+11.7%
1949	7098	5621	12719	+1071	+9.2%
1950	7666	5617	13283	+564	+4.4%
1951	7949	5592	13541	+258	+1.9%
1952	8554	5717	14271	+730	+5.4%
1953	8973	6015	14988	+717	+5.0%
1954	9385	6157	15542	+554	+3.7%
1955	9900	6289	16189	+647	+4.2%
1956	10476	6691	17167	+978	+6.0%
1957	11021	7040	18061	+894	+5.2%
1958	11713	7145	18858	+807	+4.5%
1959	—	—	17857	–1001	–5.3%
1960	—	—	17430	–427	–2.4%
1961	—	—	18566	+1136	+6.5%
1962	—	—	16232	–2334	–12.6%
1963	—	—	17115	+883	+5.4%
1964	—	—	17379	+264	+1.5%
1965	—	—	17742	+363	+2.1%
1966	—	—	18674	+932	+5.3%
1967	—	—	19793	+1119	+6.0%
1968	—	—	22240	+2447	+12.4%
1969	—	—	24186	+1946	+8.8%
1970	—	—	25730	+1544	+6.4%
1971	—	—	26805	+1075	+4.2%
1972	—	—	27328	+523	+2.0%
1973	—	—	28444	+1116	+4.1%
1974	—	—	29513	+1069	+1.8%
1975	—	—	29389	–124	–0.1%
1976	—	—	30863	+1474	+5.0%
1977	—	—	32658	+1795	+5.8%
1978	—	—	35108	+2450	+7.5%
1979	—	—	36915	+1807	+5.1%

Year Ending	Members ASHVE or ASHAE	Members ASRE	Aggregate Membership	Net Change over Previous Year	Percent Change over Previous Year
1980	—	—	39131	+2216	+6.0%
1981	—	—	41599	+2468	+6.3%
1982	—	—	44074	+2475	+5.9%
1983	—	—	45804	+1730	+3.9%
1984	—	—	45959	+155	+0.3%
1985	—	—	46730	+771	+1.7%
1986	—	—	48121	+1391	+3.0%
1987	—	—	48799	+678	+1.4%
1988	—	—	47533	–1266	–2.6%
1989	—	—	46384	–1149	–2.4%
1990	—	—	46815	+431	+0.9%
1991	—	—	46920	+105	+0.2%
1992	—	—	46880	–40	–0.1%
1993	—	—	46790	–90	–0.2%
1994	—	—	47032	+242	+0.5%
1995	—	—	53,244	+6192	+13.1%
1996	—	—	54,100	+876	+1.6%
1997	—	—	53,719	–381	–0.7%
1998	—	—	54,867	+1148	+2.0%
1999	—	—	56,246	+1329	+2.4%
2000	—	—	57,364	+1118	+2.0%
2001	—	—	56,362	–1002	–1.7%
2002	—	—	57,769	+1407	+2.5%
2003	—	—	55,857	–1912	–3.3%
2004	—	—	54,348	–1509	–2.7%
2005	—	—	53,194	–1154	–2.1%
2006	—	—	53,979	+785	+0.2%
2007	—	—	49,923	–4056	–7.5%
2008	—	—	51,695	+1772	+3.5%
2009	—	—	52,141	+446	+0.9%
2010	—	—	52,219	+78	+0.1%
2011	—	—	52,900	+681	+1.3%
2012	—	—	53,696	+796	+1.5%
2013	—	—	53,768	+22	+0.1%
2014	—	—	53,145	–623	–1.2%
2015	—	—	54,044	+899	+1.7%
2016	—	—	56,105	+2061	+3.8%
2017	—	—	56,573	+468	+0.8%
2018	—	—	56,516	–57	–0.1%
2019	—	—	56,854	+338	+0.6%

Appendix J

The Societies' Presidents

1894

ASHVE

EDWARD P. BATES

1844–1919

SYRACUSE, NY

"I now charge you, as you love the cause in which you have so recently launched your bark, to look well to your applications for membership, as the growth and perpetuity of this society rests upon this fully as much as on any other proposition." (p. 1, *H&V*, Feb. 1, 1895)

1895

ASHVE

STEWART A. JELLETT

1862–1935

PHILADELPHIA, PA

"It is always interesting to trace the growth of a spontaneous movement which leads to the birth of an organization having for its object the moral, intellectual, or physical uplifting of humanity. As the proper heating and ventilation of our homes, hospitals, schools and other occupied buildings tend to secure better health and greater comfort for their occupants, we can certainly include in the list of such organizations The American Society of Heating and Ventilating Engineers." (p. 35, *ASHVE Trans.*, 1904)

1896

ASHVE

ROLLA C. CARPENTER

1852–1919

ITHACA, NY

"Our engineering society...has doubtless prospered and can certainly be recognized as one of the great engineering societies of this country. It has established a strong foundation for a broad and noble society and is now in position to commence active work for the benefit of the science and art of heating and ventilation, and it should have and doubtless will have the confidence and support of every desirable person engaged in this work in this country." (p. 68, *ASHVE Trans.*, 1897)

1897

ASHVE

WILLIAM M. MACKAY

1855–1919

NEW YORK, NY

"The society has grown steadily...and while the qualifications for membership are placed at a high standard,...the number of applications received and acted upon each year indicates the standing of the society, the necessity for a society of heating and ventilating engineers, and the possibility of uniting and elevating the profession and also accomplishing great and lasting good for the public at large by a united effort to secure legislation, compelling the ventilation of public buildings to at least a healthful standard." (p. 256, *ASHVE Trans.*, 1897)

1898

ASHVE

WILTSIE F. WOLFE

1854–1913

PHILADELPHIA, PA

"It rests largely with this society whether we shall insist upon installing only the best [ventilating equipment], rather than the mere imitation, such as would bring discredit upon us eventually, and as engineers practically eliminate us from the profession, and whether we shall strenuously endeavor to inspire the same views and the same methods in others." (p. 8, *ASHVE Trans.*, 1899)

1899

ASHVE

HENRY ADAMS

1858–1929

BALTIMORE, MD

"While the formation of standards, and especially of tests, in connection with our branch of engineering is exceedingly difficult, I believe that the adoption of rules and regulations governing tests of heating and ventilating apparatus, and the fixing of standards will advance the interests of our society materially..." (p. 8, *ASHVE Trans.*, 1900)

1900

ASHVE

DAVID M. QUAY

1885–1937

NEW YORK, NY

"What [the society] needs now is an earnest effort...to secure new members of the right kind; namely, those heating and ventilation engineers who are willing to contribute some of their knowledge of engineering facts, or their opinions on engineering theories, to our transactions..." (p. 33, *ASHVE Trans.*, 1901)

1901

ASHVE

JOHN H. KINEALY

1864–1928

ST. LOUIS, MO

"We must work in the science as well as the art of heating and ventilating. We must experiment and determine what results should be obtained in well-heated and ventilated buildings, and then we must continue our work to determine how best to attain those results." (p. 14, *ASHVE Trans.*, 1902)

1902

ASHVE

ALFRED E. KENRICK

1851–1917

BROOKLINE, MA

"...but the most auspicious element of the time is the fact that we are in the midst of great and wonderful achievements in science and engineering, while the opportunities opening before us are simply marvelous in their possibilities." (p. 8, *ASHVE Trans.*, 1903)

1903

ASHVE

HARRIE D. CRANE

1854–1922

CINCINNATI, OH

"Truly 'Time's noblest offering is her last,' and we are most happy to-day in the possession...of an association to which it is an honor to belong, not only because it is recognized throughout the heating and ventilating engineering world as the originator of nearly all of the available literature printed in the English language on this subject, but because it enrolls in its membership almost all of the brightest minds in the world working on this line." (p. 8, *ASHVE Trans.*, 1904)

1904
ASHVE

ANDREW HARVEY
1843–1912
DETROIT, MI

"I must congratulate the members on having accomplished one of the most important acts this past year that has ever been obtained by this Society since its organization. That is the adoption by the New York Legislature of a State law last April for the proper construction and ventilation for school buildings, which is...surely a very creditable accomplishment and adds much to the reputation of the Society." (p. 11, *ASHVE Trans.*, 1905)

1905
ASRE

JOHN E. STARR
1861–1931
NEW YORK, NY

"It has fallen to my lot to have the honor of making the first of doubtless a continuous series of annual addresses before an organization which I firmly believe is destined to be a power and an honorable and important influence in a field of applied science that is widening beyond bounds that were only dreamed of two decades ago." (p. 37, *ASRE Trans.*, 1905)

1905
ASHVE

WILLIAM KENT
1851–1918
SYRACUSE, NY

"Why are such tests and researches not made? The answer is that all our heating and ventilating engineers are too busy to make them. We have no national laboratory of research...and the imperfectly equipped laboratories in our technical colleges are scarcely as yet prepared to undertake such researches." (p. 14, *ASHVE Trans.*, 1906)

1906
ASRE

W. EVERETT PARSONS
1860?–1940
NEW YORK, NY

"Our Society, just celebrating its second anniversary has already attracted widespread attention among those who are interested in refrigeration and ice making. We started as a national society—now we are international." (p. 43, *ASRE Trans.*, 1906)

1906
ASHVE

JOHN GORMLY
1850?–1929
PHILADELPHIA, PA

"If we hold our faces, in the future, to the commercial grindstone as we have done in the past, we will never attain that scientific perfection in heating and ventilation which will abolish...the wasted energy of our present cumbrous and expensive systems. The art of heating is in its infancy." (p. 11, *ASHVE Trans.*, 1907)

1907
ASRE

DAVID S. JACOBUS
1862–1955
NEW YORK, NY

"In none of the sciences is there greater need of a thorough understanding of the theories and underlying principles than in refrigerating engineering...there is no profession in which a little theory, not well understood, may lead to more disastrous results than in refrigerating engineering." (p. 42, *ASRE Trans.*, 1907)

1907

ASHVE

Charles B. J. Snyder

1860–1945

New York, NY

"I most heartily congratulate the members upon the work already accomplished and trust that in the meeting now before us there will be a united effort to broaden and extend the scope and influence of the Society by observation, experiment and research..." (p. 14, *ASHVE Trans.*, 1908)

1908

ASRE

Edgar Penney

1845–1913

Newburgh, NY

"A refrigerating engineer should be competent in all the branches of his art. The upward trend of the Society should be to help its members to become representative refrigerating engineers in its broadest sense..." (p. 57, *ASRE Trans.*, 1908)

1908

ASHVE

James Mackay

1853–1911

Chicago, IL

"The Society is to be commended for the position it has taken upon the subject of proper and necessary ventilation, and for what it has done toward promoting the same, through legislative enactment and otherwise." (p. 11, *ASHVE Trans.*, 1909)

1909

ASRE

Louis Block

1850–1926

New York, NY

"We [refrigerating industries] are no longer in our infancy. We have now grown to vigorous manhood and have arrived at a more conservative age...anyone who wants to keep up with the refrigerating industries must travel fast." (p. 31, *ASRE Trans.*, 1909)

1909

ASHVE

William G. Snow

1866–1930

Boston, MA

"We should keep clearly in mind the objects set forth in our charter. With these objects in view, backed by enthusiasm on the part of members, a large field of useful effort spreads out before us and our achievements will benefit not only our members but the public at large." (p. 12, *ASHVE Trans.*, 1910)

1910

ASRE

Roderick H. Tait

1865–1939

St. Louis, MO

"It is I who have to express thanks for the honor you have done me in making me your President for the past year and for the large attendance at our meeting. We have had a good meeting full of interest; that is what brings members together." (p. 32–33, *ASRE Trans.*, 1910)

1910

ASHVE

JOHN D. HOFFMAN
1868–1938
LAFAYETTE, IN

This year, more than ever before the science of the subject [heating and ventilating] is regarded with greater respect; especially is this true concerning the ventilation of buildings." (p. 12, *ASHVE Trans.*, 1911)

1911

ASRE

EDWARD N. FRIEDMANN
1864?–1939
NEW YORK, NY

"The field of refrigerating engineering is widening from day to day and new problems are coming up more frequently than ever; and it is not only desirable, but absolutely necessary, that all members of the engineering fraternity work in hearty co-operation." (p. 20, *ASRE Trans.*, 1911)

1911

ASHVE

REGINALD PELHAM BOLTON
1856–1942
NEW YORK, NY

"The subject of fuel is of fundamental importance to the heating engineer, and the economic utilization of available materials constitutes a most important part of the service of our profession, not only to our own clients, but to the community." (p. 57, *ASHVE Trans.*, 1912)

1912

ASRE

THOMAS SHIPLEY
1861–1930
YORK, PA

"My position in the battle we are fighting is in the manufacturers' corps of the army, and that corps is always on the firing line, where action and initiative are necessary to keep one from being swept off his feet and buried among the failures." (p. 41, *ASRE Trans.*, 1912)

1912

ASHVE

JOHN R. ALLEN
1869–1920
ANN ARBOR, MI

"It would be perfectly proper for our Society to endeavor to interest persons or institutions of large means in establishing an experimental laboratory in which matters pertaining to heating and ventilation and allied subjects could be investigated." (p. 62, *ASHVE Trans.*, 1913)

1913

ASRE

PETER NEFF
1869–1930
CANTON, OH

"Refrigerating engineering has always suffered from a lack of basic standards of positive value. The Society has taken the lead in having these standards determined... We are now standing on the threshold of what refrigeration can do for the comfort and happiness of humanity..." (p.33, 35, *ASRE Trans.*, 1913)

1913

ASHVE

John F. Hale
1870–1942
Chicago, IL

"There has come to my mind the advisability of a committee for a symposium...in which the manufacturer, the contractor, the architect and the engineer each have an opportunity to set forth their position so as to bring about a better understanding of the position of each..." (p.10, *ASHVE Trans.*, 1914)

1914

ASRE

Henry Torrance
1870–1967
New York, NY

"...a purchaser can obtain considerably more refrigeration with less first cost and less upkeep and running expense...This decrease in cost...has largely been brought about by the influence of this Society..." (p.44, Jan. 1915, *ASRE Journal)*

1914

ASHVE

Samuel R. Lewis
1878–1964
Chicago, IL

"The responsibility of designing heating and ventilating equipments for buildings in this country is really in the hands of comparatively very few men. When the designing engineer has more to do with the operation of the plants he designs, there will be an improvement in design. I speak from experience..." (p. 37, *ASHVE Trans.*, 1915)

1915

ASRE

Louis K. Doelling
1871–1935
New Rochelle, NY

"The finances are in good condition, and the value and circulation of The Journal are increasing, and it is being recognized as one of the leading scientific publications in the art of refrigeration." (p. 75–76, Jan 1916, *ASRE Journal)*

1915

ASHVE

Dwight D. Kimball
1884–1958
New York, NY

"We are fast approaching...the point toward which we have been striving...when we shall be able to place our initiation fees in a separate fund for the purposes of research and committee work. Such a fund would be of value to the entire membership of the Society." (p. 10, *ASHVE Trans.*, 1916)

1916

ASRE

Theodore O. Vilter
1857–1919
Milwaukee, WI

"If we haven't co-operation our individual efforts are of little avail, but we certainly want a live organization, and with your co-operation we will make it so." (p. 72, Jan. 1916, *ASRE Journal)*

1916

ASHVE

HARRY M. HART

1878–1963

CHICAGO, IL

"I wish to make a few remarks concerning two points that we, as a Society, should constantly keep in mind, namely: Co-operation and Standardization." (p. 14, *ASHVE Trans.*, 1917)

1917

ASRE

NICOLAI H. HILLER

1868–1963

CARBONDALE, PA

"The creation of branch associations in four cities...will...add greatly to the interest in our Society and stimulate its growth... The interest that the branch meetings will arouse in such members may lead them into channels dealing with refrigeration... thus increasing our size and scope." (p. 427, Jan. 1918, *ASRE Journal*)

1917

ASHVE

J. IRVINE LYLE

1874–1942

PLAINFIELD, NJ

"[The government believed] that all business organizations, and especially all professional and technical societies should continue their work and...do everything possible to increase the industrial efficiency of the country as a whole...the members...entered into the spirit with the deepest and most sincere enthusiasm..." (p. 319, *ASHVE Trans.*, 1917)

1918

ASRE

EZRA FRICK

1856–1942

WAYNESBORO, PA

"The greatest and most horrible of all wars is practically ended, and in assisting in the favorable termination the refrigerating engineer, the refrigerating and allied industries are entitled to a share of credit...our industry has been engaged principally in taking care of Government business..." (p. 304, Jan. 1919, *ASRE Journal*)

1918

ASHVE

FRED R. STILL

1867–1940

DETROIT, MI

"Shortly after our country entered into the war, the services of this Society were offered to the various branches of the government in any capacity in which it could serve. It was not long before we were called upon to aid in solving many difficult problems..." (p. 146, April 1919, *ASHVE Journal*)

1919

ASRE

GEORGE E. WELLS

1875–1942

ST. LOUIS, MO

"...the refrigerating engineer of the future will carry on the work to a point that we cannot conceive...[we] have lived through an age of wonderful mechanical achievement. We can remember the appearance of the electric light, the electric motor, the automobile, the wireless and air craft, also the development of the modern ice plant and the great cold storage industry." (p. 289, Jan. 1920, *ASRE Journal*)

1919

ASHVE

WALTER S. TIMMIS

?–1928

NEW YORK, NY

"As a Society we should be interested in legislation for protection of health and comfort; for the regulation and establishment of standards; for the national support of a general engineering bureau of research...; for the recognition of standards...; for the placing of engineers in public positions..." (p. 198, March 1920, *ASHVE Journal*)

1920

ASRE

F. E. MATTHEWS

1877–1942

LEONIA, NJ

"In the refrigerating industry, [there is the] continuance of the general movement from steam to electric power for refrigerating and ice-making machines; a continuation...from natural to manufactured ice, and...from distilled water to agitated raw water ice...and most important of all, the household refrigerating machine." (p. 325, Jan. 1921, *ASRE Journal*)

1920

ASHVE

E. VERNON HILL

1876–1950

CHICAGO, IL

"I think it is well to call your attention...to the work of the Research Laboratory particularly, that you stop and think over the importance of [it]. It is not a side issue of this Society any more. It is, as I view it, the very heart of our organization." (p. 198, March 1920, *ASHVE Journal*)

1921

ASRE

FRED OPHULS

1876–1966

NEW YORK

"An accurate knowledge of the properties of the refrigerants used is not of greater importance in the design of refrigeration systems than is an accurate knowledge of the performance of the various machinery and apparatus which forms a part of it." (p. 349, Jan. 1922, *ASRE Journal*)

1921

ASHVE

CHAMPLAIN L. RILEY

1877–1937

NEW YORK, NY

"The Guide will prove a great help in financing the Society's many activities. The project as a whole is of such merit as to command the enthusiastic interest of every member of the Society." (p. 1, Nov. 1921, *ASHVE Journal*)

1922

ASRE

HARRY SLOAN

1869–1961

MILWAUKEE, WI

"We must not pass without calling attention to the added interest and activity now taking place in research work. It has been said that in research we have the element of romance of engineering. We are continually working in the light of past and present knowledge..." (p. 24, July 1922, *RE*)

1922

ASHVE

JAY R. MCCOLL
1867–1936
DETROIT, MI

"Aside from the importance of the Research Laboratory which has already assumed a position of great magnitude...we have another piece of work...the construction of a new Code of Heating and Ventilating." (p. 199, Mar. 1923, *ASHVE Journal*)

1923

ASRE

WILLIAM S. SHIPLEY
1879–1951
BROOKLYN, NY

"If we could imagine an upheaval that destroyed every trace of equipment we now have, the body of experts we have trained in the past twenty years would be able to reproduce it and have the entire industry going along again about as usual in a comparatively short time." (p. 350, May 1923, *RE*)

1923

ASHVE

H. PAUL GANT
1884–1973
PHILADELPHIA, PA

"In our profession most of us are so intent on the details of engineering that our analytical minds lose sight of the fact that every time we definitely determine a new coefficient of heat transfer or a critical velocity in a pipe, we have...shown future generations how to conserve a pound of coal or a pound of steel and this conservation...is cumulative." (p. 186, Feb. 1924, *ASHVE Journal*)

1924

ASRE

GEORGE A. HORNE
1877–1959
NEW YORK, NY

"The engineer by training and by occupation is peculiarly adapted to accept this social challenge...It is his exalted privilege to interpret the findings of science and translate them into practical ways of usefulness for the benefit of mankind." (p. 200, Dec. 1924, *RE*)

1924

ASHVE

HOMER ADDAMS
1873–1953
NEW YORK, NY

"Our representative and substantial membership of able and skilled engineers is now undoubtedly on a plane that compares with the standards set by any of the great engineering societies..." (p. 178, March 1925, *ASHVE Journal*)

1925

ASRE

VAN. R. H. GREENE
1883–1964
NEW YORK, NY

"Less than twenty years ago refrigeration employed a rule of thumb method in calculating requirements. Today it has developed into a mathematical exactness." (p. 418, June 1925, *RE*)

1925

ASHVE

SAMUEL E. DIBBLE

1882–1970

PITTSBURGH, PA

"The Research Laboratory of the Society is in better shape now than it ever has been in its history...Interests other than those in the heating and ventilating field are beginning to look with expectancy toward our Laboratory, which shows that we must not fail to produce fundamental data..." (p. 195, March 1926, *ASHVE Journal*)

1926

ASRE

L. HOWARD JENKS

1862–1939

PITTSBURGH, PA

"A recent development in the refrigerating field has been the household machine. This...is not new, and it is interesting to note that one of the papers read at the First Annual Meeting...twenty-one years ago, was entitled 'Requirements of Small Refrigerating Plants of Less Than One Ton Capacity.'" (p. 414, June 1926, *RE*)

1926

ASHVE

WILLIAM H. DRISCOLL

1879–1950

SYRACUSE, NY

"Above and beyond all of the things that our Society...has ever done has been the establishment of the Research Laboratory...From a scientific standpoint, the work done at the laboratory has been of the highest order and...its results have been of immeasurable value." (p. 149, March 1927, *ASHVE Journal*)

1927

ASRE

WILLIS H. CARRIER

1876–1950

NEWARK, NJ

"Thus we see that the economic, industrial, and engineering problems of the Heat Engineer and the Refrigerating Engineer are becoming more... interlocked...They are both engaged in the pursuit of the elusive thermal unit. Their engineering processes and methods of analysis are identical. Some day...they will be joined in a common Society, the Society of Thermal Engineers." (p. 149, March 1927, *ASHVE Journal*)

1927

ASHVE

F. PAUL ANDERSON

1867–1934

LEXINGTON, KY

"Isn't it...a fitting thing for this Society, although we may be interested...in one of the narrower fields of human interest, to be the sponsor for [Benjamin Franklin] who represents the ideals that are at the very basis of this government?" (p. 210, March 1928, *ASHVE Journal*)

1928

ASRE

GEORGE B. BRIGHT

?–1956

DETROIT, MI

"It is safe to predict that the greatest economies of the future use of power lie in the combined heating and refrigerating principles...Our Society has an important duty to perform in the future development of refrigeration—the most essential of the world's necessities." (p. 19, Jan. 1929, *RE*)

1928

ASHVE

DR. ARTHUR CUTTS WILLARD

1878–1960

URBANA, IL

"Ever since its establishment, the Research Laboratory has had the loyal and untiring support and cooperation of the members of the Society. From their inception, the Research activities of the Society have included the cooperation...of many universities and scientific institutions as well as government agencies." (p. 2, 3, *ASHVE Trans.*, 1947)

1929

ASRE

ARTHUR J. WOOD

1874–1931

STATE COLLEGE, PA

"Progress in mechanical refrigeration was retarded until we had available tables on the properties of refrigerants. The ammonia tables developed [earlier] have been of immeasurable value in their time...but now the engineer demands certainty and he turns with a sense of security to the tables of the properties of ammonia, bearing the stamp of the Bureau of Standards and sponsored by this Society." (p. vi, Jan. 1930, *RE*)

1929

ASHVE

THORNTON LEWIS

1887–1945

NEWARK, NJ

"There are hundreds of splendid engineers who are not in our ranks and who ought to be with us...to advance the aims for which the Society was organized. Our Society can only be maintained in a healthy condition by a constant infusion of new blood, of good quality, and this infusion must come from the younger men in the profession." (p. 336, Aug. 1929, *ASHVE Journal*)

1930

ASRE

HARRY D. EDWARDS

1886–1970

NEW YORK, NY

"The development of domestic mechanical units has brought about a more detailed knowledge of not only the physical and chemical, but the other properties of refrigerants when used in the presence of oils, moisture and in different metals." (p. 73, March 1930, *RE*)

1930

ASHVE

LOUIS A. HARDING

1876–1953

BUFFALO, NY

"The day is apparently not far distant when all structures designed to house human beings will be equipped with automatically controlled heating, ventilating and air conditioning systems, which will produce a comfortable and healthful atmosphere the year around..." (p. 439, May 1930, *ASHVE Journal*)

1931

ASRE

ALVIN H. BAER

1879?–1954

CARBONDALE, PA

"We are all familiar with the general purpose of our organization—the advancement of all matters pertaining to refrigerating engineering—but I doubt if many members stop to think of the very important place the Society holds in its field or of the important part they can play in its further advancement." (p. 114, Feb. 1931, *RE)*

1931

ASHVE

Willis H. Carrier

1876–1950

Newark, NJ

"An effort has been made to eliminate the rule of thumb craftsmen who by virtue of years of experience and cut-and-try methods, can arrive at tolerable results with uncertain and unforeseen materials and methods, and to replace him with standardized methods and materials which give, in effect, their own control." (p. 335, April 1931, *ASHVE Journal)*

1932

ASRE

Glenn Muffly

1884–1972

Detroit, MI

"Kitchen refrigerators will not be combined with air conditioning systems, but the latter may be combined with heating systems for year-round comfort control of temperature, humidity and air quality." (p. 326, June 1933, *RE)*

1932

ASHVE

Frank B. Rowley

1882–1965

Minneapolis, MN

"Three days of interesting meetings are in prospect. The benefits to be derived from attending are obvious and the cost is in keeping with present day conditions...The rate of dues for 1933 has been set... the work that can be carried on by the Society for the benefit of members is proportionate to the amount of money received." (p. 326, June 1933, *RE)*

1933

ASRE

Alfred W. Oakley

1890–1967

New York, NY

"No plant is built, no building rises, but could be improved upon. We look back on the work of a few years ago to see momentous changes. The compressors of years ago seem cumbersome and slow... But to look ahead—do we stop to think our stuff will one day look antiquated too?" (p. 187, Oct. 1935, *RE)*

1933

ASHVE

William T. Jones

1883–1947

Boston, MA

"Let us, therefore, always keep before us the fine ideals of this Society; let us all work to the common end of making this industry a better industry because of our efforts; let us prove ourselves worthy of the great age in which we live, and unite in this Society to strive for constantly higher standards and higher ideals." (p. 3, *ASHVE Transactions,* 1934)

1934

ASRE

Alexander R. Stevenson, Jr.

1892–1946

Schenectady, NY

"[The] matter of cooperation...is within the whole industry. The American Society of Refrigerating Engineers has more or less led in a cooperative effort...in getting out their safety code...The engineering societies are of great benefit in promoting proper cooperation..." (p. 258, April 1931, *RE*)

1934

ASHVE

CHARLES V. HAYNES

1868–1962

WATERBURY, CT

"The thermostatic trap...must be made from a metal that will not break, stretch or lose its tension, in operation, so that over a period of time the trap will function perfectly...The trap situation is one that the Society should take up and check...the Society should set a standard which the manufacturer should equal or better if possible." (p. 107, *ASHVE Trans.*, 1923)

1935

ASRE

HARRY HARRISON

1885–1985

PHILADELPHIA, PA

"There is hardly a trade or craft in the technical or business field which refrigerating engineering does not utilize; there is hardly a human, commercial, or industrial activity which it does not in some way affect. Therefore refrigerating engineering offers wide scope for achievement." (p. 222, Oct. 1935, *RE*)

1935

ASHVE

JOHN HOWATT

1880–1949

CHICAGO, IL

"The most important asset of this Society is its membership and while the membership is not large when compared with some national organizations, because of the character and interest of the members, it has an effectiveness far beyond that which is accounted for by numbers only." (p. 2, *ASHVE Trans.*, 1936)

1936

ASRE

LOUIS S. MORSE

1873?–1956

YORK, PA

"The principal means for [promoting the arts and sciences connected with refrigerating engineering] are the meetings for the presentation and discussion of technical papers, and the dissemination of engineering knowledge and data through publications." (p. 378, June 1936, *RE*)

1936

ASHVE

GUSTUS L. LARSON

1881–1953

MADISON, WI

"The research division of our organization has passed through some trying experiences in recent years, but...activities are being resumed that had to be dropped through lack of funds...we are once more getting into position where we can pay our way in connection with co-operative research..." (p. 2–3, *ASHVE Trans.*, 1937)

1937

ASRE

HARRY M. WILLIAMS

?–1958

DAYTON, OH

"However, we believe that it is the duty of our members to present papers...In this way up-to-date developments can be made public and others...can have the advantage of such information. Very few outstanding developments or discoveries have ever been made by one person...these presentations have great value. We are all interested in the advancement of our industry." (p. 5, July 1936, *RE*)

1937

ASHVE

DAVIS STUART BOYDEN

1872–1945

BOSTON, MA

"Rapid growth has taken place in the industry during the past year and particularly [in] that branch referred to as air conditioning. Business conditions throughout the country during the last year were better than for several years, which has contributed to the success of the Society." (p. 1–2, *ASHVE Trans.*, 1938)

1938

ASRE

CROSBY FIELD

1889–1972

BROOKLYN, NY

"In planning for the future...we must take heed of the past, and predicate our plans thereon. We have nothing to be ashamed of in our history of the past twenty years. Refrigeration has maintained its steady pace of technological advance, and that pace has equalled the pace of technological advance in other...industries." (p. 7, Jan. 1939, *RE*)

1938

ASHVE

E. HOLT GURNEY

1882–1954

TORONTO, CANADA

"I have difficulty in finding words to express my great appreciation of the complete and enthusiastic cooperation I have had from everybody throughout my year, and I also wish to pay tribute to the men and women in the employ of the Society for both their ability and their remarkable loyalty." (p. 3, *ASHVE Trans.*, 1939)

1939

ASRE

GARDNER POOLE

1877–1940

NEW YORK, NY

"The development of industrial refrigeration in the United States has expanded to a point far beyond the conception of the early pioneers, and the refrigerating machine may well rank with the steam engine, the internal combustion engine, and with electricity, as among the principal agencies in the development of human progress and prosperity." (p. 69, Feb. 1935, *RE*)

1939

ASHVE

JAMES F. MCINTIRE

1882–1951

DETROIT, MI

"Modem air conditioning commenced in the Victorian era and was first referred to by that name in a book by Stuart Cramer. The art reached a high stage of development for industrial uses, but did not attract public attention until the early 1920's when the new application to comfort was announced. At the present time the importance of air conditioning to health is engaging much attention and a substantial part of the Research activities sponsored by the...Society." (News Release, 1940)

1940

ASRE

GEORGE E. HULSE

1877–1965

NEW HAVEN, CT

"A successful refrigeration system for freight cars must...have... ample cooling capacity...a supply of energy... a minimum of moving parts...[a] design... to withstand the shocks which it will receive in service." (p. 41, Feb. 1929, *RE*)

1940

ASHVE

FREDERICK E. GIESECKE

1869–1953

NEW BRAUNFELS, TX

"...the greatest source of error in making an estimate of the heat requirements of a building occurs in allowances made for air infiltration. A calculation shows that if the air change method, based upon Table 3, Chapter 6, of The 1935 Guide, were followed, even allowing only one air change per hour, the heat requirement estimate would be considerably larger than indicated [in this study]." (p. 344, June 1936, *ASHVE Journal*)

1941

ASRE

L. LOGAN LEWIS

1887–1965

SYRACUSE, NY

"Just one thing – the hearty, intelligent and unselfish cooperation of national and sections officers, of committee chairmen and members, of individual members and of the staff at headquarters – has made [a successful Society] possible." (p. 395, Dec. 1941, *RE*)

1941

ASHVE

WALTER L. FLEISHER, SR.

1888–1959

NEW YORK, NY

"During the October Council meeting in Washington, I tried to summarize the contribution of the Society to national defense, and it was a revelation to find how...the research of the Society has contributed considerably to the development of the implements of war...There is...not a single phase of production for defense in which the work of the Society is not playing a prominent part." (p. 4, *ASHVE Trans.*, 1942)

1942

ASRE

WILLIAM R. HAINSWORTH

1896–1971

NEW YORK, NY

"Now let us take a quick look at events in 1942. A Government Relations Committee was appointed. Standards were promoted and approved. Our technical papers and publications assumed an even greater importance in helping dispel the fog...Services of the Society were offered to various branches of the Government." (p. 20, Jan. 1943, *RE*)

1942

ASHVE

EVERETT O. EASTWOOD

1876–1960

SEATTLE, WA

"Practically every activity of war, whether manufacturing, transportation, combat, construction, or destruction, is of an engineering nature. This influence is reflected in the activities of the... Society...Our members are serving in government work and in the Army and Navy. Our research activities have been influenced along lines of service in war...Comfort, efficiency, economy, and health, under rationing conditions, are of great importance to the public." (p. 2, *ASHVE Trans.*, 1943)

1943

ASRE

CHARLES R. LOGAN

1896?–1979

PHILADELPHIA, PA

"Refrigeration has a very definite and important part in this...In many contacts with government officials at Washington and in the field, we of the A.S.R.E....realize the tremendous tasks at hand...This is the time for unity, standardization and true unselfishness to a cause." (p. 368, Dec. 1941, *RE*)

1943

ASHVE

MERRILL F. BLANKIN

1898–1972

PHILADELPHIA, PA

"The 50th Annual Meeting of the Society marks an outstanding milestone in the life of a great, scientific organization. In the midst of the greatest war of all time we are met here in New York these three days to celebrate our glorious history, consider the present, and prepare for the future." (p. 2, *ASHVE Trans.*, 1944)

1944

ASRE

ALPHEUS B. STICKNEY

1903–1961

CHICAGO, IL

"I am deeply conscious of the smallness of the part that any one man can play in such an organization as ours. I am grateful for the fine spirit of cooperation, and for the number and quality of men who have taken an active part in Society affairs." (p. 465, Dec. 1944, *RE*)

1944

ASHVE

S. H. DOWNS

1898?–1980

KALAMAZOO, MI

"The Society and its members have continued to support the prosecution of the war by every possible means; and a great deal of our present planning will contribute largely to conversion to peacetime pursuits." (p. 2, *ASHVE Trans.*, 1945)

1945

ASRE

JOHN F. STONE

1900?–1977

NEW YORK, NY

"It does not seem an exaggerated hope that the engineering societies can advance a general understanding among peoples by not only broadening their professional contacts with foreign engineering but also by increasing their knowledge of and acquaintance with foreign engineers." (p. 521, Dec. 1945, *RE*)

1945

ASHVE

CHARLES-EDWARD A. WINSLOW

1877–1957

NEW HAVEN, CT

"The principal problem before the Council this year has been that of finding permanent quarters for the Research Laboratory...we were able to purchase [a] property... it is a place in which the work of the Laboratory can go forward actively and successfully..." (p. 2, *ASHVE Trans.*, 1946)

1946

ASRE

CHARLES S. LEOPOLD

1896–1960

PHILADELPHIA, PA

"The volunteer committees demand the greatest amount of work and offer the greatest opportunity to serve the Society." (p. 509, June 1946, *RE*)

1946

ASHVE

ALFRED J. OFFNER

1888–1979

NEW YORK, NY

"Our Research Laboratory is unique among engineering societies, in that we are the only national engineering Society to own and operate such facilities. It deserves the full support, not only of industry, but of every member of the Society." (p. 5, *ASHVE Trans.*, 1947)

1947

ASRE

R. H. MONEY

?–1982?

CINCINNATI, OH

"In the design, testing and development of various war products the refrigeration engineer certainly is among the best...qualified. He is a pinch hitter in all and a specialist in most [engineering] subjects...[He] is well equipped to deal with more than his normal job of cooling something...[which] leads to one reassuring conclusion—that the refrigeration engineer is in effect one of our secret weapons, a weapon in which we know we are many times stronger than our enemies." (p. 69, Aug. 1942, *RE*)

1947

ASHVE

BALDWIN M. WOODS

1887–1956

BERKELEY, CA

"The wide participation in the work of the Society by its members, chapters, committees, Council, staff and officers emphasizes more than ever the importance of teamwork. The year just passed has seen evidence of unusually high performance to meet this requirement." (p. 7, *ASHVE Trans.*, 1948)

1948

ASRE

CLIFFORD F. HOLSKE

1901–1977

BROOKLYN, NY

"By the early nineteen hundreds an adequate ice supply and a supply of desirable food products which required refrigeration were both available and from that time the distribution of refrigerating equipment progressed rapidly." (p. 149, Sept. 1936, *RE*)

1948

ASHVE

GEORGE L. TUVE

1896–1980

BERKELEY, CA

"Among the year's accomplishments...Payment of the mortgage on our Research Laboratory...we have been able to increase our publications program... cooperation with other groups of engineers [and others]...Our research program has been broadened..." (p. 1, *ASHVE Trans.*, 1949)

1949

ASRE

BURGESS JENNINGS

1903–?

EVANSTON, IL

"Air sterilization, one of the newer fields of engineering and medicine, presents a real challenge to the combined efforts of the engineering and medical professions. Something must be done to reduce the toll of airborne disease which afflicts many millions in this country...The engineer's role in this problem is that of reducing the number of pathogenic organisms in a given space to such a small amount the chance of cross infection becomes remote." (p. 323, Oct. 1948, RE)

1949

ASHVE

Alfred E. Stacey, Jr.

1885–1975

New York, NY

"We have grown since 1935 from a membership of less than 2000 to our present gratifying membership of 7700. This is a gain of approximately 400 percent." (p. 2, *ASHVE Trans.,* 1950)

1951

ASRE

Paul B. Christensen

1910–1950

New York, NY

"It is our hope that close liaison and coordination can be developed during the coming year between...committees so that the work of each will both supplement and complement the work of the others." (p. 179, Feb. 1951, *RE*)

1950

ASRE

John G. Bergdoll, Jr.

1898–1983

York, PA

"The best way to hold our membership is to make contributions to the industry as a whole and to the public through the medium of our...papers...if we could reach that ideal condition where each author feels that he has no right to take time...unless he really has something constructive to give—then there would be no question as to the continued growth in membership." (p. 271, Oct. 1944, *RE*)

1951

ASHVE

Lauren E. Seeley

1898–1968

Durham, NH

"The key to the success of our Society rests in the generous, voluntary services of many of our members and the continued friendly and cooperative spirit of the whole membership. When all is said and done the greatest single asset of our Society is the friendly spirit which animates it so universally." (p. 130, March 1952, *ASHVE Journal*)

1950

ASHVE

Lester T. Avery

1896–1978

Cleveland, OH

"...I feel that in the Chapter meetings we have our greatest new opportunity to serve the public, the nonmember public of interested engineering and business people...We should take time to... invite those groups who might be interested in some particular subject." (p. 113, March 1951, *ASHVE Journal*)

1952

ASRE

Edward Simons

1903–1988

San Fransisco, CA

"The time of election of your officers is concurrent with that for the voting on the constitutional amendments. Let us perform these duties and rights of voting to the fullest extent in order that men may well say, 'This Society knows itself.'" (p. 1097, Oct. 1952, *RE*)

1952

ASHVE

ERNEST SZEKELY

1888–1956

MILWAUKEE, WI

"...but we, who are actively interested in air conditioning... feel that the fire protection engineers have become unduly panicky about hazards produced...by air conditioning installations. This probably explains why rules and regulations are being promulgated which...will make the first cost of air conditioning systems prohibitive and thus may...hinder...healthy development of a new industry. We feel keenly on this point because our observations do not indicate that air conditioning systems...have contributed greatly to the fires reported." (p. 573, *ASHVE Trans.*, 1939)

1953

ASRE

RICHARD C. JORDAN

1909–2002

MINNEAPOLIS, MN

"Any great engineering organization, such as the American Society of Refrigeration Engineers, has but one real asset—the technical contributions of its members...The members...and their contributions constitute the Society." (p. 185, Feb. 1953, *RE*)

1953

ASHVE

REGINALD F. TAYLOR

1889–1974

HOUSTON, TX

"Since I joined the Society in 1915, when it had 500 members and but 3 chapters, it has grown to over 9300 members with 56 chapters, 9 student branches and a special branch in Zurich, Switzerland. The Society's membership growth has been paralleled by the growth of its publications." (p. 1, *ASHVE Trans.*, 1954)

1954

ASRE

ARTHUR J. HESS

1904–1981

LOS ANGELES, CA

"Because of the rapidly expanding growth of the refrigerating industry, particularly the development of new fields, it has been felt necessary to expand the scope and number of the technical committees." (p. 386, April 1952, *RE*)

1954

ASHAE

LOUIS N. (NAT) HUNTER

1903–1974

JOHNSTOWN, PA

"One important action taken by the membership this past year was changing the name of the Society to American Society of Heating and Air-Conditioning Engineers, Inc. This in no way changes our purpose and we will continue to promote all of the objectives provided for in our Charter." (p. 161, March 1955, *ASHAE Journal*)

1955

ASRE

LEON BUEHLER, JR.

1899–1993

CHICAGO, IL

"Honesty is of course expected of everyone, but the member of a profession needs a higher standard of honesty than is generally expected from others." (p. 43, April 1955, *RE*)

1955

ASHAE

John E. Haines

1903–1967

Minneapolis, MN

"Our improved publicity and public relations program has provided people with a better knowledge of what the Society does and a greater appreciation of what is being done by so many Society members for the advancement of the profession." (p. 169, March 1956, *ASHAE Journal*)

1956

ASRE

Carlyle M. Ashley

1899–1993

Syracuse, NY

"During the year, the ASHAE-ASRE Committee on Cooperation was reconstituted and was directed by the Councils of both Societies to explore further areas of cooperation and the problems which might be involved in possible eventual merger." (p. 46, May 1957, *RE*)

1956

ASHAE

John W. James

1907–1994

Chicago, IL

"The strength of an organization such as ours is dependent on the influx of engineers from all segments of our profession who have the zeal to advance the arts and sciences of heating, ventilating and air conditioning for the benefit of all mankind." (p. 190, Jan. 1957, *ASHAE Journal*)

1957

ASRE

Herman F. Spoehrer

1903–1968

St. Louis, MO

"Our aim at all times should be to increase the prestige of the Society and to keep all of its activities on a high technical plane...Those who use our products and services are entitled to the best we can give them in quality, performance, economy, safety and comfort." (p. 61, July 1957, *RE*)

1957

ASHAE

Peter B. Gordon

1907–1973

New York, NY

"I believe the area of Society activities that encompasses 'technical information available to all' to be the most important single activity in the Society's framework of operations...[Society publications] provide for a free and open exchange of information about design and operations..." (p. 174, March 1958, *ASHAE Journal*)

1958

ASRE

Cecil Boling

1908–1992

New York, NY

"That there should be positive and strong-minded expressions of viewpoint with regard to the proposed merger of ASRE and ASHAE is, in my opinion, a definite indication that our members are giving serious consideration to this important subject." (p. 49, July 1958, *RE*)

1958

ASHAE

ELMER R. QUEER

1904–?

STATE COLLEGE, PA

"...in recent months, I have devoted my message to keeping you supplied with information on this merger...There are two...reasons for doing this. One is the conviction that this merger...is the most important...item of business now under consideration... The second...is...that the membership be kept continually and accurately informed...as details...are worked out. Without knowledge the members cannot vote thoughtfully and with due consideration when the time for voting comes." (p. 154, *ASHAE Journal*, Sept. 1958)

1959

ASHAE

ARTHUR J. HESS

1904–1981

LOS ANGELES, CA

Mr. Hess served as president of ASHAE from the evening of January 28, 1959 until the consolidation of the two Societies became effective on January 29, 1959. (p. 7, *ASHRAE Trans.*, 1959)

Jan. 1959–June 1959

ASHRAE

CECIL BOLING

1908–1992

NEW YORK, NY

"...let us approach the future of ASHRAE with the idea of how much we shall contribute as individuals to the possible progress of our Society, of our companies, of our associates and of ourselves." (p. 97, *ASHRAE Journal*, March 1959)

June 1959–Jan. 1960

ASHRAE

ARTHUR J. HESS

1904–1981

LOS ANGELES, CA

"As your new President, even though slightly tarnished from use, I wish to express my thanks to you for your confidence in my ability to do the work of this highest office at your command. I also wish to express our thanks to Cecil Boling who preceded me...performed a Herculean task during the very trying period of transition." (p. 69, *ASHRAE Journal*, July 1959)

Jan. 1960–June 1960

ASHRAE

DANIEL D. WILE

1902?–1984

LOS ANGELES, CA

"We must never lose sight of the fact that we are a technical society... We are a nonprofit organization of engineers devoted to advancing our particular arts and sciences." (p. 57, *ASHRAE Journal*, June 1960)

June 1960–Feb. 1961

ASHRAE

WALTER A. GRANT

1904–1990

SYRACUSE, NY

"While experienced leaders in any organization necessarily will be buffeted by the eddies and crosscurrents of events and opinions, in the long run they are obliged to determine a wise and consistent course in tune with the membership in order to make constructive progress." (p. 47, *ASHRAE Journal*, July 1960)

Feb. 1961–June 1961

ASHRAE

ROBERT H. TULL
1904–1973
MORRISTOWN, NJ

"The importance of our profession provides the opportunity and the challenge to build a great engineering society. But its greatness will be determined by how well it serves the interests of its members and the general public." (p. 45, March 1961, *ASHRAE Journal)*

June 1961–June 1962

ASHRAE

JOHN EVERETTS, JR.
1905–1981
PHILADELPHIA, PA

"We are a strong, healthy and vigorous Society and, now that the interim period of merging is over, we must devote our interests and energies to promoting our aims and objectives as a Technical Society. If we will do this in a spirit of cooperation and with unity of agreement, our progress will be inevitable." (p. 75, July 1961, *ASHRAE Journal)*

June 1962–June 1963

ASHRAE

JOHN H. FOX
1903–?
TORONTO, CANADA

"Growth and change...the pattern that has been characteristic of ASHRAE and its predecessor societies since their inception 68 years ago...were unusually dominant in Society activities...we have sought...new challenges in order to improve our services to members, to industry, and to the public." (p. 44, Jan. 1963, *ASHRAE Journal)*

June 1963–June 1964

ASHRAE

FRANK H. FAUST
1905–1995
TYLER, TX

"Substantial progress has been made since the merger...Despite [an] impressive list of accomplishments there are still a number of problems... Some of these include the necessity of fulfilling our obligations to the United Engineering Center Fund, the necessity of rebuilding contributions from industry for research, continued improvement of editorial content in and increased advertising income from our Journal...and the acceleration of membership growth." (p. 23, July 1963, *ASHRAE Journal)*

June 1964–June 1965

ASHRAE

JOHN E. DUBE
1905–1983
ST. LOUIS, MO

"A satisfactory system of communication must be responsive in both directions, and it is the region and chapter route which offers the individual member the best opportunity to participate in the forming of Society policy...A member without chapter affiliation misses much more than chapter programs and local sociability. He is deprived of a vital line of communication which, in turn, depreciates the full value of his national membership." (p. 31, Nov 1963, *ASHRAE Journal)*

June 1965–June 1966

ASHRAE

JAMES W. MAY
1907–2008
LOUISVILLE, KY

"Communication is an area in which we must maintain constant vigilance...ASHRAE is a society made up of individual members, and good communication is absolutely essential for a well-knit organization." (p. 27, July 1965, *ASHRAE Journal)*

June 1966–Sept. 30, 1966

ASHRAE

LINCOLN BOUILLON

1900–1966

SEATTLE, WA

"Membership of 25,000? Why not! This would mean an increase in each chapter of approximately 40%...Many of us have felt...that for every member of ASHRAE, there is another person making his living in the heating, refrigerating or air-conditioning business, who is not a member...We also feel that most of this group of non-members are not necessarily holding out; they simply have never been contacted properly or maybe 'pushed' a little towards membership." (p. 62, April 1966, *ASHRAE Journal)*

Sept. 30, 1966–June 1967

ASHRAE

WILLIAM L. MCGRATH

1911–1988

SYRACUSE, NY

"It may be that engineers are conditioned by an environment of problems and therefore may be uneasy when things are running smoothly. Nevertheless, we are happy to predict continued progress and comparable prosperity..." (p. 93, Jan. 1967, *ASHRAE Journal)*

June 1967–June 1968

ASHRAE

P. N. VINTHER

1901–1988

DALLAS, TX

"...if, in beginning our new fiscal year and in approaching our 75th anniversary, we look over our shoulders in search of clues to the future, that which will impress us most deeply is the element of change. Some of the change is sudden and unavoidable...Other changes occur...gradually...ASHRAE is now 73 years young, vigorous and growing. But make no mistake, the very essence of growth is change." (p. 45, July 1967, *ASHRAE Journal)*

June 1968–June 1969

ASHRAE

WILLIAM L. HOLLADAY

1901–2001

LOS ANGELES, CA

Presidential Theme: Lifelong Learning

"I refer to the obligation each of us has to continue educating oneself, keeping abreast of an ever-advancing technology...First, listen to your fellow engineers...The second way is to study...A third way is to go back to school...A fourth way, of course, is membership and active participation in ASHRAE." (p. 63, July 1968, *ASHRAE Journal)*

June 1969–June 1970

ASHRAE

WILLIAM G. HOLE

1910–2002

MONTREAL, CANADA

Presidential Theme: ASHRAE... Man and His World

"Man and His World—that really is what ASHRAE is all about. The activities of our members are all related in some way with man's environment and well being, his living and working conditions, his food supplies, his comfort in his surroundings." (p. 57, July 1969, *ASHRAE Journal)*

June 1970–June 1971

ASHRAE

FRANK H. BRIDGERS

1922–?

ALBUQUERQUE, NM

Presidential Theme: Excellence: The Quest of the Engineer

"If each Committee could outline its goals for the decade, I believe that ASHRAE's activities will be more effective...I feel that we can reap rich rewards from establishing our short- and long-range goals. I am convinced that it will help us in achieving our overall goal for the Seventies—'To strive for excellence—the quest of the engineer.'" (p. 69, July 1970, *ASHRAE Journal)*

June 1971–June 1972

ASHRAE

STANLEY F. GILMAN

1921–1983

LOUISVILLE, KY

Presidential Theme: Personal Involvement: The Impact of Individual Effort

"We have problems of air pollution, water pollution, thermal pollution, and noise pollution, among others. But air, water, heat and noise are just the things ASHRAE members 'cut their teeth on.'" We simply cannot stand on the sidelines of the pollution problem. We have so much talent that it is our responsibility, indeed our duty as professionals, to lend our aid." (p. 55, Aug. 1971, *ASHRAE Journal)*

June 1972–June 1973

ASHRAE

WALTER F. SPIEGEL

1922–2012

JENKINTOWN, PA

Presidential Theme: Meeting New Challenges

"'Meeting New Challenges' will extend to all facets of our many activities, including research, membership growth, improved services to members, expanding publications policy, and increased attention to developing technology for the benefit and survival of mankind." (p. 73, June 1972, *ASHRAE Journal)*

June 1973–June 1974

ASHRAE

RODERICK R. KIRKWOOD

1920–2010

SEATTLE, WA

Presidential Theme: Optimum Energy Utilization

"ASHRAE's membership is concerned about utilization of energy, not with its production. We, as engineers, designers, manufacturers and technicians, can help to reduce the shortage of energy by using our technology to assure that the utilization of energy is optimized. If we don't take the forefront in this, we must expect others to take over." (p. 57, June 1973, *ASHRAE Journal)*

June 1974–June 1975

ASHRAE

DAVID RICKELTON

1916–?

PINEVILLE, NC

Presidential Theme: International Year of Progress and Cooperation

"It is quite evident that the economic welfare of all nations is becoming increasingly dependent one upon the other...As the interdependence of nations increases, so must cooperation and exchange of information..." (p. 46, Aug. 1974, *ASHRAE Journal)*

June 1975–June 1976

ASHRAE

WILLIAM J. COLLINS

1915–2006

OKLAHOMA CITY, OK

Presidential Theme: Commitment

"...only by committing ourselves can we accomplish a job well done. Ingenuity, pride and hard work are the real answers to the problems of today's energy conscious world...for not only do we have challenges; we also have opportunities." (p. 1, *ASHRAE Trans.*, pt. 2, 1975)

June 1976–June 1977

ASHRAE

WILLIAM P. CHAPMAN

1919–2002

MILWAUKEE, WI

Presidential Theme: Continuing Excellence: Requirement for Change

"By all the standards for measuring professional excellence in a society, ASHRAE excels. We have striven for excellence; we have achieved it...For ASHRAE to remain the outstanding organization that is, we must assess our strengths and our weaknesses...To foster excellence, to nurture leadership, requires change. We cannot be static; we must be dynamic..." (p. 31, 32, June 1979, *ASHRAE Journal)*

June 1977–June 1978

ASHRAE

BRUNO P. MORABITO

1922–2015

SYRACUSE, NY

Presidential Theme: Involvement Beyond Ourselves

"...change is necessary to meet today's evolving needs. The change-with-meaning that has been recently brought to our Society has been impressive. This emerging spirit—this Involvement: Beyond Ourselves—needs to be encouraged and continued." (p. 13, July 1977, *ASHRAE Journal)*

June 1978–June 1979

ASHRAE

MORRIS BACKER

1927–2006

SYRACUSE, NY

Presidential Theme: From Strength to Greater Strength

"...with continued dedication and enthusiasm, our membership will fulfill ongoing and future goals. We have great strength in our members, our organization, and our pursuits. Let us build on this sturdy foundation and move forward, From Strength To Greater Strength." (p. 23, Aug. 1978, *ASHRAE Journal)*

June 1979–June 1980

ASHRAE

HUGH D. MCMILLAN, JR.

1925–2006

HOUSTON, TX

Presidential Theme: ASHRAE's Future: Commitment

"I have come to realize that ASHRAE is unlike any other society I know. I have given careful thought as to why this is true—why this esprit de corps exists in ASHRAE. The answer is best described by one word—Commitment." (p. 30, Aug. 1979, *ASHRAE Journal)*

June 1980–June 1981

ASHRAE

CHARLES F. SEPSY

1924–2004

COLUMBUS, OH

Presidential Theme: Continuing Growth Through Professional Development

"In the next decade, we will see technological changes in our industry of a magnitude not yet encountered. Energy generation, conservation and utilization will remain ASHRAE's most active battleground." (p. 22, Aug. 1980, *ASHRAE Journal)*

June 1981–June 1982

ASHRAE

JACK B. CHADDOCK

1924–2015

DURHAM, NC

Presidential Theme: Technical Leadership

"The overriding goal which I ask you to adopt for this Society year is: 'The advancement of technical leadership through a strengthening and broadening of the applied sciences, engineering practices and communication skills which are the basis of the engineering profession.'" (p. 10, Aug. 1981, *ASHRAE Journal)*

June 1982–June 1983

ASHRAE

CLINTON W. PHILLIPS

1919–2010

WASHINGTON, D.C.

Presidential Theme: *Effectiveness of ASHRAE*

"...ASHRAE's accomplishments...have been brought about by the personal commitment of the people who make up ASHRAE. It is the dedication and commitment of people who see a value to themselves and to their fellow human beings and perhaps the enhancement of the preservation of the commercial value of what they do that makes ASHRAE work." (p. 8, Aug. 1982, *ASHRAE Journal)*

June 1983–June 1984

ASHRAE

RICHARD P. PERRY

1923–2014

VANCOUVER, CANADA

Presidential Theme: Growth and Improved Technology Through International Cooperation
"All of you, as members of ASHRAE, are world leaders. The members domiciled on the North American continent are just as much international members of this unique organization as members from Europe, the Far East or Australia. We all share a common purpose. We are all stimulated by the desire to learn from each other. We all wish to advance our profession. ASHRAE allows us to do this..." (p. 9, Aug. 1983, *ASHRAE Journal)*

June 1984–June 1985

ASHRAE

ROBERT O. MCDONALD

1929–2006

ARLINGTON HEIGHTS, IL

Presidential Theme: Professional Excellence: Building the Future
"First, we must make a concentrated effort to advance engineering education...Second, we must provide our chapters with means for their future development...Third, we must make substantive progress in the development of ASHRAE's internationalism...And fourth, we must continue development of energy standards and energy management programs..." (p. 26, Aug. 1984, *ASHRAE Journal)*

June 1985–June 1986

ASHRAE

DONALD R. BAHNFLETH

1927–2016

CINCINNATI, OH

Presidential Theme: Committed to Serve
"ASHRAE is committed to serve...ASHRAE is committed to serve its membership, industry and the public through research...ASHRAE is committed to serve its membership through continuing education...ASHRAE is committed to serve the public...ASHRAE is committed to serve [in the area of energy efficiency]..." (p. 14, 16, Aug. 1985, *ASHRAE Journal)*

June 1986–June 1987

ASHRAE

FREDERICK H. KOHLOSS

1922–

HONOLULU, HI

Presidential Theme: Develop Our Human Resources
"The broad scope of ASHRAE's efforts affords opportunity to enhance individual technical competence. We will encourage ASHRAE members to develop and mature, to take their places in advancing our Society's technical and research efforts. In this way, we will develop our human resources." (p. 21, Aug. 1986, *ASHRAE Journal)*

June 1987–June 1988

ASHRAE

H.E. "BARNEY" BURROUGHS

1935–

ATLANTA, GA

Presidential Theme: ASHRAE Technology and the Human Destiny
"Yes, there have been challenges and we have conquered them. Yes, there are challenges before us even now...and yes, there are even more lurking ahead. Not without risk, not without investment of dollars and time and effort, and not without dedication and commitment...But ASHRAE, its technology, and you, its members, will shape the human destiny." (p. 21, Aug. 1987, *ASHRAE Journal)*

June 1988–June 1989

ASHRAE

LOUIS F. FLAGG

1914–1999

MINNEAPOLIS, MN

Presidential Theme: Communications: A Formula for Progress
"Communication is our formula for progress. Having no goals, no dreams, no stars to reach would be a true tragedy for our Society. But...with the vision of its members, ASHRAE is faced with vast opportunities." (p. 20, Aug. 1988, *ASHRAE Journal)*

June 1989–June 1990

ASHRAE

DAVID S. BUTLER, SR.

1939–2012

JACKSON, MS

Presidential Theme: Volunteers Advancing Environmental Technology

"We have covered the what and the how, and now the question is who. Who is going to venture past the possible into the impossible? This answer...is simple. The very same committed, dedicated member volunteers and professional staff members of ASHRAE who have unselfishly and untiringly led the way in HVAC&R technology the past 95 years!" (p. 12, Aug. 1989, *ASHRAE Journal)*

June 1990–June 1991

ASHRAE

A. DAMON GOWAN

1936–2016

HOUSTON, TX

Presidential Theme: *P*rofessional Development through Participation

"Meeting...challenges and building upon ASHRAE's strengths in education, technological development and communication is 'what's in it' if you will for every ASHRAE member, and it lies at the heart of 'Professional Development through Participation.'" (p. 14, Aug. 1990, *ASHRAE Journal)*

June 1991–June 1992

ASHRAE

DONALD G. RICH

1929–

SYRACUSE, NY

Presidential Theme: Quality: Our Ongoing Challenge

"Engineers have high public credibility. A recent poll revealed that engineers have the highest credibility of all professional groups...The message here is clear. ASHRAE has responsibility to speak on issues in which we have expertise. And if we speak, the public will listen. If we don't, others less qualified will speak for us." (p. 14, Aug. 1991, *ASHRAE Journal)*

June 1992–June 1993

ASHRAE

RICHARD A. CHARLES

1931–2013

SAN FRANSISCO, CA

Presidential Theme: Sharing Resources Globally

"I believe that one of ASHRAE's secrets to success has been the diversity of its membership, which includes educators, engineers, design professionals, manufacturers, service people, contractors and salespeople. Each person brings a variety of experience and needs to the ASHRAE community." (p. 22, Aug. 1992, *ASHRAE Journal)*

June 1993–June 1994

ASHRAE

NEIL R. PATTERSON

1929–2007

LA CROSSE, WI

Presidential Theme: ASHRAE: The Bridge to Professional Growth

"Engineers have always been builders. And this year we must build the bridges that will attract new members to advance technology and bring our expertise to bear on creative solutions to the challenges facing our industry. It's these new bridges that will open the doors to leadership development and professional growth." (p. 19, Aug. 1993, *ASHRAE Journal)*

June 1994–June 1995

ASHRAE

BILLY R. MANNING

1934–2014

BIRMINGHAM, AL

Presidential Theme: Building on the Shoulders of Giants

"ASHRAE members have always been doers and we must continue that tradition. Our mission as members is to turn innovative ideas into real products and systems that provide simple solutions to the problems that people encounter—problems in their everyday lives and problems they meet as they push into the new frontiers that technology presents..." (p. 14, Aug. 1994, *ASHRAE Journal)*

June 1995–June 1996

ASHRAE

Richard B. Hayter

1943–

Manhattan, KS

Presidential Theme: Sharing the Vision

"Just as HVAC&R technology is growing exponentially, so are communication technologies. Today 30% of US households have a personal computer, and 50% of all computer sales are for home use. Also, 38 million people now have access to the information superhighway through Internet compared with 8 million just 2 years ago." (p. 32, Aug. 1995, *ASHRAE Journal*)

June 1996–June 1997

ASHRAE

James E. Hill

1942–

Moneta, VA

Presidential Theme: Service to Members is Our Strategy for Success

"Leaders shouldn't rely on beliefs and perceptions as a basis for decisions about the Society's direction. But rather, they should rely on hard data or 'knowledge' about members' needs and preferences. To get that data requires that we, the Society's leaders, have access to a continual stream of information from you, the Society's members." (p. 46, Aug. 1996, *ASHRAE Journal*)

June 1997–June 1998

ASHRAE

Donald E. Holte

1936–2002

Edmonton, Alberta, Canada

Presidential Theme: Technology for a Better Environment

"We must become proactive in what we do so as to lessen the impact our technology has on the environment. We must become the link between the indoor built environment and the outdoor global environment. We must strive to do more with less. We must be willing to reward people for designing and building buildings that are energy efficient and which do not adversely affect the environment." (p. 40, Aug. 1997, *ASHRAE Journal*)

June 1998–June 1999

ASHRAE

George A. Jackins

1934–

Birmingham, AL

Presidential Theme: ASHRAE's Bridges to the Future—Learning-Unity-Visibility

"It's going to take a commitment to learning-L-so that our members have the knowledge and skills to design, build and operate buildings that are energy efficient, have healthy indoor environments and don't harm the outdoor environment. It's going to take a unified effort...-U. It is going to take not only leadership, but also visibility-V." (p. 31, Aug. 1998, *ASHRAE Journal*)

June 1999– June 2000

ASHRAE

Harley W. Goodman, Jr.

1928–

Little Rock, AR

Presidential Theme: ASHRAE in the New Millennium's Global Community

"If we really want to commit to the global environment, economy and community, then our focus, our structure and the way we do business must change. We also must make stronger efforts to involve engineers from other countries and consider not only the needs of the U.S. market, but also the needs and resources of HVAC&R markets around the world." (p. 37-38, Aug 1999, *ASHRAE Journal*)

June 2000– June 2001

ASHRAE

James E. Wolf

1941–

Arlington, VA

Presidential Theme: Engineering for Tomorrow's Quality of Life

"Climate change will be a defining issue for the future of ASHRAE. It offers us an opportunity to be 'proactive' rather than 'reactive' on an issue of pressing environmental concern. Our business environment is changing and to flourish we need to consider and try new ideas." (p. 32, Aug. 2000, *ASHRAE Journal*)

June 2001– June 2002

ASHRAE

William J. Coad
1931–2014
Saint Louis, MO

Presidential Theme: Accepting the Challenge
"We must advance the technology, not perpetuate it. The very premise of the challenge is that if society is to survive, change is inevitable. So if we are to advance technology, we must rely heavily on those activities that tend to do so." (p. 28, Aug. 2001, *ASHRAE Journal*)

June 2002– June 2003

ASHRAE

Donald G. Colliver
1952–
Lexington, KY

Presidential Theme: *Building a Better World*
"Passion is our fuel. People being passionate about learning new information and better methods and then sharing them with others. People being passionate about development of their skills and talents, passionate about mentoring and nurturing, and passionate about making the world a better place to live." (p. 17, Aug. 2002, *ASHRAE Journal*)

June 2003–June 2004

ASHRAE

Richard H. Rooley
1940–
Slough, England, UK

Presidential Theme: The Community of ASHRAE
"Ask an HVAC&R engineer anywhere in the world about ASHRAE. Every one of them...knows about ASHRAE, identifies with the technical community and has an opinion about it....They will talk of technology, they will talk of the systems, they will talk in a common language, which soon progresses from shared technology to shared humanity." (p. 16, Aug. 2003, *ASHRAE Journal*)

June 2004– June 2005

ASHRAE

Ronald P. Vallort
1942–
Elmhurst, IL

Presidential Theme: Refrigeration: Technology for Survival
"Refrigeration should be more economical and foolproof both to construct and operate, while still being friendly to the environment. ASHRAE's mission will continue to increase in importance.... Planet Earth has a long future ahead—ASHRAE can and must contribute to this future." (p. 17, Aug. 2004, *ASHRAE Journal*)

June 2005–June 2006

ASHRAE

Lee Burgett
1939–2014
La Crosse, WI

Presidential Theme: Advancing ASHRAE Technology and Our Future
"The breadth of issues has never been wider from mold to energy conservation, and the level of need has never been greater. At the same time, ASHRAE's ability to respond has never been better." (pg. 15, Aug. 2005, *ASHRAE Journal*)

June 2006–June 2007

ASHRAE

Terry Townsend
1949–
Chattanooga, TN

Presidential Theme: The ASHRAE Promise: A Sustainable Future
"Because of the concept of sustainability, we must go outside of our current areas of membership and seek to include facility managers, owners and architects because they are also involved in the sustainable design process. ASHRAE has what they need." (p. 15, Aug. 2006, *ASHRAE Journal*)

June 2007–June 2008

ASHRAE

KENT PETERSON

1963–

LONG BEACH, CA

Presidential Theme: Greater Efficiency Today, Blue Skies Tomorrow: Innovation for a Sustainable Built Environment

"I dream of the day when the building industry realizes that what is possible is far beyond the minimum performance the general market demands today; I dream that we unleash the spirit of innovation to break through existing boundaries and deliver the elegant sustainable buildings society is beginning to demand." (p. 12, Aug. 2007, *ASHRAE Journal*)

June 2008–June 2009

ASHRAE

WILLIAM A. HARRISON

1943–

LITTLE ROCK, AR

Presidential Theme: Maintain to Sustain: Delivering ASHRAE's Sustainability Promise

"The time has passed when we can shake our head and walk away saying 'this isn't my problem.' Every day we observe installations and operating practices that are wasting our precious energy and water resources, draining power from the grid, increasing the emissions from our generating plants." (p. 21, Aug. 2008, *ASHRAE Journal*)

June 2009–June 2010

ASHRAE

GORDON HOLNESS

1939–

DETROIT, MI

Presidential Theme: Sustaining Our Future by Rebuilding Our Past

"We should remember that 75% to 85% of all of the buildings that will exist in urban areas in 2030 exist today. If we focus our technology solely on that 2% of new construction, it would probably not get us to the much-needed worldwide reduction in energy consumption that we have been striving for." (p. 16, Aug. 2009, *ASHRAE Journal*)

June 2010–June 2011

ASHRAE

LYNN G. BELLENGER

1949–2011

ROCHESTER, NY

Presidential Theme: Modelling a Sustainable World

"Building modeling is a growing segment of our industry, with modeling projects often assigned to men and women just entering the field. Those few of us who have been modeling for decades must share our expertise with a new generation. And, the most valuable lesson we can share is that buildings operate as systems rather than a collection of components." (p. 20-21, Aug. 2010, *ASHRAE Journal*)

June 2011–June 2012

ASHRAE

RON JARNAGIN

1946–

RICHLAND, WA

Presidential Theme: Sustaining ASHRAE through Leadership

"We have owners and people that procure property and buildings that don't get what they want or what they need. This means that engineers have to do a better job in their designs, contractors have to do a better job putting designs together, and commissioning agents need to make sure everything works as intended. And we've got to make the sure the owners are trained as well." (p. 24, Aug. 2011, ASHRAE Journal)

June 2012–June 2013

ASHRAE

THOMAS WATSON

1944–

STAUNTON, VA

Presidential Theme: Broadening ASHRAE's Horizons

"Do we need complicated buildings? We need to focus on impact, making sure the advanced technology is used through-out the life of the building, not just installed as showpiece to win an award, then not used. We need to have buildings that remain viable for years to come. We need to use innovation that works." (p. 17-18, Aug. 2012, *ASHRAE Journal*)

June 2013–June 2014

ASHRAE

WILLIAM P. BAHNFLETH

1957–

UNIVERSITY PARK, PA

Presidential Theme: Shaping the Next
"Our goals should address our world—using our talents and resources for the benefit of the general public, as our governing documents charge us with doing. In order to achieve these goals, we must also set goals for ourselves—developing a workforce that is capable of meeting the challenges of the future, and for our work—what we do, how we do it, and with whom we do it." (p. 23, Aug. 2013, *ASHRAE Journal*)

June 2014–June 2015

ASHRAE

THOMAS H. PHOENIX

1952–

GREENSBORO, NC

Presidential Theme: People, Passion and Performance
"We need more of our best minds talking to each other. Collaborating, sharing, mentoring, learning. Instilling the passion in all of us.... We will be successful because our people, our passion and our performance will make ASHRAE better in the future than it is today." (p. 20, Aug. 2014, *ASHRAE Journal*)

June 2015–June 2016

ASHRAE

T. DAVID UNDERWOOD

1941–

OAKVILLE, ONTARIO. CANADA

Presidential Theme: Making Connections
"Volunteerism is at the heart of ASHRAE....Making connections has been foundational in building ASHRAE's reputation as the industry leader. But we won't rest on our laurels; we will move forward with even bolder steps. We will make sure today's discoveries become tomorrow's design standards." (p. 14, 19, Aug. 2016, *ASHRAE Journal*)

June 2016–June 2017

ASHRAE

TIMOTHY G. WENTZ

1953–

LINCOLN, NE

Presidential Theme: Adapt to Shape Tomorrow
"Adapting our ever-changing technology such that it transforms our lives, our Society, our communities is one of our core values. Our core values must never change, for they are the bedrock upon which our Society rests....Make a difference locally in order that ASHRAE can make a difference globally." (p. 22, Aug. 2016, *ASHRAE Journal*)

June 2017–June 2018

ASHRAE

BJARNE W. OLESEN

1947–

KONGENS LYNGBY, DENMARK

Presidential Theme: Extending our Community
"Why should we be more global? How do members here in the U.S. and around the world benefit from a more global Society? The answers to these questions should serve as the foundation of a new global strategy that addresses challenges facing the global building industry today." (p. 15 Aug. 2017, *ASHRAE Journal*)

June 2018–June 2019

ASHRAE

SHEILA J. HAYTER

1967–

GOLDEN, CO

Presidential Theme: Building Our New Energy Future
"ASHRAE will actively engage in the rapidly growing wellness community. The increased connectivity of the future brings more opportunities than just those in energy. Human wellness and wellbeing within the built environment is an area of significant opportunity, and ASHRAE members are well positioned to be at the forefront..." (p. 22, Aug. 2018, *ASHRAE Journal*)

June 2019–June 2020

ASHRAE

Darryl K. Boyce

1951–

Kemptville, Ontario, Canada

Presidential Theme: Building for People and Performance. Achieving Operational Excellence
"ASHRAE needs to work with building owner-operator organizations to develop strategies that will prepare the operators to effectively operate the building through enhanced training, effective use of the building automation system and analytical and other operational tools. [...] We can do better. We will do better for those who operate our buildings. People must succeed within the buildings we create. Let's ensure we take the steps to achieve effective operational performance and enhance the operator experience." (p. 17, 18, Aug. 2019, *ASHRAE Journal*)

Appendix K

125 Papers from the ASHRAE Archives

Technological progress does not come in measured steps. There are periods of rapid advancement where scientific breakthroughs are followed by nearly immediate application, just as there are periods of prolonged refinement. In some years, progress follows a straight path, in others a detour is taken. Always, the application of technology responds to external factors, with emphasis shifting from need to need as society dictates.

A review of ASHRAE's literature is a journey through our century. Successes are described as well as failures—some would not be known until years later. The literature of ASHRAE tells the story of how researchers, practicing engineers and equipment designers learned to control the environment and respond to the public's needs—whether it be in 1894, 100 years later, or 125 years later. In many ways, these needs have never changed.

This appendix presents 125 selections from ASHRAE's archives—one from each year of the Society's existence. Some papers were chosen because they heralded a new era of development, others because they best captured the demands of the period, yet others because they described the current state of the art, and some because with the advantage of hindsight we simply find them interesting.

The selections of the papers were made by panels of distinguished ASHRAE members. The panel that selected papers from ASHRAE's first 100 years included the following:

Louis F. Flagg, Chairman	Donald E. Nichols
Dr. Raymond Cohen	Joseph B. Olivieri
Guy W. Gupton	Ronald L. Shelton
George B. Hightower	Dr. Hans O. Spauschus
Gershon Meckler	

The panel that selected papers from ASHRAE's most recent 25 years included the following:

Eric Sturm, Chairman	Steven F. Bruning
Charles E. Henck	James E. Hill
Gordon Holness	David Knebel
Ronald Shelton	Branislav Todorovic
David Underwood	

Each selection appears with an abstract. Abstracts, whenever possible, are drawn from the words of the author using the language and grammar of the period. The Basis of Selection for the first 100 papers was prepared by the selection panel.

The authors' names appear in this appendix as they are shown on the original papers. In the early years of ASHVE and ASRE literature, the locality of the author was shown. We have reproduced this style for those years. Likewise, membership grade appears (or does not appear) as it does on the paper at the time of its publication.

The Course of History

The principal activity of the American Society of Heating and Ventilating Engineers during the early years of its existence was the convening of annual meetings, and later semiannual meetings, at which papers were presented. The volume of papers was such that parallel sessions were not necessary, so all meeting attendees were able and in fact were expected to participate in the discussion which followed each paper. Today, these discussions, which were published in their entirety in *ASHVE Transactions,* are often more informative than the paper on which they comment.

During the Society's first decade, the papers presented at its meetings indicate there was greater interest in application than in system design and equipment manufacture. Many were discourses on how not to do something or reviews of what went wrong. But soon the focus turned to new ideas and solutions to problems. Perhaps some impetus for this change in direction came from the accelerated pace of urbanization and industrialization which characterized the turn of the century.

The second decade of ASHVE literature and the literature of the American Society of Refrigerating Engineers' first ten years are rich with papers on heating with natural gas, use of ammonia and ethyl chloride as refrigerants, heating and ventilating cars (the rail type), ozone as an order controller, and charts for sizing steam plants. If a single topic stood out among the heating and ventilating engineers during these years, it was their perceived need for ventilation standards for schools and public buildings.

In the years leading up to World War I, many papers reported that the new research and applications of the era were not so new after all, but rather were refinements of earlier work. During and after the war, the first of several periods began when there was intensive interest in conservation of fuel sources - both for heating and refrigeration.

The 1920s and early 30s can be characterized as a period of discovery and growth in the refrigeration field. As new industries flourished and people for the first time experienced leisure time, industrial demand for controlled environments exploded.

In the years leading to World War II, attention shifted to advances in controlled environments for buildings, largely because the U.S. Government let contracts for many large building air-conditioning systems during this era. The science of heating and cooling leaped forward. It was the era in which practicing engineers gained an understanding of dehumidification and developed techniques to rate cooling coils to predict performance. Solar energy, while discussed at ASHVE meetings prior to World War I, now was explored in depth, as was thermal storage. But as had happened to a previous generation of engineers, the nation's resources became focused on the war effort, and the commercial market for improved technology evaporated. Further commercial innovation would need to wait until the 1950s.

Pent-up demand and an inventory of technical advances waiting for investment created an explosion of activity in the 1950s. Sales of window air-conditioning units soared, as did home refrigerating appliances. Designs for large building air-conditioning systems built upon the fundamentals learned a decade earlier enabled Sunbelt cities to grow and prosper.

The 1960s and 70s saw tremendous interest in the further definition of thermal comfort. There was a flurry of activity in the enhancement of heat transfer surfaces, and the computer became a factor both in research and system design. As governmental guidelines dictated improved noise control, researchers investigated equipment improvements.

The literature published in the late twentieth century is marked by contributions which improved calculation of heating and cooling loads, enabled engineers to accurately predict and measure energy use, and advanced design for fire and smoke control. The need for improved ventilation standards for indoor air quality was as important a concern as it was a century earlier. And since the mid-80s, the archives reflect heightened awareness of environmental issues.

In the years following ASHRAE's Centennial in 1994–95, a new source of literature was added: *International Journal of Heating, Ventilating, Air-Conditioning and Refrigerating Research* became ASHRAE's vehicle for the publication of archival research. In 2015, the journal's name was changed to *Science and Technology for the Built Environment*.

In addition, ASHRAE expanded the number of technical conferences that it organized, further increasing the volume of technical information available to members.

ASHRAE literature traces many things. The growth of two societies dedicated to the advancement of technology, the growth of industries which enabled control of the environment to advance the quality of life and, most fascinating of all, the ability of engineers to meet the demands of consumers, whether they be the general public or commerce and industry.

The papers described in this appendix capture the idealism and the keen intelligence of the members of ASHRAE. The legacy of the members who volunteered their time and talent for the Society's benefit is a sound foundation upon which the contributions of succeeding generations of members can rest as ASHRAE begins its second century.

1895

Heating and Ventilation of School Buildings

By T.J. Waters, Chicago, Ill.

(Member of the Society.)

The introduction in 1867 of the first steam heating and mechanical ventilating apparatus in a Chicago public school is discussed. The apparatus operated for seven years, when it became necessary to remove old coils, owing to pin-hole leaks caused by rust. The coils would have lasted much longer had they been placed in a perfectly dry basement or kept in constant use. The next apparatus consisted of wrought iron staggered pipe radiators, one being placed at the base of each duct. In addition, wall coils were placed around the exposed walls under windows. Later, switch dampers were placed in ducts, enabling the teacher to regulate the air temperature without decreasing its volume.

Basis for selection: Amazing to see the progress that had been made in ventilation and heating of schools from 100 years ago.

Source: *ASHVE Transactions*, Vol. I, p. 78-100

1896

Forced Blast Warming with Furnaces

By Geo W. Kramer, New York

(Non-member of the Society. Presented to the Society on request.)

For the majority of churches the so-called hot air furnace is the only recourse. The furnaces in a church described were to heat 1,000,000 cubic feet of air per hour to 70°F. The manufacturer recommended using four to six furnaces, but there was only room for three. With 1,500 people in attendance at the dedication and the thermometer 10 degrees below zero, the animal heat created was such that two-thirds pure cold air had to be mixed with the warm air from the furnace. The distribution, supply and air temperature were deemed perfect.

Basis for selection: Good coverage of an early forced warm air system.

Source: *ASHVE Transactions*, Vol. II, p. 144-171

1897

Circulation of Steam for Heating Purposes At or Below the Pressure of the Atmosphere

By Reginald Pelham Bolton, C.E.

(Non-member of the Society. Presented by request.)

The Webster combination system comprises primarily an automatic outlet valve to each part requiring drainage, a connection of it to a suction apparatus, such as a pump or an ejector, the abstraction of all air and gases from the heating system, and the return of the condensed water into a heater wherein the water and gases freely dissociate in a chamber sealed from the atmosphere, and where the temperature of the condensed water, plus that of any additional fresh supply found to be necessary, is raised by direct contact with a proportional amount of exhaust waste steam, and finally the return of the whole automatically to the boiler. The operation of this apparatus can be brought to any degree of automatic regulation, its control is entirely in the engineer's or fireman's discretion, while leaving the control of each individual radiator or coil absolutely in the hands of the tenant or occupant, by means of one hand valve only. A remarkable result due to this arrangement is the ability to reduce the total temperature of any separate coil or radiator by reducing the amount steam admitted to it, without water logging or hammering, a result unknown with any combination of steam heating apparatus.

Basis for selection: Solid coverage at such an early date of steam distribution problems for heating.

Source: *ASHVE Transactions*, Vol. III, p. 155-186

1898

Heating and Ventilating Church and Parish Buildings by Forced Draft

By B.H. Carpenter, Wilkes Barre, PA.

(Member of the Society)

In designing and carrying out this system it was necessary, in order to ensure its success, to obtain the following results: First, to heat the buildings by the gravity system at all times; second, to heat and ventilate the buildings when necessary by mechanical means; third, to avoid drafts of any nature; fourth, to prevent objectionable noises.

Basis for selection: One of the earliest extensive systems using forced air distribution.

Source: *ASHVE Transactions*, Vol. IV, p. 231-243

1899

The Relation Between the Architect and the Heating Engineer

By T.N. Thomson

(Associate Member of the Society)

It is unfortunate for the advancement of heating and ventilating interests that so little consideration is given to the scheme of installation while a building is in the embryonic condition. An architect is asked to provide plans even though the owner and his wife have not decided on all the details to be included; they have not even chosen a system of heating. The draughtsman, having decided on structural requirements of the design, now turns his attention to the location and size of the smoke and heating flues, provision for which must be made in the walls. The building is constructed and the owner is notified that a heating system must be selected, otherwise the plastering will be delayed. Heating and ventilating engineers are called in, but the job will be difficult. An indirect steam or indirect hot water system would be ideal, but installation in a half-finished building will present many difficulties at a great expense. The old direct radiation method may have to be used. I wish that all the architects in the United States could have an opportunity to read this paper so that they might be reminded of the fact that a world of difference exists between the "forethought" job and the "afterthought" job.

Basis for selection: Early public acknowledgment of the difficult relationship that still exists.

Source: *ASHVE Transactions*, Vol. V, p. 108-116

1900

Dangerous Air Ducts

By John Gormly

(Member of the Society.)

In such cities as New York, intake shafts for ventilating apparatus are often near drainage systems or water closets, but it would be no better to have intake shafts above the roof, exposed to exhaust and smoke flues. Other examples are given of poorly designed or placed air-intake shafts and of wire screens blocked by all manner of foreign matter. Dwellings located on burials grounds, swamps, and refuse dumps are described. Air ducts underground in such locations must be constructed to remain air tight. The author advocates filtration and disinfection of all air used in ventilating apparatus. It is recommended that a board of sanitary experts, who are also heating engineers, should approve all proposed systems of heating and ventilation prior to their installation. Yearly inspections of heating appliances are encouraged.

Basis for selection: Discussion of indoor environment problems before we knew what they were all about.

Source: *ASHVE Transactions*, Vol. VI, p. 59-68

1901

Some Notes on Central Station Heating

By William H. Bryan

(Member of the Society.)

Heating from central plants is not new, although the subject has only recently begun to attract extended notice. Nevertheless, the outlook is one of great promise. It is, of course, only feasible in cities of some magnitude, where large commercial buildings or residences are concentrated, and so located as to be readily reached from a central station. The author examines available literature on central station heating, finding much of it written by promoters of particular systems, and, thus, was not impartial. Many data were faulty and misleading. Although many methods of central station heating have been employed, they have been reduced to practically two: steam and hot water. Experiments with hot air, gas, and electricity were not very successful, had limited application, or showed the system to be costly and inefficient.

Basis for selection: Good examination of problems with early central heating systems.

Source: *ASHVE Transactions*, Vol. VII, p. 97-131

1902

Hospitals For Contagious Diseases and Their Ventilation

By Thomas Barwick

(Member of the Society.)

Hospitals for treating contagious diseases should be constructed without the cost of construction or cost of operation being the first requisite. The general health of the public should be considered first and above all other circumstances. In supplying air to such a building, it is necessary to have a very large volume, so that the percentage of vitiated air will be kept to a very low degree. For buildings of this class I should recommend not less than 5,000 to 6,000 cubic feet of air per hour for each occupant. The vitiated air from the various rooms should be collected through vertical flues carried down to the basement connecting into sealed ducts formed of brick or terracotta, and the inside of each flue and duct should be enamelled or finished in similar manner to the heat flues. The vitiated air should be collected into a receiving chamber and passed through a disinfector, in which the air should be burned.

Basis for selection: Early disclosure of the need for very clean air (the clean-room concept).

Source: *ASHVE Transactions*, Vol. VIII, p. 61-73

1903

COOLING AN AUDITORIUM BY THE USE OF ICE

BY JOHN J. HARRIS

(MEMBER OF THE SOCIETY.)

Two days prior to commencement at a high school in 1901, the author was asked to devise a method to keep the auditorium temperature comfortable. The auditorium was 80 feet by 80 feet by 20 feet high. A rack to hold about 8 tons of ice was constructed in the fresh air inlet. The ice was staggered so that the air had to pass around and between the cakes of ice until it was discharged by the fan through the flues into the auditorium above. The flues were located at each side of the stage and above the dressing rooms. Foul air exited through registers in the floor of the aisles. The outside temperatures was 90 F and the inside temperatures was maintained at 76 F. The humidity did not reach the point of saturation. Over 3 nights the amount of ice melted was 38,400 pounds. Calcium chloride was used to control the humidity.

Basis for selection: Fascinating example of the early use of ice for comfort cooling.

Source: *ASHVE Transactions*, Vol. IX, p. 179-187

1904

THE NECESSITY OF MOISTURE IN HEATED HOUSES

BY R.C. CARPENTER

(MEMBER OF THE SOCIETY.)

The human body requires a higher temperature to be comfortable if the relative humidity of the air is lower. Dry air removes moisture from furniture and shrinks woodwork. The air in heated houses can have a relative humidity as low as 12 to 15 percent, which is drier than that in deserts in Asia and Africa. It would be an interesting question to know what effect the dry air in our inhabited rooms has upon the health of the occupants. Mr. W.W. Johnson, of Milwaukee, has invented an instrument that he terms "the humidistat" which automatically supplies the necessary moisture for maintaining a constant degree of humidity. In the circular issued by the Johnson Service Company, who are putting this instrument on the market, we find the following statements regarding the effect of dry air: Medical authorities tell us that the physiological symptoms of an atmosphere too dry are parched lips and tongue; a dry, feverish condition of the skin; baldness and the breaking and splitting of hair.

Basis for selection: Ahead of its time in advocating humidification.

Source: *ASHVE Transactions*, Vol. X, p. 129-136

1905

GAS AS A FUEL FOR HOT-AIR HEATING

BY R.S. THOMSON

(MEMBER OF THE SOCIETY.)

For cleanliness, convenience of management and economy of labor, gas is the ideal fuel. I believe the day is not far distant when the householder would no more think of fitting his cellar with coal in order to supply his house with heat than he would of putting a slaughter house in his cellar in order to supply his family with meat. To use gas successfully and economically in hot air heating, the following are necessary: Use a burner that ensures complete combustion and does not permit the production of carbon monoxide; provide sufficient surface to reduce the products of combustion to a temperature below 212F before they leave the furnace to condense the steam; pass sufficient air through the furnace to remove heat efficiently from the products of combustion; and remove the condensed water, which contains such corrosive products as sulfuric acid. I have been called to "sick furnaces" where the trouble was that the lower flues had become completely filled with water.

Basis for selection: Early recognition of use of natural gas as a fuel for heating residences.

Source: *ASHVE Transactions*, Vol. XI, p. 52-63

1906

HORSE POWER PER TON OF REFRIGERATION OF AMMONIA COMPRESSION MACHINES

BY THOMAS SHIPLEY, YORK, PA.

(MEMBER OF THE SOCIETY.)

It is important that the engineering fraternity adopt standard conditions under which a ton of refrigeration shall be calculated. Until such a standard is adopted no standard of power required per ton of refrigeration can be arrived at. Every manufacturer, every expert and every owner has a standard of his own; to wit, his own likes and dislikes. Some of the specifications that have come to my notice should be framed as monuments of either the ignorance or the dishonesty of the men who got them up. We are standing in our own light if we do not do everything we can to advance the profession we have adopted, and every fact and item of data made public makes it harder for the "quack" expert, whether in the guise of manufacturer, salesman or consulting engineer to fool a purchaser.

Basis for selection: Discussion of the lack of standard conditions for the measurement of the horsepower required per ton of refrigeration for ammonia.

Source: *ASRE Transactions*, Vol. II, p. 154-176

1907

Heating and Ventilating of Cars

By E.R. Swan

(Non-member of the Society. Presented by request.)

In building ventilation there is never a fixed point to work from. The wind is changeable. With a car it is different. We are always sure of the air entering the inlet if it faces in the direction the car is moving. The reason car ventilation has not been more successful is the ventilation engineer had not been called upon to solve the problem. One cent for each passenger carried on the railroads for one year would ventilate every passenger car in the U.S. The deck is of no use as a ventilator. An apparatus can be installed in each car which automatically controls the volume of air which enters and exits the car. Surely the poor man or woman who is obliged to ride in the coach is as much entitled to pure air to breathe as is the wealthy passenger who resides in the Pullman. Fresh air is too cheap and the supply is too large to be stingy of it.

Basis for selection: Early consideration of methods for the heating and ventilation of railroad cars.

Source: *ASHVE Transactions*, Vol. XIII, p. 169-186

1908

Ethyl Chloride Refrigeration

By C.C. Palmer, New York, N.Y.

(Member of the Society.)

Ethyl chloride approaches nearer to the ideal chemical for refrigeration than any other now in use. This is on account of its stability and the ease with which it can be handled in a machine, and also that in the very near future it will be manufactured from denatured alcohol, free from Government tax, which will make its cost practically the same as several of the other chemicals used in mechanical refrigeration. Ethyl chloride belongs to that class of chemicals in which the work must be done under partial vacuum, and consequently, the machine must be correctly proportioned and the compressor so constructed that there is no possibility of air being taken into the system.

Basis for selection: Early discussion of the use of ethyl chloride as a refrigerant.

Source: *ASRE Transactions*, Vol. IV, p. 73-88

1909

The Value of the "Flooded System" and Its Application to Ice-Making and Refrigerating Plants

By H. Rassbach, Milwaukee, Wis.

(Non-Member of the Society.)

The flooded system defines a method of supplying liquid anhydrous ammonia to the freezing coils or other vessels in which the evaporation of the refrigerant takes place. The flooded system is especially adapted for plants in which a large number or set of coils are operated in unison-an arrangement which we generally find in all ice manufacturing plants and which may readily be provided for refrigerating plants used for other purposes. The mechanical appliances necessary for the successful application of the flooded system must consist of a reservoir inserted into the suction line of a refrigeration apparatus, in which the entrained liquid, returning from the freezing coils, is intercepted-a cooling device by which the temperature of the liquid supply, while held under high pressure, is reduced to that which conforms to the low pressure of the system, and a pipe connection between the elevated accumulator and the supply or distributing header connecting the freezing coils, through which the liquid will flow by its own gravity to freezing coils.

Basis for selection: Interesting description of the original "flooded ammonia system" which was used for many later years.

Source: *ASRE Transactions*, Vol. V, p. 95-128

1910

Heating and Ventilation of Federal Buildings

By Nelson S. Thomson

(Member of the Society.)

In all buildings equipped with a plenum fan the practice is to install an air washer, as such devices are looked upon as the most essential feature of a successful ventilating apparatus. Many of the old ventilating apparatuses were a failure on account of the inability of the dry-air filter to cleanse the air properly. When funds are available a first-class automatic temperature-controlling apparatus is installed in the larger buildings. Aside from comfort, a saving of not less than 10 percent in the coal pile is secured. The simple one-pipe gravity return steam-heating system operating at atmosphere pressure has given us the best service. In large buildings, where an electric generating plant is to be installed, our practice is to install a vacuum system with a pump or injector. These devices are a valuable and economical adjunct to such a plant.

Basis for selection: Description of heating and ventilation systems of the early 1900's.

Source: *ASHVE Transactions*, Vol. XVI, p. 266-288

1911

Standards of Ventilation

By W.A. Evans, M.D.

(Non-Member of the Society, Presented by Request.)

A standard should be "such that no inhabitant should be harmed immediately or ultimately by the air of the place ventilated." In order that this may be brought about it is necessary that every factor be standardized. A standard of ventilation must consist of many standards: dust content, humidity, temperature, carbon dioxide content, odor, feel of the air, volume of air per inhabitant, cubic feet of space per inhabitant, air currents, and bacterial content.

Basis for selection: Development of the earliest standards (codes) applicable to heating and ventilating systems.

Source: *ASHVE Transactions*, Vol. XVII, p. 126-148

1912

Relative Humidity – Its Effect on Comfort and Health

By J.I. Lyle

(Non-Member of the Society, Presented by Request.)

The anti-tuberculosis movement has alerted the public to the danger of procuring contagious diseases from dust. This has lead to the development of means for dust elimination such as air washers. Simple, reliable methods for accurate humidity regulation have also been developed. After a review of the literature on humidity, the author concludes: (1) there is probably not an exact humidity that should be maintained for health and comfort, although extremes should be avoided; (2) low humidities require higher temperatures for comfort; (3) low humidities are detrimental to health; (4) high humidity in cold weather can cause excessive condensation on windows that runs down over woodwork and wall decorations; (5) in cold weather, the relative humidity should be maintained between 35 and 45 percent; (6) cooling by evaporation can make a building more comfortable in hot weather than the natural conditions; (7) physicians and scientists should investigate to determine the relative humidity and temperature best suited to the comfort and health of most people.

Basis for selection: Early reference to the impact relative humidity has on comfort and health.

Source: *ASHVE Transactions*, Vol. XVIII, p. 106-127

1913

Ozone and Its Applications

By Dr. M.W. Franklin

Ozone will reduce the odors in a way that ventilation cannot. There are cases, of course, where the thing can be taken care of entirely by proper ventilation; but there are cases, many of them in shops and in factories, where no system of aspirating the atmosphere from the room will destroy the odor. In tunnels, glue factories, rendering plants, fertilizer plants, intestine dealers' plants, and slaughter houses only the use of ozone can produce the result that is aimed at; namely destruction of the odor. The steamship Imperator which will be launched in May, the greatest steamship in the world, bigger than the Titanic, is equipped from stem to stem with an ozone system. Ozone is injected into the air so that the amount of forced ventilation required is reduced greatly. Ozone destroys and in nowise masks offensive odors.

Basis for selection: Discussion of the "almost magical" ability of ozone to control odors.

Source: *ASHVE Transactions*, Vol. XIX, p. 128-140

1914

Flow of Steam in Pipes

By W.F. Verner

In making a careful study of the flow of steam in pipes, the author learned that several equations have been evolved for use in such calculations, but unfortunately have been seldom used due to the difficulty of solution. The author put these fundamental equations and put them in such a form that logarithmic charts may be made, as by so doing the solution of various problems is made much simpler.

Discussion: I would say a word more. I appreciate very much what has been brought out by this paper. That is one reason why I gave it - I wanted it cut to pieces. And I hope that they will keep on cutting it, and I hope it goes into the record with some scars on it, and I hope it will be brought up again. We need work in this subject.

Basis for selection: Early tabulation of the flow of steam in various sizes of pipes and corresponding friction losses. The data, although updated, are still used today for sizing of steam pipes.

Source: *ASHVE Transactions*, Vol. XX, p. 151-185

1915

A Theory of Cooling Towers Compared with Results in Practice

By B.H. Coffey and George A. Horne, New York, N.Y.

(Associate Members of the Society)

A mathematical expression of evaporation in cooling towers due to free contact with the atmosphere is presented. In discussion Edwin Burhorn comments that instead of taking enormous numbers of daily readings, as was done by the authors of this paper, better results could be obtained by using recording instruments, which would make a daily chart, showing all variations. Such instruments are obtainable for recording water temperatures, dry and wet bulb temperatures, ammonia pressures, etc. The principle of cooling towers is pretty well understood. We find refrigerating plants operating with enormous water bills or very heavy coal bills due to excessive pumping, etc. The trouble is that engineers have not taken sufficient interest in the subject of cooling towers and have not sufficiently studied the question of under what conditions will a cooling tower be a profitable investment.

Basis for selection: First quantification of cooling tower performance problems predicting and proving cooling tower performance still exist.

Source: *ASRE Journal*, Vol. 1, No. 2, p. 71-89

1916

Can We Standardize the Requirements for Ventilation?

By J.J. Blackmore, New York

(Member)

It may be possible to arrive at a standard for the factors of ventilation by contrasting the air in buildings with that of the air outside and by comparing the relative humidity and the lack of air movement in different buildings. One thing seems apparent, and that is the constant changing of all the factors that enter into the problem of ventilation. It may that one of the reasons for the healthfulness of the outside air is the constant changing in the air movement, humidity, temperature, sunlight, etc., that continually take place in the aerial envelope or atmosphere that surrounds the earth. Good ventilation involves cleansing the air, regulating the relative humidity, regulating the temperature, providing adequate air movement, and removing odor.

Basis for selection: One of the first efforts in the standardization of design parameters.

Source: *ASHVE Transactions*, Vol. XXII, p. 375-399

1917

Synthetic Air Chart

By E. Vernon Hill, Chicago, Ill.

Member

The synthetic air chart allows comparison of different installations so that engineers can tell when improvements have been made in equipment. It is a means of charting progress in equipment design.

Basis for selection: Introduction of the Synthetic Air Chart, which considered psychrometric principles and air quality parameters.

Source: *ASHVE Transactions*, Vol. XXIII, p. 225-230

1918

The Argument Concerning Mechanical and Natural Ventilation

By Dr. E. Vernon Hill, Chicago, Ill.

Member

There is no more quarrel between natural and mechanical ventilation than there is between natural and mechanical water supply. There are places, particularly rural, where natural ventilation is satisfactory, when the space per occupant and window area are adequate, the outside air is uncontaminated, and the noise is not excessive. Other places require mechanical methods of ventilation. Tests for the quality of ventilation made by the Ventilation Division of the Chicago Health Department show that the antiquated and inefficient "so called natural methods" are not always best. Man's skin does not provide adequate protection from the elements, but he is endowed with a brain, which he is expected to use for correcting and improving his condition.

Basis for selection: Discussion of the case for mechanical ventilation versus that for natural or "open window" ventilation.

Source: *ASHVE Journal*, Vol. 24, No. 5, p. 737-742

1919

Code for the Regulation of Refrigerating Machines and Refrigerants

The code, presented to several municipalities, applies to every refrigerating machine employing ammonia, carbon dioxide, ethyl chloride or sulphur dioxide as a refrigerant. Section 3 requires automatic by-pass valves. Section 5 requires emergency means for discharging the refrigerant in case of fire. Section 8 requires helmets and respirators for certain refrigeration plants. Section 9 excludes flames, arc lights and gas jets from refrigerating machine rooms using ammonia or ethyl chloride. Section 10 requires rooms for refrigerating machines to have direct exit to the open air or to a room or hall from which gases can be excluded. Section 11 requires cylinders containing refrigerant to be stored in cool, well ventilated places, remote from fire danger.

Basis for selection: Presentation of the first safety code for mechanical refrigeration.

Source: *ASRE Journal*, Vol. 5, No. 4, p. 310-316

1920

Refrigeration in Air Conditioning

By Lee Nusbaum, Philadelphia, Pa.

Before the perfection of air conditioning apparatus, or what is also known as air washers or air humidifiers, the only method of reducing the temperature of a room was by means of refrigeration. The refrigerating machinery required for this work ran into large sizes and the costs were such as to make the proposition impracticable commercially. The advent of air conditioning apparatus changed all this. To reduce the temperature of a room from 90 to 70 F could now be done for less than 20% of the cost of the refrigerating apparatus. But the advantages of the use of refrigeration in connection with air washers was quickly recognized because the capacity of the air washer soon became limited by the temperature of the spray water, so that in warm weather the results were cut down. By applying refrigeration to cool the water, the air washer is able to further reduce the temperature of the air and regulate the humidity. It is my belief that every properly designed air conditioning apparatus should be equipped with refrigeration in order to achieve the maximum results and to make it more effective in summer.

Basis for selection: Discussion of the use of refrigeration to make air conditioning more effective.

Source: *ASRE Journal*, Vol. 7, No. 2, p. 170-172

1921

A Plea for Better Air Distribution in Ventilating Systems

By J.R. McColl, Detroit, Mich.

Member

Ventilating engineers now know air movement and humidity are important factors along with temperature in getting rid of body heat. Good air distribution is vital in crowded rooms, such as school rooms, where persons sit for hours at a time where they must be kept comfortable and efficient. Two forces distribute air in a room: gravity and projection. The old blast system distributes air by gravity. In the other, air is distributed by virtue of its velocity. Some systems, like for the Detroit school system, are a combination of both. My experience is that a system deliberately laid out as a gravity system or a projection system or as a combination of the two gives far better uniformity in distribution than systems which are haphazard in their means of control. Ventilating engineers will eventually recirculate a large portion of the air in their schools. Also, I believe that something will be done on what might be called intermittent ventilation. Instead of maintaining continuous and uniform distribution, systems will be designed to give intermittent flow of air, making the maximum delivery velocities much higher than are now in vogue for continuous operation and tapering off to practically nothing before the next impulse.

Basis for selection: Recognition of the role of air motion in human comfort (and discomfort) with a plea for better design of air handling systems.

Source: *ASHVE Journal*, Vol. 27, No. 4, p. 417-419

1922

Cooling of Theatres and Public Buildings

By Fred Wittenmeier, Chicago, Ill.

No one would think of building a theater or a public building without calling in a good heating and ventilating engineer and making sure that the best equipment is installed in order that in cold weather the occupants may be comfortable. Yet it is only comparatively recent that there has been anything more than an occasional attempt at making buildings more comfortable during the hot summer months. Proprietors of theaters have always had to reckon with the falling off of patronage during the summer, and since this often meant a financial loss, steps were finally taken to remedy conditions. Systems in which a spray of ordinary well water was an important part were first tried. But it soon became evident that more flexibility was necessary, so it was at this point that the refrigerating engineer was finally called in. The development of the CO_2 system has helped considerably to make the installation of air-cooling apparatus, possible and profitable.

Basis for selection: Presentation of design parameters for cooling of theatres and public buildings.

Source: *Refrigerating Engineering*, Vol. 9, No. 4, p. 115-118, 132

1923

Determining Equal Comfort Lines

By J.R. F.C. Houghten, Pittsburgh, Pa. (Member) and C.P. Yagloglou, Pittsburgh, Pa. (Non-Member)

Three principal factors affect the loss of body heat: temperature, humidity and air motion. From a consideration of these factors, it is concluded that certain combinations of temperatures, humidities, and air velocities exist that produce the same total body heat loss by radiation, convection and evaporation, and therefore, the same feeling of comfort or discomfort. Lines passing through such air conditions are called equal comfort lines. A study to determine these lines is being conducted at the A.S.H.V.E. Research Laboratory. Four hundred forty similar tests were conducted and the corresponding lines were drawn on the standard psychrometric chart. The angles between these lines and the dry bulb temperature lines were plotted against the dew-point at their intersection with the saturation curve. These points form a definite shape approximating a parabolic curve.

Basis for selection: Exploration of the concept of the comfort zone with lines of equivalent temperature.

Source: *ASHVE Journal*, Vol. 29, No. 2, p. 165-176

1924

Modern Trend in the Science of Ventilation

By Perry West, Newark, N.J.

Member

The basic idea of ventilation today is quality rather than quantity, or the proper conditioning and distribution of a small quantity of air by efficient compact means rather than poor conditioning and distribution of larger quantities with cumbersome apparatus too expensive to be kept in operation. The starting point of the modem trend of ventilation in this country can be traced to the presentation by Dr. W. A. Evans of the Chicago Health Board and Dr. Luther H. Guilick of the Russell Sage Foundation at the 1911 meeting of A.S.H.V.E. It was forcibly brought to light that the great majority of mechanical ventilating systems installed in hospitals, schools, public buildings, etc., were not efficacious and did not produce the comfort and healthful indoor air conditions desired. While the heating and ventilating engineers had been continuously improving and refining the mechanical apparatus and were in a position to furnish most any condition of indoor atmosphere desired, the doctors and physiologists had made little or no progress in the matter of determining just what atmospheric conditions were best suited for the maintenance of proper indoor ventilation. It is now felt that proper ventilation depends on a number of factors which may best be stated in the order of their importance: Air supply, air temperature, air cleanliness, sanitation, relative humidity, distribution, air motion, freedom from odors, freedom from other injurious substances, and freedom from monotony.

Basis for selection: Description of the progress made in designing a ventilating system using scientific methods.

Source: *ASHVE Journal*, Vol. 30, No. 6, p. 421-438

1925

Effective Temperature with Clothing

by C.P. Yaglou (Member) and W. Edw. Miller (Non-Member)

Clothing helps the human body maintain a constant temperature by insulating against heat loss. Heat loss by radiation and convection is reduced, but heat loss by evaporation may increase because of the greater surface afforded by the clothing. The rate clothing transfers heat depends upon the material and its thickness, mesh size and condition of wetness or dryness. The experiments were performed using garments of medium thickness and mesh size. Equivalent conditions of temperature, humidity and air movement were determined with normally clothed individuals who were slightly active. Considerable effort was made to present the results in a simple, practical chart that could be used by those not proficient in the use of psychrometric charts or complicated figures. The human thermometric chart may be used to determine the sensible or effective temperature for normally clothed individuals from measurements of the dry-bulb and wet-bulb temperature and the air velocity.

Basis for selection: Early discussion of the concept of effective temperature, which helped engineers design comfortable systems.

Source: *ASHVE Transactions*, Vol. 31, p. 89-99

1926

Forced Hot Water System Heats Ford's Twin Cities Plant

by E.H. Whittemore, Boston, Mass.

Member

Millions of cubic feet are warmed by a forced hot water heating system using both cast-iron radiation and pipe coils, with one room in the office section using unit heaters. The total heat loss for the building is 123,338,000 B.t.u. per hour. To compensate for this loss, approximately 480,000 sq. ft. of direct radiation was installed: 440,000 sq. ft. in 1 1/2 pipe coils and 40,000 sq. ft. in cast-iron radiation of both column and wall type. A large part of the heating surface was placed overhead in the roof trusses to compensate for large heat losses through the roof and overhead sash areas and to avoid interfering with the installation of machinery.

Basis for selection: First known use of forced hot water in a large industrial plant.

Source: *ASHVE Transactions*, Vol. 32, p. 49-58

1927

Ten Fundamentals of Unit Ventilation and Their Application

by A.J. Nesbitt, Atlantic City, N.J.

Member

There are several important requirements to be met in the design of a unit system. First, to obtain the best results, the unit should be placed along the outside wall and in the center of the wall. Second, care should be used in locating the vent flue or vent outlet so that it is not on a direct line opposite the ventilating unit. Third, vent flue areas should be restricted to 20 sq. in. cross section of flue area per 100 cu. ft. of air. Fourth, where thermostatic control is used it is important that the thermostat be located as nearly as possible on a direct line opposite the ventilating unit. Fifth, where conditions permit, use the blast system, and in no case provide sufficient radiation to heat the room independent of the ventilating unit.

Basis for selection: Early history of the use of classroom unit ventilators.

Source: *ASHVE Transactions*, Vol. 33, p. 319-331

1928

Refrigeration as Applied to Air Conditioning

by R.W. Waterfill, Newark, N.J.

Non-Member

Air conditioning, including dehumidification, passed out of the experimental stage long ago. While the refrigerating requirements for air conditioning involve the same basic principles as for other refrigerating work, there are differences which make it desirable to treat air conditioning refrigeration from a different point of view than that considered in ice making or other low temperature work. The differences are primarily that air conditioning refrigeration requires very large heat capacitates, which need to be handled only at low temperature heads. Ice making and other low temperature work ordinarily require that the heat be pumped through a much greater temperature range. The analogy to which this might be compared is the use of fans for handling large volumes of air at low pressure differences, as against compressors designed to handle small quantities of air but at relatively high compression ratios.

Basis for selection: Discussion of the use of refrigeration for cooling and dehumidification instead of for making ice.

Source: *ASHVE Transactions*, Vol. 34, p. 503-517

1929

Air Conditioning System of a Detroit Office Building

By Hiram L. Walton and Leslie L. Smith, Detroit, Mich.

Members

The Bank and Trust Co. were not oblivious to the comfort of their customers, and it was recognized than an air conditioning installation would also have some advertising value for these institutions, but it was believed that comfort for their employees and working conditions that would contribute most to their health and efficiency were considerations that gave the greatest opportunity for return on any investment that might be made. It was further recognized that there was some element of perfection in having air conditioning, and which would not be out of keeping with the building and its appointments, and the standard of business conducted in it. All features considered, it was concluded that it was well worthwhile to have the air conditioning at the investment and operating costs that would be incurred. The additional investment was estimated at $130,000. The operating costs, exclusive of maintenance were estimated at $9,600 per year. Allowing annual fixed charges, including maintenance at 11 per cent, the total annual cost of the air conditioning feature over that which straight ventilation would have cost, amounted to $23,900. It will be noted that the operating costs do not include any time for attendance, it being concluded that the air conditioning would not result in any additions to the operating force.

Basis for selection: Installation of a combined cooling, dehumidification, and heating system in a high-rise building.

Source: *ASHVE Transactions*, Vol. 35, p. 377-398

1930

Air Conditioning for Summer and Winter Comfort

By W.H. Carrier, Newark, N.J.

Member

The author predicts that the future of air conditioning lies not in the application to theaters, department stores and office buildings, but to the home. Here is where a great part of a person's time is spent. Extremes of temperature and excessive variability should be prevented. Extreme dryness in winter is to be avoided. Relief from the torrid days of summer is desirable when it can be afforded. The ordinary steam or hot air heating system of today is somewhat crude, as it is designed primarily for the lowest first cost rather than for either comfort or the best economy. It seems inevitable that someday the average householder will be able to press a button in winter and produce a climate in his home rivaling the pleasant days of Florida, and press another button in the summer to bring the invigorating and bracing air of the mountains and the seashore to his abode.

Basis for selection: Stresses the comfort air conditioning provides in summer and winter.

Source: *ASHVE Journal*, Vol. 2, No. 9, p. 783-787

1931

Utilization of Hot Springs for Heating in Iceland

By Ben Gröndal, Reykjavik, Iceland

Member

If Iceland's natural heat sources were properly utilized, this North Atlantic Island would not need to import any fuels. Farmsteads, school buildings and a sanitorium are now heated by water from hot springs or subterranean steam. Plans are now underway to heat buildings in Reykjavik, the island's largest city.

Basis for selection: Early use of geothermal energy.

Source: *ASHVE Journal*, Vol. 3, No. 2, p. 174-178

1932

Field Studies of Office Building Cooling

By J.H. Walker, S.S. Sanford (Members) and E.P. Wells (Non-Member), Detroit, Mich.

Sunshine through the window glass is apparently the most important factor to contend with in the cooling of a room. At times it may account for as much as 75 percent of the total cooling necessary. Because of the importance of the sunshine, cooling systems should be zoned so that the side of the building on which the sun is shining can be controlled separately from the other sides of the building. Consideration should also be given to shadows from nearby buildings which may cover part of the sunny side of a building. If buildings were provided with awnings so that the window glass was shielded from sunshine, the amount of cooling required would be reduced and there would also be less difference in the cooling requirements of the different sides of the building.

Basis for selection: A report on how successful some early office buildings air conditioning systems were.

Source: *ASHVE Journal*, Vol. 4, No. 2, p. 125-137

1933

Natural Gas Engine Power in the Refrigerating Plant

By C.T. Baker

The natural gas engine has contributed a great measure of help in lowering the cost of producing a ton of ice or a ton of refrigeration, as well as lowering the cost of producing electric power. Recent years have seen a dedicated increase in natural gas distribution from all of the gas producing fields, and natural gas is now available at attractive prices in many sections of the country. This has led to a wide use of the gas engine as a prime mover in ice and cold storage plants as well as in municipal and privately owned electric power stations in localities where gas is available. This paper discusses a few installations in Georgia.

Basis for selection: Early discussion of the use of natural gas as fuel for an engine-driven refrigeration plant.

Source: *Refrigerating Engineering*, Vol. 26, No. 2, p. 65-67, 102

1934

Thermodynamic Properties of Moist Air

By John A. Goff (Non-Member), Urbana, Ill.

The heating and ventilating engineer already possesses sufficient information, mostly in the form of psychrometric charts, to enable him to deal effectively with most problems in his field involving properties of atmospheric air. This being true, it may appear quite unnecessary to attempt a further contribution on this subject. Still, much of the information, although capable of yielding approximate results of practical value, is, in some cases incorrect and sometimes leads to impossible conclusions if used without discretion. Consequently, an attempt to work out a thermodynamically consistent treatment of the properties of atmospheric air based on best available thermal data written in the language of thermodynamics, but yet reduced to a form which allows quick and easy application may possibly find favor with even the more practical-minded engineer.

Basis for selection: Important contribution to the science of psychrometrics.

Source: *ASHVE Journal*, Vol. 6, No. 3, p. 117-123

1935

Heat Absorbing Glass Windows

By W.W. Shaver, Corning, N.Y.

Non-Member

A reduction in the cooling load varying from 9 to 28.5 per cent was observed in a test house equipped with heat-absorbing heat-resisting glass used as an outside window with ordinary glass in the inside sash and from 16 to 24 percent with a single heat-absorbing glazing. With air conditioning equipment in operation, maximum recording thermometers with blackened bulbs, suspended inside the windows in the sunshine, averaged 10.4 F lower when heat absorbing glass was used. Heat required in a 10-day period in a winter test was approximately 9 percent more in a test house having double windows with heat-absorbing glass in the outside sash as compared with a similar house having ordinary window glass in the outside sash.

Basis for selection: Report of pioneering research on the use of heat-absorbing glass to reduce the impact of solar heat gain on a building and its air conditioning system.

Source: *ASHVE Transactions* Vol. 41, p. 287-298

1936

Progress in Air Conditioning in the Last Quarter Century

By W.H. Carrier, Newark, N.J.

Member

In retrospect we have seen the progress of air conditioning development marked off in decades. 1901 marks the end of what might be termed The

Azoic Age of air conditioning. Ten years later, in 1911, air conditioning was acknowledged as a new art by the engineering profession. By 1921 the first successful modern type of installation for public comfort was designed. The beginning of the development of unitary equipment extending the benefits of air conditioning to small users came in 1931. Without thought of prophecy the year 1941 can be anticipated as marking the probable beginning of commercial success and public acceptance of complete air conditioning in the residential field.

Basis for selection: Historically significant summary of air-conditioning progress during a seminal twenty-five year period in the development of cooling coils, psychrometrics, refrigeration equipment, and air-conditioning installations.

Source: *ASHVE Transactions* Vol. 42, p. 321-348

1937

Performance of Fin-Tube Units for Air Cooling and Dehumidifying

By G.L. Tuve and C.A. McKeeman, Cleveland, Ohio

Members

This paper compares several methods used for expressing the cooling and dehumidifying capacities of surface coils. Test results indicate that many of the simple methods of calculating surface-coil ratings are only approximations. It is also demonstrated that accurate ratings call for much experimental work of a very precise nature and for involved calculations to interpret the results. It is because this accuracy requires more time than the practicing engineer or the manufacturer can devote to the problem that a program of cooperative research along these lines has been undertaken.

Basis for selection: Summary of important research on fin-tube cooling coils. Based on test data from ASHVE labs, criteria are defined for selecting and rating cooling coils for temperature control and dehumidification.

Source: *ASHVE Transactions* Vol. 43, p. 367-388

1938

Effects of Artificial Lighting on Air Conditioning

By Walter Sturrock, Cleveland, Ohio

Non-Member

For lighting systems employing the usual type of luminaries placed below the ceiling, it is mechanically possible to install a ventilating system with air ducts to the units so that the maximum of about one-third the total generated energy can be removed. With the so-called built-in types of lighting equipment where a free circulation of air is provided around the lamp, the amount of heat carried off will depend upon the heat transmission characteristics of the glass through which the light enters the room. If none of the energy generated by the lighting is carried off by the ventilating system, it is estimated that from 50 to 90 percent of it will eventually become a part of the cooling load. In the author's opinion, the cost of an elaborate auxiliary ventilation system for this purpose is not economically justified for the present standards of lighting.

Basis for selection: Early discussion of the interaction of lighting and air conditioning. Description of the first installation to exhaust air through lighting fixtures to remove heat.

Source: *ASHVE Transactions* Vol. 44, p. 213-244

1939

Application of Summer Weather Data in Design

By John Everetts, Jr., New York, N.Y.

Member

The practical application of weather design data in air conditioning is demonstrated. Following determination of the transmission load, ventilation load, solar radiation load, and internal load, the air conditioning apparatus is chosen. The choice is influenced by the dry-bulb, wet-bulb and dew point temperatures, depending on the system selected. An air washer system, which is affected only by the wet-bulb temperature, need only be designed for a total heat removal from entering to leaving wet-bulb. A chemical dehumidifying system is affected by both wet-bulb and dew-point. Cooling coil capacities are affected by dry-bulb, wet-bulb and dew-point temperatures. The dry-bulb affects the mean effective temperature between the air and coil surface; the total heat removal of the coil reflects the wet-bulb; and the dew-point varies the transfer rate of the coil by changing the sensible-latent heat ratio.

Basis for selection: Report of pioneering work on the selection of weather data and procedures to use in sizing different types of air-conditioning apparatus for economy and adequate performance.

Source: *ASHVE Transactions* Vol. 45, p. 431-440

1940

Chemical Dehumidification Agents

by F.R. Bichowsky, (Member), Ann Arbor, Mich.

Selection of a drying agent for chemical dehumidification requires consideration of several balancing factors. A comparison of various solid absorbents is given, showing amount of water absorbed at varying relative humidities. Equipment suitable for the use of solid absorbents utilizing the stationary and movable bed principles is described. Engineering data are outlined for absorbents in solution and for concentrations necessary to maintain constant relative humidities. Dehydration may be combined with evaporative cooling, refrigeration, and solvent recovery to give a great number of combination systems.

Basis for selection: First comprehensive paper on desiccant dehumidification as applied to air conditioning that discusses and compares the whole range of desiccant dehumidification options, liquid as well as solid.

Source: *ASHVE Journal,* Vol. 12, No. 10, p. 627-632

1941

Panel Cooling and Heating Analysis

by B.F. Raber and F.W. Hutchinson, Berkeley, Calif.

(Members of ASHVE)

A rational method is outlined of analyzing panel heating problems and setting up general equations leading to a determination of the mean radiant and inside air temperatures corresponding to a fixed panel temperature and a known outside temperature. It is shown (1) that the air temperature in a radiant conditioned room is a function of the MRT and cannot be arbitrarily fixed if comfort is to be realized; (2) that the MRT can be calculated by solving simultaneously the heat balance equations for each different type of interior surface and for the ventilation air; and (3) that the error likely to result from application of equations for a simple ideal system to a complex real system may be great.

Basis for selection: Important early paper on analysis and methodology for designing radiant heating and cooling systems.

Source: *ASHVE Transactions,* Vol. 47, p. 285-308

1942

Use of Cold Accumulators in the Air Conditioning Field

by R.W. Evans (Member) and C.J. Otterholm, Minneapolis, Minn.

The cold accumulator was first developed to store refrigeration effect to meet the short refrigeration demands of the dairy industry. Many types of air conditioning work have similar needs for a refrigeration storage battery. Data for the determination of peak cooling demand are insufficient for the selection of accumulator equipment, which is dependent upon the total cooling demand in a 24-hour period. New factors, such as accumulated degree-hours and accumulated sun intensity values, are introduced for accurate determination of the total cooling load. The performance characteristics of one type of cold accumulator, its application to air conditioning loads of several types, and economies obtainable with this method of cooling are discussed.

Basis for selection: First ASHVE paper on the application of ice thermal storage to air-conditioning systems.

Source: *ASHVE Transactions,* Vol. 48, p. 123-144

1943

Controlled Air Supply for Supercharger, Carburetor and Engine Testing - Adsorption Dehumidification and Sensible Cooling by Well Water and Refrigeration

by Charles S. Leopold, Philadelphia, Pa.

An apparatus was designed for and installed at Ranger Aircraft Engines to deliver air to the test blocks at any required dew point at or below saturation. The apparatus provides for 25,000 lb per hour of aviation standard air at 60 F and –45 F dew point, of which 12,500 lb can be cooled to –67 F without visible condensation or frost. Low temperature refrigeration is not required for the production of standard air. The process involves precooling and dehydration by silica gel, with 3-stage low temperature refrigeration for further cooling as required. Dry conditions are used for the major portion of the air treatment. The use of antifreeze sprays, rectifiers, and electric or other reheat is avoided. The electrical demand for the method is less than for an all-refrigeration method.

Basis for selection: Early analysis comparing silica gel desiccant dehumidification with low-temperature refrigerated dehumidification for industrial process air conditioning.

Source: *Refrigerating Engineering,* Vol. 46, No. 2m p. 85-87, 118

1944

Description and Performance of Two Heat Pump Air Conditioning Systems (Using Well Water and Outside Air as the Heat Source)

by Philip Sporn and E.R. Ambrose (Member), New York, N.Y.

The authors compare air and water source heat pumps operated in Ohio. They conclude that the heat pump, properly engineered and installed from an application and design standpoint, is even now a wholly practical device to furnish year-round all-electric air conditioning service. Its further development should make it even more so.

Basis for selection: Documentation of the performance of early heat pump installations for building heating and cooling.

Source: *ASHVE Transactions,* Vol. 50, p. 405-424

1945

Airborne Perishables Need Temperature Control

by Dr. Spencer A. Larsen, Wayne University, Detroit

Tests comparing the transport of perishables by air and by rail were conducted. The perishables were evaluated for such factors as appearance, eating quality, Vitamin C content, and sugar content. Even in the transport by air, the need for refrigeration is emphasized. Fruits and vegetables that are to be shipped by air can be allowed to ripen on the vine, but they must be carefully wrapped and packaged.

Basis for selection: Emphasizes the need for refrigeration of perishables, even with speedy transportation by air.

Source: *Refrigerating Engineering,* Vol. 50, No. 1, p. 17-20, 54

1946

Dehumidification: Methods and Applications

by John Everetts, Jr., San Fransisco, CA

Prior to World War II, the use of sorbents in the air conditioning industry was secondary. During the war, use of sorbents received tremendous impetus. Today, industry is recognizing the importance and economic value of dehumidification. Charts are presented for determining relative costs of sorbents vs. refrigeration. Dehumidification is primarily an engineering subject. No credence should be given to rule-of-thumb methods now being used.

Basis for selection: Discussion of how more efficient use of sorbents was predicted to make dehumidification an industry.

Source: *ASHVE Journal,* Vol. 18, No. 12, p. 121-124

1947

Conditions for Comfort

by Charles S. Leopold (Member), Philadelphia, Pa.

The definition of comfort is the absence of discomfort or annoyances due to temperature and atmospheric effects indoors. The definition includes the effects of radiation, air temperatures, water vapor, odor and air motion. In this definition, considerations of health, deliberate stimulation and lowering of activity are not primary factors in optimum comfort or minimum discomfort. Interpretations and limitations of comfort charts and their revisions are discussed, along with the discomfort chart.

Basis for selection: First known report on a comfort zone psychrometric chart with backup data.

Source: *ASHVE Transactions,* Vol. 53, p. 295-306

1948

Friction Equivalents for Round, Square and Rectangular Ducts

by R.G. Huebscher (Member), Cleveland, Ohio

The design of a ventilating or air conditioning system requires the use of rectangular duct work. Friction loss data on the ducts are essential for design purposes. Air friction charts for round ducts are available. This paper presents a relationship between rectangular and circular ducts enabling the design engineer to better estimate the resistance of rectangular ducts in terms of their circular equivalents and the new friction chart. The paper also gives the results of an investigation using three ducts of different form, each of 8 in. equivalent diameter: 8 in. round, 8 in. square and 4.5 by 36 in. rectangular (8:1 aspect ratio). Air velocities ranged from 300 to 9310 fpm. For most practical purposes, the three ducts were identical in flow resistance at equal velocities.

Basis for selection: Presentation of an essential design tool for air duct design that saves a lot of time.

Source: *ASHVE Transactions,* Vol. 54, p. 101-118

1949

Psychrometric Factors in the Air Conditioning Estimate

by C.M. Ashley (Member), Syracuse, N.Y.

The author's method of estimating summer air conditioning load and selecting equipment is presented and compared with other methods. The author discusses the approach to the estimate, sensible and latent heat, sensible heat factor, apparatus dew point and chart, coil bypass factor, airside coil performance, overall coil performance, problems due to outside air, and calculation of the air conditioning estimate. Appendixes cover derivation of the bypass factor and derivation of the sensible heat, latent heat, total heat, and sensible heat factor.

Basis for selection: Discussion of the psychrometric factors that affect the final calculated cooling load.

Source: *ASHVE Transactions,* Vol. 55, p. 91-110

1950

Physiologic Examination of the Effective Temperature Index

by Nathaniel Glickman (Member), Tohru Inouye, Robert W. Keeton, M.D. (Member) Chicago, Ill., and Maurice K. Fahnestock (Member), Urbana, Ill.

In recent years, investigators have indicated that the effective temperature index places too much emphasis on the influence of relative humidity in determining sensations of warmth and coolness at temperatures customarily encountered in heating and ventilating practice and too little emphasis at the high temperatures. Fifteen healthy young adult male students, clothed in 90 percent cotton union suits and wood sandals, were subjects for the experiments. Each of the subjects was exposed to two ambient environments having the same effective temperature, although only seven subjects comprised a group for study at each effective temperature. In general, the results suggest that the present effective temperature index is adequate for subjects in the dynamic state except for correction at the higher temperatures. For subjects in a steady state room, the present effective temperature index places too much emphasis on the influence of relative humidity for the range of ambient conditions studied.

Basis for selection: Examination of new thoughts and data on current effective temperatures still in use today.

Source: *ASHVE Transactions,* Vol. 56, p. 51-74

1951

Transportation Heating and Air Conditioning Systems and Controls

by Norman O. Kirkby, Chicago, Ill.

Even though it is not a high mass production, highly competitive industry, the field of transportation heating, ventilating and air conditioning has offered valuable contributions to this field of engineering. More and more applications of individual engine generator sets on passenger cars are being made to solve the problems of increased electrical loads. Propane engines are used on some railroads for generating electrical energy and also for air conditioning. Much work is being done on diesel engine generator sets and in some cases, the waste heat from the diesel engine is being recovered. Modem street cars make use of otherwise wasted heat from dynamic brakes and by means of thermostatically controlled dampers, either reject the heat or admit it into the car body.

Basis for selection: Discussion of the status of heating and air conditioning systems used in various modes of transportation.

Source: *ASHVE Transactions,* Vol. 57, p. 275-286

1952

Performance of a Warm-Air Radial-Feeder Perimeter-Loop System in a Residence

by M.E. Childs, R.W. Roose (Associate Member) and S. Konzo (Member), Urbana, Ill.

The construction of homes provided with a concrete slab floor laid on the ground has introduced such difficulties as cold floor surfaces and condensation on these surfaces. The use of conventional warm-air heating systems has not completely solved the problem of cold floors. On the basis of research obtained with four separate arrangements for the radial-feeder perimeter system it was evident that such a system should be designed so that (1) feeder ducts extend into exposed comers of the floor, (2) the total air-flow distances from the subfloor plenum to the registers are relatively short, and (3) relatively high air-flow rates are maintained in all sections of the perimeter ducts.

Basis for selection: First test data from a laboratory installation of a warm-air radial-feeder perimeter-loop system

Source: *ASHVE Transactions,* Vol. 58, p. 235-258

1953

The Shape of Things to Come: The Past, The Present, The Future

by W.J. Donald, Walter M. Timmerman and Glenn Muffly

Past, present and future viewpoints of household refrigeration is presented. A basic question of the day is: does the public want a separate refrigerator and a separate freezer or a combination refrigerator and freezer in one unit. A major challenge of the day is: how to convince consumers to purchase new refrigerators every 12 years or so instead of waiting for 25 or 30 years to replace their units. A prediction for the future is: Just like the family car which stands out in front where all the neighbors can see it, the refrigerator will no longer be hidden away in the kitchen - if the refrigerating engineer puts sufficient pride of ownership into design of the product.

Basis for selection: Discussion of the contribution of past records, present design, and the estimation of future trends to the successful manufacture of refrigerators.

Source: *Refrigerating Engineering,* Vol. 61, No. 1, p. 45-49, 106, 108

1954

Availability and Utilization of Solar Energy

by R.C. Jordan (Member) and J.L. Threlkeld (Member), Minneapolis, Minn.

This paper is divided into three parts: (1) solar energy availability for heating in the U.S.; (2) utilization of solar energy for house heating; (3) design and economics of solar energy heat pump systems. Because of the steady depletion of our fossil fuel reserves, new sources of energy must be utilized. The use of solar energy for space heating is realizable and the sun's supply of energy is virtually inexhaustible. The desirable orientation for a solar energy collector appears to be a south-facing vertical position. The paper presents a rational design procedure for estimating collector area, heat storage volume, heat pump specification and auxiliary heating capacity. This procedure may be used for any locality for which the proper solar statistics are available. The main problems associated with the development of solar energy heat pump systems involve solar collectors and heat storage systems.

Basis for selection: Early study of solar energy.

Source: *Refrigerating Engineering,* Vol. 61, No. 1, p. 45-49, 106, 108

1955

Ventilation Requirements for Cigarette Smoke

by C.P. Yaglou (Member), Boston, Mass.

Until recently when an association was found between smoking and lung cancer, physicians considered nicotine to be the most potent poison in cigarette smoke. It is now generally believed that many substances contribute to its toxicity. An outside air supply of 35 to 40 cfm per smoker was required in order to remove objectionable odors of fresh cigarette smoke. Non-smoking subjects who merely inhaled the smoke in the air considered as acceptable an outside air supply of 25 cfm per smoker. The smokers themselves were incapable of perceiving the smoke odor regardless of air flow. But they were more susceptible to irritation of eyes, nose and throat than the non-smokers or observers when the ventilation became deficient. Distinctly unhealthful conditions resulted when the air supply was reduced to less than 15 cfm per smoker, with headaches, smarting and watering of the eyes, irritation of the nose and throat, a feeling of depression, and a loss of concentration power for reading among both smokers and non-smokers. There is no way to ascertain now whether the ventilation requirements for controlling smoke, odor and irritation effects are in fact adequate to protect a non-smoker from possible effects of nicotine and of other poisonous smoke ingredients of unknown toxicological thresholds.

Basis for selection: Recognition of health hazards associated with cigarette smoke.

Source: *ASHAE Transactions,* Vol. 61, p. 25-32

1956

Combining Gamma Radiation, Refrigeration

By L.E. Brownell, Member ASRE, and S.N. Purhoit

This "new" food process in which high gamma radiation is combined with refrigeration has been proposed to increase the storage life of cooked meats, blanched vegetables and other foods packaged in plastic bags. Loss due to spoilage of fresh meats and produce could be eliminated if retail sales were made within a few weeks. Commercial development of the process probably would greatly increase use of refrigeration both in commercial handling of food and storage in the home. Housewives might use an additional refrigerator solely for storage of foods kept for two or three months or longer. Foods could be stored at 40°F cheaper than at home freezer temperatures, and the thawing waiting period would be eliminated. This additional use of nuclear-power reactors may hasten the day when nuclear power will be able to compete with electric power from fossil fuels.

Basis for selection: Early recognition of the value of combining gamma radiation and refrigeration for food preservation.

Source: *Refrigerating Engineering,* Vol. 64, No. 6, p. 39-49, 98

1957

Criteria for Room Noise from Air Conditioning

By Carlyle M. Ashley (Member), Syracuse, N.Y.

Consumer surveys indicate the need for improved noise control in room and home air-conditioning systems. Many people doubt whether an objective criterion for the noise levels can be set up, but several criteria have been proposed. This paper considers the characteristics of noise that make it acceptable or unacceptable, examines the noise criteria further, and suggests a simplified criterion and a more refined method for evaluating the quality of noise. Recommendations for room noise levels and typical noise levels from air-conditioning equipment are given. Noise criteria form a starting point for establishing standards of acceptable room noise. A new method has been presented for determining the sound-power level requirements of the air-conditioning noise of certain types of rooms directly without having to go through the sound-pressure level.

Basis for selection: Presentation of guidelines for the level of room noise from air conditioning.

Source: *ASHAE Transactions,* Vol. 63, p. 355-366

1958

Performance of a Solar Heated Office Building

By F.H. Bridgers (Member), D.D. Paxton (Member), and R.W. Haines (Member), Albuquerque, N.M.

What is believed to be the first solar heated office building in the world, located in Albuquerque, was occupied in August 1956. The building uses flat plate solar collectors with a net collector area of 750 sq ft. A 6,000-gal insulated underground water storage tank stores collected solar heat for cloudy weather and night-time use. A nominal 7 1/2 ton package water chiller is used as a heat pump in winter and for cooling the building in summer. With the present cost of fuels for heating, the savings in fuel costs do not justify the necessary first cost expense for a solar heating system in most localities in the U.S. However, there are some areas where the high fuel cost would make a solar heating system economically sound. With the continual depletion of fuel reserves, the solar heating system with a heat pump may be economically attractive over a large part of the U.S. in a relatively short time.

Basis for selection: Description of the first solar heated office buildings and the total energy concept.

Source: *ASHAE Transactions,* Vol. 64, p. 83-96

1959

Digital Computer Applied to Compressor Design Analysis

By H. Soumerai (Member), T. Kusuda (Member), and J. Dittfach

The computation of the forces acting on various components of reciprocating compressors can be performed accurately and economically on a digital card-programmed computer (CPC). The cost of setting up and utilizing the computer programs developed in this paper has been fully justified. The CPC program allows rapid and economical study of the effects of various parameters on compressor component design, and frees the engineer from time-consuming, repetitive computations.

Basis for selection: Early application of the digital computer to compressor design.

Source: *ASHRAE Journal,* Vol. 1, No. 7, p. 43-49

1960

An Air-Cooled Absorption Cycle

By R.H. Merrick (Member) and R.A. English (Member)

A newly developed air-cooled absorption cycle for use in 3-ton and 4.5-ton gas-fired air-conditioning equipment that comprises an outdoor, air-cooled water chilling section is described. Ammonia-water is the refrigerant-absorbent combination. Unusual features of the cycle include the use of a hermetic transfer device to circulate solution and a solution- cooled rectifier piped in parallel with the heat exchanger to improve cycle efficiency. The air-cooled, hermetic absorption cycle was developed following a review of familiar cycles that disclosed their limitations.

Basis for selection: Pioneer paper on a residential absorption system.

Source: *ASHRAE Journal,* Vol. 2, No. 8, p. 39-41

1961

Psychrometrics and Modern Comfort

By Ralph G. Nevins (Member)

The history of environmental research and the contributions by ASHVE and ASHRAE are reviewed. Future research will attempt to provide the complete comfort chart. In addition to comfort aspects, ASHRAE is interested in the effect of the thermal environment on learning rate and achievement and on productivity. The development of the psychrometric specifications for the comfort zone and optimum comfort line is summarized. It is interesting to note the shift in the optimum conditions since 1900 and the reluctance of some researchers to define a line, preferring to specify a range or zone of comfort.

Basis for selection: Classic paper on comfort.

Source: *ASHRAE Transactions,* Vol. 67, p. 609-621

1962

Refrigerating Capacity and Performance Data For Various Refrigerants, Azeotropes and Mixtures

By R.C. McHarness and D.D. Chapman

The performance of a variety of refrigerants, azeotropes and mixtures has been studied in a calorimeter unit. Comparative capacity data have been obtained over a range of temperatures typical of refrigerating and air-conditioning applications. These studies show that the use of mixtures is both feasible and practical and that definite and reproducible operation can be obtained with them. Actual operating information provides a basis for further consideration by refrigerating engineers. This practical demonstration of the use of mixed refrigerants provides almost unlimited possibilities for varying the capacity of refrigerating systems. Design engineers will have greater flexibility in studying new applications and problems and in selecting compressor size and speed.

Basis for selection: Excellent report of the performance of refrigerant mixtures.

Source: *ASHRAE Journal,* Vol. 4, No. 1, p. 49-58

1963

Adiabatic Single and Two-Phase Flow in Small Bore Tubes

By Edward P. Mikol

Two-phase flow as it occurs in small bore tubes such as those used as refrigerant restrictors was studied to (1) determine the most appropriate friction factor correlation for liquid flow through small bore tubes, (2) develop an understanding of the physical realities of adiabatic two-phase flow using visual and photographic studies, (3) determine the flow model that most accurately represents the mode of flow for which refrigerant restrictors should be designed, (4) determine the friction factors for two-phase flow, and (5) study the flow limiting phenomenon known as choked flow as it applies in two-phase flow.

Basis for selection: Examination of the fundamentals of flow through small tubes (capillaries).

Source: *ASHRAE Journal,* Vol. 5, No. 11, p. 75-86

1964

Evaluation of Refrigerant 502 in Integral Horsepower Commercial Refrigeration Compressors

By Henri Soumerai

Member ASHRAE

R 502 over R 22 is cooler compressors. Differences of 30° to 40° are on the conservative side. With liquid injection, the compressor can operate with R 22 at equally safe temperatures as with R 502, however, with some penalty in performance. Compressor capacity gains from 5 to 15% can be expected with good low temperature hermetics when converted from R 22 to R 502 without liquid injection on either refrigerant. Total compressor capacity gains from 10 to 30% can be realized when substituting R 502 without liquid injection for R 22 with liquid injection. R 502 is a welcome addition to the family of refrigerants for single-stage, low temperature refrigeration applications or heat pump winter operation.

Basis for selection: Basic study of R-502 that lead to its widespread use.

Source: *ASHRAE Journal,* Vol. 6, No. 1, p. 31-40, 83

1965

The Analog Computer as a Product Design Tool

by L.W. Nelson

Associate Member ASHRAE

Analog computers can be used to evaluate thermal performance of heating-cooling systems. This means that the complete air-conditioning system can now be simulated. Variations in component design are readily evaluated by computer techniques to get maximum control performance with minimum cost. Time can be speeded up or slowed down for convenient analysis (a 24-hour heating-cooling day required just 14.4 sec on the analog computer).

Basis for selection: Discussion of the usefulness of computers in solving design problems.

Source: *ASHRAE Journal,* Vol. 7, No. 11, p. 37-45

1966

Air Pollution and Chronic Respiratory Disease

by I.T.T. Higgins

There has been a steady increase in the mortality rate for emphysema in the U.S. since 1950. Evidence that general air pollution affects health is examined, including acute episodes and chronic effects of pollution. Current studies are described. The author concludes that there is evidence from rational mortality and morbidity rates and from specially designed surveys that atmospheric, industrial and personal (smoking cigarettes, cigars and pipes) air pollution are associated with increases in the number of people who have respiratory disease and respiratory disability.

Basis for selection: Early discussion of IAQ, even before the term IAQ became popular.

Source: *ASHRAE Journal,* Vol. 8, No. 8, p. 37-45

1967

Calculation of Thermal Comfort: Introduction of a Basic Comfort Equation

by P.O. Fanger

This paper presents a new method of approach in which the mean skin temperature and sweat secretion (both functions of the subject's activity level) can be used as basic conditions for thermal comfort. Based on these basic conditions, existing physical and physiological knowledge has been used to derive a comfort equation with the following principal variables: air temperature, humidity (partial vapor pressure), mean radiant temperature, relative air velocity, activity level (internal heat production), and insulation value of clothing. All combinations of these variables that satisfy the comfort equation should give thermal comfort.

Basis for selection: Classic paper on comfort.

Source: *ASHRAE Transactions,* Vol. 73, Pt. 2, p. III.4.1-III.4.20

1968

Thermal-Electric Expansion Valve

by Alan A. Matthies

A method of controlling refrigerant flow with electrical response has been developed following more than three decades of basic thermal refrigerant control. The thermal-electric expansion valve for capacities up to 7.5 tons with R-22 provides air-conditioning manufacturers with a control component that can function as either a constant superheat or constant pressure control. In the valve, an increase in voltage increases the refrigerant flow, a decrease diminishes the flow or closes the valve. The changes in voltage can be established by employing various temperature, pressure or liquid refrigerant sensors. Therefore, the function of the valve can be changed instantly by switching from one sensing device to another. This expands the scope of the valve well beyond that of conventional expansion valves. Possible applications suggested are bi-directional heat pump control, uni-directional heat pump control, and evaporator capacity for temperature control.

Basis for selection: Chosen for fun, since it may be a pioneer paper on the field of electronically controlled expansion valves.

Source: *ASHRAE Journal,* Vol. 10, No. 1, p. 71-76

1969

Heat Transfer Characteristics of the Air Curtain

by F.C. Hayes (Associate Member) and W.F. Stoecker (Member)

The research reported concentrates on the thin, high- velocity, non-recirculatory type of air curtain. The objective of the investigation was to develop a satisfactory model for predicting the rate of heat transfer across the air curtain. This model should indicate the effect of outlet velocity as well as the discharge angle and nozzle opening. Availability of such a model will aid in the design of air curtains and should even permit the determination of the combination of outlet velocity, discharge angle and nozzle opening which results in the minimum heat transfer rate.

Basis for selection: Definitive scientific work on air curtains.

Source: *ASHRAE Transactions,* Vol. 75, Pt. 2, p. 153-167

1970

Development and Evaluation of a General Method for Design of Small Acoustic Filters

by Raymond Cohen (Member ASHRAE)

The research reported concentrates on the thin, high- velocity, non-recirculatory type of air curtain. The objective of the investigation was to develop a satisfactory model for predicting the rate of heat transfer across the air curtain. This model should indicate the effect of outlet velocity as well as the discharge angle and nozzle opening. Availability of such a model will aid in the design of air curtains and should even permit the determination of the combination of outlet velocity, discharge angle and nozzle opening which results in the minimum heat transfer rate.

Basis for selection: Definitive work on the measurement of the acoustic impedance of mufflers connected to 1/4 in. tubing such as those internal to compressors.

Source: *ASHRAE Transactions,* Vol. 76, Pt. 1, p. 38-51

1971

Use of an Absorber Heat Exchanger in the Absorption Refrigerating Machine

by E.P. Whitlow (Member ASHRAE)

Much work has been done to improve absorption refrigerating machines which date to the 18th century. This paper considers methods of improving the performance of the absorption machines primarily by means of an "absorber heat exchanger," which takes some of the heat of absorption that is normally dissipated and returns it to the generator to yield a significant increase in the coefficient of performance.

Basis for selection: Example of work done in the important area of absorption.

Source: *ASHRAE Transactions,* Vol. 77, Pt. 2, p. 166-173

1972

Problem Areas in Mathematical Modeling and Simulation of Refrigerating Compressors

by E.B. Qvale, M.J. Stevenson, J.P. Elson, and D.A. Coates (Member ASHRAE)

Mathematical simulation models of refrigeration compressors have great advantages over other types of mathematical models and have proven themselves to be very useful to the practical designer. However, recent developments and studies of simulation models have made it clear that there are still numerous basic and refinement problems associated with mathematical simulation. It is apparent that the major difficulties both in the prediction of cyclically steady performance characteristics and in mathematical simulation models arise from the lack of understanding of the basic fluid mechanics, heat transfer, and thermodynamics of the detailed processes. In addition, in mathematical simulation modeling the computational requirements may easily exceed available computer capabilities, economic resources, or available manpower.

Basis for selection: A discussion of the caution that must accompany the skyrocketing use of digital computers.

Source: *ASHRAE Transactions,* Vol. 78, Pt. 1, p. 75-84

1973

Reducing Fuel Consumption with Night Setback

by Lorne W. Nelson (Member ASHRAE)

Systematic lowering of heating temperatures at night can help save substantial amounts of fuel. Here is a study conducted by analog computer simulation to determine maximum reduction of space heating requirements and minimum loss of comfort conditions. In general, the greater the amount of setback, the greater the potential for savings. Thermostat setback can be achieved by simply turning the thermostat back 5 to 10 degrees before retiring and turning it back up on arising in the morning. However, systems are available to change the thermostat setting automatically at the desired time, relieving the occupant of the necessity of performing this task manually.

Basis for selection: Illustration of one response to the energy crisis.

Source: *ASHRAE Journal,* Vol. 15, No.8, p. 41-49

1974

In-Duct Fan-Sound Power Measurements Systems

by Dr. Malcom J. Crocker (Member ASHRAE) and Dr. John Song Pen Wang

The International Organization for Standardization (ISO) has been developing Standard ISO/TC 43/SCI, "Sound Measurement Procedures for Air Moving Devices Connected to Either a Discharge Duct or an Inlet Duct," and ASHRAE has been developing Standard 68P, "Method of Testing Sound Power Radiated into Ducts from Air Moving Devices." The ISO and ASHRAE drafts offer solutions to the practical problems of in-duct fan sound measurement systems. It would seem that sufficient theoretical and experimental work has been accomplished to justify the adoption of an in-duct fan sound power measurement standard now that a sampling tube is commercially available.

Basis for selection: Discussion that led to a new standard method for measuring noise from large fans that replaced an old AMCA standard.

Source: *ASHRAE Transactions,* Vol. 80, Pt. 2, p. 82-97

1975

An Investigation of the Importance of Air Flow in Control of Post-Operative Infections

by Carl Eugene Intag (Associate Member ASHRAE), Dr. Henry A. Wiebe, and Dr. C. Leon Partain

This paper shows strong correlations between bacteria in the air and post-operative infection rates; between air flow rates and bacteria in the air; and between air flow rates and post-operative infections. The high correlation between airflow rates and bacteria in the air cannot be attributed to quantity of air supplied alone, but must take into account the efficiency of the filtering system and the direction of the air currents. The high correlation found between bacteria in the air and the post-operative infection rates provides a convincing argument for guarding against airborne contaminants. It appears that the combination of factors applied to maintain the lowest number of airborne contaminants also will result in the lowest post-operative infection rates.

Basis for selection: A superb investigative report on the importance of HVAC in the health care industry.

Source: *ASHRAE Journal,* Vol. 17, No. 2, p. 27-33

1976

An Experimental Determination of Shading Coefficients for Selected Insulated Reflective Glasses and Draperies

by Prof. Clayton A. Morrison, P.E., Member ASHRAE; James M. Wheeler, Jr. and Dr. Erich A. Farber, P.E.

This report contains shading coefficients based upon experiments covering five commercially available reflective insulating glass panels and three representative draperies. The experimental results formed the basis for the following conclusions: (1) the solar optical properties of the draperies have less effect on shading coefficients as the glass panel solar transmittance decreases; (2) for a given panel with a reflective film on the inside surface of the glass, the shading coefficient will be less than if the same film were on the outside surface of the inside glass; (3) values for shading coefficients given by the 1972 ASHRAE Handbook of Fundamentals averaged 19 plus/minus 5% above experimental results for the glass panels with reflective film on the two-side films and about 1 plus/minus 16% different from the experimental results for glass panels with three-side films.

Basis for selection: Significant investigation related to mitigating the effect of solar radiation on building cooling loads.

Source: *ASHRAE Transactions,* Vol. 82, Pt. 1, p. 38-59

1977

Comparison of Cooling Load Calculations

by William Rudoy, P.E., Member ASHRAE, and L.M. Robins

A method for calculating cooling loads was developed in an ASHRAE research project that appeared to be more consistent and accurate than previous methods. It was therefore of interest to compare the results of that method with a more sophisticated computer routine, NBSLD, developed by the National Bureau of Standards. The NBSLD program is unique in that fewer assumptions are made regarding the loads. All load sources are applied simultaneously. The resulting cooling loads and temperatures reflect the interdependence of the loads and do not require the assumption of superposition. The simpler method does yield results that can be used with great confidence for design day cooling load and for equipment selection.

Basis for selection: Comparison of methods for a fundamental task of HVAC engineers, the calculation of loads.

Source: *ASHRAE Transactions,* Vol. 83, Pt. 1, p. 38-50

1978

A Review of the Attenuation of Sound in Straight Lined and Unlined Ductwork of Rectangular Cross Section

by Dr. István L. Vér

Ductborne noise is the unwanted by-product of ventilating and air-conditioning system operation. The incorporation of interior lining into duct systems is frequently the most economical control of ductborne noise because, while attenuating noise, the lining serves as a thermal insulator and introduces only a slight increase in pressure drop. Both of these nonacoustic properties of duct lining are vital in modem system design, which strives to conserve energy by minimizing operating cost. As the volume of new building construction grows and with it the need for some kind of interior duct lining to attenuate to acceptable levels ductborne fan noise in HVAC systems, ASHRAE has realized the need to improve the accuracy of information to permit optimal noise control design of HVAC systems. This ASHRAE research paper is a critical review of the state of current knowledge in predicting the attenuation of sound in straight lined and unlined ductwork of rectangular cross section with airflow up to 4000 fpm. In addition, acoustical design information has been generated that allows the HVAC engineer to predict the sound attenuation in straight rectangular ducts more accurately than with current methods.

Basis for selection: A review of a fundamental problem, the attenuation of sound.

Source: *ASHRAE Transactions,* Vol. 84, Pt. 1, p. 122-149

1979

The Calculation of House Infiltration Rates

by G.T. Tamura

Member ASHRAE

The equations for calculating house infiltration rates given in this paper give values which agree reasonably well with the measured values of two single-story houses with oil fired central systems located in a residential district. The calculation procedure takes into account the motive forces (wind action, stack action and furnace operation), house characteristics and wind exposure. The paper identifies areas where additional test data are required so that the proposed method can be applied to houses of various design, construction and location.

Basis for selection: Excellent experimental effort to define air infiltration in houses.

Source: *ASHRAE Transactions,* Vol. 85, Pt. 1, p. 58-71

1980

An Experimental Validation of a Rational Model for Dynamic Responses of Buildings

by Dr. D. Paul Mehta, Member ASHRAE, and
Dr. James E. Woods, P.E., Member ASHRAE

Energy balance methods can be used to derive a rational model to predict dynamic conditions inside occupied spaces. The rational model has been shown to be modular in nature so that it can used to develop models which can describe dynamic interactions between the building envelopes, HVAC systems, building occupants and the exterior environments. The rational model has been used to develop three models of environmental controls systems: A heating system for a single family residence, a fan coil system for a classroom, and a constant volume dual duct system for an office buildings.

Basis for selection: Significant investigation of a building's response to heating and cooling loads.

Source: *ASHRAE Transactions,* Vol. 86, Pt. 2, p. 497-520

1981

Revised Noise Criteria for Design and Rating of HVAC Systems

by Warren E. Blazier, Jr., Member ASHRAE

Current methods of rating the noise produced by HVAC systems are reviewed. The failure of these ratings to correlate with subjective opinion in many cases is explained. A new method of assigning noise ratings is proposed and is expected to provide a significantly better correlation between objective measurements and subjective responses. The proposed rating method uses a revised set of noise criterion curves (RC curves). The technical considerations leading to the development of the RC curves as a replacement for the NC curves used in the past are discussed. The NC tangent-contour method of rating addresses only one attribute of noise-level. The RC noise rating contains two terms: a number corresponding to a measure of the speech communication (or masking) properties and a letter designating the quality or character of the sound. Examples demonstrating how RC ratings are determined are given for neutral, rumbly, and hissy background noises and for background noise with tonal components.

Basis for selection: Presentation of improved noise criteria.

Source: *ASHRAE Transactions,* Vol. 87, Pt. 1, p. 647-657

1982

Degree-Days Method for Simplified Energy Analysis

by R.D. Fischer, P.E.; L.J. Flanigan; S.G. Talbert, P.E. (ASHRAE Members); and D. Jaffe

The degree-days method of energy analysis has been an attractive approach to residential energy analysis when time does not permit the use of computer energy-analysis procedures. Buildings today are using more insulation, storm windows, and weather stripping, and builders are generally upgrading the quality of construction relative to air tightness and heat loss. In addition, more energy-consuming household appliances are used in homes and there has been a nationwide effort to adjust thermostat settings to further reduce energy consumption. This paper presents one year of energy consumption and weather data to update the degree-days method. The research shows that the mean heating and cooling base temperatures for homes constructed in 1970 was about the same as the 18.3C (65F) base temperature in use for many years. Seasonal heating loads for occupied homes were predicted with an absolute error of about 38% and a coefficient of correlation of about 0.83 using a constant correction factor of 0.51 applied to the load computed with the degree-days procedure. The error dropped to about 31% and the correlation improved to 0.88 when different correction factors were used. For cooling, with a constant correction factor of 0.76, the absolute error increased to 66% and the coefficient of correlation dropped to 0.42.

Basis for selection: Discussion of a method for improved, simplified energy analysis.

Source: *ASHRAE Transactions,* Vol. 88, Pt. 2, p. 522-571

1983

Air Quality in Buildings During Smoking and Nonsmoking Occupancy

by B.P. Leaderer and W.S. Cain (Associate Member)

Ventilation requirements have been derived primarily from those for odor control and secondarily from criteria for concentrations of air contaminants. This study looked at criteria for the control of occupancy odor and tobacco smoke odor. The study also examined steady state concentrations of two contaminants in sidestream cigarette emissions (total suspended particulates and carbon monoxide). Under nonsmoking conditions between 5 and 10 cfm (2.5 and 5 L/s) of fresh air per occupant should satisfy 75% of the visitors and between 15 and 20 cfm (7.5 and 10 L/s) should satisfy 80% of the visitors. None of the conditions in this study satisfied even two-thirds of the nonsmokers, but smokers found the odor of the environment generally acceptable during and after smoking. From other field studies, it is calculated that 35 to 53 cfm (17.5 to 26.5 L/s) would be required to satisfy 75 to 80% of the occupants. Smoking increased the particulate burden of nonsmokers considerably, even at the highest practical ventilation rates, from 3 to 40 times above background.

Basis for selection: Presentation of new data on air quality in buildings.

Source: *ASHRAE Transactions,* Vol. 89, Pt. 2B, p. 601-613

1984

Vent Capacity Data for High-Efficiency, Condensing Type, Gas-Fired Appliances

by D.W. DeWerth (ASHRAE Member), S.G. Talbert (ASHRAE Member), S.M. Connelly, and D.D. Paul

Consumers are demanding more efficient heating equipment because of increased awareness of the need for energy conservation and of increasing energy costs. Manufacturers have responded with new appliances that operate with efficiencies as high as 95%. In order to obtain these high efficiencies, almost all of the heat from the combustion process must be utilized. Thus, the temperatures of the flue gases vented from these high efficiency alliances are much lower than in conventional appliances. These temperatures are low enough to cause condensation of the water vapor in the flue gases. Because the flue gases are so cool, mechanical venting means are needed. This paper provides guidelines and design tables for high-efficiency gas fired heating equipment to be used by manufacturers and installers. These data should be included in the ASHRAE Handbook and appropriate ANSI standards.

Basis for selection: Discussion of new engineering data for gas-fired equipment.

Source: *ASHRAE Transactions,* Vol. 90, Pt. 2B, p. 555-572

1985

Variable Flow in Hydronic Systems for Improved Stability, Simplicity, and Energy Economics

by W.J. Coad, P.E. (ASHRAE Fellow)

Variable flow rates to accommodate variable thermal loads imposed upon hydronic heating and cooling systems are one of two options available to designers. This paper explores the advantages of the variable flow concept over variable temperature range, some of which include greater simplicity, control stability and improved energy economics. These systems use finesse rather than energy muscle and are therefore less forgiving of maladjustment or misunderstanding. The three design characteristics worthy of particular note are, first, the two-way valves must be high quality control valves, carefully selected for capacity C_V shutoff and shutoff head, and the temperature controllers operating these valves must be high quality industrial-type devices. Second, check valves should not be used at any point in the system, except in the pump discharge lines. Third, overpumping of load circuits will only result in raising the supply water temperature available to the loads. The biggest problems experienced in the application of these systems has been that many operators (and designers) have the preconception that if they want more capacity for a specific load they need only provide a bigger pump. With this type system, overpumping a load circuit results in increased supply water temperature and a reduction in cooling capacity.

Basis for selection: Great basic coverage of a subject that is often misunderstood.

Source: *ASHRAE Transactions,* Vol. 91, Pt. 1B, p. 224-237

1986

Energy-Integrated HVAC Systems Use Nonrefrigerated Cooling Techniques

G. Meckler, P.E. (ASHRAE Member)

Historically energy for air conditioning has been supplied almost exclusively by utility-generated electricity energizing vapor compression refrigeration. Two approaches are reviewed to use non-refrigerated techniques to significantly reduce utility energy requirements. One approach eliminates the need for using refrigeration to dehumidify by shifting latent cooling to a desiccant dehumidification system and regenerating the desiccant with heat from a selective-energy system incorporating cogeneration, solar energy, and thermal storage. A second approach uses non-refrigerated techniques to remove solar heat gain through glass before it impacts the vapor compression refrigeration system and to use the recovered heat as needed.

Basis for selection: Extremely well-written article describing energy-conserving HVAC systems for maintaining comfort conditions under nonrefrigerated cooling conditions.

Source: *ASHRAE Transactions,* Vol. 92, Pt. 1B, p. 887-900

1987

Models for Variable-Speed Centrifugal Chillers

J.E. Braun, P.E.; J.W. Mitchell, Ph.D., ASHRAE Member; S.A. Klein, Ph.D., ASHRAE Member; and W.A. Beckman

A mechanistic model of a centrifugal chiller with variable speed control is described. The model utilizes mass, momentum and energy balances on the compressor, evaporator, condenser, and expansion device. Given a chilled water setpoint temperature and entering chilled and condenser water temperatures and flow rates, the model determines both the required compressor speed and power consumption. It may also be used to estimate, for any given set of conditions, the chiller capacity at a specific speed or power consumption or the compressor speed at which compressor surge develops. Results from the model are compared with performance data for the variable-speed centrifugal chiller at the Dallas-Fort Worth Airport. The best chiller performance occurs at part-loads of between 35 and 70% of the design capacity of 5500 tons (19.3 MW), depending upon the temperature difference between the leaving water streams. The power requirement of a particular chiller depends primarily upon two variables; The chilled water load and the temperature difference between the leaving condenser and chiller water streams. This is a useful result for correlating performance data for centrifugal chillers. The use of different refrigerants was also investigated, with R-12 showing about a 5% improvement over the current choice of R- 500 at part-load conditions.

Basis for selection: Information is provided for estimating energy consumption.

Source: *ASHRAE Transactions,* Vol. 93, Pt. 1, p. 1794-1813

1988

The HVAC Costs of Increased Fresh Air Ventilation Rates in Office Buildings

By J.H. Eto, P.E., ASHRAE Member, and C. Meyer

ASHRAE Standards Project Committee 62-1981R is in the process of revising ASHRAE's standard for indoor air quality. This study reports on the changes in annual energy operating costs and in equipment sizing that result from increased minimum outside air ventilation rates. The results suggest that higher minimum outside air ventilation rates will affect equipment-sizing decisions relatively more than they will affect annual building energy use. Increases in annual energy operating costs were small (less than 5%) because electricity is the dominant component of cost and electricity is used primarily for non-space conditioning purposes. Estimates of the increase in HVAC first cost suggest that higher ventilation rates will have small effects (less than 0.5%) on total building construction costs.

Basis for selection: Investigation into the cost implications from the use of more outside air.

Source: *ASHRAE Transactions,* Vol. 94, Pt. 2, p. 331-345

1989

Improving Gas-Fired Heat Pump Capacity and Performance by Adding a Desiccant Dehumidification Subsystem

By B.K. Parsons; A.A. Pesaran, Ph.D.; D. Bharathan, Ph.D., P.E.; and B. Shelpuk

This paper examines the merits of coupling a desiccant dehumidification subsystem to a gas-engine-driven-vapor-compression air conditioner. A system is identified that uses a rotary, silica gel, parallel-plate dehumidifier. The dehumidification subsystem processes the fresh air portion and handles the latent portion of the load. Adding the desiccant subsystem increases the gas-based coefficient of performance 40% and increases the cooling capacity 50%. This study supports the addition of a desiccant subsystem to a thermally activated heat pump system for particular climates and favorable gas and electricity rates.

Basis for selection: Describes an innovative combination of using the desiccant dehumidification subsystem and the gas-fired heat pump with promise for economic use.

Source: *ASHRAE Transactions,* Vol. 95, Pt. 1, p. 835-844

1990

Central Heating and Cooling Plant Economics for the College Campus

By E.E. Friberg, P.E., Fellow ASHRAE

In the preparation of a facility master plan for a university, the feasibility of providing a new central heating and cooling plant was examined. A new plant and the required distribution system would cost $758,000 less than replacing individual building water chillers. Operating costs were also compared and cost estimates were made for the new utility distribution system. The net additional cost of the new system was estimated to be $2,440,790. Cost savings with the central plant were calculated for a 25-year period, and price escalation considerations were made. The 25-year cash flow analysis operating cost savings with the central plant will provide a positive cash flow during the fifth year. The total cumulative savings at the end of 15 years are projected to be $978,338 and, at the end of 25 years, $7,253,105.

Basis for selection: Shows how fully economic analysis can be integrated with engineering design practice.

Source: *ASHRAE Transactions,* Vol. 96, Pt. 1, p. 936-945

1991

Indoor Air Quality Assessment in an Office-Library Building: Part I–Test Methods & Part II–Test Results

By C.Y. Shaw, Ph.D., P.E., Member ASHRAE; R.J. Magee; C.J. Shirtliffe, P.E. and H. Unligil, Ph.D.

The measurement methods for assessing the indoor air quality of a fully air-conditioned eight-story office/library building are discussed. Based on results of the study, it was postulated that complaints of occupants on the first floor could be caused by (1) lack of outdoor air supply through the HVAC system due to an outdoor air damper that was never fully opened and (2) unsatisfactory thermal comfort conditions. On the sixth floor, complaints could be caused by higher-than-normal concentrations of total volatile organic compounds, unsatisfactory thermal comfort conditions, and contaminated water in the HVAC systems.

Basis for selection: Presents an authoritative description of analysis methods for indoor air contaminants. Comprehensive discussion of results provides a model for other investigators concerned with indoor air quality assessment.

Source: *ASHRAE Transactions,* Vol. 97, Pt. 2, Test Methods - p. 129-135 and Test Results - p. 136-145

1992

The CFC Controversy: Issues and Answers

By F. Sherwood Roland, Ph.D., D.Sc.

The problem of mold, mildew and other humidity-related problems in hotels is examined. Buildings and furnishings can be kept dry by using a desiccant dehumidifier to remove excess humidity from the air. Dry air, in turn, removes excess moisture from building materials and furnishings, which prevents the growth of mold and mildew. A gas-fired desiccant dehumidification system that incorporates a heat pipe is being field-tested at a low-rise hotel in West Palm Beach, Florida. The system is dehumidifying the outside air, which is the source of 90% of the moisture that enters a typical hotel. The hotel has two wings. One wing is using a desiccant-based dehumidification system, while the other is using a direct-expansion cooling and reheating system. The preliminary results of this field test demonstrate the desiccant-based system maintains lower humidity levels, which has eliminated musty odors and rust on the ceiling tile grid, and also uses less energy than a properly sized cool/reheat system.

Basis for selection: Addresses in full detail the most significant scientific and technological issue currently impacting the air-conditioning and refrigerating industry.

Source: *ASHRAE Journal,* Vol. 34, No. 12, p. 20-27

1993

Measuring and Calculating Laboratory Exhaust Diversity–Three Case Studies

By D.T. Hitchings, P.E., CIH, Member ASHRAE, and R.S. Schull, P.E., CIH, Associate Member ASHRAE

Diversity in laboratory exhaust systems can theoretically be used to downsize equipment and reduce capital and operating costs. This paper provides a method for analyzing and reporting laboratory diversity data and applies this method to three facilities. Results indicate that substantial diversity exists in real operating facilities providing three key motivators are effectively in place: (1) facility design and function, (2) training, and (3) monitoring and enforcement. It is suggested that the fume hood to personnel ratio may predict the facility diversity provided these motivators exist.

Basis for selection: Presents an innovative method for analyzing diversity in laboratory exhaust systems.

Source: *ASHRAE Transactions,* Vol. 99, Pt. 2, p. 1059-1071

1994

A Steam Systems Primer: Low Pressure Steam Heating Systems

By Roy C.E. Ahlgren, Associate Member ASHRAE

Steam has been used for many years to transfer heat. The principles involved in using steam were developed long ago. The technology which makes low pressure steam an excellent heat transfer medium is reviewed, with old and new installation practices and components described.

Basis for selection: Excellent description of a technology which has involved ASHRAE members for nearly all of the Society's 100 years.

Source: *ASHRAE Journal,* Vol. 36, No. 1, p. 56-64

1995

Evolution of Building Energy Simulation Methodology

By Edward F. Sowell, Ph.D., P.E., Fellow ASHRAE, and Douglas C. Hittle, Ph.D., Fellow ASHRAE

Public domain building load calculation and energy analysis programs developed along two major paths with respect to calculating air conditioning loads. One approach used the so-called weighting factor method, which calculates instantaneous space energy gains and then smears them out over time using weighting factors. The other approach relied on a surface-by-surface heat balance. In this scheme, a radiative, conductive, and convective heat balance is done on each room surface (both inside and outside). The air conditioning load is determined by computing how much energy is convected into the room air from surfaces, lights, people, and equipment. Both methods have advantages and disadvantages, especially with respect to the connection between air conditioning load calculation and system performance simulation.

Source: *ASHRAE Transactions*, Vol. 101, Pt. 1, p. 525-527

1996

BACnet™: Integrating Building Automation and Control Products Using the BACnet Protocol

By H. Michael Newman, Member ASHRAE

This paper describes the main features of BACnet, the motivation for developing the protocol, and the impact the protocol will have on manufacturers and users of building automation products.

Source: *ASHRAE Journal*, Vol. 38, No. 11, p. 36-42

1997

Legionnaires' Disease: Seeking Effective Prevention

By J. Donald Millar, M.D., D.T.P.H. (Lond.), George K. Morris, Ph.D., Member ASHRAE, and Brian G. Shelton, M.P.H.

Describes the two forms of legionellosis—classical Legionnaires' disease (LD) and Pontiac fever. Estimates the annual number of fatalities from LD in the USA. Explains how LD is an environmental disease, the implications of this, how it is amplified and how it may be prevented. Outlines and illustrates schematically an effective preventive strategy in buildings. Discusses how the current approach to legionellosis compares with this model. Criticizes the existing officially sanctioned approach and calls for a truly integrated national prevention strategy.

Source: *ASHRAE Journal*, Vol. 39, No. 1, p. 22-29

1998

450 Golden Gate Project: BACnet's First Large-Scale Test

By Martin A. Applebaum, P.E., Member ASHRAE, and Steven T. Bushby, Member ASHRAE

States that the adoption of BACnet as the standard protocol for integrating building control products has forever changed the industry and has opened the door to new innovation in building control technology. Describes the Phillip Burton Federal Building and U.S. Courthouse in San Francisco, selected for the first large-scale commercial demonstration of the BACnet standard. States the project is unique because of its large size—22 storeys, 130,000m^3 (1.4 million ft^2)—the involvement of multiple vendors and the inclusion of more than just HVAC control. States this project will significantly affect way the largest landlord in the world—the U.S. General Services Administration—will manage its buildings in the future. Presents an overview of the project design, the demonstration team's experiences to date and recommendations for engineers and building owners considering BACnet in their future automation projects.

Source: *ASHRAE Journal*, Vol. 40, No. 7, p. 23-30

1999

Milton Ward Garland, Refrigeration Engineer, and a Case History of Manufactured Ice

By Harry M. Will, Member ASHRAE

This paper recognizes the accomplishments of Milton W. Garland, engineer and inventor and leader in the refrigeration industry, honored in 1998 by the President as the Oldest Working American. It touches on the history of the Frick Company, where Garland has worked for 78 years, focusing on his renovation of the Waynesboro Ice and Cold Storage plant, originally built in 1901.

Source: *ASHRAE Transactions*, Vol. 105, Pt. 1, p. 1177-1185

2000

Smoke Movement for Sprinklered Fires

By Gary D. Lougheed, Ph.D. Member ASHRAE, Cam McCartney, and Bruce C. Taber

This paper presents the initial results of a project initiated by ASHRAE and the National Research

Council of Canada to investigate smoke movement resulting from a sprinklered fire in a communicating space into an adjacent large open area such as an atrium or retail mall. Recent research on the interaction of sprinkler spray with a smoke layer is also reviewed. In addition, information in the literature from full-scale fire tests of mercantile and office occupancies is discussed. As part of the joint project, a large-scale test facility was established to investigate smoke flow for sprinklered fires. This facility is described in the paper. The results of steady-state fire tests using a propane burner system are discussed. These tests indicate that two smoke flow regimes can occur depending on the fire size. For fires with low heat release rates, the smoke temperature was uniform over the height of the compartment opening and was near ambient. Under this condition, the smoke was nonbuoyant and accumulated near the opening. With higher heat release rates, a two-zone air and smoke flow regime resulted. The smoke exited the compartment in the hot upper layer. The fire test results were used to determine approximate limits for the smoke flow regimes. Preliminary tests were conducted to investigate the effectiveness of opposed airflow systems in limiting smoke flow between the test compartment and the adjacent area. Initial results are also provided for this portion of the investigation.

Source: *ASHRAE Transactions*, Vol. 106, Pt. 1, p. 605-615

2001

Advances in Residential Wall Technologies—Simple Ways of Decreasing the Whole Building Energy Consumption

By Jan Kosny, Ph.D.

The main objective of this paper is to document the most common thermal improvements in several wall technologies. The improvement results are analyzed based either on the R-value comparisons or on whole building energy consumption reduction. This paper is focused on small material configuration changes made in the clear wall scale of wall technologies. These changes are expected to bring significant whole building energy consumption reductions.

Source: *ASHRAE Transactions*, Vol. 107, Pt. 1, p. 421-428

2002

Responding to Thermal Sensation Complaints in Buildings

By Rodney A. Martin, Clifford C. Federspiel, Ph.D., and David M. Auslander, Ph.D., P.E.

Computer simulation methods were used to compare two different strategies for responding to thermal sensation complaints in buildings. The baseline strategy involved changing the space temperature setpoint in the appropriate direction and leaving it there until another complaint occurred. The alternative strategy involved changing the setpoint in the appropriate direction for a finite time and then resetting it to a value expected to produce the fewest complaints on average. A complaint model recently proposed by Federspiel (2000) was used to simulate complaint behavior. A building heat transfer model that included a multi-layer wall, heat accumulation by furnishings, meteorological weather data, time-varying internal disturbances, temperature sensor dynamics, and a proportional plus integral (PI) temperature controller was used to model the building. A grid search was used to determine the optimal values of the setpoint change and duration for the resetting strategy. The optimization indicates that setpoint changes greater than 2°F and longer than two hours are most effective. A comparison of the resetting strategy and the base-line strategy shows that resetting the setpoint significantly lowers both the complaint rate and the complaint recovery period.

Source: *ASHRAE Transactions*, Vol. 108, Pt. 1, p. 407-412

2003

Temperature Control and Zoning in Underfloor Air Distribution Systems

By Kenneth J. Loudermilk, Associate Member ASHRAE

The use of underfloor air delivery systems in conjunction with raised access floors has had rapid growth in the past few years. Underfloor systems are capable of improving air quality and occupant comfort levels as well as extending the service flexibility of the raised floor platform to encompass the mechanical services to the space. However, care must be afforded during the design of these systems to avoid unnecessary obstructions in the floor (service delivery) cavity if the flexibility of the raised floor system is to be optimized. Temperature control and zoning strategies that provide superior occupant comfort yet maintain the integrity of the open floor cavity should be favored. This paper discusses many of the issues and available alternatives to accomplishing this. Particular emphasis is directed toward the differences in controlling interior and perimeter zones.

Source: *ASHRAE Transactions*, Vol. 109, Pt. 1, p. 307-314

2004

Development and Testing of the Characteristic Curve Fan Model

By Jeff Stein, P.E., Member ASHRAE, Mark M. Hydeman, P.E., Member ASHRAE

This paper describes the development and testing of the characteristic curve fan model—a gray-box model. This model produces fan efficiency as a function of airflow and fan static pressure. It is accurate, relatively easy to calibrate, and could be easily incorporated into commercial simulation programs. Also presented is an application of an existing model to predict fan speed from airflow and fan static pressure. These models were developed as a part of a larger research project to develop design guidelines for built-up variable air volume fan systems. The models have been successfully employed in comparative analysis of fan types, wheel diameters, fan staging, and analysis of supply pressure reset.

Source: *ASHRAE Transactions*, Vol. 110, Pt 1, p. 347-356

2005

Advanced Energy Design Guide for Small Office Buildings

By Donald G. Colliver, Ph.D., P.E., Presidential Member/ Fellow ASHRAE, and Ronald E. Jarnagin, Member ASHRAE

A group of organizations led by ASHRAE recently completed the *Advanced Energy Design Guide for Small Office Buildings*. The *Advanced Energy Design Guide* series is designed to extend the lead in energy-efficient standards into the arena of advanced energy-efficiency recommendations.

Source: *ASHRAE Journal*, Vol. 47, No. 3, p. 22-27

2006

Some Quantitative Relations between Indoor Environmental Quality and Work Performance or Health

By Olli A. Seppänen and William Fisk

Poor indoor environmental quality (IEQ) has been related to increases in sick building syndrome (SBS) symptoms, respiratory illnesses, sick leave, and loss in productivity. Calculations indicate that the cost of poor IEQ can be higher than energy costs FOR space conditioning and ventilation and that many measures taken to improve indoor IEQ will be highly cost-effective when accounting for the monetary savings resulting from improved health or productivity. To enable building professionals to select of building designs and operating practices that account for effects on health and productivity, we need models for quantifying the health and productivity benefits of better indoor environments. Therefore, we have reviewed the literature on the effects of indoor environment on health and performance and used existing data, when possible, to develop some initial models. Based on the best available evidence, we present quantitative relationships between ventilation rates and short-term sick leave, ventilation rates and work performance, perceived air quality and performance, temperature and performance, and temperature and SBS symptoms. We also show that a relationship exists between SBS symptoms and work performance.

Source: *HVAC&R Research*, Vol. 12, No. 4, p. 957-973

2007

Net Zero Energy Building Case Study: Science House

By Jason Steinbock, David Eijadi, FAIA, and Tom McDougall, PE

The challenge of the Science House at the Science Museum of Minnesota was to create habitable, cold-climate architecture that would result in a net zero energy building and to get it built in a "low bid" environment. The design team used scientific evaluation to resolve design integration conflicts between functionality, aesthetics, and performance. The team significantly reduced annual energy consumption, beginning with expectations of use by the owner and architectural form and then by adding a renewable energy source. The defining question became, "How much building, with fixed program requirements, can we build and generate power for with the given budget?" The resulting building uses passive solar design, daylighting, ground-source heat pumps, and photovoltaic (PV) panels as the major design strategies. This paper documents the predicted energy use and actual monitored performance, comparing to a calibrated DOE-2 model. It shows the extent of load reduction achieved with passive solar design. A challenge for getting to "real zero" is the difference between expected performance and actual building performance. This paper illustrates how measured data are used to trace the causes to unexpected equipment performance, heat pump behavior, and off-line PV panels. Assumptions regarding occupancy and building use during the design phase often differ from their actual use; this makes operating a building for zero energy an additional challenge beyond just designing one. Overall, the actual building is exceeding the design goals, using on average 22,385 Btu/ft^2·yr (0.71 kWh/m^2·yr) annually and generating 30,864 Btu/ft^2·yr (0.97 kWh/m^2·yr) to result in a building that generates more energy than it uses.

Source: *ASHRAE Transactions*, Vol. 113, Pt. 1, p. 26-35

2008

Smoke Control and Occupant Evacuation at the World Trade Center

By Michael J. Ferreira, PE, Member ASHRAE, Steven M. Strege, PE, Member ASHRAE, Richard D. Peacock, and Jason D. Averill

This paper examines smoke control and occupant evacuation in WTC 1 and WTC 2 on September 11, 2001, focusing on the impact region and above for each tower. Approximately 2,000 individuals were at or above the area of impact in WTC 1 and WTC 2 who did not successfully evacuate. NIST found that the smoke management (smoke purge) systems in WTC 1 and WTC 2 were not initiated on September 11, 2001. Had the smoke purge sequence (required by the BCNYC for post-fire smoke venting) been initiated in WTC 1 or WTC 2, it is unlikely the system would have been capable of operation, due to damage caused by aircraft impacts. Even if fully operational, none of the hypothetical potential smoke management approaches evaluated would have prevented smoke spread given the damage caused by aircraft impact. During the events occurring on September 11, 2001, stair pressurization would have been ineffective in improving conditions for occupants trying to exit the building due to the extensive damage to the stair shafts. Installation of combination fire/smoke dampers in HVAC ductwork, which was not required in WTC 1 or WTC 2 at the time the WTC was constructed, may have acted to slow the development of hazardous conditions on the uppermost floors of the building, but would likely not have had a significant effect on the ability of occupants to egress the building due to the impassibility of the exit stairways.

Source: *ASHRAE Transactions*, Vol. 114, Pt. 2, p. 151-158

2009

Sustaining Our Future by Rebuilding Our Past: Energy Efficiency in Existing Buildings: Our Greatest Opportunity for a Sustainable Future

By Gordon V.R. Holness, P.E., Fellow/Life Member ASHRAE

The majority of buildings that will exist in the year 2030 have already been built, says ASHRAE's 2009-2010 President, Gordon V.R. Holness in his inaugural address. Holness describes ASHRAE's path forward on addressing energy efficiency in existing buildings. While existing buildings present great challenges, they offer us a greater opportunity to significantly impact our overall national energy demand, reduce our dependence upon imported oil and gas and minimize our carbon footprint.

Source: *ASHRAE Journal*, Vol. 51, No. 8, p. 16-21

2010

Low Reynolds Number Air-Flow Heat Transfer in Trapezoidally Corrugated Perforated Plate-Fin Ducts

By O.A. Huzayyin, Student Member ASHRAE, M.A. Jog, PhD, and R.M. Manglik, PhD, Member ASHRAE

The performance and size of refrigerant-to-air heat exchangers (evaporators and condensers) is mainly limited by the relatively low air-side heat transfer coefficients. This warrant that both surface area and convective coefficient on the air -side of the heat exchangers be increased substantially. While traditional solutions include adding high-density fins on the air-side surface, the goal of the design proposed in this study is to complement this by employing a novel trapezoidally corrugated perforated plate-fin core. It alters the convective behavior such that an increase in the heat transfer coefficient is accompanied by a substantial reduction in the friction factor. This allows the heat exchanger to be much more compact with both a smaller volume and frontal area. To highlight this, results of computational simulations for velocity and temperature fields in typical trapezoidally corrugated perforated plate-din ducts are presented. Low Reynolds number ($10 < Re < 1000$) flow of air ($Pr = 0.72$) passing through inter-fin passages, where fin walls have perforations that are equally spaced along the length of the duct, is considered and a parametric study of the effects of the duct geometry. This includes variation in fin spacing or fin density and period length of corrugation, with fixed trapezoid inclination angle and perforation spacing. Fin-surface porosity, or perforations is shown to promote the unusual behavior of increasing the heat transfer coefficient while reducing the friction factor relative to its unperforated counterpart, primarily due to surface transpirations, which lend to better flow mixing, and consecutive boundary-layer disruption.

Source: *ASHRAE Transactions* Vol. 116, Pt. 2, p. 339-346

2011

Optimizing Design and Control of Chilled Water Plants , Part 1: Chilled Water Distribution System Selection

By Steven T. Taylor, P.E., Fellow ASHRAE

This is the first in a series of articles based on the research used to support a new ASHRAE Self-Directed Learning Course on the design and control of chilled water plants. System selection is discussed and a simple application matrix is included. The next installment of the series will be in the September edition and will cover the selection of condenser water distribution systems.

Source: *ASHRAE Journal*, Vol. 53, No. 7, p. 14-25

2012

Using Building Mass To Heat And Cool: Thermo Active Building Systems (TABS)

By Bjarne W. Olesen, Ph.D., Fellow ASHRAE

Thermo active building systems (TABS) are embedded water-based surface heating and cooling systems, where the pipe is embedded in the central concrete core of a multi-story building's construction. This article describes how TABS work, how to avoid condensation issues, and best strategies for installing them.

Source: *ASHRAE Journal*, Vol. 54, No. 2, p. 44-52

2013

Manitoba Hydro Place: Energy Efficiency 2.0

By Tom Akerstream, Alexander Knirsch, and Mark Pauls, P.Eng.

Manitoba Hydro Place is among the most energy-efficient office buildings in North America. The building's high performance has its roots in an integrated design process, but the expected results were only achieved after an intensive optimization phases. Situation in Winnipeg, Canada, where temperatures range from –35°C (–31°F) to +35°C (95°F) annually, a unique climactically-responsive design was constructed to take advantage of passive energy opportunities. For example, the building form is oriented with solar gains in mind, with a wide exposure to the exact south, and a reduced facade area in the north. These strategies, with the support of energy modeling as a design tool, were intended to reduce energy at Manitoba Hydro Place by 60% compared to the Model National Energy Code of Canada for Buildings. Upon building completion, an optimization process began, which included the key engineers from the design team. The optimization process considered data from hundreds of energy meters and made comparisons with the as-built model. Discrepancies were identified, and several modifications were made to mechanical and control systems.

Source: *ASHRAE Papers CD: 2013 ASHRAE Winter Conference*

2014

Celebrating 100 Years of ASHRAE Standard 15

By Douglas T. Reindl, Ph.D., P.E., Fellow ASHRAE

In November 1914, a committee comprised of engineers from the American Society of Refrigerating Engineers began consulting with fire department officials from New York City to develop a regulation aimed to enhance the safety of refrigerating plants in the city. Out of this initial effort grew the nation's first refrigeration safety code, which eventually become Standard 15.

Source: *ASHRAE Journal*, Vol. 56, No. 11, p. 36-43

2015

Develop a Radiant System Module for the Simulation and Analysis of Spaces and Systems

By Charles S. Barnaby and Curtis O. Pedersen

ASHRAE Research Project 1383-RP, Develop a Radiant System Module for the Simulation and Analysis of Spaces and Systems, produced analysis procedures that allow calculation and display of comfort conditions at any point within a room. These procedures are implemented in a PC-based application called Radiant Performance Explorer (RPE), an enhanced version of the ASHRAE Comfort Tool. The project developed a method for calculating view factors from an arbitrarily-positioned occupant to all surfaces of an arbitrarily-shaped space. With this general ability and knowledge of room surface temperatures, mean radiant temperature (MRT) can be calculated for any occupant position. This in turn allows derivation of common comfort measures, such as PMV and PPD. Other radiant values, such as radiant temperature asymmetry, are also calculated. RPE displays these results in a computer-graphics based visualization screen. RPE can import and display data generated by the 3D drawing tool SketchUp, the building energy simulation application EnergyPlus, or other sources. Export of comfort results is available. The project also enhanced EnergyPlus to more flexibly model controlled-temperature panels.

Source: ASHRAE Research Project RP-1383 Final Report

2016

Assessing Effectiveness of Ceiling-Ventilated Mock Airborne Infection Isolation Room in Preventing Hospital-Acquired Influenza Transmission to Health Care Workers

By Deepthi Sharan Thatiparti, Student Member ASHRAE, Urmila Ghia, PhD, and Kenneth R. Mead, PhD, member ASHRAE

Exposure to airborne influenza (or flu) from a patient's cough and exhaled air causes potential flu virus transmission to the persons located nearby. Hospital-acquired influenza is a major airborne disease that occurs to health care workers (HCW). This paper examines the airflow patterns and influenza-infected cough aerosol transport behavior in a ceiling-ventilated mock airborne infection isolation room (AIIR) and its effectiveness in mitigating HCW's exposure to airborne infection. The computational fluid dynamics (CFD) analysis of the airflow patterns and the flu virus dispersal behavior in a mock AIIR is conducted using the room geometries and layout (room dimensions, bathroom dimensions and details, placement of vents and furniture), ventilation parameters (flow rates at the inlet and outlet vents, diffuser design, thermal sources, etc.), and pressurization corresponding to that of a traditional ceiling-mounted ventilation arrangement observed in existing hospitals. The measured data shows that ventilation rates for the AIIR are about 12 air changes per hour (ach). However, the numerical results reveals incomplete air mixing and that not all of the room air is changed 12 times per hour. Two life-sized breathing human models are used to simulate a source patient and a receiving HCW. A patient cough cycle is introduced into the simulation and the airborne infection dispersal is tracked in time using a multiphase flow simulation approach. The results reveal air recirculation regions that diminished the effect of air filtration and prolong the presence of flucontaminated air at the HCW's zone.

Source: *ASHRAE Transactions*, Vol. 122, Pt. 2, p. 35-45

2017

Sustainability In Energy And Water: Air-Cooled Versus Water-Cooled Heat Rejection

By Omar Hawit, PE, Member ASHRAE, Trevor Jaffe, PE, Member ASHRAE, and Coral Pais, EIT, Member ASHRAE

While water-cooled systems often reduce building energy use, there has been a dramatic improvement in air-cooled chiller performance. Fresh water scarcity results in increased water treatment plant operational cost and distribution infrastructure maintenance cost, all of which lead to higher customer charges.Simultaneously, major growth of renewable energy generation in the grid energy mix affects both process water used and greenhouse gases emitted. The market's demand for sustainability through both energy and water efficiency must be weighed carefully as competing interests continue to evolve rapidly over the next several years. This parametric study evaluates the impacts of water-cooled chiller plants versus air-cooled chiller plants and identifies trends inenergy and fresh water consumption.

Source: *ASHRAE Papers CD: 2017 ASHRAE Winter Conference*

2018

Understanding Climate Change Impacts On Building Energy Use

By Arfa N. Aijazi, Student Member ASHRAE, Gail S. Brager, Ph.D., Fellow ASHRAE

Adaptation, which describes a building's resilience to respond to climate change related hazards, is generally not part of the design process, but is equally important. This article serves as a supplement for "A Conversation on Adaptation in the Built Environment," an industry round-table moderated by the authors of this technical feature.

Source: *ASHRAE Journal*, Vol. 60, No. 10, p. 24-32

2019

Advancing Occupant Modeling for Building Design and Code Compliance: Parts 1, 2, and 3

By William O'Brien, PhD, PEng, Associate Member ASHRAE, Sara Gilani, PhD, Associate Member ASHRAE, and Mohamed Ouf, PhD, PEng, Associate Member ASHRAE

In buildings with a high degree of automation, occupants often override controls or use buildings in ways never conceived of by the designer. Advanced occupant modeling that achieves a higher level of precision can help to avoid some of these problems. These articles update the building design and energy modeling community with recent progress on occupant modeling.

Source: *ASHRAE Journal*, Vol. 61, No. 2, p. 22-29; *ASHRAE Journal*, Vol. 61, No. 3, p. 28-36; *ASHRAE Journal*, Vol. 61, No. 3, p. 30-40

Appendix L

Technical Committees, Task Groups, Technical Resource Groups, and Multidisciplinary Task Groups

(As of July 1, 2019)

TECHNICAL COMMITTEES

SECTION 1—FUNDAMENTALS AND GENERAL

1.1 Thermodynamics And Psychrometrics
1.2 Instruments And Measurements
1.3 Heat Transfer And Fluid Flow
1.4 Control Theory And Application
1.5 Computer Applications
1.6 Terminology
1.7 Business, Management And General Legal Education
1.8 Mechanical Insulation Systems
1.9 Electrical Systems
1.10 Combined Heat And Power Systems
1.11 Electric Motors And Motor Control
1.12 Moisture Management In Buildings
1.13 Optimization

SECTION 2—ENVIRONMENTAL QUALITY

2.1 Physiology and Human Environment
2.2 Plant and Animal Environment
2.3 Gaseous Air Contaminants and Gas Contaminant Removal Equipment
2.4 Particulate Air Contaminants and Particulate Contaminant Removal Equipment
2.5 Global Climate Change
2.6 Sound And Vibration
2.7 Seismic, Wind and Flood Resistant Design
2.8 Buildings Environmental Impacts and Sustainability
2.9 Ultraviolet Air and Surface Treatment
2.10 Resilience and Security

SECTION 3—MATERIALS AND PROCESSES

3.1 Refrigerants And Secondary Coolants
3.2 Refrigerant System Chemistry
3.3 Refrigerant Contaminant Control
3.4 Lubrication
3.6 Water Treatment
3.8 Refrigerant Containment

SECTION 4—LOAD CALCULATIONS AND ENERGY REQUIREMENTS

4.1 Load Calculation Data And Procedures
4.2 Climatic Information
4.3 Ventilation Requirements And Infiltration
4.4 Building Materials And Building Envelope Performance
4.5 Fenestration
4.7 Energy Calculations
4.10 Indoor Environmental Modeling

SECTION 5—VENTILATION AND AIR DISTRIBUTION

5.1 Fans
5.2 Duct Design
5.3 Room Air Distribution
5.4 Industrial Process Air Cleaning (Air Pollution Control)
5.5 Air-to-air Energy Recovery
5.6 Control Of Fire And Smoke
5.7 Evaporative Cooling
5.9 Enclosed Vehicular Facilities
5.10 Kitchen Ventilation
5.11 Humidifying Equipment

SECTION 6—HEATING EQUIPMENT, HEATING AND COOLING SYSTEMS AND APPLICATIONS

6.1 Hydronic and Steam Equipment And Systems
6.2 District Energy
6.3 Central Forced Air Heating and Cooling Systems
6.5 Radiant Heating and Cooling
6.6 Service Water Heating Systems
6.7 Solar and Other Renewable Energies
6.8 Geothermal Heat Pump and Energy Recovery Applications
6.9 Thermal Storage
6.10 Fuels and Combustion

SECTION 7—BUILDING PERFORMANCE

7.1 Integrated Building Design
7.2 HVAC&R Construction and Design Build Technologies
7.3 Operation and Maintenance Management
7.4 Exergy Analysis For Sustainable Buildings
7.5 Smart Building Systems
7.6 Building Energy Performance
7.7 Testing and Balancing
7.8 Owning and Operating Costs
7.9 Building Commissioning

SECTION 8—AIR-CONDITIONING AND REFRIGERATION SYSTEM COMPONENTS

8.1 Positive Displacement Compressors
8.2 Centrifugal Machines
8.3 Absorption and Heat Operated Machines
8.4 Air-to-Refrigerant Heat Transfer Equipment
8.5 Liquid-to Refrigerant Heat Exchangers
8.6 Cooling Towers and Evaporative Condensers
8.7 Variable Refrigerant Flow (VRF)
8.8 Refrigerant System Controls and Accesories
8.9 Residential Refrigerators and Food Freezers
8.10 Mechanical Dehumidification Equipment and Heat Pipes
8.11 Unitary and Room Air Conditioners and Heat Pumps
8.12 Desiccant Dehumidification Equipment and Components

SECTION 9—BUILDING APPLICATIONS

9.1 Large Building Air-conditioning Systems
9.2 Industrial Air Conditioning and Ventilation
9.3 Transportation Air Conditioning
9.4 Justice Facilities
9.6 Health Care Facilities
9.7 Educational Facilities
9.8 Large Building Air-Conditioning Applications
9.9 Mission Critical Facilities, Data Centers, Technology Spaces and Electronic Equipment
9.10 Laboratory Systems
9.11 Clean Spaces
9.12 Tall Buildings

SECTION 10—REFRIGERATION SYSTEMS

10.1 Custom Engineered Refrigeration Systems
10.2 Automatic Icemaking Plants and Skating Rinks
10.3 Refrigerant Piping, Controls and Accessories
10.5 Refrigerated Processing and Storage
10.6 Transport Refrigeration
10.7 Commercial Food and Beverage Refrigeration Equipment
10.8 Refrigeration Load Calculation

TECHNICAL RESOURCE GROUPS

TRG4.IAQP—INDOOR AIR QUALITY PROCEDURE DEVELOPMENT

TRG9.CCD—COLD CLIMATE DESIGN

MULTIDISCIPLINARY TASK GROUPS

MTG.ACR—AIR CHANGE RATE

MTG.ASEC—AVOIDED SOURCES ENERGY CONSUMPTION DUE TO WASTE HEAT RECOVERY AND HEAT PUMP TECHNOLOGIES

MTG.BD—BUILDING DAMPNESS

MTG.EBO—EFFECTIVE BUILDING OPERATIONS

MTG.HCDG—HOT-CLIMATE DESIGN GUIDE (MTG Under Development)

MTG.HWBE—HEALTH AND WELLNESS IN THE BUILT ENVIRONMENT

MTG.IAST—IMPACT OF ASHRAE STANDARDS AND TECHNOLOGY ON ENERGY SAVINGS/ PERFORMANCE

MTG.LowGWP—LOWER GLOBAL WARMING POTENTIAL ALTERNATIVE REFRIGERANTS

MTG.OBB—OCCUPANT BEHAVIOR IN BUILDINGS

Appendix M

Standards and Guidelines

This list includes all active committees as of June 2019. Some committees are just organizing; some are actively engaged in preparing drafts; others are about to conclude their activities. Standards and guidelines designated with a "P" are proposed; those designated with an "R" are existing standards and guidelines being revised.

Guideline 1.2 (Gdl 0.2)	*Technical Requirements for the Commissioning Process for Existing HVAC&R Systems and Assemblies*
Guideline 4	*Preparation of Operating and Maintenance Documentation for Building Systems*
Guideline 10	*Interactions Affecting the Achievement of Acceptable Indoor Environments*
Guideline 11	*Field Testing of HVAC Controls Components*
Guideline 13	*Specifying Building Automation Systems*
Guideline 14	*Measurement of Energy, Demand and Water Savings*
Guideline 21-2012R (IEEE 1635-2012)	*Guide for the Ventilation and Thermal Management of Batteries for Stationary Applications*
Guideline 22	*Instrumentation for Monitoring Central Chilled-Water Plant Efficiency*
Guideline 27	*Measurement Procedures for Gaseous Contaminants in Commercial Buildings*
Guideline 29	*Guideline for the Risk Management of Public Health and Safety in Buildings*
Guideline 32	*Sustainable, High Performance Operations and Maintenance*
Guideline 34	*Energy Efficiency Guideline for Historic Buildings and Structures*
Guideline 35	*Method for Determining the Energy Consumption Caused By Air-Cleaning and Filtration Devices*
Guideline 36	*High Performance Sequences of Operation for HVAC Systems*
Guideline 37	*Guidelines for the Application of Upper-Air (Upper Room) Ultraviolet Germicidal (UV-C) Devices to Control the Transmission of Airborne Pathogens*
Guideline 38 (formerly Standard 175)	*Guideline for Using Metal Pressure Vessels to Test Materials Used in Refrigeration Systems*
Guideline 41	*Design, Installation and Commissioning of Variable Refrigerant Flow Systems*
Standard 15	*Safety Standard for Refrigeration Systems*
Standard 16	*Method of Testing for Rating Room Air Conditioners, Packaged Terminal Air Conditioners and Packaged Terminal Heat Pumps for Cooling and Heating Capacity*
Standard 17	*Method of Testing Capacity of the Thermostatic Refrigerant Expansion Valve*
Standard 20	*Methods of Laboratory Testing Remote Mechanical-Draft Air-Cooled Refrigerant Condensers*
Standard 23.1	*Methods of Testing for Performance Rating Positive Displacement Refrigerant Compressors and Condensing Units That Operate At Subcritical Pressures of the Refrigerant*

Standard 23.2	*Methods of Test for Rating the Performance of Positive Displacement Compressors That Operate At Supercritical Pressures of the Refrigerants*	**Standard 24**	*Method of Testing for Rating Evaporators Used for Cooling Liquids*
Standard 25	*Methods of Testing Forced Convection and Natural Convection Air Coolers for Refrigeration*	**Standard 26**	*Mechanical Refrigeration and Air Conditioning Installations Aboard Ship*
Standard 28	*Method of Testing Flow Capacity of Refrigerant Capillary Tubes*	**Standard 30**	*Method of Testing Liquid Chillers*
Standard 32.2	*Methods of Testing for Rating Pre-Mix and Post-Mix Beverage Dispensing Equipment*	**Standard 33**	*Methods of Testing Forced Circulation Air Cooling and Air Heating Coils*
Standard 34	*Designation and Safety Classification of Refrigerants*	**Standard 35**	*Method of Testing Desiccants for Refrigerant Drying*
Standard 37	*Methods of Testing for Rating Electrically Driven Unitary Air-Conditioning and Heat Pump Equipment*	**Standard 41**	*Standard Methods of Measurement*
Standard 51 (AMCA 210-07)	*Laboratory Methods of Testing Fans for Certified Aerodynamic Performance Rating*	**Standard 52.2**	*Method of Testing General Ventilation Air Cleaning Devices for Removal Efficiency By Particle Size*
Standard 55	*Thermal Environmental Conditions for Human Occupancy*	**Standard 62.1 (Gdl 42)**	*Ventilation for Acceptable Indoor Air Quality*
Standard 62.2 (Gdl 24)	*Ventilation and Acceptable Indoor Air Quality in Residential Buildings*	**Standard 63.1**	*Method of Testing Liquid-Line Refrigerant Driers*
Standard 64	*Methods of Laboratory Testing Remove Mechanical-Draft Evaporative Refrigerant Condensers*	**Standard 70**	*Method of Testing for Rating the Performance of Air Outlets and Air Inlets*
Standard 72	*Method of Testing Open and Closed Commercial Refrigerators and Freezers*	**Standard 78**	*Method of Testing Flow Capacity of Suction Line Filters and Filter-Driers*
Standard 84-2013R	*Methods of Testing Air-to-Air Heat/Energy Exchangers*	**Standard 90.1**	*Energy Standard for Buildings Except Low-Rise Residential Buildings*
Standard 90.2	*Energy Efficient Design of Low-Rise Residential Buildings*	**Standard 90.4**	*Energy Standard for Data Centers and Telecommunications Buildings*
Standard 94.2	*Method of Testing Thermal Storage Devices With Electrical Input and Thermal Output Based On Thermal Performance*	**Standard 97**	*Sealed Glass Tube Method to Test the Chemical Stability of Materials for Use Within Refrigerant Systems*
Standard 100	*Energy Efficiency in Existing Buildings*	**Standard 105-2014R**	*Standard Methods of Determining, Expressing, and Comparing Building Energy Performance and Greenhouse Gas Emissions*
Standard 111	*Measurement, Testing, Adjusting and Balancing of Building Heating, Ventilation and Air-Conditioning Systems*	**Standard 113**	*Methods of Testing for Room Air Diffusion*
Standard 116	*Methods of Testing for Rating Seasonal Efficiency of Unitary Air-Conditioners and Heat Pumps*	**Standard 118.1**	*Method of Testing for Rating Commercial Gas, Electric, and Oil Service Water Heating Equipment*
Standard 118.2	*Method of Testing for Rating Commercial Gas, Electric and Oil Service Water Heating Equipment*	**Standard 124**	*Methods of Testing for Rating Combination Space-Heating and Water-Heating Appliances*
Standard 127	*Method of Testing for Rating Air Conditioning Units Serving Data Center (DC) and Other Information Technology (ITE) Spaces*	**Standard 128**	*Method of Rating Portable Air Conditioners*

Standard 130	*Laboratory Methods of Test for Air Terminal Units*
Standard 133	*Method of Testing Direct Evaporative Air Coolers*
Standard 135 (Std 135.1 and Std. 223P)	*BACnet—a Data Communication Protocol for Building Automation and Control Networks*
Standard 140	*Standard Method of Test for the Evaluation of Building Energy Analysis Computer Programs*
Standard 143	*Method of Testing for Rating Indirect Evaporative Coolers*
Standard 145 (Std. 145.1 and Std. 145.2)	*Test Method for Assessing the Performance of Gas Phase Air Cleaning Equipment*
Standard 146	*Methods of Test for Rating Pool Heaters*
Standard 147	*Reducing the Release of Halogenated Refrigerants From Refrigerating and Air-Conditioning Equipment and Systems*
Standard 150-2000R	*Method of Testing the Performance of Cool Storage Systems*
Standard 153	*Method of Test for Mass Flow Capacity of Four-Way Refrigerant Reversing Valves*
Standard 154	*Ventilation for Commercial Cooking Operations*
Standard 155	*Method of Testing for Rating Commercial Space Heating Boiler Systems*
Standard 158.1	*Methods of Testing Capacity of Refrigerant Solenoid Valves*
Standard 158.2	*Methods of Testing Capacity of Refrigerant Pressure Regulators*
Standard 160	*Criteria for Moisture-Control Design Analysis in Buildings*
Standard 161 (Gdl 28)	*Air Quality Within Commercial Aircraft*
Standard 164.4	*Method of Test for Commercial and Industrial Adiabatic Humidifiers*
Standard 169	*Climatic Data for Building Design Standards*
Standard 170	*Ventilation of Health Care Facilities*
Standard 174	*Method of Test for Rating Desiccant-Based Dehumidification Equipment*
Standard 180	*Standard Practice for Inspection and Maintenance of Commercial-Building Hvac Systems*
Standard 182	*Method of Testing Absorption Water-Chilling and Water-Heating Packages*
Standard 184	*Method of Test for Field Performance of Liquid-Chilling Systems*
Standard 185 (Std 185.1 and 185.2)	*Methods of Test to Inactivate Microorganisms in HVAC Systems With UV-C Lights*
Standard 188 (Gdl 12)	*Legionellosis: Risk Management for Building Water Systems*
Standard 189.1	*Standard for the Design of High-Performance, Green Buildings Except Low-Rise Residential Buildings*
Standard 189.3	*Design, Construction and Operation of Sustainable High Performance Health Care Facilities*
Standard 190	*Method of Testing for Rating Indoor Pool Dehumidifiers*
Standard 191	*Standard for the Efficient Use of Water in Building, Site and Mechanical Systems*
Standard 193	*Method of Test for Determining the Airtightness of HVAC Equipment*
Standard 195	*Method of Test for Rating Air Terminal Unit Controls*
Standard 196	*Method of Test for Measuring Refrigerant Leak Rates*
Standard 198	*Method of Test for Rating DX-Dedicated Outdoor Air Systems for Moisture Removal Capacity and Moisture Removal*
Standard 200	*Methods of Testing Chilled Beams*
Standard 204	*Method of Test for Rating Micro Combined Heat and Power Devices*
Standard 205	*Standard Representation of Performance Simulation Data for HVAC&R and Other Facility Equipment*
Standard 207	*Laboratory Method of Test of Fault Detection and Diagnostics Applied Commercial Air-Cooled Packaged Systems*
Standard 208	*Method of Test for Determining Hydronic System Balance Valve Capacity*
Standard 210	*Method of Testing for Rating Commercial Walk-in Cooler and Freezer Equipment*
Standard 211	*Standard for Commercial Building Energy Audits*

Standard 212	*Method of Test for Determining Energy Performance and Water-Use Efficiency of Add-On Evaporative Pre-Coolers for Unitary Air Conditioning Equipment*	**Standard 213**	*Method for Calculating Moist Air Thermodynamic Properties*
Standard 215	*Method of Test to Determine Leakage of Operating HVAC Air-Distribution Systems*	**Standard 216**	*Methods of Test for Determining Application Data of Overhead Circulator Fans*
Standard 217	*Non-Emergency Ventilation in Enclosed Road, Rail and Mass Transit Facilities*	**Standard 218**	*Method of Test for Lubricant and Refrigerant Miscibility Determination*
Standard 219	*Method of Testing the Ability of Liquid Line Filter Driers Or Absorbents to Remove Organic Acid*	**Standard 220**	*Method of Testing for Rating Small Commercial Blast Chillers, Chiller-Freezers, and Freezers*
Standard 221	*Test Method to Measure and Score the Operating Performance of An Installed Constant Volume Unitary HVAC System*	**Standard 222**	*Standard Method of Test for Electrical Power Drive Systems*
Standard 224	*Standard for the Application of Building Information Modeling*	**Standard 225**	*Method for Performance Testing Centrifugal Refrigerant Compressors and Condensing Units*
Standard 300 (Std 202, Gdl 0, Gdl 0.2, Gdl 1.1, Gdl 1.4, Gdl 1.5, Gdl 1.6)	*Commissioning*		

Appendix N

Snapshots

Images in Words and Photographs from ASHRAE's Past

PRESIDENT'S PAGE

The real meaning of ASHRAE

CECIL BOLING

Frankly, I am not greatly impressed by numbers. One hundred million people can be as wrong as they could be right or vice versa. If numbers alone counted India and China would be of greater significance in the world of today than is our own country.

ASHRAE is far more than the nearly twenty thousand people engaged in a more or less common activity using closely related engineering principles for the consummation of their individual goals.

First, ASHRAE is opportunity – to improve upon things as they are, to broaden the horizons of accomplishment and to insure more efficient and economical use of materials, energies, resources and efforts.

Second, it is figuratively a larger and more easily opened door for the man who has chosen engineering as a career and heating, refrigerating and air conditioning or ventilating as his field for activity.

Third, it is a challenge that we make the most of the inherent possibilities created by this now more broadly enveloping professional society.

Perhaps that sounds rather idealistic; you might have hoped that I would spell out in terms of specific things that would be personally rewarding to you. I do not think that to be the way that a professional society should function nor the way that an engineer should approach his membership in such an organization.

It requires no great study to realize that over the longer interval we must give in order to get and that, in the final sense, the more we give the more we get.

So let us approach the future of ASHRAE with the idea of how much we shall contribute as individuals to the possible progress of our Society, of our companies, of our associates and of ourselves.

Many of us know of the long hours put into the development of Standards, the furthering of the work of committees, the preparation of meetings papers and other lesser chores which may seem to go unrewarded and little noted. I do not think that they are ever purposeless or lacking in true effectiveness. The question is did we give enough to make the activities worthwhile?

As the first president of the American Society of Heating, Refrigerating and Air Conditioning Engineers, I feel that my part presently is to expedite organizational phases of the new Society for the sooner we establish ASHRAE as an operating entity the sooner we may proceed to those broader accomplishments which I envision for 1959 and later years. Other days will present other problems but if we have built well the future will be all that you and I have hoped in even our most optimistic moments.

MARCH 1959

Admissions Committee Meets

Admissions Committee meets at headquarters in New York each month. At the November meeting were (left to right) Martha Flaherty; T. R. Kearney; C. F. Holske, chairman; C. F. Kayan; T. J. Phillips

1955

Columbus Section Formed

Among those at the speakers' table at the formation meeting of Columbus Section were Al Chadburn; Jim Kelly, temporary chairman; George S. Jones, Jr., of ARI at the rostrum; Jim Snyder; Eddie Graff. Ed Note: Jim Kelly submitted the petition, constitution and temporary list of officers to Council at the 51st Annual ASRE Meeting at Atlantic City and they were accepted as legal sections of the Society

1955

ELECTION TELLERS COUNT BALLOTS

Tellers of election, left to right, W. I. Freeman Jr., E. R. McFarlan and K. M. Fajans, convene at headquarters to count ballots for election of national ASRE officers and directors.

1956

Among those present were: Andrew T. Boggs III; François L'Anglais; ASHRAE President John E. Dube; B. J. Horsburgh; and Les Single

Letters and wires of congratulations and wishes for success have been received from all over the continent by the Atlantic Provinces Chapter which received its Charter on March 15. B. J. Horsburgh, Region II Chairman presided over the Charter Proceedings, assisted by President John E. Dube, Treasurer John Ross and Associate Secretary Andrew T. Boggs III. Several prominent members of neighboring Canadian Chapters also participated.

Murray Malloy, who was instrumental in the formation of this eleventh ASHRAE Chapter in Canada, gave the background to the development of the Chapter, from the selection of the Montreal Chapter Sponsoring Committee to the election of officers on February 16 and Charter Night.

Mr. Dube addresses the newly-formed chapter

President Dube, who presented the Charter to Chapter President Les Single, welcomed the new Chapter to ASHRAE and discussed the role of chapters within the national organization.

The new Chapter has 48 paid-up members, 14 applications in process and 6 applicants awaiting application forms.

1965

ASHRAE CONTRIBUTES TO PRESIDENT'S PEOPLE-TO-PEOPLE PROGRAM: GUIDE AND DATA BOOKS GO TO IRAN

Over the past few years, ASHRAE has contributed early volumes of the society's Guide And Data Book to the Engineers and Scientific Committee of the President's People-To-People Program. The program, in effect since 1958, has been sending up-to-date technical literature to universities and libraries in Balkan, Nead and Middle Eastern countries. The engineering journals and technical books collected through voluntary donations supply engineers and students from Yugoslavia, Turkey, Lebanon, Syria, Iraq and Iran with the knowledge needed for the building of roads, raising of power stations, and construction of buildings and dams.

ASHRAE has already sent a total of 2900 Guide And Data Books.

The Engineers and Scientists program is an integral part of a nonprofit People-To-People communication inaugurated nationwide in 1956 to establish lasting two-way relationships between Americans and their counterparts in countries all over the world.

At right, students from the University of Tehran, Iran, examine one of the ASHRAE Guide And Data Books their school has received

ASHRAE JOURNAL *February 1966*

president's page

P. N. VINTHER
Vice President ASHRAE

Who is responsible to whom

ASHRAE is a membership organization, operated by its members both for member benefit and of the public-at-large. By their vote, the members of ASHRAE adopted by-laws according to which they are governed. These by-laws establish, among other things, a plan for the administration of Society affairs through a Board of Directors and committees. The by-laws specify the duties of the Board, as well as the number and qualifications of its members. They also specify committees, delineate their respective spheres of authority, state how each is to be constituted, and the number and qualifications of their personnel.

The accompanying chart illustrates the lines of authority and communication among these bodies. It shows by varied shading that there are four types of bodies: (a) Membership, at both national and chapter levels, participation in which is voluntary; (b) Officers and Directors, who, with the exception of the Executive Secretary, are elected by the membership; (c) Committees which, with three important exceptions, are appointed by the President with the consent of the Board of Directors; and (d) Staff, who are employed persons operating under the direction of the President. The personnel currently in office in each of these categories, except (d), appear on pages 90 and 91 of this issue of the Journal.

There are five elected officers: President, President-Elect, two Vice Presidents, and Treasurer. The Board of Directors consists of these officers and 16 Directors, of whom six are elected at large and one is elected from each region for the remaining 10. Each of these also serves as Regional Chairman for his region. Officers are elected for a one-year term. Directors are usually elected for a three-year term, with terms staggered to introduce new Directors at as uniform a rate as possible.

In order that each administration may retain control of the activities for which it is responsible, Presidential appointments to committee membership are for a period of one year. To effect continuity in committee work from year to year, however, those appointed are usually re-appointed by succeeding Presidents for two additional years. Thus, approximately one-third of the total membership of all appointed committees in any one year represents new members.

One of the three exceptions to Presidential committee appointment is the Nominating Committee. This Committee consists of 16 members, each elected for a one-year term, six by the Board of Directors and 10 by the chapters themselves, operating through their Chapters Regional Committees, and is chaired by the most recent Past President available to serve. To insure some degree of continuity of thought and information from year to year within the Nominating Committee, it is required that one of the six members elected by the Board for any year shall have served on a previous Nominating Committee.

The second exception is the Research and Technical Committee and its related groups. The Research and Technical Committee, itself, consists of 12 members elected, after solicitation along prescribed lines from specified sources for qualified nominees, by secret ballot by the Board of Directors for a three-year term. To maintain continuity in the work of the Committee, the by-laws require the election of four members each year.

The third exception is the Regions Central Committee, which is composed of the 10 elected Regional Chairmen, with the President-Elect as Chairman and the two Vice Presidents as Vice Chairmen.

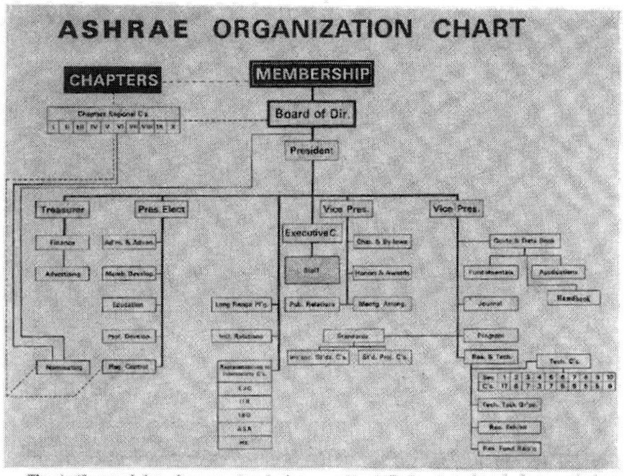

The significance of these three exceptions is that appointment or election to service in each of these committees is reserved, insofar as possible and in truly democratic fashion, to the Society membership as a whole: a majority of the Nominating Committee is chosen directly by the membership; the Regional Chairmen are elected by it; and Research and Technical Committeemen are elected by the Board, of whom the Regional Chairmen constitute a majority. Thus, what are perhaps the three most important facets of the life of the Society are safeguarded against domination by a single influence or interest.

In order that there be liaison and a channel of communication between the President and the Board of Directors, on the one hand, and the several committees, on the other, one of the officers is assigned as Directing Officer to each of the committees, becoming an *ex-officio* member thereof, but without vote. The Treasurer is assigned, quite naturally, to the Finance Committee and to the Advertising Committee, which is a sub-committee of Finance. The President-Elect is Directing Officer of Regions Central Committee, as well as its Chairman, and, in addition, serves as Directing Officer of a group of appointed committees whose interests are general and Society-wide. A Vice President is assigned to each of the two other groups of committees whose interests are specific, one in generally technical areas and one in generally non-technical areas. The President personally retains contacts with those committees and appointees whose activities lie, in general, outside the Society. In this way, the lines of authority and communication run among the membership, the Board, the officers and the committees, all represented by the heavy lines on the chart.

An equally important channel of communications, and leverage, runs from the membership through chapters to Chapters Regional Committees, and from there to the Board and to the Regions Central Committee, all as represented on the chart by the dotted lines. This channel is implemented when groups of membership, operating as chapters, designate representatives to become members of the Chapters Regional Committee for each region, when each Chapters Regional Committee designates a representative to become a member of the national Nominating Committee and provides him with a list of names to be offered for consideration for nomination as officers and Directors; and finally, after their election the Regional Chairmen come together under the chairmanship of the President-Elect as the Regions Central Committee. Along this line, any individual or any chapter has access through the Regional Chairman to the Board of Directors, either directly as illustrated or through his representation on the Regions Central Committee to the President-Elect and the Board. It is the duty of the Regional Chairman to facilitate this access. It is in this way that every member of the Society is afforded the means of presenting his thoughts before the Board, whether in suggestion, praise or criticism.

In addition, any member is welcome to attend a meeting of the Board or any committee at any time that it is not in executive session. He is privileged to seek an audience with any one of these bodies, with the expectation of being heard courteously and attentively, thus cutting across all other lines of communication. For, in a membership society, the administrative personnel are the servants, not the masters.

research page

PAUL R. ACHENBACH
Fellow ASHRAE

ASHRAE contributions to environmental engineering in buildings

Leaders in the building industry are currently giving much attention to performance requirements in the design and construction of buildings, and the associated mechanical systems. Under this concept, a building component or system is evaluated in terms of its ability to fulfill the important requirements of the user, without regard to the specific properties or arrangement of the materials involved. The recent adoption of ASHRAE Standard 55-66 on Thermal Comfort Conditions is a significant contribution to the performance concept with respect to thermal environment for human occupancy.

Although this Standard sets forth comfort conditions principally for sedentary individuals, it is applicable to most residential and commercial occupancies and to others involving a minimum of physical activity. The Standard is based on a long history of ASHRAE physiological research and sets forth acceptable limits of dry-bulb temperature, relative humidity, mean radiant temperature, air motion and ventilation rate in the occupied space of a building and the permissible maximum rate of change of temperature and humidity, without regard to the type of building construction or air-conditioning system involved.

For the first time, a leading professional society has provided performance criteria for the heating or air-conditioning of buildings which can be used by architects, engineers, builders and federal housing agencies. If used, this Standard could upgrade the quality of a large segment of heating or air-conditioning installations and serve as a foundation for a much broader pattern of environmental criteria in buildings.

Both private industry and construction agencies of the Federal government are experimenting with the use of a broad description of the air-conditioning, acoustic, illumination and structural performance of buildings based on user requirements as a means of stimulating new developments in integrated systems.

The key position of performance criteria for thermal comfort conditions in buildings is emphasized by the fact that most buildings are built for the express purpose of providing a more favorable thermal environment for a particular activity than would otherwise be possible. In most municipalities the structural, safety, health, and sanitation requirements for buildings are set forth in legal codes that are based on model codes and on a substantial body of technical information or experience. No corresponding support has existed for the equally-important functional requirements of buildings related to environmental performance and durability.

It is well-known that the interior thermal environment of a building depends not only on the design and application of the heating or air-conditioning equipment, but also on the design and arrangement of materials for the building and on the processes and activities carried out inside the structure. However, responsibility for the interrelationship between the performance of the heating or air-conditioning equipment, the thermal aspects of the building enclosure, and the heat generation within the structure has not always been fully accepted by designers and builders.

Furthermore, the increase in illumination levels provided in many buildings, the prevalent generation of noise and vibration by heating, air-conditioning and ventilation equipment, and the relatively large use of electric energy by this equipment has made it necessary for the air-conditioning engineer to become better informed about, and collaterally responsible for, lighting systems, noise and vibration control, and electrical distribution systems in buildings.

Thus, the growing integration of the heating or air-conditioning system in a building with the electrical and lighting systems, the structural elements of the building, and the acoustic treatment of the structure has focused attention on the desirability of authoritative performance criteria for the several environmental characteristics of buildings and has broadened the scope of the ASHRAE research program.

A large number of the current ASHRAE research projects are concerned with human comfort studies, air distribution, noise evaluation and control, particulate and toxic contaminants in indoor air, calculation of dynamic heating and cooling loads, and control systems for air-conditioning systems, which may produce technical information relevant to environmental performance criteria.

Paul R. Achenbach is Head, Section 6B, Air-Conditioning Equipment and Application, of the ASHRAE Research and Technical Committee.

Proposed amendment to ASHRAE By-Laws to be placed on the June 1967 ballot

This amendment will be voted on at the 74th Annual Meeting of the Society in Minneapolis, Minn., June 26-28, 1967.

The section for which amendment is proposed appears, first, as it presently stands and, second, in the form of the proposed amendment. Changes to the present section are italicized.

Sec. 5.6

PRESENT

The terms of all Officers and Directors, except as otherwise provided in this section, shall commence upon their installation during the Annual Meeting and shall continue until their successors have been elected and installed. The President-Elect shall automatically succeed to the office of the President at the conclusion of the President's term in office. If the President dies, resigns or is removed from office, the President-Elect shall immediately become President and shall serve for the remainder of the term of his immediate predecessor. If the time served is less than six (6) months, he shall also serve as President for the next Society year. If the President-Elect dies, resigns, or is removed from office, the Board of Directors shall elect a successor from one of the other elected officers. If there is a vacancy in the offices of both President and President-Elect, the Vice President in the order of his seniority as a member of the Society shall act as President until the next Annual Meeting. If another elected officer dies, resigns, or is removed from office, the Board of Directors, at its first meeting thereafter, shall elect a successor from one of its members not currently serving as an officer. If a Director dies, resigns, or otherwise vacates his office, the Board of Directors shall elect a successor to complete such Director's unexpired term.

PROPOSED

The terms of all Officers and Directors, except as otherwise provided in this section, shall commence upon their installation during the Annual Meeting and shall continue until their successors have been elected and installed. The President-Elect shall automatically succeed to the office of the President at the conclusion of the President's term in office. If the President dies, resigns or is removed from office, the President-Elect shall immediately become President and shall serve for the remainder of the term of his immediate predecessor. If the time served is less than six (6) months, he shall also serve as President for the next Society year. *If the President-Elect dies, resigns, is removed from office, or becomes President in accordance with the foregoing provisions hereof, the office of President-Elect shall remain vacant until the next Annual Meeting.* If there is a vacancy in the offices of both President and President-Elect, the Vice President in the order of his seniority as a member of the Society shall act as President until the next Annual Meeting. If another elected officer dies, resigns, or is removed from office, the Board of Directors, at its first meeting thereafter, shall elect a successor from one of its members not currently serving as an officer. If a Director dies, resigns, or otherwise vacates his office, the Board of Directors shall elect a successor to complete such Director's unexpired term.

ASHRAE NATIONAL MEETINGS AHEAD	1967	1968
	June 26-28 74th Annual Minneapolis, Minn.	February 5-8 Semiannual Columbus, Ohio June 24-26 75th Annual Lake Placid, N. Y.

78 ASHRAE JOURNAL *April 1967*

Nine chapters presented a total of $16,667 for ASHRAE research. Each contribution was for $1000 or more. Pictured are ASHRAE Director of Research Royal S. Buchanan; J. E. Copeland, Philadelphia; Henry Buffolow, Jr., San Jose; C. J. Bruechert and D. C. Powell, Atlanta; R. Friedman, Golden Gate; W. M. Green, New Orleans; S. E. Ammons, Dallas; and W. Dudek, Puget Sound. Absent are the representatives from Southern California and North Piedmont

44 ASHRAE JOURNAL March 1970

Life Members pose for the photographer at their semiannual luncheon

1970

BOSTON "TEA" PARTY with Thayer Francis, Sr ; President & Mrs. C. M. Ashley and Mr. & Mrs. P. K. Barker

1957

INFORMAL COMMITTEE SESSION

Business and pleasure were mixed at meeting of Admissions committee at "Kayan's Acres" in Katonah N. Y. Enjoying the proceedings are, left to right, Prof. Carl Kayan, Assistant to Treasurer Martha Flaherty, Thomas J. Phillips, Secretary Emeritus M. C. Turpin, Assistant Secretary Herbert Tinning and Donald McCuaig.

1956

Delegates to the Region VIII Conference included, front row: Andrew T. Boggs III, ASHRAE Associate Secretary; Jack Thompson, Director and Regional Chairman of Region VIII; Edwin C. Kennedy, President of the East Texas Chapters; and Warren Spofford, General Chairman of the Conference and member of the East Texas Chapter. ASHRAE President W. L. McGrath was also present at the meeting.

1967

Report: Air Disinfection in Hospitals

SCOTT A. SPENCER
Member ASHRAE

Editor's Note: At the request of Executive Secretary Andrew T. Boggs, Scott A. Spencer represented ASHRAE at the Meeting on Air Disinfection on May 10 at the Johns Hopkins School of Hygiene and Public Health, Baltimore, Md. This meeting was co-sponsored by Johns Hopkins and the National Tuberculosis Assn. Mr. Spencer's report follows:

THE purpose of the meeting was to discuss the practical aspects of the installation of ultraviolet radiation for the control of airborne bacteria in hospitals. Earlier, a committee of the National Tuberculosis Assn (NTA) had recommended that the air in potentially hazardous areas be disinfected by ultraviolet to eliminate the possibility of cross infection and thus permit the treatment of tubercular patients in general hospitals.

Co-chaired by Dr. Richard Riley of The Johns Hopkins University Dept of Environmental Medicine and Dr. James E. Perkins of the National Tuberculosis Assn, the meeting was attended by almost 100 representatives of medical and public health organizations, hospitals, equipment manufacturers and professional societies.

While considerable research on ultraviolet air sanitation had been done in the past by Dr. Riley and his associates and by the major manufacturers of ultraviolet equipment, most such studies have been based on upper air irradiation of occupied areas by the installation of ultraviolet fixtures high on the sidewalls to disinfect the air immediately below the ceiling. Such installation depends on natural or induced room circulation between upper and lower levels to bring the total room air contents within the influence of the radiation source. Installations in areas of more or less continuous occupancy have been inhibited by reports of the possible human hazards of over-exposure, the required degree of installation maintenance and metering supervision and by the adverse effects of radiation on some materials such as plastics, paints, and textiles.

Recent research has been directed towards concealment of the ultraviolet source exposing to radiation, to the maximum extent, the air in the area to be disinfected. A current experimental installation at The Johns Hopkins University consists of a room of approximately 120 sq ft with a louvered egg-crate ceiling installed at a height of about 9 ft above the floor leaving, due to the room's physical dimensions, a space of close to 4 ft between the ceiling and the slab. Across the full width of the middle of the room, between ceiling and slab, a barrier has been installed in which a propeller fan is mounted to draw the air from one half of the room through the ceiling and return it to the other half. Ultraviolet lamps, mounted on their channels, are installed directly on top of the egg-crate ceiling, their output directed upwards, in sufficient number and pattern to provide the desired amount of radiation but so located that their back-up channels and the effective line of vision cut-off provided by the egg-crate configuration prevents any direct radiation to the room below.

To obtain the desired degree of disinfection of the room air, the rate of air movement through the irradiated space above the hung ceiling has been determined as 100 complete cycles per hr of the entire air contents of the treated room. Assuming the ceiling to have approximately 80% free area, such air circulation results in air velocities at the ceiling between 20 and 30 fpm with correspondingly lower velocities in the room below.

In addition to the many comments concerning the practicality of the experimental installation, from areas of interest other than ASHRAE, relative to its lack of reality in available ceiling height compared to the current squeezed down designs to meet construction costs; the added equipment and electric service requirements; operating and housekeeping costs; air and motor noise; etc., it was pointed out that no such massive movement of the air contents of a conditioned space could be considered independently of the conditioning system. Because an air-conditioning system depends for its satisfactory functioning on the complete and continuous diffusion of the conditioned air supply throughout the treated space and the air circulating disinfecting system likewise depends on continuous recirculating of the entire room air, it is obvious that the two systems, to be practical, should be combined to avoid conflict and the possible negation of one system by the other.

Several suggestions for combining germicidal units with air-conditioning or ventilating equipment were discussed at the meeting. As the objective is to disinfect the air as close as possible to the source of infection, the treatment of the room supply air (non-recirculated) need not be considered, but individual room air recirculating equipment such as terminal induction units should be adaptable.

Further study is to be made of the experimental installation to ascertain its functioning within practical floor heights; to investigate its effects on other air systems; to minimize installation and operating costs and eliminate any radiation hazards. However, it appears at this time that the forced air disinfection system will prove to be impractical and installations, where medically advisable, will return to the previous sidewall and curtain type of ultraviolet fixtures located within the treated space with improved safeguards against the hazards of improper installation.

S. A. Spencer is a consulting engineer in New York City.

68 ASHRAE JOURNAL July 1968

DINNER DANCE round table group—"Big Chief" John Dube—upper right

1957

When the Life Members Club, guided by E. K. Campbell, met for its luncheon meeting, there were 21 qualified members present

1961

Attending this meeting was a substantial delegation from the ASHRAE Purdue University Student Branch. Professor Frederick B. Morse had these students under his guidance. President John Kaman headed the group. Trip expenses were defrayed variously by the gifts of individuals and of organizations. The group attended both the Meeting and the Show

1961

ASHRAE journal May 1967

American Society of Heating, Refrigerating and Air-Conditioning Engineers

THE SOUND OF OUTDOOR EQUIPMENT
TWO PAPERS FROM THE DETROIT SYMPOSIUM: BLAZIER; MELING

Winners of Distinguished Service Award, from left to right: front row – J.D. Lovely, R.S. Buchanan receiving for H.P. Soumerai, J.R. Schreiner, R.S. Stover and J. Barrie Graham; center – R.L. Eichhorn, W.P. Chapman, L.R. Smith and A.B. Newton receiving for A.L. Hesselschwerdt, Jr.; rear – C.W. Phillips, C.F. Kayan, T.J. White and S.P. Soling

1969

At the Mardi Gras Party officers received the gold keys to Bourbon Street and certificates of citizenship in New Orleans from J. T. Knight, General Chairman of the New Orleans Section Arrangement Committee. Here are Cecil Boling, J. T. Knight, Jr., D. D. Wile, R. H. Tull, Elmer Queer and R. C. Cross

1958

A New TC is Born: TC 4.4 – Industrial Air Cleaning

WILLIAM J. COLLINS, JR.
Fellow ASHRAE

AIR pollution has become a subject of increasing interest to the public, the industry, and ASHRAE. At the 1967 Semiannual Meeting of ASHRAE, the Research & Technical (R & T) Committee directed its Chairman to "appoint a Task Group whose first responsibility will be to define the role of the Society in the area of air pollution control and correction. . . ." This Task Group reported to R & T at the Annual Meeting in June of 1967 and, based upon that report, the Board of Directors formulated a policy on the Society's role in this area. The policy was set forth in the September 1967 issue of ASHRAE JOURNAL (p. 56).

One of the items included in the policy was that "ASHRAE shall encourage and sponser research to discover improved methods to deal effectively, economically, and without contributing to the pollution of our water supply, with those aspects of air pollution control and correction of particular interest to its members and those they serve in a professional society."

At a meeting of the Task Group on Air Pollution in December 1967, it was noted that existing Technical Committees (TCs) were slanted towards elimination of pollutants in air admitted into buildings, rather than elimination in that air exhausted. Three existing TCs touch on such matters: TC 4.3—Industrial Environment; TC 6.3—Industrial Air Conditioning; and TC 9.4—Air Cleaning and Purification Equipment. It was felt that the Society should be more concerned with collectors, scrubbers, and other air cleaners, especially as related to air exhausted from buildings.

The possible need for a new Technical Committee in this area was presented to the R & T Committee at the ASHRAE 1968 Semiannual Meeting in February. After investigation and discussion with the TCs previously mentioned, the R & T Committee, at a meeting in March 1968, under provisions of its Operational Guide, voted to establish TC 4.4—Industrial Air Cleaning. [illegible] M. Kane, consultant, Jeffersontown, Ky., will serve as Chairman.

Note that activities of the TC will be in the area of "those aspects of air pollution control and correction of particular interest to its members and those they serve in a professional capacity," and that ASHRAE "shall not undertake to concern itself with the control of effluents from processes, chemical reaction, and similar operations not historically associated with ASHRAE endeavors, except as such effluents may indirectly become a part of the enclosed space exhaust or enclosed supply air."

TC 4.4 will be responsible for advising the R & T Committee on research and technical matters arising from, or related to, its area of interest. It shall be concerned with the request and support of a needed standard through the Standards Committee and shall be responsible for review and revision of the GUIDE AND DATA BOOK Chapter on Industrial Air and Gas Cleaners. The TC shall also maintain close liaison with other pertinent societies and agencies to assure that its efforts will supplement rather than duplicate the activities of the organizations.

The new TC will also bring a much needed addition to the ASHRAE R & T structure, and help to further the Society's objectives.

W. J. Collins, Jr. is president, Collins [illegible] Ohio. Mr. Collins was former head of Section 4.0—Ventilating and Air-Handling, ASHRAE Research & Technical Committee.

ASHRAE JOURNAL August 1968

TENNESSEE VALLEY RECEIVES CHARTER; ASHRAE EXECUTIVES ATTEND

Mr. Boggs, Mr. Wilson, Mr. Hardy, Mr. Nichols, Mr. Goodman, John Germ (Chapter Organizational Chairman), Mr. Tate, Mr. Bridgers, Mr. Kelso and Mr. Tallon

1971

ASHRAE charters new chapter

ASHRAE chartered its 138th chapter, the Tri-Cities Chapter of Upper East Tennessee and Southwest Virginia, on Sept. 9th. Present for the ceremonies were (left to right) Andrew T. Boggs, ASHRAE executive vice president; Clint Phillips, ASHRAE president; Chip Bailey, president of the Tri-Cities Chapter; and David Butler, ASHRAE Region VII Chairman.

1982

SEPTEMBER 10, 1969
ASHRAE 75th ANNIVERSARY

CHAPTERS URGED TO HOLD MONTHLY MEETINGS ON THIS DATE

On September 10, 1969, ASHRAE will officially recognize its founding 75 years ago by 75 dedicated engineers. This recognition not only honors an organization which is respected internationally, but pays homage to all the countless thousands of Society members who contributed their technological skills to the progress of the air-conditioning, heating, refrigeration and ventilation industries.

Frank H. Bridgers, President-Elect and Chairman of the 75th Anniversary Committee, urges each ASHRAE Chapter to hold its monthly meeting on this historic date – September 10 – to reflect on the past and consider the future.

Mr. Bridgers suggests that each chapter should invite and honor all past presidents and charter members and that special efforts be made to make the occasion memorable such as: a scholarship award to a deserving student; award to member who has contributed most significantly to chapter activities; award to member who has been most active in local community affairs.

In addition, each chapter is requested to circulate news releases to the local press, informing the public about the achievements of ASHRAE and, in particular, about the contributions of local chapter members to the community – in terms of technological knowledge and benefits of increased environmental control.

In order to encourage record attendance, the Board of Directors has authorized a plaque to be given to the chapter who has the highest percentage of attendance for this meeting. There will be a Large Chapter Division (Chapters having 150 members or more) and Small Chapter Division (Chapters having less than 150 members). The count on chapter members will be based on the National Headquarters records as of July 1, 1969 with a correction applied for national members assigned to the chapter who are not dues paying members of the local chapter. Computed will be only 50% of members in this category assigned to the chapters. The reason for this is to try to encourage the attendance of this type of member to this special meeting of the chapter.

There have already been some wagers made among Regional Directors as to where the plaques will go. This is a great opportunity to start off each chapter for a banner year this fall.

The Emerging Importance of the Computer

WILLIAM P. CHAPMAN
Section Head — 10.0 (Auxiliary Equipment) Research & Technical Committee

ONE of the subtle, overlooked facts of our time, reflected in the program at ASHRAE's 1968 Annual Meeting at Lake Placid in June, was the emerging importance of the computer. The Symposium on Energy Requirements, and the Forum on Computer Applications, helped to illustrate the increasing significance of computational techniques.

The two distinct, but often confused, applications for computers in our industry are design and operation of equipment, and it is this area to which I want to direct my remarks.

The operation of equipment in accordance with design precepts is the first step in optimizing performance. If the operational characteristics of the equipment are included in the mathematical model used in the design, then the system can be expected to operate within the parameters set by the design. This concept, although unrealizable, does not have the necessary data to describe the dynamic characteristics of the equipment in our air-conditioning systems.

The need for such data was described years ago. In May 1958, a conference was held in our former laboratory in Cleveland for the sole purpose of discussing the need for research on dynamic performance of mechanical equipment. In 1951, an ASHRAE research contract was set for RP-5—Air-Conditioning System Control, and today this work has progressed into RP-51—Dynamic Response of a Refrigeration Evaporator and RP-52—Air-Conditioning System Control Application. Several papers have been published and some excellent work has been done.

However, much more must be done, for with the growing awareness of the capabilities of computers, consulting engineers and manufacturers will demand the publication of mathematical expressions that will permit the modeling of entire systems—from the building and piping to the boiler and pump. By employing computers, it would be feasible to simulate climatic variations and predict operating cost and performance for several proposed systems of a structure.

The comparison of these several proposals would yield a truly optimum combination. In addition, the results of the simulation would also yield the operating schedule. Then it might become feasible to put a computer on-line in the control loop.

One might ask, why is it not possible, or at least practical, to do this today? The answer, as stated above, is simply that the dynamic properties of structures and equipment are not known. Apparently, though, the work reported at Lake Placid indicates that soon we will be able to write a transfer function for a structure. Or, at least, we can approximate one with sufficient accuracy to use it in a model. Aside from the work done on coils, shell and tube heat exchangers, and expansion valves, practically nothing has been done on the mechanical elements.

Rather than belabor the point further, I would like to invite the comments of the ASHRAE membership on a suggestion for a study group which would prepare a work statement for research in the field of Dynamic Response of Mechanical Equipment. This would be an ad hoc group charged with the responsibility of defining the work to be done, either privately or by ASHRAE, so that designers could simulate entire systems over the whole load spectrum. The completion of this work, coupled with the work being done by the Task Group on Energy Requirements for Heating and Cooling, should enable the air-conditioning engineer to break at last with the design concept of thermal equilibrium. He should then be able to deal with the real environment of transients rather than the ideal, fictitious criteria of equilibrium. Although he will be forced to employ more powerful techniques, we can still see the economic picture pointing toward computers. Manual computation soon will be as archaic as manual bookkeeping. Computers will be as common as typewriters and calculation sheets as rare as longhand letters.

The suggested study group may begin with a review of the available data and then contact cognizant Technical Committees (TCs) for suggestions on how further data may be obtained. For those areas where no information is available, research effort would seem to be required. Possibly this study group would evolve into a Task Group or TC, but this could best be determined after experience and discussion. What seems to be important now is that a knowledgeable group be assembled to look today at tomorrow's needs.

W. P. Chapman is vice president—operations, Johnson Service Co. Milwaukee, Wis.

ASHRAE JOURNAL September 1968

Society of Environmental Engineers

WILLIAM L. HOLLADAY
Presidential Member ASHRAE

A MAJOR interest of ASHRAE has always been related to environmental control within spaces. For some time the ASHRAE Board of Directors has been concerned by the proliferation of organizations using the word "environment" in their names. Due to this increasing encroachment, the Board directed that a study be made of the use of the word "environment," and the Long Range Planning Committee was charged with the responsibility of developing a program that would preserve the name "Society of Environmental Engineers" for future appropriate use.

Society legal counsel conducted a copyright survey, and determined that over 50 organizations already have "environment" in some form, in their registered names. The survey indicated these groups varied from interior decorators to hi-fi installers. Certainly these do not relate to the "environment" of concern to ASHRAE.

As directed, counsel developed incorporation papers, and the Society of Environmental Engineers Inc (SEE) is now a fact. It should be stated, however, that it is *not* a legal segment, division, or branch of ASHRAE. SEE is a separate entity, with its own incorporation papers, Bylaws, Board of Directors, and opportunity to serve the engineering fraternity with interest in the control of environment in enclosed spaces.

At the organizational meeting on January 19 in San Francisco, the following officers and Board of Directors were elected:

President –
William L. Holladay
Vice President –
Axel Marin
Treasurer –
Earle K. Wagner
Secretary –
Andrew T. Boggs III
Directors –
Albert A. Giannini
John W. James
James W. May
William L. McGrath
P. N. Vinther

Since there is a tie to ASHRAE objectives, suggestions for future programs of SEE would be welcome. Such suggestions will be published in ASHRAE JOURNAL, and it is hoped that with your help SEE may become an effective platform for all those with interests in this specialized field.

SEE BYLAWS AVAILABLE

We shall be happy to send anyone interested a set of the SEE Bylaws. Membership is limited to individuals actively engaged in the practice of engineering. If you are interested in charter membership in SEE, please address your inquiry to: Andrew T. Boggs III, Executive Secretary, SEE, c/o ASHRAE, 345 E. 47th St, New York, N.Y. 10017.

It is hoped, also, that this announcement will answer the questions about any imminent plans to change the name of ASHRAE.

W. L. Holladay is chairman of the Board, Holladay, Eggett & Helin, Engrs & Consultants, Los Angeles, Calif.

ASHRAE JOURNAL March 1970

Why Study Energy Consumption?

HERBERT T. GILKEY
Section Head – 2.0 (Heating and Cooling Loads)
Research & Technical Committee

BEFORE it is successfully completed, the work of the Task Group (TG) on Energy Requirements for Heating and Cooling will have consumed several years of time and thousands of dollars. Much of the time will have been given to ASHRAE by its dedicated members who serve on the TG, its subcommittees, and the Technical Committees which plan and monitor research projects related to this particular project. Some of the money spent will come from ASHRAE general research funds; *most* of the money will have to come from sources outside the Society.

The energy consumption study is the most comprehensive project ever undertaken by ASHRAE. Parts of it involve highly theoretical considerations and sophisticated mathematical solutions to apparently commonplace problems. At the same time, final results must be practical – readily applicable procedures and data.

The members of ASHRAE have the right and responsibility to know about the research projects for which their money is being spent. At the same time, it is important to realize how easy it is to overlook and to undervalue significant parts of a comprehensive study.

Learning what the study has already accomplished and what is projected for the future will aid understanding of what is going on. Guidance to answer the question "Why study energy consumption?" must come from those who most clearly see needs and can best evaluate benefits.

At the 1968 Annual Meeting at Lake Placid, preliminary copies of Procedures for Determining Heating and Cooling Loads for Energy Calculations were distributed to interested members of the Society for review and comment. This bulletin, prepared by the Subcommittee on Heating and Cooling Loads and published without direct cost to ASHRAE, utilizes the newly developed response factor technique of load calculations.

A second publication, Proposed Procedures for Simulating the Performance of Components and Systems for Energy Calculations, was released for review and comment at the 1969 Annual Meeting in Denver. This booklet was prepared by the Subcommittee on Systems and Equipment.

Each of these publications, after a period for review, comment, and final revision, will be released for general distribution as an ASHRAE Bulletin. The first, Procedures for Determining Heating and Cooling Loads for Computerized Energy Calculations, is to be available in 1970.

These two books are important to successful completion of the energy consumption study, for they form a major part of the basic theoretical foundation upon which other, seemingly more "practical" phases of the study will be based. For example, the TG has selected four buildings in widely separated locations for field studies. It hopes to instrument these buildings and to check and validate the calculation procedures in them. This will provide the essential proof-of-the-pudding evaluation needed to justify their use by heating and air-conditioning engineers.

Other phases of the program are also well underway. Existing programs on load calculation and energy consumption are being studied and compared by the Subcommittee on Overall Program Logic. This study is identifying the different approaches which have been taken to similar problems by different people and is evaluating the significance of individual components of thermal load.

Research on thermal properties of building materials and assemblies is underway. The response factor technique of load calculation evaluates transient heat flows which could not heretofore be calculated routinely. New types of thermal property data are required and they are being obtained under the direction of TC 2.4, Thermal Insulation and Moisture Barriers.

Weather is all around us, yet its characteristics must be evaluated in different ways if weather effects on energy consumption are to be known. Furthermore, the data must be presented in such a way that they can be used in programs required for energy consumption calculations.

A lot of activity, a lot of research, a lot of time, and a lot of money – all of these are involved in the work of the TG. But why expend this effort? Why study energy consumption?

This question can be answered in a number of ways:

1. To observe the general interest in the work of the TG – overflow crowds at the TG meetings and near-capacity crowds at Forums and Symposiums sponsored by the TG, and the scramble for copies of preliminary procedures when they are distributed.

2. To listen to those most deeply involved in estimating energy consumption for heating and cooling, and to understand the problems they face in attempting to provide answers to questions which cannot yet be stated clearly and completely. The information needs of these engineers are great; the work of the TG provides the best possibility of getting this information.

Recently a member of a subcommittee of this TG commented on the value of the TG work as he sees it. He pointed out that the energy consumption calculation will allow one to make a choice of fuels or a choice of systems based on the cost of operation. The accuracy of the entire calculation procedure must be very high for this application. Improved accuracy of calculation procedures is the TG's primary objective and justifies its continued quest for the best and most accurate procedure that can be conceived. These "ultimate" procedures must be the goal, even though experience may later prove that certain components can be simplified.

The member also pointed out other applications of the overall calculation procedures. Temperature control simulation may permit air-conditioning system control by anticipation of system requirements, rather than by reaction to changing load conditions. This should be an application of major interest in design and operation of the system.

System operation simulation will allow system-design evaluation and checking before construction. It can help avoid inherent faults in operating characteristics which can result in unacceptable environmental conditions and sometimes unacceptable operating procedures. It would also allow checking of actual system operation against the design intent after the system is constructed.

Design load simulation will be used to make optimum equipment selections at design conditions. It could also be used to optimize system component selection for both design and partial load operation. Above all, this simulation must be a design tool tailored to the needs of the engineer.

In effect, this member of a TG subcommittee is saying that the energy consumption study must be successfully completed if the members of ASHRAE are to have the tools they need to make the best decisions related to system selection, system design and system operation.

Study energy consumption? Yes, because it is itself an important engineering consideration and because, in the course of studying it, procedures and data necessary to better solve the problems related to other phases of air-conditioning system selection, design and operation will be developed.

H.T. Gilkey is research director, Waterloo Register Div, Dynamics Corp of America, Cedar Falls, Iowa.

ASHRAE JOURNAL February 1970

ASHRAE JOURNAL February 1970

89

ASHRAE chartered its 137th chapter, the East Central Illinois Chapter, on May 25. Present for the ceremonies were (left to right) Andrew T. Boggs, ASHRAE executive vice president; Jack B. Chaddock, then ASHRAE president; Donald Leverenz, president of the East Central Illinois Chapter; and Philip Dugan, ASHRAE Region VI chairman.

1982

When We Voted to Become ASHRAE

Counting the votes. John Dube and Past Presidents Leon Buehler, Crosby Field and Glenn Muffly check the ballot box contents after proxy and personal votes were cast

1958

New Brunswick Chartered in October

A new ASHRAE Chapter, New Brunswick (Canada), was chartered on October 13 with 80 members and guests as participants and well wishers. Society Officers who attended included ASHRAE President Walter F. Spiegel, Executive Director Andrew T. Boggs III, and Director and Regional Chairman of Region II Jacob Klassen. Also lending their support were President of the Halifax Chapter (sponsoring Chapter) James Scriven, the Major of Moncton (N.B.) Leonard C. Jones and representatives of the Montreal and Ville de Quebec Chapters.

Mr. Klassen gave a history of the events leading up to this Charter night and paid tribute to the individuals involved in the Chapter's organization. He then presented the Charter to New Brunswick Chapter President Kirk Bavis and installed the slate of officers—Vice President Robert Macpherson, Secretary Kenneth Perry, Treasurer Brian Hildreth and Governors Glen Cowan, Joseph Slemin and John MacLean. Mr. Boggs presented an ASHRAE banner to the Chapter.

Messrs. Perry, Hildreth, Bavis, Macpherson, Cowan and Slemin share first night glory with Mr. Spiegel and Mr. Boggs

President Spiegel addressed the assembled celebrants regarding the importance of ASHRAE in the HVAC&R industry. He encouraged all members to get personally involved to assure the success of the New Brunswick Chapter. An explanation of ASHRAE research was also given.

1973

EASTERN MICHIGAN CHAPTER CHARTERED IN MAY; ASHRAE OFFICERS ATTEND

May 24 was the Charter Night of the new ASHRAE Eastern Michigan Chapter. On hand to extend an offical welcome to the Society were President Roderick R. Kirkwood, Director and Regional Chairman of Region VI Joseph B. Olivieri, and Secretary and Executive Director Andrew T. Boggs.

Leaders of the new Chapter are President Eugene A. Marino, Vice President Dar Johnson, Secretary Ed Naretto, Treasurer Tony Krapek, Governors Robert McGovern and Bernard Darenkamp.

Messrs. Kirkwood and Boggs observe as Mr. Olivieri (second from right) presents gavel to Mr. Marino

ASHRAE JOURNAL August 1974

We Started—Let's Finish

25,000 Members by July 1969, 50,000 by 1994

DIXON A. ERVIN, JR.
Chairman
Membership Committee

IN the fall of 1965, then President-Elect Lincoln Bouillon returned from an ASHRAE Membership Committee meeting and called the officers, board of governors, and the membership committee of the Puget Sound Chapter together for a discussion. He announced that he had made a small wager with W. J. Collins, Jr. of the Central Oklahoma Chapter that the Puget Sound Chapter could increase its membership by 40% before the Oklahoma Chapter could. The challenge was met enthusiastically and plans for the drive were started immediately. The results are now well known. Both Chapters, within about six weeks, exceeded their goals and, according to Executive Director A. T. Boggs, the contest was a draw!

This started something! The next chairman of the Membership Committee, William Taylor of Columbus, Ohio, took over and set forth a goal of 25,000 members by July 1967. The goal, unfortunately, was not reached. However, we did realize an increase of 6% in 1966-67 and an increase of 12% in 1967-68. Our total membership as of September 30, is about 23,000. (In October 1965, our membership was 18,062.) Let's get those 2000 more members!

What are some of the ways to start and carry out a successful membership drive? Let's borrow some ideas from ASHRAE Chapters. The Iowa Chapter, for instance, exceeded its quota of a 25% increase by a lot of hard work and excellent organization. The membership drive was under the leadership of Wayne H. Allen, the first recipient of the Lincoln Bouillon Membership Award for the most outstanding work in increasing the membership of the Society.

First, the Chapter drew up a prospect list of over 200 names. Letters were then sent enumerating the benefits and activities of ASHRAE, along with application blanks.

A few weeks later, follow-up letters were mailed; these contained the personal testimony of R. W. Flanagan, then Membership Committeeman for Region VI, regarding the benefits of ASHRAE. Along with the letters, calling teams were organized and visits arranged to firms of contractors and engineers for presentation about the benefits and activities of membership in ASHRAE.

The results of this type of energetic and enthusiastic drive are now history; the Iowa Chapter showed an increase of more than 60%.

Along with the efforts at the local level, national headquarters now has some aids available. These are: a presidential letter to be sent to individual prospects; a membership kit of promotional materials for use by membership recruiters; and a bulk rate for Society jewelry, which may be given to new members as a "bonus."

All of this is of very little value, however, unless the individual members and the Chapters make a commitment to themselves and to the Society to START and FINISH this membership drive.

Let's examine where we are now and what we must do to finish the job.

As of September 30, 1968, the Society membership totaled about 23,000. This represents approximately a 40% achievement of the increase necessary to reach our goal of 25,000. This increase was accomplished by only about 10% of the Chapters reaching their prorata share. About 90% of the chapters must still FINISH their jobs.

Now let's set out our immediate and our long range goals.

First: FULFILL our immediate goal of 25,000 members by July, 1, 1969, the 75th anniversary celebration of our Society.

Along with attaining our goal of 25,000 members, we want to EMPHASIZE the need for "upgrading" of the present membership. ENCOURAGE student membership through close cooperation with Chapter manpower and education committees and local educational institutions. ELIMINATE "unpaid" members (make paid members out of them!).

Second: Develop a long range program to at least DOUBLE our membership by the 100th anniversary of our Society. Sounds impossible! Not at all. Actually, a very nominal NET growth of 3% per year will achieve this goal of 50,000 by 1994. This, I would consider to be the minimum growth in order to keep pace with the growth of our industry and everything else around us these days.

Every member must make a personal *commitment* to do his share.

We all know the old adage: "Don't start something you can't finish!"

Well, we have STARTED—now let's FINISH.

D. A. Ervin, Jr. is a partner of Kane & Ervin, Seattle, Wash.

ASHRAE JOURNAL November 1968 63

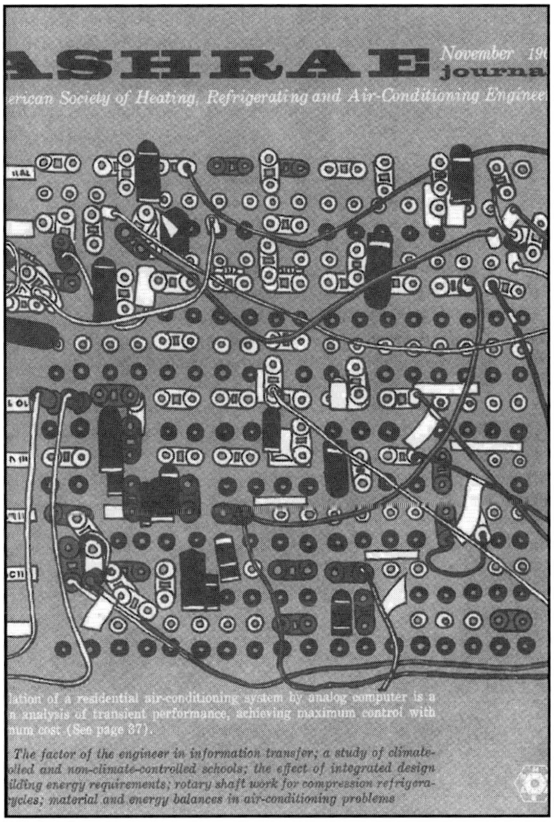

DELAWARE CHARTER PRESENTED; ASHRAE OFFICERS AMONG 118 ATTENDING

The Delaware Chapter of ASHRAE made its debut with a Charter Night fete November 18. Among the 118 members, guests and Society officers attending were ASHRAE President Frank H. Bridgers, Vice President Walter F. Spiegel, Treasurer Gayle B. Priester, Executive Director Andrew T. Boggs III, Director and Regional Chairman of Region III Robert J. Evans, and visitors from the Philadelphia, Baltimore and National Capital Chapters. Representing Philadelphia were John Seelaus, Chairman of the Region III Fund Raising Committee, and Glenn Davidson. Attending from Baltimore was Mr. Priester, and from National Capital were Chapter President C.W. Phillips, Chapter Vice President James E. Shea, and Chapter Secretary Shiga Hiratsuka.

Mr. Bridgers presented the Charter to Delaware Chapter President John W. Burkert, Sr. The Society officers each spoke briefly. Mr. Bridgers gave a short talk on the State of ASHRAE. Mr. Evans reviewed the genesis and development of the Delaware Chapter. Chapter officers were introduced by President Burkert: Vice President, Edward A. Strauss; Recording Secretary, John P. Fallon; Corresponding Secretary, Donald Grier; and Treasurer, John Renninger. Governors are Robert B. Barefoot and Bernard A. Schneider.

Mr. Bridgers congratulates Mr. Burkert as the gavel is presented

ASHRAE Officers and Chapter Officers: seated—Mr. Spiegel, Mr. Burkert, Mr. Bridgers, Mr. Strauss; standing: Mr. Boggs, Mr. Schneider, Mr. Evans, Mr. Fallon, Mr. Renninger

1971

ASHRAE AND METRICATION

C. W. PHILLIPS
Fellow ASHRAE
Chairman, ASHRAE Metric Committee

WHAT is ASHRAE doing about the change to the use of metric units? Many professional societies have already committed themselves to a deadline for conversion and some have already completed the process. ASHRAE, like several other organizations, has begun to educate its membership on conversion and, according to policy set by the ASHRAE Board of Directors in June, 1972, will pattern ASHRAE's conversion to metric usage after the official United States position.

The U.S. Congress presently has before it several metric conversion bills. These bills differ slightly, but all have the following criteria in common:

- Conversion to the metric system will be voluntary;
- The government will participate in an organized program;
- A definite deadline, probably 10 years, will be recommended for conversion;
- The system of units to implemented will be the International Metric System, frequently referred to as the SI system after the internationally-accepted "Système International d'Unités."

C. W. Phillips is in the Thermal Engineering Systems Section, National Bureau of Standards, Washington, D.C.

SI BASE UNITS

Quantity	Unit	SI Symbol
length	meter	m
mass	kilogram	kg
time	second	s
electric current	ampere	A
thermodynamic temperature	kelvin	K
amount of substance	mole	mol
luminous intensity	candela	cd

Supplementary units are:

Quantity	Unit	SI Symbol
plane angle	radian	rad
solid angle	steradian	sr

Among the derived units of major interest to ASHRAE are:

Quantity	Unit	SI Symbol	Formula
acceleration	meter per second squared	...	m/s^2
angular velocity	radian per second	...	rad/s
area	square meter	...	m^2
density	kilogram per cubic meter	...	kg/m^3
electric capacitance	farad	F	A·s/V
electrical conductance	siemens	S	A/V
electric resistance	ohm	Ω	V/A
electromotive force	volt	V	W/A
energy	joule	J	N·m
entropy	joule per kelvin	...	J/K
force	newton	N	$kg \cdot m/s^2$
frequency	hertz	Hz	(cycle)/s
power	watt	W	J/s
pressure	pascal	Pa	N/m^2
quantity of heat	joule	J	N·m
specific heat	joule per kilogram-kelvin	...	J/kg·K
thermal conductivity	watt per meter-kelvin	...	W/m·K
velocity	meter per second	...	m/s
viscosity, dynamic	pascal-second	...	Pa·s
viscosity, kinematic	square meter per second	...	m^2/s
voltage	volt	V	W/A
volume	cubic meter	...	m^3
work	joule	J	N·m

In anticipation of a formal United States program, the Metric Committee is encouraging gradual increase in the use of SI units in ASHRAE publications. During the transition period it is likely that "dualiaztion" will be employed, with both conventional units and SI units being given; this practice is now being implemented. For example, the 1972 ASHRAE HANDBOOK OF FUNDAMENTALS and the 1972 ASHRAE GUIDE AND DATA BOOK contain SI conversion units. The Standards Committee will use SI units in standards under development. (Note: The International Standards Organization now requires use of SI units.) Several technical committees are converting technical data into SI units. In addition, ASHRAE is a participating member of the American National Metric Council and of the Engineers Joint Council Metric Commission, both groups being concerned with systematic U.S. conversion to the International Metric System.

ASHRAE members are encouraged to begin using SI units in this fashion to develop the important value-awareness which will make the final transition easier. To facilitate the use of correct units, ASHRAE has made available two documents to each standard and technical committee and task group whose work output involves the use of SI units. These documents are "Metric Practice Guide E380-72" and "Instructions to ASTM Technical Committees on Metric Conversion," both published by the American Society for Testing and Materials. ASTM E380-72 (ANSI Z210.1—1973) is recognized as a current authoritative reference for conversion to working units in the SI/International Metric System.

Additional units, conversion factors, and methods for utilizing units in documentation are included in ASTM E380-72.

Under SI, some of the more familiar units become:

- joules in place of Btu (1 Btu equals 1055 joules);
- watts in place of Btu/hr (1 Btu/hr equals 0.2930 watts);
- watts in place of "tons of refrigeration" (1 ton of refrigeration equals 3517 watts or 3.517 kilowatts);
- joules in place of "ton-hours" (1 ton-hour equals 1.266×10^7 joules or 12.66 megajoules);
- cubic meters per second in place of cubic feet per minute (1 cubic foot per minute equals 4.719×10^{-4} cubic meters per second or 471.9 cubic centimeters per second);
- kilograms in place of pounds-mass (1 pound-mass equals 0.4535 kilograms);
- cubic meters per second in place of gallons per minute (1 gallon per minute equals 6.309×10^{-5} cubic meters per second or 63.09 cubic centimeters per second);
- pascals in place of pounds-force per square inch (1 pound-force per square inch equals 6894 pascals or 6.894 kilopascals);
- pascals in place of inches of water (1 inch of water equals 248.8 pascals);
- kelvin (or Celsius) temperature in place of Fahrenheit temperature ($F = 1.8K - 459.7$, $F = 1.8C + 32$, $K = \frac{F + 459.7}{1.8}$, $C = \frac{F - 32}{1.8}$)
- difference in temperature in kelvins (or degrees Celsius) in place of degrees Fahrenheit (a difference of one degree Fahrenheit is equal to $\frac{K}{1.8}$ or $\frac{C}{1.8}$).

Conversion to the International Metric System can be "soft" or "hard." "Soft" means changing the descriptive units to SI terminology without redesigning or altering the item described. "Hard" means redesigning the product to conform to a selected metric dimension. The selection of "soft" or "hard" conversion is a matter for individual judgment.

The ASHRAE Metric Committee is continuing to work toward the determination of answers to important Society questions about conversion to SI units: Should ASHRAE convert? How soon? What "special units" are needed? How should the educational process be accomplish? The Committee requests comments and recommendations from ASHRAE members concerning this important matter. Please write to the Editor, ASHRAE JOURNAL. □□

ASHRAE and the Consumer

LLOYD A. STAEBLER
Section Head — 8.0 (Domestic Refrigerators and Small Refrigeration Equipment)
Research & Technical Committee

ASHRAE members are aware of the increasing concern shown by the various trade, government and consumer organizations in initiating and promoting action to protect the interest of the consumer, a movement popularly known as "Consumerism." Your Society has a similar concern: product safety and consumer protection keynoted ASHRAE's 1968 Annual Meeting at Lake Placid[1] and set the stage for continuing discussions.[2, 3]

At Lake Placid, participants in a forum on the subject, Providing Serviceable Products, unanimously recommended to the Board of Directors that the President of the Society appoint a Task Group to "explore the role of ASHRAE in matters pertaining to the quality and reliability of products." Immediate Past President Holladay determined that the matter was properly one for consideration by the Research & Technical (R & T) Committee and referred it to R & T Chairman J.R. Schreiner. The following is a report of the Committee's deliberation and a statement of policy submitted to the Board of Directors at the 1969 Annual Meeting in Denver.

ASHRAE RESPONSIBILITY

The R & T Committee feels that the Bylaws of the Society clearly define ASHRAE's responsibility to the consumer. Section 1.2 states: "The object of the Society is to advance the arts and sciences . . . for the benefit of the general public." Section 8.8.20, in defining the functions of the R & T Committee, states that its activities shall be devoted to the "public welfare" and "general benefit." Paragraph 2.1.6 of the Operational Guide of the R & T Committee, in speaking of the objectives of Society research, is even more specific: "The results of Society research should contribute to standards of health and safety, improved application, performance and reliability of equipment and systems, and economic gains for the benefit of the general public and the enrichment of the professions represented by the Society."

L.A. Staebler is manager, Refrigeration Products, Appliances, Research and Advanced Engineering, Philco-Ford Corp, Philadelphia, Pa.

In view of the foregoing the R & T Committee agreed that ASHRAE has a definite responsibility to both the industry and the public for the generation and dissemination of information relevant to equipment and/or systems reliability, durability and serviceability and that ASHRAF should take appropriate affirmative action to meet such responsibility.

LIMITS OF RESPONSIBILITY

It is obvious, however, that ASHRAE cannot indulge in any form of commercialism or attempt to police the industry without violating the fundamental precepts of the Society. For this reason, it was generally agreed that ASHRAE must confine itself to the development and dissemination of information without: (a) specifying reliability, durability and serviceability requirements: or (b) sponsoring or engaging in field studies for the purpose of establishing failure rates of commercial products, systems and installations. These are presumed to be the prerogative of industry and appropriate trade associations and not a proper function of a technical society.

IMPLEMENTATION OF POLICY

The R & T Committee recommends the following means of implementing this policy (note that virtually all segments of the Society are involved):

A. The R & T Committee shall instruct the various Technical Committees and Task Groups to consider the general area of reliability, durability and serviceability as one of their important responsibilities in:

1. Developing information for ASHRAE GUIDE AND DATA BOOK, particularly the Equipment and Systems volumes.
2. Planning Forums and Symposiums relating to equipment and systems.
3. Requesting and supporting the need for appropriate Standards.
4. Recommending appropriate research projects.

B. The Guide And Data Book Committee shall include two new chapters in forthcoming editions:

1. Reliability Considerations (HANDBOOK OF FUNDAMENTALS).
2. Preventive Maintenance

C. The Program Committee shall encourage and sponsor Technical Sessions, Symposiums and Forums relating to the general area of reliability, durability and serviceability.

D. The Standards Committee shall develop test procedures as required for determining product reliability and durability characteristics.

E. With Board of Directors implementation, the various General and Special Committees of the Society shall cooperate with other organizations such as Refrigeration Service Engineers Society (RSES), Air-Conditioning & Refrigeration Institute (ARI), Assn of Home Appliance Manufacturers (AHAM), etc., in areas of mutual interest relating to reliability, durability and service. This may involve the following General Committees of the Society:

1. Education (development and training of manpower, particularly for service and maintenance).
2. Standards (development of test procedures and standards).
3. R & T Committee (continuing liaison on a working level).

F. With Board of Directors implementation, suitable publicity shall be accorded through ASHRAE JOURNAL and other appropriate means to make known Society policy and contributions in the field of product and system reliability, durability and serviceability.

APPROVAL BY BOARD OF DIRECTORS

At its meeting on Sunday, June 29, during the 1969 Annual Meeting, the Board of Directors approved the recommendations of the R & T Committee and requested that other committees cooperate with R & T in furthering those objectives which will benefit consumers.

REFERENCES

1. Consumer Protection Keynotes ASHRAE 1968 Annual Meeting, ASHRAE JOURNAL, August 1968, Vol. 10, No. 8, p. 60.
2. C.W. MacPhee, Is Preventive Maintenance the Responsibility of ASHRAE Engineers? ASHRAE JOURNAL, November 1968, Vol. 10, No. 10, p.65.
3. H.O. Spauchus, Preventive Maintenance (Letters to the Editor), ASHRAE JOURNAL, February 1969, Vol. 11, No. 2, p. 4.

At left, ASHRAE Executive Secretary Robert C. Cross thumbs through one of a recent shipment of Guide And Data Books donated to the international People-to-People Engineers and Scientists Committee. Warehouse below holds books awaiting shipment to countries all over the world

G.E. MAKES CONTRIBUTION TO ASHRAE RESEARCH

Members of ASHRAE receive a Contribution to their research program from the General Electric Company. From left to right are Joseph H. Gauss, Vice President and General Manager, Air Conditioning Products Division, General Electric, Louisville, KY; Walter F. Spiegel, President ASHRAE 1972-73; Frank H. Faust, Presidential Member and Consultant to ASHRAE's Technical & Financial Outreach Committee; Andrew T. Boggs, Secretary and Executive Director; and Mel Cole, Marketing Manager, Air Conditioning Division, G.E.

1953

The Blackmore Family—Heating Engineers

The accompanying photograph shows four generations of the Blackmore family, three of whom are members of the A.S.H.V.E., and the youngest, born September 15, 1936, is a prospect.

J. J. Blackmore is a Charter Member of the Society and was granted Life Membership in 1931. He became secretary of the Society March 24, 1914, and served until February, 1915. He was a pioneer in the heating industry and was associated with J. L. Mott Iron Works up to the formation of United States Radiator Corporation in 1910, when he served as secretary of that organization. During the World War, he manufactured chemical equipment and since his retirement has devoted a great deal of time to world travel. He keeps in excellent physical condition with golf, which is his chief recreation and hobby. He tries to play three games a week and he has a record of having played on 650 different golf courses in various countries.

Of late he has been spending his winters in Florida and now at the age of 81 he is hale, hearty and enjoys life. When he is in New York he makes his home at the Engineers Club, 32 West 40th St.

F. H. Blackmore joined the Society in 1923 in St. Louis and was active in the local chapter. He is now located in Detroit and is a member of Michigan Chapter. He entered the heating field at West Newton, Pa., in 1901 with the United States Radiator and Boiler Co. and in 1910 was manager of the Corry, Pa., plant, when the United States Radiator Corp. was formed. Since that time he has been in charge of the West Newton, Pa., and the Edwardsville, Ill., plants of the company. Since 1928 he has been in the general office of the United States Radiator Corp. as manager of the manufacturing division.

J. J. Blackmore II was graduated from the University of Illinois in 1932 and in 1935 opened an office as manufacturers' representative in St. Louis and represents Bell & Gossett Co. and McDonnell & Miller in the eastern Missouri and southern Illinois territory. He resides in Edwardsville, Ill., and takes a great interest in outdoor activities, being scout master of a large boy scout troop. He joined the Society in February, 1937, and is a member of St. Louis Chapter.

J. J. Blackmore III was born September 15, 1936, and, while he has not announced his desire to join the Society, family custom indicates that he will become a member as soon as he is eligible.

This will carry out the advice of his great grandfather, who, at the Semi-Annual Meeting of the Society in 1916 at Detroit, said to the members present: "Don't you know that in giving up something for the general good you will get more real satisfaction than you would in making dollars? The fact that you have contributed something to help along the field of Heating and Ventilating Engineering will be a lasting source of satis faction to anyone who accomplishes anything good. . . Each member should do all he can to induce those who are engaged in the industry to become members."

1937

ASHRAE contribution in the development of engineering facilities for survival shelters

The National Fallout Shelter Survey has disclosed that the addition of ventilation facilities is the single most important step toward the creation of 60 million more shelter spaces in addition to the 70 million already identified.

What is the role of the heating and air conditioning engineer in the development of these facilities? Probably a very considerable one, says Henry S. Wakabayashi, ASHRAE Member and Chief Mechanical Engineer of the Architectural and Engineering Development Division of the Office of Civil Defense.

To train engineers for the task of designing mechanical systems for survival shelters, the Office of Civil Defense has started a number of courses throughout the country, where practicing mechanical engineers are studying the art and science of making shelters habitable.

These courses are being presented in cooperation with ASHRAE. Two of the basic references being supplied to the participants are copies of the Guide And Data Book Chapter on Survival Shelters developed by the Society's Task Group on Survival Shelters, and the bulletin of the Symposium on Survival Shelters presented at the 69th annual meeting of ASHRAE in 1962.

The Course of Instruction was developed by the University of Florida, under direction of the Office of Civil Defense. Over half of the instructors and participants of the Pilot Course, given last August, were ASHRAE members.

The first two courses being presented to qualified practicing engineers have been sponsored in cooperation with the ASHRAE Chapters in Philadelphia and New York where two groups of approximately 70 men each are participating.

Both these series are given for three hours during one night each week for 10 weeks. The Course Director for these two courses is Mr. Walter F. Spiegel, P.E., Chairman of the ASHRAE Task Group on Survival Shelters. In Philadelphia, the course is being conducted at the University of Pennsylvania, while in New York at the United Engineering Center Building. The attendance has been excellent, with extracurricular activities in fundamentals being particularly beneficial to the participants. A final examination will terminate the course. Those who successfully complete the course will receive recognition from the Department of Defense.

With this specialized training in Environmental Engineering these men will be better qualified to serve the needs of this program as it is expanded, or if the need for its use becomes acute.

Similar courses will be given in the Cleveland, Chicago, Long Beach and Washington, D.C., areas. J. Raymond Carroll and Gilbert Engholm, both ASHRAE Members, will be involved in directing courses in the mid-west area. Quentin R. Thompson, ASHRAE Member, will conduct the Long Beach course; Francis Govan, ASHRAE Member, of the National Academy of Sciences, the Washington, D.C., course, and Joseph R. Ackerman, ASHRAE Member, the Cleveland course.

The Committees of the Philadelphia and New York Chapters who assisted in promoting the publicity for this national federal activity are to be commended for the success of this venture, which Walter Spiegel reports has been most eagerly participated in by practicing engineers, many of whom have subsequently requested membership in our society.

The Federal Government has in committee a bill to consider spending 192 million dollars on a participating program, with local funds to further the development of creating habitable fallout shelter spaces. ASHRAE's support to date is proving a most significant contribution to this important phase of this country's National Defense Program.

1964

President Kirkwood, right, is inducted into the Kiowa Indian Tribe by ASHRAE Associate Member Elmer T. Saunkeah

1974

Idaho Becomes ASHRAE's 134th Chapter

Idaho was established as ASHRAE's 134th chapter in ceremonies held September 12th at the Crystal Ballroom of the Hoff Building in Boise, ID. Keith Robertson, second from right, the chapter's acting president, received the charter from ASHRAE President Charles F. Sepsy. Also present were Andrew T. Boggs, left, ASHRAE executive vice president, and J. Lee Mutum, right, chairman for Region IX.

1980

Bill Moser receiving Region IX trophy from Robert D. Pagliasotti, President Kirkwood and James A. Beach, Jr., Chairman of ASHRAE's Membership Committee

1974

ASHRAE Establishes Air Pollution Task Group

Because the problem of air pollution abatement lies so deeply within the main channel of ASHRAE endeavor, the control of environment by means of heating, refrigerating, air conditioning and ventilation, and because of its own growing concern with atmospheric pollution, the Society has established a Task Group on Air Pollution.

Acting upon a decision of the ASHRAE Board of Directors, the Chairman of the ASHRAE Research and Technical Committee, John F. Sandfort, has appointed Herbert F. Laube to head the Task Group. The group is made up of 13 members representing four of the Society's Technical Committees with specific interests in air pollution control and correction. These four committees are: TC 1.4 Physiology and Human Environment; TC 1.6 Odor Causes and Control; TC 4.3 Industrial Environment; TC 9.4 Air Cleaning and Purification Equipment.

The Society's interest in the causes and control of air pollution, stems from the majority of its members who are also greatly concerned with inhibiting its results by conditioning of indoor air. In its newly published Handbook of Fundamentals, ASHRAE defines air conditioning as "the process of treating air so as to control simultaneously its temperature, humidity, cleanliness, and distribution to meet the requirements of the conditioned space." Thus, control of many contaminants, including bacteria, odors, toxic gases, smoke, and other contaminants is involved in the control of air cleanliness for its effect on human health and well-being.

Appointed to the ASHRAE Task Group on Air Pollution are:

Herbert L. Laube, Chairman, Senior Consultant, Climate Control Division, The Singer Company, Auburn, N.Y.

Robert L. Boyd, Secretary, Engineering Consultant, Climate Control Division, The Singer Company, Auburn, N.Y.

C. M. Bosworth, Engineering Consultant, Carrier Air Conditioning Company, Syracuse, N.Y.

Dr. Arend Bouhuys, John B. Pierce Foundation, New Haven, Conn.

John H. Clarke, Engineering Design Supervisor, Air Conditioning and Power House, Union Carbide Corporation, Food Products Division, Chicago, Ill.

Thomas C. Elliott, Engineering Editor, Heating, Piping and Air Conditioning, Chicago, Ill.

Crosby Field, President, Flakice Corporation, Brooklyn, N.Y.

Wesley C. Hemeon, Hemeon Associates, Pittsburgh, Pa.

R. J. M. Horton, Health Effects Research Program, National Center for Air Pollution Control, Cincinnati, Ohio.

G. B. Priester, Baltimore Gas and Electric Company, Gas and Electric Building, Baltimore, Md.

Kenneth E. Robinson, Ventilation Engineer, Industrial Hygiene Department, General Motors, Corporation, Warren, Mich.

E. N. Seiler, Department Chief, Plant Service, Western Electric, New York, N.Y.

H. O. Spauschus, Section Head, General Electric Company, Appliance Park, Louisville, Ky.

To be considered by the Task Group are the sources and control of air pollution, the effect of air pollution on people and materials, and the means for removing air pollution in order to maintain maximum satisfactory indoor levels.

Specific questions requiring answers by the Task Group include:

What are the chief areas of ASHRAE interest, authority and responsibility regarding air pollution?

What physiological, medical and psychological effects do odors have on people? What are the means for minimizing these effects?

What are the most severe outside levels of vapor and gaseous contaminants likely to be encountered today? What means are available for removing such pollutants?

What are the Threshold Limit Values and Quality Standard Levels presently in effect for specific air contaminants (indoors and outside)?

What means are presently being used in actual practice to remove air contaminants?

ASHRAE JOURNAL *April 1967* 79

Paul Addams, left, with Fernando Duran, center, recipient of the ASHAE-Homer Addams award, and his mentor Professor William Rudoy of the University of Pittsburgh

1974

Mad hatters who attended the Monday night Mad Hatter ASRE party were Mrs. and Mr. J. G. Bergdoll of York Corp., J. R. Chamberlain of York, and Walter Beline of American Locomotive.

1952

ASHRAE and NCEC to Co-Sponsor Energy Management Seminars

WALTER F. SPIEGEL
Presidential Member ASHRAE

SAMUEL W. MILLER, JR.
Member ASHRAE

A considerable portion of ASHRAE resources and efforts during the last 5 years has been spent on meeting the technical challenges of energy conservation in the operation of buildings. The recent energy "crisis" points out the need to develop a method whereby people who actually operate buildings and industrial facilities can be oriented on workable energy management plans. Such plans involve both technical and management principles.

If ASHRAE is to become visible in local communities it must participate in providing usable, informational programs to business and energy managers who control the energy consumption in the millions of industrial plants and buildings in the U. S. and other countries.

To help businessmen solve the energy management problem and to overcome the everwidening energy crisis "environment gap," executives of several companies and representatives of labor and educational institutions have recognized the urgent need for independent, neutral, private sector activity. Early in 1974 they banded together to form the National Council for Energy Conservation with a goal of creating a forum for information exchange on more effective utilization of energy; their Secretariat is at the University City Science Center in Philadelphia.

As one of its functions, NCEC conducts energy management workshops where local businessmen learn to maintain their facilities at normal production and environmental levels with less energy usage, applying little or no capital investment. Since such savings translate to lower operating costs, it is an appealing concept even if energy conservation were not an over-riding consideration.

ASHRAE and NCEC have recently agreed to jointly sponsor several local seminars during the Spring of 1974. Generally patterned after energy management seminars already conducted by NCEC, these meetings should serve as prototypes for similar seminars which can be scheduled by other ASHRAE Chapters later in 1974.

The Spring 1974 ASHRAE/NCEC Seminars will be devoted primarily to energy managment in building operations and maintenance. ASHRAE Chapter members will be encouraged to bring guests who are responsible for plant and building operations. Joint efforts with local Chambers of Commerce are also expected to result in participation by business leaders. These full-day seminars will feature a panel of energy experts who will discuss the realities of the current energy shortage, Federal Energy Office activities in the region, how to establish an energy management program; how to conduct internal energy audits; how to evaluate the financial aspect of energy management; and how to contact knowledgeable experts in the heating, refrigerating and air-conditioning fields. Afternoon sessions will be devoted to studies of case histories—how other companies have achieved significant energy-use reductions in their operations. Another program feature will be individual discussions in small groups, conducted by industry, NCEC, and ASHRAE discussion leaders.

With this type of format, it is hoped that a major impact can be made by ASHRAE and NCEC on the energy-using community, utilizing the organizational capabilities of both sponsoring groups.

The registration fees will be budgeted at approximately $10 per person.

The results and program format of these prototype sessions will be reported in future issues of ASHRAE JOURNAL and in the ASHRAE Newsletter. For immediate information contact Executive Director Andrew T. Boggs at Society Headquarters. □□

W. F. Spiegel is President of W. F. Spiegel, Inc. Jenkintown, PA.

MEA CULPA
Proper identification in the form of a caption under Walter F. Spiegel's photo was inadvertently omitted on page 42 of the March, 1974 issue of ASHRAE JOURNAL. Couldn't have happened to a nicer man. Our sincere apologies.

ASHRAE JOURNAL May 1974

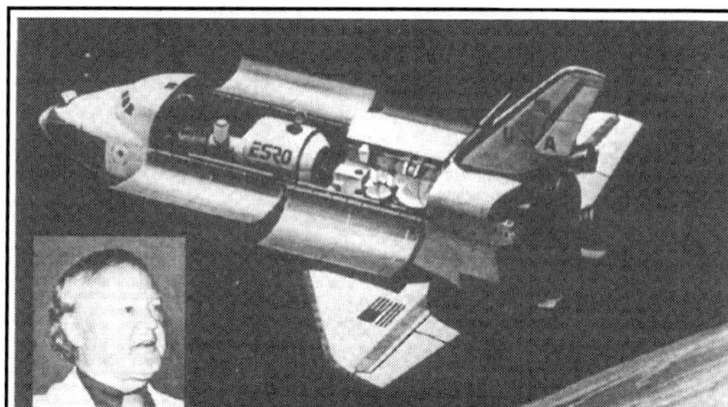

The Space Shuttle: Today's System For Tomorrow's World

Excerpted from Plenary Session address by Col. John L. Fisher, Director, Space Systems Group, Rockwell International, Downey, CA, at ASHRAE 1980 Annual Meeting In Denver, CO.

TWO decades ago, the space age dawned and awakened us to a realm of technological possibilities beyond any we had imagined. Since then, we have linked continents with communication satellites, sent probes to other planets, and see men on the moon.

During the next two decades, we will establish the foundation for the 21st Century's accomplishments in space. The Space Shuttle vehicle will be the cornerstone for that foundation, providing economical opportunities for space exploration and utilization.

The Space Shuttle vehicle is composed, in part, of the fully reusable orbiter, which is designed to fly more than 100 missions with minor refurbishment. The orbiter is about the size of a DC-9 airplane. It can transport a 65,000-pound payload into low earth orbit and can support satellites that are in orbit. Two reusable solid-propellant rocket boosters (SRB's) complete the Space Shuttle vehicle.

The atmospheric revitalization subsystem (ARS) provides the flight crew and passengers with a conditioned environment that is both life supporting and comfortable. The ARS is operated continuously during all mission phases to provide the crew with atmospheric pressure control, humidity, carbon dioxide, odor, and temperature control, and avionic equipment temperature control. In addition, the ARS cools the garments of two crew members before and after extravehicular activity (EVA) and sends conditioned air to manned payloads (carried in the payload bay).

Food, water, and waste management subsystems are designed to support hot- and cold-food preparation; provide sterilization, storage, and dispensing of hot and cold potable water; and collect and store condensates, disinfected urine, and feces for return to earth. The smoke detection and fire suppression subsystem is designed to detect smoke in the avionics bays and the crew compartment and extinguish fires with Freon 1301. Portable fire extinguishers are also available in the crew compartment. Fixed fire extinguishers located in each avionics bay are actuated from the flight deck.

Active thermal control subsystem (ATCS) provides thermal control for several subsystems during mission phases. The ATCS consists of the following major assemblies: freon heat transfer loop, radiator system, ammonia evaporative system, flash evaporator system, and coldplates.

The airlock support subsystem pressurizes and depressurizes the airlock, recharges EVA equipment, transfers waste water, and supports prebreathing and emergency breathing. These functions operate on demand during all orbital phases.

Purge, vent, and drain (PVD) subsystems include the window cavity conditioning and hazardous gas detection subsystems. These five subsystems control the environment of the orbiter's unpressurized structural cavities. Since the crew module is the only pressurized structure of the orbiter, these five subsystems must provide for nearly the entire orbiter structure, including purging and venting of payloads.

The reusability of the orbiter is the most significant factor in the economy of the STS. Essential to this reusability is the thermal protection subsystem (TPS), which protects the orbiter's aluminum skins from on-orbit and entry temperatures ranging from -250 to 2700 F (-157 to 4182° C). Like the orbiter it protects, the TPS will be used for about 100 missions. The design of a system with this capability posed one of the major challenges in the development of the Space Shuttle.

The Space Shuttle vehicle's design is economically adaptable to a wide spectrum of advanced missions substantially more demanding in their requirements than envisioned when the Shuttle's requirements were delineated. This economical growth potential—along with the basic capabilities introduced by the Shuttle for payload recovery and reuse, on-orbit construction, assembly, maintenance and repair, and other complex functions—is expected to result in an extended program lifetime. We can anticipate rapid evolutionary growth of operational space mission capabilities during this program.

As we begin to use the Shuttle to meet technological challenges, we will become increasingly aware of its value in earth resource, navigation, communication, scientific, and industrial projects. The benefits will far overshadow the costs, for the Space Shuttle holds the promise of solutions to the problems and needs of mankind—a promise that cannot be ignored. □□

ASHRAE JOURNAL August 1980

Dateline Washington

News of the technology/government interface provided through the ASHRAE-NSPE Liaison Program.

SHIFT TO EMPHASIS ON CONSERVATION NOTED ON WASHINGTON ENERGY POLICY SCENE

Definite shift to more emphasis on conservation clearly evident on Washington energy policy planning scene. Administration's energy and economic programs for coming year reflect basic governmental thrust to cut foreign oil imports and push for more funding in development of renewable energy sources. Increased attention to geothermal resources, for example, spotlighted in President Ford's economic message to Congress in October and in Project Independence energy program.

Congressional interest in renewable energy sources reaffirmed by Geothermal Energy Research, Development, and Demonstration Act of 1974 (H.R. 14920). Signed into law by President Ford at same time as historic Solar Heating and Cooling Demonstration Act, new law establishes Federal management team to honcho programs demonstrating commercial feasibility of using geothermal steam for power production. Act guarantees loans of up to $20 million to develop geothermal power facilities.

HVAC&R Implications: *Congressional and Federal agency inclusion of geothermal in national energy policy planning — and funding — should begin buildup of geothermal R&D and applications industry similar to what is already under way in solar, although on much more modest scale. HVAC&R sector opportunities likely to increase in both geothermal R&D and commercial applications in direct proportion to speed and success of NASA-directed program to determine overall effort needed to develop and exploit U.S. geothermal resources.*

FEA PUSHES VOLUNTARY GUIDELINES FOR ENERGY CONSERVATION IN BUILDINGS

FEA has kicked off yet another energy conservation program. Directed at commercial and industrial building owners, managers, and tenants, set of voluntary guidelines produced by energy agency is published under title of Lighting and Thermal Operations: Energy Conservation Management Programs. Project based on case studies of Federal Energy Reduction Program (FERP) which has been successful in reducing Federal government's own energy usage by average of 26% or 75 million barrels of oil in nine-month period. FEA estimates that identification of readily gained savings from "skimming off the top" of present wastage could save "several hundred thousand barrels of oil per day," with next year's possible savings double this winter's achievement. Specific recommendation for thermal, lighting levels are included in plans presented for industry and commercial use with special emphasis on thermostat levels and non-uniform task lighting. Operation, like many others from FEA, is aimed at immediate energy savings for quick impact on oil importation and trade balance woes, as well as improving fuel allocation situation for winter.

Recent speeches by energy advisors have demonstrated concern for conservation as major weapon to fight fuel supply problems. Guidelines, available from FEA regional offices, will not include recommendations for any significant retrofitting. However, FEA is now completing review of retrofit study for commercial buildings and expects to test guidelines on demonstration buildings early

22 ASHRAE JOURNAL December 1974

this winter. Retrofit report, prepared by Dubin-Mindell-Bloome Associates, will be in two sections: 1)easily complied with suggestions for building owners and managers to cut down energy usage with minimal capital investment, requiring only minor modifications; and 2) technical guidelines for engineers and architects which will mean major modifications of existing structures and significant investment levels.

ENGINEERING SOCIETIES MAKE INPUT TO PROJECT INDEPENDENCE HEARINGS

Project Independence public hearing in Philadelphia this fall included joint engineering society statement on national energy policy planning endorsed by ASHRAE, ASME, ASCE, AIIE, IEEE, and NSPE. Statement, presented at hearing by NSPE President Leslie Gates, stressed need for comprehensive technical manpower considerations in any national energy scenarios involving large-scale increases in energy production or conservation.

Philadelphia sessions of Project Independence hearings also heard strong case made for development of solar energy by Dr. Peter Glaser, vice president, Arthur D. Little, Inc. Glaser, ASHRAE member and long-time solar enthusiast, testified that solar climate control "could contribute to the national goal of energy independence within 15 years, and by the year 2000 annual energy savings could be two million barrels of oil daily." In interview with Washington Dateline, Glaser emphasized necessity of insuring that public is not oversold on any one solution to U.S. energy problems. "ASHRAE has an important role to play in solar development," Glaser said, noting that the society should help "dispell the ambiguities" about solar technology, stress hard facts, and take a definite part in standards setting. "The solar energy industry will be a hundreds-of-millions-of-dollars industry by 1980, according to some estimates," he said, "with a great need for standards and performance criteria."

OSHA NOT WINNING POPULARITY CONTESTS IN WASHINGTON, EITHER

Labor Secretary Peter Brennan currently having large difficulties with Congress over OSHA management. Joint Senate labor subcommittee and General Accounting Office study includes 17 "issue papers" pointing to areas of management problems. In letter to Secretary Brennan, Senate Labor and Public Health Committee Chairman Harrison Williams charges that "some of our findings would seem to necessitate the immediate application of corrective measures if OSHA is to have any meaningful effect on the safety and health conditions of the American workplace." Study finds that after three years of record-collecting, OSHA has failed to develop necessary statistical information by which to measure OSHA's impact on safety and health. Senator Williams also charges that "there seems to be no uniform application of guidelines covering the issuance of citations in circumstances where there is employer unawareness of hazardous conditions."

FEDERAL APPLIANCE LABELING PROGRAM AN EXPANDING UNIVERSE

Voluntary labeling program for water heaters will soon be added to list of Commerce Department energy conservation efforts. Commerce sources indicate February or March publication of proposed guidelines in Federal Register for public comment. Department already has underway optional program for manufacturers of room air conditioners and is awaiting response to its proposed labeling for refrigerators, freezers, and combination refrigerator/freezers. New labeling, unlike air conditioner EER approach, would show: 1) kilowatt-hours used on monthly basis; 2) monthly cost of operation, stressing dependence on varying regional rates; and 3) comparison with kw range for similar units. Across town in Washington, Federal Trade Commission now finalizing proposals for mandatory labeling of room air conditioners and awaiting public comment. FTC also working on mandatory refrigeration labeling.

ASHRAE JOURNAL December 1974 23

The Cup presented to Past President Alfred E. Kenrick at the Annual Dinner of The American Society of Heating and Ventilating Engineers, January 23, 1907, "In Recognition of a Service Rendered."

L. N. Hunter, Crosby Field, John H. Fox, John Everetts, Jr. and P. B. Gordon enjoy a pre-taping moment at the TV studio

ASHRAE Notables Appear on Television Hour

Starting at 11 p.m. on January 17, in an hour-long presentation over television Channel 13—WNDT, moderated by ASHRAE President John H. Fox, Presidential Members L. N. Hunter, Crosby Field, John Everetts, Jr. and P. B. Gordon told a varied story covering the ASHRAE fields of endeavor.

The hour, The Engineer and Environment, forming ASHRAE's portion of Channel 13's Science and Engineering Television Journal, was opened with brief remarks by President Fox elucidating the extent of Society interests and member makeup, followed by introduction of the four topical speakers: L. N. Hunter on Physiological Aspects of Heating, Crosby Field on Refrigeration and Cryogenics, John Everetts, Jr., on Ventilation and Man's Environment and P. B. Gordon on Man and Control of His Environment through Air Conditioning.

L. N. Hunter reviewed the physiological aspects of heating to clarify, through understanding, our need for heat and its effect upon us, sketching in the body's metabolic processes, vasomotor regulation and the role of artificial heat in the body's functioning. With reference to the ASHRAE Guide And Data Book, he reviewed the concept of Effective Temperature and psychrometric charts and related these to engineering applications in home and commercial heating systems.

Colonel Crosby Field outlined the scope and theory of "cooling below normal human environmental temperatures", tracing the history of refrigeration from earliest times to the present in its ramifications and uses as well as the variety of its processes. Especially explored by Colonel Field was the field of cryogenics "the science of the behavior of materials under temperatures approximating absolute zero".

The topic, Ventilation and Man's Environment, brought to life by the exposition of John Everetts, Jr., followed a detailed historical survey and led to an analysis of the discoveries of research projects concerned with odors, and building infiltration leading, finally, to discussion on relative contents of the air we breathe within enclosures.

P. B. Gordon talked about the effect of heat and humidity on human life and on industrial processes, concluding, in part, that "Considerable basic research to provide for a better understanding of man's reaction to his thermal environment is still needed . . . ". By way of illustration, Mr. Gordon cited studies under way on: an analogue computer to analyze human temperature regulation; responses of human beings to rapid changes in environmental temperatures; the hypothalamus as a temperature regulator and mechanism of temperature regulation in human paraplegics.

These talks were illustrated with pertinent chart displays and interspersed with questions posed by President Fox and answers given by the participants.

FEBRUARY 1963 71

Harry Phillips introduces Charles Logan at record meeting of Chicago Section. Left to right—Ben Seamon, Colonel Field, Mr. Logan, Mr. Phillips, Wm. Bodinus, Hal McPherson, A. B. Stickney

1943

Dr. Kusuda shows ASHRAE emblem to SHASE President Mr. Uichi Inoue

1978

Students gather for view of Charter

NYC Community College, 1978

MONTREAL SPONSORS DESIGN COMPETITION

The Montreal Chapter Education Committee organized an HVAC system design competition for senior mechanical engineering students at McGill and Concordia Universities and Vanier and Ahuntsic community colleges. Anthony Kovic at Vanier College won first prize. A special award for best presentation went to Student Members Jean-Claude Provost and Normand Lafortune, at Ahuntsic College. Winners pose with 1976-77 Chapter President Morton Slone and Chairman of the Education Committee Mal Turaga (third and fourth from right, seated)

1978

Above: Directors Benny Bootle (left), Robert McDonald and Fritz Traugott listening to Keith Massart. Below: The Board in session, showing Clinton Phillips (left), Assistant to the Executive Vice President Doris Flandorffer, Morris Backer, Executive Vice President Andrew Boggs, Hugh McMillan, Jr., and Charles Sepsy.

1978

Argentine associate AAF celebrates 50th anniversary

The Argentine Association of Refrigeration (AAF), an international associate of ASHRAE since 1974, celebrated its 50th anniversary at its 1982 annual meeting, October 18-20 in Buenos Aires. Representing ASHRAE was Victor W. Goldschmidt (fifth from right), professor of mechanical engineering, The Ray W. Herrick Laboratories, Purdue University, and a member of the ASHRAE International Activities Committee. Goldschmidt reviewed the development of ASHRAE Standards 90 and 100, energy conservation in new building design and in existing buildings, and spoke on ASHRAE research on losses in reversing valves and transient effects in heat pumps. AAF consists of some 90 members and produces Boletin Tecnico, a periodical of news and technical features.

1983

ASHRAE Energy Awards displayed in Washington D.C.

An exhibit of the 1985 ASHRAE Energy Awards was recently on display at the Department of Energy offices in Washington D.C. Present were ASHRAE President Robert O. McDonald and Donna Fitzpatrick, principal deputy assistant secretary of the U.S. Department of Energy.

Sunny Spain visited by Solar '83 planning committee

The International Planning Committee for Solar '83 met in Palma de Mallorca, Spain, October 7-11 to plan the symposium and to visit the locations that are available to hold the symposium. Those attending the meeting were: (standing, left to right) M. Rivera—ATECYR, J. Benito—president of ATECYR, L. Rios—ATECYR, R. Hughes—ASHRAE, A. Alaman—ATECYR, W. Stethem—ASHRAE, G. Barcelo—committee chairman, N. Gomez—ATECYR, (seated) J. Rovira—ATECYR and J. McClung—ASHRAE. Abstracts were approved and written notice has been given to those approved for the writing of manuscripts. The International Planning Committee will meet again at the ASHRAE Semi-Annual Meeting in January.

August, 1929 REFRIGERATING ENGINEERING 19

STUDENT RESEARCH PRIZES

for

PAPERS ON RESEARCH OR INDIVIDUAL STUDIES

PAPERS TO BE PRESENTED *at the* FIRST SESSION *of the* 25th ANNIVERSARY MEETING, DECEMBER 4 - 7, 1929.

Cash Prizes Totalling $300 and Certificates to be Awarded

Time Limit Extended to First of November

THE announcement of this contest was made some months ago. Since that time the response has proved very satisfactory. However, the Research Committee—desiring a few more papers of a representative type—have extended the time limit to the first of November. This will enable the participation of a larger group of students. Those who contemplate submitting papers, at this date, are asked to notify the Committee. Address all communications to the Society office.

TYPES --- SUBJECTS --- CONDITIONS

THE type of research is not closely restricted. The Committee recognizes its scope as wider than that of the organized research institution, assuming that "individual" research—field or library investigations—are permissible and to be encouraged. The various types may thus include:

a. Descriptive technical studies of industrial processes—where refrigeration is a fundamental factor—and their developments.

b. Library studies coordinating existing data.

c. Tests of refrigerating apparatus under normal or laboratory conditions.

d. Laboratory investigations on behavior of refrigerating media.

e. Theoretical studies—application of existing principles to design of apparatus or to the measurement of its performance, or to new applications.

EVERY technical college student, whether working for a first degree or an advanced degree (and in the latter case, no matter whether the student is at the same time doing instructing work) is invited and urged to enter into this competition.

Contestants are permitted to receive advice and guidance from their instruction staff—to the same extent as such assistance is given in preparation of a thesis for graduation or for an advanced degree.

This is in every way desirable and to be encouraged.

The suggested topics are "live" issues and should prove interesting as well as valuable.

Any student is privileged to write to the Committee asking for suggestions and advice as to the scope of any of the subjects it has listed.

The Committee also invites all contestants to use the Committee freely for advice and counsel.

THE awards will be based upon originality, consistency, clarity of presentation and value of the paper as an engineering document. Inasmuch as they will be presented at the 25th Anniversary Meeting, unusual publicity and recognition will be given to the winning papers.

The American Society *of* Refrigerating Engineers

37 West 39th Street New York, N. Y.

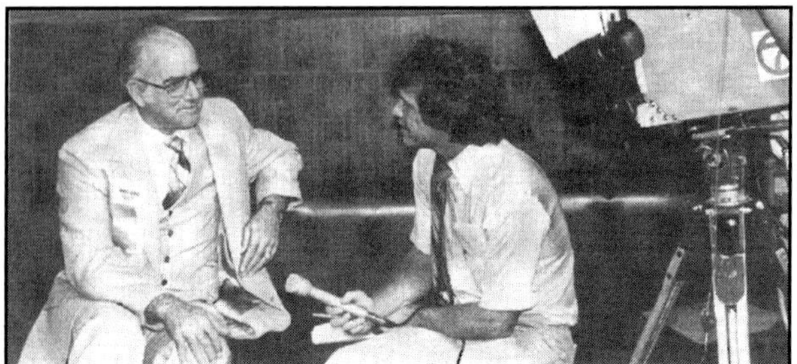

Newly installed President Morris Backer (left) explaining to the Albuquerque press the significance of ASHRAE's role in energy conservation efforts.

1978

Chicago Chapter celebrates 25 years

The Chicago Chapter of ASHRAE was recently presented with a certificate commemorating its 25th anniversary. A number of the chapter's past presidents were present at the ceremony. Pictured are: (front row, left to right) Ron Vallort, 1977-78; John Levenhagen, Region VI chairman; Robert Gray, 1979-80; Richard Krause, current chapter president; (middle row, left to right) Tom Brady, 1984-85; John Sanchez, 1981-82; Bill Richards, 1960-61; Herman Krantz, 1974-75; (back row, left to right) Raymond Swanson, 1980-81; and Ron Schmalz, 1983-84.

1986

September, 1923 REFRIGERATING ENGINEERING 109

THE AMERICAN SOCIETY OF REFRIGERATING ENGINEERS

35 WARREN STREET, New York, N. Y.

September 25, 1923

To the Members of the A. S. R. E.:

The Educational Committee is now engaged in preparing the first section of the material for the A. S. R. E. Data Book and it will be issued shortly. These tables, charts, diagrams, etc., will be supplied to the membership of the Society only, without charge. Additional material will be issued from time to time as it is prepared.

The size of the page will be 8½" x 11", except folders. The folders, when folded, will conform to the 8½" x 11" page.

Many of the members of the Society probably have a loose leaf binder, which they are now using, that will accommodate the Data Book material. However, that every member may have a substantial binder in which to keep the material as sent out, and at the same time have the pages in a form that will be very convenient for ready reference, the Society has made arrangements to supply the members with a special flexible cover loose leaf binder in fine imitation black leather, with the words "A. S. R. E. Data Book" stamped in gilt letters on the front cover, as can be noted from the illustration printed herewith, Figure 1.

Figure 1

The other illustration, Figure 2, shows the simplicity of inserting and removing pages from the binder.

This binder has all of the better advantages of the loose leaf idea and at the same time practically all of the advantages of a bound book. It is flexible as to capacity, holding one sheet or 400 sheets in perfect alignment. It is very light in weight and of simple construction.

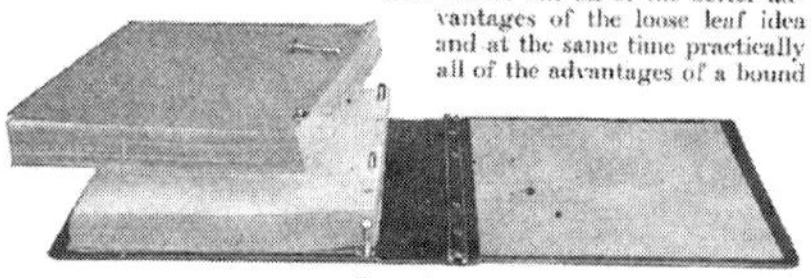

Figure 2

All weights and grades of paper may be bound in this binder, from brittle enamel book to thin multi-copy paper.

The size of the binder, holding a sheet 8½" x 11" admits of the insertion of the pages from all standard size trade papers with very slight trimming.

The price of the binder is $2.00 delivered to any member in any part of the world. Every member is urged to send in his order promptly that we may know how many binders to order. Binders will not be sold to non-members.

Very truly,

William H. Ross, *Secretary.*

Judges pore over winners in ASHRAE regional competitions to select the 1988 Energy Award winners in both new and retrofit energy engineering projects. The annual competition requires energy consumption data for 12 months of operation to demonstrate the effectiveness of the HVAC system.

NIST recognizes researchers for "landmark" paper

National Institute of Standards and Technology (NIST) researchers Mark O. McLinden, Chemical Engineer, NEL, and David A. Didion, Supervisory Mechanical Engineer, NEL, have been recognized by NIST for their research in the paper "Quest for Alternatives," which was published in the ASHRAE Journal *in December of 1987. The paper addressed the tradeoffs and limitations involved with developing new refrigerants in the advent of an international agreement to limit the production of refrigerants that are potentially harmful to the atmosphere. The NIST called the paper a "landmark contribution to the field of chlorofluorocarbons and industrial refrigrants."*

Dinner Served in Furnace to Minnesota Chapter

1930

Progress Is the Outgrowth of Research

Shown on This and the Facing Page Are Typical Examples of Research Exhibits Conducted to Further the Art and Science of Refrigeration and Air Conditioning

AT the 49th Annual Meeting of the American Society of Refrigerating Engineers held in Washington, D. C., December 6 to 9 twenty-six exhibits of research equipment and techniques were on display. These exhibits covered such diverse fields as quick freezing techniques to preserve life, early models of refrigerating equipment, speed-up life test equipment, heat transfer calculation models, etc. On this and the facing page, 13 of the exhibits are pictured. Photos of other of the exhibits not shown here were published in the November 1953 issue of this magazine.

The exhibit program of the Society was started at the Atlanta, Georgia, Spring Meeting of ASRE in 1952. A research exhibit was held at the Annual Meeting of the Society in New York City in 1952 and the third and most recent exhibit was at the Annual Meeting in Washington, D. C. It is planned to continue to hold research exhibits at future Annual Meetings of the Society.

Chairman of the 1953 Research Exhibit Committee who was particularly responsible for the exhibits shown on these pages was S. J. Williams of International-Harvester. Chairman of the 1954 Exhibit Committee is A. P. White of Spencer Thermostat Division.

R. A. Line and T. R. Kearney of Ansul Chemical stand behind the test setup that gives a visual method of checking moisture in a refrigerant while W. H. Mullin on the left inspects the equipment.

A. P. White of Spencer Thermostat examines the Audiffren refrigeration machine which was probably the first hermetically sealed unit and was invented by a French monk in 1913.

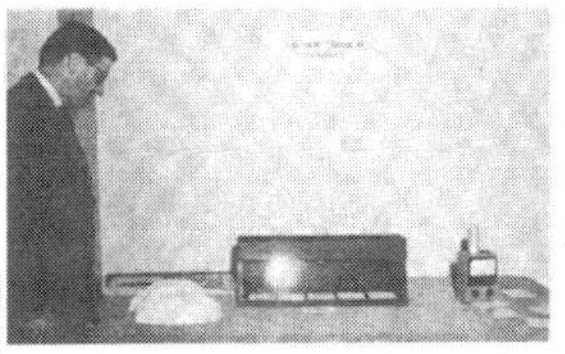

The Dow Chemical exhibit showed how a two-color dusting technique reveals the presence of positive or negative charges on polystyrene plastic parts. Harold Stults, patent attorney, looks on.

The Purdue University exhibit was a box containing three separate compartments, one sealed, one unsealed and vented, and one unsealed and unvented. The third cell fills up with water.

Refrigerating Engineering

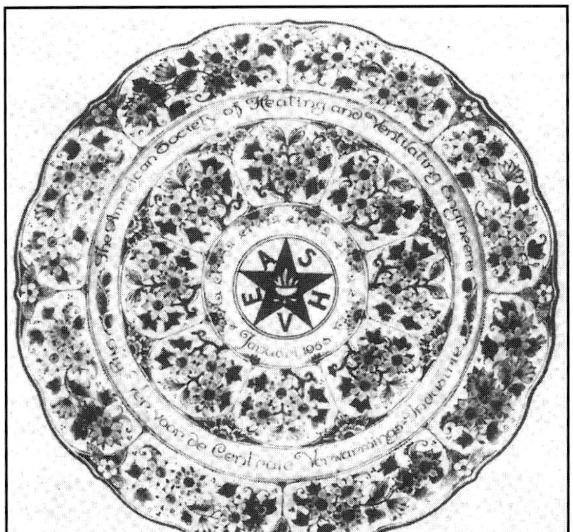

1955

Part of the merry St. Louis contingent of ASRE showed up at the costume party in the genuine uniforms of the St. Louis Browns. Shown here, l. to r., are J. A. Wilkerson, Dole Refrigerating Co.; J. H. Spence, Hussmann Refrigeration; J. T. Barry, Sporlan Valve; W. F. Wischmeyer, Sporlan Valve; D. M. Lawson, Sporlan Valve; J. R. Caulk, Hussmann; and Hermann Spoehrer, Sporlan Valve.

One of the best laugh-getting costumes at the masked ball was that worn by ASRE vice president Arthur J. Hess shown with Mrs. Hess. His number spells a naughty word upside down.

Who would suspect that these two bold characters (left) are P. B. Christensen, former ASRE president, and M. C. Turpin, secretary of the Society?

P. B. Christensen shakes the hand of B. C. D'Antoni, chief engineer of Standard Fruit & SS Co., who donated the bananas which graced each dinner table at the party.

1952

Gateway to Energy Awards

The 1982 ASHRAE Gateway to Energy Conservation Awards were presented to three firms at a recent meeting of the American Society of Heating, Refrigerating and Air Conditioning Engineers, Inc. Jim Cubbage of Blackmore & Glunt, Awards Committee chairperson, presented the awards, sponsored to promote the conservation of energy in the design of new and existing buildings. Awards were presented to (from left) Danny Brouillet, Midwest Refrigeration, for Ritepoint Pen Co. in the existing project over 25,000 sq. ft. category; Les Penn, William Tao & Associates, Inc., for McDonnell Douglas Automation Center in the new project over 25,000 sq. ft. category; and Edward A. Kriege, E.D.M., Inc., for Wyneken Hall Concordia Seminary in the category of existing projects under 25,000 sq. ft. Judges were Don Guilfoy, City of St. Louis water commissioner; William P. Norris, former ASHRAE chapter president; Vernon Kofron, vice president of Vactec, Inc.; and William Kountz, William Kountz & Associates, Architects. *Photo by DeRanek*

Numbering System Offered to Aid Refrigerant Identification

The Du Pont Company has offered to make generally available a simplified numbering system developed over the last quarter century to identify chemical compounds used as refrigerants.

Acceptance of the proposal, made initially to The American Society of Refrigerating Engineers, would eliminate confusion existing in the refrigeration industry due to similarity of fluorinated halo-hydrocarbon refrigerants. A common numbering system, it explained, not only would simplify equipment designers' and manufacturers' work but would greatly assist refrigeration servicemen in identifying and using the proper cooling agent in repair work, regardless of the source of the material.

The proposal already has been accepted by the Standards Committee and Council of The American Society of Refrigerating Engineers and will be incorporated into an ASRE Standard on refrigerant designation for approval by the general membership of the scientific group in the near future.

Specifically, Du Pont has announced that it will not look upon use by the refrigerants industry of the generic term "refrigerant" followed by code numbers based on Du Pont's numbering system to constitute infringement of its trademarks. Such trademarks consist of a combination of "Freon" or the letter "F" with such numbers, as in the case of "Freon-11," "F-11," "Freon-22," "F-22," etc. However, the announcement made it clear that Du Pont reserves to itself the exclusive use of its trademarks.

The numbering system, based upon the chemical structure of compounds used as refrigerants, was first developed by "Kinetic" Chemicals, Inc., then a jointly-owned subsidiary of Du Pont and General Motors Corporation, in 1930. The first of a family of "Freon" fluorinated or halo-hydrocarbon compounds had just been introduced to replace more toxic, flammable, or explosive chemicals then used as cooling agents. The "Freon" type refrigerants are credited with making mechanical refrigerators, freezers, and air conditioning systems completely practical from a public safety standpoint, and are used today in nearly all home cooling equipment as well as a sizable portion of commercial and industrial refrigeration and air conditioning systems.

From 1930 until 1952, "Kinetic" Chemicals, which became a division of Du Pont's Organic Chemicals Department in 1950, was the only U. S. manufacturer of fluorinated hydrocarbon refrigerants. In the early 1950's the General Chemical Division of Allied Chemical and Dye Corporation entered this field with "Genetron" fluorinated hydrocarbon products. Pennsylvania Salt Manufacturing Company has announced it will introduce later this year a third brand of fluorinated hydrocarbon compounds under the trademark "Isotron."

In making this offer of its numbering system to The American Society of Refrigerating Engineers, R. J. Thompson, Director of Sales of the Du Pont Company's "Kinetic" Chemicals Division, observed that an ASRE Task Committee has been studying the problem of designation of refrigerants for the last several years in order to avoid the problems created for users and equipment manufacturers if refrigerant manufacturers adhered to or adopted different numbering systems.

Mr. Thompson expressed the hope that Du Pont's proposal would eliminate presently-existing confusion and would be beneficial to the whole refrigeration industry.

NEW BIRMINGHAM SECTION

Herbert P. Tinning, National Assistant Secretary, chats with members of newly-organized Birmingham, Ala., Section. Left to right, are, E. B. Miller, Chairman; Tinning, Frank L. Vaughn, first vice chairman; J. C. Malone, second vice chairman; Sam Lawrence, secretary, and J. G. Woodroof, Regional Director.

August 1956

RESEARCH PAGE

Disposal of ASHRAE Laboratory Facilities and Equipment

E. P. PALMATIER

Chairman ASHRAE Research and Technical Committee

As announced in the January issue of the ASHRAE JOURNAL, the Society's Research Laboratory at 7218 Euclid Ave., Cleveland 3, Ohio, is being deactivated. Concurrently, steps are being taken to accelerate and expand sponsored work at universities and other laboratories.

One of the responsibilities of the Research and Technical Committee is the development of policies and procedures by means of which the facilities and equipment of the Laboratory may be liquidated. At first, this might seem like a simple task, but to do the job with proper consideration of the Society's research objectives and with complete fairness to potential recipients represents quite a challenge.

Actually, there are two parts to the problem. First, there is the question of relocating two major facilities which have been designed and erected for executing specific programs. Second, there is an inventory of general purpose instrumentation and equipment that might be of value to almost any laboratory.

MAJOR FACILITIES

One of these is the Controlled Environment Room, which has been used for the past few years to investigate the reaction of healthy subjects to various thermal and radiant environments. Negotiations are essentially completed, as this is being written, to relocate this facility at Kansas State University, where it will be used to carry on the program described in the January JOURNAL.

The second major facility is the Solar Calorimeter, which has been used for many years to study the solar heat gain through glass and other structural components, and the influence of shading devices on heat gain. Laboratories interested in acquiring this facility should address an inquiry to ASHRAE Research Laboratory, 7218 Euclid Ave., Cleveland 3, Ohio, to the attention of Assistant Director of Research Clark M. Humphreys. It will help to indicate the type of program contemplated for use of the facility, the staffing suggested procedures for working cooperatively with the Society (see April JOURNAL Research Page), the probable annual budget contemplated and the portion of this budget expected to be covered by grants from ASHRAE. The communication should also identify the individual with whom negotiations should be concluded and whether this person will be available at the ASHRAE 68th Annual Meeting in Denver on June 26-28. All inquiries will be evaluated by committee at that time and a recommendation will be submitted to the Board for action.

It is the intention to donate this facility, with its associated instrumentation, with the understanding that the recipient will handle rigging and trucking to its destination. Rigging to its present location on top of a one-story building was done with a small crane years ago at a cost of about $20. Today's cost might be $50. It can be shipped by flat-bed truck; weight is estimated at 1500 lb.

GENERAL PURPOSE INSTRUMENTS AND EQUIPMENT

An inventory has been prepared of this equipment, as shown on the facing page. Those interested in acquiring items should submit bids separately identified by item numbers to the attention of Mr. Humphreys at the ASHRAE Research Laboratory, 7218 Euclid Ave., Cleveland 3, Ohio. The deadline for consideration of all bids will be June 1, at which time the successful bidders will be notified. The equipment may then be picked up at the Laboratory or it will be packed and shipped at the bidder's expense price after June 15.

Any equipment that is not sold in this manner will be given away on a first-come-first-served basis. On July 1 the remainder will be sold in one lot or scrapped. Anyone wishing to inspect or evaluate the laboratory inventory may do so without prior notification.

ASHRAE JOURNAL

1961

ASHRAE President Frank H. Faust, assisted by Dr. Nevins, officially opens KSU Institute with a snip of the shears

Institute for Environmental Research dedicated at Kansas State University

"The formal opening of the Institute for Environmental Research and the dedication of the KSU-ASHRAE Environmental Laboratory at Kansas State University is an event of great interest and significance to the more than 17,000 members of the American Society of Heating, Refrigerating and Air-Conditioning Engineers . . . to Kansas State University, the State of Kansas, and to the general public, who will ultimately be the beneficiaries of the research that will be performed here." Thus stated ASHRAE President Frank H. Faust, addressing the dedication ceremonies of the Institute for Environmental Research at Kansas State University on November 7. The opening and dedication took place at 4 p.m., preceded by an open house of the facilities from 10 a.m. to 3 p.m.

Dr. Ralph G. Nevins, Director of the Institute, presided at the dedication. A Member of ASHRAE, Dr. Nevins also is Head of the Department of Mechanical Engineering at Kansas State. Other speakers on the program were: Dr. Everett J. Dennis, Minister of Education, First Methodist Church, Manhattan, who delivered the Invocation; Dr. James A. McCain, President of Kansas State, who welcomed those attending and introduced the special guests; William F. Danenbarger, who extended greetings on behalf of the Board of Regents; Clark M. Humphreys (Fellow ASHRAE), Division of Occupational Health, U. S. Public Health Service; and Mr. Faust.

In his address, Mr. Faust outlined ASHRAE's interest in environmental research at Kansas State. He pointed out that research was one of the basic objectives of the Society when it was formed in 1894. This objective was implemented by a research program in 1917, which has been in operation continuously since that time with a total expenditure of approximately $3,800,000. According to Mr. Faust, a significant portion of this research, although not a major one, has been concerned with physiological reactions of humans in their environments. However, despite the extensive amount of basic knowledge that has been established in this area, Mr. Faust stated, there are still many needs for consolidating and improving technological knowledge in the field of environmental control. Among these are methods of measuring radiant heat transfer to and from the body, the effect of radiant heating and cooling and humidity on comfort, and thermal environment as it affects health, comfort, learning and productivity.

When ASHRAE decided to close its Cleveland Laboratory in 1961, the ASHRAE Environmental Laboratory was presented to Kansas State. Some of the reasons for choosing Kansas State, according to Mr. Faust, were that: the University has shown interest in research in this field and had a staff engaged in such work; Dr. Nevins had been an active member of various technical committees of the Society interested in and directing research on physiology and human environment; the University was willing to erect a new building to house the facility; and the University is in an excellent position to develop its graduate education courses and to attract an outstanding staff.

In conclusion, Mr. Faust predicted that: "Kansas State University and the State of Kansas will benefit in a number of ways from the KSU Institute for Environmental Research and the KSU-ASHRAE Environmental Laboratory. It will help establish KSU as an authority in this field. Facilities of the Society provide a means for publication of the results of research and their presentation to engineers who are in a position to apply the results for the better design of products and systems to the overall benefit of the general public. This activity should enhance the economic future of the State of Kansas and the area in which the University is located."

President Faust also delivered a message over the KSU radio station.

December 1963

A. S. R. E. Members Meeting Jointly With A. S. H. V. E. Enjoy Splendid Technical Sessions and Expertly Arranged Social Program

THIS issue contains reports of part of the technical sessions at the Cleveland meeting, the rest of which will appear in later issues. The various meetings went forward as announced in the program appearing in the last issue, and all were well attended. The Wednesday afternoon meeting featuring the papers by Brizzolara and Milener was the best attended with more than 250 men on hand. The joint sessions at the Cleveland Auditorium filled the floor and part of the gallery both mornings, with an attendance of some six hundred.

On Wednesday the high spot was the address on acoustical problems by Dr. V. O. Knudsen. At the session put on the next morning by the A. S. R. E. a similar address was heard from Dr. Prescott, who gave an appealing and scholarly treatment of bacteriology in its relation to refrigerating engineering. In this session A. R. Stevenson's paper on heating and cooling with refrigerating machinery, printed in REFRIGERATING ENGINEERING last month, marked the high point of the engineering part of the whole program. This paper drew very valuable comment in the way of discussion from the audience. Mr. Willis H. Carrier, past president of the A. S. R. E. who was on the platform representing the A. S. H. V. E., outlined some new determinations of suitable temperatures for air conditioning which depart from past assumptions.

The student prize sessions enjoyed a very able address by President Wickenden of the Case School, who defended a plan for strengthening the professional ties in a paper to appear here later. The three students who presented papers in competition for prizes amounting to three hundred dollars, donated by the Frick Company, had three subjects of different purpose and scope, all interesting, all well presented. The committee of judges headed by Mr. Harrison, who acted as chairman of the session on Tuesday evening when the papers were heard, scored each paper on the announced bases and found the three contestants tied. These men were Lewis Elmer, Jr., of Cornell University, Lewis H. D. Fraser, Jr., of M. I. T., and Henry F. Irving of the University of Illinois, while awards in the form of certificates also went to Joe McEachern and Charles R. Lucas, both of the class of 1931 of the University of Tennessee. Colleges were well represented at the convention, delegations being on hand from several Middle Western campuses.

The whole program was run off in three days instead of the usual four, but with a number of inspection trips arranged for those who stayed over the fourth day. The inspection trip of Wednesday, a trip to Akron, was somewhat interfered with by rain, which prevailed the first three days of the week. The chief side show was of course the Heating and Ventilating Exposition, which was a great success and well attended. The refrigeration end of the show was prominent, several of the booths finding their squads of representatives busy at all hours for the whole week. The comment regarding the advisability of having the A.S.R.E. represented in the joint convention as well as the exposition was decidedly favorable.

The Cleveland Committee under D. F. Keith had full charge of the arrangements outside the actual presentation of technical papers. This group in making its initial plans assumed that its experience was to be somewhat unique, since this was the first meeting to be held under such auspices away from the Society headquarters. It desired not only to do a first-class job in running the convention but if possible to establish a record which would add to the experience of the Society in future events so managed. The objective was amply realized, and many of the methods established will undoubtedly stand as a precedent for other meetings outside of New York. Each man on the committee, noted below, had charge of a definite job and the group worked together well. The entertainment of about twenty-five out-of-town ladies was in charge of Mrs. Keith, who with Mrs. Timmerman and Mrs. Scott made each day interesting with its prearranged events.

1932

ORANGE EMPIRE — ASHRAE'S NEWEST CHAPTER — RECEIVES CHARTER MARCH 25

ASHRAE's first National President, A. J. Hess, presents the Charter to K. H. Watts, Orange Empire's first President. Pictured from left to right are: W. L. Holladay, National President-Elect; Mr. Hess; A. T. Boggs, National Executive Secretary; Mr. Watts; and V. J. Burke, Chairman, Region X.

1968

GUIDE AND DATA BOOK Series Completely Indexed in Each Volume for Easy Reference

1968

Solar Home Viewed in Central Indiana

In June, members of the Central Indiana Chapter were guests at the BDP Company's Solar Demonstration Home. Hosts Alan Nelder, right, and Dick Chang, second from right, said twenty tons of common river rock (shown in picture behind the demonstration window) heated by solar energy can keep a home warm up to 11 hours, even on cloudy days. Observing the bin of pebbles are (L-R) Donald O'Keefe, chapter president; Russel Peek; Lee Kennedy; and Reason Biddle.

1980

First Region XI CRC Held in Alaska

Above are some of the participants in the first annual general meeting of Region XI held recently in Anchorage, AK. Among those present were 1979-80 ASHRAE officers including Hugh D. McMillan, Jr., president; Martin McDougall, Region XI chairman; Richard P. Perry, treasurer; and Steve Singleton, membership manager.

ASHRAE JOURNAL September 1980

Astronaut James A. Lovell, center, whose topic at the Welcome Luncheon was Why a Trip to the Moon?, chats with Walter Cooke and President Faust

1964

Air Conditioning Progress in Great Britain

BERNARD C. OLDHAM, prominent British refrigerating engineer, addressed the Institution of Heating and Ventilating Engineers in London in April on the "Application of Refrigerating to Air Conditioning." This is an elaborate paper going into the essentials of refrigerating machinery as well as air cooling equipment. Much of this material is familiar to refrigeration through the author's previous writings in these pages and elsewhere, while for heating engineers this is an excellent compendium for reference.

Comments on the air cooling theme are indicative of the present state of the art in England. Air conditioning, Mr. Oldham says, accounts for 40% of the inquiries coming to refrigerating machinery manufacturers, but only 1 to 2% of the orders. In citing some of the reasons for this, attention is called to criticism of recirculation, which appears to have been more common there than here. The rest of this review quotes from the original.

"There appears to be a natural reaction in some quarters against the use of refrigeration because recirculation of the majority of the air is necessary for reasons of economy. The increase of CO_2 content is one line of argument; deprivation of oxygen is another.

"The removal of the added CO_2 should be provided for in every air-conditioning plant for auditorium or theatre conditioning. The absorption and subsequent liberation of CO_2 is quite a simple matter which should be economically carried out. In the conservation of perishable foods, refrigeration goes further than to condition the air for purity and humidity; the constituents of the atmosphere are changed to produce optimum storage conditions.

"For air conditioning human beings, the removal of CO_2 would appear to be a ready means of answering criticisms antagonistic to refrigeration on account of recirculation. Washed, refrigerated, recirculated air can be purer than any other.

"The almost negligible percentages of CO_2 increment and oxygen deprivation are shown by the following comparison, the unit being the requirements of one person.

Case I.—No recirculation.

1,800 ft.^{3}/hr. of fresh air per person.

Case II.—Two-thirds recirculation.

1,200 ft.^{3} recirculated air, 600 ft.^{3} fresh air — per hour per person.

with 85% efficiency of CO_2 removal.

"Assume the initial condition for both cases to be a specific volume 13.5 ft.^{3}/lb., absolute humidity 56 grains/lb., CO_2 content 0.04% by volume, which equals 0.06% by weight.

"The total weight of one hour's supply of air under this condition is therefore 133⅓ lb., comprising

CO_2	0.080 lb.	Also traces of ozone, argon, etc. Proportion of oxygen to nitrogen by weight 23:77
H_2O	1.067 lb.	
O_2	30.403 lb.	
N_2	101.783 lb.	
	133.333 lb.	

"Assume for each person a production of 0.1 lb. CO_2/hr., which involves a deprivation of 0.073 lb. O_2 and an addition of 0.1 lb. water vapor. The final composition of the air in the two cases is therefore as follows:

	Example I. (Continuously)	Example II. (At end of 12 hr.)
CO_2	0.180 lb.	0.300 lb.
H_2O	1.167 lb.	1.167 lb.
O_2	30.330 lb.	29.821 lb.
N_2	101.783 lb.	101.783 lb.
	133.460 lb.	133.071 lb.

"Proportions:

CO_2	0.090% by volume.	0.150% by volume after 12 hr. 0.075% average.
$O_2 : N_2$	22.957 : 77.043	22.66 :: 77.33

Comparative oxygen deprivation 1.3%

"These figures should suffice to clear up any doubts that may exist concerning the absence of vitiation of air due to recirculation, particularly as 0.3% of CO_2 (twice that cited above) is frequently found in rooms after only a few hours' occupation; and 0.5% of CO_2, according to a Medical Research Committee in London in 1920, can exist without producing any noticeable effects."

The Samuel Wylie Miller medal, awarded annually by the American Welding Society for meritorious contributions to the science and art of welding, has been presented to H. H. Moss of New York for his achievement in the application of fusion welding and oxy-acetylene flame cutting.

1933

Student branches formed in Kansas and Wisconsin

A total of 93 students, members of the Kansas City Chapter and guests attended as the Kansas State University Student Branch, Manhattan, Kansas, received its charter. Pictured with the banner are (left to right): branch officers Keith Davis, vice president; Mike Lorenz, president; Todd Bickel, secretary; Kansas City Chapter president Jerry Osborne; and Region IX Education Chairman Steve Ivesdal.

Students in the air conditioning technology program at District One Technical Institute in Eau Claire, Wisconsin, have formed a student branch of ASHRAE. Sponsored by the La Crosse Area Chapter, the branch has enrolled over 40 members. Pictured are the members and Professor Timothy Mentink, faculty advisor (bottom left).

1985

ASHRAE RESEARCH PROJECT ON FROSTING OF FINNED COILS NOW IN PROGRESS AT OHIO STATE UNIVERSITY

A discussion on the objectives, procedure and results of the ASHRAE research project on Forced Convection and Frosting of Finned Coils in Cross Flow of Air (RP-47), being conducted at Ohio State University, was led by the project director, Professor Charles F. Sepsy, at a recent luncheon at the Faculty Club.

Present at the time were representatives of companies which have contributed directly to this and other projects sponsored by the Technical Committee on Heat Transfer and Fluid Flow (T.C. 1.3).

After the luncheon, the test facilities of the University were observed while tests were made by graduate students.

The objective of project RP-47 is to study the phenomena of heat and mass transfer for tube and fin heat exchangers. The study is being made on finned surfaces that are dry, wet and at various stages of frosting. Data, to be made available, will be applicable to the design of tube and fin coils utilized in air conditioning, heat pump, and refrigeration units.

Of particular interest to manufacturers of heat pumps will be the rate of frost formation for different air flow rates, fin surface temperatures and air moisture content. The relationship between frost thickness and air side pressure drop are also determined.

It is the intention of the experimenters to produce useful and vital information for the industry. However, the program has been designed as a basic research project in heat and mass transfer and is not a test program for a specific manufacturer's coil design.

Professor Charles Sepsy (Member ASHRAE) describes one of many coil configurations used in the ASHRAE Research Project RP-47. Looking on are ASHRAE Members William R. Strutz, Gerald C. Smith and William Melnyk and also John Ehinger

ASHRAE JOURNAL *October 1965*

REGION VIII

CENTRAL OKLAHOMA ENERGY CONSERVATION TEAM

The Energy Conservation Committee of the Central Oklahoma Chapter: Seated: George W. Gilroy, Chairman Richard J. Stone, William J. Flynn, Jr.; Standing: Charles D. Callahan, William H. Orr, Thomas C. Moore, John H. Carnahan

1974

INVOLVEMENT IS...

providing technical leadership in assisting with local environmental problems.

Pollution of any or all sorts is the current "in" thing. When a subject like "environmental pollution control" becomes so popular in so short a time, everybody wants to get into the act. The result is inevitably confusion, much of it caused by pressures for action now and technical and economic analyses later. Witness the ups and downs of phosphate detergents!

Part of the problem is that many who have involved themselves are just not knowledgeable in vital aspects of pollution control. This is why you can make significant contributions in your local or regional areas, either as an individual or as the representative of your ASHRAE chapter. You can be very effective, at a town meeting for example, by helping less knowledgeable people to understand the technical and economic factors that bear on the problem at hand. In other words, you can explain, in a logical fashion, the "whole picture."

As you well know from your engineering experience, a "quick-fix" to a problem can be worse than the problem itself. Hence, such counselling needs the objectivity and enlightenment that you, as an engineer, can provide to dispel misinformation, while offering suggestions for corrective actions.

Also, your engineering training is ideally suited for appraising the proliferation of suggested solutions, standards and directions to be taken; analyzing their merits and limitations, and proposing logical courses of action.

Stan Gilman

1972

Central Oklahoma Chapter celebrates 50th anniversary

ASHRAE Past President Robert O. McDonald (left) accepts a Kiowa ceremonial bonnet from Bud Saunkeah. The presentation was made at the Region VIII CRC and 50th anniversary of the Central Oklahoma Chapter.

1985

A good time was had by all at the Bal Masque, including Masquers Mrs. William Wallace, William Wallace, Secretary of the Life Members Club, Mrs. John E. Dube, John E. Dube, Mrs. H. G. S. Murray, and John Everetts, Jr.

1964

December speakers at the Michigan Chapter pictured above were Robert G. Coughey, Joseph B. Olivieri, Joseph S. Bobbio, Bruce A. Dean and Edwin G. Siegel

Michigan Chapter Past President David S. Falk (right) is shown receiving the Chapter's Certificate of Appreciation from Chapter Vice President William M. Dull

1964

chapter news

SAN JOSE CHAPTER RECEIVES CHARTER NOVEMBER 1

Representatives from every California chapter were present at the San Jose Charter Meeting, November 1. The 140 in attendance saw Chapter President Alex Boome receive the new charter from National President James W. May.

As a token of cooperation and friendship, the Golden Gate Chapter presented San Jose with a gavel. ASHRAE President-Elect, Lincoln Bouillon, presented the new chapter with another gavel, from National.

Former Region X Director, T. J. White, was also at the meeting.

The new chapter was welcomed with many congratulatory telegrams and letters from all over the United States and Canada.

Chapter President Alex Boome accepts gavel from National President-Elect Lincoln Bouillon

National President James W. May (right) presents charter to Chapter President Boome

F. Adams, Governor; J. Wilson, Vice President; D. Aronoff, Treasurer; A. Boome, President; and M. Scofield and G. Greene, Governors; pose with their new charter

1965

Cleveland Chapter Meeting Arrangements Committee and guests—Standing left to right—R. Wilson, Chairman, Golf Committee; J. Calafato, Chairman, Sessions Committee; R. Halverstadt, Chairman, Entertainment Committee; R. B. Myers, Cleveland Convention and Visitors Bureau; J. Lushbaugh, Chairman, Housing Committee, and Hugh McNair, Chairman, Finance Committee. Seated left to right—W. Mussun, Jr., Chairman, Reception Committee; W. Bush, Chairman, Field Trip Committee; B. Schwirtz, Chairman, Publicity Committee; V. Coe, Chairman, Banquet Committee; S. Bowen, General Chairman; and Julia Szabo, ASHRAE Assistant Secretary—Meetings. Not pictured are R. Rubin, Chairman, Ladies Committee, and W. Farr, Jr., Chairman, Transportation Committee

1964

The Board of Governors of newly-elected East Tennessee chapter and visitors. Seated: B. Marnet, Burt Lomax, Jr., John E. Dube, James W. May, ASHRAE Associate Secretary Andrew T. Boggs, III, and R. Forde. Standing: R. E. Vandius, W. L. Montgomery, R. Crawford, E. H. Hall, J. T. Bailey, and F. Vaughn.

Pictured are chapter members present at the East Tennessee Charter Meeting in Knoxville, Tenn.

1965

president's page

CARL F. KAYAN
Chairman, ASHRAE Education Committee

Let's look at our image

You hear it on every side, in business, in politics, "What Image are you building?" What face do you put on for the public-relations department to win friends and influence people?

We, as engineers, do not have to turn to Madison Avenue; we do not have to jerry-build an Image. We have a real one of our own; one which has been building itself for at least the last hundred years—and one which can well serve to bring "new blood" into our ranks.

We, as members of ASHRAE, are concerned with the translation of fruitful concepts of science and technology into useful purposes in the general fields of heating, refrigerating and air-conditioning engineering. These fields are concerned with general personal well-being, on one hand, and with the specific demands of industry, commerce and defense, on the other.

We, as engineers, are by the very nature of our work concerned with fundamentals, not with superficial gimmicks. We are concerned with exploration, research and development over a broad spectrum of temperatures, not only on land and sea and in the [illegible], but now even in outer space. We deal with the design, manufacture, and operation of individual components—in the field of refrigeration for example—ranging from refrigerant compressors and heat exchangers to electronic controls and thermoelectric devices. As system design engineers we follow up with the application of the separate elements to an integrated, often automated, system. For this ultimate system we are then concerned with the overall control, operation, and sustained-performance maintenance. And all this must be in terms of reasonable economic philosophy.

We work from bare concepts to finished products—from dreams to realities—from the rough calculations on the back of an envelope to the formal detailed specifications. There are probably no more versatile people on earth! Our heads have to be in the clouds but our feet have to be on the ground. We not only have to think "what," but we have to think "how" and "when." Is it a good idea, is it feasible to manufacture from the economic angle, and is it practical to do it now? And then we further our creative objectives via logic, analysis and computation, seeking to achieve our ultimate results by different feasible mathematical and computer means including analog and digital schemes.

Because of us and our predecessors, people in New England towns eat vegetables all the year round. We survive the rigors of winters in comfortably heated buildings. People in Arizona and Saudi Arabia live in tolerable comfort because of our air-conditioning equipment. Remote fishing villages are now economically solvent because they can ship their catches to processing plants and to markets via modern methods of refrigeration. Fishermen in Iceland can sell not only to their own townspeople but to people in Kankakee and Houston, to people in Vienna and Turin.

All these things in the past have been accomplished by an extraordinary group of pioneers. We must not be unmindful of our responsibility to recruit as their successors the best of the coming crop. Statistics tell us that we have the largest group in history waiting to be educated in our colleges. We represent a technologically-elite group. We shall welcome to our ranks creative, imaginative and enthusiastic recruits, who can take their appropriate place in the different echelons of our activity. . . . We must imbue them [illegible] excitement of the new worlds still to conquer.

Let us make our prospective candidates aware of the romance of our profession. Let them know of the joy and satisfaction in the design and creation of equipment and systems that fulfill their destiny and thereby add to the intrinsic richness of our civilization, with commensurate recognition and monetary rewards.

Much can be accomplished in talking to a younger group in terms of "case histories." These could be on unusual and challenging problems that had to be solved, and therein relating how dreams were translated into realities. Such talks can well be bulwarked by field trips for small groups to exciting installations to highlight the "from-dreams-to-reality" format.

Finally, Chapters might well try to develop a program of summer "cadetships" in different fields with the candidate serving as the "man-Friday" assistant to an enthusiastic creative engineer. (The latter might well receive Chapter recognition for his educational contribution.) Thus might the cadet be innoculated with enthusiasm . . . and it could be contagious to his own fellow students!

ASHRAE JOURNAL *December 1964*

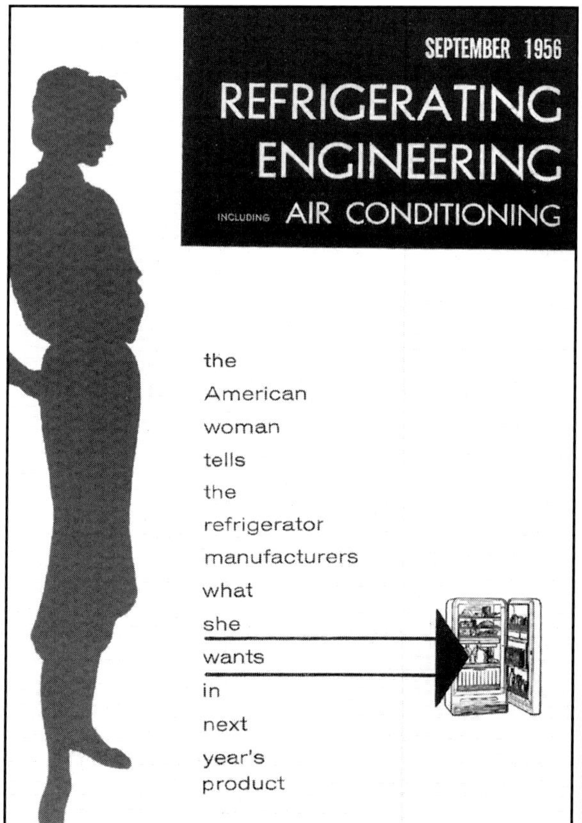

New York college students and their teachers are shown during the presentation of engineering achievement awards by the New York Chapter of ASHRAE. They are: H. I. Klee and Professor William Vopat, Cooper Union; Assistant Dean F. K. Teichmann, NYU; Alfred Greenberg, New York Chapter of ASHRAE and member of ASHRAE's national Education Committee; R. P. Pollack, NYU; Professor Carl F. Kayan, Chairman of ASHRAE's national Education Committee, and P. A. Ulvad, Columbia; Joseph M. Pennesi, President of the New York Chapter of ASHRAE; Professor A. Repetto and P. J. Lukovits, CCNY; R. Motylenski and Professor J. Quadrini, Pratt Institute; and B. G. Seberg and Professor P. Chaikin, Brooklyn Polytechnic Institute.

1964

NEW ORLEANS INSTALLATION

Pictured at installation ceremonies for new officers of New Orleans Section are, left to right, seated, E. K. Strahan Sr., Regional Director; Fred DuPre, chairman; Al Lusch, secretary; J. F. Albright Jr., first vice chairman; standing, E. K. Strahan Jr, retiring chairman; W. W. Taylor, treasurer, and J. S. Burke, second vice chairman.

1956

1994

PAST PRESIDENTS' NIGHT FETE IN SHREVEPORT

The January meeting of the Shreveport Chapter featured Past Presidents' Night with 1948 Past President William Fitzgerald outlining the Chapter history. Among the anecdotes, Mr. Fitzgerald told how he had to use the American Society of Heating and Ventilating Engineers (ASH&VE) GUIDE as a text for air conditioning course when he was a Texas A&M University student in 1934, because the GUIDE was the only authorative publication available at the time.

A technical talk followed by Watt Light from Vitaulic Co, who discussed the grooved coupling concept of joining piping and fittings and stressed the advantages of this concept.

A talk titled Energy Conservation in Pumping Systems was presented by Gilbert Carlson, Director of Technical Services, ITT Bell & Gossett. Speaker Carlson emphasized that the designer of the pumping system exercises greater control when it comes to energy savings than the pump manufacturer. He stressed that properly applied pumping systems can save in operation costs. Ways to apply pumps and match flow and gpm for different systems were discussed.

Past Presidents: Howard Angle (1966), Harold Scott (1956), Farrell Adams (1963), Ed Kneipp (1957), William Harrison (1972), George Jambor (1967), Robin Hood (1952), and Mr. Fitzgerald

ASHRAE JOURNAL April 1975

MONTREAL EXECUTIVES INSTALLED AT MAY MEETING

Seated: Messrs. Goupil, Bertrand and Bruce; standing: Messrs. Quessy, DeBroux, Paulin, Past President John Dugan, Messrs. Slone, Sharples, Bozzer and Dufresne

Mr. Betrand

Mr. Hole, Dalton McIntyre

Mr. Paul Gaudette, Mr. Murray

ASHRAE JOURNAL October 1973

CENTRAL OKLAHOMA ACKNOWLEDGES PAST PRESIDENTS; HANDBOOK EDITOR GUEST SPEAKER

Chapter President Robert E. Estep introduced the 15 Past Presidents who gathered at the April meeting of the Central Oklahoma Chapter for the Annual Past Presidents Night. Three who served twice were Earle W. Gray (1938 and 1945), John H. Carnahan (1942 and 1951) and Louis C. Nettleship (1968 and 1970).

Past Presidents of the Central Oklahoma Chapter: L. C. Nettleship, W. J. Collins, Jr., L. L. VonTungeln, E. R. McKinney, E. W. Gray, A. R. Morin, L. E. Wickline, J. H. Carnahan, W. W. Frankfurt, William R. Johnson, R. R. Ellis, H. E. Rountree, L. Loeffler, Jr., and C. D. Miller (R. E. Swan was present but not in photo)

Speaker of the evening Carl W. MacPhee, Editor of the ASHRAE HANDBOOK & Product Directory at ASHRAE Headquarters in New York, NY, explained his two-fold purpose in visiting chapters: To provide a better understanding of the HANDBOOK volumes, what they can do for the members and how the members and chapters can help in continuously updating the information in the HANDBOOK. Beginning with a brief history of our predecessor societies' volumes, Mr. MacPhee stated the purpose of each of the current four volumes and the new Product Directory section. He described in detail the processes of revision and the work performed by Technical Committees, Revisers, HANDBOOK Committee, and the editing and printing. Speaker MacPhee told how individual members and Chapters may participate in revisions and encouraged participation through service on Technical Committees, chapter programs, and educational seminars.

For the Technical Session, H. Glenn Logsdon, member of ASHRAE TC 2.6, Sound and Vibration Control, presented a program on Air Distribution Devices — Selection, Types, and Limitation. Mr. Logsdon is Vice President, Engineering, Aeronca Inc. Environmental Control Group, Pineville, NC. Illustrating his talk with slides, Mr. Logsdon defined the basic groupings of air distribution devices and showed pictures of all types of air outlets. It was also pointed out that mixing air rapidly at leaving outlet provides less temperature variation between floor and ceiling.

1975

ENGINEERING SOCIETY FORMED IN SPAIN; JOINS ASHRAE AS INTERNATIONAL ASSOCIATE

The recently formed Spanish Technical Association for Heating, Refrigerating and Air Conditioning (ATECYR) has joined ASHRAE's growing ranks of International Associate Societies. L. to r. are some of the founding members of ATECYR: Francisco Arredondo y Verdu; Rafael de la Hoz Arderius; Vicente Mortes Alfonso, president of the Society; Manuel Estada Girauta; Jaime Nieto Sanchez; and Gabriel Barcelo Rico-Avello. Other founding members not pictured are: Francisco Vighi Arroyo; Jose Laorden Jimenez; Aurelio Alaman Simon; Jeronimo Cabot Jaume; and Rafael Urcido Aramburu. The new Society has a potential of some 100 members.

1975

ASHRAE & ENERGY CONSERVATION

This article is from the address made by Dr. McNall at the Conference on Energy Conservation held on August 23, 1973, at Henniker, NH.

DR. PRESTON E. McNALL, JR.
Member ASHRAE
Chairman, ASHRAE Research and Technical Committee

ASHRAE is a technical society, and not a trade association, as some people assume. It is concerned with all aspects of environmental control for people, as well as for plants and animals; the latter relate to food production and processing. Although mechanical engineers are the largest group of members, other technologies are also well represented, such as chemistry, material science, medicine, physiology, psychology, etc.

ASHRAE is unique in many ways but, of importance here, is its research program. Yours is the only society which funds and conducts a sustaining research program. A portion of each member's dues is allocated for research. Industry and individual contributions and the income from the ASHRAE-ARI co-sponsored International Air-Conditioning, Heating, Refrigerating Exposition are also expended for research. Currently, the annual effort is about $300,000. This is not large by federal standards, but it is precious to ASHRAE. The Research and Technical Committee allocates it to various projects. The results must be non-proprietary and in the public domain.

This research effort started in the early 1920's and over the years has been reduced to practice in the ASHRAE HANDBOOK & Product Directory, now a four-volume set. To do this job are technical experts numbering over 800, serving on over 80 separate committees, including energy utilization and energy conservation. Energy conservation is no newcomer to ASHRAE. Our first research was concerned with measuring and predicting heat flow through walls and other building components!

CURRENT RESPONSIBILITY

ASHRAE's responsibility in the current U.S. energy situation is as follows:

- Approximately 20% of U.S. energy is used in the heating and cooling of spaces occupied by people (homes, factories, offices, schools, etc.). This is primarily gas and oil with some electricity.
- Approximately 5% of U.S. energy is used in refrigeration associated with foods, from processing plants, storage, transportation, etc., to the household refrigerator. This is primarily electric, with some gas and oil.

Therefore, 25% of U.S. energy is used in the equipment and systems designed, built and installed with ASHRAE knowledge. This is a significant amount and, therefore, significant savings are probable.

"FREE RIDE"

If ASHRAE is as knowledgeable as I have claimed, why can these savings occur? Why haven't architects and consulting engineers already designed and built optimum energy systems? There are many reasons, but two significant ones have to do with our past nearly "free ride," so far as energy cost is concerned, and our business practices with speculative builders. Recent studies have shown that for a typical commercial building, only 10-15% of the annual cost is energy related. Another 10-15% is for maintenance and the lion's share remaining (70-80%) is for capital cost. Economics dictates that first cost and interest rates are far more important than energy. The speculative builder will sacrifice a "quality" job and sell out to the ultimate owner, leaving him with a "low dollar" energy wasting system. Even the non-speculative builder will tend to make similar decisions until he sees the "energy crisis" coming.

This explains the many existing energy wasting systems, such as the reheat system, which cools all the system air to, say 55 F, and then heats it up as needed, with double energy costs in some cases. Past economics said "OK" to such systems, which give very good comfort performance. Remember, comfort is what its all about. A tenant paying $7-$10 per square foot per year demands comfort, and it was easy this way. There are many other examples, and I don't mean to suggest that other systems don't also waste energy. The important point is that it was not significant enough in the past to get the attention it deserves today.

Therefore, significant energy savings can be made in the short-range by modest investments in "tuning-up" or adding to existing systems, with existing hardware and technology. ASHRAE members can do this now.

There are also many computerized control systems already in use and these could be considered for some larger existing systems. This relatively new technology, applied to heating and air-conditioning systems, allows a much more efficient operation by providing almost instantaneous data for operators to use in controlling the systems. Even more sophistication, already available, provides pre-programming the computer with control strategies so that operating efficiencies can be even further increased, past man's capability to continuously react to all his decision variables. A large water chiller, for example, could have a significant increase in efficiency if the chilled water could satisfy the load and be 1 F. warmer!

The President's goal of 5% should be easy to attain by the above means, without any of the more drastic measures suggested by some people.

PENNY-WISE . . . ?

One of those "easy" suggestions is changing thermostat settings. It is true that considerable savings could be realized with lower winter and higher summer control points; this can be done today, a short-range saving. However, before we implement this, we should consider the consequences. ASHRAE has sponsored comfort research for 50 years. Our present data shows the following. Lightly clothed people in an office or residential environment prefer 75 F. This seems to be true, winter and summer, regardless of national origin or weather climate around the world. Quality of life is largely dependent on our environment. If we remove the stress caused by people fighting their environment, we release more energy for man's higher pursuits. It is part of the well-documented energy use per capita vs living standard correlation. Therefore, we need to cause people to wear more clothing at cooler winter temperatures, or their performance will surely suffer. In the summer, the limits of decency on clothing have perhaps been reached. I believe caution should be exercised on the consequences of "hip-shooting" edicts here!

As an aside, it may have occurred to some that we might save energy by limiting or controlling "labor saving" appliances or machines. Let's put this in perspective. A healthy young male, who is doing heavy physical labor, (ditch-digging for example) can produce equivalent watt-hours of energy in an eight-hour day of less than 10 cents worth of electrical energy! Clearly, increased reliance on manual labor is no practical answer!

30% SAVINGS POSSIBLE

Over the last 25 years, ASHRAE has documented energy saving systems which have been built, in some cases, as demonstration projects. These involve heat pumps, heat recovery systems, solar heating and cooling systems, etc. Much of this information is now being used in some projects in recent years and some now being designed and built by a few "enlightened" owners. Many will take advantage of such existing knowledge and will benefit in the future. Savings in energy use of up to 30% should easily be possible in new construction, just by taking advantage of knowledge and without resorting to exotic to yet-to-be developed hardware.

Why don't we do it? In my opinion, the main deterrent to employing our extensive existing know-how to energy conservation is a lack of incentive for the people who are in the decision-making positions—the present building owners—(homeowners to those owners of large building complexes). I believe, with proper incentives, present and near-future savings could approach 20-30% easily, without a significant effect on living standard or comfort.

PEOPLE-ORIENTED SYSTEM

Now to the somewhat longer range. Remember, 20% of our energy is used to heat and cool people. A person metabolizes at the rate only about 400 Btuh on the average. This is a relatively small amount. A family of four could heat and cool itself with about $15 worth of natural gas per year, if 100% efficient! Recent research at Kansas State University has indicated that a liquid or air-cooled hood, covering the head and neck, can effectively cool a person working in a hot environment. At the same time, it allows good freedom of movement and permits the rest of the body to sweat efficiently, which entire body cooling with air jets or liquid-cooled suits tend to inhibit. Energy could be provided with a small refrigeration system, similar to that of a household refrigerator. The energy savings of such a future "people oriented" system could be dramatic. I simply chose one example with which I am familiar; there are countless others.

I have confined my remarks to the here-now-and-useful-tomorrow technology. For this we don't need "breakthroughs" that the Pollyanna's hope for, in nuclear fusion, coal gasification, etc. Even if successful, the impact would be 10-20 years in coming.

In summary, ASHRAE has know-how available, today, to make a great impact in energy conservation. However, a building system is just that—a complex system, including:

Architectural and structural details
Weather-climate environment
Building usage—(hotel, office, etc.)
Heating and cooling system
Control methods and strategy
Available energy sources, rates, etc.

There are obviously thousands of combinations of the above six variables available. It is equally obvious than an optimum energy conservation system is difficult to design. It is not a game for amateurs; it is not a game for "quick-draw" solutions, like "don't heat with electricity"; nor is it a game for "instant experts" who leap on the energy bandwagon. It needs to be done by professionals who understand the total concept of these complex systems.

To conclude, ASHRAE has considerable know-how, not being optimally used at present because of inadequate incentives. For the future, ASHRAE's organization of experts serving on its technical committees can provide some of the nation's best stewardship for the massive research effort needed in this important area. How can we better utilize this expertise? □□

Dr. P.E. McNall, Jr. is Director of Engineering, Johnson Service Co, Milwaukee, WI.

ASHRAE JOURNAL February 1974

ASHRAE JOURNAL February 1974

GOLDEN GATE'S PRESIDENT INSTALLED

Newly-elected President (1974-75) of the Golden Gate Chapter Richard A. Charles (left), President of Charles & Braun Consulting Engineers, accepts symbolic gavel from past President Lewis S. Pollock. Mr. Charles is the 38th President of the Chapter. The gavel represents the responsibility of the office.

1974

The Board of Directors (BOD) Luncheon preceding the BOD meeting gave ASHRAE directors and regional chairmen an opportunity to socialize before getting down to business. Seated, from left, are Frederick J. Pearson, chairman, Region III; James A. Story, chairman, Region IV; Robert W. Crosby, chairman, Region V; Cyril G. Hansen, chairman, Region X; Charles D. Callahan, chairman, Region VIII; standing, from left, are ASHRAE President-elect Louis F. Flagg; Billy R. Manning, director at large, Region VII; Raymond C. Thornton, chairman, Region VII; and Laurance S. Staples, Jr., outgoing chairman, Region IX.

1987

WESTERN NEW YORK CHAPTER HOST TO SWEDISH ENGINEERS

Guests of the Western New York Chapter (II) in Mid-February, 26 members of the Swedish Association of Heating and Ventilating Engineers visited Niagara Falls, participated in tours of the nearby American Standard stamping plant and the main works of the Buffalo Forge Company, and inspected the heating, ventilating and air conditioning facilities in the plant of the Buffalo Evening News and the offices of the Bethlehem Steel Company. Hosts and guests are here shown at the brink of the Falls.

APRIL 1959

The newly-formed Ozark Chapter, Region IX, in Springfield, Missouri, held its chartering ceremonies earlier this year, with 1985-86 ASHRAE President Donald R. Bahnfleth in attendance. Bahnfleth delivered an address to the chapter and presented its charter. Chapter officers and board members present at the event were. (front row, left to right) Jack Climer, second vice president; Donald R. Bahnfleth; Will Nopper, 1985-86 chapter president; Max Porter, treasurer; Steve Houston, research promotion chairman; (back row, left to right) Bob Bernard; Craig McMichael, publicity chairman; Dave Edie, first vice president; Larry Gritz; Bob Snell, 1986-87 chapter president; Randy Nelson; and Dick Petterson.

1986

ASHRAE cosponsors air systems seminar with Colombian international associate

"This meeting not only surpassed the expectations of the organizing committee, but most important it surpassed the expectations of those in attendance. The large number of favorable correspondence we have received from participants encourages us to continue working towards the development of the professionals in our industry."

These are the words of Hernando Clavijo, referring to the conference on Air Movement Systems cosponsored by ASHRAE and Asociación Colombiana del Acondicionamento de Aire y de la Refrigeración (ACAIRE), of which Clavijo is president. ACAIRE is an International Associate of ASHRAE.

Held in Bogotá, Colombia, the two-day seminar was conducted by Dr. Victor W. Goldschmidt, ASHRAE Fellow and a professor at Purdue University, West Lafayette, Indiana, and Dr. J. Barrie Graham, owner, Graham Consultants, Santa Fe, New Mexico, also a Fellow of the Society.

Goldschmidt echoed Clavijo's sentiment of success. "We were extremely delighted to run out of application forms for prospective ASHRAE members!"

Close to 70 persons participated in the conference which included an exhibit of air conditioning and refrigerating companies.

The sixth General Assembly of ACAIRE Members also held their elections for 1986-87 officers during the meeting. Elected were: president, Hernando Clavijo; vice president, Alvaro Patarroyo; secretary, Juan Carlos Camargo; and treasurer, Jose Francisco Guerrero.

ACAIRE President Hernando Clavijo (second from left) welcomes participants to the air systems seminar in Bogota, Columbia. Meeting participants (from left) are ASHRAE member Dr. Victor W. Goldschmidt, past ACAIRE president Alvaro Tapias, and ASHRAE member J. Barrie Graham. Attendance was high.

1986

Tennessee Valley installs new officers

ASHRAE's Tennessee Valley Chapter recently held its annual officer installation ceremony with ASHRAE immediate past president Frederick H. Kohloss, seated, left, conducting the event. Raymond Thornton, seated, right, past chairman of Region VII, was also present. Elected for 1987-88 were, standing, from left, Bill Ross, president-elect; J.W. Weeks, president; Darlene Tyson, treasurer; Chuck Koptis, Region VII director; Terry Townsend, outgoing president; and John Richardson, secretary. During the ceremony, Townsend presented Kohloss with a certificate from Chattanooga Mayor Gene Roberts, designating Kohloss an Honorary Citizen of the city. Townsend also presented Thornton with a plaque of appreciation for his chapter support during his tenure as regional chairman.

1987

CFC issue brings ASHRAE's Government Affairs activities into the spotlight

By William M. Dillard
Government Affairs Chairman

Why is participating in government affairs on a chapter level important to ASHRAE members as engineers, designers, contractors, manufacturer's representatives, manufacturers, and building owners or operators? If you have been following the articles published recently in *Insights*, you have read where the Oregon Legislature considered banning all types of chlorofluorocarbon refrigerants; in another instance, a small municipality took initial steps toward banning mechanical air conditioning in their local jurisdiction. Would similar actions affect your business if it happened in your local chapter area? Dramatically!

ETAC and chapter activities

The close coordination between the Society-level Energy and Technical Affairs Committee (ETAC) and the Government Affairs Committee (GAC) sets an example for similar cooperation at the local chapter level; we are encouraging chapters to be involved with their local, state and provincial levels of government.

The Society's ETAC has responsibility for implementing and nurturing chapter government affairs activities. The GAC has the responsibility for (1) setting and monitoring the procedures by which we conduct those activities; (2) identifying (both on a Society and a local level) emerging issues; and (3) acting as a conduit from the chapters to Washington, and vice versa.

Local chapter's role

First and foremost, establishing an active government affairs program working in concert with your ETAC committee is extremely important.

Next, making contacts with local government will require following some simple rules that are spelled out in a recently revised Government Affairs Manual for Chapters and a complementing set of guidelines; those documents are distributed through your ETAC Regional Vice Chairman. ASHRAE has certain rules which must be followed (as a not-for-profit organization) regarding overly aggressive actions directed at influencing legislation. Get this information at your regional CRC, review it with your local chapter leadership, develop a written plan of action, and work the plan. All of these steps are similar to successful business endeavors in the private sector.

The real fruits of this endeavor will be establishing local government contacts. What you will find is that local governments are often in need of objective technical expertise; and if relationships are properly developed, having ASHRAE as a resource in the local community when needed is a tremendous asset to governmental staffs and officials.

Working with Washington office

By participating in local government affairs activities, you and your chapter may also have an opportunity to work with our Washington office, whose knowledge of national issues may be of great benefit to you particularly when your local technical issues are related to national issues and you can draw on that expertise.

The Washington office staff will assist your chapter as resources permit. This interaction may help to maintain contacts made by you and track issues with which we, as a technical society, must come to grips at an ever increasing pace. We are in the information age. We, as an engineering society, have to be ready to act, instead of react.

Keeping a governmental awareness in Washington and by the chapter at the local government level is part of that process. The Energy and Technical Affairs Committee has a major role to play in this regard, and the Government Affairs Committee is prepared to assist.

Government Affairs award

Any successful program has a plan and a means of measuring the success of that plan. Accordingly, a Government Affairs Award is being considered by the Society leadership to formally recognize chapters for their efforts in conducting successful government affairs activities. Success in establishing contact, providing technical assistance, acting as a conduit for emerging issues (that may affect all ASHRAE members) with local government along with continuity of efforts will all be recognized by the Government Affairs Award. Most important of all, this new award is a Society award to recognize "chapter" efforts.

1988

Student Branch Chapter chartered at Wilkes University

The Anthracite Chapter established an ASHRAE Student Branch chapter at Wilkes University and presented the charter to the chapter officers and the faculty advisor. Pictured is: (seated L to R) Dr. Daniel Pindzola, faculty advisor; and Richard Nanes, regional vice chairman of education and chapter programs; (standing L to R) Ed Gall, student vice president; Gina Marie Aleo, student secretary/treasurer; Michael Fortnell; Holly Pitcavage, student chapter president; Johnathon Dambek; David Bonomo; Joseph Galletta, chapter education chairman; Paul Dreater, chapter president; Dan Mello, chapter vice president; and Dr. Umid R. Nejib, dean of science and engineering at Wilkes University.

1990

Fort Worth Chapter Conducts Teach-in

Scott Harris of Johnson Controls illustrates "out of control" in explaining the use of automation in controlling the comfort system to Glenn Harmon Elementary School student in Arlington, Texas. James Hall, Judy Tribble, Scott Harris and Bob Marks participated in explaining to students math courses required for an engineering degree and how an HVAC project is started and completed, using CAD design and a simulation of comfort control to explain the examples.

1992

Society Honors Contributors to ASHRAE Research

The ASHRAE Research Golden Circle and special recognition awards were presented at the Chicago Winter Meeting. Golden Circle member are contributors investing $10,000 or more to the research program. The company or organization is presented with a sculptured award at the President's Luncheon the first year this level of giving is achieved. This year's Golden Circle includes Honeywell, Carrier and SMACNA. All are longtime contributors.

Special recognition is given to corporate or organization contributors that invest $10,000 or more as a one-time contribution. These contributors also are presented a plaque. This year's special recognition awards were presented to the Air Diffusion Council and the Spiral Duct Manufacturer's Association of America (SPIDA).

Clockwise from left: George L. "Butch" Welsch (left), president, SMACNA and president of Welsch Furnace Co., and Dave Bevirt, SMACNA director of technical research, display their Golden Circle plaque; Honeywell representatives accepting Golden Circle plaque from ASHRAE President Louis F. Flagg (far right) are (l to r) John Bailey, vice president and general manager, Building Controls Division, Joe Chenoweth, president, Home and Building Automation and Control, and Donald L. Flamm, vice president and general manager, Residential Division; Carrier representatives with President Flagg (third from left) included Keith Eisberg, John Jacobs, John McNeley, Thomas Kassouf, George Powers, Fred Honnold and Richard English accepting the Golden Circle plaque; Fred Kimmel (left) of SPIDA accepts the Special Recognition Award from President Flagg; and Air Diffusion Council's Marvin A. Koerber, vice president (left), accepts the Special Recognition Award.

AGA donates check to ASHRAE Research

George H. Lawrence (middle) president of the American Gas Association, presents a $5,000 check for ASHRAE Research to the National Capital Chapter. Accepting the check is Brian Alexander (far left), president of the National Capital Chapter. Also present is Donald Heim, chairman of the Washington Gas Light Company and incoming chairman of the American Gas Association.

1989

ASHRAE charters India Chapter-at-Large

President David S. Butler, Sr., (left) present the India Chapter's charter to chapter president Prem C. Jain (center) and V.K. Rastogi at an installation ceremony held in Delhi, India.

1990

President Bush Kicks-Off National Engineers Week Student Campaign

President George Bush greeted leaders of the National Engineers Week Discover "E" Program at the White House's Oval Office in February to help kick-off this nationwide campaign. More than 5,000 engineers from all sectors went into junior and senior high schools through the United States during National Engineers Week, February 18-24. The nationwide "teach-in" was aimed at inspiring student interest in math and science and in engineering and technical careers and goals. Pictured is (L to R): Richard Truly, NASA Administrator; Stephen D. Bechtel, Chairman of the Bechtel Group, Inc., and Engineers Week Honorary Chairman; David S. Butler, Sr., P.E., ASHRAE President and Engineers Week Chairman; George Bush, President of the United States; Louise Hicks, Science Department Chair of Thoreau Intermediate School in Vienna, Virginia; Rita Torres-Tucker, P.E., Young Engineer of the Year; and Anthony Wyatt, ninth grader and Friendship Education Center in Washington, D.C.

1990

ASHRAE Foundation Created

The ASHRAE Foundation, established by the Society to financially support the work of ASHRAE, has been approved by the U.S. Internal Revenue Service as a tax exempt organization.

The Foundation's goal is to build an endowment by which investment income will support ASHRAE's mission to advance the arts and sciences of HVAC&R through the permanent funding of scholarships, research projects and grants-in-aid.

Four endowment funds, which will be administered by the Foundation, have been established: education, honors and awards, research and unrestricted. Individuals and companies will be able to contribute to these funds through financial donations, grants, wills and other means.

The Foundation was formed as a result of a recommendation by a Presidential ad-hoc committee, chaired by Presidential Member William J. Collins, Jr. P.E. Mr. Collins also serves as a Foundation trustee along with chairman A. Damon Gowan; Richard P. Perry, P. Eng.; Benjamin T. Bootle, Jr., P.E.; Frank M. Coda; Louis F. Flagg; George B. Hightower, P.E.; Hugh D. McMillan, P.E.; and Fritz A. Traugott, EUR Ing.

For more information about the Foundation, named awards, or financial estate and gift planning ideas, contact the ASHRAE Foundation Manager at ASHRAE Headquarters.

1994

The Trane Company Contributes $100,000 for A Student Scholarship Fund and Research

Jim Schultz (left), executive Vice President, Trane Commercial Systems Group, presents a $25,000 check to ASHRAE Executive Director Frank M. Coda for ASHRAE's research program. Mr. Schultz also presented Mr. Coda with a $75,000 check to establish ASHRAE's Reuben Trane Scholarship named after the company's first president. The scholarship, which will be presented this year, provides $5,000 per year for two years. Also pictured are Neil R. Patterson (middle right), director of market development and product planning, Trane Commercial Systems Group and ASHRAE Treasurer, and Tom Kikulina (right), vice president of marketing, Trane Commercial Systems Group.

1992

Region VIII Conducts CFC News Conference

During the Region VIII Spring CRC, a news conference was held on the CFC issue.

Participating in the news conference were Donald Bivens, engineering fellow, DuPont Chemicals, who spoke on CFC replacements; James Wolf, chairman, the Alliance for Responsible CFC Policy and ASHRAE Director-at-Large, who spoke on industry action; ASHRAE President Donald G. Rich who spoke on ASHRAE research, Bill Goodman, director and Regional Chairman, Region VIII, who chaired the news conference; Jim Cox, ASHRAE Director of Government Affairs, who spoke on ASHRAE's refrigerant-related standards; and Jean Lupinacci, chief, Technology and Substitutes Branch, U.S. EPA, who updated the U.S. Clean Air Act, ozone depletion, and global warming. Many local print and broadcast media attended.

Among the comments presented, Ms. Lupinacci said, "Developing an accelerated research program to identify and test refrigerant alternatives, especially for R-22, is a high priority. This should not be considered a time of 'panic,' but rather a time of cooperative accelerated research between industry, government and professional organizations like ASHRAE to quickly address and solve environmental and engineering problems."

News conference participants were (left to right) Donald Bivens; James Wolf; Donald G. Rich; Bill Goodman; Jim Cox; and Jean Lupinacci.

1992

Members of the Michigan chapter dine at the finish of the annual A.S.H.V.E. derby in 1930. In the foreground is the prize banner of the Michigan chapter won in the National Membership Campaign, 1929.

Milt Garland (right) unveils the Centennial plaque dedicating the site and exact time one hundred years ago when the Society was founded. Assisting Mr. Garland is Alfred Greenberg, the general chair of N.Y. Centennial event. The plaque unveiling took place September 10, 1994 at 3:00 p.m. at the corner of Broadway and East 3rd Street in New York City.

PHILADELPHIA -- Refrigeration technology sealed in a time capsule 40 years ago at the Franklin Institute is examined by Philadelphia Mayor Edward Rendell (right) and officials of the American Society of Heating, Refrigerating and Air-Conditioning Engineers (ASHRAE) (from left) Walter Spiegel, a past president of the Society, Billy R. Manning, Society president, and Milt Garland, 99-year-old member of the Society. The capsule was opened in recognition of ASHRAE's centennial anniversary being celebrated this year. Among the contents were microfilmed copies of technical handbooks, the November 1954 issue of "Refrigerating Engineering" magazine, copies of special 50th anniversary programs, and photographs of special refrigeration industry historical exhibits.

President Rich opened the IAQ session to a standing-room-only crowd. Seated are the session panelists: (l-r) Kevin Teichman, Robert Axelrad, Philip Morey and Hal Levin.

1992

THE BENJAMIN FRANKLIN

honoring a great name

J. BRUCE ROGERS
Manager

CHESTNUT STREET AT NINTH
PHILADELPHIA 5

TELEPHONE WALNUT 2-8600

RECIPE A.S.R.E. SAZERAC

Sol Strahan

Into one (1) ten ounce chilled glass put two dashes absinthe, add two cubes of ice, pour one teaspoon of simple syrup over ice, add two drops of Peychaud Bitters, two drops of Angustora Bitters, and pour one ounce of rye, or bourbon whiskey over ice after the bitters have drained to bottom of the glass. Stir and remove ice. Cut a sliver of lemon peel and rub rim of glass with inside of peel then squeeze the peel over mixture so peel oil sprays over the mixture. Sip the drink slowly.

The last paper added to the 1954 ASRE Time Capsule. (See page 26)

ASHRAE Garners Top Ranking vs. Other Societies

Membership Gives ASHRAE High Marks in Survey

ASHRAE members rate their Society higher in overall satisfaction than do members of comparable engineering and scientific groups. The survey, conducted by the Council of Engineering and Scientific Society Executives (CESSE), polled the members of these societies to determine member satisfaction.

The results of this survey are very similar to the results of ASHRAE's member/non-member survey conducted in November 1993. A detailed summary of these results appeared in the May 1994 *ASHRAE Insights.*

In the CESSE study, ASHRAE was rated the top society in four categories — Overall Satisfaction, Local Chapter Activities, Member Benefits and Building Public Image. ASHRAE rated very high in the other four categories, which were National or Regional Meetings, Publications, Trade Shows or Product Service Exhibits and Professional Licensing and Standards.

Member satisfaction in each of the eight categories was measured on a scale of 1 to 10; 1 being very poor and 10 being excellent. The Society was compared with other societies of comparable size and with all the societies participating in the survey.

The Overall Satisfaction category averaged the ratings of the other seven categories. The Society rated 7.61, which was the highest rating among all participating societies and societies with a membership size more than 12,500.

The Local Chapter Activities category assessed member satisfaction with information and topics discussed at local chapter meetings, networking opportunities with peers and convenience of meeting schedules. ASHRAE led in this category with a rating of 7.38.

The Member Benefits category measured satisfaction with personal benefits of membership, value for the money, career services, responsiveness to individual members, support for local chapters and inter-Society coordination. ASHRAE also led in this category with a rating of 6.74.

In addition, ASHRAE led in the Building Public Image category, with a rating of 6.61. The Society's advocacy role with governmental agencies, building the public image of the profession, outreach programs to schools and college/university programs were looked at in this category.

The National or Regional Meetings category evaluated member satisfaction with conference themes, relevancy of presentations, organization and format of conferences and socialization. ASHRAE's rating was 7.44.

The Publications category measured satisfaction with the quality and relevance of technical or scientific and professional or applied publications, access to information, publications as a forum for exchange and publication format. The members rated the Society at 7.68.

Member satisfaction with technical knowledge of company representatives at trade shows, format for exhibiting products and services, representatives of different companies at Society trade shows and "hands-on" experience at trade shows were examined in the Trade Shows or Product/Service Exhibits category. The rating was 7.72.

In the area of Professional Licensing and Standards, the survey appraised satisfaction with the Society's promotion of uniform registration requirements across states, promotion of uniform continuing education requirements, proactive posture in setting technical standards, continuous dialogue and coordination during standards development process and promotion of uniform standards internationally. Membership satisfaction in this category was rated at 6.95.

CESSE is a membership organization of technical and scientific society staff members. The survey was conducted in 1993 and reported at the 1994 CESSE annual meeting.

1995

Society President Billy R. Manning, PE, celebrated the East Tennessee Chapter's 30th Anniversary with a visit to Knoxville on November 17. Pictured are 9left to right) first row: Billy Manning, Earl Graham, Bob Slusher, Bob Forde, Leonard Payne, second row: Wayne Rose, Bob Crawford, Charles Sexton, Jr., Philip Breman, Charles Swan, A.B. Fuller and Don Gwyn.

ASHRAE Centennial Celebration

Winners Announced in Historical Systems and Equipment Competition

What do the Saenger Theater in Mobile, Ala., Waynesboro Ice and Cold Storage in Waynesboro, Pa., Central High School in Omaha, Neb., and the St. Louis Steam Loop in St. Louis, Mo., have in common? These HVAC&R systems were judged by ASHRAE to be the most unique and interesting systems or equipment of historical value, which are still operational.

The Society recently announced the winners of the ASHRAE Historical Systems and Equipment Competition, which was held as a part of ASHRAE's year-long Centennial Celebration. The entries will be displayed at ASHRAE's Centennial Meeting in Chicago, January 28—February 1, 1995.

The St. Louis Steam Loop has been part of St. Louis' heritage since the 1904 World's Fair. It consists of a 22-mile network of underground pipe encompassing a 400-square block area in the city's downtown district. The loop is supplied by the Ashley Street Steam Plant. This plant, which was built to serve the growing city's needs and to supply power the World's Fair in 1904, has undergone several major modernization projects, and is in excellent condition. The history was submitted by the St. Louis Chapter, Region VI, and written by Hank Sauer.

Central High School in Omaha, Neb., sits on Capitol Hill, and is listed on the National Register of Historic Buildings. Prior to becoming the state's first high school in 1859, the site served as the second territorial capitol building. The current facility was constructed one wing at a time during the period of 1900 to 1912, and was renovated in the early 1980s. The history was submitted by the Nebraska Chapter, Region IX and written by William Koperski.

Waynesboro Ice and Cold Storage was built in 1901 by the Frick Company in Waynesboro, Pa., but the oldest remaining ammonia compressor was installed in 1914. This compressor has continued to operate 24 hours a day for more than 80 years. Through the years, when other ice makers went out of business, Waynesboro Ice and Cold Storage was able to evolve with the refrigerating industry through mechanical retrofits and to respond to changing markets and customer base. The history was submitted by the Baltimore Chapter, Region III, and written by Harry Will.

The original air-conditioning system installed in the Saenger Theater in Mobile, Ala., was a "spray water" system, which sprays chilled water into the supply air stream to both cool and dehumidify the air. It was installed in 1926 along with a centrifugal refrigerating machine, both of which were invented by Willis H. Carrier. The spray water systems is still in use today on a regular basis. The original centrifugal unit was replaced in 1956 with Westinghouse reciprocating compressors. The history was submitted by the Mobile Chapter, Region VII, and written by D.C. Edwards.

The Historical Equipment Contest also attracted other entries from throughout the United States and Canada. The following entries were submitted:

- History of St. Peter's Catholic Church HVAC System, submitted by the Memphis Chapter, Region VII, and Rhett Hailey
- Synopsis of the Development of Steam Heating Systems and the Contributions of Mr. Edgar C. Wiley to the Development of the Variable Pressure Orifice System, submitted by Edgar B. Boynton
- 1952 Hotpoint Refrigerator-Freezer, submitted by the Cincinnati Chapter, Region V, and Norbert J. Menke
- Room Heater, Stove, and Water Pump, submitted by the Cincinnati Chapter, Region V, and Norbert J. Menke
- The Tennessee Theater, submitted by the East Tennessee Chapter, Region VII, and Ron Shelton
- Banquet Dairy York Ammonia Compressors, submitted by Central Indiana Chapter, Region V, and Robert Newton
- Day/Night Control, 1930s Version, submitted by the Ottawa Valley Chapter, Region II, and Paul Baker
- Southern New England Ice Co. Ammonia System, submitted by the Connecticut Chapter, Region I, and Gordon Root, Sr.
- The Westinghouse Building, submitted by the Pittsburgh Chapter, Region III, and David Glenn

1995

The ASHRAE Museum

The ASHRAE Museum, created especially for the Centennial meeting, offered attendees a look at the history of the Society and the industry and how HVAC&R technology has improved the quality of life. The museum included modular exhibits, featuring numerous photographs and descriptions, a wall of the 100 papers from ASHRAE's archives which capture the idealism and dedication of Society members to the advancement of HVAC&R technology, and a theater, which showed the History of ASHRAE video series and full length interviews of distinguished members. A high point in the museum was the display of materials sealed in a time capsule by The American Society of Refrigerating Engineers in 1954, which was opened in a special ceremony in October 1994 for ASHRAE's Centennial.

1995

Artist's rendition of ASHRAE President Billy R. Manning, PE, delivering the State of the Society Address at the 1995 Centennial Meeting.

ASHRAE Time Capsule Dedication Comments

ASHRAE President Billy R. Manning, P.E., delivered the following dedication comments at the sealing of the ASHRAE Time Capsule at The Franklin Institute, Philadelphia, Penn., on June 6.

"When the ASRE time capsule was formally transferred to The Franklin Institute on April 8, 1955, Edward Simons, a past president of ASRE, delivered the dedication. Over the years, Mr. Simons' message has proven its lasting value just as the contents of the ASRE time capsule have. I believe Mr. Simon's comments are appropriate for today's rededication of the ASHRAE time capsule. I present this dedication:

'In the serenity of this great hall we are met to entrust to the years a record for the future. Within the emplaced capsule are held the records of our own years and of the years from which we, foundationwise, have spurred our efforts. Here are held the gains achieved and the traceries of things to come as the light of new knowledge finds day within the heart of man.

Words may not wholly tell of challenges accepted and met; of moments of doubt and ultimate triumph; of faith in principle and trust in those who trod before; of devotion to the task and the kindly respite of the fleeting moment when one's own inner peace senses that the ideal has become real. The heart of man knows of these things; and he who has served best knows best.

The work here emplaced in record has been accomplished toward the betterment of mankind. Dedication lies within the very doing. We here, and those for whom we stand, hold ourselves ready for the years to come and solemnly pledge ourselves to work truly and well that there may be those who shall give of themselves to the fullness of their talents in the growing of this age. We, with faith in the dignity of mankind and belief in the powerful Goodness of Almighty God, pledge ourselves to this high calling in which we shall not fail. In the eyes of the world and in the quietness of our own hearts we stand, so dedicated.

For half a century, then, O Guardian Through Time, keep safe that which we have sealed in thee. Stay at thy place until thy day is come again!'"

Contents of the ASHRAE 1995 Time Capsule

(to be opened in the year 2045)

- Centennial Status Report
- ASHRAE 1995 Centennial Ball Program
- A piece of paper used as HEPA Filter Media
- Capsules of R-11 and R-12
- *Proclaiming the Truth: An Illustrated History of ASHRAE* (hard copy plus microfilm)
- The types of seismic snubbers used to protect HVAC + electrical components from earthquake damage
- 1995 ASHRAE CD-ROM
- Standard 135—BACnet™
- Newspaper with an article about an ASHRAE field of interest
- Standards 90.1-1989 and 90.2-1993 and Energy Policy Act (with reference to Standard 90)
- ASHRAE Pocket Guide (I-P and SI)
- Plastic ice trays
- A programmable thermostat
- Bill Holladay's K&E Log-Log DeciTrig slide rule & instructions
- A programmable calculator
- Standard 62-1989
- Standard 15-1994
- All position papers/statements
- ASHRAE Vision Statement and ASHRAE Strategic Plan
- Video—A January 1995 Reenactment of the Founding of The American Society of Heating and Ventilating Engineers, September 10, 1894; script; and a picture of the actors
- Centennial Research Medal
- Paperweight from Centennial Plaque Commemoration
- *Heat and Cold: Mastering the Great Indoors*
- Ductulator
- *1993 ASHRAE Handbook—Fundamentals* (I-P)
- Milton Garland's two ASRE pins and Design Notebook for Frick, 1923
- Philadelphia Chapter 1995 Directory
- Philadelphia Chapter Newsletter from October 1994
- President Billy R. Manning's comments at the Time Capsule sealing on June 6, 1995
- Pictures taken on June 6, 1995 of the Time Capsule Closing Ceremony

1995

The Niagara Frontier Chapter celebrated its 75th anniversary along with the Society's 100th year celebration. Pictured are chapter members who attended not only the chapter's 75th anniversary but its 50th celebration as well. Front row (left to right): Gary Bullen, Bob Dailey, Ed Kinkle, Ed Halady, William Howe, Bob Jorgenson, Paul Dupernell.

World Wide HVAC&R Info Highway Open

ASHRAE Launches Home Page on World Wide Web

ATLANTA—Type http://www.ashrae.org on your computer to learn about the latest HVAC&R technology, news and standards through ASHRAE's Home Page on the World Wide Web.

The information is a small part of what's being offered by ASHRAE on its new home page. "The ASHRAE Home Page will enable practitioners in the HVAC&R industry to easily access information about ASHRAE and HVAC&R technology," said ASHRAE President Richard B. Hayter.

To learn more about ASHRAE and its services and how to participate is the focus of the ASHRAE Home Page. The Home Page main menu ranges from in-depth technical information to an electronic version of *ASHRAE Journal*. For example, web browsers can find the entire technical program for ASHRAE's 1996 Winter Meeting, *ASHRAE Journal* departments such as letters, Washington Report, Meetings and Shows, Call for Papers, selected news items, an abstract of the feature of the month, and the Editorial Calendar.

In addition, there are course descriptions and schedules for ASHRAE seminars, a subject listing of ASHRAE standards and guidelines and on-going research. There's also scholarship information, chapter service descriptions, news releases and ways to participate in the Society.

The ASHRAE Home Page will be updated often to provide additional information and future software and hardware enhancements, planned by ASHRAE, will allow search capabilities of files for interactive meeting registration and publications ordering. Forms and files on the ASHRAE Home Page currently can be downloaded or printed.

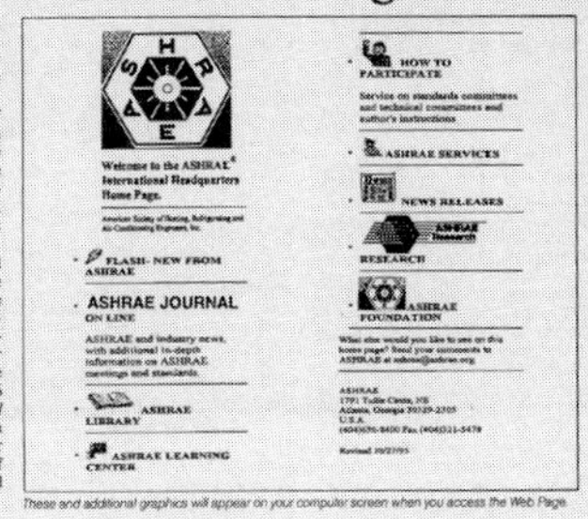

These and additional graphics will appear on your computer screen when you access the Web Page

The ASHRAE Home Page is currently organized into 10 menu selections so information can be quickly located. Some of the menu topics and contents follow.

***ASHRAE Journal* On-Line**

This section has many of the news stories and features that appear in ASHRAE's monthly magazine. Included are industry news, an editorial calendar, an expanded calls for papers and meetings section, a Washington Report and classified advertising.

FLASH — New from ASHRAE This section showcases new features and additions, and directs browsers to the proper locale on the ASHRAE Home Page. This month's "flash" showcases a compilation of 18 papers that describe ways to integrate artificial intelligence techniques into HVAC design. Also provided is a link to the information on ASHRAE's 1996 Winter Meeting.

ASHRAE Research

This section has a list of research projects that are ready to bid, a list of current projects organized by category and a description of ASHRAE's research promotion program.

ASHRAE Library

The "bookshelf" has a publications catalog, a publications order form and information about how to order photocopies of ASHRAE papers. Also included is ASHRAE's International Journal of HVAC&R Research. ASHRAE plans to add software that allows browsers to interactively order publications.

Learning Center Information in this section includes Professional Development Seminar descriptions and self-directed learning courses, and a link to the technical program for ASHRAE's 1996 Winter Meeting.

How to Participate

This section presents various ways to participate in ASHRAE. Included are guidelines for authors to submit articles to ASHRAE publications, meeting paper preparation, a list of technical committees and subjects covered, an ASHRAE standards subject index, a list showing the titles, purposes and scopes of ASHRAE standards, and other topics that describe ways HVAC&R professionals can get involved.

ASHRAE Foundation

There are numerous ways to support HVAC&R industry and this section describes how to set up an endowment and other ways to give. These funds will be used to support the goals and mission of ASHRAE.

News Releases

What's new? You'll find it in this section which has all the news about ASHRAE that's fit to transmit.

Take a look at the new ASHRAE Home Page, and let us know your comments. Send your comments to Anthony Giometti, editor of the ASHRAE Home Page, by mail to ASHRAE Headquarters or e-mail to giometti@ashrae.org.

See World Wide Web
continued on page 4

1995

Carrier Corp., McQuay International, The Trane Co.

Three Companies Contribute $650,000 to ASHRAE Foundation

Carrier Corporation, McQuay International and The Trane Co. have contributed a combined $650,000 to the ASHRAE Foundation, an organization founded to administer permanently endowed funds ASHRAE.

The ASHRAE Foundation launched an endowment campaign in January 1995 to acquire $5,000,000 within two years. The purpose of the campaign is to provide permanent financial support for the Society's educational and training efforts, said ASHRAE Foundation Chairman Damon Gowan.

"Through the financial support of companies and individuals in the HVAC&R industry, the ASHRAE Foundation will be positioned to meet the future educational and training needs of the environmental control industry," he said. Future plans call for establishment of a training institute.

Carrier Corporation donated $250,000 to the ASHRAE Foundation. The Carrier donation is being formulated to fund ASHRAE scholarships and research grants to graduate students at Purdue University.

The Trane Company contributed $300,000 to the Foundation to support four two-year undergraduate ASHRAE scholarships of $5,000 each.

McQuay International pledged $100,000 to the Foundation to help meet the Society's future education and training goals.

In recognition of their contributions, the three companies were presented with an ASHRAE Foundation Industry Award at the Society's annual meeting held June 24-28 in San Diego, Calif.

ASHRAE President Billy R. Manning (left, in each photo) presented the first three awards to (below) Richard Ertinger, director of engineering for Carrier Corp., (middle) Tom Mikulina, vice president of marketing, The Trane Co., and (right) William Mudge, vice president of global marketing communications, McQuay International.

Also recognized at the meeting were Damon and Carolyn Gowan, Hugh and Dorothy McMillan and Donald Nichols, the first people to receive the Foundation's lapel pin, given in recognition to donors who have made gifts of $10,000 or more.

For more information about the ASHRAE Foundation, contact Bob Peach, ASHRAE Foundation manager, at ASHRAE Headquarters.

Presidential Member Hugh McMillan and his wife, Dorothy, receive from Billy Manning a framed certificate. The McMillan's initiated a challenge fund with a $10,000 personal contribution to establish a Region VIII scholarship. At press time, ASHRAE was notified of Mr. McMillan's death. An obituary will appear in the October issue.

Forums

continued from page 4

design and building industry's fee structure, especially when private funding is obtained. In addition, there is a very low understanding among design disciplines about the benefits of sharing information and among investors about the financial and social benefits of Total Building Design.

The participants agreed that the best way to address these issues is through education. They recommended that ASHRAE take a leading role in educating design professionals, building owners, investors and lending institutions about the benefits of Total Building Design and what is required to design and build a building using this approach. They also recommended that ASHRAE work with other industry organizations to create a more favorable environment for Total Building Design.

Status of GPC 10P—Criteria for Achieving Acceptable Indoor Environments

This forum updated participants on the status of this proposed guideline and solicited their comments on the work of the committee. The discussion began with an overview of the fundamental design issues facing engineers in achieving acceptable indoor environments. These issues include problems related to interactions among differing requirements and the potential hazards of designing

See Forums
continued on page 7

1995

Champlain Valley Chapter Celebrates Its 25th Anniversary

The Champlain Valley Chapter celebrated 25 years of chapter involvement. Ninety-five people attended the event. Among them were chapter members from the present and the past, including 19 of the 25 past chapter presidents, whose residences span from California to Maine. Festivities included a slide show presentation of chapter activities over the last 25 years. Opening remarks were made by Region I Director Joe Ting, followed by recollections of memorable chapter events reported by each of the past presidents.

The evening concluded with a presentation of a 25-year anniversary ribbon for the chapter banner by Mr. Ting (right) to Chapter President Leo Ioannou. Closing remarks were made by ASHRAE Executive Director Frank Coda.

1995

Richard Hayter, PhD, visited the Idaho ASHRAE industries, communities, and the world. Arden Davis, Region RVC Programs, gave Hayter a tour of the Boise and Meridian growth area which included stops at Micron, St. Luke's Hospital, and Hewlett Packard. The Tour ended with a visit with Idaho Gov. Philip E. Batt. Batt (seated) is shown with Hayter (left) and Davis (right) (1996).

Region I Dedicates Heritage Capsule

As a finale to its celebration of ASHRAE's Centennial, Region I dedicated a Heritage Capsule on December 5, 1995 at the General Society of Mechanics and Tradesmen (#20 West 44th Street, New York, N.Y.), Region I Historian Walter Bishop, P.E., organized the event, which was hosted by the New York Chapter. The capsule will be unveiled again in the year 2020 during ASHRAE's 125th anniversary year.

The capsule, which is more like a display, includes items depicting the history of the ASHRAE, Region I and the New York Chapter, including:

- Region I banner sponsored by the Region's 15 chapters (Bi-State, Boston, Central New York, Champlain Valley, Connecticut, Granite State, Long Island, Maine, New York, Niagra Frontier, North Jersey, Northeast, Rhode Island, Rochester and Twin Tiers)
- Photographs of the ASHRAE's first past presidents (Edward F. Bates, the American Society of Heating and Ventilating Engineers; John E. Starr, American Society of Refrigerating Engineers; and Cecil Boling, ASHRAE's first president following the merger of the ASHRAE's two predecessor societies)
- The books *Proclaiming the Truth*, which highlights significant moments in ASHRAE's history, and *Heat and Cold: Mastering the Great Indoors*, which tells the story of the people and inventions that changed the way people live indoors
- Photograph of ASHRAE President Richard B. Hayter, Ph.D., P.E.
- Gubernatorial proclamations from the eight states (Connecticut, Maine, Massachusetts, New Hampshire, New Jersey, New York, Rhode Island, Vermont) where the 15 Region I chapters are located

The capsule initially was housed in a street-level window display at the General Society of Mechanics and Tradesmen for public viewing during the month of December before it was moved to its permanent location on the Society's museum floor.

Among those attending the dedication were Mechanics Institute Past President Joseph Healy and First Vice President William Fryer; Region I Director and Regional Chairman Joseph K. Ting, P.E.; Regional Historian Walter Bishop, P.E.; North Jersey Chapter President Julian Ocejo, P.E.; and from the New York Chapter, President Kevin Hoey; Chapter Historian Alfred Greenberg, P.E.; Chapter Research and Promotion Chair Richard Batherman and Chapter Student Activities Chair Carl Howard.

The General Society of Mechanics and Tradesmen was founded as a guild in 1785, and is one of the oldest technical societies in the United States. Through the Mechanics Institute, which was incorporated in 1820, the Society provides free evening continuing education and training for persons in the construction trades. Among the courses offered is a four-year course in HVAC&R.

Participating in the Region I Heritage Capsule Ceremony were (left to right): Alfred Greenberg, P.E., chapter historian; Richard Batherman, research promotion chair; Carl Howard, student activities chair; Al Schroeder, member; Julian Ocejo, P.E., North Jersey Chapter president; Kevin Hoey, New York Chapter president; Cyril Butler, member; Joseph K. Ting, P.E., Region I DRC; William F. Fryer, general society 1st vice president; Walter P. Bishop, P.E., regional historian; Joseph Healy, Heritage Center Society past president; and Terrence Hoey, member.

1996

President's Outreach

James Hill

ASHRAE has approximately 15,000 Registered Professional Engineers in the United States among its 50,000 members. The requirements for our U.S. members to maintain registration or obtain new registration may be changing.

Last month I represented ASHRAE at the Annual Meeting of the National Society of Professional Engineers (NSPE) in Boston. A major recommendation to come before their Board was the approval of a national model for engineering licensing and registration.

NSPE formed a task force in 1994 to study the licensure process for engineering graduates in the United States. They had been concerned for some time that only one in five graduate engineers become licensed professional engineers and this situation may not be serving the best interest of public safety. The task force had representatives from NSPE, the American Society of Engineering Education (ASEE), the National Council of Examiners for Engineering and Surveying (NCEES), the Engineering Dean's Council (EDC), and the Accreditation Board for Engineering and Technology (ABET). After two years of work, the task force made its recommendation to the NSPE Board in Boston.

The major features of the model are for the candidate seeking a license to (1) have an ABET/Engineering Accreditation Commission (AEC) accredited baccalaureate degree in engineering, and (2) pass a new Fundamentals Exam (FE) that consists of a half-day test on engineering fundamentals and a half-day test on disciple-specific subjects such as Mechanical Engineering. As now, this first exam could be taken immediately following graduation. If the individual passes, he/she becomes a Registered Engineer (RE). After four years of "appropriate and acceptable experience", the individual can take the Professional Licensing Examination which consists of questions on ethics and ethical practice, codes and standards, and related governmental, legal, and public policy issues. There would be no testing of technical knowledge as part of this second exam. Upon passing this second exam, the individual becomes a Licensed Professional Engineer (LPE). The model also includes requirements for mandatory continuing education in order to maintain an active LPE license.

The debate around this new model was hot and heavy, both before the NSPE meeting and at their Board meeting. The main areas of debate centered around the use of the term Registered Engineer after passing the first exam, and the mandatory requirement for continuing education to maintain the LPE license. Surprising to me was that there was only token opposition in Boston to the lack of testing for technical competence during the second exam. A strong case was made that State Boards of Engineering Registration hardly ever take disciplinary action against professional engineers for lack of technical competence; but rather for lack of ethical practice.

The new model passed the NSPE Board by voice vote and now will be considered individually within each state for adoption. The debate on these changes over the next year or two should be very interesting. I encourage ASHRAE members with a Professional Engineers (PE) license or those considering obtaining such a license to get involved in this upcoming debate within your state. The outcome will undoubtedly affect your future status as a PE or a LPE.

1996

Fred, Peggy Kohloss Donate $1 Million to the ASHRAE Foundation

The contribution of Presidential Member Fred Kohloss, P.E., and his wife, Peggy, to the ASHRAE Foundation through a charitable gift annuity offered benefits to both the Society and the Kohloss's.

A charitable gift annuity is a retirement plan that allows ASHRAE members to make significant contributions to the ASHRAE Foundation (minimum gift of $10,000), while retaining a guaranteed fixed income for life and, if married, for their spouse's lifetime. It also affords members a number of tax benefits, including an immediate tax deduction on federal tax returns, partial avoidance of capital gains taxes on appreciated investments, tax-free income as a part of each annuity payment over the life expectancy, and a reduction in potential estate taxes.

Since 1949, Mr. Kohloss has been an active member of ASHRAE, including serving as Society president in 1986-87.

His theme for his presidential year was: "Develop Our Human Resources." His goal was to encourage ASHRAE members to develop and mature and to take their places in advancing the Society's technical and research efforts. He offered his personal encouragement to ASHRAE members during visits to 61 chapters.

Mr. Kohloss graduated from the University of Maryland in February 1943. He served in the Army Corps of Engineers in Europe and the Pacific until his release from active duty in September 1946.

He joined the American Society of Refrigerating Engineers (ASRE) in 1949, while teaching at George Washington University. As an assistant professor, he taught mechanical engineering courses during the day and attended law school at night. He received his law degree from the university in 1949. He also attended the University of Delaware, receiving a master of mechancial engineering degree in 1951.

In 1954, he joined the American Society of Heating and Ventilating Engineers (ASHVE) while working for Lester T. Avery, at Avery Engineering Co. in Cleveland, Ohio. Avery is a past president of ASHVE.

Mr. Kohloss attributes his good fortune to being one of the first consulting mechanical engineers in Hawaii, having moved there in 1955. A year later he became principal of Montgomery & Kohloss, and in 1961, he formed Frederick H. Kohloss & Associates. At times, the firm had branch offices in Melbourne, Australia; Guam; Tucson, Ariz.; San Francisco, Calif.; Cleveland, Ohio; and Denver, Colo.

"As I got older I closed the branch offices," said Mr. Kohloss, "and in 1991 my Honolulu firm merged with an Australian firm to form Lincolne, Scott & Kohloss." Presently, he is chairman of Lincolne, Scott & Kohloss, Inc.

He also attributes his success to his wife, Peggy, a native of Washington, D.C. The Kohloss' were married in 1944.

"Above all else, Peggy is responsible for whatever I have accomplished. In our early years she raised our three daughters, which allowed me to teach at the George Washington University during the day and to go to school at night. When I opened my engineering firm in Hawaii, she became the firm's secretary," said Mr. Kohloss.

"Throughout my career," he said, "I have realized again and again that there are so many fine people and such an infusion of knowledge that it is imperative for those in our industry to be a members of ASHRAE." Since there was not then sufficient technical information in Hawaii, he regularly attended Society meetings and served on various technical committees, beginning in 1962. In 1970 he helped form ASHRAE's Hawaii Chapter, and was president of the chapter in 1989-90.

He also has served on numerous Society committees. Most recently, he served as chair of the Special Publications Committee in 1990-94.

Mr. Kohloss is a member of many engineering societies and has received several awards, including ASHRAE's Distinguished Service Award in 1977. He was elevated to the grade of Fellow ASHRAE in 1973, and in 1995 he became a Fellow of the Australian Institute of Refrigeration, Air-Conditioning and Heating (AIRAH).

Of his nearly 50 years as a member of ASHRAE, Mr. Kohloss said, "Participation in ASHRAE gives you life-long friendships that you wouldn't have any other way. Also, most engineers understand their first duty is to the public. ASHRAE members feel a proprietary interest in the Society, because it is so people driven and committed to advancing HVAC&R technology for the benefit of the public."

The ASHRAE Foundation supports ASHRAE's educational and training programs. It provides stewardship of permanently endowed funds raised from individuals, corporation and foundations, and complements the ASHRAE Research Program. The ASHRAE Foundation also provides planned giving services to ASHRAE members.

1996

Florida West Coast Chapter 1996-97 Officers and Board of Directors installed: ray Patenaude, M.C. (podium); Tim Citek, President (stage right); Floor level; Howard Blankenship, President Elect; John W. Wells, III, Secretary; Collen Smith, Treasurer; Joe Griner III, Second Vice President; Ted Hansen, Governor; Mark Smith, First Vice President; Gary Stenlund, Governor; Juan Soler, Governor.

The Honorable Edward G. Rendell, (right) mayor of Philadelphia, Pa., presented ASHRAE President James E. Hill, PhD, with the proclamation that made the week of January 25-29, 1997, ASHRAE Convention and Expo Week in Philadelphia.

Open Board Meeting Encourages Member Participation

OSTON—The special invitation to mem-ers to attend ASHRAE's Board Meeting Boston on Sunday, June 29, encouraged e attendance of a number members who rought forth a variety of issues. Even ough Board meetings have always been pen for visitation by the membership, very w members have taken the opportunity to ddress the Board in the past few years. utgoing President James E. Hill, Ph.D., resented the idea to the Board at the 1997 Winter Meeting in Philadelphia and the oard unanimously approved the idea to ncourage comments and questions from e membership.

Approximately 15 people commented to e Board during the hour long session on sues ranging from the Society's work in ergy conservation through selection of SHRAE's Hall of Fame recipients. An pdate on 90.1 was provided along with mments on ASHRAE's expertise and ork in residential HVAC design. In the ea concerning service to members there ere comments to consider giving students ice breaks on ASHRAE's educational fferings, more use of research grants for inority groups, and concerns about support eded for the international membership.

Outgoing ASHRAE President, James E. Hill, Ph.D., responds to a point raised during the open session of the Board meeting on Sunday, June 29.

"For a Standard to have impact it must be written in code language"

Ron Jarnagin

"Review the bid process for ASHRAE Research"

Chet Sandberg

"Be mindful of the need for diversity"

Victor Goldschmidt

"Use grants to foster minority participa-tion"

Harmohindar Singh

1997

ASHRAE Foundation Funds Distinguished Lecturers Program

The purpose for creating the ASHRAE Foundation in 1994 was to endow a permanent source of funding for ASHRAE programs which benefit the membership and support the future education and training needs of the HVAC&R industry. With the presentation of a $10,000 check to the Society on October 23, 1997, to help fund the ASHRAE Distinguished Lecturers Program (see photo), the Foundation has taken its first step (outside of scholarships) in fulfilling its mission.

The Foundation's endowment fund now grants over $40,000 annually for technical, undergraduate and graduate scholarships. With the continued support of Society members and the HVAC&R industry, the Foundation anticipates the continued growth of its scholarship funds and hopes to provide funding in the future for other Society education and training programs.

Society members can support the ASHRAE Foundation with gifts from their estates, charitable trusts and gift annuities. Call Bob Peach, RP/Foundation Manager, for more details.

Pictured are Foundation trustees Don Nichols, treasurer (left) and Damon Gowan, chairman (second left) presenting a $10,000 check to Society officers George Jackins, president-elect (second right) and Frank Coda, executive vice president.

1997

Stay Cool!

ASHRAE and ARI Team Up for Exhibition on Air Conditioning in America

The story of how air conditioning transformed the way Americans live is the subject of a major exhibition to be held at the National Building Museum in Washington, D.C., May 1, 1999 through January 2, 2000. ASHRAE and the Air-Conditioning and Refrigeration Institute (ARI) are providing major funding and technical support. The exhibit is entitled "Stay Cool! Air Conditioning in America."

Newspapers around the United States are calling the exhibit the first to portray "a defining technology of the twentieth century." *The New York Times*, in describing "Stay Cool!", reported that air conditioning spurred the invention of new forms of architecture and interior design, altering the way Americans live, work and play. From glass skyscrapers, enclosed shopping malls and suburban tract houses to Disney's indoor theme-park rides, high-tech manufactured clean rooms and pressurized modules for space exploration, many of the nation's modern structures and industries would not exist without the invention of what newspapers term "man-made weather." Bernard Nagengast, a member of the Society's Historical Committee, is serving as a technical consultant and as ASHRAE's representative to the museum for the exhibit.

photo courtesy of Lenox Industries

"Stay Cool!" will encompass several distinct viewing areas.

In "Life before Air Conditioning," visitors will see illustrations of how office and factory work was subject to the conditions of the outside air. Seasonal patterns needed to be respected; indoor theaters closed during the summer; and official government ceased to function. Industries, such as printing, suffered from inconsistent manufacturing abilities.

The "hot" section of the exhibition leads to a cool installation, evoking the interior of a 1920s motion picture palace – the first place where the public encountered air conditioning. The theater installation features a short film presentation combining stills and moving images to document the industrial and commercial uses of air conditioning at the time.

After leaving the theater, visitors walk into a recreated suburban living room and kitchen. The objective is to show that air conditioning was sold to the public as an essential component of modern living. When air conditioning was adapted to the home, it was truly democratized – as one

Stay Cool! . . . Continued on page 7

1997

Society Approves Establishment of ASHRAE Learning Institute

CHICAGO —To meet the need for life-long HVAC&R education, the ASHRAE Board of Directors approved the establishment of the ASHRAE Learning Institute (ALI) at the 1999 ASHRAE Winter in Chicago.

The Institute will centralize, coordinate and present learning programs for the industry and offer training for new engineers, providing the transition from theories presented in formal education to making contributions in a work environment. In addition, the ALI will provide continuing education courses for established professionals, while working to increase the public's awareness of the professionalism and proficiency of ASHRAE and the HVAC&R industry.

ASHRAE President George A. Jackins, P.E., said the Institute will become a major center through which traditional and innovative educational programs will be available for students of all ages and educational levels to prepare some for careers in HVAC&R, while for others advancing proficiency in the arts and sciences of HVAC&R. "The Institute will encompass the Society's current educational programs, including Professional Development Seminars, self-directed courses and short courses," Jackins said. The Institute will use the model of virtual classroom delivery using electronic delivery techniques such as satellite and web-based training.

The ALI will replace the Education Council, which currently oversees the Society's educational programs with a structure that is more flexible and proactive. ASHRAE Vice President and Education Council Chairman Don Colliver, Ph.D., P.E., Fellow ASHRAE, of the University of Kentucky, said, "The Institute's Board of Trustees will be more proactive in recommending course development and curriculum. Its members will represent a cross section of industry, consulting and education sectors of the ASHRAE membership."

1997

Pictorial Review of Toronto Meeting Events

ASHRAE President Donald E. Holte, P.Eng. (right), presented Presidential Member, Fellow ASHRAE and Life Member Frederick H. Kohloss, P.E. (left), with the Louise and Bill Holladay Distinguished Fellow Award in recognition of his many achievements in the HVAC&R industry and continuing preeminence in engineering and research.

The Poster Session featured nearly 30 presentations of the results of research on fundamental concepts and basic theory. John J. Meyer, Ph.D. (right), explains some of the finer points of his research. His poster, entitled "New Insights into the Behavior of the Metastable Region of an Operating Capillary Tube," was based on an article published in the January 1998 issue of HVAC&R Research Journal and was co-authored by William E. Dunn, Ph.D., P.E.

On behalf of the 1997-98 Board of Directors and the Society's membership, 1998-99 ASHRAE President George A. Jackins, P.E., presented a Citation to Donald E. Holte, P.Eng., acknowledging his many contributions as ASHRAE's president to standards, technology and the indoor environment.

The ASHRAE Book Store offered attendees the opportunity see what's new from ASHRAE and to update their technical libraries. The bookstore featured a number of new publications as well as CDs.

ASHRAE's international and diverse membership was well represented by nearly the 2,200 people who attended the Society's 1998 Annual Meeting in Toronto. Attendees came from 33 countries.

The Technical Program featured 141 papers and more than 140 presentations on topics ranging from indoor air quality and comfort, refrigeration, systems and applications to computers and software.

Presidential Member and ASHRAE Foundation Chairman Damon Gowan (right) recognized Henry Adams, Inc. of Baltimore, Md., for endowing an undergraduate engineering scholarship for $3,000 each year in the name of their founder, Henry Adams.

The 1998-99 slate of officers and directors were installed at the President's Luncheon on Monday, June 22, including (left to right) Vice President Ronald P. Vallort, P.E., Fellow ASHRAE; Vice President Raymond E. Patenaude, P.E.; Vice President Lynn G. Bellenger, P.E., Fellow ASHRAE; Vice President Donald G. Colliver, Ph.D., P.E., Fellow ASHRAE; Treasurer James E. Wolf; President-Elect Harley W. Goodman, Jr., P.E., Fellow ASHRAE and Life Member; and President George A. Jackins, P.E., Fellow ASHRAE.

President Donald E. Holte, P.Eng, was among the diverse panel that spoke at The Public Session, "Green Buildings: It's Not Easy Being Green." The session provided insights into the challenges and issues surrounding green building technology and high performance buildings worldwide.

1998

ASHRAE Brightens Solar Decathlon

WASHINGTON—ASHRAE helped enlighten the future of engineering through its volunteerism and sponsorship of the 2009 Solar Decathlon held in October.

"The Solar Decathlon was amazing," said ASHRAE president-elect Lynn Bellenger, who represented the Society at the event. "I expected the houses to look similar to one another and was surprised by the variety in style and appearance. The houses were all designed to be net-zero-energy buildings, and this was the first Decathlon where they were grid connected rather than relying on battery backup."

As part of the Solar Decathlon, ASHRAE hosted a student reception.

The Decathlon is a competition in which 20 teams of college and university students compete to design, build and operate the most attractive, effective and energy-efficient solar-powered house.

The first-place winner was Team Germany (Technische Universität Darmstadt); second-place was the University of Illinois at Urbana-Champaign; and third-place was Team California (Santa Clara University, California College of the Arts).

Sixteen ASHRAE members served as Solar Decathlon Observers, observing two to four houses each to manage the 10 contests that make up the entire competition. ASHRAE observers dedicated eight days to serve in this capacity.

As part of its role as a supporting sponsor, ASHRAE also hosted two work-

See Solar Decathlon, Page 4

1998

"Stay Cool! Air Conditioning America" Exhibit Showcases Technology's Transformative Power

"Stay Cool! Air Conditioning America" the first major exhibit in the United States on the transformative power of air conditioning opened at the National Building Museum in Washington, D.C., May 1. The exhibition sponsored by ASHRAE and ARI investigates how the century's defining technology spurred the invention of totally new forms of architecture, forever altering the way people live, work and play. The exhibit will be open through January 2000.

In comments opening the exhibit, ASHRAE President George A. Jackins, P.E. said, "Much of America takes air conditioning for granted these days. With the cooling season now upon us in much of the country, we are moving from air-conditioned homes to air-conditioned cars to air-conditioned offices, theaters, malls and arenas. But those of us here tonight know full well the impact that our industry has had on our comfort and on the development of agricultural and manufactured goods that define our lifestyle in the 20th century."

Jackins also noted that the Society's early parallel of work through ASHVE and ASRE beginning in 1894 and continuing into the early 1900s yielded a spurt of technological development marking the true start of air conditioning as we now define it. Since then, steady progress has made the 1900s the first air-conditioned century. As we approach the start of a new century — and indeed a new millennium — air conditioning has evolved from a curiosity to a necessity, literally transforming the way that much of the world lives.

This General Electric Monitor Top refrigerator being examined by a visitor to the Stay Cool! Exhibit at the National Building Museum was manufactured from 1925 to 1936 and featured a unique, truly hermetically-sealed household refrigerating machine that was mounted on the top of the cabinet. Domestic refrigerators were marketed as early as the 1890's.

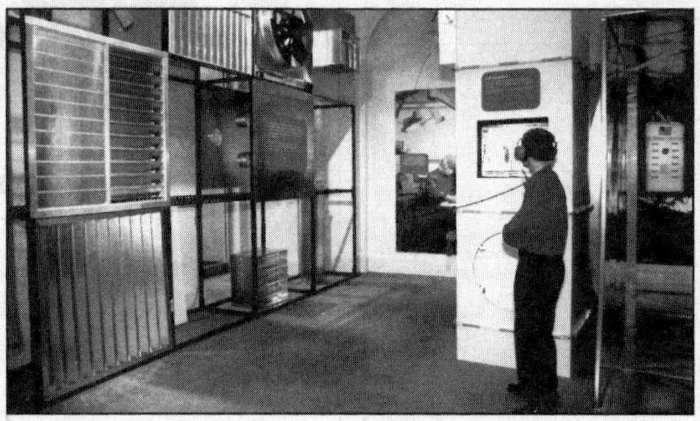

This visitor to the Stay Cool! Exhibit enjoys listening to the dialog accompanying a two-minute film with live footage describing aspects of the science of air conditioning. In addition, key terms used in the film footage is presented at the kiosk for the visitor.

The "Stay Cool! Air Conditioning America" exhibit recreates a series of revolutionary environments, including: a 1920s indoor movie theater, the first place millions of Americans were introduced to air conditioning; a centrally air-conditioned 1960s suburban living room, separated from its outdoor patio by only a thin layer of sliding glass; and a contemporary inflatable structure supported by its own air-conditioning system featuring visionary projects such as R. Buckminster Fuller's scheme to cover midtown Manhattan with a dome and Frank Lloyd Wright's 1957 design for Fiberthin Airhouses commissioned by U.S. Rubber Company.

The exhibit also includes television commercials and advertisements, clips from feature films, and interactive displays of air-conditioning equipment. Stay Cool! features models of skyscrapers that incorporate energy-efficient and environment-friendly mechanical systems, including New York's Times Square Building with its innovative underfloor air distribution network, and images of scientific installations, including the 3.15-acre Biosphere outside Tucson, Ariz.

ASHRAE Member Bernard Nagengast served as technical consultant and as ASHRAE's representative to the museum for the exhibit.

One benefit of the display is the attention it has brought to the air-conditioning industry in the popular press. Extensive reviews have appeared in The New York Times and Washington Post and on ABC News and National Public Radio.

The Museum is located at 401 F Street, NW, Washington, D.C., at the entrance to the Judiciary Square Metro station on the Red Line. The Museum's hours are Monday through Saturday 10 a.m. to 4 p.m., and Sunday 12 p.m. to 4 p.m. Admission is free.

1999

In recognition of ASHRAE's co-sponsorship of National Engineers Week, ASHRAE Executive Vice President Frank Coda (center) was presented with a sculpture of the Thinker at an event held during the 1999 festivities. Presenting the award were Earnest W. Deavenport, Jr., (left), honorary chair of National Engineers Week 1999 and chairman and CEO, Eastman Chemical Co. and Stephen D. Bechtel, Jr. (right), chairman emeritus, Bechtel Group.

Ottawa Valley Chapter Board of Governors

The Ottawa Valley Chapter Board of Governors for 2000-2001 are from left front row: Jason Mac Murdo, treasurer; Frank Bean, president-elect; Mike Swayne, president; Lan chi Nguyen Thi, secretary. Second row from left: governors Glenn Maclean, Peter Dunlap, Jay Doshi, Gary Hartmann, Robert Kilpatrick and Joel Primeau, past president.

2000

Milton W. Garland, "Mr. Refrigeration", Dead at 104

Milton Ward Garland, recipient of numerous ASHRAE Awards and the holder of over 40 patents of refrigeration related items, passed away at the age of 104. He had been one of America's oldest active workers beginning his career in the refrigeration industry in 1920 at the Frick Company (now part of York International) in Waynesboro, PA. He was working there through May of this year when he suffered a heart attack.

Garland was an ASHRAE Fellow and Life Member. He was the recipient of the Distinguished Service Award, F. Paul Anderson Award, and the Louise and Bill Holladay Distinguished Fellow Award. He received a special 100-Year Old Member Centennial Award at ASHRAE's Centennial Celebration in Chicago in 1995.

Milton Garland was known as "Mr. Refrigeration" in honor of his pioneering work in refrigeration systems for gold mines in South Africa and in the ice cream factories of Philadelphia. He contributed numerous articles to *ASHRAE Journal* and published a number of meeting papers in *ASHRAE Transactions* .His patents ranged from ice makers to screw compressor volume controls. His work in refrigeration aided in the construction of the Hoover Dam for which he designed systems to cool the water, sand and rock used to make the concrete to build it. It was said that without these systems that it would have been impossible to pour the concrete for the dam.

2000

Sign Up Now!

Personal "members.ashrae.org" E-mail Address Now Available to Members

A new ASHRAE e-mail service that automatically forwards e-mail to your personal account is now available for members to sign on. The ASHRAE e-mail alias account, free to ASHRAE members, has the potential to eliminate many volunteer hours now spent maintaining chapter, TC and committee e-mail routing lists.

The ASHRAE e-mail alias program allows members the option of signing up for an ASHRAE email address through the ASHRAE Members Only Section of the website at http://members.ashrae.org/memberalias. ASHRAE members sign up using a "firstname.lastname@members.ashrae.org" e-mail address. Since this system is an email forwarding program which passes messages through to a forwarding address, ASHRAE members then indicate an existing email address where they want their ashrae.org mail to be sent.

In addition, ASHRAE members can choose to be listed in the ASHRAE e-mail directory, where their e-mail address will be searchable by name. Only ASHRAE members with valid member numbers and PIN numbers will have access to the directory.

The intent of the ASHRAE e-mail alias system is to foster member communication. When a member who has signed up for the service changes his or her personal e-mail address either because of a change of employment or Internet service provider, members only need to change the forwarding address for their ASHRAE e-mail address account instead of sending out numerous individual messages to a personal directory.

Members must read the license agreement and accept it to start the service. The ASHRAE server will start re-directing members' ashrae.org mail to their commonly used address. Members who use the system are responsible for seeing that their hardware, software and e-mail (to which ASHRAE e-mail is forwarded) are protected from viruses. The ASHRAE e-mail address may not be used in advertisements nor for commercial promotion.

To open your account, go to http://members.ashrae.org/memberalias/.

2001

Students tour the control room of an icing tunnel at NASA where they learned about the types of experiments performed in the tunnel (2002).

ASHRAE CD Provides International Weather Data

The successful estimation of energy performance of buildings depends on obtaining accurate weather data, which is especially difficult for international locations.

The new ASHRAE *International Weather for Energy Calculations CD* contains typical weather files suitable for use with building energy simulation programs for 227 locations outside North America. The information was developed as part of ASHRAE Research Project 1015, Typical Weather Years for International Locations.

"Typical weather year files are commonly used as input to building energy simulation software to estimate the average annual energy consumption of buildings," Didier Thevenard, Ph.D., principal investigator, said. "But for locations outside North America, they are often hard to obtain, and their format and method of derivation varies from one country to the next. With this new CD, typical weather files in a common format and quality become widely available for a large number of international sites."

The files are derived from 18 years of DATSAV3 hourly weather data originally archived at the National Climatic Data Center. The weather data is supplemented by solar radiation estimated on an hourly basis from earth-sun geometry and hourly weather elements, particularly cloud amount information.

The geographical distribution comprises 12 sites in Africa, 49 in Asia, 19 in South America, five in Central America,

See CD, Page 2

2002

Dennis O'Keefe, secretary of the North Piedmont Chapter, explains how natural gas is compressed for use in trucks. Dr. H. Singh, faculty advisor at NCA&T State University (far left) watches the demonstration (2001).

ASHRAE: Keeping History Alive

Boiler ad (left) and engraving of ice delivery (right) are some of the rare offerings of the ASHRAE library.

History Channel, Others Turn to ASHRAE Archives

While ASHRAE prides itself on its technological advancements, organizations have turned to the Society since 1990 for its rare historical offerings.

Most recently, several images were sent to The History Channel for its program, *Fire and Ice*, part of the Modern Marvels series. ASHRAE Historical Committee Chair Mohinder Bhatti and former chair Bern Nagengast were interviewed for the program about the history of HVAC&R. *Fire and Ice* aired in April.

A video tape of the program may be purchased from www.historychannel.com. Also, you may check the site's monthly schedule for future airings.

Old photos and ads also were provided to DuPont Suva® refrigerants as part of its 200th anniversary. An exhibit with the images was displayed at the DuPont booth at the AHR Expo in Atlantic City.

ASHRAE librarian Emily Sigman said the library is primarily a center for print documents, including the acquisitions of a collection from member Gershon Meckler in 1994 and very old documents from the now-defunct Engineering Societies Library. One rare library offering is an 1895 copy of Metalworker, which announced the formation of ASHVE, a predecessor society of ASHRAE.

A patented car warmer from Baker, Smith & Co.

"We have materials at ASHRAE headquarters that do not exist anywhere else in a collected format," Sigman said.

Many library patrons, like architect Michael Henry, spend hours looking through rare books about HVAC systems. Henry, who works on historic buildings, finds bits and pieces of old systems

See History, Page 2

2002

Fourth-graders at Winding Creek Elementary School learn about engineering in the "Great Egg Drop" challenge (2002).

The 2003 National Engineers Week Future City Competition winners with project, from left: Mitchell Laski, Teacher Susan Hester, Megan Horton, and Casey Laski of Mission Middle School in Bellevue, Nebraska.

Roadmap Leads to E-ASHRAE

Electronic Communications Staff Section to Implement Roadmap, See Page 3

Electronic communications are transforming all aspects of ASHRAE, including meetings, publications, operations, member services, and public review. Like other organizations, ASHRAE is attempting to make use of new and emerging electronic technologies.

Some examples of recent initiatives include a weekly eNewsletter, an online paper review system, a news release list server and an e-mail alias system.

The Board approved the *Roadmap for the ASHRAE Web Site* at the 2002 Annual Meeting. In addition, the Board adopted *Key Principles for Development of the ASHRAE Web Site* as the Society's official document for development of programs for the site. The Board also agreed that responsibility for maintaining the roadmap be assigned to the Special Publications Committee.

The intent of the roadmap is to provide background information and a discussion of issues related to integration of ASHRAE Online with all of the functions and operations of the Society. This document seeks to articulate a vision for an integrated e-ASHRAE that provides:

- Centralized operations with an integrated database and Web site;
- International access through the Web;
- Reduced operating costs through reduction of paper, postage and handling;
- Reduced burden on staff and volunteers by streamlining operations through Web-based planning, deployment and data gathering;
- Increased revenue through new marketing mechanisms and increased outreach;
- Increased visibility by offering better access to technical information; and
- New and improved services to membership.

The roadmap is available at www.ashrae.org/ABOUT/spcom.htm.

2002

Finding Information Easier On Redesigned Web Site

A newly designed Web site launched by ASHRAE makes it easier for visitors to find the information they need.

The site, www.ashrae.org, features improved navigation as well as a new Resource Center, which combines the publication sections into one shopping area.

Material on the site has been grouped into three major areas:

- HVAC&R Information, home to the Resource Center, *ASHRAE Journal, International Journal of HVAC&R Research* and other published news and resources from ASHRAE;
- Activities & Membership, a section devoted to Society information and the grassroots work of ASHRAE members, including committee participation and membership services;
- HVAC&R Marketplace, an area where companies can reach the HVAC&R audience with product and service information, including classified ads and a product and service directory.

The new Resource Center provides the ability to search for a topic throughout ASHRAE's publications. For instance, a keyword search on "humidity control," yields materials from *ASHRAE Journal*, various meeting papers, and books. Most papers and articles can be purchased as

See Web, Page 2

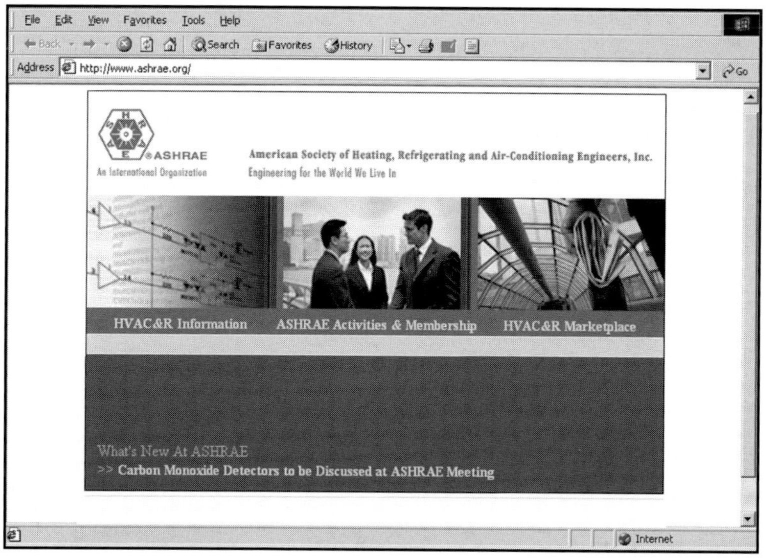

2002

Region II CRC Visits Deep Lake Cooling Facility

Attendees of Region II's Chapters Regional Conference tour Enwave, which includes deep lake water cooling supply. The Toronto Chapter hosted the conference, which also featured a technical field trip to Air Canada Center's mechanical room. Shane Pospisil, assistant deputy, Ontario Ministry of Energy, spoke on the supply and conservation of Ontario's current and future energy source and conservation strategies. Doug Cochrane and Jim Oven served as co-chairs under the direction of Jean Bundock, Region II director and regional chair.

2004

Bill Bissmeyer of the Central Indiana Chapter organized a basketball tournament for area HVAC companies. Teams from three states participated in the competition. Pictured are Bob Newton (left), Marty Stevens (top), Vince Rago (right), and Bill Bissmeyer (center) (2003).

See Main Story, Page 1

Summary of Organization Changes

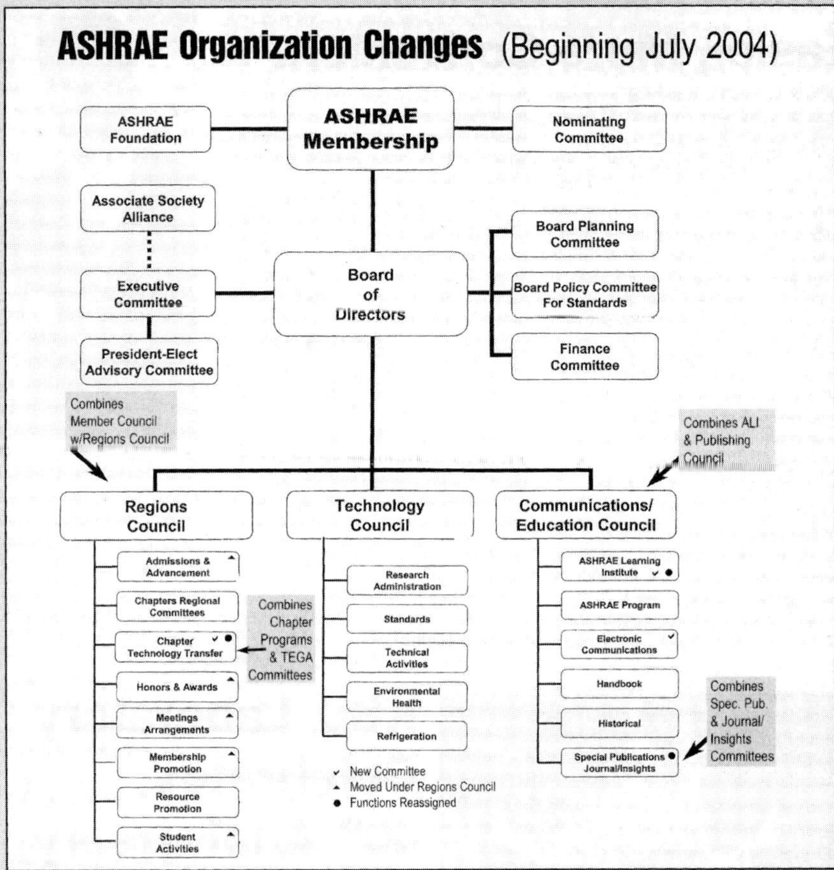

Councils

• Combining Publishing Council with ASHRAE Learning Institute to create a new Communications/Education Council. ASHRAE content can be easily cross-purposed. ASHRAE's continuing education programs benefit from marketing, communication and production capabilities available through ASHRAE publications.

• Combining member services from Member Council with Regions Council to provide improved grassroots communication and coordination of member-related services.

With these changes, the Society hopes to improve services to members by focusing on the areas of member services (Regions Council), technology development (Technology Council) and information dissemination (Communications/Education Council).

New Committees

• Creation of the ASHRAE Learning Institute Committee under Communications/Education Council. It will develop, manage and implement ASHRAE's continuing education programs. It combines the functions of the ALI Board of Trustees with the Course Development Committee.

• Creation of the Chapter Technology Transfer Committee under Regions Council. It will provide educational resources to assist chapters in the professional development of members and communicate member needs to the Society. It combines the Technical, Energy and Government Activities (TEGA) Committee with the Chapter Programs Committee.

• Creation of an Electronic Communications Committee under the Communications/Education Council. It will recommend policy on all aspects of electronic communication.

Committees with Functions Reassigned

• Accreditation Activities. ASHRAE will continue to provide ABET assistance. Staff with the Learning Institute Committee will manage a group of program evaluators for HVAC technology programs.

• Chapter Programs and TEGA. Responsibilities will transfer to the new Chapter Technology Transfer Committee to focus technology transfer for chapter programs, chapter seminars and government activities through a single grassroots committee.

• Charter and Bylaws. These functions will be provided by staff and coordinated with Regions Council. The Society rules function will be handled by the Board.

• Course Development. Responsibilities will transfer to the new ASHRAE Learning Institute Committee.

• Journal/Insights. Functions will merge with the Special Publications Committee under Communications/Education Council.

Realignment of Existing Committees

• Admissions and Advancement, Membership Promotion, Honors and Awards, Meetings Arrangements and Student Activities are moved under Regions Council to focus member and chapter services under one council.

Proposed timeline

• Annual Meeting 2003. Board approves reorganization plan that takes effect July 2004.

2003

First Affiliate Member Is Approved

Sinha

Joining ASHRAE under the new Affiliate Member grade was a "logical step" for Rajeev Sinha as a young professional.

"The benefits seemed to be appropriate for me, as I already have access to the ASHRAE *Handbooks* and other publications that would be required for design," said the 22-year-old. "This membership grade made it affordable for our small, family-owned, growing business, Contech Design Inc., to purchase the membership at a very reasonable price for the first three years, and then transfer to an Associate membership until I have enough experience to be considered a full Member.

"I fully intend to pursue this course of action as ASHRAE is the most appropriate society for my chosen profession. I believe that the decision to offer this category of membership is a very wise move on ASHRAE's part, and I believe it will draw in members like me who want to join the society at an 'entry-level' until we've worked our way up."

Sinha was the first person to join ASHRAE under the new Affiliate Member grade. ASHRAE members approved the new grade in June, as part of efforts to attract additional younger members and meet the needs of members worldwide. The grade is open to new members under age 30 and can only be held for up to three cumulative years. Annual dues are $40.

Sinha has worked in the HVAC industry since he was 14. Originally hired as draftsman and file clerk for Contech Design, he now serves as vice president and director

See Affiliate, Page 2

2004

Peggy Fritz and Lynne Frye, both of the Atlanta Chapter, and Dee Lord of the Tennessee Valley Chapter volunteered at a Girl Scout science camp in 2004. Forty Girl Scouts ages 8–12 participated in the week. Shown is Peggy Fritz with the girls.

In 2004 the Cincinnati Chapter presented a check to Ursuline Academy, an all-girls high school, to further its engineering program, affiliated with Ohio State University. Shown left to right are Jeff Hetzel, engineering class instructor, Carol Obert, science department coordinator, Joanne Dearing, Cincinnati Chapter president, Dr. Diane Castelli, Ursuline Academy president, and Karen Hadden, director of major and planned gifts.

Stamps Honor ASRE Pioneers

ATLANTA—Their names are synonymous with technological breakthroughs related to refrigeration and air conditioning.

Now the faces of Clarence Birdseye, Willis Carrier, Mary Pennington and Gardner Voorhees are being made "famous" as well, via postage stamps commissioned by ASHRAE.

U.S. postage stamps bearing the likenesses of these four industry pioneers have been created as part of ASHRAE's celebration of the 100th anniversary of the founding of The American Society of Refrigerating Engineers (ASRE). ASHRAE also has created a fifth stamp, which is a replica of a poster being displayed as part of the centennial.

ASHRAE is encouraging that the stamps be used during Refrigeration Appreciation Week. As part of the centennial celebration and ASHRAE's 2005 Winter Meeting in Orlando, Fla., Orlando Mayor Buddy Dyer has signed a proclamation designating the week of meeting, Feb. 5-9, as Refrigeration Appreciation Week, to "honor the work of engineers who have harnessed this technology to provide innumerable benefits in improving the quality of life for people throughout the world."

"People around the world enjoy the benefits that stem from the accomplishments of these pioneers – foods that are safe, foods that last longer, vaccines provided worldwide, life giving blood, tissue and organ transplants, and comfortable homes and workplaces," said ASHRAE

See ASRE Stamps, Page 2

ASRE Stamps, From Page 1

President Ron Vallort, P.E. "Featuring them on a stamp gives proper recognition to those who make our life easier today."

The pioneers include:

- Carrier, former president of ASRE, who is associated with many "firsts" during the infant stages of air conditioning.
- Pennington, first female member of ASRE, who was regarded as the foremost American authority on home refrigeration. An ASRE Fellow, she developed milk and dairy standards that were adopted throughout the United States and recommended standards for construction and insulation of refrigerator cars.
- Voorhees, whose design for air conditioning at the St. Louis World's Fair in 1904 marked the first time the public-at-large was exposed to the comforts of mechanical cooling. Voorhees was a charter member of ASRE. He will be inducted into the ASHRAE Hall of Fame at the 2005 Winter Meeting.
- Birdseye, who invented, developed, and commercialized a method for quick-freezing food products in convenient packages without altering the original taste.

The stamps are 37-cent first-class and are sold in sheets of 20 at a cost of $15 per sheet. The stamps are recognized by the U.S. Postal Service for mail delivery but are manufactured by a private contractor.

Other celebratory activities planned for Orlando include:

- A refrigeration museum paying tribute to ASRE and the industry through posters, audio visual and papers.
- Two seminars focusing on refrigeration applications and refrigeration components over the last 100 years.
- A live reenactment of papers presented at early ASRE meetings at the meeting of the members, 3:15 p.m., Saturday, Feb. 5.
- A cocktail reception hosted by the Refrigeration Committee from 5-6:30 p.m. Monday, Feb. 7.

2004

Connecticut Chapter President Michael Rocchetti sees a snow cannon at work.

Snowmaking Cool for Connecticut Chapter

By Michael J. Rocchetti, P.E., Connecticut Chapter president

HARTFORD, Conn. —After a January 2003 program on snow melting systems, the members of the Connecticut Chapter thought that it would be interesting to borrow on that winter theme for their January 2004 meeting — but with a slightly different twist — snowmaking systems.

So, the chapter held its meeting at a local ski resort for a day of fun on the slopes, a tour and demonstration of a snowmaking system, and a presentation on the physics and chemistry of snowmaking.

While most of us who live in the cold climates of the north think of snow as something that needs to be plowed, removed and melted, skiers think of snow as something that you should be able to make, especially if there isn't enough natural snowfall. Most of the ski resorts in the Northeast have snowmaking systems that can cover 100% of their skiable terrain with snow.

These snowmaking systems are a marvel of modern mechanical engineering technology. A good example of this technology can be found at Connecticut's premier ski

See Conn. Chapter, Page 2

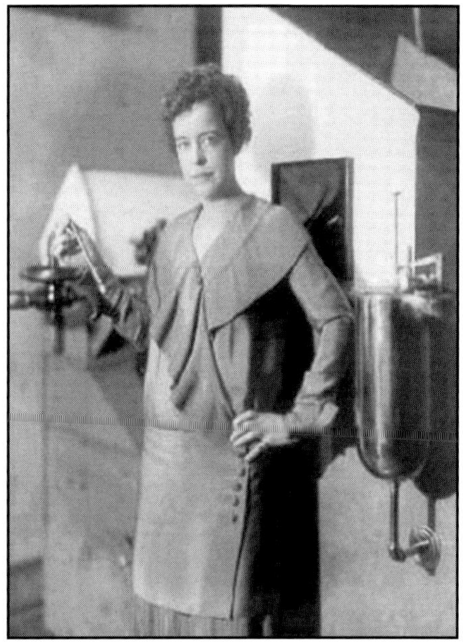

In 2005, a new student residence hall at the University of Kentucky was named after Margaret Ingels, one of the first female members of ASHVE.

Jean Bundock, Region II director and regional chair (center) and his wife Dyane reached the summit of Mount Kilimanjaro, the highest mountain in Africa, on November 2, 2005.

Interactive CD for Handbook

Electronic Version Has New Tools

An enhanced CD-ROM provides greater access to the technical guidance in the *ASHRAE Handbook*.

The ASHRAE HandbookCD+ 2002–2005 is the Society's first four-volume HandbookCD with electronic enhancements.

"The CD provides users with the most complete and useful HVAC&R reference available," said Mark Owen, *ASHRAE Handbook* editor. "The CD+ contains all *Handbook* chapters with the latest updates in a searchable electronic format, featuring interactive and supplemental tools."

The tools include:

- Spreadsheets demonstrating the radiant time series (RTS) method of load calculation;
- Expanded climatic design data tables from the *2005 Handbook — Fundamentals;*
- NAIMA 3E Plus software for calculating insulation thickness;
- A desiccant wheel performance estimator;
- Video clips of kitchen hood airflows;
- Animations of equipment;
- Interactive charts;
- Supplemental examples and text;

See HandbookCD+, Page 2

- Additional links to organizations and data;
- Color graphics for improved understanding, surpassing the presentation possible in the black-and-white print volumes; and
- Links to commercial resources that allow users to locate products and services related to the topic of each chapter.

The CD+ contains PDF files of chapters in all four current volumes: *2005 Fundamentals; 2004 HVAC Systems and Equipment; 2003 HVAC Applications; and 2002 Refrigeration.*

The more than 3,100 pages of PDFs are searchable across all the volumes, in both the I-P and SI unit editions.

The cost of the Handbook CD+ is $499 ($249, ASHRAE members). Prices are for a single user. A multiuser network license and a network HandbookCD+ also are available.

To order, contact ASHRAE Customer Service at 1-800-527-4723 (United States and Canada), or 404-636-8400 (worldwide); fax 404-321-5478; by mail at 1791 Tullie Circle NE, Atlanta, GA 30329; or visit the bookstore at www.ashrae.org.

2005

The Southern Alberta Chapter celebrated its 50th Anniversary and Past Presidents Night on October 19, 2007, with a gala dinner. The celebration was attended by four chapter charter members and 22 past presidents. Special guests included ASHRAE president-elect Bill Harrison, Region XI DRC Traci Hanegan and Region XI Historian Ivan Hall.

ASHRAE Adorns Times Square For Earth Day

NEW YORK—ASHRAE's image is larger than life in the building industry, but for a few days recently, it was literally larger than life—in New York's Times Square.

As part of the Society's public relations campaign centered around Earth Day, April 22, the ASHRAE logo, along with a news headline, appeared on the Reuters billboard in Times Square for four days surrounding Earth Day.

ASHRAE's materials were displayed several times each day during the morning and evening rush hours.

The display was in conjunction with an Earth Day package with PR Newswire, which entailed distributing a feature article with consumer-oriented energy-saving tips for the summer months.

The article, bundled with other environment-related Earth-Day articles, was also sent to reporters and editors through a separate news distribution service.

The article has appeared in the *Tampa Tribune*, among other outlets.

The ASHRAE message was presented to the estimated 1.6 million people who pass through Times Square each day.

2008

ALI Launches eLearning Library

Course Listing on Page 4

The ASHRAE Learning Institute (ALI) has launched the eLearning library, an online, on-demand HVAC&R educational experience.

The eLearning library provides subscribers access to a range of long and short eLearning courses for a period of twelve months. During that time, subscribers are able to access 19 full length courses and 50 stand-alone short courses.

Full courses comprehensively cover a broad subject area in a structured manner, using short course modules on specific topics. Short courses can be completed in convenient time frames, typically two to four hours.

Courses currently available in the eLearning library include *Fundamentals of HVAC Systems*, *Fundamentals of Standard 90.1*, *Fundamentals of HVAC Controls Systems* and *Standard 90.1 for Architects*. Some 15 courses are scheduled to be added to the library in 2008.

Any number or combination of the Web-based courses in the ASHRAE eLearning library can be taken anywhere, any time at the user's own pace. For more information, or to order, visit www.ashrae-elearning.org.

ASHRAE eLearning Library Courses

Participants in eLearning courses may take these courses now with ongoing access for 12 months.

- **Fundamentals of HVAC Systems (I-P and SI)**
- **13 Short Courses from HVAC Systems (I-P and SI):**
  1. Intro to HVAC Design
  2. HVAC Systems: An Introduction
  3. HVAC Systems: Thermal Comfort
  4. HVAC Systems: Ventilation & IAQ
  5. HVAC Systems: Intro to Zones
  6. HVAC Systems: Single-Zone Handlers & Unitary Equipment
  7. HVAC Systems: Multiple-Zone Air Systems
  8. HVAC Systems: Hydronic Systems
  9. HVAC Systems: Hydronic System Architecture
  10. HVAC Systems: Central Plants
  11. HVAC Systems: Controls
  12. HVAC Systems: Energy Conservation Measures
  13. HVAC Systems: Special Applications
- **Fundamentals of ASHRAE Standard 90.1**
- **Standard 90.1 for Architects**
- **Fundamentals of HVAC Control Systems (I-P and SI)**
- **12 Short Courses from HVAC Control Systems**
  1. HVAC Controls: Introductions to HVAC Control Systems
  2. HVAC Controls: Basics of Electricity
  3. HVAC Controls: Control Valves and Dampers
  4. HVAC Controls: Sensors and Auxiliary Devices
  5. HVAC Controls: Self- and System-Powered Controls
  6. HVAC Controls: Electric Controls
  7. HVAC Controls: Pneumatic Controls
  8. HVAC Controls: Analog Electronic Controls
  9. HVAC Controls: Control Diagrams and Sequences
  10. HVAC Controls: DDC Introduction to Hardware and Software
  11. HVAC Controls: DDC Networks and Protocols
  12. HVAC Controls: DDC Specification, Installation and Commissioning

Participants in ~~eLearning courses may take all these courses~~ coming in 2008 until the end of their subscription:

January
- Fundamentals of ASHRAE [illegible] Air Quality)
- Advanced Energy Design for Small Office Buildings
- Advanced Energy Design for Small Retail Buildings

February
- Standard 62.1 for Architects
- Fundamentals of Refrigeration (I-P and SI)

March
- Refrigeration Equipment (I-P and SI)

April
- Refrigeration Applications (I-P and SI)

May
- Electrical Systems for HVAC (I-P and SI)

- **Second Quarter of 2008**
- Thermal Guidelines for Data Processing Environments
- Datacom Equipment Power Trends and Cooling Applications
- Design Considerations for Datacom Equipment Centers
- Liquid Cooling Guidelines for Datacom Equipment Centers

Third Quarter of 2008
- Energy-Saving Systems for Green Buildings (I-P and SI)
- Fundamentals of Psychrometrics (I-P and SI)
- Air Conditioning System Design

2008

ASHRAE Heard In Washington

WASHINGTON, D.C.—ASHRAE's work in providing energy guidance was highlighted by ASHRAE President Kent Peterson, P.E., in Congressional testimony and in a series of media interviews with the D.C. press corps.

Peterson spoke May 14 at a hearing, *Building Green, Saving Green: Constructing Sustainable and Energy-Efficient Buildings*, before the Select Committee on Energy Independence and Global Warming of the U.S. House of Representatives. Also speaking were Ed Norton, actor and trustee of Enterprise Community Partners; and Gavin Newsom, mayor of San Francisco. Photos and more information are available at http:// globalwarming.house.gov.

"As Congress examines all sources and causes of global warming emissions, it must consider how the buildings we work and live in can contribute to reduce the impact of climate change," said Rep. Edward Markey, D-Mass., chair of the committee. "ASHRAE's standards offer a foundation for energy-efficient buildings, and the committee is interested in how building codes can be used to increase the number of green buildings throughout the nation."

Peterson discussed ASHRAE's role in writing standards for adoption into building codes and its work in developing guidance that goes beyond minimum requirements in building codes.

While in Washington, D.C., Peterson also conducted a media tour. He met with general and trade media reporters from outlets such as *The Washington Post*, *Roll Call*, *Environment and Energy Daily*, *ClimateWire*, and *Environmental Science and Technology*. Peterson also held a briefing on net-zero-energy buildings at the National Press Club. An interview with E&ETV is available at www.eenews.net.

2008

Service Life, Maintenance Data Included

Engineers are asked to advise building owners and managers on strategic decisions involving the life cycle and functionally of buildings.

In the past, lack of valid data has left engineers without a solid basis for making these decisions.

A new free online database from ASHRAE provides engineers with equipment service life and annual maintenance costs for a variety of building types and HVAC systems. The database can be accessed at www.ashrae.org/database.

It contains more than 300 building types and more than 38,000 pieces of equipment with service life data.

The database allows users to access up-to-date information to determine a range of statistical values for equipment owning and operating costs. With this, ASHRAE is providing the necessary methods and information to assist in using life-cycle analysis techniques to help select the most appropriate HVAC system for a specific application.

"Life-cycle evaluations provide the most effective method for determining the best value of HVAC system alternatives," said Lynn Bellenger, chair of ASHRAE's Technology Council. "In order to facilitate the use of life-cycle analysis techniques by decision makers, the necessary data must be available, current and correctly applied. This database provides that needed data."

As part of the project, users are encouraged to contribute their own service life and maintenance cost data, further expanding the utility of this tool. Over a period of time, this input will provide sufficient service life and maintenance cost data to allow the comparative analysis of many different HVAC systems types in a broad variety of applications. Data can be entered by logging into the database and registering, which is free.

Database, From Page 1

Information from the database also is used to update the ASHRAE Handbook.

Chapter 36, "Owning and Operating Costs," of the *2007 ASHRAE Handbook—HVAC Applications*, contains median equipment service life data from the first 163 commercial buildings that were used to seed the database, with updates to come as the database grows.

The database is the result of ASHRAE research project 1237, Interactive Web-based Owning and Operating Cost Database, sponsored by ASHRAE's technical committee 7.8, Owning and Operating Costs.

2008

Michael Bobker (front), director of the Building Performance Lab, City University of New York, leads ASHRAE President Bill Harrison along a ledge of the Empire State Building (2009).

Presidential Member Kent Peterson and Thassanee Wanick, former Green Building Council Brasil Board chair, display the translated Standard 90.1. Standards 90.1 and 189.1 were translated into Spanish and Portuguese for the South American market in 2010.

ASHRAE Updates

College of Fellows Celebrates 10 Years

The ASHRAE College of Fellows is celebrating the 10th anniversary of its 1998 founding.

The College was founded to enhance the Society's technical image internally and in the community at large.

"The College serves as an ambassador supporting ASHRAE through many different pathways," said Richard Rooley, FREng, Presidential Member/Fellow ASHRAE, president of the College of Fellows. "Our Fellows are leaders in the their fields who support ASHRAE at the highest levels through activities such as transferring ASHRAE technology and knowledge; mentoring students, engineers and educators; and communicating ASHRAE-recommended practices to resolve industry issues."

Membership in the College of Fellows is open to anyone holding ASHRAE Fellow member grade. Fellow ASHRAE honors distinction in the arts and sciences of HVAC&R and is earned through achievement as a researcher, designer, educator or engineering executive. Approximately 500 of ASHRAE's 50,000 members are Fellows.

Among the projects undertaken by the College is review of the annual ASHRAE Handbook volume. Members of the College also served as resources in the U.S. Department of Energy's 2007 Solar Decathlon, of which ASHRAE served as a title sponsor. The group answered technical questions submitted by the student teams who participated.

For more information on the College of Fellows, visit www.ashraecof.org.

2009

Approximately one dozen Young Engineers in ASHRAE (YEA) members met for a paintball game of epic, and colorful, proportions (2009).

New Report Provides Energy Policy Roadmap For the New U.S. Presidential Administration

WASHINGTON—As the federal government adjusts to the presidential transition, it faces challenges in dealing with increasingly complex issues and new directives from the Obama administration and the new Congress, especially concerning energy issues. A new report from ASHRAE provides a potential roadmap for addressing the nation's dependence on foreign energy sources and its greenhouse gas emissions while growing the economy.

"Buildings are often overlooked as an opportunity to reduce energy consumption and offer an excellent opportunity to achieve national energy goals and shape policy," said ASHRAE President Bill Harrison. Buildings are responsible for 40% of the United States' energy consumption—more than transportation and industry—and represent 38% of the U.S.'s greenhouse gas emissions.

People in the U.S. spend approximately 90% of their time indoors—many of them in schools and office buildings. The entire U.S. construction industry employs an estimated 10 million people including manufacturing, and with increased focus on improving energy efficiency within buildings, that number can be expected to rise.

ASHRAE's report provides detailed recommendations on shaping energy policy. Some of the suggested provisions include:

Energy Policy and Climate Change

ASHRAE suggests requiring annual updates of building energy use, providing funding and direction for data collection and analysis regarding energy use in buildings. ASHRAE recently launched an effort to form a domestic building energy labeling program that will "grade" buildings on their energy consumption.

Federal Incentives

The report offers ideas for government incentives for energy-related activities, particularly commissioning, re-commissioning and retro-commissioning; education and training for operations and maintenance personnel; realistic depreciation schedules; and long-term tax deductions.

Research and Development

ASHRAE recommends increased research and development efforts in the built environment, particularly for on- and off-site renewable energy, net-zero-energy building technologies, and increased governmental support for private -sector R&D.

Federal Agency Activities

ASHRAE recommends providing adequate financial and technical resources to federal agencies to meet new energy requirements and promoting the use of tools such as building information modeling and integrated design for federal construction projects.

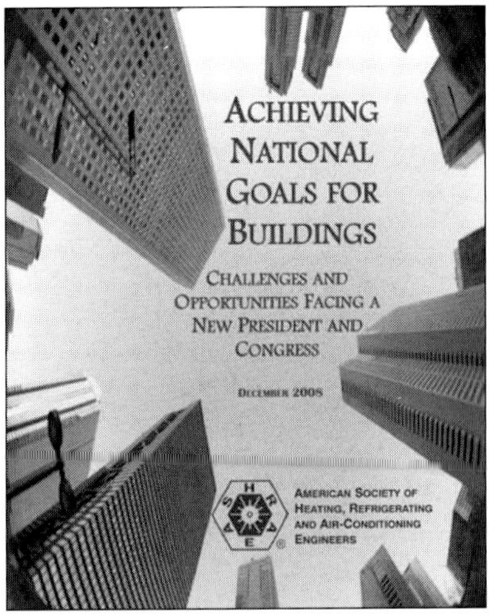

The 12-page report is available at www.ashrae.org/advocacy.

Education

The report stresses the importance of supporting educational programs focused on student competence in STEM fields, and providing funding for "green-collar" job training programs.

To read the report, visit www.ashrae.org/advocacy.

2009

Florentino Roson displays copies of Standard 189.1 and the translated version of the standard, 2010.

New Brand and Logo

ASHRAE Announces Changes At 2012 Winter Conference

CHICAGO—Throughout its 117-year history, ASHRAE has been the go-to source in the HVAC&R industry for standards, education and other resources for engineers. As the role of HVAC&R has progressed to incorporate many facets of building design, construction and operation ASHRAE also has changed.

ASHRAE recently announced an evolution of its brand to reflect those changes. Elements of the repositioning include a refreshed logo, a new tagline and a change to using only its acronym.

The announcement was made at the Society's 2012 Winter Conference.

"ASHRAE's original commitment to HVAC&R engineering excellence remains resolute even as the Society continues to expand its influence into all facets of building design, construction, reconstruction and operation," said ASHRAE President Ron Jarnagin. "Just as integrated design is the cornerstone of sustainable buildings, ASHRAE members create an integrated body of knowledge to make buildings as high-performing as possible."

The repositioning of the ASHRAE brand evolution is an acknowledgement of ASHRAE's broadening scope beyond HVAC&R to include standards, research, publications and educational resources relating to total building design, energy efficiency and sustainable building technologies, otherwise referred to as the "total building environment," said Jarnagin.

The new logo incorporates the ASHRAE name and the traditional hexagon shape. The logo transitions from "ASHRAE blue" to green from left to right.

The most visible change is the refreshed logo, which was originally created in 1959 when the American Society of Refrigerating Engineers and the American Society of Heating and Ventilating Engineers merged to form ASHRAE.

"We want our logo to reflect that we are

See Brand, Page 3

Brand, From Page 1

looking ahead," said Tom Watson, chair of the logo ad hoc committee. "In creating this logo, we wanted to pay homage to our HVAC&R origins by keeping the familiar hexagon and traditional shade of blue, while looking forward to a more sustainable future."

Along with the new logo, ASHRAE also has a new tagline: *Shaping Tomorrow's Built Environment Today*. The tagline serves as a promise to members, and the industry, that whatever the future brings in the built community, ASHRAE will be at the forefront for research and guidance.

Lastly, the Society is doing business as "ASHRAE" vs. using its full legal name of the American Society of Heating, Refrigerating and Air-Conditioning Engineers. Use of ASHRAE reflects the Society's worldwide membership and that services will continue evolving globally.

2012

Participants in the 2013 YEA Leadership Weekend in Vancouver enjoyed networking and learning opportunities.

Panelist Jim Kelsey, moderator Jennifer Gladstone, panelist Dru Crawley and panelist Chris Mathis during the Assessing Building Energy Performance webcast (2013).

ASHRAE 'Best Association'

WASHINGTON, D.C.—ASHRAE has received the U.S. Green Building Council's (USGBC) Best of Building award for Best Professional Association.

"ASHRAE is proud to be recognized as the Best Professional Association in the Best of Building Awards," said ASHRAE president Tom Phoenix. "ASHRAE strives to set an example for the industry in sustainability through efforts such as increasing the stringency of its standards, developing guidance that will lead to high-performing buildings and offering resources to professionals in the building industry to keep them up to speed with the latest sustainable technology. We look forward to building on our foundation as future industry issues come to the forefront."

The Best of Building Awards celebrates the year's best products, projects, organizations and individuals making an impact in green building. Nominees and winners were selected exclusively by the members of USGBC, a vibrant and diverse community of nearly 13,000 of the world's leading organizations invested in sustainability.

"USGBC's membership represents a diverse community of leaders that have made significant contributions to the advancement of green building," said Mahesh Ramanujam, chief operating officer, USGBC. "We congratulate ASHRAE as these peer-chosen awards reflect new and innovative achievements that are to be commended."

There are 30 peer-selected awardees selected for 48 individual categories in the competition. Awardees were selected based on their region, size and area of specialization and are designed to showcase the most progressive, innovative organizations in the fields of green architecture, landscape, engineering, interior design and manufacturing.

A full list of winners can be viewed at www.usgbc.org.

2014

First Electric Refrigerator Comes to HQ

ASHRAE has added a piece of history to its headquarters in Atlanta, with the display of the first successful electric household refrigerator manufactured 100 years ago.

The DOMestic ELectric REfrigerator (DOMELRE) marked the first attempt to mass-market a simple, inexpensive household refrigerator. It was also the first successfully manufactured air cooled system, and the first to be easily portable, being designed as a ready plug in refrigerator unit that could be added to an ice box, instantly converting it to an electric refrigerator.

It was developed by Fred Wolf Jr., who was a charter member of the American Society of Refrigerating Engineers (1905), a group that merged with the heating and ventilating engineers to form ASHRAE in 1959.

The DOMELRE condenser, evaporator and motor from 1916 was installed on the first floor of ASHRAE Headquarters on June 19.

"The piece comes from the Frigidaire collection where it had resided since the 1920s," said Bern Nagengast, the ASHRAE historian who arranged for the donation. "As far as I know, it's the only one in existence. It is a significant piece of both industry and ASHRAE history, being the first successful automatic electric refrigerator and invented by Fred Wolf Jr, a charter ASRE member."

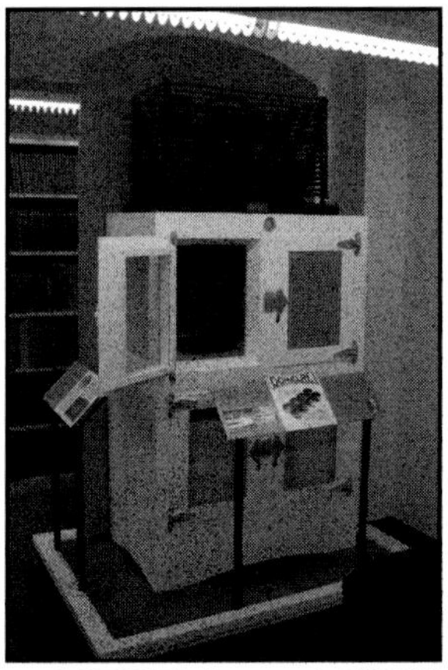

The DOMELRE display at ASHRAE headquarters

Interesting Facts About the DOMELRE

- **It was designed to be inserted into a homeowner's existing ice box.**
- **The plug was designed to screw into a light socket for homes that might not have another electric outlet.**
- **It was advertised as the first "portable" refrigerator.**
- **It was one of the first refrigerators to have a space for an "ice tray"—originally a muffin tin.**
- **The refrigerant originally used was sulfur dioxide.**

Wolf was inducted into the ASHRAE Hall of Fame in 2014 for his contributions. To learn more about his work, visit www.ashrae.org/halloffame.

2015

Nearly 11,000 View 'Net Zero' Webcast

Some 10,800 viewers worldwide logged in to watch ASHRAE's recent webcast, "Making Net Zero Net Positive: Solving the Efficiency & Cost Paradox."

ASHRAE chapters, companies and other organizations were among the 588 group sites around the world that hosted the webcast.

Viewers from dozens of countries and six continents accessed the three-hour live broadcast via the Internet. Hundreds of viewers also took advantage of the online on demand replay of the program, which was made available for two weeks following the live webcast.

The Webcast featured industry experts who defined the importance of, and why we should strive for, net zero in the built environment. Viewers were able to identify behaviors that create more effective ownership, design and construction teams, and recognize the value of a collaborative process in building design and the impact on costs. With a strong emphasis on real-world applications, the program discussed the primary technical and financial challenges in achieving net zero buildings, and where such a design approach can best be applied.

The presenters were Marc Brune, P.E., senior associate and mechanical engineer, PAE, Portland, Ore.; Philip Macey, AIA, national director of collaborative delivery, JE Dunn Construction, Denver; and Paul Torcellini, Ph.D., P.E., principal engineer for commercial building research, National Renewable Energy Laboratory, Golden, Colo.

Presenters and others involved in the Webcast included (back row, from left) Rob Laneve, CTTC chair; Bert Phillips, CTTC past chair; Leslie Jonsson, CTTC vice chair; Nathan Hart, CTTC Webcast Chair; and Andy Cochrane, CTTC Vice Chair. (front row from left) Marc Brune, presenter; Jennifer Gladstone, moderator, Paul Torcellini, presenter, and Phil Macey, presenter.

The subject for the April 2017 ASHRAE webcast is "integrating control technology and analytics for optimal building performance."

ASHRAE Insights and www.ashrae.org/webcast will provide more information regarding the date, program details and registration for next year's webcast.

2016

Portal Shares ASHRAE Knowledge

New Online Repository Gives Members Access to Decades of Published Works

More than 2,000 ASHRAE Journal articles and final research reports are available for free to ASHRAE members through a new Technology Portal.

The new technology portal can be accessed at www.ashrae.org/technologyportal and is available for ASHRAE members.

The ASHRAE Technology Portal serves a central body of knowledge for ASHRAE technology and research products. It provides access to more than 1,700 Journal articles published since 1997 and 600 plus final reports from ASHRAE research projects issued since 1958.

Final Reports of projects conducted by ASHRAE are available in the Technology Portal. This includes ASHRAE sponsored investigations at universities, laboratories, government agencies, and consulting firms that yield non-proprietary research that benefit practitioners and suppliers. ASHRAE members have free access to reports in PDF format in this repository.

Also, the Technology Portal includes the complete archive of ASHRAE Journal Issues starting from January 1997. ASHRAE members can download ASHRAE Journal articles in PDF format for free.

ASHRAE Technology Portal features a robust search feature for easy retrieval of required Journal articles and research reports. The users can search for the required publications using keywords, article title, report title, description, and research report codes.

The portal is one of ASHRAE President Tim Wentz's major initiatives for the year, and is part of a larger goal to "adapt ASHRAE technology to produce an immediate, direct benefit to members and society."

"Since 1959, ASHRAE has invested over $150 million in today's dollars in research that impacts the HVAC&R industry," Wentz said. "But how do we access this wealth of information in a timely, easy fashion? This portal will ensure our members are always on the cutting edge of technical advances and have immediate access to ASHRAE technology."

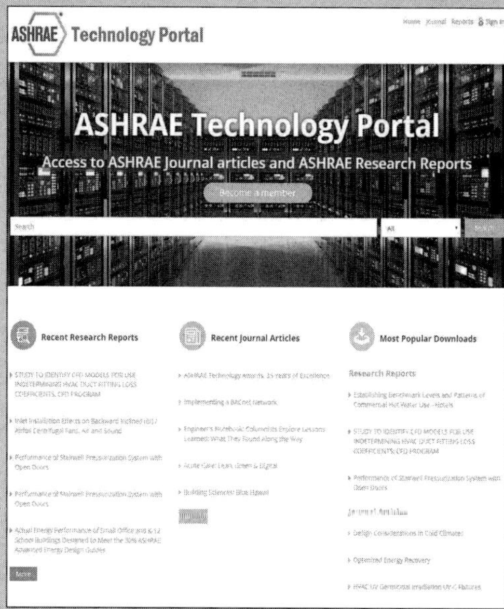

A screenshot of the Technology Portal, showing key features such as the search function, access to research reports and articles from ASHRAE Journal, as well as a link to become an ASHRAE member.

2017

ASHRAE President Bjarne W. Olesen, Ph.D. (4th from left) led the ceremonial ribbon cutting of the new ASHRAE Global Training Center.

ASHRAE Global Training Center Officially Launched In Dubai

ASHRAE celebrated the grand opening of its new Global Training Center in Dubai with a ribbon cutting ceremony and reception Sept. 19. The Global Training Center will serve ASHRAE members and other building systems professionals in the Persian Gulf Region and surrounding areas.

"ASHRAE and our members are working tirelessly toward our goal of extending our global community to better embrace our industry's shared needs and objectives," said 2017–2018 ASHRAE President Bjarne W. Olesen, Ph.D. "Dubai was an intentional and obvious location to establish the ASHRAE Global Training Center. In doing so, we hope to ensure the technical guidance we produce for all members continues to strengthen through global diversity. This center will empower our members in the Middle East with the knowledge they need to better serve the needs of their local communities."

The focus of the ASHRAE Global Training Center is to make curricula-based training conveniently available on a regular schedule. The training offered in the center is customized and scalable based upon climate, culture, suppliers, energy sources, prices, codes and construction practices. The center's instructors are engineers familiar with the intricacies of the Middle East.

To commemorate the opening, ASHRAE hosted a day of events, including a ribbon

See Global Training Center, Page 2

2017

ASHRAE, UNEP Partner on Successful eLearning Course

Oscar Quiroz displays his Certificate of Completion for the refrigerants course.

By Mary Kate McGowan, Associate Editor, News

ASHRAE and United Nations Environment Programme paired up to launch a new eLearning course to help developing countries better understand and implement Montreal Protocol regulations.

ASHRAE President Bjarne W. Olesen, Ph.D., Fellow/Life Member ASHRAE, announced the course, "Refrigerants Literacy," at the 39th Meeting of the Open-ended Working Group, held the week of July 11 – 14 in Bangkok, Thailand.

UNEP commissioned ASHRAE to develop the course based on ASHRAE's subject matter expertise and knowledge base.

During the meeting, participants could ask questions about and try out the course. The feedback will be used in future revisions of the course and other ASHRAE

See eLearning Course, Page 2

2017

LowDown Showdown Again Going Down at SimBuild

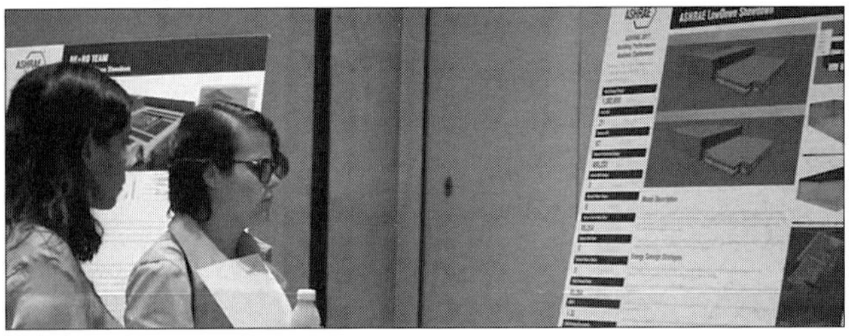

Each year, ASHRAE hosts its annual LowDown Showdown modeling competition, which showcases the work of four teams to use their design and modeling skills to create a near net-zero energy building.

The 4th Annual ASHRAE LowDown Showdown will be held in conjunction with the 2018 Building Performance Analysis Conference and SimBuild, which is co-organized by ASHRAE and IBPSA-USA.

The conference will be held Sept. 26–28 in Chicago.

The focus of the 2018 Building Performance Analysis Conference and SimBuild is the adoption of new techniques and workflows to advance modeling and simulation to meet the growing challenges faced by today's designers and modelers. In that spirit, the 2018 LowDown Showdown challenges teams to go beyond just achieving an energy efficient building, and use their ingenuity to include elements of conference themes into their design and analysis.

Getting to "near net zero" will be a part of the model building baseline. That in and of itself will be a challenge, as the model building for 2018 is a 60,000 ft^2 (5574 m^2) museum (new construction) located in Denver, and to include retail space and a full-service restaurant.

The goal of the 2018 competition is to engage participants in a collaborative and fun learning experience that explores new advances in building science, modeling and technology.

Each team will create and submit a poster of their building design, a performance analysis model and results spreadsheet, and write a one-page narrative on project workflow. Participants will also be required to submit graphics to Project StaSIO, an online crowd sourced repository of modeling graphics and images.

Modeling and calculation workflow, building designs, systems and control strategies should be creative without being implausible from a cost standpoint. To that end, one of the requirements will be a cost per square foot spending limit. However, each team may include two (2) elements in its project that are not required to be included in the project costs. Teams will be judged in two phases. Phase 1 will be based on their initial entry. Phase 2 judging will occur at the conference after teams have presented their projects. Teams will be judged on seven categories: creativity, innovative approaches, workflow, energy use, calibration, teamwork and presentation.

Questions and comments can be emailed to Christopher Preyor, cpreyor@ashrae.org.

2018

Members of the Pakistan Chapter listen to a presentation.

ASHRAE Journal and the Origin of Pakistan Chapter

Before there was an ASHRAE Pakistan Chapter, there was the ASHRAE Journal Club.

In December 2002, about 40 people attended the first ASHRAE Journal Club meeting in Karachi, Pakistan–about a year before the ASHRAE Pakistan Chapter was formed. Fifteen years later, the club continues to discuss technical features from the Journal in addition to other chapter activities.

Two of Pakistan's senior ASHRAE members—Ainul Abedin, Fellow/Life Member ASHRAE, and the late Humayun Zaheer, Associate Member ASHRAE—formed the ASHRAE Journal Club because "there was no source of technical information relating to HVAC, which could be disseminated to practicing engineers within the country," said Mohammad Abbas Sajid, P.E., Member ASHRAE, who has served as president of the ASHRAE Pakistan Chapter and sub-regional chair for ASHRAE's Region-At-Large.

Pakistani ASHRAE members wanted to provide technical activities to encourage young engineers, but the members initially had difficulty garnering enough support to apply to become a chapter, he said. So, the ASHRAE Journal Club was born to provide technical information to those members.

2018

New ASHRAE Jordan Chapter Celebrates Inauguration and Installation

ASHRAE Region-at-Large officials and chapter members celebrated the beginning of the ASHRAE Jordan Chapter. The chapter's inauguration and installation took place on May 1 in Amman, Jordan. The chapter was added during the 2018 Fall Members Council Meeting. Photographed are ASHRAE Vice President Farooq Mehboob, P.E., Fellow/Life Member ASHRAE; ASHRAE Region-at-Large Director and Regional Chair Ahmed Alaa Eldin, Ph.D., Member ASHRAE; and ASHRAE Jordan Chapter officers and members.

2019

The first of ASHRAE's Datacom books, *Thermal Guidelines*, was published in 2004. Authored by ASHRAE TC 9.9, the series has grown to 14 books.

ASHRAE Vice President Farooq Mehboob, P.E., Fellow/Life Member ASHRAE; ASHRAE Region-at-Large Director and Regional Chair Ahmed Alaa Eldin, Ph.D., Member ASHRAE; ASHRAE Falcon Chapter President Liju Thomas Eapen, Member ASHRAE; and other members and officials celebrate the chapter's anniversary.

ASHRAE Falcon Chapter Celebrates Anniversary

Since the ASHRAE Falcon Chapter was established in 2003, the chapter has grown to include about 520 members. The chapter celebrated its 15th anniversary in April in Dubai, UAE.

2019